A CULINARY TOUR OF INDIA

Experts' Views

"Finally we have a chef/author/professor who has chosen the least documented and most complex cuisine in the world to put it down on paper. Yogesh has exceeded expectations remarkably. Young and established chefs alike who are away from home finally have a "La rousse" to refer to. As an NRI food artist myself who is exploring the modern possibilities with Indian cuisine, I have a factual book as guidance. Kudos to *'A Culinary Tour of India'* which truly lives up to its name".

Aarthi Sampath
Chef De Cuisine
American Gymkhana
Orlando (U.S.)

"There are several books in market but most of them contain recipes, whereas this book focuses on history, food habits and brief information of famous dishes of that region. *'A Culinary Tour of India'* cover almost all states of the country and I hope will be useful for students, learners and others. We have different climatic conditions, availability of raw materials and our food habits have been shaped according to them. We need to escalate the research work to explore untouched diverse information on different regional cuisine of India and this book is an important step in that direction".

A.K. Singh
Principal
Institute of Hotel Management
Mumbai

"Encapsulating the depth of Indian cuisine in the format of a solitary publication has always been a near to impossible task. Nevertheless, some authors accomplish the goal with pride and honour, the very traits that underline the ethos and culinary heritage of India and this book is one of them. The author takes us on a journey throughout the length and breadth of the country covering majority of cuisines and general cooking etiquette. The book is well structured and easily comprehensible, making it a must read for culinary enthusiasts and students alike".

Bhavjit Singh Channa
Leading Hospitality Entrepreneur
Former Corporate Chef - Cirios Hotels Ltd.

"A Culinary Tour of India- with an enormous culinary detail in every possible culture and in every possible culinary region of India is a wonderful trail of traditional Indian Food. The book answers the question of what is so popular, so diverse and so delightful across the various states of India. The author Chef Yogesh Singh has included the best feasts for a culinary tourist across the country. The book provides a valuable and absorbing window into almost all regions which are for most of us inaccessible in terms of cuisine philosophy. Chapters like basic gravies and detailed introduction to Indian cuisine are noteworthy besides other chapters having insight of specific regions and food of India. *'A Culinary Tour of India'* is a perfect culinary book and travelogue".

Navdeep Sharma
(Principal/Secretary)
President- Indian Culinary Forum
Punjab & Chandigarh Chapter
Food Craft Institute
Hoshiarpur

A CULINARY TOUR OF INDIA

Yogesh Singh
Senior Faculty
Institute of Hotel Management (IHM), Kurukshetra
(Affiliated to NCHMCT, Noida)

ISBN: 978-93-89520-57-6

Edition: 2020

Printed at: Rekha Printers

I dedicate this book to

My mother Mrs. Shashi Singh
My father Mr. Hari Nath Singh
My brother Mr. Shailesh Singh
My wife Dr. Sarita Singh
and
My lovely son Aaryaveer Singh

Foreword

It gives me immense pleasure and excitement to write foreword for "A Culinary Tour of India" by Yogesh Singh.

The students, professionals, connoisseurs of food and cultural historians were waiting for a long time for such a work. This book is an in-depth research on Indian culinary art and history. There are not many such books and I am sure Yogesh's book will meet the requirement. In this book, the author has taken us to a pan-India tour of Indian cuisine.

The book is divided into three sections. **First section** deals with food habits in different eras starting from ancient days of Ramayan, Mahabharat and Vedas; ingredient produced and consumption with their classification at that time and also with various influences of religions which were defining factors in cooking and eating; and the festivals celebrated in various states of India and also the preparation of food during such festive seasons. This segment highlights, how the influence of rulers and invaders, who came to India from different parts of world, have influenced and enriched Indian cuisine. Underlining the various catering trends of food service from *dhabas* to 5 star hotel's restaurants and medicinal relation of food is an important feature.

Second section is the soul and heart of this book and focuses on the crucial culinary details and trends of almost every state of India; total twenty-eight states have been covered. It brings the finer aspects of food habits of different states of India, their staple diet and specialty dishes. This section also explains various specialty dishes from each state with brief description.

India is a country of diversity with a variety and vividness in customs and communities. Salient features of cuisine of different communities beside Hindus and Muslims, e.g., Parsi, Bohri, Chettinad, Iyengars, Malabaris, and so on, with their food habits are described.

The third and last section highlights the spices, gravies, breads and rice preparation of various states of India. This part also highlights beverages and kitchen equipment used in making Indian food.

Author has kept in mind how over a period of time Indian cuisine shaped itself with various adaptations and changes. Origin and use of kitchen equipment and their development particularly tandoor, spices and mixed spices, gravies and their various uses, making of various Indian beverages, etc., are important segment in this section.

I am sure this book will not only benefit the students of culinary art but will also immensely benefit and help professionals and historians who are researching and working on development of Indian cuisine.

My heartfelt thanks and congratulations to Yogesh Singh.

Ranjit Chaudhury
Principal
Institute of Hotel Management, Kolkata
Former Sous Chef and General Manager
India Tourism Development Corporation

Preface

India is enriched with huge diversity, glorious history and delightful cuisine. Indian cuisine is undoubtedly a miscellanea of flavourful regional cuisine each having its own identity, attributes and uniqueness. Each state of this land gasconades of their specific cuisine and all regional cuisine collectively combine together to form divine "Indian cuisine".

This country has been flooded with persons who have been blessed with refined epicurean senses in every era and this has contributed to the overall growth and formation of this lovely cuisine with incredible gastronomic perspectives and fundamentals.

India is a country with 29 states and each state has its own cuisine which portrays distinct features in respect to cultivation and availability of ingredients, climatic conditions, cooking styles, eating habits, speciality dishes and varied culture.

Nonetheless of such vividness, complexity and brilliance, its cuisine has been documented in a limited periphery. In fact, it has remained unexplored in the world of documentation and this has inspired me to pen down this cuisine in a book dedicated entirely to Indian cuisine.

Indian cuisine is ambrosial and nectarous in its nature. No one can remain without being spell bounded by the magic, flavour, charm and taste it is blessed with. This book is a sincere effort to demystify this cuisine and document it as well.

This book has been divided in three parts.

The first segment ***Indian Cuisine – A Broad Perspective*** would take the reader on the journey of Indian cuisine with a broader aspect.

- It focuses on food and ingredients that were produced and consumed in different eras. It also has references from the ancient eras like Vedas, from Ramayan and Mahabharat, etc., and a few historical references as well.
- It then describes various classification of food based on groups, nature, nutrients and so on.
- It also focuses on how the religion has been a very defining factor, in context to food, and special dishes prepared in all main religions of India. It also shows how the various religions have defined and shaped the Indian cuisine.
- It also highlights all the important festivals celebrated in India, and special dishes prepared during such celebrations. It also describes festive foods in detail.
- It also comprehends about various catering trends like dhaba (eating joints), roadside eateries, restaurant and 5-star hotels.
- It also highlights in brief about the relation of Ayurveda and Indian trends of eating and its food.

The second segment ***Regional Cuisine- A Gastronomic Overview*** is the soul and heart of the book and focuses on the crucial culinary details and trends of almost every state of India.

- It brings into light the finer aspects of culinary system, the eating trends and patterns, the staple diet, the speciality dishes as well. This section focuses on only the various regional cuisines of India and puts forward the culinary viewpoint and food pattern of each state of India. It explains the speciality dishes of each state with a brief description.
- The states included in this section are: Awadh (Uttar Pradesh), Bengal, Bihar, Goa, Gujarat, Haryana, Himachal Pradesh, Hyderabad (Andhra Pradesh), Karnataka, Kashmir, Kerala, Madhya Pradesh, Maharashtra, North Eastern states (Assam, Arunachal Pradesh, Manipur, Meghalaya, Mizoram, Nagaland, Tripura), Odisha, Punjab, Rajasthan, Sikkim, Tamil Nadu and Uttarakhand.
- India is a land which is a home to many communities like Parsi, Bohri, Chettiyar, Iyengars, Malabari and so on. This section also tells reader about various salient features of different communities with respect to food habits and their special dishes as well.

The third and last segment ***Significant Topic – Soul of Indian Cuisine*** highlights various other aspects of Indian cuisine like spices, different gravies, tandoor, biryanis and pulaos; breads, sweets, beverages and kitchen equipment, etc.

- It mentions various spices and their roles in Indian cuisine, and various combinations of spices popularly used throughout the country.
- The breads prepared in India, their region, their classification depending upon ingredients or methods of preparation.
- The various main gravies, their preparation, various dishes that can be prepared.
- It speaks about tandoor in brief - its origin, its development, its equipment, and its operation.
- It has brief description about biryani and pulaos.
- The various Indian sweets, their description based on ingredients used and on the region and their salient features.
- The various Indian beverages consumed and prepared throughout the country like *jal jeera, shikanji, lassi, chaach, thandai,* etc.
- The various kitchen equipment used in India.

This book has been enriched with noteworthy ***quotations*** related to food of some remarkable persons. Such quotations have been placed below the title of each chapter.

Each chapter of the book is brought to an end with ***Culinary Trivia*** which is nothing but an interesting detail attached with Indian cookery.

Yogesh Singh

Acknowledgements

Penning down a book is genuinely a gratifying and enriching experience. Many people have contributed a lot in accomplishing this task and so I would like to pay gratitude to all from the bottom of my heart.

I pay a huge sense of gratitude to God – "The Supreme Almighty" for giving me the strength and blessings to work on this project.

This mammoth project would not have been accomplished without the honest guidance of Mr. A.K. Singh, Principal, Institute of Hotel Management, Mumbai and Mr. Rajiv Mehrotra, Principal, Institute of Hotel Management, Kurukshetra.

I owe a tremendous debt of gratitude to Mr. Ranjit Chaudhury, Principal, Institute of Hotel Management, Kolkata for adding a grace to the book by writing a sincere Foreword for it.

I am forever in debt to all my reviewers: Mr. A.K. Singh, Mr. Navdeep Sharma, Chef Aarthi Sampath and Chef Bhavjit Singh Channa for taking time of their busy life schedule and writing review for this book.

Special acknowledgements to Mr. Priyadarshan Lakhawat, Sr. Faculty, Institute of Hotel Management, Gurdaspur and Chef Satya Prakash Pandey, Executive Chef, Country Inn by Carlson, Saket, New Delhi.

Heartfelt thanks to Shailesh Singh, Seema Singh, Inderjit Singh, Shailja Singh, Gaurav Amit, Bhamini Singh and Rajeev Amit (Rishi) for their huge support and immense motivation.

I would also like to thank Vikas Mohan, Sanjay Kumar (Librarian- IHM Kurukshetra), Rajneesh Bhadana, Saurabh Kataria, Sonal Sajwan, Gaurav Kashyap, Ashish Sharma, Jatin Kumar, Mukul Khera and Manu Muralidharan.

Sonal, Sheetal, Kajal, Adityaveer Singh and Aaryaveer Singh all deserve special thanks.

The photographs used in this book have been taken from Google images and hence I thank all the original source persons of the all such photographs for this contribution.

I owe so much to my parents, my in-laws and my wife Dr. Sarita Singh for extending unending and everlasting support in writing this book.

Yogesh Singh

Contents

Part C: The Soul of Indian Cuisine

COLOUR PHOTOGRAPHS of dishes discussed in the book

India: A Brief Introduction

"India is not, as people keep calling it, an underdeveloped country, but rather, in the context of its history and cultural heritage, a highly developed one in an advanced state of decay." – Shashi Tharoor

India, a subcontinent in Asia, is the seventh largest country in the world. It has one of the oldest civilizations of the world, almost more than 5000 years old. It is known by different names like *Aaryavrat*, *Bharat*, *Bharatvarsh*, and *Hindustan*.

It stretches from Kashmir (North) to Kanyakumari (South) and Gujarat (West) to Manipur (East).

It is surrounded by Himalayan mountains in the north and has Arabian Sea on its west, Bay of Bengal on its east and Indian Ocean on its south.

Its neighbouring countries include Pakistan on its west, Bangladesh and Myanmar on its east, Tibet and China on its north. Sri Lanka is an island located at its southern tip.

Its population consists of 72% Indo-Aryan, 25% Dravidian, and 3% Mongoloid.

India is a country with probably the largest and most diverse mixture of races. All the five major racial types – Australoid, Mongoloid, Europoid, Caucasian and Negroid – find representation among the people of India, who are mainly a mixed race. In short, India is a country with diverse ethnic groups of people.

The two important races that segregate India are Aryan and Dravidian. Aryans were the inhabitants of North India and Dravidians were the inhabitants of South India.

At various periods of India's long history, successive waves of settlers and invaders including the Aryans, Parthians, Greeks and Central Asians, Jews and Zoroastrians or Persians came into the country with their food culture and merged with the local population. This explains the variety of racial types, cultures and languages in India.

India is a country with a varied culture and it believes in the notion *Atithi devo bhava* meaning- the guest is treated like God and hence the guest is given due **respect** and **regard** and is treated with ultimate **hospitality**. These three words define our culture and showcase our hospitality in front of the entire world which gives us pride.

India is a secular and democratic country where all religions are given the same importance and are treated as one.

It is a land of beliefs and religions, customs and traditions, saints and scholars, gods and goddesses, customs and cultures, languages and dialects, beauty and purity.

It is the land of festivals, fairs and celebrations, where cricket is a new religion and *bollywood* outlines the new definition of the entertainment for the whole world.

It is an agriculture based country where the livelihood of $2/3^{rd}$ of the entire population is based upon agriculture. This is in spite of the fact that agriculture is uncertain in India as it is purely based upon the blessings of the monsoon.

India can be compared with a **sea**. A sea allows all the water bodies to merge in it and then also it never loses its identity, and it even maintains the identity and dignity as a sea with a great strength. India is like a sea so versatile in its nature that it has absorbed all the culinary goodness of its invaders, flavours of endless ingredients, and subtle aromas of varied regions without losing the sheen and peculiarity of its own. India, by its nature of generosity is imparting new dimensions to its cuisine. It is a land of taste, flavour, aroma, spices, curries and an amazing cuisine.

Indian cuisine offers an extravagant platter piled up with numerous scrumptious delicacies that enthral the genuine epicurean personality. Fasten the seat belt for a voyage to experience the ultimate celestial and pristine cuisine through *A Culinary Tour of India*.

India

AFGHANISTAN
PAKISTAN
CHINA
NEPAL
BHUTAN
BANGLADESH
MYANMAR
SRI LANKA
JAMMU & KASHMIR
Srinagar
Jammu
HIMACHAL PRADESH
Shimla
Chandigarh
PUNJAB
Dehradun
UTTARAKHAND
HARYANA
DELHI
New Delhi
UTTAR PRADESH
Lucknow
Jaipur
RAJASTHAN
SIKKIM
Gangtok
ARUNACHAL PRADESH
Itanagar
Dispur
ASSAM
NAGALAND
Kohima
Shillong
MEGHALAYA
Imphal
MANIPUR
Agartala
TRIPURA
Aizawl
MIZORAM
BIHAR
Patna
JHARKHAND
Ranchi
WEST BENGAL
Kolkata
Gandhinagar
GUJARAT
Bhopal
MADHYA PRADESH
DAMAN & DIU
Daman
Silvassa
DADRA & NAGAR HAVELI
Mumbai
MAHARASHTRA
Raipur
CHHATTISGARH
ODISHA
Bhubaneswar
TELANGANA
Hyderabad
BAY OF BENGAL
ARABIAN SEA
Yanam (Puducherry)
Panaji
GOA
KARNATAKA
ANDHRA PRADESH
Bengaluru (Bangalore)
Chennai
PUDUCHERRY (Pondicherry)
Mahe (Puducherry)
LAKSHADWEEP (INDIA)
Kavaratti
KERALA
TAMIL NADU
Karaikal (Puducherry)
Thiruvananthapuram
Palk Strait
ANDAMAN & NICOBAR ISLANDS (INDIA)
Port Blair

Part A
Indian Cuisine: A Broad Perspective

1 Shaping up of Indian Cuisine

"I love Indian food - it's my favourite cuisine. I love the mixture of spices and the subtle flavours. It's really exotic; the spices are so sensuous." – Joe Perry

An **era** is a specific period marked by distinct classifiable features, characters, events, and changes and modifications on the earth reckoned and delineated from a particular point or event.

In simple words, eras refer to longer interval of time or period. When an era is stretched to a calendar system, it is referred to as a calendar era. In Indian culture, eras are known as yugas.

The Pre-Ancient Era

Referring to the plethora of references on what man used to eat, fruits appears to have been his main dietary item during the Eolithic (early phase of the Stone Age) period. With the passage of time, meat began to enter the meal of *homo stabilis*. During the early Stone Age, man searched and killed animals and as his hunting accomplishment improved, the consumption of meat increased considerably.

Around 10,000 BC, the development and slight inclination towards agriculture changed the dependence on hunting for animal foods. Within a few millennia, meat consumption declined gradually and the shift toward vegetarian food increased.

The approach that characterizes the kind of food man consumed during that particular period can be deduced from certain evidences such as tools used and survival of old tales through generations.

About 2,50,000 years ago, during the Paleolithic (second phase of the Stone Age) period, man preferred to use tools like heavy clubs, cleavers and axes to bludgeon animals and these have been unearthed from various sites in India. During the Middle Stone Age (about 50,000 years ago), tools like pointed stones, axes, spears, knives clearly support the fact that the man used to have meat as its main diet.

During the New Stone Age or Neolithic times, the tools got more polished and refined. Such tools have been found all over the country and again these indicate indirectly the fact that meat was an indispensible diet.

There is a huge uncertainty about how fire originated. Still there is a question mark about the context when and where fire came into existence. It is assumed that the earliest use of fire by human being may have appeared as early as 1.4 million years ago. According to the available evidences, it is considered that the origin of fire might have resulted from natural causes. The roasting of meat might have occurred unintentionally due to sparks produced from self-generated friction resulting to forest fires. Also, it has been assumed that the method used for cooking was only roasting, and the boiling method came much later as a concept.

About 7000 years back, clay boiling pot was discovered and about around 5000 BC man became an agriculturalist. Around 3000 BC, with the egression of the Metal Age, man changed his tools, started cultivating and growing food and led a comparatively settled life. Around 5000 BC, tools unearthed in India indicate that a crucial change appeared when transition from a food-gathering to a food-cultivation stage and from a wandering life to a settled life took place.

Food history in India is as ancient as perhaps the creation of man.

The Ancient Era

In India, this era was referred as *Praachin Yug*.

The Ancient Era can be said to be a period from 2500 BC to AD 350.

It begins from the Indus Valley Civilization which flourished for a thousand years and is the earliest known civilization of South Asia, corresponding to the Bronze Age cultures.

It has been examined carefully and methodically that even before Indus Valley civilization, cultural evolution had taken place in the north and north-west of India and it brought a lot of prosperity.

During the Harappan period, when Indus Valley civilization witnessed its peak places like Harappa, Mohenjodaro, Chanhudaro, Kalibangan and other areas were buzzing and clamouring with the trading activities. Even then fruits like *ber* and dates were common, and several wild animals were treated as food. Various animals like sheep, buffalo, and horses were accustomed to be used in various aspects. At least four varieties of wheat and barley were raised as a basic diet. Pulses like peas, *chana*, bengal gram also find references. It is also evident from certain facts that during this period, sesame seeds and rice were also found and used. Cereals and pulses would have been in abundance and this is the reason for the elaborate arrangements for mass storage of food grains, and hence were the inseparable part of this ancient civilization. It is still a matter of curiosity whether in which form these cereals were consumed in those days. Flat metal and clay plates resembling modern *tawa* have been found in plenty at Harappan sites, suggesting that the baked *chapati* may have been known.

It is apparent from the boiling pots recovered from excavation sites of that period that cooking was done by boiling on *chulhas*. Many other pots and pans of copper for cooking and frying and the cups, ladles, kitchen knives, clay plates and other tools excavated disclose the fact that even then, the passion for cooking and eating were enjoyed.

The Harappans took delight in meat dishes and alcoholic drink called *sura* was consumed and savoured.

It is evaluated from the excavation of a piece of jewellery and other earthenware that, most probably, coconut, pomegranate, lemon leaf, lotus flower were already in existence because these earthen pots resemble such items mentioned.

Originally, the Harappan civilization was an urban one and flourishing trade was carried on between different countries by sea and land routes. Items and commodities such as cotton and cotton goods, barley, sesame and linseed oils, a variety of woods, gems, stones and copper, etc., were exported and traded.

The Harappans knew the domestic fowl, but are now few and insignificant in number. The jungle fowl is believed to be the forerunner of poultry in the world. The poultry were used for function of food, eggs, and even cock-fighting only after 600 BC.

Cooking operations used during those days were:

- *Thalanam* (drying),
- *Kvathanam* (par-boiling),
- *Pachanam* (cooking in water),
- *Bhavita* (seasoning),
- *Apakva* (frying),
- *Putapaka* (baking),
- *Svedanam* (steaming),
- *Bharjanam* (dry-roasting),
- *Thanduram* (grilling).

Devices for these operations developed in collimate along with these cooking methods.

It is still a big question and one can only speculate about how cereals were consumed and in what form. It has been proved from Harrapan sites that the people in that period used to use flat metals plates and clay metal plates which has a huge resemblance to *tawa* (griddle). Such plates were found in plentitude during excavation. Along with this, many circular ovens were also found at the Indus Valley sites. Both, above- ground and underground mud hearths (*tandoor*) were also found in area of Kalibangan. Not only this *chulhas* carrying knobs with one to three openings have also been unearthed at several sites.

Indian cooking educes its history from about 4000 years old timeline during which culture has changed tremendously; geographical boundaries have changed significantly, leading to perplexing terms such as sub-continental cuisine, while other parts of a region want a separate culinary identity.

Most people are of the opinion that the Ayurvedic tradition of cooking, which is an entire holistic (emphasizing the organic and functional relation between parts and the whole) approach to cooking is contemporaneous with this era. This lays the foundation of the concept that everything we eat affects both our body and mind; therefore the food should be pure derived from nature and balanced.

During this era, Aryans invaded our country and made Dravidians to shift to the southern part of India. At this time, the cuisine was largely vegetarian. The roots of Hinduism are moulded and shaped at this point; the Vedas or the religious texts were developed at this point as in the *Mahabharat*. The caste system was developed and along with it was developed the division of the food habits, for example, the Brahmins were made vegetarians while Kshatriyas were suggested as non-vegetarians.

Thus, the ancient era is strongly marked by Hinduism which was followed by all including Aryans and Dravidians.

The Medieval Era and Modern Era

In India, the medieval era is referred as *madhyakaalinyug* and the modern era as *adhunikyug*.

The Medieval Era, also called the Middle Age, lasted from about AD 350 to AD 1450.

The adjective medieval comes from the Latin words for this term, *medium* (middle) and *aevum* (age).

The Modern Era commenced after AD 1450.

No single event is considered to define the end of the Ancient Era and the beginning of the Middle Age. In fact, no one who lived in what is now called the Middle Age ever thought of themselves as living in it. In the Middle Age, people thought they were living in modern times, just as people do today.

Hinduism was the central religion which was being followed by Aryans and Dravidians from the Ancient Era itself.

The Medieval Era saw the booming of two crucial religions shaping India, namely, Buddhism and Jainism. The later has a marked influence on the cuisine in some parts of the country. Jains were strong believers in non-violence. Traditional Jain cuisine, apart from being cooked without meat, was also cooked without onion and garlic.

This period was the period of several North Indian dynasties, including the Gupta Dynasty, which was noted for its love of the arts. Several travellers visited India during this time. This was also known as the Golden Age of Indian Art, in which several travellers visited India and carried with them knowledge and products like tea and spices.

This era was marked by the booming and flourishing of diverse religions and during this era, few religions actually got their shape and structure in India. India has also witnessed the conquest of rulers like Mughals from west and thus came Islam in India.

Almost at the end of this era and at the dawn of the Modern Era, Sikhism also boomed. Europeans invaded India and ruled for a longer duration of time and hence their cuisine has also created an impact on Indian cuisine to a large extent.

Each religion has a culture of its own and so is its cuisine. Indian food has been influenced from time to time, by invaders, the people of other regions, by the customs and culture adopted by various religions and groups of people, who made India their home.

Various Food References from Vedas/ Ramayan/Mahabharat/Royal Kings

• Food Culture of Aryans

The Aryan civilization followed the Harappan civilization, and it inherited practical and theoretical knowledge. Yet the whole distinctive spirit of the culture changed. The Aryans brought the knowledge of agriculture with them and the Vedic civilization developed as an agricultural, pastoral and philosophical one. The Aryans set the agricultural pattern of food production that still persists in India.

During the Aryan civilization, the four vedas written between 1700 BC to 800 BC, documented Aryan foods and drinks in an elaborate and descriptive manner, along with the culture of that period.

The four vedas are - Rigveda, Samaveda, Yajurveda and Atharveda.

Rigveda, which is the oldest of the four vedas, (1700 – 1500 BC) describes barley as the chief staple diet of that period. It contains no references about rice and wheat. This justifies the fact that only barley was consumed, by and large, by all, at that time. Rigveda has a special description of a unique drink made by the concoction of honey, curds and ghee called *madhuparaka*. This drink was served to the guest as a mark of hospitality.

It was the period when animals were kept as pet and were domesticated for products like milk and milk products, curds, butter, *ghee* (clarified butter), *paneer* (cottage cheese) and ripened cheese. All the commodities were in plenty. Milk was used fresh, boiled or mixed with some juice.

Yajurveda, which is documented to exist during 1500 BC to 800 BC, mentions wheat and rice, along with barley as the main staple diet of that period. It also has the citation of sesame as an oilseed and *mugda* (*mung*), *masha* (*urad*), *masura* (*masur*), *kalaya* (*peas*) as the main pulses eaten along with plenty of animal meat. The Aryans were great cultivators and hence they were expert in raising auxiliary foods, like a diverse variety of vegetables such as pumpkins, gourds and mangoes. They also cultivated spices like turmeric, ginger, garlic and fenugreek. Peppers and cardamoms came from South India, and asafoetida from Afghanistan. Salt has been mentioned in the later vedas. It was a rarity but had an important and revered place in the performance of sacred rites.

Few other fruits and vegetables such as dates, *bael*, *ber*, *amla*, Indian fig, *jamun*, coconut, banana, jackfruit, palm, *phalsa*, *karonda* and several citrus species were described and noted in later vedas. Vegetables like lotus stem, cucumber, bottle gourd, bitter gourd and *mahua* flowers were much in use. During this time, honey was the main sweetening agent. Vinegar was made from a variety of fruits and was used as a preservative. Sugar cane finds mention in the later vedas. The Aryans were people with great taste with excellent dining habits and hence enjoyed fruit beverages as refreshing drinks, and consumed a variety of meat dishes and even alcoholic drinks.

Thus, barley was the major staple grain used by the Aryans. It was fried and consumed in the form of cakes dipped in ghee, or as sweet cakes called *apupa*. The modern-day preparations of *malpua* from Bengal preserve its name from this term apupa.

Later, rice entered and dominated the Aryan food system and it was cooked with either water or milk or with *dal* (pulses) or along with curds, honey or meat. It was consumed with almost all preparations.

Lajah, a variety of parched rice, was a regular food item. It was either soaked in milk, or perhaps mixed with some seasoning. Whereas *chipita* was the flattened rice, which is the modern *chivda*, consumed in those days.

Somras was an alcoholic beverage, which had a significant role and place in rituals.

The Aryans had a huge predilection for cooking meat items. They cooked meat dishes in seven ways. The seven different methods adopted by them included fancy and imaginative cooking. The technique of roasting, frying, stuffing, mincing, shaping the meat pieces into different shapes, cooking meat with rice, and cooking meat with sour fruit juices were all popular even in those days.

An ancient cookery book *Sushrutha Samhita*, mentions and describes all the seven types of meat preparations in ancient India carried out by the Aryans give an account of cooking as follows:

- The first was the preparation of meat with the inclination towards sour taste. It was prepared using ingredients like ghee, curds, rice, gruel soured by fermentation, acid fruits, and pungent and aromatic ingredients.
- Roasting of dried meat yielded *Parisukamamsam*.
- The third type of cooking was minced meat, *Ulluplamamsam*.
- Frying of fresh meat was known as *Bharjita*.
- The meat that had been ground and then shaped into patties or balls were termed *Pishtha*.
- When the meat was roasted on charcoal fire along with proper bating with ghee it yielded *Pratapta*.
- The seventh and the last type was *Vesavara* and it was frequently used for stuffing. In order to make it boneless the meat was first boiled, and then ground fine, and cooked with such ingredients as ghee, molasses, black pepper and ginger in several of tastes and flavours.

Thus, we see that even during the early period items like shaped meat roasted on skewers, and ground, shaped meats were in general use.

Food in the Aryan belief was not only a means of sustenance and nourishment of the body, but it was also a part of a cosmic universal moral cycle.

The above statement can be strongly justified by the sentence mentioned in the Upanishads - "from earth sprang herbs, from herbs food, from food seeds, from seeds man. Thus, man consists of the essence of food, from food, thus, all the creatures are produced, and by food they grow. The self consists of food, of breath, of mind, of understanding, of bliss."

The food was further classified as Tamasic, Sattvic and Rajasic. This classification was largely based on the Aryans' concept of hot and cold food beliefs which represented five elements - Earth, Water, Fire, Air and Sky. That is why, Indian scholars in the field of medicine recommended food according to the season, climate and the region. Gradually, this food ethos of the Aryans influenced the whole of India and they became Indian food beliefs. Food was a part of spiritual, secular and temporal life.

The dishes prepared and eaten by the Aryans during those days are equally popular in India even today, with slight changes in the methods of cooking.

Barley was the major grain consumed by the Aryans. It was fried and consumed in various ways. It was eaten in the form of cakes dipped in ghee or as sweet cakes called *apupas* which was fashioned out of barley flour boiled in water or fried in ghee and then dipped in honey.

Mandaka, now called *mande*, was a large *paratha* stuffed with a sweet pulse paste and then baked on inverted *tawa*.

Pua or malpua, a modern Bengali sweet still preserves both the name and the essentials of the preparation.

Bhatka was the boiled rice.

Kshira was *til* rice and here rice was boiled in milk with sesame seeds.

Krasara was a *khichdi* made from rice and *dal*.

Lajah was the parched rice.

Chipita was flattened rice, today's *chidva*.

Kheel was puffed rice.

Vataka was *wada* made of *urad dal*.

Rasala, sugared and spiced curds, was a popular home item.

Shirkarini was modern *shrikhand*.

Chittrana was a dish of several cereals cooked together.

Moreandaka made from *khoa* was shaped like a peacock egg.

Honey has been the most earliest and ancient sweetener. In Rigveda, it is mentioned that the product derived from small bees was better than that from large ones.

Sugar cane has not been mentioned in Rigveda, but has been described in Atharveda. The thickened sugar cane juice was referred as *phanita*, and which on further concentration yielded *guda*.

By the Buddhist period, the use and importance of honey receded, and it had been replaced by *guda* and sugar as common sweetening agents. *Guda* was the base for numerous and almost all sweet preparations. Sesame seeds were mixed with *guda*, was shaped to give *palala*. Wheat flour was fried in ghee and then mixed with milk to prepare *samyava*, which was often flavoured with cardamom, pepper or ginger; whereas ground barley or wheat mixed with jaggery yielded *abhyusa*. *Modaka* or *madhugolaka* was a sweet preparation of rice flour. Rice cooked in milk and sugar yielded *payasa*, a popular sweet even now.

Fruit beverages were developed at a very early phase of the Aryan life as refreshing drinks. The juices of ripe mango, *jamun*, banana, grapes, *phalsa*, coconut and others were prepared and relished with great zest.

The history of Indian cuisine cannot be complete, if the foods from the early days are not discussed, right from the epic days to the Mughal and the European periods. The ancient Indians wrote books not only on religion and philosophy, but they also wrote a book on the art of cookery called *Supasastra*. There are many works on cookery in Sanskrit and other languages from the southern parts of India.

The most dependable and authentic sources of getting information are:

- The books which were written by saints or *rishis*.
- The chronicles and descriptions given by historiographers.
- The books or diaries that were written by the kings themselves.
- The memoirs, essays, and descriptions of the royal hospitality scripted by many travellers or foreigners who visited India from time to time since time immemorial.
- Last but not the least, Sanskrit and regional literature written on this topic, or which includes this topic.

It is mentioned in the book *Nalacharita*, the term *nalabhima pakam* refers to the preparation of food by the two cooks Nala and Bhima, who lived in different periods, who are known for their splendid culinary accomplishments. It also has references of cook Nala cooking a dish (Hundika). The king after being satisfied with the dish presented gifts to Nala comprising ornaments, a lakh rupee and 500 villages, for his culinary achievement. This depicts how crucial were food and culinary arts even during those periods of antiquity. It is of interest to mention that though women do cooking at homes today but the two men Nala and Bhīma are remembered as great cooks.

Indian epics of great honour like the *Ramayan* and the *Mahabharat* portrays the Kshatriya princes who used to enjoy lavish and sumptuous meals of rich and expensive dishes prepared with a variety of meats.

The *Ramayan* describes that Rama and Lakshmana while in exile in the Dandakaranya forest hunted animals for the pot, and a dish most liked by Sita was called *mamsabhutadana* which was a delicacy of rice cooked with the combination of deer meat, vegetables and spices. There is a reference that at the sacrificial banquet of King Dasharatha, myriad delicacies of meat of all kinds, meat of lamb, chicken, pig, and peacock were served. These dishes were cooked in fruit juices, or were sauté fried in butter or had spices, seeds and lentils simmering in them.

Even the most unique feast arranged in the accolade of Saint Bharadhwaj lists the dishes prepared with pig and fowl meat and which stimulates the appetite. In *Ramayan*, the meat of hare, hedgehog, porcupine, and tortoise are apparently mentioned.

Two spicy concoctions, *supa* and *nisthana*, which were popular in Ayodhya in Rama's time, were made by cooking pork and mutton in fruit juices. A pepper-flavoured decoction of a tree bark, *mesashringi* was also popular during this period.

The *Mahabharat* mentions *pishthaudana*, a dish of rice cooked with minced meat and it was liked most by Duryodhana. The Pandvas while in forest ate meat of many kinds of deers. There is a reference that King Yudhishtra fed ten thousand brahmins with pork and venison, besides preparation of milk and rice mixed with ghee and honey, and fruits and roots. Elsewhere in the epic, besides roasted birds, swine, donkey, camel, and sheep meat are also mentioned. Meat in those days was cooked in various ways. It was roasted on spit fire, cooked as curries with the sauce made of tamarind, pomegranates/mangoes, along with spices, fragrant herbs, asafoetida, and ginger.

The cooking of meat along with sour tasting fruits is noteworthy throughout the historic literature, but at the present time, this practice has disappeared. Now, only use of tamarind is in vogue. Pomegranate and mango are used in the cookery, but in the seed and powder form respectively.

In *Valmiki Ramayan*, there is description of Rama and Lakshmana bringing home huge quantity of dead beasts (wild boars and 3 or 4 varieties of deer). It also mentions about their favourite family diet which consisted of spike-roasted meats (*shalyapakva*). It also provides the information that Lakshmana roasted the meat on fire.

In one reference, when Yudisthira opened the banquet spread, there were hills of food cooked by Bhima. He served innumerable dishes which included 18 kinds of barbecued meat, wild rice and sesame seeds in 30 kinds of sauces, grains boiled in milk and butter, hot candies of sugar, ginger and pepper, sour and sweet preserves, fresh and dry fruits, 70 kinds of vegetables — raw and cooked, 93 soups, 11 stews, 29 kinds of fish cooked in 51 ways, unleavened bread baked and refried, 100 kinds of pie and cake, and curds, raw sugar, roots, salty fried leaves, boiled nuts, honey light and dark, and oceans of wine and clear water of rivers and lakes of milk.

Alcoholic Beverages

Somaras finds a special mention in the beverages during the ancient period. It was a juice of some plant, not known today, had a very significant role in life and religious ceremonies of early vedic Aryans. The drink was offered to the gods, and imbibed by the priests and proponents of sacrifice. It was clearly distinguished from a mere alcoholic stimulant. An individual who imbibed *soma* was gladdened beyond his natural powers, and the juice itself was described as being primordial, all powerful, curative of all diseases, super-liked by riches, loved by the gods, even the Supreme Being. In order to get its juice the *soma* plant was sprinkled with water and ground on stone. The mass was collected on a cowhide and then strained through a woollen cloth. The filtered liquid was mixed with milk, curds or fruit juice for consumption.

Several attempts have been made to recognize the *soma* plant, but none seems really satisfactory. The assumption includes a leafless shrub called *somalata*, an American milkweed, Indian *bhang* plant and mushroom of deep red colour with white spots.

Much of the description seems to fit the description of the mushroom *Amanita muscarita* which is an old world species. It exercises the quality of producing hallucinogenic effects of the kind described in the vedas and contains *muscimol* and *muscarine*.

Rigveda has an elaborate and vivid description of *Somaras*, boiling or stewing.

Among the Kshatriyas, drinking alcohol was an accepted standard practice. Sita has promised the River Ganga a thousand jars of wine if her exiled party returned home safely. She kept her promise when all returned safely. After they did so, Rama served her with his own hands with *maireya* (a liquor, probably distilled, flavoured with tree bark of *mesashringi* with *guda*, pepper, *triphala* and spices added to it), a spiced wine. In *Mahabharat*, Krishna too enjoys drinking freely with Arjuna, and the Yadavas are finally killed in a drunken brawl.

• Food Culture of the Dravidians

The reference of food culture of the Dravidians is new and novel as compared to the food culture of the Aryans.

South India was exposed to a wide variety of enriching influences during its development. There was a connection with Africa through Gujarat, and a land bridge existed. Similar tools were in use at both the places some 2,50,000 years ago. Some similarities can be traced through food also. Many food plants also might have been transferred. Many Tamil words for certain products like coconut, banana, betel, etc., appear to have been assimilated ones. There is a likelihood that before the Aryans reached the South around 600 BC, the Harappan people had already found their way there. Early Tamil script resembles early Gujarati. Archaeological surveys show the existence of cultivations in South India along with the cotton growing and weaving into a cloth. By 750 BC, the staple food was rice, cattle, sheep, and goats. The domestic fowls were used as sources of meat. Huge tanks were built in order to supply both domestic and irrigation water to grow rice.

Food was rich and varied in South India in the first few centuries AD. Five varieties of rice were eaten, boiled with aromatics sprinkled on it or with tamarind dressing, sesame seeds, sugar, pulses, meat or ghee. Tamil literature is full of references from processing to cooking dishes like *appams*, *idlis*, *dosas*, *adai*, *modak*, and *naiappam*. A variety of vegetables like brinjals, bitter gourds, unripe bananas, tubers and several leafy vegetables were eaten by the common man. There was a fairly wide variety of fruits like jackfruit, mango, banana, *amla*, *jamun*, fig, lemon, pomegranate and coconut. Tamarind and *amla* were combined in making a drink. Pepper was the prize spice of the South, sought after all over India and overseas. It was grown in today's Kerala. Other flavouring agents were turmeric, ginger, cloves, cardamom, tamarind and lemon. Tender mangoes were pickled. Chewing the betel leaf was a custom. Since the cattles were raised, milk and milk products like cream, butter, curds, buttermilk and ghee were in much use. Curds were spiced with pepper, cinnamon and ginger.

The pre-Aryan southerners had no restrictions and inhibitions about eating meat or fish, or even consuming liquor. Beef was in wide use all over. People savoured pork and buffalo meat. It is also mentioned that even elephant meat was dried and stored for consumption. Fishermen relished fish at a meal. Plain rice was served with curried crabs and vegetables. There were many ways in which animal meat based foods were cooked.

Kari word has actually come to stay from south India. Jaggery was a common sweetening agent. Honey was a prized product and was exchanged in bartar for fresh oil or *toddy*. Alcoholic drinks were consumed at all levels of society by both men and women. Salt in South India was a well-known commodity and was an important item of trade. Earlier, paddy and salt were the principal measures of value, but later on pepper became a major product. Here, rice and wheat were the staple diet.

Two southern kings of 12th and 18th centuries have given detailed accounts of the food consumed by the South Indian royal families.

King Someshwara of Kalyana in Central India and King Basavaraja of the Keladi Kingdom (now in Karnataka) have given a concise and succinct account of food culture prevailing in South India in the books written by them.

King Someshwara, in his book *Manasollasa*, mentioned about *mandakas* made from wheat flour, which was obtained by washing wheat, drying it in sun, grinding and then sifting on a sieve. The flour was mixed with ghee and salt and made into balls, flattened in palms. This flattened roll were first cooked pottery and then roasted on live coals before eating. It could very well be stuffed with various fillings and enjoyed. Honey was stuffed to yield *madhumestak* and *madhushirshaka*, jaggery to yield *polikas*, and savoury stuffing yielded *angarapolikas*. *Kasara* was a wheat flour delicacy prepared by frying in ghee, with milk, sugar and spices added to the dough.

Vidalapaka was made from a mixture of five pulses flours like *chana*, *rajmah*, *masoor*, *mung* and parched *thuvar*, seasoned with salt, asafoetida and turmeric and then cooked on low fire. *Vatakas* were the fermented *urad vadas*. It also mentions various types of *vadas* like *manahvataka* and *kshiravata*. Blending of the pulses along with vegetables and meat to make curries was practised. Thus, *mung dal*, pieces of lotus stalk, and *chironji* seeds were seasoned with asafoetida and green ginger pieces, fried in oil, and boiled to a curry, to which fried brinjal pieces and mutton might have been added, and finished with black pepper and dry ginger.

Manasollasa also mentions sweet dishes like *kshiraprakara* which was made by adding sour substances to boiling milk, after which the precipitate was separated and was mixed with refined flour, fashioned in various shapes, fried in ghee and coated with sugar. Sweet balls prepared with rice or pulse flours and sugar were termed *laddukas* or *modakas*.

King Basavaraja in his book *Sivatattvaratnakara* mentioned that only gold vessels were used by the king for eating. Drinks and *rotis* (bread) were placed on the left of the plate, rice in the middle, and greens and vegetables below. Sweet items were served first, followed by sour and salty items, and finally bitter, pungent and astringent items were served.

All pulses were used for making *supa* (broths) which were described as a wholesome accompaniment to rice. Milk was reduced to various degrees by boiling to yield *panapaka* (to half), *lehyapaka* (to one-third), *ghutipaka* (to one-sixth) and *sharkarapaka* (to one-eighth, a solid product now called *khoya*).

One of the earliest works from Gujarat, the *Bimalprabhandha* of Lawanyasamay of about AD 1200 describes that milk was widely used in western India to yield *thakra* (buttermilk) *themanam* (*kadhi*) *kshiraprakara* (*chenna*) *kurchika* (*mawa*) *shikarini* (shrikhand) and *sarkara* (*dudhpeda*).

Similarly, there were four sugar syrups of different consistencies, termed *mrdu*, *madhyama*, *khara* and *sarika*. A popular confectionery called *varselapaka* was prepared by adding milk, cardamom, saffron and camphor to *khara* syrup.

For centuries, relishes of different kinds have been important part of our meals because they add pungency to our simple meals of *dal*, rice and vegetables. King Basavaraja of Keladi (now Karnataka) mentions in his book *Sivatattvaratnakara* written around AD 1700 that relishes were called *upadamsha* and were made in five ways, without cooking, by boiling in water, by mixing and heating in oil, by direct heating without water or oil, and by cooking in a vessel.

The *idli*, *kadubu*, *dosai*, *appam* and *vadai* of southern India have each had a long history, though not every detail can be clearly traced. *Idli* seems to be first mentioned in a Kannada work of AD 920, as one of eighteen items served as refreshment to a *brahamachari* who visited a home of a lady. Thereafter, it is frequently mentioned in Indian treatises. It is clear from all the writings that *idli* is made of *urad dal* but the elements of modern *idli* are missing that use of two parts of rice with one part of *urad dal*, long process of grinding and the overnight fermentation of the mix and the steaming of the batter.

In Karnataka, 13th century literature describes *idli* as being 'light, like coins of high value'. In Tamil literature *idli* (*ittali*) is first mentioned in the writings of AD 17th century. In AD 1485 and AD 1600, the *idli* is compared to the moon, which suggests that rice was in use. Yet, the reference shows that many other moon like products were made but only from *urad* flour. The *manasollasa* written in Sanskrit about AD 1130 describes *idli* (*iddarika*) to made of fine urad flour, fashioned into small balls, fried in ghee and then spiced with pepper powder, *jeera* powder and asafoetida.

It is likely that the name *idli* continued to exist even though its character and attributes changed with the passage of time. There is a suggestion that perhaps the fermentation technique came from Indonesia as Indonesians ferment many edible items. They have something which is fermented and steamed and are called *kedli*. Perhaps the cooks of the Hindu kings brought this technique back with them and perhaps rice was necessary to be used along with pulse for the yeast and enzymatic reaction.

The *kadubu* is quite similar to *idli* but this is steamed on leaves as slab. It was first mentioned in the Kannada writings in AD 1430. *Uradkadubu, kadubu* made from vermicelli and from *rava* or *channa* and containing bamboo shoots get mention. Now it is steamed as a slab on leaves or in a metal tray and then sweet or savoury stuffings are placed between layers of *kadubu,* and the resulting sandwich cut into smaller pieces for consumption.

The *Tosai* (*dosai* or *dosa*) is first noted in the Tamil *Sangam* literature of about the AD 6th century. It was perhaps then a pure rice product, shallow fried in a pan, while the *appam* of similar vintage was heated without fat, on a shallow clay *chatti*. Today even *dosa* is a fermented product, almost of the thinner batter of *idli,* but slightly changed in proportion of pulses and rice. It has a slight variation in its preparation depending upon the region in which it has been made. The *dosa* of Tamil Nadu is a soft, thick product while that of Karnataka is thin, crisp and large. These days, it is stuffed with spiced potato mash to yield the popular *masala dosa*. It is this version of *dosa* that is liked by almost everyone.

The *appam,* circular in shape, is mentioned in the 5th century writings along with the *idi-appam*. Both products seem to have remained unchanged to this day. The *appam* batter is fermented overnight using *toddy*/yeast and baked in a clay pan to prepare a product with a thick, soft, spongy centre and lacy, crisp, brown edge. Heating on a metal plate held over boiling water yields *kalappam*. Steaming in a banana leaf packet with jaggery, grated coconut, and jackfruit pulp added to the rice batter, yields *yelle-appam* (leaf *appam*).

Vata and *vataka* are first mentioned in the *Sutra* literature of about 500 BC andD regularly thereafter. The Tamil literature does not seem to carry it till quite late. The modern *vadai* is generally a deep fried snack in which *urad dal* (yielding *meduvada*) and *chana dal* (the *ambada*) pulse flours are generally employed and occasionally *tuvar* and *masur* are employed too to make the *vadas*. The *urad vataks* were once placed only in milk, buttermilk and curds, but at present only the *dahivada* steeped in spiced curds have survived. In Karnataka, between Bangalore and Mysore, about eight decades back, a special kind of vada has been developed. It is made of *rava* mixed with a plenty of fried onions, chopped cashew nuts and green chillies.

Languages have always been a crucial element in knowing the culture of any place. In India, Sanskrit is believed to be the oldest language, which is in record from about 1500 BC. The Rigveda was composed during this period in Sanskrit.

Another language which was spoken in India mainly in South India was Tamil. These two languages have given many words used today in the context or food and Indian cuisine.

This also gives a clear indication that these ingredients existed since long as they have been discussed in early languages used.

Few important culinary words from Sanskrit and in Tamil taken from earlier periods are as below:

- Rice: *chomla* and then *chaval*
- Ragi: from raga, red in Sanskrit
- *Mung*: *mudga*
- *Masoor*: *masura*
- *Sarson*: *sarshapa*
- Brinjal: *vantingana, vartaka* and *vrntaka*
- Pumpkin: *alabu*
- *Tinda*: *tundi*
- *Panwal*: *patola*
- Jackfruit: *panasa*
- Banana: *kadali*
- Roseapple: *jambu*
- *Jamun*: *jambula*
- Lime (*nimbu*): *nimbuka*
- Orange: *nagaranga* (*narangi*)
- Coconut (*nariyal*): *narikela*
- Ghee: *nai*
- Butter: *vennai*
- *Haldi*: *haridra*
- *Arhar*: *adhaki*
- *Pan*: *parna*, sankrit for leaf
- *Peach*: *chinani, nashpati*
- Jaggery/*Gur*: *guda*
- Rock sugar: *khand*
- Crystal sugar: *sharkara*
- Camphor: *karpura*
- Curry: *kari* in Tamil
- *Mulligatawny*: pepper water in Tamil
- Oil: *ennai* in Tamil
- Sesame oil: *elluennai* in Tamil
- Coconut oil: *thengaennai*
- Groundnut oil: *nallennai*
- Ginger: *inji* in Tamil
- Pepper: *milagu* or *miriyam* in Tamil
- Fish: *meen* in Tamil
- Hopper: *appam* in Tamil
- Mango: *amra*/*ambah* in sanskrit and *ma*/*mangga* in Tamil
- Ladyfinger: *vendekayi* in Tamil.

Such sporadic references would help anyone to have a crisp idea about Indian cuisine from earlier periods to modern day. It has undoubtedly matured and got refined with the passage of time and experiments that have been done on it.

Thus, Indian cuisine has descended a lot from the earlier eras to attain and achieve its current status. No cuisine is fashioned in a short period of time and Indian cuisine is no exception to this. Its long history and long existence has made its culinary features more divine. It has experienced a vast change or can be said that it has refined repeatedly over a long period of time to be what it is today.

Culinary Trivia: Honour of Guest in the Vedic Era

Guests had a respected rank in the vedic society, only below that of father, mother and teacher. On arrival, a guest was ceremoniously received, given water for washing and then offered the beverage *Madhuparaka,* made of five ingredients ghee, curds, milk, honey and sugar. *Madhuparaka* was an auspicious ritual beverage. In early vedic times, if the guest was an honoured *brahmin* or a king, a large bull or goat would be sacrificed in his honour, even if the host himself was a vegetarian. Later on, this ritual became symbolic.

2 Classification of Food

"Food is everything we are. It's an extension of nationalist feeling, ethnic feeling, your personal history, your province, your region, your tribe, your grandma. It's inseparable from those from the get-go." – Anthony Bourdain

Food is that divine substance which helps us to satisfy our appetite. Along with this it helps us to meet basic bodily needs. It also supplies energy to maintain the body temperature and to perform all activities.

A food group is a collection of foods that share similar nutritional properties or similar nature, or biological classification.

Thus, food has been classified in various groups on this basis and they are:

Based on nature: This classification describes the nature and characteristics of the food.

Based on groups (*vargas*): This classification segregates the food on the basis of its group.

Based on nutrients: This grouping of food is done on the nutrient contents of the food.

The first two methods or classification of food was done in the ancient period. Food grouping on the basis of *vargas* is now more refined according to the convenience of the modern society.

The latter classification is done in the modern era and is more emphasized today.

Classification of Food Based on Nature

According to the *Bhagavad Gita*: *Sattvic* foods are morally wholesome, nutritive and palatable, conducive to serenity and placidity, tranquillity, easy to digest, and support spirituality. It is light, unctuous, nourishing, sweet and tasty. It escalates the energy of the mind, produces cheerfulness and mental clarity. A person of *sattvic* nature likes to eat foods that prolong life, purify one's inner being, and give strength, health, happiness and satisfaction. Such foods are juicy, oily, fatty, wholesome and pleasing to the heart. It is also referred to as *yoga* diet or sentinent diet.

Examples of these are milk and its products, jaggery, honey, fruits, vegetables, almonds, sprouts, barley, wheat, etc.

The spices mostly used are turmeric, ginger, cinnamon, coriander, fennel and cardamom.

Lord Vishnu, the preserver, represents and exemplifies the *sattvic* temperament.

Tamasic foods are cold, stale and highly spiced, making the eater slow, sluggish and slothful. It is not at all beneficial for the health. Stale, tasteless, decomposed, putrid and leftover foods are dear to a person of *tamasic* nature. It is also referred to as sedative food or inactive food.

Examples of such foods are pork, beef, non-scaly fish and strong brews. It also includes alcohol, preserved food and fermented foods.

Lord Shiva, the destroyer, exemplifies the *tamasic* temperament.

Rajasic foods are bitter, sour, salty, pungent, dry and burning. They stimulate a person and make him restless. This food is fresh but heavy. Such foods cause distress, misery and disease. It is nutritious and may contain a little more oil and spices compared to *sattvic* food.

Examples are non-vegetarian food like meat, fish, eggs and chicken, all whole pulses and *dals*, pungent vegetables like hot peppers, and garlic and onion.

Lord Brahma, the creator, exemplifies the *rajasic* nature.

Depending upon the character and effect it creates on the mind and body, the food is callled Sattvic, Tamasic or Rajasic.

Thus, this classification is not just about the qualities of food, but is also a way of life.

Classification of Food Based on Vargas

Food materials were classified into various *vargas*, which correspond fairly closely to the divisions in use today;

- *sukhadhanya* (cereals),
- *samidhanya* (pulses),
- *shakna* (vegetables),
- *phala* (fruit),
- *supyam* (spices),
- *payovarga* (milk products),
- *mamsavarga* (animal meats) and
- *madhyavarga* (alcoholic beverages).

However, in ritual terms, a different concept prevailed. A classification was also done on the basis of how the foods were cultivated.

- ***Anna/Kristapachya:*** Foods that were grown using plough, like rice, wheat, barley and lentils were termed *anna* or *kristapachya*.
- ***Phala/Akristapachya:*** Food items that grew without cultivation (*akristapachya*) like wild grains, vegetables, and fruits, were broadly termed *phala* and these fell into a different category.

At certain auspicious ceremonies, or for men who had taken *sanyaas*, only the latter categories of food were permitted. Thus, the starchy yam or water-chestnut (*singhada*) would qualify not as *anna* but as *phala*, which were permitted during a fast. Items such as flowers (*pushpa*), roots (*mula*), bulbous tubers (*kanda*), leaves (*patra*), fruits (*phala perse*) and some pods or legumes (*shimbi*) are also considered *phala*.

Lentils (*masur*) qualify as *anna*, and therefore, *chana* (chickpea) is not classed as an auspicious grain.

Milk and ghee are ritually pure, especially auspicious and therefore extremely flexible in use as food ingredients.

Ghee is quite different, ritually, from cooking oil. Frying food in the former constitutes a superior ritual act, not comparable to frying in vegetable oil. An outcome of these ritual distinctions is the two major classes into which cooked foods fall, namely, *kaccha* and *pucca*. *Kaccha* foods are basically those foods which are cooked in water, like rice, *dal*, and *khichdi* whereas *pucca* foods are those which are cooked with fat or ghee.

Talking in terms of modern scenario, the foods are nowadays classified as given below:

- Dairy products
- Meat products
- Vegetables
- Fruits
- Cereals and grains.

Classification of Food Based on the Nutrients

All food items contain some of the nutrients. But the nutritive value of each food is different and each food has mixed nutrients. Some nutrients dominate in certain foods while other nutrients are found in major quantities in other foods. Food provides us with six essential nutrients, viz., carbohydrates, proteins, fats, vitamins, minerals and water. So, depending upon the nutrient it contains, foods can be classified as below:

- **Carbohydrate-rich foods:** Cereals and cereal products, starchy roots and tubers, sugar and its related products, and fruits with high pulp content.
- **Protein-rich foods:** Pulses, legumes, nuts, eggs, milk, certain milk products, meat, fish, and poultry.
- **Fat-rich foods:** Butter, cream, oils, ghee, *vanaspati* ghee, full-cream milk and its products, egg yolk, meat, poultry, seafood, nuts, and oilseeds.
- **Vitamin-rich foods:**

  Vitamin A: Liver (especially beef, fish and chicken), organ meats, fatty fish, fish liver oil, dairy products, and green leafy vegetables such as *amaranth*, colocasia, turnip greens, curry leaves mango, apricot, papaya, orange, raspberries, carrots, tomato juice, and broccoli.

  Vitamin D: Cod liver oil, fatty fish, oysters, salmon, mushrooms, milk, butter, egg yolks, beef liver, cheese, and most importantly sunshine.

  Vitamin E: Wheat germ oil, oils, margarine, green leafy vegetables (spinach and turnip greens), broccoli, tomato paste, whole grains, organ meats (liver), egg yolks, nuts and oilseeds.

  Vitamin K: Dark green vegetables, legumes, oils and fish, spinach, brussels sprouts, broccoli, asparagus, cabbage, cucumber, peas, and margarines.

  Vitamin B_1 or Thiamin: Husk/bran and germ of whole grains, yeast, pork, ham, tuna, beans, legumes, nuts, and sunflower seeds.

  Vitamin B_2 or Riboflavin: Liver, dried yeast, milk, cottage cheese, curds, yogurt, egg, fish, turkey, chicken, beef, ham, and almonds.

  Vitamin B_3 or Niacin: Beef, liver, chicken, tuna fish, halibut, cod, mushrooms, and sunflower seeds.

  Vitamin B_5 or Pantothenic Acid: Beef liver, mushrooms, sunflower seeds, dairy products, fish, eggs, whole grains, potatoes, tomatoes, broccoli, and coffee.

  Vitamin B_6 or Pyridoxine: Liver of beef and chicken, tuna, turkey, beef, pork, chick peas, halibut fish, herring fish, turkey, chicken, meat, tomato, potato, bananas, sesame seeds, and sunflower seeds.

Vitamin B_7 or Biotin: Cooked eggs, liver of all animals, fish, eggyolk, cheese, soybean, peanut, cauliflower, and whole grains.

Vitamin B_{12} or Cyanocobalamin: Liver of beef and chicken, tuna, turkey, beef, pork, and chick peas.

Vitamin C or Ascorbic Acid: *Amla*, goose berry, guava, cashew nut, lime, orange, sweet lime, strawberry, raspberry, papaya, pineapple, drumstick leaves, amaranth, cabbage, raddish leaves, capsicum, and bitter gourd.

- **Mineral-rich Foods:**

Calcium: Milk, cheese, curds, *lassi*, *khoya*, broccoli, chard, and colocasia leaves.

Phosphorous: Dairy products, meat, poultry, seafood, and nuts.

Sodium: Salt, processed food, seafood, milk, meat, green leafy vegetables, lotus stem, litchi, and musk melon.

Chloride: Salt, processed food, meat, milk, and eggs.

Potassium: Unprocessed fruits, vegetables, milk, and certain grains.

Iron: Meat, fish, seafood, poultry, green leafy vegetables, bengal gram leaves, mustard leaves, and radish leaves.

Iodine: Iodized salt and seafood.

Nowadays, the food has also been classified on the basis of functions it performs in the body. In this respect, the foods are classified as:

- **Body-building foods:** Foods rich in protein play a crucial role in this function of food.
- **Regulatory foods:** Vitamins, minerals, phyto-chemicals, fibres all act as regulatory food. Example – *Bael*, pineapple, cabbage, lotus stem, green leafy vegetables, beans, and legumes.
- **Protective foods:** Citrus fruits, vegetables, orange, red and purple coloured vegetables.
- **Energy giving foods:** Carbohydrates, protein, and fats all provide energy to the body for performing various activities.

Culinary Trivia: Food Eaten According to the Four Seasons

In ancient India, it was believed that food to be eaten should be chosen according to the four main seasons of the country, particularly in the areas where seasonal variations in the climate are extreme, e.g., North India. Even now, foods are chosen on the basis of ancient Hindu food beliefs.

During spring: Heavy and cold foods are avoided in this season and pungent foods are preferred. During *Vasant Ritu*, i.e., mid-March to mid-May, heavy, sour, oily and sweet foods are to be avoided. In the past barley, wheat, flesh of stag and hare, quails and partridges and a certain kind of liquor were advised.

During summer: Ancient Indian doctors like *Sushrutha* and *Charaka* suggested that cold and sweet foods should be the choice of the people because the strength and digestive fire are weak during summer period. With the advent of *Grishma*, i.e., mid-May to mid-July, cold, oily and fluid foods such cold preparations of barley with milk and sugar, milk itself, rice, ghee and deer meat were the proper foods in the past. Salty, sour and pungent foods were taboo. Liquor was also to be avoided.

During the monsoon season: *Varsha* and *Sharad Ritu*, i.e., mid-July to mid September call for hot foods in the conceptual sense because the digestive system is considered to be weak during this season. In *Varsha Ritu*, strong meat was banned. Venison with a boiled sauce, barley, wheat and old rice were taken.

Liquor diluted with water and honey was recommended. Autumn is a time to avoid ghee and other fats. Bitter foods are preferred. 'Eat moderately' should be the motto in these months.

During winter: Hot foods are considered to be the best. Dry fruits (coconut, almonds, peanuts, sesame and cashew nuts) based delicacies and sweets rich in fat are available all over the northern Indian markets in the winter and are liberally consumed. It is believed that strength and the digestive fire are strongest in the winter. During *Hemantha* and *Shishira*, i.e., from mid November to mid-March, man's strength is at its peak. He can also digest sour and salty meats, birds and fowls, new rice, milk preparations and sweets like rich *halwas*, *ladoos*, *pinnies* and a variety of *chikkies*.

In fact, no diet was specified for a strict vegetarian.

3 Impact of Religion on Indian Cuisine

"Food has no religion but each religion has its distinct food" – Yogesh Singh

Hinduism

According to Hinduism food is certainly a gift of Lord Brahma to humanity, the creator (*annam parabrahma swaroopam*). Being a gift from the God, it should be treated with great respect and reverence. The gross physical body is called *annamayakosh* or the food body, because it (the body) is nourished by food and grows by engrossing the energies from the food. Puritan Hindus offer food to the God mentally before eating.

Hinduism emphasizes its followers to be more careful and cautious about the food to be consumed, because what people eat decides their physical well-being as well as their mental makeup. It believes in the fact that men are what they eat. Eating very egregious foods like animal meat and heavy or intoxicating food, may lead to the strengthening of animal instincts and lethargy. This is one reason why Hindus do not prefer to eat non- vegetarian food and remain vegetarian. Another reason of being attached to the vegetarian nature is that they are of the belief that killing innocent and helpless animals for the purpose of filling one's stomach is a bad *karma* (bad task) with harmful consequences.

Apart from consuming non-vegetarian food, orthodox Hindus also avoid eating spicy food, onions, garlic, mushrooms, intoxicating juices, very sour food, and some bulbs and tubers.

It is not that all Hindus avoid eating meat. A large sect of Hindus prefers to consume it. In ancient India, even the brahmins were said to have eaten certain types of sacrificial meat. Hindu law books do not prohibit the eating of meat, in general, but only definite types of meat are inhibited.

Food is attached with moral values and is associated with many religious activities too. Food is constantly offered to the God during the very start of the most of the religious ceremonies. On specific days in a year, food is offered to departed souls. Food is also distributed to people at the end of many religious ceremonies. Many Hindu temples distribute food freely, every day, to the visiting devotees. Hindus believe that serving food to the poor and the needy or to a begging mendicant is a very good *karma*.

The main foods eaten by migratory dwellers included fruits, meat, and fish. They also picked wild berries as part of their diet.

The earliest Indians (called the Harappans) dined on meals that primarily consisted of wheat, lentils, and rice. Sometimes, they relied on the meat of chickens, goats, sheep, cows, and pigs.

Early Indians would take some of their wheat and transform it into soups and stews. They also made flat breads with it (called *chapatis*).

Rice, wheat, barley and barbecued animals flavoured with spices and fruits formed the basis of the cuisine of rich Indians in the past. Then, as today, it is rice which formed the basis of most meals. The type of rice determined depended on how it was to be prepared. Short-grained rice was pounded into flour and then used to make the pancakes known as chapatis which are still a very important part of the Indian cuisine. Long-grained rice was generally mixed with vegetable broth to form a kind of gruel (porridge). Medium-grained rice was the most commonly used as the basis for meals. Indian households reverberated to the sound of regular beating of mortar and pestle as rice was separated from its husks, before being sorted and then rinsed. It was then cooked in water, brought to boil. This rice could be a meal in itself, and often was for the poorer people who would be grateful enough for it. Alternatively, it could be served flavoured with ghee or mango juice or *garam masala* or other spices.

Rice was agglomerated on a plate and cooled with fans so that people could eat when they were ready. The most common side dish served with rice was the kind of curds that are served today in northern India and elsewhere. Beans, barley and wheat were other staples which were used to create basic dishes, flavoured with the three base spices, to accompany the rice. The presence of meat varied depending on religious belief and caste. The Kshatriya caste was, in general terms, the only caste rich enough to be able to have meat on a regular basis and they had never forbidden it. The animals and fish could be prepared in various ways: those of a substantial size could be roasted on a spit, basted with ghee and marinated with spices, while others might be boiled with fruit or bitter herbs, tamarind or sorrel. Milk-giving animals (cow and buffalo) were generally not killed, although exceptions were made for gazelles. The fear of lack of food remained constant and hence there was very little waste. Spices formed an appetizer between dishes and these also provoked and aggravated thirst.

The purpose of all cooking of course is to convert potentially edible material into a palatable form that is *Ahara*. In the Hindu spirit, it is an essential requirement that food should be both auspicious and ritually pure for those who would eat it.

It is clearly stated in vedic references that a balanced meal should include almost 50% food in its raw form. This is the reason why the salads of raw leafy vegetables, sprouts, roots, fruits and nuts, *chutneys* made out of fresh greens along with dry fruits, nuts and seeds, and the pickles, made of vegetables and fruits are relished and enjoyed by all the religious groups and communities on all occasions. In fact, Indian pickles are considered a kind of preserves. Since the olden times up to this 20th century, many pickles or *chutneys* have still been made without fire. Vegetables or fruits are mixed with spices and oils are kept under the sun for a few days till they are ready for consumption.

Moreover, this fact cannot be ignored that in ancient times, *rishis* and *munis*, meditating in the deep woods and forests, used to survive on this natural food, cooked without fire. They used to enjoy an excellent health and lived much longer. Food cooked without fire or assembled in certain ways is still being used in India as one of the natural cures, as a medicine for many diseases since time immemorial. But this kind of treatment is generally given for a specific period. After recovering from illness, the patients start taking cooked food with fire too, but only in a certain proportions.

Hinduism advocated the medicinal system of approach, *Ayurveda*, and tried to inculcate its philosophy in it with genuine sincerity.

Buddhism and Jainism

• Buddhism

Buddhism and Jainism are the two important religions shaping themselves from the Hindu connection of the vedic period. Therefore, the basic structure of food did not change as compared to that of Hinduism.

Buddhism spread the philosophy of vegetarianism in India and hence the influence of vegetarianism flourished all over. Buddhism as compared to Jainism is very practical in its approach to consumption of food. For the ardent followers of Jainism, restrictions of food are far more severe than those of the orthodox Hindus. Eastern India, Bengal and Assam felt the breath of Aryanism much later than the rest of the country, perhaps only after the spread of Buddhism.

The early literature of the Buddhists and Jains mentions the food practices and concepts of the followers of Buddha and Mahavira, in detail.

Staple diet during that period was **rice**, either boiled, or cooked with sesame seeds, or made into gruel, or even cooked as a sweet dish. Pulses used at that time were peas, *arhar*, *chana*, *mung* and *urad*, etc. Pulses were eaten as soup (*supa*), *vadas* (*vatakas*) and *papads* (*parpatas*). Milk and milk products were used freely. Many sophisticated sweets like *mondaka*, *madhusarika*, *moreandaka* and *ghratpura* were made. *Payasa* (*kheer*) was the most popular one. Vegetables like lotus stem, cucumber, bitter gourds, water chestnuts, gourds, fenugreek, yams, spinach, ginger and radish were used. Fruits like mango, Indian fig, *jamun*, bananas, jackfruit, grapes, *phalsas*, *karonda*, citrus fruits and coconut also find mention. Spices were used and salt was a rarity. Honey was replaced by jaggery and sugar. Even brassica leaves were used as a tasty relish. Mustard seeds were used as a spice and as a powerful agent to ward off evil spirits. Sesame and safflower seeds are mentioned as sources of oil in early Buddhist literature.

Buddha allowed his followers to consume animal flesh on occasions when the killing had been unintentional and not deliberate. Consumption of this meat was permitted when the monks were sick. However, the meat eaten had to be 'blameless' in three ways: the killing should not have been seen or heard, or suspected by the monk *cadrastam*, *asrutam*, *aparivirtakam*. It was the responsibility of the person giving the food as donations to ensure this.

Few popular dishes of the Buddhist era were the following:

- *Tilaudana*: *Til* cooked with rice.
- *Krasara*: Rice cooked with milk.
- *Ladduka*: *Laddoos* made with *til* and jaggery syrup.
- *Shaskuli*: Todays *tilkut*, sesame seeds powder compounded with coarse rice flour and jaggery.

Sesame was used in various forms. It was used as a seed and these seeds were cooked with vegetables.

Rice was used to make sweets. It was also roasted, pounded and mixed with vegetables to be rolled as *parpatas* (*papads*).

In fact, with them arrived the different methods of cooking – concepts of using new Indian ingredients and also new ways to combine many fruits and dry fruits with milk, milk products, cereals, pulses and meats to prepare unique delicacies.

It was suggested to all Buddhist monks that they should consume solid foods only between the period of sunrise and noon. They were advised not to eat anything between noon and sunrise. This would suppress their passions and would help them to gain and achieve spiritual strength. When it came to beverages, eight drinks were allowed to Buddhists and they were the juices of the ripe mango, *jamun*, banana, grape, edible water-lily, coconut, *phalsa* and diluted honey. These juices could be consumed after the last (noon) meal of the day. Pure rainwater was recommended for drinking. The beverages that accompanied the meal were cold or warm water, whey, buttermilk, or fermented sour rice gruel (*kanjika*). At the end of the meal, betel leaves with fragrant spices were served with the purpose to help digestion and also make the mouth fragrant.

• Jainism

The practices were very obstinate and rigid in Jainism and hence eating meat was strictly prohibited. They could not even think of eating meat. The prohibited list included not only 22 eatables but 32 things which are religiously restricted as they were believed to have uncountable life germs in them, e.g., underground roots or tubers or pickles (more than three days old). Fruit beverages were however allowed.

The guidelines related to food in Jainism were strictly confined to the principle of asvoiding injury to life. It was suggested to everyone not to eat after dark (*aratri-bhojana*), preferably, all round the year, but it was mandatory during the four monsoon months when insects bred and propagated.

Even the pulses that split into two parts were not permitted to be consumed. Brinjals, any fruit (such as the five kinds of figs) with abundant small seeds, green turmeric, ginger, carrots, the tender green leaves of any vegetables, and tender tamarind fruit before the seeds had formed were not allowed.

Honey was also banned, because when it is extracted from the comb it leads and connotes the death of bees, and therefore consumption of honey would destroy self-generated creatures originating from it.

It is stated that water has to be boiled, and re-boiled every six hours mandatorily. All liquids have to be strained before drinking, be it water, fruit juice or milk. During the occasions of various fasts, certain permitted foods are also restricted which may include milk, curds, ghee, salt, oil and sweetmeats. It would sound strange but Jain monks are not allowed to eat a permitted fruit if it has fallen from the tree, or fruit that is kept for sale in shelves in shop.

Judaism

Jews are among the ancient and oldest of the many people acknowledged in history. Their origin dates back to at least 3000 years, and perhaps even further back.

During this relatively prolonged period, Jews have colonized in all parts of the world and have had an impact on many civilizations. The Jewish religion, Judaism, has made great efforts to influence not only its own adherents but far beyond it, and Islam accepted many of the traditions, doctrines, principles and practices of Judaism. By and large, Jews in India pursue the dietary laws set out in the legal document *Old Testament*.

Certain things are followed by them all across the world:

- The prohibition on eating of pork
- Slaughtering the animal by the jugular vein (a blood vessels that carries blood from the capillaries towards the heart).
- They are not supposed to eat the shell fish or seafood as they do not have scales. Orthodox Jews mostly do not consume meat at the same time when dairy products are also consumed.
- They use separate utensils and vessels for preparing food of different nature and characteristics.

The history of Jews in India has been of extremely chequered in the ancient times. India has been abode to Jews, for many centuries. The three major groups of Jews found in India are the Cochin Jews, the Bene Israel and the Baghdadi Jews.

The Cochin Jews have settled in India for not less than a millennium in Cochin, a port city in Kerala. They were educated, prosperous and sophisticated clusters who were connected with trade, mostly of spices.

Kerala has always been a spice abundant state and hence the Cochin Jews had extraordinarily great pungent spicing in their cuisine. The 3 c's — cardamom, cinnamon and cumin — along with coconut oil found in plentitude have found a special place in Jewish cuisine. A very popular snack among them is *bonda*, which is a fritter coated with chickpea flour and then fried. It is prepard in both savoury and sweet varieties. In Cochin, a different version is made with coconut and raisins replacing potato in *bonda*.

When British rule commenced in the 19th century, the Baghdadi Jews inhabited Bombay (currently Mumbai) and then Calcutta (currently Kolkata). They made tremendous wealth due to huge economic avenues and this abundant wealth is reflected in their food. Baghdadis have developed an outstanding cuisine using local spices and ingredients. They have a special liking for *pulaos* and *biryanis*. *Aloo makalla* is a potato dish, which is the most famous Jewish dish in India. This delicacy depicts a combination of Arabic and Indian cooking patterns in which whole potatoes are simmered for long in hot oil. It is served with fenugreek *chutney*, spicy chicken, curried vegetables and other rice dishes. *Machboz* is a pastry preparation stuffed with dates, walnut and cheese. They use sesame and nuts in their cuisine, which reflects and speaks about Middle Eastern influence.

The Bene Israel group is the largest and influential group of Jews in India. *Gulab jamun* which is milk based dumplings soaked in sugar syrup is popular among them during *Hanukkah*. The group often ends its Yom Kipper fast with *padhar*, a coconut filled crepe. *Purim* is associated with *malpua*, a sweet pancake made with bananas, pineapple and other fruits and served with syrup. *Laddoo* is a small ball-shaped snack made up of flour and sugar which is also common among the Bene Israeli ceremonial rite known as *Malida*. At the centre of the ceremony is a dessert called *malida*, which is made of pressed rice flakes called *poha*, which is often intensified in quality by addition of ingredients like coconut, cardamom, almond and pistachios. *Malida* is displayed on a round platter that has fresh fruits and flowers. In addition, goat, chicken or lamb meat may accompany the *malida*, symbolizing a temple offering.

Christianity

Christianity is the most widely scattered religion of the world and it has significant representation in all the populated continents of the globe and India is no exception to it.

Christianity is the religion which emerged out of Judaism (Jewish religion).

The Christians in India are of two types:

- Syrian Christians of Kerala who were spiritually reborn by the Apostle of St. Thomas.
- Catholics who came to Kerala and Goa due to Portuguese exploitation.

Syrian Christians are prejudiced with certain prohibitions regarding food, but, over a period of time, have developed some preferences for local food available.

The fusion and unification of Portuguese cuisine with the crude raw material of Goa created undoubtedly, a distinctive and more of a regional Goan cuisine. This is how the Goan cuisine has been characterized.

Portuguese Christians in Bengal not only influenced and but also dominated the preparation of "sweets" culture in a very noticeable manner. In Pondicherry, it was only due to French influence for 400 years that a variety of breads, pork-based sausages, pates, stews, fried meat balls, steamed fish served with mayonnaise, fish croquettes and many desserts became popular.

The creative influence of the Christians introduced the native Indians to versatile techniques of cooking meat and fish. Indian food now has incorporated many local ingredients and cooking techniques from European influences. Indian cuisine now mirrors European customs and traditions, and its items such as rum-flavoured cake or sandwiches describes the authentic and traditional culinary practices of the Christians. The Christians never had any inhibitions on the type of meat for consumption.

It is only because of influence of the Christians that the Indian food habit tends to incorporate various new kinds of tastes and delicacies. In fact, the Indian cuisine has been benefited and enriched by their cuisine. In years to come, the food that was a consequence of Christian influence on Indian cuisine became popular as Anglo-Indian cuisine. The Britishers incorporated many novel food delicacies to Indian meal such as soups and salads. The Christian influence on Indian food has been rather very huge and creatively good. Indian food has witnessed and experienced a notable and appreciable change by the time the English left India. The eating habits in the dining hall have also seen changes due to influence of eating habits of the Christians. Dining table came into use and entered India in place of kitchen floor. Porcelain dishes replaced the banana leaf as the utensil used to dine. Kitchen utensils were modernized. Indian cooks collected information about many Christian dishes such as cutlets, croquettes, sausages, cakes, pudding, jams and biscuits and started working on it. Indian beverages were also not left out, but these also experienced a change with the coming of the Christians.

The Syrian Arab Christians came to India and took shelter in Kerala. They too created a rather visible impact in the sector of Indian cuisine, which goes a long way in describing the prevalence of non-vegetarian food in typical Kerala dishes. Syrian Christian dishes are undoubtedly rich flavoured. Foods such as fish, seafood, duck, lamb and chicken dishes are among the delicacies produced in this region.

The typical culinary art of the Syrian Christians is referred to as Kerala Syrian Christian cuisine. This cuisine is known for offering few delectable meat preparations such as lamb stew and *piralen*, a stir-fried meat which is marinated in the marinade of vinegar and spices. The most favoured dish of Kerala Syrian Christian (or Saint Thomas Christian) is the stew which is made by bringing chicken and potato to a slow boil in a creamy white sauce seasoned with black pepper, cinnamon, clove, green chillies, lime juice, shallots and coconut milk. This appetizing stew can be made with chicken, lamb or duck.

Few noted delicacies of Kerala Syrian Christian cuisine include fiery *vindaloos*, *meat thoran*, dry curry prepared with shredded coconut, sardines and duck curries, and *meen moilee* which is a spicy stewed fish. This stew is generally consumed with *appam*, which are rice flour pancakes with soft, thick white spongy centres and thin, golden, crisp lace-like edges. Other well-known preparation of this community is beef cutlet with *sallas* (a salad made of finely cut onions, green chillies and vinegar) and *peera pattichathu* (a dry fish delicacy with grated coconut). *Meen mulakittathu* or *meen vevichathu* (fish in spicy red chilli sauce) is another preferred item. Wine is an essential part of Syrian Christian cuisine.

Another interesting feature of the cuisine is the liberal use of coconut oil, mustard seeds, curry leaves and coconut milk in their preparation.

Islam

In North India, many merchants and invaders came around AD 998. By the 10th century, the Turkish Muslims began aggressively attacking and capturing India and bringing the Islam to India along with them. The Ghaznavis, an influential dynasty from eastern Afghanistan, began a series of raids into northwestern India at the end of the 10th century.

Succeeding them, the Mughal dynasty was established by the Afghan Babar which rose to glory and prominence during Emperor Akbar and they ruled the country for two centuries. This had an intense and fundamental impact on Indian cuisine.

Dietary laws and commands are derived both from *Quran* and *Sunnah*, which are the recorded words of Prophet Mohammad.

It makes very clear in its description that the animal to be consumed had to be killed by *halal*. In spite of this, swine meat was strictly restricted and alcohol was a complete no-no, but seafood was allowed. The Muslims were of the belief that precaution should be taken not to waste the food, even left-overs were eaten (contradicting the Hindus who use to throw the left-over food, away for birds and animals) and the necessity to share food with others. They emphasized and introduced community eating.

The holy book, *Quran* has made special recommendation for commodities like dates, figs, honey, olives, milk and milk products. The Mughlai cuisine has added a new dimension to the Indian cuisine by adding a diverse variety of delicacies like *pulaos*, *biryani*, *soolas*, *haleem*, a variety of *kebabs*, *tikkas*, *naans*, *sherbets*, *phirni* and *seviyan*. The Muslims relished the dishes prepared by fish, like their Hindu counterparts and this was a matter of similarity with Hinduism.

The Muslims were good in preparation of sweets like *kheer*, *laddu*, *jalebi*, *halwas*, *burfi*, *sohan halwa*, *raitas*, *chutneys*, *morabbas* and *pickles*. These delectable delicacies constituted the integral part of their main diet. The historical etiquette and food habits of the mainstream, recognized throughout by all were the salient features which added charm to their cuisine.

The two historians of the Sultanate period were (AD 1253 - 1325) Amir Khusro and Ibn-e-Battuta (AD 1325 to 1354). The Mughal period was very well recorded and documented by the emperors themselves. Emperors, Babar and Jahangir were fantastically superb in writing their diaries. Emperor Akbar was uneducated and hence his affairs were minutely chronicled by his court historian Abul Fazal in the document *Ain-i-Akbari* and *Akbarnama*. The Muslims influenced largely the style and materialistic approach of Indian food. The Hindu dining ambience was hugely based on the principles of austerity but the Muslims ornamented the Indian cuisine by bringing a much refined and courtly etiquette and sophisticated mannerism. Eating was done by hand. Spoons and knives were used for service and for carving.

The best part of Islamic rule in Indian cuisine was that the Indian cuisine was introduced to rich gravies, *pilafs* and non-vegetarian fare such as *kebabs*, as well as fruits such as apricots, melons, peaches, and plums.

The Mughals were great patrons of cooking. Extravagant and lavish dishes were prepared during the reigns of Jahangir and Shah Jahan. The Nizams of Hyderabad were no behind than any other Mughal ruler and they meanwhile developed and perfected their own style of cooking. The most notable dish was *biryani*. *Biryani* is considered by many connoisseurs and food experts to be the finest of the main dishes in India.

Sir Thomas Roe, a British ambassador to the court of Emperor Jahangir, noted that the Mughal nobles kept luxurious dining tables decorated with about twenty to fifty dishes.

The Arabian travellers were enthusiastic chroniclers and acute observers. Many other Arabians also left their impressions through their writings. Later on Europeans and Italians also started visiting India during the Mughal period. They have made observation about Indian crops, fruits, vegetables, pulses and cereals, spices, availability of seafood and a variety of meats, plentitude of milk and milk products, and the food habits of common people of India and the ruling class. Their writing details are so vivid that an apparent visualization of India's yester-years is sketched well. India has always been overflowing with a plenty of food commodities and ingredients and this factor always attracted people worldwide. Exotic and great dishes have been prepared in India right from the beginning, that is why, those who stayed in India were left with no option but to get mesmerized by the Indian food.

Zoroastrianism

Parsis or Parsees are the ardent and staunch followers of the ancient Persian religion known as Zoroastrianism. They were the inhabitants of India, Iran and Pakistan. Their ancestors fled Persia (Iran) in the 7th and 8th centuries to avoid inhuman sufferings by Muslim invaders and came to India from Iran – first near Gujarat and then in the entire mainland.

Parsis also had certain food restrictions but they voluntarily adopted some Hindu customs and traditions. They accepted the principle of prohibiting beef consumption. Their dishes themselves are a huge reflection of both Iranian ancestry in its strong non-vegetarian components and local vegetarian Gujarati cuisine.

Iranian influence can be easily visualized and felt by the wide and varied use of nuts, raisins, and *sultanas*, whereas the Gujarati impact of *chutneys*, *morabbas* and snacks can be apparently seen in the Parsi cuisine.

Parsi dishes are adorned and characterized by the preparations like sweet fried noodles called *sev*, *falooda* drinks, and barbecued mutton called *shoojan*, different kinds of *pulaos*, *dhansak*, baked fish in banana leaf packet, eggs cooked with different ingredients like potatoes, tomatoes, almonds, raisins, and cream and butter. Each dish has its own individuality and taste.

Like Gujaratis, Parsis also consider coconut with a dab of vermillion as an auspicious item and use its tender pulp in cooking.

Sikhism

Sikhism is a major religion of India founded by Guru Nanak in the 15th century. Like Buddhism and Jainism, Sikhism (500 years ago) has also been shaped from the Hindu connection of the vedic period and is based on the principle of indigenous faith. Punjab is the historic main homeland of Sikhism, but it has also extended to other parts of northern India. A significant diaspora exists in Europe and North America.

Therefore, when it comes to food principles, Sikhs have all the features in similarity with the Hindu distinctive spirit. Their holy book *Guru Granth Sahib* was compiled by the fifth and the tenth guru, Guru Arjun Dev and Guru Gobind Singh respectively (this is a collection of writings by twenty authors who spanned six centuries, with those of six Gurus forming the bulk). Nowhere in this holy compilation had the gurus described and pointed out any dietary law and command, though many have emerged in practice. The *khalsa* tradition is embodied in the *Rahatnamas* or codes of conduct complied by several contemporaries of Guru Govind Singh. In practice, alcohol is strictly forbidden and so is beef, but not pork. It is suggested to refrain from the use and consumption of tobacco in any form. Slaughtering of animal to be consumed is performed by *jhatka*. It is clearly stated for the Sikhs, that the meat of an animal killed by ritual is totally banned for them, as saying prayers over the slaughtering of an animal does not make the meat pure and it also states that it would be dangerous to eat any meat bought from a shop where the history of the slaughtering is unknown. It is also recommended for the Sikhs, that they should consume only healthy food and drinks that are nutritious and good for the body and that causes no harm to the body. At any happy or sad occasion Kaval Prasad (a special wheat *halwa*) is prepared, which is served to all attending the ceremony as a *prasad*, followed by Langar (people of all religions sit together on the floor in rows and a meal is served). Sikhs eat meat of lamb and call it *mahaprasad.*

They enjoy and relish poultry and seafood too.

• Invasions by Europeans

The eating habits and the eating patterns of Indians have been largely influenced by the Europeans. Earlier in India, the main meal used to be in the afternoons but later on, mid-day meals became lighter and the main meal shifted, to seven or eight in the evening. This has been described by Mrs. Fay in the 18th century.

There was a shift of emphasis from quantity to quality. The kind and variety of food served had also clearly altered. With the arrival of British memsahibs, the distinctive feature shifted to English style soups, roasts, baked pies and puddings. Since Indian ambience could not be avoided and as a result, a myriad of complex dishes were raised up between the English lady and her Indian cook. Windsor soup, *patna* rice, broth of *dal, burdwan* stew, *kebabs,* fish *moilee,* curry *chutney* and *byculla* soufflé, are a few examples of such great combinations. From *toddy* and distilled *arrack,* punch emerged and became a popular drink.

Keeping aside the food items, few unique Anglo-Indian terms rose to prominence in the sector of food and became an inseparable feature of Indian food terminology, e.g., punch, *toddy,* peg, rice *canjee, kedgeree,* rice cakes, *mullugatwany* soup, *dumpukht,* curry, *moilee* and a tiffin.

In this context, the word tiffin which originally meant Anglo Indian luncheon became a late afternoon snack meal of South India, especially, when dinner became a heavy evening meal, light snack lunch (tiffin) became accustomed.

Culinary Trivia: Eating Rituals and Ceremonies

In olden days in India, food was never to be eaten standing up, lying down, moving about or from plates on the lap. In ancient India, food was taken in the following manner:

- One had to eat sitting on the ground, alone, facing East or North, in total silence.
- Morsels (small quantity) of the meal were to be cast into the fire as an oblation and prayers offered to various deities and one's ancestors.
- Portions of food were reserved for brahmins, serpents, dogs and insects and laid outside for crows, who were believed to be messengers to the world of the departed spirits.
- Prior to eating, a few drops of water would be sprinkled on the leaf for purity, and, on the rice that had been served, a few drops of ghee. Every item placed on the leaf had its exact position and ritual eating order. Drinks and *bhakshyas* (chewed items, like rotis) were placed on the left of the plate, rice in the middle, and greens and vegetables were placed below. Sweet items were served first, then sour and salty foods, and finally bitter, pungent and astringent items. Today, these practices have become region specific.
- Only the right hand was supposed to be used for eating, reserving the left for other functions outside eating.

4 Catering Trends in India

"Food is your body's fuel. Without fuel, your body wants to shut down." – Ken Hill

Every region, every territorial division, every state and every country has its own culinary pattern and style defined by distinctive eating trends. Similarly, their catering trends are also altogether varied and different. India is no exception. India has depicted its catering trends based on people's preferences which keep on changing with the passage of time, with accumulation of sufficient money and newer lifestyles as well. The catering trends in India have developed over a period of time and have got refined as compared to earlier periods. Here, eating at the roadside is a fun fare. Eating in a *dhaba* is a different experience altogether, whereas those dining in five-star hotels have a different sense of sophistication.

The various catering trends are versatile and are presented below:

Roadside Food

The concept of roadside food is very old in India. It has its own specialities, features and charm. It is often a one-man show, where the seller himself is generally the cook too. He prepares a few snacks or specializes only in one item and sells whatever he prepares. Mostly, he stations himself on a particular place and buyers start recognizing him for the quality of his preparation. The buyers approach him during his time of operation and do the purchasing for consuming the delicacies prepared by him. Generally, the diners come with the intention to consume the item in the shop, but nowadays, they are gifted with the privilege to get the food packed by the seller and take it to their homes for consumption at their own convenience.

The highlights of this kind of food are:

- Roadside food sellers generally prepare snacks and the choice is limited and not varied.
- Since the seller is on the roadsides, no rent has to be paid for the shop, and so the food is of low cost, hence affordable.
- Roadside snacks differ from state to state and are relished with great vigour, e.g., *wada pav, batata wada* or *bhajias* in Maharashtra; *bread pakoda, chole bhature, fried fish, sheek kebabs, chaat, kulfi,* ice cream and a variety of *pakodas* in North India; *medu wada, idli* and *dosa chutney* in South India.
- This kind of food is handed over, generally on a piece of paper or at the most, in a paper plate.
- Mostly, the sellers of roadside food stations themselves near the bus stops, railway stations, parks, schools or colleges, cinema houses, residential areas, and markets.

Dhaba Food

Speaking without exaggeration, a *Dhaba* means an eating house located near the edge of the road. It is a kind of fast food joint located along side highways to cater to the needs of travellers. The concept of *dhaba* was born out of necessity. It originated in the northern parts of India, when vehicular movement and transportation of items by road facilitated long-distance travel.

A *dhaba* then meant a small shack (small crude shelter) serving as a kitchen, located invariably near a fresh-water well or river, and a few camp-cots arranged randomly under large shady trees where the travellers could break their journey, rest for a while, satisfy their appetites and restore their energies for the onward grind. It was supposed to be, and was, a simple fare. There was nothing pompous about it like the modern-day motel. It served only the basic needs and that too, at an affordable price, a *dal, subzi* and roti, to be washed down with, naturally, cold water from a nearby well or river.

Though there is no dearth of real-sense *dhabas* all over the country, yet in recent times the concept of *dhaba* is experiencing a paradigm shift. It has now attracted entrepreneurs, leading to a large number of *dhabas* springing up in the cities, aided by modern technological developments. These stylized *dhabas* are now a part of big hotel chains, and vast amounts of money are spent in their design and decoration. However, to keep the essence of a 'real' *dhaba* layout, an urban *dhaba* is manual in operations and rich like ornate eateries. Needless to say, the prices charged in such eating places makes it expensive and out of reach of the commoners. In the current scenario, the one with a substantial amount of money in his pocket and looking for a variety, can frequent such *dhabas*.

Notwithstanding, there are some rudimentary differences between restaurants and *dhabas* notwithstanding their location:

- A *dhaba* always has an open visible kitchen unlike the restaurants, where the cooking is always done behind closed doors and out of sight of the customers. Only live kitchen restaurants are an exception.
- A restaurant has an arrangement of tables and cushioned chairs whereas the visitors to a *dhaba* are made to use cots for informal sitting and eating. But now luxurious *dhabas* also have laid-out seating arrangements.
- Unlike restaurants, the food in *dhabas* is served without cutlery. Only serving spoons are provided, to encourage the actual eating with hands (which can really be a great pleasure).
- Decor and ambience of the *dhaba* is deliberately kept simple. In a poorman's *dhaba*, it happens automatically (to keep the establishment costs to the minimum possible), but in made-up *dhabas*, all care is taken to duplicate the natural ambience of roadside *dhabas*, even if that demands heavy expenditure.
- Real *dhabas* serve only the essential fare. Even in the made-up *dhabas*, the menu is not complicated. Whereas, restaurants have a very elaborate menu depending upon the clientele and locality.

Five-Star Hotel Food

Along with certain available options of eateries like roadside *dhabas*, fast food and the restaurant food, the concept of the five-star food, too, has created a niche for itself in India. Even though this concept is comparatively new, it is not new to the sophisticated society. Presently, even the upper middle class people have started availing the services of five-star hotels in India. Since the food in five-star hotels is very expensive, it is affordable only to the well-to-do people of the society, the employees of bigger organizations/multinational companies, the businessmen, the corporate class, the bureaucrats, and the foreigners.

The facts about five-star foods in India are listed below:

- The food in five-star hotels is prepared by the professionals graduating from the catering colleges and such other training institutes. Therefore, right from the cutting of vegetables/meats, preparation of dishes, their appearance, taste and presentation, all is taken care of by the professionals employed by the hotel industry.
- The food here is more innovative in quality since it is cooked on order (a la carte).
- The food is supposed to be more hygienic. Nowadays HACCP (Hazard Analysis Critical Control Point) has taken care of these aspects in almost all classified star hotels.
- Here the food is served in a pleasant and decent atmosphere, especially created for the client.
- The food is served in several courses, with all etiquettes and mannerisms in the finest of crockery and cutlery. This is the reason why the bigger organizations hold their seminars and conferences in five-star hotels. The wealthy hold their private parties, kitty parties, wedding functions and other social gatherings in these hotels to get the five-star services.
- It is basically, the comfort, the service, the atmosphere, the elegance, the glamour, the class, the status, and the style which attract the people to the five-stars hotels.

Fast Food

The concept of fast food originated in America, and gradually it spread out all across the world. With the origin of fast food, the traditional ways of serving, eating, and enjoying the food has lost its sheen. Avenues have been opened for more informal and unconventional methods. After the industrial revolution all over the world, working culture is on the rise. Thus, people (irrespective of sex, caste and creed) are always on their toes and everyone is compelled to travel a lot. No individual is left with enough time to sit down, relax and eat. In fact, they are left with no option but to grab something which can be just rolled, assembled and handed over, so that they can enjoy it even when on the move and that satisfies their appetite as well. The main advantage of this style of catering is that by the time they finish off paying the bill for the food items, their choicest food is ready.

Since this culture has grabbed the entire world, it has become fashionable in India, too, to patronize such fast food joints which provide the snack food of one's choice. All kinds of food items right from the pizzas, rolls, burgers, frankies, and chicken and mutton preparations, are available in almost every nook and corner, every town in India.

Though the concept of fast food is recent, it is not that Indians are exposed to it recently. From the good old days to the modern era, Indians have always sold certain products which people used to buy and enjoy just passing by or standing on one side of the road. *Chaat, bhelpuri, chole kulche, chole bhature, sheekh kebab, kati kebabs,* fried fish, *kulfi, biryanis, vada pavs* and number of sweet items are examples of this concept.

Culinary Trivia: Custom of Eating with Hands

Indians love to eat with their hands because they find it convenient to mix various curries, vegetables, *papad,* pickles, *chutneys,* relishes and *dals* with rice. For hygiene purpose, they have strict rules about washing hands and mouth before and after meals. This rule is followed alike by the poorest villagers and the richest urbanites.

Though all Indians love to eat food with hands, yet the method of 'eating with hands' is not the same throughout India. Northerners use only their finger tips to eat their food and get upset when they see someone soiling more than the top section of his fingers with food. They are allowed to use their both hands. They use their left hand to hold roti or papad and right hand to eat. Southerners use their entire palm of the right hand, from finger tips to wrist, to eat the food, and left hand is reserved for baser functions outside the meal. Certain communities in South India are allowed to soil their hands up to the elbows. In Western India, people are allowed to use only right hand for eating, and like North Indians they use only finger tips. In East and West Bengal, people use their fingers to mix and palm to make rice balls and transport them from *thali* to mouth.

In short, as a thumb rule, Indians eat with their right hand and reserve left hand to drink water and serve themselves.

5 Festive Foods of India

> "Food, in the end, in our own tradition, is something holy. It's not about nutrients and calories. It's about sharing. It's about honesty. It's about identity." – Louise Fresco

India is undoubtedly a land of festivals and celebrations. Here festival is like a religion and each religion has its own distinctive festivals. India is one of the few countries in the world that can boast of people from different backgrounds and different religions living together and enjoying and celebrating festivals of each other with the same enthusiasm as they celebrate their own. Each festival speaks volumes about the gaiety, celebrations, happiness, brotherhood, companionship, about delicious delicacies and mouth-watering preparations associated with each festival.

A festival is a gala event ordinarily staged by a local community, which centres on and celebrates some unique aspect of that community and that is marked with a series of celebration, feasting and gaiety.

The varied religions provide India with a lot of unique festivals that are celebrated all year long. These festivals offer a great opportunity to people from different religions to enjoy the traditional delicacies that are cooked using the traditional recipes, which have been passed on from generation to generation.

Each and every festival brings with it the joy of the festival, jubilation of epicurean senses and hence of ceremonious food that is awaited all year long. Every festival in India has a different approach towards food and hence food is treated with varied trends and fashion in various festive occasions. Few festivals are about observing fasting attached with religious sentiments whereas a few festivals are all about eating and feasting all day long. For instance, the festival of Karwa Chauth is about staying hungry for the entire day from early morning till late night whereas the festival of Holi brings a huge opportunity to relish some of the best spicy as well as sweet food throughout the day. Our country gains its colorful profile with a celebration so vivid in different states, even though they have been bonded in a single mode of similarity. Thus, festivals are considered a single common platform to express happiness, break the monotonous journey of life, and make it more interesting by offering "wonderful tasty dishes in the platter of life".

Below are the distinguishing features of festivals with their special delicacies.

Baisakhi or Vaisakhi

It is simply the harvest festival of Northern India. This festival blesses people who express their gratitude to Mother Nature for ascertaining a good and desired crop in the ensuing season.

Baisakhi is commemorated on the first day of Vaisakh month as per the Nanakshahi (Sikh Calendar). According to English calendar, Baisakhi is observed on 13th or 14th April every year. Baisakhi festivity happens at the same coincidence with Rongali Bihu in Assam, Naba Barsha in Bengal, Puthandu in Tamil Nadu and Pooram Vishu in Kerala.

In Punjab and Haryana, Baisakhi embarks the beginning of the new year, for the entire farming community, as *rabi* crop is harvested during this time. On this auspicious day, farmers express their gratitude to God for the excellent crop and pray for booming and flourishing times ahead. The event is associated by the purchase of new clothes, singing, dancing and enjoying good food which comes under celebration.

On this occasion, the people of the Sikh community and Punjabis visit Gurudwara and extend prayers, to have a good harvest, year after year. At the end of the *ardas* (prayer meet), the followers are offered specially prepared *kara* prasad (sweet prepared with semolina). Then they proceed to a community lunch where all sit cross-legged on the floor in rows and are served food. The atmosphere is filled with gaiety and every kitchen in the northern states of India, especially Punjab, is filled with the aroma of authentic Punjabi recipes. People indulge themselves in preparing numerous delicious delicacies for the festival.

- **Delicacies Prepared During Baisakhi**

Choley bhature: *Choley bhature*, the mouth-watering and spicy recipe is a distinctive dish of Punjab. It is a combination of two preparations, i.e., *choley* (gravy preparation of chick peas) and *bhature* (fried leavened breads that resemble *puri*), which are mostly eaten together for breakfast or lunch, and is accompanied by *lassi*. The dish is served with onion rings and pickles.

Coconut ladoo: Coconut *ladoo* is a delicate sweet dish. It is a real joy for the taste buds of the people with an inclination towards sweet taste. Coconut *ladoos*, as the name indicates, are balls made out of coconut, which is combined with *suji* (semolina) and sugar.

Kheer: *Kheer* is an authentic Indian sweet dish, which is originally made by boiling rice in milk, sugar and it is also flavoured with cardamom, and saffron. Dry fruits are also added in excess as a garnish in this rice preparation.

Makki ki roti: *Makki ki roti* is the most loved dish of Punjab. The roti is made of corn flour served straight off the griddle and is topped with fresh dollops of homemade butter. *Makki ki roti* is compulsorily to be accompanied by *sarson da saag* — the twosome makes a grand and standard breakfast and is consumed also for lunch.

Sarson ka saag: In Punjab, *makki ki roti* and *sarson ka saag* is a great combination of corn bread with mustard green delicious vegetable. The duo makes a heavy breakfast as well as a sumptuous lunch. It is a special treat for the people living in the northern parts of India, where wheat is one of the staple foods. It has become so popular that it is the dish which comes to mind when Punjabi cuisine is talked about.

Pindi chana: *Pindi Chana*, the dry preparation of white chick pea (*kabuli channa*) is served with lemon juices and onion rings on it.

Puri: It is made of wheat flour dough flavoured with *ajwain*. It is a traditional fried Indian bread, served with a variety of side dishes, such as *aloo ki subzi* (potato curry), and *chole* (chick pea curry).

Til ka gajak: *Til ka gazak* is a sweet preparation prepared by sesame seed and sugar or jaggery. It is an indigenous dish that is relished on festivals like Baisakhi and Lohri.

Til ke ladoo: These are small round balls prepared using *til* (sesame) as the main ingredient, along with sugar or jaggery.

Pongal

Pongal, also known as Tamizhar Thirunal is undoubtedly the most important festival celebrated in South India. This festival declares the end of winter season and is around the time when the sun proceeds towards the north. The period is referred to as Uttarayan Punyakalam and is considered very auspicious.

This festival is celebrated during 12th-15th January, of which *Pongal* day is specifically on 14th January. It is celebrated across Tamil Nadu, Andhra Pradesh and Karnataka. The term *Pongal* is derived from the name of the dish *Pongal* which is cooked compulsorily on this day and offered to the Gods, thanking them for the harvest and their blessings. Each day has its own rituals and significance.

The first day is known as the Bhogi Pongal. On this occasion, abodes are cleaned, washed and beautifully ornamented. Doorways are adorned with garlands of leaves and flowers. Indra, the Rain God also known as Bhogi is worshipped on this festivity.

The second day is referred to as Surya Pongal or Perum Pongal on which people worship Surya, the Sun God. A bonfire is lighted in the evening and old goods are given to the fire, as a mark to burn all evils and hence it marks a new start. There is a very unique tradition of boiling fresh milk early morning and allowing it to boil and flow over the vessel as it is considered to bring happiness and prosperity to the family. It is celebrated by boiling rice with fresh milk and jaggery, in new pots, which are later topped with brown sugar, cashew nuts and raisins early in the morning and allowing it to boil over the vessel. This tradition gives *Pongal* its name. The very moment the rice boils over and bubbles out of the vessel, the tradition is to shout of "Ponggalo Ponggal!" collectively accompanied by blowing the *sangu* (a conch). It is a custom practised during the festival to announce that it is going to be a year blessed with a good bearing. Then, new boiled rice is offered to the Nature during sunrise, a gesture which symbolizes the expression of thanks to the Sun and Nature for providing prosperity. It is later served to the people present in the house for the ceremony. People also prepare savories and sweets such as *vadai, murukku, payasam* and visit each other and exchange greetings.

On the third day, known as Mattu Pongal, there is an old tradition, prevailing even today, to worship the farm animals and cattle. They are bathed properly and then decorated with garlands. *Kumkum* is applied on their foreheads and they are fed with sweet rice.

The fourth day is Thiruvalluvar day or Kaanum Pongal. On this last day of celebration, people visit family, friends and relatives. Women perform pujas for their brothers. People leave cooked rice on the plantain leaves allowing birds to eat it, as it is considered auspicious. This day is originally meant to thank relatives and friends for their support in the harvest.

• Delicacies Prepared During Pongal

Avial: Avial is a mélange preparation of vegetables with contrasting colours such as carrot, beans, elephant yam, plantain, drum sticks and pumpkin are chosen, sliced evenly into thin one inch long pieces, and cooked to a crunchy consistency. It is a thick mixture of vegetables, curds and coconut, seasoned with coconut oil and curry leaves.

Coconut Rice: Coconut rice is a traditional rice preparation of South India which with a combination of *chana dal*, grated coconut and cooked rice makes a scrumptious serve. It is finally tempered with curry leaves, mustard seeds and some spices.

Lemon Rice: This pleasant dish comprises cooked rice, seasoned with mustard seeds, peanuts, *urad* (black) and *channa* (gram) *dal* and flavoured with lots of lemon juice. At few places, lemon zest is grated and added for giving a more dominating flavour to the dish.

Puli Pongal: 'Puli' means tamarind in Tamil. The principal ingredients of this traditional dish are broken raw rice and tamarind. It is simply a sour rice preparation.

Salt Pongal: It is also referred as Ven Pongal. This is basically a rice preparation with *moong dal* and tempered with cumin seeds, cashew nuts and spices.

Sarkkarai Pongal: It is prepared in an earthen pot, on the second day of Pongal. Sarkkarai Pongal is a very simple and easy-to-make dish, which gives a mouth watering taste.

Sweet Pongal: This dish sweetens the celebration and sets the festive mood. It is relished with great gusto by everyone during the festive occasion.

Ariselu: It is a sweet preparation from Orissa and Andhra Pradesh. Arisa or Ariselu is a Telugu word which means rice. It is also called *kajaya* in Kannada. A similar sweet in Tamil Nadu called *adhirasam* is prepared for pujas. It is a traditional dish and is made from rice flour, ghee and jaggery or granulated sugar.

Bobabtulu: Puran Poli or Puran Puri or Boba-bttulu or Holige or Obbattu is a traditional type of sweet flatbread made in India in the states of Maharashtra, Andhra Pradesh, Karnataka, Gujarat and Goa. It is a shallow fried stuffed bread preparation with the stuffing of *chana dal* or a mixture of *dals* in wheat flour.

Jantikulu: This savoury preparation is very similar to *murrukku* and is made with chick pea flour. It Maharashtra, it is referred as *chakli.*

Palakayulu: Palakayalu is a rice based, dry and crispy snack very common in Andhra Pradesh which can be made both sweet and spicy.

Semiya Payasam: Semiya Payasam is a delicious vermicelli-milk pudding that is flavoured with cardamom and saffron.

Paramannam: Also referred as Annam Payasam or Paramannam (food of the Gods) it is a sweet dish similar to *kheer* which is prepared as an offering to the God in almost every home in Andhra Pradesh.

Pulihora: Puliyodhara/Chitrannam is a very common preparation in Andhra Pradesh, Karnataka, Tamil Nadu. Puli means tamarind. Pulihora is also referred to as sour rice. Other names are tamarind rice or lemon rice. It is given as *prasadam* in temples. Devotees queue to get Pulihora after having a glimpse of the God.

Masala Vada: The two deep fried lentil dumpling delicacies are *ulundu vadai* and *paruppu vadai. Medhu vadai* is also known as *ulundu vadai* in Kerala. It is basically *urad dal* ground into a batter and deep fried. It is generally had with *sambhar.*

Til Polis: It is made by stuffing sesame seed mixture in wheat flour dough and then shallow frying it. Many a times, jaggery is also used as the stuffing ingredient in this shallow fried flatbread.

Makar Sankranti

Makar Sankranti is a widely celebrated festival in India. In South India, Makar Sankranti is called Pongal, in North India it is called Lohri, while in Western India, particularly Gujarat, it is celebrated by flying colourful kites. Hindus assemble on auspicious places and pray to the Sun God on this occasion.

Literally Makar means Capricorn and Sankranti means change. Astrologically, there is a Sankranti every month when the sun passes from one zodiac sign to the next one. Since there are 12 zodiac signs there are 12 Sankrantis. Each of these Sankrantis has its own importance but Mesh (Aries) Sankranti and Makar (Capricorn) Sankranti are considered to be more important.

Makar Sankranti is the changeover of the sun from Sagittarius to Capricorn, during winter. From this day, the period of Uttarayana starts and it continues for six months. Makar Sankranti is celebrated in the Hindu month of Magha. After Sankranti, the days get longer and warmer.

• Delicacies Prepared During Makar Sankranti

Bajra Khichdi: Bajra (millets) is ground into flour to make rotis or is coarsely crushed to make porridge like *khichdi* that is eaten with a dollop of ghee or sesame oil in the cold desert winters. Pickles, curds, *papad* and jaggery also accompany this dish.

Til Gajak: Til Gajak is made especially during the cold North Indian winter months since *til* (sesame) is believed to warm the bodies due to its warming properties. It is a popular sweet for Diwali as well.

Til Chikki: Til Chikki is very nutritious because of the combination of sesame seeds and jaggery, both of which are good sources of iron.

Payesh: Payesh is a Bengali version of *kheer*. It is a rice pudding, which is a traditional South Asian sweet dish. It is made by boiling rice or broken wheat with milk and sugar, and flavoured with cardamom, raisins, saffron, cashew nuts, pistachios or almonds. It is typically served during a meal or also consumed alone as a dessert.

Kurmure Ladoo: These sweet round *laddoos* are made with puffed rice and jaggery.

Aate ki Pinni: Aate ki Pinni is prepared from wheat flour and lots of sugar and dry fruits. This sweet is made in the Baisakhi festival.

Bandaru Laddoo: The main ingredient in this delicacy is gram flour mixed with sugar. Pounding is called *tokkatam* in Telugu and hence the name Tokkudu Laddu. These *laddoos* are famous in Bandaru (Machilipatnam) a place in Andhra Pradesh and hence called so.

Pesarattu: Pesarattu is a crepe-like bread unique to Telugu cuisine that is similar to *dosa*. It is made with batter of green gram (*moong dal*), but unlike a *dosa*, it does not contain *urad dal*. Pesarattu is eaten both for breakfast and as a snack. It is typically served with ginger or tamarind chutney. Green chillies, ginger and onions are the various ingredients used in various versions of this snack.

Rasse ki Kheer: Rasse ki Kheer is a delicious dish in which rice is cooked for hours in fresh sugarcane juice.

Til Polis: It is made by stuffing sesame seed mixture in wheat flour dough and frying it. Many a times, jaggery is also used as an ingredient of stuffing in this shallow fried flatbread.

Mahashivratri

Mahashivratri is one of the occasions which is celebrated throughout the county. People believe that Shivratri was the day when Lord Shiva and goddess Parvati tied the nuptial knot. It falls in the month of February or March (in the Falgun Maas as per the Hindu calendar). The occasion is celebrated by keeping fast among men, women and children. By midnight, devotees perform puja and offer fruits, flowers and *bel patra* (leaves of bel tree) on the Shiva Linga. It is a belief that the *bel patra* is essentially required to execute prayers on this day. It is customary to give bath or put abhishek to the Shiva Linga with milk, curds, ghee, flowers and cow dung. Followers of Lord Shiva perform singing and dancing activities to the tunes of the devotional songs all through the night in the Shiva temples.

During this festive occasion, people participating religiously refrain from food made with grains like rice, pulses or wheat. However, the ardent followers may observe *phalahar* by taking fruits and milk, tea or coffee during the fast, if they have not observed *nirahar vrat* (fast without the consumption of any form of foodstuff). In the evening, after performing the puja, they would break the fast by eating rotis made of *singhare ka atta* (*kuttu ka atta*) and *sabudana ka kheer* (dessert made of sago). *Sendha namak* (rock salt) is the seasoning used to cook food for the fast. Special dishes are prepared in order to offer it to the deity such as potato pumpkin pancakes, *lauki ka halwa* (sweet dish made of bottle guard), *thandai*, etc. Potato curry, sweet potato *chaat*, *paneer* and *aloo chaat*, *sabudana vada*, potato and *kuttu atta pakodi* in curds, raw banana *vadas* are the few preparations prepared especially for this festivity period of Mahashivratri.

• Delicacies Prepared During Mahashivratri

Singhade ki Roti: It is a roti made of *kuttu* flour or *singhada* (water chestnut) flour. During fasting days in North India, only certain flours are used. e.g., *singhare ka atta* (water chestnut flour), *kuttu ka atta* (buckwheat flour), *rajgira ka atta* (amaranth flour), *sama ke chawal ka atta* (barnyard millets flour) and arrowroot flour.

Singhade ki Kadhi: It is a *kadhi* preparation made with *singhada* flour and curds.

Aloo Chaat: It is prepared by frying cubes of potatoes in oil and adding spices and *chutney*. It is a North Indian snack which can be served as a potato salad or a light meal.

Badaam Halwa: It is made by grounding almond which is soaked in water for about 6-7 hours and then sautéing it in *desi ghee* with addition of sugar. It is garnished with other nuts.

Daliya: It is a porridge made out of *sama ke chawal* (millets flour) along with ingredients like bottle gourd and paneer.

Holi

Undoubtedly, one of the most popular festivals in the country associated with loads of fun and gaiety is Holi. The festival centres on the legendary story of Bhakt Prahlad and King Hiranyakashap. Prahlad worshipped God Vishnu and rebelled against his father Hiranyakashyap who instructed his entire kingdom and ordered everyone to worship only him. When Prahlad disobeyed this order, the king's sister Holika suggested burning Prahlad alive, in order to teach him a lesson. But in an attempt to burn Prahlad, Holika herself got burnt.

The other mythological story indicates that people celebrate this festival to signify the story of Radha and Krishna playing Holi. Shri Krishna was advised by his mother Yashoda to colour Radha's face to darken her complexion.

From ancient times, people have been observing two auspicious days of Holi in the Falgun Maas, i.e., a day before Holi and the main day. The celebrations begin with bonfire and organizing Holi get together and playing with colouring dyes (*rang* and *gulal*). Water balloons, *pichkaris* and *rang* and *gulal* form a part of the celebration for playing Holi.

Holi is also enjoyed along with several interesting delicacies. Sweets are the vital elements of Holi celebrations in any part of India. In fact, the festival of Holi is renowned for the multitudinous range of sweets prepared on the occasion.

The most popular desserts of Holi is *gujiya*, prepared for the occasion. Then there are *papris* and *dahi vade* or *dahi-bhalles* that are prepared in majority of Indian homes on the occasion. The intoxicating *bhang ke vade* and *thandai*, the *saunf* and *bhang sharbat* are the peculiar recipes reserved for the Holi celebrations.

• Delicacies Prepared During Holi

Jaljeera: Jaljeera literally means cumin water and a popular drink in North India is used as an appetizer due to its digestive properties. It has cooling properties and is an ideal drink during hot Indian summers.

Onion Bhajia: Also known as Vengaya Bhaji, is a type of fritter made with vegetables especially onions, deep fried with seasoned batter. It is consumed with a spicy green *chutney*.

Aloo Chaat: It is prepared by frying cubes of potatoes in oil and adding spices and *chutney*. It is a North Indian snack which can be served as a potato salad or a light meal.

Papri Chaat: It is a North Indian fast food. *Chaat*, an Indo-Aryan word which literally means lick, is used to describe a range of snacks and fast food dishes. It is topped with very scrumptious *chutneys* of different tastes and colours.

Bhang: Bhang is the local name for cannabis or marijuana, which for centuries has been used for recreational and medicinal purposes in India. People also eat bhang mixed with *pakoras* that are balls of fried paste made from gram flour. It is also eaten as *golees*, which are chewy little balls of bhang mixed with ghee and sugar. It creates an illusion due to its intoxicating nature on the one who consumes it and is renowned for this quality.

Vegetable Pakora: It is made of several vegetables like potato, onion, cabbage, spinach wrapped in chickpea flour or *besan*. Vegetable Pakoda is a very light snack that is served with different *chutneys* or tomato ketchup.

Gujiya: Gujiya is a traditional sweet dish prepared using refined flour, condensed milk and nut stuffing. Though the preparation of Gujiya requires a little time and effort, the taste of this delicious recipe is worth it. The packaging of Gujiya is very much like that of a *samosa*. However, Gujia has a very distinct shape. It is filled with a mixture of grated and roasted dry fruits, *khoya*, coconut and a little *suji* (semolina) to add a grainy texture.

Kanji Ke Vade: These are fried rounds of lentil batter fermented in water, mustard seeds and asafoetida.

Dahi Bhalle: These are fried balls of skinned and split white lentil preparations dipped in seasoned curds.

Thandai: Thandai or *bhang lassi* is a nutritious refreshing drink, which is the liquid derivative of marijuana, and contains the extracts of leaves and buds of cannabis in varying intensity. These are intoxicating enough to escalate the spirit of Holi. It is prepared by squeezing the buds and leaves of cannabis into a green paste, and adding it in a mixture of milk, ghee or clarified butter, almond, sugar and spices to it. It solaces the mind and keeps the body cool. The drink is a great stress pacifier, because it comprises some of the cooling agents by nature, such as watermelon seed and rose water.

Janmashtami

Janmashtami is a festival to commemorate the birth ceremony of Lord Shri Krishna. This day falls on the eighth day (Ashtami of Krishna Paksh) of a lunar fortnight, i.e., the eighth day after the festival of Raksha Bandhan. This day comes in the months of August and September according to the Gregorian calendar. The celebration spans for two days. The first day is Krishnashtami or Gokulashtami. The second day is called Kalashtami or more commonly Janmashtami. At midnight, between the first and second day, the birth of Lord Krishna is replicated with splendour and ceremony. The most important and common ceremony of Dahi Handi (breaking a pot full of milk and its derivatives) takes place on the second day.

Lord Krishna is known to have a special liking for desserts prepared with milk and curds as the main ingredients, hence he is welcomed by such several sweet dishes. Most people keep a fast on this day although, one meal is permitted. This is known as *phalhar*, which comprises meals comprising fruits, *mithai*, curds and *singhare ki puri*. Generally, the followers prepare these food items which are considered to be loved by Lord Krishna. At the midnight, all these items are kept in front of Lord Krishna and this is referred as the ritual Bhog. Later on, all these food items are distributed amongst his devotees as Prasada.

- **Delicacies Prepared During Janmashtami**

Kheer: It is a rice pudding which is made by boiling rice or broken wheat with milk and sugar, and flavoured with cardamom, raisins, saffron, cashew nuts, pistachios or almonds. It is typically served during a meal or is also consumed alone as a dessert.

Shrikhand: This is a delicious preparation by mixing hung curds, sugar and saffron with sliced pistachios on the top.

Kalakand: A popular Indian sweet made out of solidified, sweetened milk and cottage cheese. A huge pan is kept on a flame and large amount of milk is boiled stirring it continuously till it is thickened with sugar and dry fruits.

This Indian milk fudge is soft and grainy in texture. Few nuts and cardamom are added at the final stage and a delicious sweet is ready to be served.

Murukku: Murukku, also known as Chakli, Murukulu and Jantikalu, is a favourite savory snack in our homes. Murukku is a South Indian snack of savory crunchy twists made from rice and *urad dal* flour. Murukku means twisted in the Tamil language. The town of Manapparai in Tamil Nadu is particularly known for its Murukkus.

Peda: It is one of the popular sweets, usually prepared from *khoya*, sugar and traditional flavourings like cardamom seeds, pistachio nuts and saffron.

Singhare Ki Puri: This Puri is made of *kuttu* flour or *singhada* (water chestnut) flour by deep frying.

During fasting days in North India, only certain flours are used. e.g., *singhare ka atta* (water chestnut flour), *kuttu ka atta* (buckwheat flour), *rajgira ka atta* (amaranth flour), *sama ke chawal ka atta* (barnyard millets flour) and arrowroot flour.

Ganesh Chaturthi

Ganesh Chaturthi, also known as Vinayak Chaturthi, is commemorated by the Hindus as the occasion of Lord Ganesha's birthday. It usually falls between mid-August and September.

Although this festival is observed in all parts of the country, it is celebrated with maximum zest in Maharashtra.

Lord Shiva and Goddess Parvati stayed childless for very long after the birth of their first son Kartikeya. Parvati desired strongly for another son and Shiva's long absence from home accentuated her loneliness. One day, she made a clay statue in the form of her son and used her divine powers to infuse life in it. And the clay structure came to life due to this. She was tremendously overjoyed and named him Ganesha. One day, while Parvati was busy bathing, Ganesha was given the responsibility to guard the entrance of the house. Child Ganesha was not aware of Lord Shiva and he stopped him from entering. Due to this, Lord Shiva became furious and chopped off Ganesha's head and threw it away. When Parvati became aware about the entire incident, she lost her temper and ordered Shiva to rejuvenate her son's life immediately. In order to fulfil Parvati's wish, he searched for head to be replaced but was unsuccessful in his endeavour. So he promised to replace it with the head of the next living being that he came across first. Unfortunately or fortunately, he came across a baby elephant, so Shiva chopped off the elephant's head and fit it to the lifeless body of Ganesha and revived him. Then Lord Shiva bestowed upon Ganesha the powers of a God and blessed him that in future no auspicious event will begin without invoking his name and blessings. Since then, it is considered that no new venture can be completed by the Hindus without a Ganesha puja.

• Delicacies Prepared During Ganesh Chaturthi

Besan Ke Ladoo: It is prepared by frying gram flour in *desi ghee* and adding it with powdered sugar and shaping it into round balls of Besan ke Ladoo.

Kaju Ki Burfi: Burfi is a wide collection of desserts which are made with *khoya* (condensed milk as base and then set into slabs in a greased tray and then cut into attractive shapes like lozenge and square. Plain *burfi* is made by simply cooking condensed milk and sugar until it solidifies on its own. *Kaju ki Burfi* is made using cashewnut as the main ingredient and is flavoured with rose water or cardamom powder, and garnished with *chandi ka varq*.

Karanji: Karanji is the other name of *Gujiya* in Maharashtra which is a sweet dumpling made with refined flour and stuffed with *khoya*. The *Gujia* is filled with a mixture of grated and roasted dry fruits, *khoya*, coconuts and a little *suji* (semolina) to add a coarse texture.

Modak: Assumed to be loved most by Lord Ganesha, this is a sweet dumpling preparation prepared in many parts of India, with different names and with slight variations. Rice flour is made into dough by adding hot water and then this dough is rolled and stuffed with a mixture of jaggery, coconut and dry fruits. It is then made into a shape of a *potli* and then steamed.

Motichoor Ke Ladoo: Motichoor ke Ladoo is thought to be the favourite food of Lord Ganesha. It is a ritual to offer *ladoos* to Lord ganesha for offerings.

Puliyodarai: It is tasty tamarind rice tempered with asafoetida and curry leaves.

Puran Poli: It is the cooked sweet yellow gram paste preparation rolled up in a spread out dough made from wheat flour, and is consumed with *kheer*.

Rawa Ke Ladoo: It is prepared by frying semolina in ghee and adding it with powdered sugar and shaping it into round balls of Rawa ke Ladoo.

Moong Dal Ka Halwa: Halwa refers to various kinds of dense, sweet confectionery prepared from different ingredients. *Moong dal halwa* is made by soaking *Dhuli moong dal*, grinding it till it is coarse and then cooking it in *desi ghee* with addition of sugar and dry fruits in the end. It is appreciate by all.

Onam

Onam is considered to be a grand festival of the Kerala, celebrated to give a huge reception to the home returning of King Mahabali in Kerala. It is celebrated in the months of August and September. It is marked with the celebration of over ten days and begins with Atham and ends with Thiruvonam.

On the first day, people take bath early in the morning and offer prayers. In order to welcome King Mahabali, Pookalam, floral designs are prepared by women in the courtyard in the house. A grand procession is organized to represent the king's tour in the city and back to his fort.

Pookalam is made for all the ten days – it is a flower making activity engaged by the women. The second and third days are referred as Chithira and Chodi. People organize get-togethers and exchange gifts on Chodi.

On the fourth day, Visakam, a special meal called Onasadya is prepared. A legend behind the delicacies prepared on Visakam is that King Mahabali requested

God to allow him to visit his kingdom every year and the same was granted. This nine-course meal which consists of not less than 64 dishes is prepared for his very homecoming. The platter of delicacies is served in an authentic traditional manner on a banana leaf. Rice is the most important dish on the menu.

The other items on the menu consist of *papad*, salt, banana wafers, *sarkarapuratti*, ginger lime and mango pickles, *vellarika*, *pavakka*, bee troot, and *ullikitchadi*. *Kitchadi* made of pineapple and banana splits or of grapes and apples too are served. The cuisines prepared on this day are with the intention to invite the king.

The fifth day is Anizham, the day of boat race event called Vallimkali. This event is one of the major attractions for national and international tourists. The snake boats race on the rhythm of the boat songs called *vanchipattu*. An ancient story that runs around the boat race says that the snake-like boats were built to save food from robbers. This food is prepared for the Gods in the Arunmulla temple.

The sixth day is the Thriketa or the day of merrymaking. Traditional programmes including songs and dances are held to mark this carnival day.

The celebration doesn't end here and extends to the seventh, eighth, ninth and tenth days and are referred to as Moolam, Pooradam, Uthradam and Thiruvonam respectively.

Onam is also the harvest festival of the South. Another feature of Onam is the grand elephant procession. Elephants on the occasion are adorned with golden ornaments and flowers and paraded through streets.

• Delicacies Prepared During Onam

Avial: Avial is a mélange preparation of vegetables with contrasting colours such as carrot, beans, elephant yam, plantain, drumsticks and pumpkin which are chosen, sliced evenly into thin one inch long pieces, and cooked to a crunchy consistency. It is a thick mixture of vegetables, curds and coconut, and seasoned with coconut oil and curry leaves.

Banana Halwa: It is a delicacy prepared using bananas, sugar, and ghee.

Coconut Chutney: Coconut is an ingredient used in almost every South Indian preparation. Coconut sauce or *thenga chutney* is made by grinding fresh coconut and tempering it with curry leaves, mustard seeds, whole red chilli and so on.

Idli: Extremely scrumptious, light and nutritious, Idli is an ideal breakfast item. It is made by the overnight fermented batter of rice and *urad dal* by the steaming method.

Dry Fruit Kesari: A very common and lovely dessert made of *rava* (semolina) and dry fruits as the primary items. Kesari is extremely scrumptious to taste. It is prepared in a manner very similar to north Indian *Rava Halwa*, but cut in the fashion of *burfi* in different shapes once it is set.

Masala Dosa: Masala Dosa is made up of the fermented batter of rice and *urad dal* along with the stuffing of mashed potatoes. The preparation of *dosa* puts demands on time and efforts but it is worth it.

Mor Kuzhambu: Mor Kuzhambu is a popular South Indian dish which is made from buttermilk seasoned with cumin seeds, coriander seeds, turmeric powder and mustard seeds. It is very easy to make and hardly takes 15-20 minutes for preparation. It is relished with plain hot rice.

Moru Curry: It is a very simple curds curry served as a meal or had with rice.

Kozhukattai: Kozhukattai, also known as Modak, is one of the most popular recipes of Kerala. It is prepared like Modak during Ganesh Chaturthi in Maharashtra.

Palada Pradhaman: Palada Pradhaman is basically a *payasam* prepared with rice flakes, milk and sugar. Ada Pradhaman is traditionally prepared with rice, coconut milk and jaggery.

Pesarattu: A number of varieties of *dosa* (Indian pancakes made of flour) are made in the southern parts of India. Out of them, Pesarattu stands out. Prepared using *moong dal*, Pesarattu makes a very healthy and easy-to-make snack item, which can be served with coconut *chutney*.

Rice Puttu: It is a South Indian breakfast dish of steamed cylinders of ground rice layered with coconut. Puttu means 'portioned' in Tamil. Puttu is served with side dishes such as palm sugar or chickpea curry or banana, topped with ghee or oil.

It is eaten with coconut chutney, or with sambhar or with a spiced pulse-based powder called *molaga*.

Sambhar: Sambar is a lentil based vegetable stew or broth made with tamarind and is the most popular item in the cooking of southern states of India. The vegetables included in this preparation are drumstick, red pumpkin, bottlegourd, lady finger, onion and tomato.

Theeyal: Theeyal is an authentic Kerala dish which is quite similar to Sambhar. Theeyal is made from a spice mixture consisting of burnt or roasted coconut, coriander seeds, dried red chili and fenugreek. All spices are roasted and ground to a paste and cooked in tamarind water with vegetables like shallot, bitter melon, potato, eggplant, lady finger, raw mango and so on. It is had with rice.

Tomato Rasam: It is the peppery South Indian soup which is traditionally prepared using tamarind juice as a base, with the addition of tomato, chili pepper, pepper, cumin and other spices as seasonings.

Navratri/Durga Puja

Durga Puja is a Hindu festival celebrated for continuous nine days of worshipping the various forms of the Goddess Durga. 'Nav' means nine and 'ratri' means night, thus the name meaning 'nine nights' in Sanskrit.

It is commemorated five times in a year - Vasanta Navratri, Ashadha Navratri, Sharada Navratri and Poushya/Magha Navratri. But of these, Sharada and Vasanta Navratri are the most prominent.

Sharad Navratri is the most important of the Navratris and often called Maha Navratri. It is called so since it is celebrated during Sharad, i.e., beginning of winters, sometime in October - November. The Sharad Navratri concides with the festive occasion of Dussehra.

Celebrations

It is celebrated in various styles in the entire country. During these days, all the nine forms of Shakti Durga, namely, Bhadrakali, Amba, Annapurna, Sarvamangala, Bhairavi, Chandika or Chandi, Lalita, Bhavani, and Mookambika are deeply regarded and worshipped. Some people keep fast for all the nine days. The festival finally comes to an end on the occasion of Mahanavami, on which 'Kanya Puja' is done. People who do not keep fast for all nine days have the option to keep fast on the first and second or first and last or the last 2 days, as it is believed that the fasts have to be kept in pairs.

Out of nine days, the first three days are dedicated to Durga, the Goddess of Power, the next three days to Lakshmi, the Goddess of Peace and Prosperity, and remaining days to Saraswati, the Goddess of Wisdom. In order to seek blessings from the three goddesses, all the three forms of goddess are worshipped.

Navratri is characterized with performances of Dandiya Rasa and Garba, the characteristic folk dances of Gujarat. Both men and women dress in traditional attires. Dandiya Rasa is performed mostly by men. They dance in concentric circles and beat the *dandiya* sticks in rhythm while performing this event.

- **Delicacies Prepared During Durga Puja**

Aloo Posto: It is a dry preparation in which boiled potatoes are cooked with poppy seeds. It is extremely popular in Bengal.

Bandhakopir Dalna: This tasty preparation is very simple and is made by stir frying cabbage and potatoes.

Chola Dal: It is a very tasty *dal* preparation and is enjoyed most during the festive season. It is relished with rice.

Labra: Labra is a scrumptious and nutritious dish of West Bengal. It is a kind of mixed vegetable recipe made along with curry. It contains several kinds of vegetables like *sojne data* (drumsticks), raw banana and sweet potato cooked on simmered flame along with subtle spices.

Mishti Doi: Mishti Doi is made of full cream milk and sugar. It is a real fare for those who prefer to eat the sweet dishes the most. Generally used as a dessert, this is a lovely dessert preparation which requires at least about 8-12 hours for it.

Nimki: Nimki also known as 'Namak Pare' are traditional North Indian snacks. It is made up of refined flour, salt and oil as the main ingredients. They are very tasty and light crunchy snacks which can be stored for a longer period of time.

Patishapta: Patishapta Pitha, Puli Pitha, Doodh Puli and so are the large varieties of Pitha, generally popular in Bengal. The Patishapta Pitha is a sweet with its outer layer made of flour and the inner stuffing made of different savouries like coconut and dry fruits. It is generally prepared on special occasions such as Makar Sankranti, Diwali and Durga Puja.

Roshogolla: This is a delicacy which needs no introduction and is made from ball shaped dumplings of *chhena* (an Indian cottage cheese) and semolina dough, cooked in light syrup made of sugar. This is done until the syrup permeates the dumplings.

Dussehra

Dussehra is an important festival of the Hindu community and is celebrated with lots of jubilation all over India. In some parts of the country, Dussehra is also called Vijayadashmi 'Vijay', meaning victory and Dashmi meaning the tenth day. It was on this great day that Lord Rama killed the demon king Ravana of Lanka and freed his abducted wife Sita from Ravana's clutches. In other words, Dussehra is a festival that marks the triumph and victory of good over evil.

Celebrations in North India

Particularly in North India, Dussehra is celebrated by re-enacting the epic war between Lord Rama and Ravana. The stage is set and huge effigies of Ravana, brother Kumbhkarna and son Meghnath are erected in vast open grounds. Fireworks and crackers are also placed inside the effigies. Actors dressed as Lord Rama, his wife Sita and brother Lakshman enact the battle scene in front of a large audience. After the scene is enacted the character playing Rama shoots an arrow having fire on its tip at the three effigies. First the effigies are set on fire and then the crackers in them catch fire automatically. Thus, this entire show depicts that good wins over evil.

Celebrations in Bengal

Bengalis celebrate Dussehra as the last day of Durga Puja. This day is dedicated to Mother Goddess Shakti. It is considered that it was Goddess Durga who has the combined energies of Lord Brahma, Vishnu and Mahesh and all the other lords. This Goddess came when the demon king Mahishasur gained extreme power and started bothering Gods and men alike. It was then this Shakti Maa arrived and freed gods from the said demon.

On Dussehra, the idols of Goddess Durga are immersed into a water body, after nine days of continuous celebration.

Celebrations in South India

In the southern states of Tamil Nadu and Kerala, Dussehra is celebrated in a special way. This day is considered auspicious for starting education in any art form like dance, music or fine arts. Saraswati puja is also done on this day. In Karnataka, especially Mysore and Andhra Pradesh, Dussehra is celebrated with huge ostentation.

Thus, Dussehra is one of the major festivals celebrated by people across the country.

• Delicacies Prepared During Dussehra

Panchamrut: This is a delicate drink made with a combination of five ingredients, milk, yogurt, dry fruits, nuts, and sugar. The term Panchamrut literally means "nectar of five ingredients". This drink is considered to be holy and it is offered to God as well.

Puliyodharai: It is a tasty tamarind rice dish tempered with asafoetida, whole red chilli flakes, mustard seeds and curry leaves.

Coconut Rice: It is a fragrant rice dish containing large quantity of grated coconut in it and tempered with curry leaves, mustard seeds and spices.

Thayir Semia: It is a preparation with fried vermicelli mixed in curds and tempered with mustard seeds, *chana dal* and curry leaves.

Nava Dhaanya Sundal: It is a delicious and healthy stir fried preparation of nine beans for nine nights of Navaratri.

Masala Ulundhu (Urad Dal) Vadai with Rasam: It is a South Indian snack of fried savoury lentil doughnuts with spicy tomato gravy to dip or to soak in.

Sugian/Suyyian: It is a Tamil Nadu special sweet ball, made of sticky sweet coconut dipped and fried and sweetened rice with jaggery.

Paanagam: This is basically a sweet and tangy refreshing non-alcoholic beverage made with jaggery and lime juice and is enjoyed the most.

Karwa Chauth

Karwa Chauth is one unique festival which is marked by a fast kept by married women and girls likely to get married for the well-being and the long life of their husbands or would be husbands. This festival is very close to the heart of every woman and they are attached with it emotionally.

It is mostly observed by women from the regions of North Indian states.

The preparation comprises shopping for new clothes and jewellery, sweets and snacks and applying *mehendi* on the palms by the women. In Rajasthan it is known as Vat Purnima. Women here observe fast to get married to the same man as husband for all seven lives and fill mud pot with rice and wheat which are known as the Karwas. For women in Uttar Pradesh, women pray to Goddess Gauri, Moon and Sun. They draw pictures of these gods, make *karwas* and perform puja.

The festival is important for the newly-wed brides. It is a custom that they get gifts of jewellery and clothes from their mothers-in-law.

All these gifts are considered very important for the women as it symbolizes their happy marriage or *suhag*. Items like bangles, jewellery, colourful clothes and *mehendi* are all considered auspicious for this occasion. The fast starts before the sunrise and ends after the moon rise. The Baya or the *thali* (plate) which is exchanged by the women in the evening at the time of the puja is gifted by the new bride's parents to her husband. The baya contains few sweets, almonds and some gifts. Women break their fast after seeing their husbands and take a sip of water by the hand of their husbands and pray for their long life.

• Delicacies Prepared During Karwa Chauth

Aloo Chana Chaat: The Aloo Chana Chaat is a preparation which has the combination of all tastes like sweet, sour and spicy in a single dish. However, it surely is a dish that is liked and relished by people of all age groups. Aloo Chana Chaat, many times, becomes the first choice for starters as it is very easy and simple to make.

Aloo Dahi Wale: Aloo Dahi Wale is liked by all. The dish requires little preparatory work and has a finger-licking taste. It is a *urad dal* dumpling soaked in curds, topped with various *chutneys.*

Tamarind Sauce: Tamarind sauce is a tasty condiment and the best feature of the sauce is that it can be used to spice up all kinds of food items. It can be served with snacks items like *chaats, samosas, dahi vada* and *pakoras*. Tamarind sauce is a tangy and spicy sauce which makes all the senses live.

Methi Puri: Methi Puri is a very popular recipe, which is prepared with fenugreek leaves and other spices, kneaded in wheat flour. These are stuffed in wheat flour ball and then fried.

Golgappe: It is known by various names in different parts of the country, the most popular ones being *panipuri, puchka* and *gupchup*. It was basically a roadside item but nowadays, it is prepared easily at homes.

Papri Chaat: It is made up of crispy wafers crushed on the combination of potatoes, seasoned yogurt, chillies and *chutneys*.

Puri Bhaji: Puri Bhaji is a very famous dish which includes two preparations one is a potato curried dish and another is deep-fried bread made of wheat flour. Both the dishes complement each other.

Ragada Patties: Ragada patties are known to form a complete meal. They require very less cooking time. It is a type of *chaat* and is relished by all.

Diwali

Diwali, the most prominent festival of India which calls for celebration for a longer period of time is the festival of lights, crackers and sweets. It was on this special day Lord Rama returned home after defeating the demon king Ravana. Diwali, which means simply 'garland of lamps' is enjoyed by the lighting of lamps and candles (inviting the Goddess into the house), feasting, and the exchange of gifts. It is a day of fireworks, decorate the home with *bandanwars* and *diyas* and feast with family members and friends.

It is also said that on this day Goddess Lakshmi emerged from the ocean of milk and blessed mankind with prosperity and wealth. Hence, it is believed that every home cleaned and worshiping the Goddess is visited by the Goddess herself.

Five Crucial Days of Diwali

Dhanteras: Gold or any metallic object is purchased on this day, as it is believed to bring luck and prosperity.

Narak Chaturdasi: People happily light *diyas* and burn crackers on this day which is considered small (*chhoti*) Diwali.

Diwali (Lakshmi Puja): Considered main Diwali day and also referred as Maha Lakshmi puja is a day on which people light *diyas*, draw *rangolis* on their doorsteps and worship Goddess Lakshmi. Sweets are exchanged and there is also a tradition to gift the dear and near ones.

Govardhan Puja: On this day, Govardhan Puja is performed. Many years back, Lord Krishna asked the people of Brajj (*Brijj*) to perform this puja and from then it became a tradition to perform this puja mandatorily.

Bhai Duj: On this day, brothers visit their sisters to enquire about their well-being and are gifted against this. At certain places, sisters visit brothers and gift them.

Prior to Diwali, traditional dishes are prepared for the family members, visitors during the occasions. The variety on this occasion is exhaustive and varied. *Gulab jamun, gajar ka halwa, besan ke ladoo, karanji* and *jalebis* are the most commonly made sweets on this celebrated occasion.

Not only this, *dahi bhalle* and *ghathiya* are also prepared for the same. In entire India, several mouth-watering delights are prepared in various manners depending upon the exisiting customs and tastes of the family members.

• Delicacies Prepared During Diwali

Badam Phirni: A luscious preparation made using almond, rice flour and milk. It is heavy and fulfilling in nature and is enjoyed by all.

Gulab Jamun: It is basically a fried sweet soft ball dumpling made up of *khoya*, refined flour and cottage cheese and finally dipped in sugar syrup flavoured with saffron. At times, the dumplings are stuffed with cottage cheese (paneer), raisins, saffron, etc.

Peda: It is one of the common popular sweets, mostly prepared from *khoya*, sugar and traditional flavourings like cardamom seeds, pistachio nuts and saffron. Many variants of this dessert is available these days.

Besan ke Ladoo: Undoubtedly the most loved desserts, *ladoos* are small round shaped balls of fried gram flour. It has a very crucial significant place on this auspicious day as it is offered to Lord Ganesha during Laksmi-Ganesh puja.

Jalebi: It is prepared by making batter of flour, water, curds and baking powder. This batter is allowed to ferment and then it is poured in a circular motion through a thick cloth in the hot oil. The batter is poured in spirally to form the peculiar *jalebi* shape. Once it is crisp fried, it is dipped into sugar syrup flavoured with saffron.

Rasmalai: It consists of sugary white, cream or yellow coloured balls (or flattened balls) of paneer soaked in *malai* (clotted cream) which is flavoured with cardamom.

Channar Payesh: Channar Payesh is made up of condensed milk, nuts and raisins. This tasty delicacy is at its best when it is served chilled.

Karanji (Gujiya): Gujiya is a traditional sweet dish prepared using refined flour, condensed milk and nut stuffing. The Gujiya is filled with a mixture of grated and roasted dry fruits, *khoya*, coconuts and a little *suji* (semolina).

Doodh Pak: Doodh Pak is an excellent dish made up of almond and milk and is very popular in North and West India. It is a real delight for people who have a special liking for dairy products.

Kesar Kaju Barfi: Also known as Kaju Katli, it is a diamond-shaped sweet, made of cashew nuts and sugar. As this dish is moderately sweet in taste and rich with cashew-nuts, it is liked by all who do not like extremely sugary items or are diabetic.

Shakkarpare: Shakkarpare is prepared with refined flour, sugar and oil as the main ingredients. The main quality attached with this dish is its long shelf-life. It is eaten as snacks or as an accompaniment to tea.

Gajar ka Halwa: It is made by placing bright red grated carrot in a jar containing a specific amount of milk and sugar and then cooked, stirring regularly. The nuts and other items used are first sautéed in ghee (clarified butter) to add richness to the *halwa*. *Khoya* is added in the end to the *halwa* and then it is served hot.

Kheer: It is made up of rice, milk and various kinds of dry fruits. It is a very common preparation prepared in almost in every household.

Ghathia: On the occasion of Diwali, Ghathia has found a very special place. It is tasty, crunchy, savoury item which is in the shape of finger chips. It is made up of refined flour as the main ingredient.

Eid-ul-Fitr

Eid-ul-Fitr is popularly called Eid. It is the most noted Islamic festival. The term 'Eid' has been derived from the Arabic word *oud*, which means 'the return' connoting the return of the festival each year and Fitr means 'to break the fast'. It is celebrated after the end of the Islamic month of Ramadan and it symbolizes the breaking of the fasting period.

Celebrations

It is the most important festival for the Muslims across the world. The night prior to Eid is called Chand Raat literally meaning 'night of the moon'. At the very sight of new crescent moon in the evening of the last day of Ramadan, people rejoice and everyone wishes each other "Chand Mubarak, Chand Mubarak". The sight of the moon signifies an end to their month-long fasts and from here begins the great celebrations.

People wake up early in the morning, bathe and wear new clothes. They take a light breakfast, generally dates, before going to attend the special Eid prayer called Salah. The prayer is performed publicly at mosques or open areas which can accommodate a large number of people. Salah is followed by Khutbah and then Dua where people ask Allah for forgiveness. People embrace the person sitting on either side wishing them Eid.

People pay visit to their friends, relatives and acquaintances and greet each other by saying 'Eid-Mubarak'. According to the tradition, exchanging gifts on the holy festival fortifies the bond of love between people. Children are given money (Eidi) by their elders on this day.

• Delicacies Prepared During Eid-ul-Fitr

Sheer Korma: Sheer Korma literally means "milk with dates". *Sheer* is Persian for milk and *khurma* is Persian for dates. It is a must have dessert for celebrations, which is a vermicelli pudding.

Badam Phirni: It is a rich sweet dessert made of almonds, rice flour and milk. It is a delectable preparation which has the goodness of almonds, milk flavoured with cardamom and saffron. It is healthy and nutritious.

Kofta Curry: It is a famous curried preparation of dumpling prepared from various ingredients and binding agents. Mostly it is a non-vegetarian preparation, but can be made from a wide array of vegetables also.

Biryani: It is the most celebrated dish of the Muslim community which is prepared using long grained rice, lamb or chicken, dry fruits, yogurt, saffron, rose water, fried onions and so on. It can be prepared by the way of *dum* cooking. It is accompanied by *raita* and is a complete dish in itself.

Korma: Korma is basically a style of gravy preparation which is very rich in its texture. It is used to prepare mutton, chicken or paneer as well, whichever is to be prepared. It is added with a lot of cream.

Badami Gosht: It is popular Mughlai delicacy of mutton in which the gravy is enriched with almond paste. Almond dominates the taste of the gravy and also thickens its consistency.

Kathi Kebab: It is also referred as Kathi Roll, is a very popular dish which originated in Kolkata. It is basically a street food in which the skewered kebabs are wrapped in any kind of *parantha* and served. Today any filling rolled up in any kind of Indian flat bread is called Kathi Roll.

Murg Adraki: It is a preparation of chicken which is flavoured with excess of ginger in gravy and garnish. It is only because of this, the dish is named as Murg Adraki. This dish is also liked by all.

Christmas

Christmas is the most prominent festival of Christians which is considered the birth day of Jesus Christ. Most members of the Roman Catholic Church celebrate Christmas on December 25, and many celebrate on the evening of December 24 as well.

This festive season is marked by gatherings of friends, family members, holidaying, feasting and exchanging gifts. The word Christmas literally means 'festival of Christ'.

The two things that come in one's mind when Christmas is being talked about are Christmas gifts and Christmas delicacies. Christmas cakes and cookies are the most liked delicacies for all the children around the world. People all over the world enjoy these items during Christmas celebrations. A large dinner is arranged for everyone to sit comfortably and chat only after the prayers are said jointly or by holding each other's hand. Every member of the family is gifted, especially the younger ones, by Santa Claus.

• Delicacies Prepared During Christmas

Christmas Cookies: Christmas cookies can be prepared in numerous ways. This festive item for the festival stands out. It is a custom to prepare this dish during this occasion.

Christmas Pudding/Plum Pudding: The tradition of serving Christmas Pudding during the festive season of Christmas dates back to many years. It requires patience to prepare this dish, as it cannot be prepared in a single day. Various chopped dry fruits are soaked in rum and mixed with the rest of the ingredients to prepare this unique dish. Christmas puddings are traditionally made with a wide variety of dry fruits, including almonds and plum. They are baked-steamed for a long time. The sweet dish has a very long shelf-life.

Chilean Christmas Bread: This unique bread is also an essential dish to be prepared on this festive occasion.

Cake: It is this cake prepared which is loved most by small children and they desire to consume a large portion always. It is flavoured with several ingredients and hence has varied flavours.

Christmas Fudge: A unique preparation with a wide variety, this delicacy may range from main course items to desserts and also drinks as well.

Christmas Fruit Bars: It is a huge display of various fruits and displayed at fruit bars. The fruits are cut and then consumed accordingly, as per the eater's preferences.

Culinary Trivia: Mangoes in India

Mango is the king of fruits in India. India has been a country where about a thousand of mango varieties are cultivated and relished. The famous varieties of mangoes in India are given below.

Alphonso: Also known as Hapoos, is one of the most beloved varieties in India and abroad. This variety grows in Maharashtra, Gujarat and Karnataka. Its firm yet fibreless pulp ensures a smooth creamy mango while still maintaining its integrity when cut. It is superior to other mangoes in terms of sweetness, flavour and richness. The Alphonso mango is named after Afonso de Albuquerque, a Portuguese general and a great conqueror.

Banganapalli (Safeda): This variety from Andhra Pradesh and Tamil Nadu is a fibreless cultivar and it is moderately juicy and yellow variety.

Saroli/Bombay Green: It is a popular variety in North India and is found in Haryana and Uttar Pradesh. It is one of the first mangoes to appear during the season. Sweet Bombay green mangoes are packed with flavor.

Chaunsa: Its name was given by Sher Shah Suri, the Sultan of the Muslim Suri Empire from AD 1540 to 1545. Because the Chaunsa variety was his favorite, it's hailed as "the king of mangoes."

Dashehari: Incredibly, one of the most famous and loved variety of mangoes hails from Malihabad, a place close to Lucknow. Apparently the first tree was planted when a wandering mango tradesman threw a variety onto the ground in a fit of rage after getting into a fight with the monk who housed him. The community in Malihabad takes every effort to preserve the heritage of these fantastic trees. Its pulp is sweet and succulent.

Fazli: It is a mango originating in Bihar and West Bengal. This particular variety also has great taste and is loved by all.

Gulab Khas: This variety grows in Bihar and is known for its rosy flavour and its gorgeous blush.

Himsagar: A variety grown in West Bengal but not very well-known outside of this region. It's a thin-skinned cultivar with smooth, silky flesh and sweeter than most other varieties. The sugary pulp melts in the mouth. Himsagars come to season from mid June until the end of the month and hence an unfortunate short season for such a delectable variety.

Kesar: One of the few varieties exported abroad. Kesar hails from Gujarat and has an intense aroma. Its acidity and sweetness is in perfect balance, though the fruit bears irregularly, much to the dismay of farmers.

Kishenbhog: This variety grows in North Bihar and is sweet, but firm and fibrous.

Langra: Another variety that stirs great pride in Northern Indians. Its flesh is mildly fibrous and with a distinct turpentine taste. Langra also has a short season, lasting only from mid-July to the end of the month. Just as Dashehari mangoes have a mother tree in Malihabad, a Langra mother tree exists in Varanasi. This Langra tree is believed to spawn many of India's other mango varieties. The tree's original owner was lame, and thus was born the name, "Langra".

Mankurad: This cultivar is the pride and joy of Goa. In fact, this fiber less, firm-fleshed variety and often fetches a price significantly higher than the Alphonso. The quantity of fruits is heavily contingent on the temperature during the flowering period. Also, if the weather is too cold or hot during the tender stages, the fruits drop prematurely.

Neelam: It is a consistent, large-yielding variety growing thoughout India. Hyderabad in particular is famous for this variety. Neelams come to the markets in May and lasts until the end of June.

Pairi: It grows throughout Goa and coastal Maharashtra. Though the fruit doesn't keep well, its texture is fibreless and the taste is a delightful balance of sugar and acid. It is one of the best juicing mangoes, even if mixing a more flavourful cultivar is common. Pairis have a mildly spicy aroma, and they're best consumed when the fruit turns slightly yellow.

Totapari: Its small green appearance and beak at the end of the fruit resembles a parrot beak, hence its name (as *tota* means "parrot" in Hindi). Unlike other cultivars, it is acceptable to eat the skin of this variety. This variety is a bit crunchy and tangy, best served with salt and chili powder. It is not that sweet in taste.

Mallika: Technically, a newer hybrid of the Neelam and Dashehari. Its orange pulp is of excellent quality and has pleasant honey sweetness. Growers like the variety for its disease resistance and productivity. Mallika's season lasts from June to July.

Ratna: It is found in Maharashtra and its tree is moderately vigorous, and precocious. Its fruits are medium sized with attractive in colour and is free from spongy tissue. It is the hybrid variety of Neelam and Alphonso.

Amrapali: It is dwarf, regular bearing and late maturing variety. It is suitable for high density planting. It is fibreless and is a hybrid of Dashehari and Neelam.

Dudhiya Malda: It is a mango originating in Digha and Patna (Bihar) as well as in Malda (West Bengal). The first supply arrives in the first week of June. This variety of mango is very popular among all.

6 Food and Ayurveda

"When diet is wrong medicine is of no use, when diet is correct medicine is of no need." – Anonymous

Ayurveda is the native and primeval Indian system of rules of healthcare which originated in the ancient vedic civilization of India. The knowledge base of Ayurveda is recorded and documented in the form of a compendium (a concise but comprehensive summary of an extravagant work in the form of a publication) known as *Samhitas*. Samhita simply means compilation or collection of work. These compendia such as the *Charaka Samhita*, *Bhela Samhita*, *Sushruta Samhita*, *Ashtanga Hridaya*, and *Sharngadhara Samhita* are composed in Sanskrit, a language which was used in ancient days but is not in day-to-day usage among the general population in modern India.

The Sanskrit term *ayurveda* is made by the union of two words: *Ayus,* which means "life" or "life span," and *veda,* which means "knowledge," with an implication of completeness or wholeness of the knowledge. Ayurveda cannot be seen as only a system based on only knowledge of life but it can be considered a way of living with a sense of reasoning to achieve better health and with justified logic. According to the ancient Ayurvedic scholar Charaka, *ayu* comprises the mind, body, senses and the soul and Ayurveda focuses on these aspects.

The inception of Ayurveda is in *Atharvaveda,* the contents of which date from around 100 BC. Then in 200 BC a medical exposition called *Charaka Samhita* was written in Sanskrit by a scholarly sage Charaka, who re-edited *Agnivesa,* a text written earlier by a sage of the same name along with five others, outlining the science of prolonging life without illness. It deals with the origin of medical science, a detailed classification of diseases, use of herbal commodities, all natural foods and drink ingredients and details of thorough medication, the use of drugs (medicine), and facts and practices for achieving good health.

Ayurveda can be more precisely defined as a system, which uses the integral principles of nature, to help maintain health in a person by keeping the individual's body, mind and spirit in perfect balance and in equilibrium with nature.

Ayurveda is based on the premise that the universe is made up of five elements: air, fire, water, earth, and ether. These elements are represented in humans by three *doshas,* or energies or humors: *vata, pitta* and *kapha.* When any of the humors (*doshas*) accumulate in the body beyond the desirable limit, the body recedes from its balance. Every individual has a distinct balance, and our health and well-being depends on getting the right balance of the three *doshas* (*tridoshas*). Ayurveda suggests specific lifestyle and nutritional guidelines to help individuals reduce the excess *dosha.*

Ayurveda elaborates one's natural constitution (*prakrati*) in terms of three basic functional elements, physical, mental and emotional energy patterns, called the *tridosha*: namely, *vata, pitta* and *kapha.* In terms of the physique and physiological activities of the body, the modern researchers interpret *vata* as the energy of movement, *pitta* as the energy of digestion or metabolism and *kapha* as the energy of lubrication and structure. *Vata,* translated as wind, means which moves, for example, breathing and beating of heart. *Pitta* is fire *dosha* translated as bile (a digestive juice secreted by the liver and stored in the gall bladder), which digests things, including mental digestion, or the ability to perceive reality. Kapha is phlegm (inactivity due to lack of energy leading to sluggishness), which holds things together.

Harmonious and congruous balance of *vata, pitta* and *kapha* is considered the mark of sound health. Any disturbance or malfunctioning, excess or deficiencies in any of these energies upsets the usual concentration of life-sustaining elements and physiological and (bio) chemical reactions and functioning inside the body, and, therefore results in various kinds of ailments.

A healthy person, as defined in *Sushruta Samhita,* one of the primary works on Ayurveda, is "one whose *doshas* are in balance, appetite is good, all tissues of the body and all natural urges are functioning properly, and whose mind, body and spirit are cheerful..."

Ayurveda says that *ahara* (food), after going through complete digestion, gets transformed into the nutrient fluid called *rasa* and that this *rasa* is then transformed into *rakta* in *yakrit* (liver) and *pliha* (spleen). Thereafter, *rakta* enters the heart. *Prana* derived through the act of respiration follows this *rakta*. This *rakta* is then converted into *mamsa* (flesh) and other bodily tissues. On this fundamental similarity, the educated scholarly people mostly translate *rasa* as chyle (a milky fluid consisting of lymph and emulsified fats; formed in the small intestine). Similarly, pneuma and *prana* too have a very close likeness; however, the term *prana* has varied contextual meanings as well, rather than being simply *breath*.

Related with the process of consumption of food, eight main factors have been mentioned in the book *Charaka Samhita*. These are conjointly termed *astavidhahara vidhi vishesayatan*. These are subsidiary to each other and elaborately describe the process of eating. Each of them contributes to healthy or positive and unhealthy or negative effects of the food being eaten. These are:

- natural and distinguishing attributes of food;
- method of preparation of food (it is of utmost importance about who prepares the food and how and where are they are prepared, whereas, for most of us only the taste matters);
- combination of food material (various components or constituents of the food);
- amount or measure or quantity of food;
- place (at which the food ingredients are grown; where it is prepared and eaten) the seasonal effects are also included here;
- time (of preparation and consumption of food);
- the mode and technique of eating;
- the physical and mental well-being of the person who consumes it.

If people consider these factors while eating food, it would be of great help to maintain the well-being of the person following all this. The significance of the factors mentioned above is justified scientifically.

Acharya Sushruta has categorized food in terms of their gross basic properties in 12 major categories (from medical point of view) and also recommends which and what type is conducive under certain natural conditions.

- **Shita (Cold):** The food with a cooling tendency is recommended for the person suffering from acidity, heat or other plethora of disorders. It is also advised for those attenuated by extravagant sexual activity, or under toxic effect.
- **Usna (Warm):** The food with warm character is advised for those suffering from the diseases or problems of excess of *vata* or *kapha doshas*. Such food is also consumed (in small quantity) after total stomach cleansing, fasting, and so on.
- **Snigdha (Smooth or Naturally Oily):** This type of food is suitable (in limited measure) to decrease and minimize the *dosha* of *vata*. It is also suggested to those who indulge in a lot of physical activity or excess exercises. It is also beneficial in ailments like dry-skin, bony, thin or weak body.
- **Ruksa (Rugged and Arid):** It helps to keep a check and control the *dosha* of *kapha*. It is suggested to the obese people or those with a oily skin.
- **Drava (Liquid or Watery):** Such diet is highly beneficial to a person suffering from the internal dryness of the body leading to ulcers, boils, or ligament problems. This kind of food has to be taken in excess to benefit the most.
- **Shuska (Dry):** The one suffering from leprosy, *prameha* (excretion of sperm and several vital hormones with the urine), erysipelas (an acute infection leading to deep-red inflammation of skin) or wounds should be advised to eat food that is dry in nature.
- **Eka-Kalika (One-timely):** Individual suffering from loss of appetite or having weak digestive system should eat food only once a day, in order to bring back the normal appetite and also to rectify the metabolic disorders.
- **Dwikalika (Two-timely):** In proper and normal state of well-being, a healthy and disease-free person should take proper meals only twice a day.
- **Ausadhi-Yukta (Medicinal):** There are people who cannot take medicines orally due to any reason. They are advised to eat food mixed with herbal medicines. In such a case, most of the times, specific medicinal plants or herbs are also recommended as a basic ingredient of the therapy regimen for specific diseases.
- **Matrahina (Light):** Person suffering from liver problem, fever or loss of appetite should take light and easily digestible food. This may be dry or liquid, warm or cold type, depending upon the nature of the ailment and natural feature in terms of the level of tridosha.
- **Prashamanakaraka (Tridosa-Controller):** The food should be selected depending upon the nature of the season and also the level of *doshas*

Vata

Vata monitors the flow and motion in the body. *Vata* attributes to air and ether elements. This energy is generally seen as the force, which directs nerve impulses (the act of implying force suddenly), circulation, respiration, and elimination. *Vata* controls functions such as blood circulation, expansion and contraction of the lungs and heart, intestinal peristalsis (the process of wavelike muscle contractions of the alimentary tract that moves food along in it) and elimination, activities of the nervous system, the ability of contraction process in muscles, and so on. *Vata* is of prime importance and it controls the other two principles, *pitta* and *kapha*.

People with more *vata* in their physical constitution are inclined to be thin, with a delicate physique and broad joints, soft skin that is inherently dry, and dry copious hair. Such *vata* dominated personalities are quick, responsive and lively in thought, speech and action, and are best in making friends as well. There is an attribute of delicacy in their steps and a quality of sophistication in their laughter. The quality of change is synonym to their feature. They are light slumberer and are pulled towards warm environments.

Creativity and sparkling enthusiasm are trademarks of a balanced *vata*.

Vata is connected with the *guna* (attribute) *Rajas*, manifested in enthusiasm and energy, and in a love for gain through aroused action but uncertain judgement.

Disorders Due to Vata

Cracking in soles, pain in foot, foot drop, numbness in feet, pain in ankles, stiffness in ankles, cramps in calf, sciatica, tearing pain in knees, stiffness in thighs, loss of movement in thighs, lameness, pain in anus, limping, hunchback, dwarfism, stiffness in sacral region, stiffness in back, compression on sides, twisting pain in abdomen, cardiac dysfunction, shivering in chest, constriction in chest, chest pain, wasting of arms, stiffness of neck, hoarseness of voice, pain in jaw, cracking of lips, pain in eyes, pain in teeth, loose teeth, stammering, astringent taste in mouth, dryness of mouth, loss of taste sensation, loss of smell sensation, earache, hardness in hearing, deafness, stiffness in eyelids, contraction in eyelids, loss of vision, pain in eyes, twisting of eyebrows, pain in forehead, headache, cracking of scalp, facial paralysis, feeling of darkness before the eyes, giddiness, tremors, yawning, hiccups, malaise, insomnia, and instability of mind.

Pitta

Pitta commands bodily functions related with heat and metabolism, and directs all biochemical reactions and the process of energy exchange. *Pitta* pertains to fire and water elements. This *dosha* governs metabolism, e.g., the conversion of foods into nutrients. *Pitta* is also responsible for metabolism in the organ and tissue systems. For example, it regulates digestion, functions of the exocrine (a gland that secretes externally through duct) glands and endocrine (a gland that secretes hormones directly into the bloodstream) hormones, and intracellular metabolic pathways such as glycolysis (a metabolic processes that breaks down carbohydrates and sugar into acids to release energy), the tricarboxylic acid cycle, and the respiratory chain.

People with more *pitta* in their constitution are inclined to be of medium proportions, with a physique that is neither lilliputian nor huge, warm skin that is very fair or florid red and may be very sensitive as well, and fine hair that may proceed towards premature graying or thinning. They are sharp and determined in thought, speech and action. There is an element of reasoning to their movement and vividness to their voice. Ambition is usually their second name. They are moderate sleepers and are comfortable with colder atmosphere.

Self-confidence and spirit of risk-taking tendency are trademarks of a balanced *pitta*.

Pitta relates to the *guna* (attribute) Sattva, which is expressed by way of intelligence and solemn, and of pleasure attained through knowledge and regulated action.

Disorders Due to Pitta

Heating, scorching, burning, intense burning, fuming, hyperacidity, burning in the stomach and esophagus, internal burning, burning in scapular region, pyrexia (a rise in temperature of the body indicating infection), over-perspiration, foul smell in body, tearing of body parts, excessive moisture in blood, moistening of muscles, burning in skin, tearing of skin, thickening of skin, internal haemorrhage (bleeding), haemmorhagic patches, yellowness, bluishness, herpes (viral disesase causing blisters on the skin or eruption of the skin), jaundice, bitterness in mouth, bloody smell from the mouth, foetid (unpleasant) smell from the mouth, excessive thirst, loss of contentment (satisfaction in one's life), irritation in throat, eyes, and anus, inflammation in the penis, discharge of pure blood, fainting, green or yellow colour in the eyes, urine and faeces (solid excretory products evacuated from the bowels).

Kapha

Kapha monitors the construction and cohesion (intermolecular force that holds together) of the organism. *Kapha* pertains to water and earth elements. *Kapha* is responsible for growth and protection. The mucosal lining of the stomach and the cerebral-spinal fluid that protects the brain and spinal column are examples of *kapha*. It is responsible for biological strength, natural tissue resistance, and proper body construction.

People with more *kapha* in their characteristics are inclined to be of large built, with a sturdy physique and cushioned joints, thick smooth skin that may be oily, and excellent wavy hair. They are unagitated and calm in thought, speech and action, and are easy-going and supportive in relationships. There is an element of firmness in their steps, a quality of tranquillity and lack of anxiety in their smile. Loyalty has become synonym to their nature. They are long, heavy sleepers and find themselves very uncomfortable in damp and cold climate.

Calmness and pleasant temperament are trademarks of a balanced *kapha*.

Kapha represents the guna (attributes) Tamas, which, is linked with courage and gallantry, but in practice it is expressed in an indifferent, ignorant, stubborn or mechanical response.

Disorders Due to Kapha

Drowsiness (a sleepy state), excessive sleep, cold sensation, heaviness in body, lassitude (weakness due to lack of vitality), sweetness in mouth, salivation, mucous expectoration (the process of coughing up), excess dirt, excess mucous, indigestion, plastering of heart, plastering of throat, accumulation in vessels, goitre, over-plumpness or roundness of body, white luster shineness, and whiteness in urine, eyes and faeces.

as well, for both people in good health as well as those in bad health. For example, warm and sour and sweet food helps in minimizing the *vata dosha* in rainy season.

- **Vatti Prayojaka (Naturally soothing):** For the person in a good state of health, nourishing food is the one which helps maintaining and strengthening the prominent elements and stamina and which also increases the level of immunity against diseases.

Apathya (unsuitable) Food: The food which is the prime cause of any disease, ailment or any disorder of which if not treated leads to prolonged and severe state of disease comes under this categorization of food is referred as *apathya* food. The founders of Ayurveda have asserted food as the essential source of nourishing, sustenance and strengthening of health. However, they have also emphasized the fact 'what an individual eats and how?' should not be ignored and paid due importance. They stated clearly that at times food can be the reason of suffering as well. It could even prove to be toxic and poisonous. In fact, the same nature of food could have different effects, though invisible, under various conditions or for different persons. The most important factor is what kind of guidelines an individual follows in the selection, procurement and preparation of food and in their eating habits.

Charaka Samhita states the condition of unsuitability of various types of foods or medicines under different circumstances.

Factors of Non-suitability of Food

- **Place:** Sturdy or arid (lacking spirit and water) food and herbs are harmful and unsuitable in a wild land or in a desert. Cold and greasy-smooth, oily or fatty substances or preparations (including medicines) are bad for health (or have negative effects) in a wet (highly humid) or swampy waterlogged area.
- **Season:** Eatables and beverages that are cold in nature are to be avoided in winter; whereas the use of hot spicy foods and substances having characteristic to increase the body heat should be avoided during the summer and spring season.
- **Appetite:** It should be taken care of that eating food without having proper appetite is harmful. Similarly, not eating nourishing food in adequate amount even when one is feeling hungry is also not good for health and has a negative impact on the appetite and metabolic activity.
- **Combination:** There are certain combinations which are extremely harmful and should be avoided at any cost. Eating a mixture of ghee (clarified butter) and honey in equal amount causes severe toxic effect (while individually each has crucial nourishing and medicinal properties, if consumed in right quantity keeping in mind the other factors).
- **Body's adaptability:** The body gets accustomed to the habit of consuming certain kind of food for a long period of time. If one's body has got

accustomed to acrid, spicy and hot (in tendency) foods then sweet and cold (in tendency) foods would generally be incompatible to their body's adaptability.

- **Tridoshas:** The food or medicine that has properties similar to those inducing the tendencies of any of the three *doshas* (*vata*, *pitta* and *kapha*) but, that causes contradictory effects because of disharmony (with one's natural constitution, habits and physical or mental work pattern) in practice is considered to be non-compatible with respect to the *tridoshas*.
- **Utensils:** The use of utensils has also been compatible with certain commodities. Boiling milk in pure copper pot tends to be toxic in its effects. These or some other types of metallic utensils are highly unsuitable for cooking certain meals, while several types of substances are unsuitable for preparing certain chilled drinks, and desserts.
- **Eating habits:** The food with exactly opposite tendency should not be consumed simultaneously. Eating hot (in tendency) food with cold (in tendency) substances or vice versa, simultaneously or without giving substantial time break leads to harmful effects.
- **Digestive system:** Prescribing laxatives (that stimulate excretion of faeces) or strong medicines or foods to an individual with a delicate digestive system or intra-body structure is harmful.
- **Sleeping habits:** Food or medicine which heightens the *kapha* tendency is not recommended to people who are mostly slow, lethargic and slothful in their daily routine or who sleep heavily, as they might further induce lethargy, sluggishness or lassitude.
- **Routine:** Consuming food without proper excretion of urine and stools is always harmful and undesirable. Those wishing excellent natural health should avoid eating food without having real hunger.
- **Sequence of eatables:** Drinking water, eating food cold in nature or taking any medicines after drinking or eating smooth oily foodstuff leads to negative effects. (One might even vomit instantly or suffer from sour throat in such cases.)
- **Cooking:** The food which is cooked best is neither half-cooked nor overcooked and is suitable for good health. The over-fried food is also unhealthy. Similarly, the food cooked using polluting fuel should also be avoided.
- **Composition:** Drinking any preparation in which an acidic substance (including fruits) is mixed with milk is harmful to health. Curds (unless well set and fresh) and desserts prepared with fruits kept in milk for some time are also restricted in Ayurveda.

Charaka Samhita emphasizes a great deal on the impact of food on the overall health of an individual including physical, mental and spiritual health. It broadly classifies the food and nourishing substances into twelve major categories as nourishing eatables.

• Shuka Grain (Cereals)

Wheat, rice, barley, maize, millets, corn, and so on, are staple ingredients used in Indian cooking. The cereals are the natural mode of sources for nourishment of the human body. Carbohydrates are the major components of them and they also have about 6% to 12% proteins. The presence of minerals and vitamins is, however, minimal in cereals. Only vitamin B is found in greater quantity in their outer sheath. The shelf-life of these cereals ranges between one to two years after harvesting. Sprouted cereals have more nutritional value as compared to normal cereals and these are also richer in proteins and vitamins in their content.

• Shami Grains (Pulses and Legumes)

Grams and pulses fall under this categorization of grains and they are main sources of proteins. This category comprises gram, green gram, red kidney beans, red and yellow gram and lentil, black-gram, soya-bean seeds, dry peas, and so on. The protein contents and nature of metabolic activity of these are healthier as compared to those who derive proteins from non-vegetarian foods (meat, chicken, eggs, etc). The best examples include freshly sprouted whole pulses and legumes and they are highly nutritious as well.

• Kandamula (Tubers and Roots)

Potato, sweet tuber (sweet potato), carrot, beetroot, turnip, radish, and so on are chief examples of tuber and root vegetables. Carbohydrates are in plenty in them and they are significant sources of calories in our bodies and activator of metabolism. These if had in proper amount leads to a good health and energetic life as well. They are so nutritious that they are consumed in place of several cereal dishes. It is said that *kandamula* was the chief food of the *rishi-munis* during the ancient period. The word *phalahara* mentioned during fasts refers to these only.

• Phal (Fruits)

Fresh fruits have certain nutrients like vitamins, minerals, natural glucose and carbohydrates in fairly large amounts. Fruits such as apple, *amla*, bilva (wood-apple), banana, black-plum (rose-apple), dates, figs, grapes, guava, mango, orange, pomegranate, papaya, sweet-lime, and so on are easily found in almost every part of India. According to Ayurveda, fruits have been associated with certain medicinal properties. Certain fruits like apricot, cherry, pineapple, and strawberry could also be used, depending upon their availability and seasonality. Ayurveda stresses on the fact that the fruits should be consumed only in their appropriate season and it is best to consume fruits that are naturally ripened. As raw fruits are difficult to digest and over-ripened fruits are not that nutritious (in fact they are harmful), such fruits don't have the desired medicinal and nutritious properties. Nowadays, fruits are ripened using chemicals like carbide and it must be avoided entirely. They have severe harmful effects and may lead to even dangerous diseases like cancer.

- **Shakas (Vegetables)**

When it comes to the most nutritious diet, fresh vegetables are placed above all varieties of food. They are the mine of micro-nutrients like vitamins, minerals and compounds. It is even recommended by nutritionists to consume different types of green beans, bitter gourd, brinjal, cabbage, cauliflower, cucumber, green-gourd, ladyfinger (bhindi), tomato, and so on with the diet. Few types of vegetables supplement other vegetables in fulfilling the body's requirement of vitamins and minerals. It is desirable to eat vegetables in their own season and not otherwise.

- **Harit (Greens Leafy Vegetables)**

Green leafy vegetables like varieties of *saag*, spinach, coriander leaf, and fenugreek leafs, green peas, mint leafs, radish leaf, and so on come under this category. They are also highly nutritious. They have iron, calcium, and other minerals like Vitamin C and E in plentitude and they are also highly recommended in the diet.

- **Shuska Phal aur Tilahan (Dry Fruits and Oilseeds)**

Almond, cashew nut, chestnut, coconut, groundnut, peanut, pistachio, etc., are a major source of proteins. The oils of all these provide natural lubricants and fats essential for the body's mechanical and varied functions. The seeds of sesame and mustard also yield oil which is also used for the same purpose.

- **Ikshu (Glucose-Rich Substances)**

This group of food includes molasses, sugarcane, sugar, treacle, and other glucose rich substances. These are mostly used to sweeten the drinks and eatables. They contain carbohydrates in very large quantity, and hence are the main source of producing energy in the body.

- **Ambu (Watery or Juicy Substances)**

This category comprises of all edible substances which have high water content. Watermelons, contain about 90% water, and same is for the cucumbers as well, both are crucial in this group. Fresh lemon squash, and juice of watery fruits, if consumed properly and in substantial amount, also nourish us with other nutritious substances along with water.

- **Goras (Milk products)**

Milk, curds, buttermilk, cheese, etc., comes under this group. Pure cow milk and buttermilk are considered 'divine' foods and indeed the best source of nourishment. Many people are able to perform *kalpa* (long-term fasting) only with the consumption of milk or buttermilk. Curds are also very nutritious with certain medicinal properties, if taken fresh and in adequate amount in various seasons according to one's temperament (level of *tridosha*). Fresh cheese and its products (if not fried) are wholesome sources of calories. Buttermilk is also referred in Ayurveda as a significant medicinal food. Condensed milk and milk powder are popular as they are a means of preserving milk, but these are harmful to health, because of the chemical synthesis processes adopted in their preparation. Hence, the use of condensed milk, milk powder or dairy whiteners should be avoided as much as possible.

- **Sneha (Oils and Fats)**

Butter, ghee (butter clarified), edible oils and fatty substances, if taken in balanced amounts, are also part of a healthy diet. These are highly rich in calories (one gram of fat yields nine calories). They play a crucial role in lubricating the body parts (mostly joints) and also in generating energy production in the body system. They contain fat soluble vitamins like Vitamins A, D, E and K. The excess of this group has to be avoided as this may lead to obesity and certain ailments.

- **Krattana aur Yaugika (Cooked Food and Edible Compounds)**

Cooked food has been classified as an entirely different class of food, according to Ayurveda. Many ingredients can be consumed raw or sprouted. The process of cooking alters the natural characteristics of the food ingredients. But certain foods are suggested to be consumed cooked as cooking renders them to be more digestible and which helps in the metabolic processes of the body. The cooking of food as per the concept of Ayurveda was to make it edible, but in today's scenario cooking is done just to make it more tasty and delicious. Various experiments have been carried out to work upon the factor how to make food tastier and also nutritious and hence *molecular gastronomy* has found a very special place in the world of gastronomy.

The rudimentary law of maintaining good natural health was elaborated by Vagbhatta as under three terms: Hitbhuka, Mitbhuka and Ritbhuka.

- **Hitbhuk:** This term emphasizes on the principle that one should eat food that is nutritious and nourishing for one's health and not only for the sake of gaining pleasure from taste.
- **Mitbhuk:** This term stresses on the fact that one should eat moderately to sustain vigour, vitality and stamina of the body. It says one should not be a voracious eater.
- **Ritbhuk:** This term accentuates that an individual should consume only that food which is earned by morally justified and righteous means and also that is conducive with a particular season.

Culinary Trivia: Six Tastes

Six tastes are found in Indian cuisine and they are: sweet (*madhura*), sour (*amla*), salty (*lavana*), pungent (*katu*), bitter (*tikta*), and astringent (*kasaya*).

Each taste has specific therapeutic actions. The tastes increase or decrease biological humours (*doshas*), as the case may be. Everyone needs a certain amount of each of the six tastes, and relative proportions differ according to the constitutional or humour type of the particular individual. Too much of any taste is harmful to any constitutional type.

The sweet taste gives strength to the tissue elements, is good for nourishment, and harmonizes the mind. Sweet tasting products are not only those which taste sugary, but include rice, ghee and fruits. Sweet food is heavy on digestion.

The sour taste stimulates the digestive fires and enzymes and sour-tasting food, for example, lime and tamarind, are easy on digestion and good for the heart (it is only relatively recently that modern dietetics have discovered that Vitamin C is good for heart and it is found in all sour foods). By sour Ayurveda means naturally so and not manmade ones like vinegar.

The salty taste stimulates digestion, clears obstruction in the channels of the body, causes sweating, and increases the power of digestion, but tends to deplete reproductive secretions. An excess of salt causes greying and wrinkling.

Pungent tastes, as in onion, pepper and garlic, help digestion, improve metabolism and dilate channels in the body.

Foods with bitter taste eliminate bacterial elements, purify the blood and are light on digestion. Examples include bitter gourd, fenugreek seeds and lemon rind.

Substances which have a predominance of astringent taste such as potatoes, apples, betel-nut leaves, most green vegetables and food containing tannin like tea, possess the properties to heal ulcers and wounds. They dry up the moisture and fat in the body and act as water absorbents.

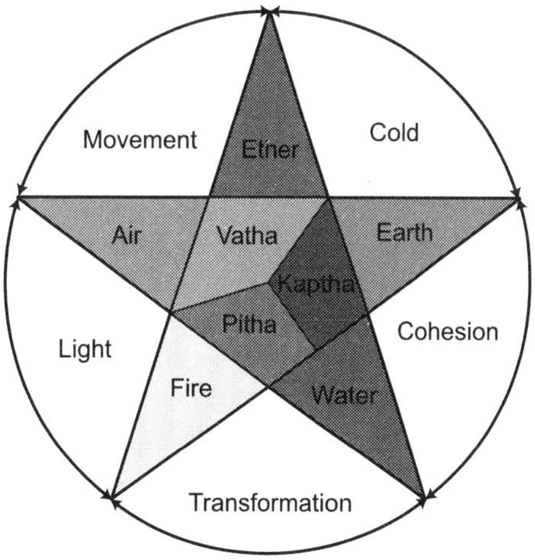

Culinary Trivia: Relation between Tastes and Doshas

Dosha	Aggravating Tastes	Pacifying Tastes
Vata	pungent, bitter, astringent	sweet, sour, salty
Pitta	sour, salty, pungent	sweet, bitter, astringent
Kapha	sweet, sour, salty	pungent, bitter, astringent

7 Brief Introduction of Indian Cuisine

"Food can be expressive and therefore food can be art." – Grant Achatz

The Indian subcontinent is the birthplace of Indus Valley Civilization, heart of cultures, cradle of a few religions, blessed with a rich heritage and therefore it is so varied in its cuisine. The cuisine of India is so diverse that it has created an influential and indelible mark on the world cuisine.

India is the divine land where the past amalgamates with the present; where almost every ingredient is cultivated and they contribute in the making of Indian cuisine. It is here in India where cuisine has risen to prominence by dominance of taste, and spices have blended with other ingredients in order to define and fabricate the Indian cuisine.

This land has experienced extensive immigration and its nature of acceptance from each stream has made it very rich in terms of its cooking traditions. The intrusion from various parts of the world has diversified its cooking culture taking it to the zenith. Notwithstanding the various influences brought into the country by various rulers, invaders and travellers, Indian cooking has never lost its identity, and rather it has got elaborated and become richer with the assimilation of the myriad influences.

The fertile land of this country is blessed with the blessings of rivers like Ganga, Yamuna, Narmada, Godavari and Brahmaputra. It also has a conducive and favourable weather in various parts of the country which favours the growth of *kharif* and *rabi* crops and thereby it is rich in terms of its agriculture. It goes without saying that the fertile land supported by irrigation and a rainy season is the best in producing seasonal crops. A place rich in terms of land output would undoubtedly be rich in its cuisine and India is no exception to it.

Religious and caste inhibitions; weather and climatic changes; location and geographical background; seasonal availability, cultivation and produce; culture and civilization; ostentatious display of culinary skill and the impact of foreigners eating style have affected the eating habits of Indians and thus its cuisine too.

It would be an impossible task, rather meaningless task to assemble the cuisine of a subcontinent without comprehending the basic and distinctive features of each state, each domain and region of the country. The country is so diverse, so varied that an old saying captures the variations in rural India perfectly, "*Kos-kos par badle paani, chaar kos pe baani*"; which translates to – at every two miles taste of water changes and every four miles the dialect (*baani*) changes. So, to bring the cuisine of such a versatile land under one single platform, it has to be started from scratch and then it would demystify itself.

The cardinal essence of Indian cooking lies in the impeccable and exact use of aromatic spices. Whenever there is a mention of Indian food, the first image which comes to mind is that of a variety of spices which are visibly perceptible by the senses, undoubtedly the characters of their colour, flavour, character and aroma. The accomplishment of the cook lies in the subtle blending of a variety of spices to enhance rather than to overpower the basic flavour of a particular dish. These spices are also used as appetizers and digestives. Each spice is characterized by its individual taste, colour, flavour, aroma and peculiarity. The spices used are incorporated in the dish in two forms, i.e., in powdered form or in whole form. It would not be unfair to state that the Indian cooking revolves around the magic of spices used in it. It is because of this very reason that, when Indian cuisine is talked about, one image that emerges in the mind of any outside individual is the spiciness. Indian cuisine has rather become synonymous to its spicy tastes.

Indian cooking is divided in three different stages. The first and foremost is to prepare the base or the gravy. This requires warming the oil and then tempering it with the spices and seasoning. The second stage involves adding the vegetables or the main ingredients and stirring it into the gravy base. The third stage is to allow the dish to simmer until completely cooked. This is the basic technique to prepare the dishes in India.

Indian cuisine is not the cuisine of a single nation but it is the resultant cuisine of many factors like seasonal availability, religions, communities, local taste and preferences, and indeed all states. The best adjective for this cuisine is only one and that it is ambrosial. It is versatile in wide-ranging tastes, diverse in varied beliefs, and practices and eating habits of the people of India. No preparation has a standard recipe. Each preparation can be prepared in different ways and methods. No recipes were written and documented in books and then prepared, but the actual recipe has been passed orally from generation to generation. The recipe of Indian cooking is prepared by *andaaz* meaning approximation and experience. The spices are never measured by the weighing scale or by any other measure but they are added by *andaaz*. This *andaaz* is achieved by regular practice and indeed experience.

Indians attribute a lot of importance to breakfast, known as *nashta*, and this is taken after the customary cup of tea or coffee which marks the beginning of the day. The drinking of tea is a custom gifted by Bristishers. While *nashta* in North India features rotis, *parathas*, a vegetable preparation, *puri bhaji*, pickles and curds, but in the southern belt it is *idli* or *dosas* accompanied by *chutney*, and in the western region it comprises *dhokla*, *pav bhaji*, *poha*, *upma* and milk.

Lunch is a significant affair of the day for every Indian and calls for elaborate preparations of at least 2-3 vegetable dishes, *dal*, rice, curds, a variety of desserts and is wrapped up with *paan*. The main dish during lunch varies from region to region but it is usually either rice or roti or both. Indian food in the evenings consists of a cup of tea or coffee with some snacks while dinner serves the purpose of bringing together the family followed by desserts which may be traditional or fruit-based. It is said in India that to be healthy and in a better state of health, eat breakfast like a king, lunch like a normal human being and dinner like a pauper. This means that, breakfast should never be skipped and should be heavy too, lunch should be normal in portion size and dinner should be very light as compared to lunch.

India can be disaggregated into various sections, in terms of culinary aspects, depending upon its similarity and commonality in a single section. One can segregate it in various directions like North, East, South and West. But as India is so wide-ranging and multifaceted that it would be unfair to do so. It has to be classified as below to have a better picture.

The segregation and division would be:

- The Himalayan Valley ranges: Jammu & Kashmir and Himachal Pradesh.
- North India: Delhi, Haryana, Punjab, Uttar Pradesh and Madhya Pradesh.
- The Gangetic plains: Bihar, West Bengal and Odisha.
- North East India: The seven sister states of India and Sikkim.
- West India: Gujarat.
- The Konkan coast: Goa, Maharashtra and Karnataka.
- The Thar Desert: Rajasthan
- The Deccan Plateau or peninsular plateau: Andhra Pradesh, Tamil Nadu and Kerala.

In the regional classification made above, few regions have some similarities. The similarities may be due to the same practices followed or due to seasonal availability of ingredients in that particular region.

Cuisine of Himalayan Valley Ranges

The availability of ingredients like *haak*, *knol khol*, *kanaguchhi*, saffron, colocassia makes some dishes very unique in this region. Kashmir is a place where *wazwan* is the aromatic celebratory banquet meal with thirty-six tasty dishes. In Himachal Pradesh the mid-day meal is referred as *dham*. The cuisine of both the regions has been very different from the rest of the Indian cuisine and same are their dishes. The Kashmiri preparations are distinguishable with delicacies like *roghanjosh*, *goshtaba*, *rista*, *kabargah*, *tabakmaaz*, *heddar*, and so on whereas the Himachali dishes are based on a huge variety of *dals* and dishes like *madrah*, *sidu*, *sepu badi*, *patande*, *maahni*, *babroo* and so on. The cuisine of this region is almost dissimilar to the cuisine of the rest of India due to atmospheric climate, local produce and its location adjacent to the Himalayan ranges.

Cuisine of North India

One unique and distinguishing feature of this region's cuisine is the gravy preparation. When it comes to Punjab, the seasonal availability and regional producc dominates strongly, hence the dishes like *sarson ka saag* with *makki ki roti* has become popular worldwide. Tandoori style cuisine also finds a revered place in the cuisine of Delhi and Punjab. Haryana is also very particular about its preparation like *raabri, bajre ki khichri, singri ki subzi, kachri ki subzi, methi gajar, bathua ka raita,* and so on. The excessive produce of milk is easily felt in the cuisine and the dishes of Haryana and Punjab are rich in butter and ghee. When it comes to the cuisine of Uttar Pradesh, Awadhi cuisine plays a key role and it becomes the centre of attraction for the whole national cuisine. The Awadh region has gifted many mouth-watering dishes to Indian cookery. The people from Madhya Pradesh do not have a distinct cuisine of their own, but is based on the cuisine of its neighbouring states. The number of dishes is not that huge here but a few are with a unique flavour and taste like *daal bafla, bhutte ki kees, chakki ki shaak, koprapak, kulsi, bundeli gosht, sighri wala kukra,* etc. It speaks about Bundelkhand cuisine which is referred as tribal cuisine. The cuisine of this area has left a huge influential mark on the Indian cuisine and it has become very popular all over. This area has been the torchbearer to popularize the Indian cuisine on the map of world cuisine.

Cuisine of Gangetic Plains

It is this region which is influenced and blessed by the benediction of river Ganga. The cuisine of Bihar is very simple and relishing too. It has unparalleled dishes like *makhuni* roti, *litti-chokha, belgrami, sattu,* and so on. The dishes are healthy and nutritious. On the other hand, Bengali cuisine is symbolized by the rice and fish preparations. Mustard oil is the main medium of cooking. The cuisines of Odisha and Bengal share a similarity and have many common features. For example, a five-spice mixture combination is used in both the cuisines and is known as *panch-phoran* in Bengal and *panch-phutana* in Odisha. The similarity is also seen in sweets of both the regions. Rasogulla originated in Odisha long back but gained popularity in Bengal. Few dishes are common like Rasmalai and Chenna sweets in both the states. It is the Jagan Nath temple of Puri in Odisha which prepares and offers Chhapan Bhog (collection of 56 delicacies) to their Almighty God.

Cuisine of North-East India

North-East India comprises eight regions which includes Sikkim, Assam, Arunachal Pradesh, Meghalaya, Nagaland, Tripura, Manipur and Mizoram. The dishes of this region are unique and different from the entire country. All the dishses are prepared with sheer simplicity and it is easily reflected in their cuisine. The paneer of yak milk is referred as *chhurpi* and is consumed with great zest. *Momos* and *thukpa* are the famous preparations and are known all over the subcontinent. Rice, being the staple diet is consumed in large quantity by the north-eastern people. Rice is also used in preparing local brew beverage. Assam is famous for its tea production. This region has also been blessed by the production of one of the spiciest chillies *bhut jolokia* and is renowned worldwide.

Cuisine of West India

Gujarat is renowned and esteemed for its vegetarian dishes all across the country. It uses very subtle spices and is relatively rich in texture. The Gujarati *thali* comprises roti, *dal, kadhi,* rice and *subzi* (*shaak*). The preparation here has a combination of sweet and sour taste as they prefer to use jaggery and tamarind in most of their preparations. Gujarat also offers an immense variety of delicious snacks called *farsan.* Basically, *farsan* means snacks which can be anything like salted, fried, and crunchy. The noted snacks of this region include *dhokla, khandvi, shev, ragda, samosa, batata vada,* and so on. Parsi is the common community here and hence dishes are mostly vegetarian due to their religious beliefs and compulsions. Non-vegetarian dish like *salli chicken jardaloo* is also famous.

Cuisine of the Thar Desert

This desert region has a marvellous history. It experienced an extreme harsh climate and war-like situations between Rajputs and Mughal which resulted in continuous immigration in the region. All these factors along with lack of availability of vegetables due to scarcity of water have been a deciding factor in shaping the cuisine of Rajasthan. The warriors here had a great passion for hunting and due to this game cooking has been popular in this region. The best of this cuisine is the combination of *dal-bati-churma* where *dal* is lentils, *bati* is baked or fried wheat ball and *churma* is powdered sweetened cereal. The mutton preparation like *lal maas, safed maas, mohan maas* and *jungle maas* are also very popular. It also offers an innumerable variety of sweet preparations as well.

Cuisine of the Konkan Coast

The state of Maharashtra has coastal as well as arid parts and hence the food varies accordingly. It is rich in myriad of vegetable preparations and rice is the staple food grain here. Few preparations are acknowledged all over like *puran-poli, modak, pandra rassa, zunka-bhakar, vada pav, shrikhand,* and so on. When it comes to Goa, the list of famous unique preparations is indeed very long like *vindaloo, sorpotel, xacutti, bebinca, dodol, cafreal,* and so on. The influence of Portuguese is also easily visible in the cuisine of Goa. The use of *kokum,* a purple berry which has a distinct sour taste is common. Ratnagiri district in Maharashtra is blessed with Alphonso mangoes which needs no introduction all over the world. Karnataka is also not far behind any state when it comes to cuisine as it has few preparations which comes from this region and are popular all over. Dishes of Karnataka include *jolada roti, akki roti, saaru, bisi bele bhaat, puliyodharai,* and so on.

Cuisine of the Deccan Plateau

The Deccan plateau covers the states of Andhra Pradesh, Kerala and Tanil Nadu. This region also has few similarities among the states it covers. It consumes coconut in every possible preparation. The cuisine of this region offers famous dishes like *dosa, idli, sambhar, poriyal,* lemon rice, curds rice, *rasam,* and so on. Generally, a special tempering is done to dishes which include curry leaves, mustard seeds, whole red chilli, asafoetida, and so on. They have a tradition of eating food on plantain leaves using hand. The communities of **Chettiyars, Iyengars, Malabaris** have also dominated the cuisine of this region.

Thus in short, the cuisine of India has been the cuisine of Aryans and Dravidians. It is the cuisine of all religions, all communities prevailing here and indeed of all states. It has a very peculiar aroma of all the spices and tastes of diverse culture and eating patterns. It is so ambrosial in nature that by just knowing about this celestial cuisine would engulf any one in its love, magic and charm it spells. No one can remain without being spell-bound by the charm of this cuisine. It is a great delight and a matter of extravagant delectation for all the food lovers all across the world. The Indian cuisine, which is grandeur in its character, extends its domain of versatility when it is explored a little further each time and a new domain erupts that is untouched and unexplored, thus the exploration never ends. It is a vast magnificent theme which is splendid, delectable and scrumptious in its taste and offers an ambrosial cuisine.

Culinary Trivia: Paan

Paan in Hindi comes from Sanskrit *parna* meaning feather. Another Sanskrit term for the quid, *vida,* is the *beeda* of common current usage. Sanskrit name for paan is *tambuli.* It is a stimulating and psychoactive preparation of betel leaf combined with areca nut and/or cured tobacco. It is the traditional betel leaf palate-cleanser-cum-digestive, dating to ancient times. It is regarded as an auspicious symbol of hospitality. It was offered as a moral and even legal commitment when an agreement was drawn up. *Paan* is chewed and finally spat out or swallowed. *Paan* has many variations. Slaked lime paste (*chuna*) is commonly added to bind the leaves. Some South Asian preparations include *red katha* (catechu) paste or *mukhwas* to freshen the breath. The skilled *paan* maker is known as a *paanwala* in North India. In other parts, *paanwalas* are also known as *panwaris* or *panwadis*. Beautiful containers of brass, copper and silver to hold the various ingredients of making a paan called *pandan,* have been crafted since time immemorial. *Pandans* come in a variety of floral, bird and animal motifs and nut crackers, called *sarotas* are fashioned after parrots, peacocks, horse riders, celestial figures and amorous couples.

A *paan* is a heart shaped, smooth, shinning and long-stalked leaf from a creeper called the *paan* creepers, grown in hot and humid climate but under shade so that direct the sunlight does not burn the leaves. Various other ingredients are added in the *paan* leaves and then folded into triangular shaped *bidas.* Now everywhere in India, almost all the communities enjoy chewing the betel leaf after meals or anytime they like. These days it may have just the traditional ingredients or a mixture of *gulkand,* dried coconut, aniseed, camphor (eatable *kapoor*), cardamom, cinnamon and cloves, peppermint, rose petal or sugar paste, fruit preserves or syrup, too. *Manasollasa* (AD 1130) written by King Someshwara of Kalyana in Central India describes *panchasugandha* as *athambula* with five aromatic ingredients, namely, the cardamom, clove, nutmeg, mace and camphor, a truly kingly concoction.

Paan leaves are commonly cultivated in Tamil Nadu, West Bengal, Odisha, Madhya Pradesh, Maharashtra and Uttar Pradesh. Betel leaves contain tannins, sugar and an essential oil which is a light yellow aromatic liquid with a sharp stringing, burning taste. It also contains a phenol called chavicol and the alkaloid arakene in it, which has similar properties compared to cocaine.

In South it was considered, "Laxmi resides in the forepart of the betel leaf, Jyestha at the bark, the Lord of speech at the right, Parvati at the left, Vishnu inside, the Moon outside, Shiva at all the edges and cupid everywhere. Yama, the lord of death resides at the root and that is why the stalk is always pinched away before the leaf is eaten".

There are three types of *paan* available in market nowadays; *meetha* or sweet paan, *zarda* paan (containing tobacco) – infamous for its teeth and sidewalk – staining properties, as the red juice is usually spit out, and *saada* or simple paan with only basic ingredients in it.

The leaves of *paan* are also given different names such as Maghareya, Chandrakala, Jalesar, Haldia, Poona, Karimpur, Sanchi, Jjagannathi, Shrirampur, Ketaki, Choorward and so on. An analysis of the betel leaf shows it to consist of 85.4% moisture,

3.1% protein, 0.8% fat, 2.3% minerals, 2.3% fibre and 6.1% carbohydrate per 100 grams. Its mineral and vitamin contents are calcium, carotene, thiamine, riboflanin, niacin and vitamin C. Its calorific value is 44.

The history of *paan* goes back to ancient times, when scholars of Ayurveda with the help of Dhanvantari invented this wonderful chewing material after doing several experiments on rats. During this research, *paan* was found to be good for digestion. Even reference of *paan* is found in *Shrimad Bhagvat* as Lord Krishna used to chew it.

Ibn-e-Batuta mentions the ritual of serving *paan* as the first thing to a guest at the time of his arrival and departure. This is one of the customs, which is still quite popular in Lucknow.

The tradition of eating *paan* was popularized by Noor-Jahan, the mother of Emperor Shahjahan who built the wonder in marble Taj Mahal. Empress Noor-Jahan discovered that by adding some particular ingredients to the *paan* and eating it gives a beautiful natural red colour to the lips. So along with its taste, the *paan* was eaten by women for reddening their lips.

Part B
Regional Cuisine: Gastronomic Overview

8 Awadhi Cuisine (Uttar Pradesh)

"Oh, the tiger will love you. There is no sincerer love than the love of food." – George Bernard Shaw

Uttar Pradesh, a state located in the northern part of India, is edged by Rajasthan on the west, Haryana and Delhi on the north-west, Uttarakhand and the country of Nepal on the north, Bihar on the east, Jharkhand on the south-east, Chhattisgarh on the south and Madhya Pradesh on the south-west. Its capital is Lucknow.

The former kingdom of Awadh (*Oudh*) is now delineated by the area in and around Lucknow (capital of Uttar Pradesh).

The cuisine of this Awadh region has reached its zenith to and indeed to the level of par excellence in the world of culinary. The Awadh region has been the land of nawabs and hence the cuisine of this region is also referred as nawabi cuisine. Awadh is renowed for two things: its culture and the cuisine. The filigreed words like *nazakat* (sophistication), *nafasat* (elegance), *tehzeeb-o-adab* (etiquettes) and *tehzeeb* (mannerism) speak volumes about the culture of this area and the image that comes forth in the mind at the mention of Awadhi cuisine is just the legendary cordial hospitality with a bouquet of culinary delights comprising *kebabs, kormas, kaliyas, mussallam, zarda, pulao* and *biryani, sheermal* and *taftan, muzzafar,* and so on. All its delicacies are genuinely captivating and a delight to all food lovers.

Lakhnawi *mehman-nawazi* (hospitality of Lucknow) can be easily depicted in Awadhi cuisine. It is widely esteemed and far famed for the sheer miscellanea it offers and for its distinct flavours and aroma. Dishes are cooked slowly over charcoal, which allows the flavours to seep in and soften the vegetables or meat naturally.

Heavily charmed by Mughlai cuisine, Awadhi cuisine is considered a distinctive cuisine of the kings (nawabs) of Lucknow. The cuisine comprises both vegetarian and non-vegetarian dishes and also has many unique and unparalleled dishes that catered to the affluent tastes of the North Indian royal class. The kitchens of Awadh had four chefs: *bawarchis*, responsible for the preparation of food only in bulk quantity; *rakabdaars*, who made food in smaller portions; *naanfus*, who had mastery in preparing rotis; and a *maharaja*, who was concerned with the onus of preparing only vegetarian dishes. The professional cooks used to receive royal clientele from nawabs and were generously rewarded for their accomplishments and services. This motivated the cooks to ascent their craft to an art form - they drew their inspiration for creativity from poetry, music, season, festival, flora and fauna. People were unintimidated to experiment and explored with unaccustomed techniques and ingredients. Their painstakingly developed recipes were blessed with careful details and hence were covetedly guarded secrets, passed on to generations by word of mouth alone.

Broadly speaking, a single cook was never given the entire responsibility to prepare the complete meal. There were specialized cooks appointed for distinct preparations. There were assistants, who assisted the specialized cooks for distinct activities that carried out specific actions. The helpers (*khidmatgars*) to cook were like the *degbos* who cleaned the utensils and vessels, the *masalchis* who just ground the spices to prepare the powdered masala, the *aabdar* who was given the responsibility to cater water to everyone, the *mehris* whose was allotted the task to carry the *khwan* or tray to spread on the *dastarkhwan*. The affuluent people of the region had a superordinate assigned in the kitchen to monitor the kitchen affairs. This officer was known as *daroga-e-bawarchikhana* or *mohtamin*. The officer was responsible for ascertaining that the quality of the food was best.

Inspired by the excellence of the Mughlai cuisine, each delicacy is fastidiously prepared with attention to minute details. The Awadhi cuisine is prepared with exotic spices and garnished with dry fruits — a symbolic representation of prosperity, affluence and royalty. Perfumes (Ittrs) perform a very significant role in meliorating the aroma of the dish and making it delicate. These perfumes are mainly made from musk deer, hunting of which is banned worldwide. The use of *chandi ka varq* is also very common in Awadhi cuisine in desserts as well as in non-vegetarian preparation like *kaliya*. This lends magnificence, grandeur and royalty to the dish in which it is used.

The Awadhi cuisine being varied in nature, the menu mostly variegates in accordance with the seasons and the festivities of the region. The cold and harsh winter months are dealt with rich food such as *paya* (which is a dish cooked overnight over a slow fire) and such items are relished with delicious hot *naans*.

The winter menu is made more exceptional by incorporating meat of birds in the dishes. Heat providing birds, like quail and partridge are more desired in the dishes during the winter season. Fish is also relished during the cold winter months, but when the rainy season arrives, fish preparations are mostly avoided. Awadh is a region where basically the fresh fishes from the rivers are preferred. Various dishes are prepared from fish and are enjoyed subsequently. One of the delectable and well-renowned fish delicacies of Awadh is undoubtedly, the fish *kebab*. Generally, a variety of Indian carp fish is used to prepare this dish and is cooked in mustard oil. One of the notable vegetables commonly used in Awadh is the green pea. This multi-used vegetable is incorporated in a varied range of dishes such as *salan, nimona, keema, pulao* or in fried vegetable dishes.

In this region, the season of spring observes the mode of festivity with a myriad variation of dishes prepared in various forms. The commonly prepared dishes are fried delicacies during this season. The crispy snacks like *phulkis* (*besan pakoras* in *salan*), *puri-kebab, birahis* (*paratha* with a stuffing of mashed *dal*), *khandoi* (*dal* balls steamed and cooked in *salan*), *lautepaute* (pancakes made from gram flour and served in *salan*), cutlet made from colocasia leaves are served with *salan*, and so on are a few of the scrumptious delicacies gifted by the Awadhi cuisine to mark a enthusiastic and bubbly season of the year. Summer months experience an entirely different list of summer recipes. For instance, raw mangoes are cooked and sweetened with sugar or jaggery and served as a dessert dish called *murabba*. Such preparations are unique authentic items of the Hindu community of the Awadh region. In Awadh, the professional cooks used to prepare *murabbas* of whole unripe small mangoes in such a style that the green outer skin maintained its original appearance. It seems to appear as if small, unripe mangoes have been plucked from the trees and made into syrup.

This region has an exceptional penchant for *pulaos* as compared to *biryani*. Seven well-renowned fragrant *pulaos* in Awadh are acknowledged. Among them are *gulzar* (the garden), *nur* (the light), *koku* (the cuckoo), *moti* (the pearl), and *chameli* (jasmine). The nawabs of this region also preferred fragrant *pulao* over *biryani*. One of the illustrious preparations in this region is Yakhani *pulao*. This preparation incorporates cuts of pieces like *nalli, puth, neck, seena,* and *chops* in it. First and foremost, the meat pieces are seared with spices and then allowed to cook in stock. Once the meat is cooked well, the *yakhni* is strained to prepare the gravy in which the rice and meat would need to be further cooked. Then, the parboiled rice, meat, browned onions, and *yakhni* gravy are all layered and the pulao is *dum* cooked for few minutes.

The dairy products like milk and yogurt have been used in abundance. In Awadh, great heed has been paid to the varied preparations from these dairy products, such as *balai*, i.e, clotted cream. Here, the topmost juicy layered portion is removed by warming the milk (in very shallow trays) over a very slow fire. Then many layers are removed simultaneously and cautiously layered one above the other until a thick *balai* is formed. *Balai* in urdu is referred as *malai*. One of the nawabs liked it very much and termed it *balai* as *bala* literally means 'above' in Persian as it also comes from the top of the milk. This word coined by him was appreciated by the masses and has became common in use.

As with the rest of India, Awadh also witnesses fervour of busting activities in the kitchen during festivals. People marked by ardent enthusiasm prepare a innumberable and delectable delicacies with the intention to serve it to their friends and family members. The women of the households generally take it as huge a responsibility on themselves to make sure that all the dishes are impeccable in taste. During the sacred month of Ramzan, when the Muslim community observes fast for the entire month, the cooks and women of the house are busy to prepare an extravagant spread of scrumptious dishes to be served at *iftari* or the meal eaten at the end of the day's fast. *Iftari* is to be shared with friends and family members along with the poor sections of the society. The festival of Eid is grandly commemorated in Awadh with a huge choice of mouth-watering and unique items specially cooked to make the occasion remembered. Huge varieties of *sewaiyan* (vermicelli) are cooked during Eid. Malida is one such similar preparation which is had during Fatiha and Niyaz. This is a sweet dish preparation which is prepared using semolina and it is so gentle that it melts in the mouth without any effort by the diners. Another festive occasion that is commemorated with a great count of tasty delicacies is the Shab-e-Barat. During this festival special *halwas* are prepared and relished with great gusto. Semolina, gram flour and various other items are used to make the *halwas*. Awadhi cuisine is not renowned to prepare special dishes only during the season of festivity, but also during the period of grief as well. An occasion like Muharram, which signifies a depressingly dark state of mind and heart, is marked by the preparation of particular dishes like *khichra* or *haleem*, which is basically a combination of various *dals*, wheat and meat, cooked together and consumed during Muharram.

Dastarkhwan

Speaking without any exaggeration, *dastarkhwan* means a meticulously and punctilious laid-out ceremonial dining spread with a great detail of perfection. The dining spread consists of the wooden table of very low height and is covered with a silk cloth. The diners sit cross-legged all around the table and the delicacies prepared by *khansamas* are brought in a bowl gilted with silver or gold and are kept on the table covered with silk cloth. It is customary in the Awadh region for three generations to sit around and share the *dastarkhwan*. Here the dinners start eating (*nosh farmana*) with pronunciation of Bismillah. This indeed is a very lavish and sophisticated setup to dine for.

The Awadhi/Lakhnawi Dastarkhwan would not be considered complete unless it had the following dishes in it mandatorily:

- *Korma* (braised meat in thick gravy),
- *Salan* (a gravy dish of meat or vegetable),
- *Qeema* (simply a minced meat preparation),
- *Kebabs* (pounded meat or a chunk of meat, fried or roasted over a charcoal fire)
- *Pasanda* (fried slivers of very tender meat, usually kid, prepared in a rich gravy)
- Rice which is cooked with meat in the form in the form of a *pulao, biryani*, or plain rice.
- An extensive and wide selection of varied rotis (breads).
- Luscious desserts which comprise *kheer, halwa, phirni* or *sheer brunj*.

Once the meal is over, water was passed to the guests in *silfachi* and *aaftaba*, the water jug and basin respectively to help them to wash their hands while sitting comfortably.

Dum-pukht

Dum means to breathe and *pukht* means to cook. In this distinctive style of cooking, the ingredients are kept in a *handi* that is plastered and sealed with dough, ensuring that all moisture remains trapped, causing the food to cook in its own steam. By this mode of cooking, flavours and fragrances are absolutely preserved, as its nutritive value. The most important element in dum cooking is the utensil *deg* in which the item is cooked. The *deg* or *degchi* is a narrow neck cooking utensil made of heavy brass metal. Since *dum* cooking desires to be taken place in an airtight utensil, over very low flame heat for longer duration of time, it is imperative that the base of the utensil is made of a thick metal. The *degchi* is sealed with dough in such a fashion that air cannot escape from the utensil and the actual flavour, aroma and nutrition remains trapped in it, which results in more flavourful dish.

In 1784, an acute famine swept across Awadh. Nawab Asaf-ud-Daulah commissioned the construction of Bara Imambara as part of food-for-work famine relief program designed to provide large-scale employment. Large *handis* or vessels of spices-infused rice were placed on hot coals and sealed to ensure that hot food was available to workers round the clock. The subtle aromas of the sealed pots evoked the interest of the royal kings and this style has since then stayed with the royal tables of the Indian cuisine. This was thought to be the birth of *dum* cooking in India. This method got more refined with the passage of time and invention of new technology, and is currently popular by the term *dum-pukht*.

This method of cooking is mostly used for meat cookery, as slow and gentle cooking is most apt logically for cooking tougher cuts of meat.

Some famous preparations that are cooked by this style of cooking are:

Dum Biryani, Raan, Shabdeg, Lahm-e-Murghan, Dum Aloo, Dum ki Subziyan, and so on.

Cooking and Flavouring Techniques

- **Dhungaar**

This is a unique technique of fumigation in which a smoky flavour is imparted to any dish. The smoke penetrates the ingredients of the dish being smoked and hence contributes a subtle aroma, thereby bestowing the quality of uniqueness to the dish. The dish may be smoked either at the final stage of the preparation or at the intermediate stage of cooking. The smoke is simply created by using a live charcoal and putting some ghee on it, which in turn produces smoke. This smoke in contact with the dish gives it a smoky flavour. The live coal may be placed on a small katori or a bowl, which in turn has to be placed in the dish to be smoked and then covered with lid. Once the dish is smoked, the coal is then removed from the

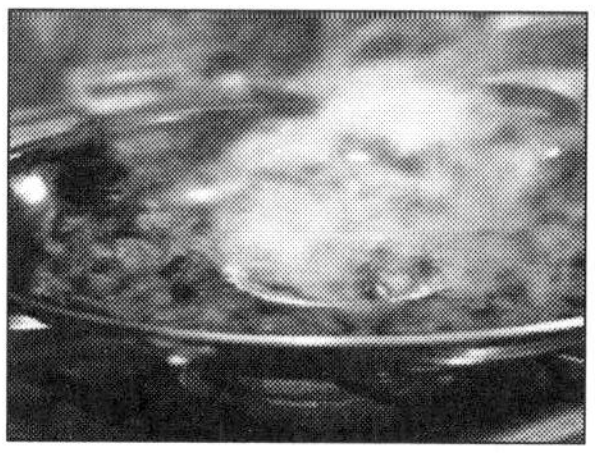

utensil and dish is ready for consumption. Fumigation is called *dhuanar* in Hindi.

- **Baghar**

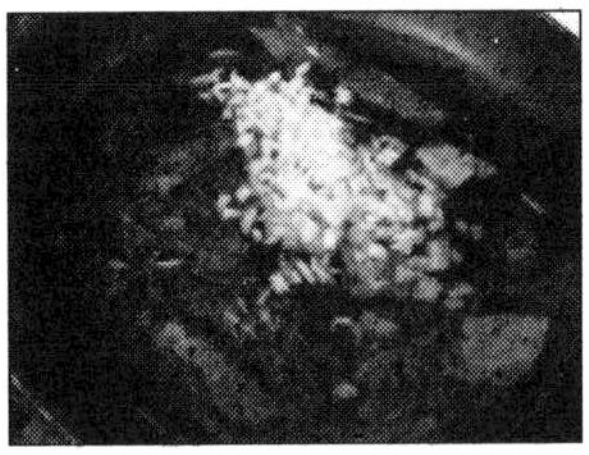

It is derived from the Sanskrit word *bhagharna*. This is a technique of tempering a dish using a cooking medium and spices. Mostly it is carried out at the end of the preparation, when the oil is heated to a very high temperature and then the spices are added to it. As soon as the spices begin to crackle, the oil is put in the cooked dish and immediately covered with a lid, so that the aroma of the spices is trapped in the dish. This method enhances the taste of the preparation.

- **Ghee Durust Karna**

This is one of the most outstanding tempering technique of improving the flavour and seasoning of the dish. The cooking medium oil is heated to a very high temperature and *kewra* water and cardamoms are added. The water evaporates gradually and once when oil cools down, it is strained through muslin cloth and used further in various preparations. Thus, it is fundamentally the tempering, seasoning and flavouring of the cooking medium with *kewra* water and cardamoms.

- **Gil-e-Hikmat**

This is one interesting method adopted for cooking which focuses on the Persian influence on Awadhi cuisine. *Gil* in Persian is referred to earth or mud and *hikmat* entails the procedure of the *hakims*. The meat or vegetable to be cooked by this method is generally taken whole and then stuffed with nuts and spices. Then the whole stuffed ingredient is enclosed in a leaf of banana or cloth and then covered properly with clay or *multani mitti* (fuller's earth) in order to seal it. It is thereafter buried in the earth almost 4-6 inches deep. On this buried content, a slow fire is placed on top for about 6–8 hours and allowed to cook, and then the food is dug out and is considered ready to be served.

- **Zamin Doz**

This is also an altogether different style of cooking. In this style, a hole is dug in the ground and the ingredients to be cooked are stuffed with certain ingredients and then placed and covered with mud. Then live charcoal or cow-dung cake fire is placed over it and allowed to cook it for about 6-8 hours. It is called Zamin Doz as the cooking ingredient is placed below the ground. This cooking technique lends an exceptional earthy flavour to the dish. Vegetables like bottlegourd and fish are prepared by this technique.

Specialty Dishes

Kaliya A very popular mutton gravy preparation cooked in brown onion gravy with addition of cream (*balai*), saffron and curds. A special mixture of spices is added at the end of preparation called *Lazzat-e-taam*, found very rarely nowadays. *Kaliya* has variation like *Mahi-kaliya, Chandi-kaliya* and *Kundan-kaliya*. The cooked mutton pieces are wrapped in gold leaf in *Kundan-kaliya* and in silver leaf in *Chandi-kaliya* and then served in a flavourful gravy.	
Do-Pyaza As the name *do-pyaza* literally means twice onions, in any of the *do-pyaza* preparation, onion is added twice to a dish. This *do-pyaza* can be made for a several kinds of ingredients like mutton (mutton *do-pyaza*), chicken (*murg do-pyaza*), ladyfinger (*bhindi do-pyaza*), jackfruit (*kathal do-pyaza*), cottage cheese (*paneer do-pyaza*), mushroom (*khumb do-pyaza*), cauliflower (*gobhi do-pyaza*), bitter gourd (*karela do-pyaza*), and so on.	
Rizala *Rizala* is a non-vegetarian preparation in which a creamy white gravy with yogurt is taken as a base and lamb meat is cooked. It is made up of onion, cashew nut, curds, saffron, *khoya* and cream. It is flavoured and aromatized with *kewra* water and *ittr*. It is fundamentally a preparation of any of the red meat in cream coloured rich gravy, which gives an unusual contrasting appeal to the dish. It is preferred to be served with *roomali* roti or *sheermal*.	

Raan

The whole mutton leg flavoured with saffron and cooked with rich nuts and freshly ground spices is a delicacy which bestows brilliance to any meal. Extreme care is taken by cooks to let no stone unturned to make sure that the whole leg is cooked properly to the right degree. This dish is made from the whole leg of lamb that is smeared with ginger-garlic paste, red chilli powder, aromatic spices and any tenderizing agent like raw papaya paste or curds and left to marinate for about 2 hours. It is then seared on a hot pan to give the colour. The *raan* is now placed in a heavy bottom pan and cooked on *dum*, till tender.

A version of it exists in the form of Parde Wale Raan in which a whole lamb leg is cooked with a blanket of flour pastry on it.

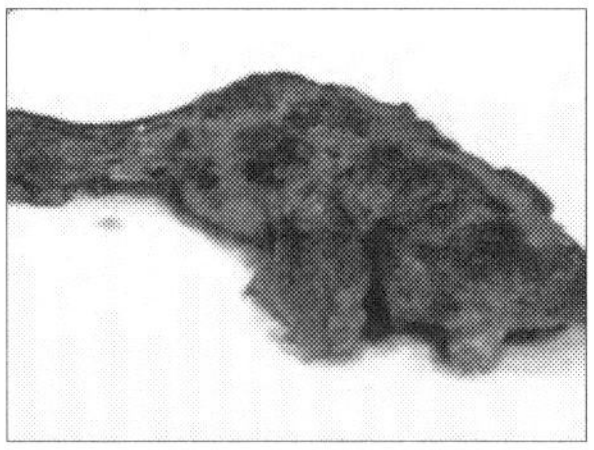

Korma

The term *korma* is derived from Urdu word 'kormah' meaning braise. Classically, a *korma* is defined as a dish where meat or vegetables are braised with water, stock, and yogurt or cream is added. The technique encompasses many different styles of *korma*. The distinctive flavour of a *korma* is based on the mixture of various spices, including ground coriander and cumin, combined with yogurt kept below the curdsling temperature and mixed slowly and carefully with the meat juices. Authentically, this would have been carried out in a pot set over a very low fire, with charcoal on the lid to provide all-round heat. A *korma* can be mildly spiced or intensely spiced and has the option to use either lamb, chicken, beef or game. There are certain *kormas* which combine meat and vegetables such as spinach and turnip.

The term *shahi* (royal), is used for few *kormas* indicating its status as a prestige dish, rather than an everyday meal, and its association with the court.

Nargisi Kofta

The delicacy which is basically a hard-boiled egg, is enclosed in a minced-spice mixture and then deep fried. When halved lengthways it resemble the eye. The poets have been describing beautiful eyes of their lover with adjectives like *nargisi aankhen*, hence the dish named Nargisi Kofta by the chefs. This delectable dish has been an essential feature in *dastarkhwan* due to its amazing beauty in the plate when served.

Shabdeg

Originally, Shabdeg is a Kashmiri preparation, which came down to Awadh from Kashmir along with forced migrated Kashmiri families. Shabdeg is a beautiful preparation made up of mutton balls, whole turnips, *ver* (Kashmiri *masala*) and spices cooked in a *deg* through the night or *shub*. The treatment of turnips with saffron, *ver*, onions, and *koftas*, cooked on slow fire in a sealed *deg* till the break of dawn, contribute this dish a special status. Extreme care is taken to make mutton balls and turnip pieces to look alike and these two are cooked in gravy, till properly done. Along with the mutton balls and turnip, the gravy is added with perfectly shaped other ingredients – mutton pieces and game birds.

Nehari

The word *nehari* derive from 'nehar' or fasting and is a famed common breakfast item with the Muslim populace. It is generally had after the first *namaz* of the day. It is originally beef, braised and then stewed overnight with spices, further prepared in the morning and eaten with *kulchas*. It is nourishing and energy-giving and hence usually had during the period of Ramadan. It is a stew consisting of slow cooked beef or lamb garnished to taste and served with cooked brain or base marrow. The word *nihar* originated from Arabic word 'nehar' which means 'morning' after sunrise prayers. It is also very popular in the Hyderabad region.

Haleem

It is a dish made from the combination of pounded wheat and mutton. In this dish, the mutton is marinated with curds and then a paste of onion (fried golden brown), poppy seeds, coconut and cashew nut is prepared. In a separate pan, the mutton is cooked slowly with spices till it shreds and then pounded wheat is added with spices and cooked properly. This preparation is also popular and common during the festive season of Ramadan. It is mostly washed down with a bowl of hot *paye ka shorba.*

Kakori Kebab

This is a *seekh kebab* very soft in texture that originated from Kakori, a place very close to Lucknow. It is mutton mince on skewers and is cooked on a barbeque of coal fire. The mince for the *kebabs* is obtained from the leg of the mutton and is added with *khoya,* black pepper and other ground spices to make patties. It is made from lamb pieces which are free from sinews and are minced many times to get the smoothness. It is minced along with fat from the kidneys and is added with certain spices and red chilli powder. The *kebab* is then skewered onto special square-shaped seekhs and grilled on an open barbeque grill. The square *seekh* is used so that the *kebab* holds better and the *seekh* does not roll over when placed on the grill.

One story attached with this delicacy is that an old aged toothless nawab wanted a lamb *kebab* that would melt in this mouth and he could enjoy the delicacy without much effort. This requirement was conveyed to the cook. Upon much research and experimentation, cooks were able to create this mouth melting delectable *kebab* for the nawab.

Shami Kebab

Referred as the king *kebab* of Awadh, and acknowledged as the best kebab of the country is made from minced meat. They are round patties of minced meat filled with spicy fillings comprising raw mango chutney or karonda, depending upon the seasonal availability of the filling ingredient. The *kebab* is extremely soft and simply melts in mouth. It is eaten with *roomali* roti also. The softness of this *kebab* speaks volumes of the cooks who prepare it.

Gilawati Kebab or Galouti Kebab

It is a *kebab* which melts in the mouth and is made without using any binding agent and is made from the use of fresh minced meat and the spices. In order to get the meat cooked properly, the *kebab* is added with a tenderizer like raw papaya paste. The word which describes this *kebab* best is mouth watering. It is cooked on a large flat utensil known as *mahi tawa. Chikana keema* from the breast of lamb is used to make this *kebab.*

Murg Mussallam

Mussallam literally means whole and hence Murg Mussallam simply means whole chicken. This delicacy is prepared by marinating the chicken with a paste of spices and ghee and then stuffing it with chopped hard-boiled egg, various dry fruits and then roasting in ghee. It is then cooked in *lagan* till well done and served garnished with silver leaves and almond slivers.

Zamin doz Machhli

This is a delicacy having a splendid earthy full-bodied flavour in which a whole fish is stuffed with spices, sealed in an earthenware case, buried in the ground and cooked for about 6-8 hours by placing cow dung cake fire on the ground above.

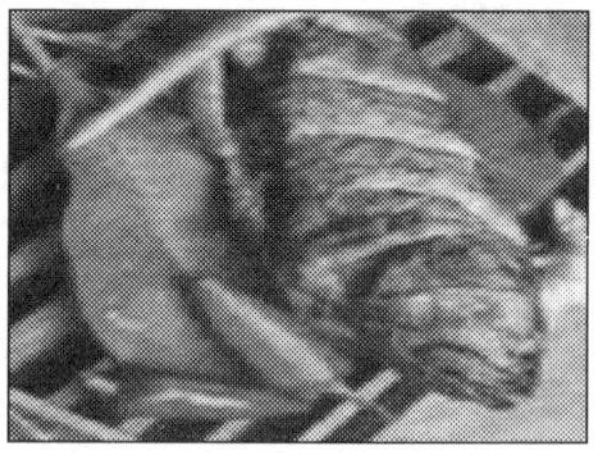

Lahm-e-Murghan It is a well-famed specialty of this region. It is prepared by marinating boneless pieces of meat in lemon juice and salt for about half an hour. The cooking process starts by heating ghee in a heavy bottom pan and frying sliced onions until golden brown. The marinated meat is added and sautéed until brown. Onion, ginger, and garlic paste; yogurt; aromatic spices and paste of poppy seeds, cashew nuts are added along with ghee. At the end, the lamb is added and the dish is cooked on slow flame. It is a delectable juicy meat preparation, relished by everyone for its distinguishing taste.	
Nimona It is a scrumptious dish made from pounded green peas, spiced *mungoris* (dehydrated lentil dumplings) and spring onions in a brown onion gravy added with asafoetida. It is cooked in winters as during this period only the fresh green peas are available.	
Lazeez Lauki This delicious bottle gourd preparation is prepared by whole gourd stuffed with khoya, curds, cashew nut and nuts cooked in a lightly spiced gravy. In this preparation, the gourd is cut lengthwise and all pits are scooped out for filling to be stuffed. Then this stuffed gourd is cooked in a mild gravy and served with *warqui parantha*.	
Badal Jaam It is a very simple preparation made of brinjal roundels deep fried and topped with a tomato mixture and flavoured curds on it. It is relished all over and looks amazingly great in presentation.	
Sultani Dal It is an unusual preparation of *arhar dal* prepared with milk, cream, curds, saffron, mint leaves and spices. It is different from the unusual normal *arhar dal* as it is enriched with the addition of milk, cream, saffron and few other ingredients. Generally, in preparation of *arhar dal* milk is uncommon and this *dal* preparation goes against the normal trend prevailing, hence it is an unusual preparation indeed.	
Zarda It is a sweet vegetarian rice preparation cooked especially during spring season in Awadh. In this preparation, cooked rice is boiled with sugar syrup and then it is *dum* cooked. At last, it is finished with pouring hot *desi ghee, bhuna khoya* and saffron in *kewra* water on it and is garnished with nuts and silver foil.	
Lucknowi Biryani A delicacy relished by all is this *biryani* in which mutton is cooked separately and then rice is also sautéed in ghee, till almost done. Then, in a *degchi* rice and mutton are layered with proper sprinkling of *kewra* water and *ittr*. It is then *dum* cooked to retain all the flavour and aroma. It is served with *boorani raita* (curds added with fine chopped garlic in it) or with *korma* gravy.	

Mutanjan

It is a unique rice preparation, very similar to *biryani*, but sweet in taste. Mutton is prepared separately and rice is also parboiled separately. Along with it sugar syrup (*kimam*) is also prepared, then all three (rice, mutton and sugar syrup) are layered and then *dum* cooking is done to make it more flavourful.

Roomali Roti

As the name suggests, this bread resembles an handkerchief in appearance. It is shaped without rolling on a board and is given the shape by flying it high with hand and finally cooked on a convex iron griddle. It can only be prepared by cooks with great expertise and skills. This difficult-to-prepare bread is a nice way to showcase showmanship of the cooks in public gathering buffets.

Sheermal

This bread was invented by Muhammadan, a top-notch bread maker. It consists mainly of flour, milk, fat and saffron. It is traditionally cooked in *tandoor* but can also be cooked in a *mahi tawa* by covering it with a lid and applying heat from top and bottom.

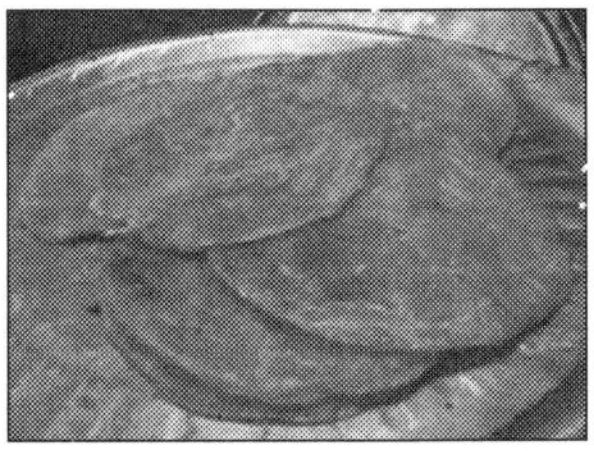

Sewain Muzaffar

It is a sweet vermicelli preparation shallow fried in ghee and then cooked in milk. It is also enriched with *khoya*, various nuts and finally garnished with silver leaf.

Taftan

It is a delicious fermented bread cooked in *tandoor* and resembles *naan*. It is accompanied by lavish *kormas* and *kaliyas* of this region.

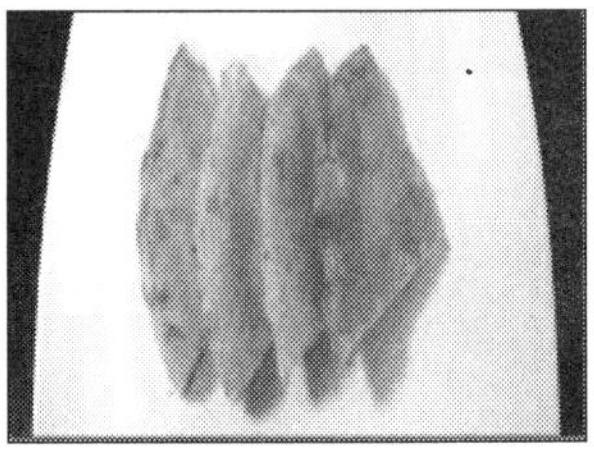

Bakarkhani

It is a very rich bread as the dough for it is prepared by mixing flour with milk, cream and cashew nut paste. Fat incorporated in the dough is also much high in quantity. The dough is allowed to rest for about an hour, and then rolled with a rolling pin and cooked in a *tandoor*.

Warqui Paratha

The Warqui Paratha or the layered paratha is cooked with lot of ghee and hence can be stored for a longer duration. It is a gourmet's pleasure to prepare this dish, and is a popular item for breakfast.

Sheer Brunj

Sheer Brunj is a variety of *kheer* in which basmati rice, milk, *khoya, ghee*, cream (*balai*), nuts and sugar are used. It is served chilled, flavoured with cardamom powder, *ittr* and *kewra* water.

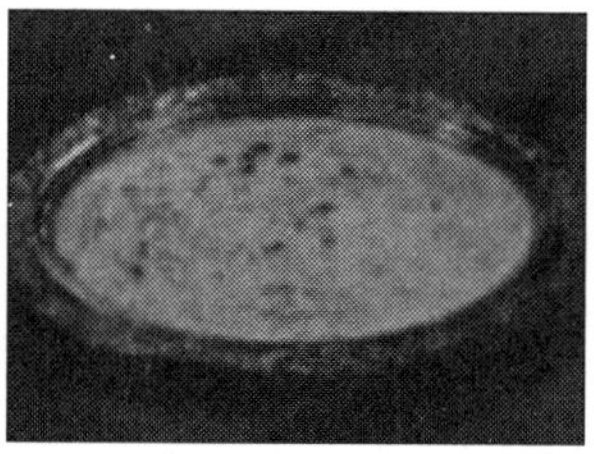

Culinary Trivia: Tunde Ke Kebab

Tunde ke Kebab is a dish made out of minced meat which is popular in Lucknow. Ingredients include finely minced lamb, plain yogurt, *garam masala*, grated ginger, crushed garlic, ground cardamom, powdered cloves, melted ghee, dried mint, small onions cut into rings, vinegar, sugar, lime and about 160 spices. It is served with *roomali roti*.

The 100-year-old Tunde ke Kebab in Chowk, Lucknow, is famous for its *kebabs*. Tunde ke Kebab is so named because it was a speciality of a one-armed chef. It was created by Haji Murad Ali.

Culinary Trivia: Chandi Ka Varq

Chandi ka Varq is an edible, stunning embellishment used as a garnish for sweets, *supari* (betel nut), *paan* (betel-leaf) and fruits in India. It is very fragile in nature, purely edible but does not have any flavour or aroma or taste. *Varq* - also pronounced as *warq, vark, varkh, varaq, varak*, is an Urdu word which means 'leaf'. Its preparation is really a back-breaking job and is prepared with great caution in workshops in India, usually Ahmedabad, Lucknow, Delhi and Hyderabad. Very minute nuggets of silver are placed between tissue paper and placed in leather pouch and beaten repeatedly with a heavy hammer until it becomes a dainty leaf fit to adorn the tops of Indian desserts or *biryani, kebabs*, and so on.

Soney ka varq is also prepared the same way using gold in place of silver.

Culinary Trivia: Ittr & Bhara Mirch

Ittr: The word *attar* or *ittr* is basically an Arabic word which means 'scent'; this in turn is believed to have been derived from the Persian word *atr*, meaning 'fragrance'. *Ittr* is natural perfume oil derived from botanical sources by natural distillation. The oils obtained from the herbs, flowers and wood are generally distilled into a wood base such as sandalwood and then aged. The aging period can last from one to ten years depending on the botanicals used and the results desired.

These all-natural perfumes are highly concentrated and therefore are usually offered for sale in small quantities and have traditionally been offered in decorated crystal cut type bottles or small jewelled decanters known as *itardans*. Most commonly they are made from musk deer, hunting of which is now banned everywhere.

Situated on the banks of the sacred River Ganges, 80 km from Kanpur in Uttar Pradesh, is the now almost forgotten ancient city of Kannauj, once the capital of the famed Emperor Harshavardhana, prides itself as the 'Attar City' or the perfume city of India. *Ittr* is used in Mughlai cuisine for added flavour and aroma.

Bhara Mirch: It is translated in English as stuffed chilli. It is a unique variety of accompaniment consumed with meals in Uttar Pradesh and Bihar. The main point to be kept in mind while preparing this is that the chilli used in it is of a red chilli variety and of large size. It is stuffed with mustard seed powder, *amchoor* powder, *panch phoran*, and so on. Seasoning is added according to the taste and then the stuffed red chillis are kept in glass jar, filled with cooked mustard oil. Then it is sundried for 2-3 days and one can consume it after 10-15 days. It is also kept for a longer period of time and is liked by all.

9 Bengali Cuisine

"Food for the body is not enough. There must be food for the soul." – Dorothy Day

Bengal, situated in the eastern region of India, is surrounded by Assam on the east, Sikkim on the north, Bihar and Jharkhand on the west and Odisha on south-west. It is also bordered by Bangladesh in east as well.

Bengal has immense and ancient culinary history and has been enriched and meliorated by various influences and encroachers; invaders and rulers. It is famous worldwide for its vivid potpourri of rice dishes and profuse miscellanea of fish delicacies; hence this great piece of land is also legendary as the land of *maach* (fish) and *bhaat* (rice).

The land of Bengal is marked by its great capability to produce, due to its rich alluvial soil and it is irrigated by none other than the water of the Ganges. Its culinary traditions are dependent on the Lucullan selection of produce, grains and seafood. Rice is a staple diet. The cuisine of Bengal is distinctly different from most other parts of India. Various immigrant communities settled in Bengal and found a closely knit populace of neighbours and hosts. There has been a very firm sense of cultural exchange between the natives and the immigrants enriching the culinary pattern of the region. In spite of this, the culinary habits and traditions have remained in its purest, authentic and undiluted form.

With a huge reliance on fish and lentils served with rice as a staple diet, Bengali cuisine is acknowledged worldwide for its subtle (yet sometimes fiery) but full-bodied flavours, its splendid confectioneries and mouth-watering resplendent desserts.

Some major historical features have influenced and shaped the Bengali cuisine, from the culinary point of view. Originally inhabited by Dravidians and Austronesians, and later further settled by the Aryans during the Gupta era, Bengal fell under the controlling influence of various Muslim rulers from the early thirteenth century onwards, and was then ruled by the British for almost two centuries (1757-1947). Bengal was ruled by Mughals for about 500 years and this is portrayed by the characteristic elements of the Bengali cuisine with rich sauce and vibrant curry. After the Mughal rule, Bengal became a hub of British rulers and even Dutch and French had some colonies in West Bengal and thus their salient features of cuisine trends impregnated the Bengali cuisine.

The cardinal culinary influence of the Christian community that influenced Bengali cuisine was the bestowal of customary practices to start the drinking of tea (introduced by the British and now recognized as the central to Bengal's identity).

One factor which has influenced Bengali cuisine and which has given it a certain specific feature is the established custom of food by widows. This contribution of the widows to the Bengali cooking cannot be ignored. The widows were prohibited many things and were not allowed even to consume onion and garlic in their food. Also non-vegetarian items like fish and meat were not allowed. They used ginger in their preparation. Their innovation and skills led to many culinary practices which were born out of the restrictions implied on them: simple spice combinations, the ability to prepare small quantities (since widows often ate alone) and creative use of the simplest of cooking techniques. The vegetarian food reached its acme of resplendency only because of the creativity and ingenuity in eating trends and restrictions on widows.

Rice is the staple diet in Bengal. Due to abundance of agricultural land, the animals for dairy products are easily available, especially buffalo. The ascent in number of domestic cattle has led to the incorporation of milk in preparation of endless number of Bengal's dessert.

Every district in Bengal has a special sweet of its own. *Langcha* and *mihidana-sitabhog* of Bardhaman, *sharbhaja* of Krishnanagar, *chanabora* of Murshidabad and so on are renowned across the country.

Bengal has a distinctive uniqueness in the cuisine of all communities and almost every one consumes fish and meat. The consumption of beef is strictly preferred only by the Muslim populace. The nature and variety of dishes found in Bengali cooking are considered to be unique and exceptional, in entire India. Fish cookery is one of its better-known elements and differentiates it from the cooking practices of the landlocked regions. The vicinity of the Bay of Bengal and Bengal's numerous rivers, ponds and lakes are accountable for various kinds of fish like *rohu*, *ilish* (hilsa), perch (*koi* or *pabda*), *magur*, sea bass (*bhetki*), clown knife fish (*chitol*), carp (*rui*), dried fish (*shootki*), mango fish (*topshe*), *bual*, *puti*, *amodi*, *mourala*, *bhola*, *phesha*, *topshe*, catfish, bass, shad or mullet, and so on. Bengalis prepare fish in multitudinous ways — steamed or braised, or stewed with greens or other vegetables and with sauces that are mustard-based or thickened with poppy seeds. Bengalis are so particular about their usage of fish that they use almost every part of the fish in their cuisine. The head of the fish is preferred most whereas the spare bits of the fish are used in flavouring *dals* and curries. The salt water fish *ilish* (hilsa) is the most popular and most consumed fish and can be said as the heart and soul of fish cookery in Bengal. It is considered that the *ilish* can be cooked in 108 distinct ways. Ilish fish obtained from the Padma river in Bangladesh is considered to be the best from the connoisseur's point of view. The list of the fish is infinite and fish such as *rui* (rohu), *koi*, *pabda*, *katla*, *shutki*, and *jhinga* are in the platter of Bengali cuisine. Depending on the texture, size, fat content and the bones, there are different cooking techniques for fish. It could be fried, roasted, cooked in a simple spicy tomato or ginger based gravy (*jhol*), or mustard based with green chillies, with *posto*, with seasonal vegetables, steamed, steamed inside of plantain or butternut squash leaves, cooked with *doi* (curds/yogurt), with sour sauce, with sweet sauce or even the fish made to taste sweet on one side, and savoury on the other.

Bengalis are not restricted only to cooking of fish but they have excelled in vegetable preparations too. The abundant vegetables the are grown throughout the year are incorporated in the cooking of Bengal and such vegetables occupy the central point among vegetarian delicacies.

The availability of vegetables, fruits and fish differ according to the six Bengali seasons - summer, rainy season, autumn, late autumn, winter and spring. Cabbage, cauliflower, carrots, beets, eggplants, tomatoes, spinach, peas and other vegetables are generally found in the winter season. A wide variety of leafy vegetables are eaten year-round. Bitter gourds or other bitter leaves such as margo are cooked and consumed mostly during the spring - as an antidote to fight chickenpox. During the summer and rainy seasons, the variety of vegetables diminishes.

Bengal has been a blessed region for the vegetable lovers as it has extraordinarily large collection of vegetables like family of gourds, roots and tubers, leafy greens, succulent stalks, eggplants, red onions, plantain, banana tree stems and flowers, broad beans, okra, jackfruit, and red pumpkins, which are available in vegetable markets (*shobji bazaar*). The Bengalis make use of their imagination and creativity to make fantastic vegetable dishes. They are relatively good at making pleasant dishes out of the rejected peels, stalks and leaves of vegetables. Their techniques are most efficient in saving fuel and they work effectively in retaining the nutritive value of the dishes. They are very peculiar about the cuts of vegetables and they have different ways of cutting vegetables for the different dish to be cooked. A cut for the *chochhori* cannot be used for the *dalna*. Each different food has its own particular cuts of vegetable, to keep with the cooking time and cooking methods of each dish. Bengal is also said to be the land of *aam* (mangoes). Mangoes are used in advised manner—ripe, unripe, or in pickles.

Bengal differentiates itself from the rest of the country in terms of usage of spices. The spices used in fish and vegetable dishes are quite extensive and includes many combinations. Examples are the onion-flavoured *kalonji* (nigella or black onion seeds), *radhuni* (wild celery seeds), and five-spice or *paanch phoron* (a mixture of cumin, fennel, fenugreek, *kalonji*, and black mustard seeds). The unique attribute of Bengali cooking perhaps is the addition of this *panch phoron*, a combination of whole spices, fried and added at the start or finish of cooking as flavouring agent to each dish. Bengalis share their love for whole black mustard seeds with South Indians, but distinctive element to Bengal is the incorporation of freshly ground mustard paste, which is used to prepare fish curry gravy or steamed fish. The paste of mustard referred as *kasundi*, is an accompanying dipping sauce popularly common in Bengal.

Meat is also enjoyed with great enthusiasm and *khashi* (castrated goat) or *kochipantha* (kid goat) meat is preferred. Some delicate dishes are cooked with *rewaji khashi*, a goat that has been specifically raised by feeding a singular kind of diet, with the intention to promote the growth of intramuscular fat, commonly known as *pardah*. Chicken is not as desired as meat and similar is the dislike for pork also. Vegetarianism is quite a common trend, especially among the Vaisnavite populace (the worshippers of Vishnu, one of the Hindu trinities). Vegetarians do not eat meat, fish or eggs, but they do eat milk products.

As rice is available in abundance and also being the staple diet, the people here are rice eaters. The productive land of Bengal produces rice of various varieties and it differs from long grain sweet-scented rice to small grained rice. Rice is consumed in various forms like well-puffed, beaten, boiled or fried, all depending upon the type of meal to be consumed. Puffed and beaten rice are used in the preparation of snacks. The other forms of rice are used for the main course preparation. *Paramannam* is a sacred preparation of rice with milk, as it is offered to the Supreme Almighty as a ritual. It is a custom that has been followed since almost 1000 years.

Rice holds a very significant position in Bengal foods and its culture. This can be observed from the fact after the birth of a child its first consumption in of solid food comes in the form of rice only and this sublime event is popularly known as *annaprasan*. Wheat preparation is not far behind rice and appears in the menu alongside rice, in different types of breads such as *luchi*, *kochuri* and *pôroṭa*. Similarly, the pulses or lentils are also similar significant ingredient of a meal. A wide variety of *dals* like *mushur dal* (*masoor dal*), *mug dal* (*moong dal*), and *arhar dal* are used commonly in varied preparations and are considered to be the best accompaniment to rice.

Shorsher tel (mustard oil) is the essential cooking medium in Bengali cuisine. The other distinct oil like sunflower oil, soybean oil, almond oil and refined vegetable oil are also used in preparations of food. However, ghee is preferably used in the preparation of dough or during frying the bread.

One of the distinctive features of the Bengali kitchen is the use of a distinct cutting instrument, the *boti*. (This instrument is also used in Maharashtra, where it is known as *vili* and in Andhra Pradesh, known as *kathi peeta* (*kathi* means knife and *peeta* means platform and in Uttar Pradesh as *Pahsul*). It is a long curved blade on a platform held down by foot; both hands are used to hold whatever is being cut and move it against the blade. This method gives excellent control over the cutting process, and can be used to cut anything from tiny shrimp to large pumpkins. Knives are rare in a traditional Bengali kitchen.

A flat metal spatula, *khoonti* is used often, along with *haata* (scoop with a long handle), *jhaanjri* (round shaped sieve like spatula to deep fry food), the *sharashi* (pincers to remove vessels from the fire), the *ghuntni* (wooden hand blender) for puréeing *dal* and the traditional wooden *belon chaki* (round pastry board and rolling pin), and the *shil nora*, which is a rough form of a mortar and pestle, or grinding stone is also commonly used. The *kuruni* is a uni-tasker, used to grate coconuts.

Classic Bengali Style of Culinary Items

The culinary terms in Bengali cuisine are the terms generally used in Bengali cuisine, and not in the other parts of India. Each term in this section is basically a description of any delicacy or a technique of cooking methods. This is used in the production of a varied list of delicacies depending on the choice of ingredients used. In all, there are six basic tastes to which the Bengali palate refers to and they are sweet, sour, salty, bitter, hot and *koshay*.

- **Ombol or Aum-bol (also known as Tok):** It is a tangy and sour dish characterized by the souring agent like tamarind pulp, unripe mango and sometimes *amla* or *amloki*. It is made either with several vegetables of one's choice or with fish, specifically fish bones. It is served at the end of the meal to aid digestion, and also to cleanse the palate.
- **Achars:** The list of the item to be picked is endless as any item can be picklesd and consumed accordingly. The item selected for the preparation of pickles is selected depending upon the taste and preferences of the diners. They are generally picklesd using ingredients like mustard oil, mustard seeds, fenugreek seeds, aniseed, caraway seed and asafoetida, or hing.
- **Bora:** Anything grated or mashed and then formed into almost round shape and then fried, generally in sharp mustard oil. It is generally served with rice as a starter, or served with puffed rice crisps as a snack. The *bora* actually has few varied versions. When potatoes are fried in a light chickpea flour batter, they are referred as *fuluri*.
- **Bhaja:** Anything salted or dipped in water-based batter and then fried are referred as *bhaja*. This section does not include croquettes, or anything fried crumb-coated items. *Macch bhaja* and *begun bhaja* are well-famed delicacies in this segment.
- **Bhapa:** The simple delicacy of either fish or any vegetable steamed with spices.
- **Bhate:** It is a unique style of preparation in which a vegetable is put inside the pot in which rice is cooked, and allowed to cook along with the rice. The vegetables used for this style of preparation include potatoes, butternut squash, raw papayas, bitter gourd, snake gourd and okra in the rice. Bengalis prefer to eat it with a slight sprinkling of mustard oil and salt. However, an acknowledged one-dish Bengali meal is *alubhate bhat*, which is potatoes boiled along with rice, and then served along with the rice. While serving, little fresh ghee or butter with salt to taste are to be mixed and mashed by hand, till it gains

the right consistency, and then eaten. Raw green chilli and a boiled egg sometimes are preferred with the dish.

- **Bhorta:** It is a segment of any vegetable, such as brinjal, potatoes, beans, sour mangoes, papaya, pumpkins or even *dal*, which is first boiled or roasted whole and then mashed. It is seasoned with red shallot, fresh chilli, mustard oil/ghee and fragrant spices.
- **Chorchori:** Basically, it is a vegetable dish with one or more varieties of vegetables cut into strips lenghtwise, and sometimes added with the stalks of leafy greens, and then slightly seasoned with spices like mustard or poppy seeds and finally flavoured with a five-spice mixture *panch phoran*.
- **Chop:** These are fried croquettes usually coated with crushed biscuit or breadcrumbs. These are served with *chutney* or any dipping sauces, depending upon the preference of the diners.
- **Cutlet:** These are typically referred to a thinly spread out dough, made generally of minced chicken/mutton, mixed together with onion, bread crumbs and chillies and then crumb-coated and fried. Generally, it is dipped in egg and coated with breadcrumb, and then fried and served along with thin juliennes of cucumber, carrots, radish and onions.
- **Chhyanchra:** A dish prepared by the assorted combination of different vegetables with portions of fish head and fish oil (entrails).
- **Chhenchki:** This style of preparation depicts the tendency of the Bengalis about how they use every part of the ingredients keeping in mind to minimize the wastage in kitchens. In this preparation the tiny pieces of one or more vegetables, generally a dice of vegetables along with general odds and ends, mostly the peels of vegetables like (potatoes, squash, gourd, pumpkin, bitter gourd, and *potol*) are used and then mostly flavoured with *panch-phoran*, whole mustard seeds or *kalojira*. Chopped shallot and garlic can also be used but hardly any ground spices.
- **Chutney:** Bengalis take the initiative to prepare *chutney* with almost everything available including preserved mango sheets, called *amshotto*. They are considered to be one who pioneered the making of *chutney*.
- **Dalna:** Simply a preparation of mixed vegetables or eggs, cooked in medium thick gravy seasoned and flavoured with ground spices, especially *gorom moshla* (*garam masala*) and served with a touch of ghee.
- **Dom:** This is a term used to denote the slow cooking of vegetables, especially potatoes, or meat, over a covered pot containing water, over a low flame of heat, slightly steaming. The word is derived from the *dum* technique well-known in Mughlai food.
- **Dolma:** It is a delicacy of vegetables, specifically *potol*, stuffed with fish, boiled, de-boned, and then cooked with five-spice powder *panch-phoran*, ginger and onions (alternately coconut-vegetable stuffing is used).
- **Ghonto:** It is a wide range of vegetables (e.g., cabbage, green peas, potatoes or banana blossom, coconut, chickpeas) are chopped or finely grated and cooked with both *panch-phoran* and ground spices. Dried pellets (dumplings) of *dal* are mostly added to the *ghonto*. Clarified butter (ghee) is usually added at the end. Non-vegetarian *ghontos* are also prepared, with fish or fish heads added to the selection of vegetables. The very popular *muri ghonto* is made with fish heads cooked in a fine variety of rice. *Ghontos* may be dry or thick and juicy, depending upon the cook's preferences.
- **Jhal:** The term *jhal* simply means hot. It is a great favourite among West Bengali households, which is made with fish or shrimp or crab, first lightly fried and then cooked in a light sauce of ground red chilli or ground mustard and a flavouring of *panch phoran* or *kalojira*. Being dry in nature, it is mostly eaten with a little bit of *dal* poured over the rice.
- **Jhol:** It is a stew style of cooking either fish or vegetables, seasoned with ground spices, like ginger, cumin, coriander, chilli, and turmeric, and with pieces of fish and long slices of vegetables floating in it. The gravy is comparatively thin, yet tremendously flavourful. Whole green chillies are usually added at the end and green coriander leaves are used to season for extraordinary fragrance. It is the very similar to a 'curry', but thinner in consistency.
- **Kalia:** It is a very lavish delicacy of fish, meat or vegetables, prepared with a lot of oil and ghee and with a sauce usually based on ground ginger and fresh shallots pasted or fried along with a tempering of *gorom moshla*.
- **Kofta (or Boras):** In this preparation, grounded meat or vegetable dumplings bounded together by spices and/or eggs are served alone or in a savoury gravy. *Koftas* are usually softer than boras which are mainly made of ground lentils, sometimes with the addition of chopped vegetables.

- **Korma:** It is a term that can also be called *qurma*, of Mughlai origin, meaning meat or chicken cooked in a mild yogurt-based sauce with ghee instead of oil. Poppy seed paste is often added to it and this addition distinguishes the Bengali *kormas* from the Mughlai *korma*. People of southern Bangladesh are known to add coconut milk to their *korma* preparation.
- **Kosha:** It means frying for a long period of time with ground and whole spices over high heat until shallot/garlic/ginger have dissolved into a thick paste. It is usually applied to preparation of meat and some shellfish.
- **Paturi:** For this dish, generally oily fish is sliced evenly, and then marinated in freshly pasted mustard with a hint of mustard oil, chilli, turmeric and salt and then wrapped in a banana leaf. It is then cooked by the steaming method.
- **Pora:** Simply, the term *pora* means burnt or charred. The vegetables used are wrapped in leaves and roasted over a wood or charcoal fire. Many roast aubergine over direct flames. After roasting, the roasted vegetables are mixed with fragrant spices and oil and consumed accordingly.
- **Poshto:** *Poshto* or *posta* refers to anything that is cooked with poppy seed paste as the main flavouring agent. *Aloo posto* is a very famed variety of this segment.
- **Torkari:** It is a general term often used in Bengal the way 'curry' is used in English. The word was previously used to refer to uncooked garden vegetables but nowadays it is also used to indicate cooked vegetables or even fish and vegetables cooked together.
- **Shukto:** A favourite Bengali palate cleanser, this dish is made with assorted motley of vegetables including at least one bitter vegetable, simmered with a hint of sugar and milk to balance out the bitterness of the fresh vegetables.
- **Shaak:** It is any kind of green leafy vegetable, like spinach and mustard greens. It is often cooked till just wilted with a touch of oil and tempering of nigella seeds.

Salient Features of Bengali Meal

An authentic and traditional Bengali meal is very distinctive and has a definite chronological sequence of food courses. The courses in meal gradually proceed generally from lighter to richer and then heavier items. A distinctive and typical demonstration of the presentation of a grand and festive Bengali dinner comprises a silver (or stainless) plate with rice (and sometimes a paratha) in the centre, with some fried vegetables and fish, surrounded by silver bowls holding different accompanying dishes.

The Bengali meal commences with a dish of bitter taste and finishes with a sweet delicacy. A slightly luxuriant Bengali meal starts with the first course or starters which are made from bitter vegetables or herbs, which acts as an appetizer. Bitter gourd is readily available almost throughout the year, hence it is used as either deep fried in oil or steamed with potatoes cut in cubes. The sizes of the portions are generally very small — a spoonful or so to be had with rice — and this course is assumed to be both a palate-cleanser and is also attached with great medicinal importance.

In West Bengal, *shukto*, a preparation comprising thick soupy mixture of vegetables including the bitter gourd (*korola*) in a pungent ginger-mustard sauce is served next after the palate-cleanser course. This bitter dish is savoured at lunch but skipped at dinner. At times, it replaces or follows the bitter item of the previous course.

Rice is undoubtedly the main component of the meal and it remains constant throughout the meal. *Bhaat* (hot steamed rice) is first served with ghee, salt and green chilli and then it is followed by *shaak* (leafy vegetables such as spinach, *palong*, fenugreek, or amaranth). The *shaak* can be served steamed or it can be cooked in oil with other vegetables such as *begun* (aubergine). Steamed *shaak* is usually accompanied by a sharp and pungent mustard paste called *kasundi*.

Then, *dal* (pulses) is served along with varied preparations of different *bhaja* (fried vegetables) or *bhate* (boiled vegetables).

Supreme mastery is revealed in the cooking of items which involves a mélange of vegetables and spices added in it with impeccable balance to produce dishes like *dalna*, *ghonto*, *torkari*, *chorchori*, and so on. These are the next series of course in Bengali cuisine, which is followed by main course which has fish preparations in it. In this, *maccher jhol*, a very light delicacy of fish with subtle spice, is served and it is followed by tremendously spiced fish preparations.

The further main course is served next which are basically the items prepared using meat. The best-loved and desirable meats of the Bengalis are *mangsho* (mutton) and *murgi* (chicken). *Kosha mangsho* or *rewazi mangsho* are the well-famed and delectable meat delicacies among the Bengalis.

This course is followed by the *ambol* or *tauk* (chutney), which acts as the palate-cleanser and refreshes the taste buds. It is essentially a piquant tangy-sweet delicacy made of pineapple, mangoes, tamarind, tomatoes, papaya or an assemblage of dry fruits and fresh fruits. *Papor* (*papadum*), a type of thin wafer made of potatoes, *shagu* (*sabo*) or *dal* is served as an accompaniment to the *chutney*.

The meal is finally finished by the next and also the last course of the meal, i.e., the dessert. *Doi* (yogurt) is served plain without any addition of ingredients or as the sweetened variety, known as Misti Doi (sweet yogurt). Misti Doi is a distinctive element of the Bengali cuisine.

Desserts

Sweets play a very pivotal and prominent role in the life and as well as in diet of Bengalis. All Bengalis have a sweet tooth. Bengalis have been blessed by the virtuoso to produce amazing and out-of-the-world sweet delicacies. It is an ancient tradition prevailing until today among Bengalis to distribute and gift sweets during festivities. The confectionery sectors have thrived tremendously due of its close connection with social and religious ceremonies.

The *Chandimangala* during the ancient period (AD 1589) mentions *kheer, rabdi, mandu, kandu,* and *nadu*. The *Chandidas Padavali* also describes various sweets (*bibidha-mishta* and *sakar mittai*). Few articles of the 16th century mentioned a huge aggregation of desserts like *chhanabura, khaja, jilebi, pishtak, malpo, sitamisri, modak, sandesh,* and so on.

The sweets of Bengal are generally made of sweetened cottage cheese (*chhena*). They generally don't prefer to use the *khoa* (reduced solidified milk) which is used commonly in the preparation of desserts in northern India. Not only this, they also use flours of different cereals and pulses to prepare desserts.

Bengal has excelled in preparing desserts and has the superior tradition of making different kinds of pan-fried, steamed or boiled sweets, known as *pithe* or the *pitha*. These tiny balls of paradise signify the arrival of winter, and the onset of a season where lavish food can be incorporated in the otherwise subtle diet of the Bengalis. An affluence lies in the creamy silkiness of the milk which is mixed often with molasses, or jaggery made of either date palm or sugarcane, and at times with sugar. They are mostly segregated into distinct categories depending on the way they are carved out. Rice flour is used generally for making the *pithe*. They are usually fried or steamed. The very common forms of these dessert cakes include *bhapa pitha* (steamed), *pakan pitha* (fried), and *puli pitha* (dumplings), among others.

The common varieties of *pithas* common here are *chandrapuli, gokul, patishapta* (thin-layered rice-flour crepes), *chitaipitha, askipithe, mugerpuli* and *dudhpuli.*

At home, Bengalis traditionally eat without using fork and knife but they prefer to eat with their skilled right hand, mashing properly the small portions of meat and vegetable dishes with rice and lentils into *lokma*. In rural areas, Bengalis traditionally eat on the ground the food being served on a large banana leaf serving as the plate.

Specialty Dishes

Shukto It is a complex bitter dish, which depicts a fine balance in myriad kinds of tastes and textures and purposed to stimulate the appetite. It has become a criterion and is often a critical measure of a Bengali housewife's abilities in the kitchen. *Shukto* is a vast mixture of diced vegetables, such as white radish, potatoes, beans, and bitter gourd or *karela*. The vegetables are lightly sautéed in ginger, mustard seed, and cumin, and then cooked with milk and water.	
Bhapa Doi This is a special sweet dish which is made up by mixing yogurt, milk, and condensed milk in a pot. Then, this pot is steamed in a double boiler or in a pressure cooker. It is then garnished with dry fruits like almonds sliver and pistachios. Then, after it is cooled in a refrigerator for about half an hour and served.	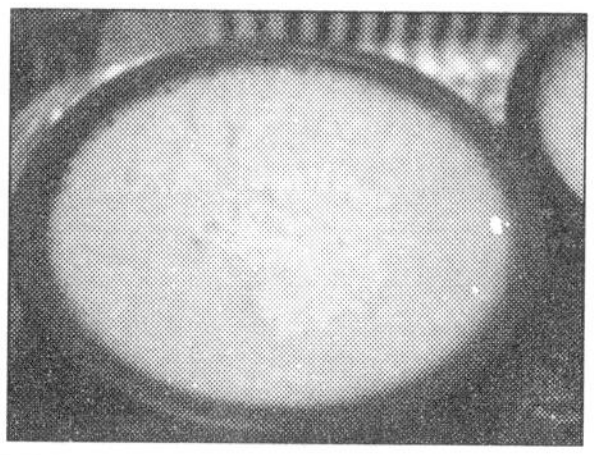
Doi Macch This is a distinctive classical preparation of Bengal in which fish is stewed in a yogurt-based gravy. This is served with rice or pulao. This delicacy has a revered place in Bengali cuisine and is relished with great zest.	

Aloo Posto

This is a resplendent preparation of potatoes, diced and cooked with freshly ground poppy seed paste and then flavoured with whole spices and turmeric. It can be eaten with *lucchi* or deep-fried *puri*.

Shondesh

Shondesh (the word means 'message' in Bengali, perhaps because it was once sent as a gift) is basically *chhenna* mixed with sugar, fried in a little clarified butter, and pressed into pretty moulds shaped like flowers, fruits, or shells. It has been very sophisticatedly developed with extreme delicacy and subtlety and now has almost hundered varieties. The varieties are *kachagolla, abarkhabo, jolbhora, indrani,* and so on that must be cautiously savoured. Another variant is the *kôrapak* or hard mixture, which blends rice flour with paneer to form a shell-like dough that has a long shelf life.

Rasmalai

The name *Rasmalai* comes from two parts in Hindi: *Ras* meaning juice/juicy and *Malai*, meaning cream.

Rasmalai is composed of white, cream, or yellow coloured balls of paneer (cottage cheese) which are dipped and soaked in sugar and *malai*. This dessert resembles the *rasogolla* greatly. Though it is not a primarily Bengali sweet and is supposed to have originated from Odisha, it is very popular in Bengal. Homemade Rasmalai is usually made up of powdered milk, all-purpose flour, baking powder and oil. These are kneaded to form dough, moulded into balls and dropped into simmering milk cream. The popularity of Rasmalai has travelled a long way all across India and has reached great heights in the world of Indian sweets.

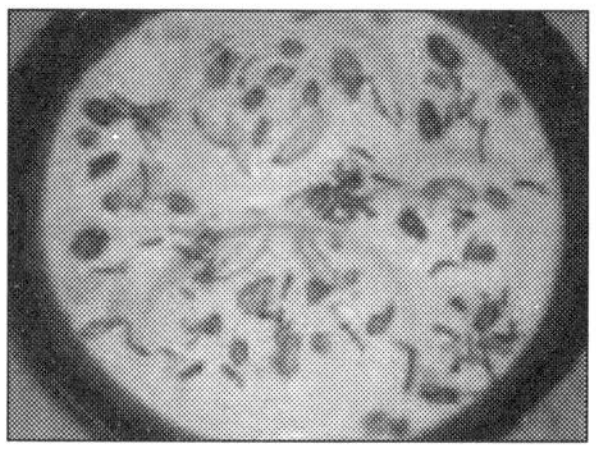

Roshogolla

Roshogolla is considered to be one dish which needs no description or introduction. It is undoubtedly the most widely consumed sweets in Bengal and is probably the identity of Bengali cuisine for the rest of India. It has become synonymous to the popularity of Bengali cuisine and also the unannounced representative of Bengali cuisine as well. The basic version has many regional variations. Many culinarian experts are of the belief that it is traditionally an Odiya sweet.

Chumchom

Chumchom (especially from Bangladesh) goes back about 150 years ago. This oval-shaped sweet delicacy is reddish brown in colour and it is of a denser texture than Roshogolla. It can also be preserved longer. It is also savoured with huge appreciation and liking by the consumer.

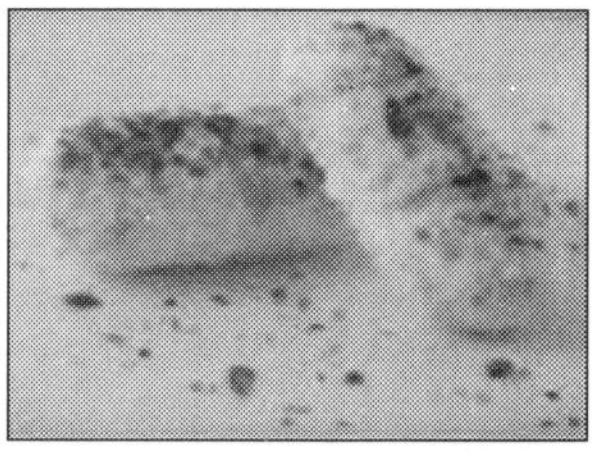

Pantua

It is somewhat similar to the Roshogolla. The only difference that distinguishes it from Roshogolla is that in Pantua the cottage cheese balls are fried in either ghee or oil until golden or deep brown before being put in syrup. They have similar taste notwithstanding being differently shaped, e.g., langcha (cylindrical) or ledikeni.

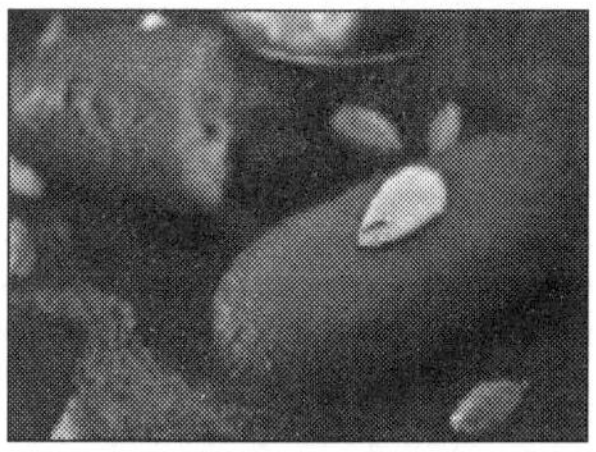

Muṛi *Muṛi* is simply puffed rice which is made by heating sand in a pot, and then throwing in grains of rice in the pot to cook in the heated sand. The rice puffs up and is separated from the sand by a strainer. *Muri* is also often used as a replacement for or in combination with regular rice. A variant of *muṛi* is *khoi*, which is popped rice. Both varieties are used to make many different snack foods.	
Jhal Muri It is the most popular snack food of Bengal. *Jhal* literally means 'hot' or 'spicy'. It is puffed rice with spices, vegetables and raw mustard oil. Many kinds of Jhal Muri are made, depending on the variation of the ingredients added, but the most common is a *bhorfa* made up of chopped onion, roasted ground cumin, black salt, chillies, mustard oil, and fresh coriander leaves.	
Moa A *moa* is especially made during winter in Bengal by taking *muri* with *gur* (jaggery) as a binder and forming it into a ball. Another popular kind of *moa* is Joynagarer moa, which uses *khoi* and *nolengur* (fresh jaggery made from the sap of date palm) as the binder.	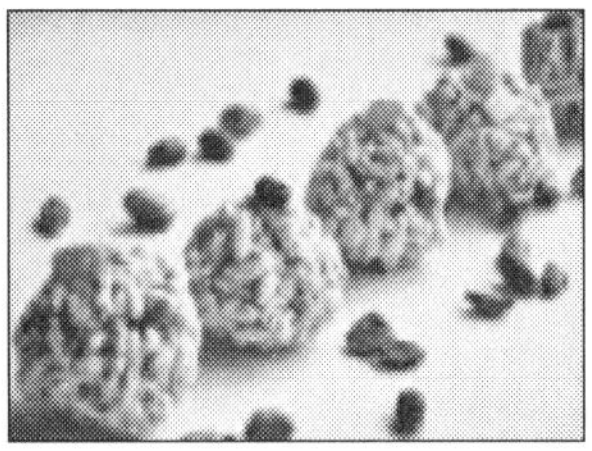
Radha Ballobhi Mostly consumed during breakfast, it is much similar to a *kachori* made in northern India. The stuffing used in it is of mashed and boiled *urad dal* and is served with potato curry known as *aloor dum*.	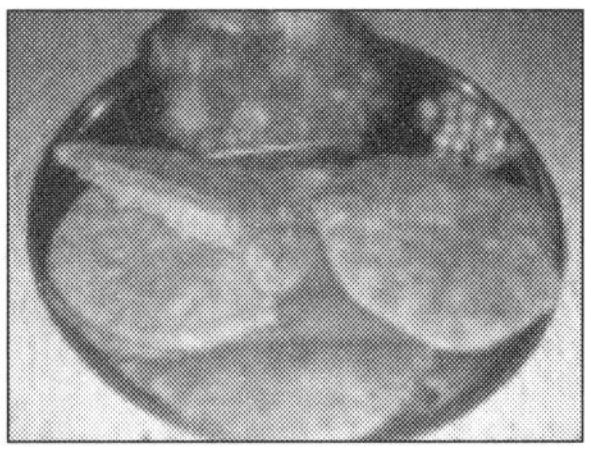
Shorshe Bata Ilish It is a lovely delicacy in which the hilsa fish is braised in mustard paste and slit green chillies. It is cooked for everyday meals or even during festivals and occasions.	
Macher Paturi The darnes of fish are marinated in freshly ground mustard paste and wrapped in banana leaves. It is then steamed and eaten with rice.	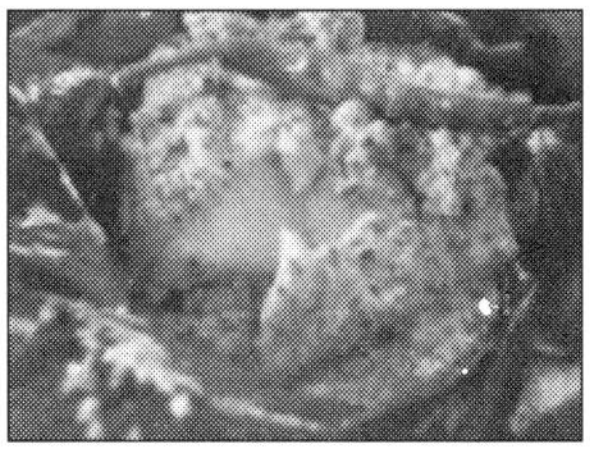
Chingri Malai Curry It is a delicacy in which small-sized prawns are stewed in a gravy made with boiled onion paste, thickened with coconut milk. The coconut milk used in it imparts a unique texture to the dish. It is cooked on festive occasions like marriages.	

Dhokar Dalna A gram flour batter is cooked with spices and then spread on a greased tray and steamed. It is then cut into small pieces and then steamed. It is then cut into small pieces in the shape of a diamond and deep-fried. Then the fried dumpings are stewed in a gravy of boiled onion paste, thickened with gram flour and whole spices.	
Kabiraji Cutlet It is a preparation which is made from chicken breast marinated in salt, turmeric, ginger-garlic paste and spices. The marinated chicken is coated with a light batter of rice flour and eggs and deep-fried until golden brown. It is served with chutney.	
Kasha Mangsho It is a semi-dry preparation of lamb meat with a unique dark colour in appearance. The dark colour imparted to this dish is due to the iron *kadhai* in which it is cooked and also due to caramelized sugar. It is consumed with deep-fried bread *luchi*.	

Culinary Trivia: Vegetables and their Classification

In culinary terms, a vegetable is an edible plant or its part, intended for cooking or eating raw. Vegetables are most often consumed as salads or cooked in savory or salty dishes.

Classification

Cole crop – Cabbage, cauliflower, brussel sprouts, knoll-khol, broccoli, and kale.

Root vegetables – Carrot, parsnip, raddish, turnip, and beetroot.

Fruit vegetables - Tomato, bell pepper, eggplant, okra, avocado, and zucchini.

Curcubits – Cucumber, pumpkin, squash, and gourds.

Leafy vegetables – Spinach, lettuce, celery, fenugreek, mustard, garlic chives, kale, turnip green, and so on.

Tuber crops – Potato, sweet potato, tapioca, taro, jerusalem artichoke, and yam.

Bulbs – Onions, garlic, shallots, and leek.

Perennial vegetables – Asparagus, rhubarb, and globe artichoke.

Leguminous vegetables – Peas, and beans.

Culinary Trivia: The Term 'Curry'

Curry is not originally Indian. Colonial rulers have never been known for their linguistic accuracy and no one knows for sure where the British got this one from. *Kari* is a South Indian word for sauce and *tarkari* is a North Indian dish, which may or may not be relevant. Clearly, the sahibs and memsahibs fell in love with the flavours of India. When they returned to the homeland, they had their cooks to grind up a mix of spices to sprinkle on their staid British staples. The world now knows this as "curry powder" and whatever is cooked with it is called a "curry."

10 Bihari Cuisine

"Food is our common ground, a universal experience." – James Beard

Bihar is located in the north of India and is bounded by Uttar Pradesh on its west and Nepal (neighbouring country) on the north, northern part of West Bengal on the east and Jharkhand on the south.

The land of Bihar is characterized by and is fortunate because of abundance of natural bounties. It is also profoundly honoured for its sacred association with Lord Buddha. Because of the much influence of the Buddhism and Hinduism ethos, the traditional Bihari society is preponderantly inclined towards vegetarianism. Notwithstanding this, non-vegetarian food is readily acceptable in certain Bihari populace and people here relish fish along with mutton and chicken. The Bihari cuisine has queerly been underestimated and has always been of low profile due to low exposure and has failed to capture the fascination of people in a considerable way.

Nature has always been partial with Bihar and has gifted it with the production of motley of assortment of seasonal fruits and vegetables. It has also been very affluent in terms of rich dairy products. The plentiful availability of dairy products has compelled everyone to like the dairy products. The ubiquity of such features has defined Bihari cuisine as the cuisine with utter simplicity and a cuisine with a bunch of fresh ingredients throughout, and healthy to consume.

The Bihari meal is packed with simplicity and hardly believes in ostentation. A usual Bihari meal comprises *bhaat* (rice), *dal* (lentil), *tarkari* (vegetable) and *achar* (pickles). Since time immemorial, the same pattern has been followed and nothing has changed with the passage of time. *Khichdi* is a unique preparation which is a kind of broth prepared using rice and lentils (*dals*) and is seasoned with spices and added with ghee to get the most-sought after flavour. It is accompanied with a variety of side dishes like curds, *chutney*, pickles, papads, ghee and *chokha*. *Chokha* is undoubtedly the most crucial and inseparable item of Bihari cuisine. It is prepared by mashing boiled potatoes and then it is seasoned with chopped onions, garlic, green chillies, salt and uncooked mustard oil. Few also add *achar* masala (pickles spices paste) in it, but it is optional and depends on the person preparing it. Bihar lacks in the well-famed preparation of chicken and mutton, but despite that it has certain non-vegetarian dishes also. It also has a good aggregation of rice based dishes in its cuisine.

Litti chokha is the signature dish of Bihar and has gathered fame and applause all across. *Chokha* is also relished with *sattu paratha*. *Sattu* (powdered gram) is an energy providing product that is used widely in Bihari cuisine. *Sattu* is used in the preparation of *litti* (as a stuffing), stuffed parathas, salty and spicy drinks, and so on. *Sattu* is one of the crucial and mandatory ingredients present in the breakfast menu in Bihar. People also prefer to drink the *sattu* based drinks in the hot and humid summer season. It is considered to be beneficial to the health and protects one from the heat waves during the summer season.

Traditionally and authentically, mustard oil is the cooking medium used sparingly all over and is considered to be a healthy option as it lowers the cholesterol. The tempering in Bihar is referred by a term *chhonk* or seasoning and is done using *panch phoran* and this adds a unique feature to the Bihari cuisine. *Panch phoran* is a five-spice mixture, which consists of five elements in equal parts, namely, *jeera* (cumin seed), *kalaunji* (mangraeel seed), *methi* (fenugreek seed), *saunf* (aniseed) and *sarson* (mustard seeds). *Panch phoran* is supposed to add a midas touch to the salient features of Bihari cuisine. *Bhoonjana* or light frying of items in different delicacies is also popular in this cuisine. Spicy and vibrant dishes are mostly liked and consumed by the people of the land.

Undoubtedly, the cuisine of Bihar is dominated by vegetarianism and hence people here are preponderantly vegetarian. Nonetheless, unlike Gujarat or some communities of South India, non-vegetarian food has also been quite preferred and is unrestricted even in the traditional abodes of Bihar. Some segments of brahmins like the Maithili Brahmins consume certain varieties of fish. Mutton or goat meat is even used as *prasad* in some type of pujas, like Devi Puja. Strangely, many Kayastha families in Bihar, generally considered to be the great admirers of non-vegetarian food, are basically vegetarian in nature.

The non-vegetarian delicacies are preferred to be cooked in a curry and are consumed with bread or at times with rice. The delicacies incorporating prawns and seafood, in certain areas, are enjoyed a lot. Bihari cuisine is renowned for a wide variety of *parathas* with a wide selection of varied stuffing. The people here popularly consume snacks line *samosa* and *kachori*, both being stuffed food items which being deep fried and then served and enjoyed with a variety of vibrant *chutneys*.

The milk-based products are a steadfast associate of the Bihari food all year round. *Dahi* (yogurt), *mattha* (buttermilk), ghee, *lassi* and butter are popularly common dairy products that the major populace of the land loves to relish with enjoyment. The scorching heat prevailing in Bihar in summers makes these products a compulsive choice of every individual of the land. The flavour and variety of this cuisine can be totally appreciated only when tried. It is likely to transform any individual into its follower.

Biharis are renowned for preparing a wide variety of a distinctive preparation like *ghoognis*. A *ghoogni* is a spicy preparation of either *matar* (green peas) or *chana* (chick peas). During breakfast, Biharis eat rotis/*parathas*/ *puris* with a *ghoogni* of *chana*/*hara chana*/*matar*/*chola*/ *kabuli chana* (chick peas).

A *namkeen puri* is usually referred to as *kachauri* here. *Kachauri-sabji* or *kachauri-ghoogni* is staple Bihari breakfast or supper. All these preparations have shaped Bihari cuisine and are liked most by all.

The people of Bihar are not far behind in preparing sweets and they too are also very fond of sweet dishes and enjoy a variety of items as dessert. The most common dessert items are *maalpua, rabri, kalajamun, motichoor ka laddu, mitha khaja, til-barfi, peda, makhana-kheer, khubi ka lai, belgrami, thekua, laktho, khurma, parwal ki mithai, postadana ka halwa, kesar,* and so on . Since Bihar is rich in dairy products, so the most common ingredient of the sweet dishes is milk-based. The sweets prepared here are simple and has no complexity in preparing them. *Makhana* (foxnut- a kind of water fruit) is prepared from lotus seeds and is taken puffed or into *kheer*, prepared with milk and sugar. *Makhane ki kheer* is a popular dessert prepared with this item.

Some of the sweets owe their proximity to city Patna like *khaja* from Silao Nalanda, *ladoo* from Maner, *kala jamun* from Vikram, *khubi ka lai* from Bakhtiarpur, *tilkut* and *kesaria peda* from Gaya, *balushahi* from Harnaut and *chena murgi* from Koelwar.

Ghee is used liberally in Bihari cuisine as it is the land abundant with its production. It is used for the preparation of food as well as desserts. Its use in seasoning transforms even the modest *khichdi* into a tempting dish with an amazing flavour.

Bihar is a prominent state and the food habits vary, depending on the season and the region. The tribals have a very distinct mode and style of cooking as compared to the rest of the population of the state. Mahua flour, maize, millets, boiled cereals, edible roots and tubers form the prime constituents of a common tribal meal in the Chhotanagpur area, which is the central area of tribal communities. The *handia*, a beverage prepared by using fermented rice, is very popular among the tribal communities.

The *wadiyaan* or *mungoris* in Bihar are referred to as 'adouri'. There are various ingredients used in the preparation of *mungoris* like rice and flax seeds. The different *mungoris* prepared with different ingredients are given names accordingly. Rice mungoris are called *ganouri*, flax seed *mungoris* are called *tisouri*, *channa dal* and *urad dal* mungoris are called *kodauri*.

Ganouri: This is prepared by soaking rice and grinding it very fine. Water is added in it and cooked till it gets thick in consistency. Then small portions of this are laid on a plastic sheet and allowed to sun-dry for 2-3 days. This paste of rice can be added with salt, black pepper powder and red chilli powder, according to taste. It can be preserved for further use. It is deep-fried and consumed with tea, when required. It is also known as *chaurouri* at a some places.

Chhath Puja: A Unique Festival of Bihar

Chhath Puja is the largest and declamatory festival of this region. The people have high regards for this festival and it is celebrated in high spirits. It is celebrated for three successive days.

On the auspicious first day Nahay Khay, after taking bath in Holy River, boiled small grain *arwa chawal* is consumed with *lauki ki subzi* and *chane ki dal*.

On second day Kharna, people take dip in the holy Ganges and take the water home to cook *kheer* (jaggery is used in place of sugar) and *puri*. It is eaten as *prasad* at night.

Next day on Daala Chhath, delicacies like thekua and *belgrami* is prepared by the women who observe fast.

After both the Arghyas, on the fourth day, these sweets along with several fruits and dry fruits are served as *prasad* and are eaten for several days.

Specialty Dishes

Litti-Choka *Litti* is a resplendent and well-famed snack food which consists of balls of wheat and *sattu* (powdered gram or lentil) formed into balls with spices, and then filled with ghee (clarified butter) via a hole. Although it is often confused with the similar prepared *Baati* (of Rajasthan), it is an entirely a different dish in terms of taste, texture and style of preparation. It may be eaten with yogurt, *baigan ka bharta, alu bharta*, and *papad*. The *litti* are traditionally baked over a cow-dung fire, but in the modern days of technological change, it may be cooked in an oven or in a wok of boiling oil to deep fry it. It has many variations like *hare matar ki litti, keeme ki litti* and all variations have their own uniqueness. All are famous all across Bihar. Special spices are used to flavour the *litti* including *ajawain, mangraeel*, garlic, red pepper, mustard oil, salt, and ginger. Tasty pickles can also be used to add a spicy flavour. It is served with *chokha* (a vegetable preparation of roasted and mashed eggplant, tomato, and potato).	
Sattu The powder of roasted *channa* is referred to as *sattu* whereas the mixture of *sattu* and barley flour is *sattuee*. It is a high energy providing foodstuff made from the concoction of a mixture of ground pulses and cereals. The dry powder is prepared in a variety of ways as a principal or secondary ingredient of dishes. It is taken mixed with water or with milk. Sometimes, *sattu* mixed with spices are used to prepare stuffed chapatis, locally called *makuni roti*.	
Pua It is unique preparation prepared from a mixture of powdered rice, milk, ghee, sugar and honey. The very popular variant of it is Malpua, not only in Bihar, but all over India.	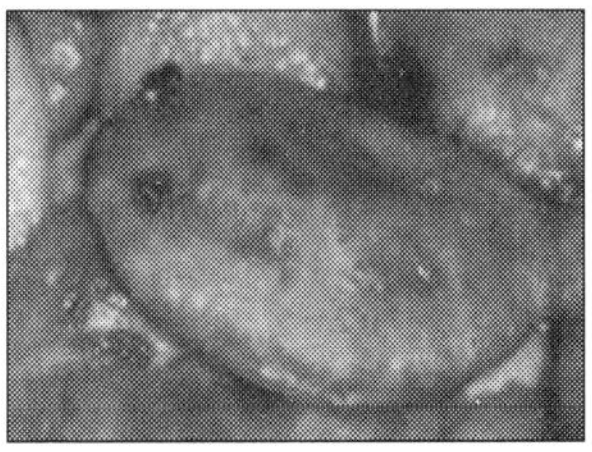
Pittha It is cooked by steaming a mixture of powdered rice.	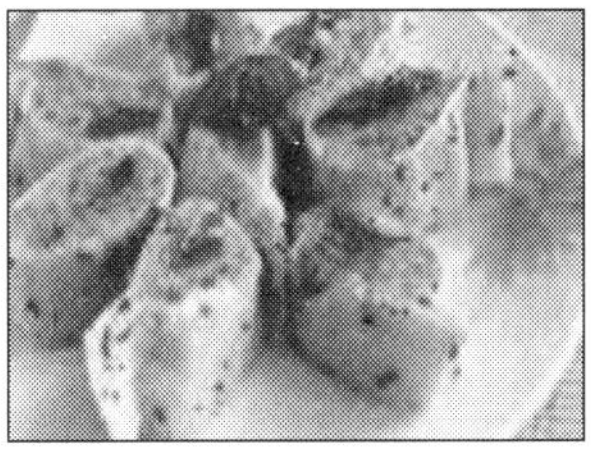
Chiwra It is simply beaten rice combined and served with a coat of creamy curds and sugar or jaggery.	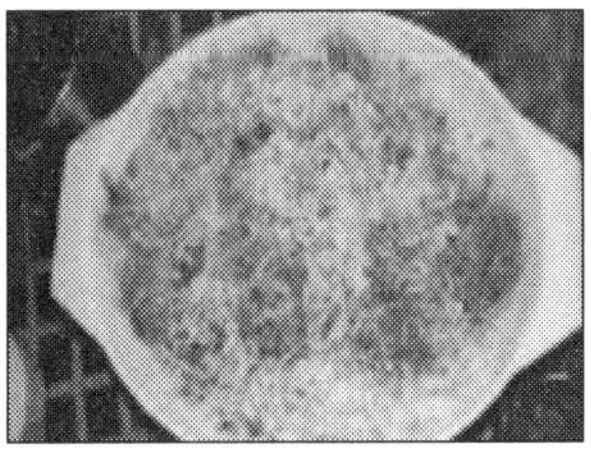

Pedukia It is prepared by mixing *sooji* or *khoa* with sugar and wrapping the mixture in thin layer made by dough of refined flour, water and ghee. The resultant delicacy is then deep fried in ghee and served. It is a sort of *gujia*.	
Thekua It is also popularly referred as *khajoor*. It is a very common and a splendid homemade dessert from Bihar and Jharkhand. It is a sweet and crispy dessert prepared with whole wheat flour, sugar and chopped coconuts. *Thekua* is an ideal dessert to carry with during long journeys as it can be stored for a few days due to its high shelf-life. *Thekua* mould is available in market and it is made up of wooden material. This mould helps to create design of *Thekua*.	
Khaja It is a sugar-coated puffy dessert made with all-purpose flour. The preparation of it requires dexterity, and ultimate skill to prepare it to perfection.	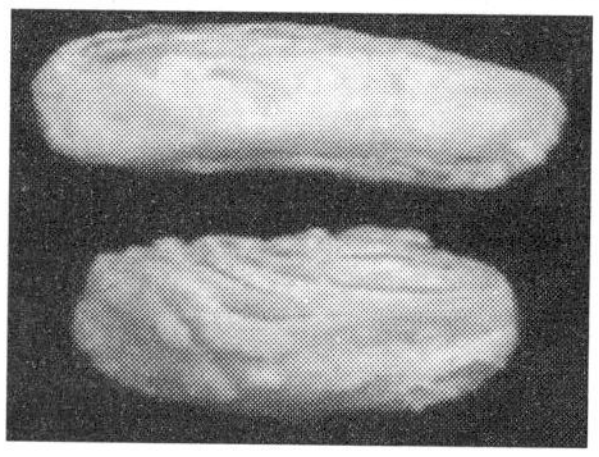
Dhuska It is a deep-fried item prepared from a mixture of powdered rice, bengal gram and ghee, but is salted. It is an irresistible dish and requires just 25-30 minutes of cooking time.	
Belgrami It is another outstanding sweet preparation of Bihar, which is made from cheese, sugar and ghee. It is famous from Udwantnagar, which falls in between Arrah and Buxar.	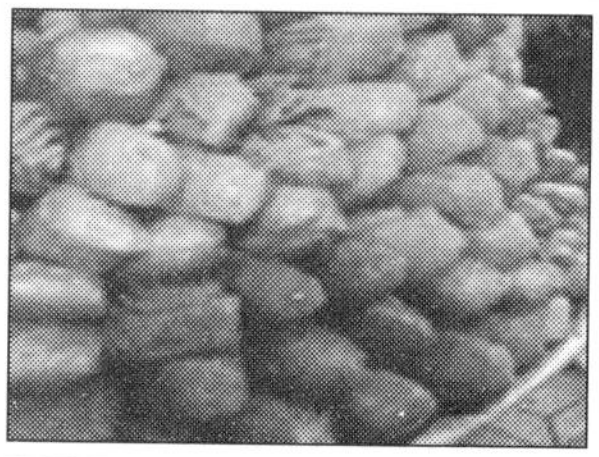

Culinary Trivia: Chulha

Chulha is a traditional Indian cooking stove used for indoor cooking.

A *chulha* is a U-shaped mud stove made from local clay. After the clay formation is complete, it is finished by covering it with a coat of clay and cow-dung mixture. The thickness of the walls is not as important as the dimensions of the fire-side are. The front of the chulha has an apron. This apron helps hold the fuel to be burnt (usually wood, sticks, cow-dung patties, straw, crop waste, and so on). Once the process of cooking is complete, the apron holds the ash, which is removed later.

To cook on such traditional stoves, one must squat on one's haunches or sit on the floor. Burning of cow-dung is supposed to purify the stove. A mixture of clay and cow-dung is routinely prepared to coat the cooking surface of the stoves.

Fuel used: Wood and animal dung patties are used as fuel for the *chulha*. Animal dung patties are called *upla* or simply dung cakes. The animal dung of domestic animals like cows, buffalos, goat, sheep, camels, and so on is mixed with finely chopped plant materials (stalks called *sarkanda* and a straw called *tuhari*). The mixture is formed into patties (about 6" diameter and 1" thick) and dried under the sun. The plant material depends on the region and the crop being harvested. In North India, mustard stalks, legume stalks, wheat straw are commonly used. The plant materials add to the density of *upla* and makes the fire last longer like charcoal.

Kerosene or ghee is used as an accelerator on the wood or dung patties to start fire.

11 Goan Cuisine

"My philosophy from day one is that I can sleep better at night if I can improve an individual's knowledge about food and wine, and do it on a daily basis." – Emeril Lagasse

Goa is located in West India and it is bounded by the state of Maharashtra on the north and by Karnataka on the east and south, while the Arabian Sea forms its western coast.

Goa is a small state and the most astonishing facet of Goan cuisine is that it offers an intriguing and challenging variety of cuisine. Similar to its habitant, the Goan cuisine is vibrant, lively and full of bright colours. The Goans have acquired from their predecessors an amazing gastronomic tradition that is distinctive, wide-ranging and a potpourri of ultimate spice combination.

It has an outstanding culinary importance and cuisine for the Christian and Hindu populaces. The cuisine of brahmins (both Hindu and Christians) is distinctly different. It has a huge impact of Kashmiri inhabitant, Muslims and Portuguese. The cuisine of the Catholic people is a complex cookery that combines Hindu lineages and Latin techniques with stimulating local flavours and ingredients from Portugal's former colonies, from Angola to Brazil. It is a culinary style which is endangered and would be on the verge of extinction due to continuous threatening by altering lifestyles and demographics. The impeccable culture blend of Arabian, Portuguese and native cultures is mirrored in the cookery of Goa, which is a distinctive amalgamation of cornucopia and simplicity. Goa is characterized distinctively by the uncontroversial combination of cuisines of the East and West existing together in a cordial and peaceful lifestyle. The resultant is an exquisite and splendid cuisine of a lavish variety of culinary styles, with each style boasting of a distinct flavour.

Authentic Goan cuisine bespeaks for enough laborious efforts and time, so as to get the most-sought after results. The process of grinding is mandatory for almost all recipes. It also believes in the fact that the better the dish, the longer it takes to prepare. The commodities used are also considerably varied as their style of being used and their nature also have an effect on each other. The gravies of each style have their own versions of describing each preparation in which they are used. The style of gravies used usually describes the style of preparation. The names used are similar, as are the ingredients used for making a delicacy, yet their aroma, flavour, taste, texture, consistency, appearance, presentation and colour can be completely different from each other. Very slight and negligible differences in ingredients or their use make the resultant recipes distinct. Thus, the cook has to be dexterous and adept in blending spices in Goan cuisine.

The cuisine of North India is generally based on tomato and onion gravy, but Goan cuisine is characterized by an abundant and generous use of kokum, coconut, coconut oil and palm vinegar, which are common ingredients found in Goa. Goan cuisine is like a bouquet in which amazing flowers of rich cultures, distinct foods, various influences, and different ingredients are involved, depending on the availability of ingredients. Thus, Goan cuisine speaks volume about the versatility, and is incredibly a multifaceted cuisine.

Rice, fish, and coconut are the basic elements of the distinctive Goan cuisine. In general, it is very common to find delicacies made from these three essential items in almost every Goan meal. Rice is consumed by all and is liked by all at both meals, but the gravies prepared in each style are entirely distinct and distinguishable. They use the same name and the same ingredients for a delicacy and yet their aromas, flavour, taste, texture and colour is completely different and delicious.

Charmed with wide-ranging seafood, the Goans are blessed with genuinely superior quality prawns, lobsters, crabs, red snapper, shark fish, pomfret, salmon, kingfish, sea bass, barakuda, squid, mullet and jumbo pomfrets along the coastline. Seafood shift are used by them in preparing innumerable variety of soups, salads, pickles, curries, and fries.

One of the basic essential ingredients used in Goan cooking is coconut, which distinguishes Goan cuisine from the rest of the cuisines. Coconut is an ingredient which acts as a captivating factor for an individual experiencing Goan cuisine. Coconut is considered by the non-brahmin Hindus a symbolism to gaiety and contentment while for the Christians it is the symbolic representation of perspicacity. Coconut is used generally in the mode of coconut milk which is obtained by grating the white flesh of a coconut and then soaking it in a cup of warm water. Coconut milk is a sweet, milky white cooking base obtained from the flesh of mature coconuts. The coconut tree bestows us with commodities like sugar, wine, vinegar, oil, water, milk, wood, and yarn. Thus, the coconut tree is truly the king among the trees, due to the versatility it offers.

Equally conspicuous in terms of significance is kokum, a sour, deep red coloured fruit characterized by sharp and sour flavour. The popular red Goan chilies have also become an inseparable ingredient in Goan cuisine, as is tamarind. Goans prepare their own version of vinegar from *toddy*. Then there are countless *chutneys* that are a salient feature of Goan cuisine. Goa lacks far behind in terms of vegetarian preparation. While Hindus are comfortable with lamb and chicken, Christians prefer pork. Pork *vindaloo*, pork *baffado* and pork *assado* are a few popular preparation of pork in Goa and are relished with great zest. Notwithstanding, both Hindus and Christians have a special liking and preference for fish and seafood than any other meat.

The populace of northern Goa prefers to grind their *masalas* and coconut separately while the southern people mostly grind them together before squeezing out the extract through fine muslin cloth. The Christians prefer vinegar while the Hindus use *kokum* to give tang and piquancy to their respective cuisine. The Hindus have a cuisine which is almost similar to the cuisine of the Konkan region but meliorated with certain classic dishes and local touches.

Normally, a Goan kitchen is traditionally equipped with basalt hand-held grinders of different sizes and shapes for peculiar uses, bamboo sieves, wood burners, and a vast display of earthen pots. There is substantial space in the kitchen with a high ceiling. Here, cooking is generally done in earthern pots and ladles made of coconut shells. The fuels chiefly used in the kitchen are firewood, dry coconut leaves, coconut husks, and so on. The food cooked on a simmering flame fed by coconut husk using earthen pots and coconut shell ladles gives them special flavours, which sets them a class apart.

The bona fide conceiver of Goan food were the locals, formerly Hindu women with an imagination capable of producing amazing ideas regarding the delicacy preparation, but nothing was lettered and noted down. Chiefly rice consumers, they didn't eat beef or pork and prefer to use green chillies which are also spicy and special on elaborate party days. With mingling of Christianity, the Hindu populace were bestowed with the choice to take beef or pork, they stood socially disoriented, and were expelled from the community. Acknowledged facts that they could not possibly alter, but they transformed the old taboos and restrictions into new freedoms and trends.

Breakfast: Ambil, a maize porridge is a pack of nutrients, but sour in taste. It is made by soaking porridge and grinding it to a thin batter and then cooking it with incorporation of jaggery. It is mostly consumed during breakfast. Banana fritter is also a popular item eaten during breakfast which is prepared by splitting open the bananas and then frying and finally sprinkling sugar after taking it out from the frying pan. A unique plantain called Moira plantain is used for this preparation. Moira is a village located in North Goa and the bananas here are comparatively quite large.

Brunch time is mostly referred as Canji time and Canji is a basic meal in Goa. Canji is a gruel (thin porridge) of rice. It requires a great deal of patience to prepare Canji and the resultant item is worth it. The paddy for the rice to be used is grown in one's own fields. It is parboiled in the backyard of the house, in huge pots that have been in the family, made up of selected wood with utmost attention with copper or brass rims at both ends, by servants who have been with the family for generations. Canji is then dried over large bamboo mats and finally stored in containers made up of termite resistant wood. It is a typical preparation requiring much indulgence.

Along with Canji, the leftovers of kitchen from the previous day, the curries condensed to a thick paste in shallow earthen pots called *kudnis*, and the meat diced and fried with onion rings and chilly over fires of rice husks, fresh shrimps and prawns — boiled or fried, dried shark in tamarind sauce, and pickles of all kinds, prepared by the females in the house — are all served.

Certain preparations served during brunch time along with Canji are the *prawn balchao, sukin sungtam*, Bombay ducks, and so on. The *prawn balchao* is one of the most prominent delicacies prepared from prawns. Sukin Sungtam is dried salted shrimps, roasted on a griddle and fried Bombay ducks are also served with Canji.

Rissois are snacks or starters, which are made from prawns, fried in pastry shells are also served during brunch.

Lunch: Lunch commences with a nutritious soup known as Sopa Grossa. It is basically a thick beef or chicken broth in which certain vegetables are boiled, with addition of fine rice, macaroni, and rounds of homemade sausages. Fish is an essential component of lunch. Rice and curries are compulsorily incorporated and are followed by sweets and fruits.

There are not less than 5 types of curries made in a typical Goan home for each season and purpose. They are **Sorak**, **Rosachi**, **Ambot-tik**, **Xir** and **Sambrachi**.

Sorak is a curry with utter simplicity and needs no ornamentation in its presentation.

Rosachi is lavishly rich, made from Ros (Konkani for juice, coconut milk in this case). The Goans have wide varieties of *rosachi,* i.e., fish *rosachi,* chicken *rosachi* or prawn *rosachi.*

Ambot-tik is basically a sour and spicy style of curry. It is generally made up of shark fish or ray fish. It is a fish curry.

Xir literally means slice, which is essentially a curry prepared during summer and the chief component is sliced mango. Goan curries are essentially red pepper curries with green chillies added for flavour. In Xir exactly the opposite happens.

Sambrachi which is referred as Madras curry by the Portuguese is a curry for special occasions and it tastes excellent when made of salted and dried prawns.

An authentic Goan curry is prepared by using coconut, dry coriander, cumin seeds, garlic, tamarind and turmeric ground to fine paste, dissolved in water and then cooked in an earthen pot on a slow fire. In this gravy, prawns or wide varieties of fishes are added to increase its taste and flavour. In Goan prawn curry, dry mango slices are added to enhance its flavour and Solan, a multi-purpose Goan preserve may also be added. In Goan fish curry, dry *kokum* are added. Certain vegetables like drumsticks and lady finger are also added to the prawn curry. If neither prawn nor fish is added to the curry, it is called Saurak (Sorak). A seasoning of onions is added in it, to which ground *masala* and spices are used.

The curry and rice in Goa are served with an array of side-dishes like fried fish and shrimps. Some of these are Recheado (stuffed) and Tisreo (clams) cooked in their own juices with grated coconuts.

Solantlem mass, salted and fatty pork cooked with *kokum* peels, and fried oysters in season (if not big, with rounds of onion and chopped garlic) are also served with curry and rice preparation. The Goans have the tiger prawn cooked in a dozen distinct methods, boiled with kokum peels and a red pepper. Fried Recheado, stewed in white gravy of onion and garlic, roasted on ambers of fire woods, diced, fried and pickled in a paste of vinegar and chilli may also be served during lunch time.

Kuswar

Kuswar is a term which is broadly used to describe a collective distinct Christmas goodies, which are also an essential and inseparable part of the cuisine of the Goan Catholic community and the Mangalorean Catholic community of Karnataka. The collection is huge and has at least 22 different traditional recipes in this assemblage. Kuswar originally comes from Goa.

Goan Catholic's Kuswar comprises about 22 different traditional recipes. Perada (Guava cheese) are a concoction made from mouth-watering green guavas and sugar. Kidyo or Kulkuls are semolina-based delectable delicacies flavoured with coconut and cardamom. Neuero or Neuries are a scrumptious dish prepared from a dough mixed with assortments like coconut, cashew nuts, raisins and cardamom and then deep fried. Bebinca is a multi-layered baked dessert, which is prepared using refined flour, coconut milk, sugar and ghee. Doce is a sweet item made using chickpeas and coconut. Marzipan is a confectionery concoction comprising mainly of sugar and almond. Bolinhas are simple coconut-baked cookies made with grated coconut, sugar, semolina, egg yolks and butter. Baath is an appetizing and moist rich coconut tart baked in a large round shape with pastry framework with ornamental design work on top, mildly flavoured with cardamom and currants. Once baked it is cut into pieces and served surrounded with the other sweets on the festive sweet tray. Kormolas are sweet scrumptious coconut pastry rolled out, then cut in squares and hand shaped into flower buds. Pinarg (Pinaca) are mouth-watering cutlets like sweets prepared from jaggery and crushed rice. Tuelinnas (Tuelinnas de Coco) are a sweet preparation made from scrapped coconut. Dodol are a unique preparation made by using jaggery and rice pudding. Dos de Grao is a well-famed and commonly prepared sweet concoction made by baking gram flour together with grated coconut and sugar. It has a thick firm crust with a soft and chewy centre.

Feni: The Signature Liquor of Goa

Feni is Goa's undoubtedly most venerable and well-famed triple, double distilled into an impeccably crystal-clear and alarmingly potent liquor. This is a drink which certainly is worthy of profound respect. It is an accompaniment to mitigate the effect of all spicy Goan food. Goans are excessively attached with their sentiments and emotions about their *feni,* as they are about their cuisine.

Basically, *feni* is of two types, both derived from local ingredients. Coconut or palm feni is prepared from the sap (solution) drawn from the cut-off shoots on a coconut tree. In Goa, this is referred as *toddy,* and the men who collect it are called *toddy* tapers. *Toddy* tapers at work are seen frequently crouched in the umbrella-like shade of the palm tree, they collect the terracotta pots, which have been filled with creamy white sap and then cut the shoots to ease further collection. They tie a new pot over the top, and descend to move to the next tree. *Toddy* can be collected throughout the year, and thus Palm Feni is in abundance at all times.

Cashew or Caju Feni, can only be collected during the cashew season in late March and early April. Cashews are a significant crop in Goa and one can have a sight of it during early spring all across Goa. The cashew apple, when ripe, turns into yellow-orange colour and the nut ripens inside it. When the fruit is gathered after harvesting, the nuts are set apart from the apples, and are allowed to dry in the sun. The apples collected meanwhile are placed in a pit and stomped by foot in order to collect the juice.

Both Palm Toddy and caju juice can be drunk fresh as soon as they are collected and are found to be delectable and scrumptious. When left for just a few hours, it begins to ferment.

Specialty Dishes

Goan Fish Curry

Ambot-tik is the most famous version of fish curry which translates without exaggeration to sour-spicy. It is made distinctive due to the sour and spicy combination of taste merging into each other. It derives its sour taste from the petals of the tart *kokum. Kokum,* the red purple coloured fruit, is the real king of ingredient in Goan cuisine and is well-acknowledged for its cooling and medicinal features. The fish curry paste is prepared by making a paste of ground coconut with red chillies, black peppers, cumin seeds, coriander seeds, turmeric powder, garlic and ginger. This paste is then after added with sliced onions, tamarind juice and green chillies with a cup of water and salt. This mixture is further cooked with extra addition of *kokum.* At last, the fish is added and cooked till done.

One of the renowned Goa's poets writes in his poem to Yama, the God of Death: "Please Sir, the God of death, don't take it my turn today. Not today, Sir, there is a fish curry for dinner...." From this message, the fondness for Fish Curry by the Goan people can be easily realized.

Putte

Putte is a delicious and nutritious delicacy prepared from the paste of rice flour, grated coconut, and jaggery, wrapped in a jackfruit leaf to resemble a cone. It is then steam cooked. It is a preparation generally made by the Hindus during the festive occasion of Naag Panchami. When the same preparation is made by stuffing the mixture in a turmeric leaf, it is called Patoleo.

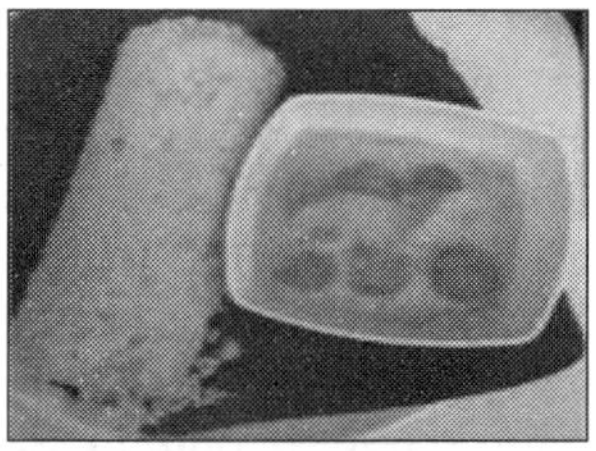

Caldo Verda

This is a distinctive Goan soup that is thickened by adding mashed potatoes and is garnished by juliennes of spinach.

Christmas Pudding

It is a kind of pudding with utter simplicity prepared during the Christmas festive season. In this dish, milk is boiled on a double boiler and then added with sugar, cocoa and gelatin. It is then removed and added with nuts, salt and vanilla essence to mould and then it is refrigerated. It is served along chilled with cream.

Leitao Assado

It is an authentic delicacy prepared during the festive occasion of Christmas. A suckling (fed by lactation) pig is marinated with Portuguese white chillies, ginger-garlic paste, and *feni*. The whole pig marinated is roasted in the oven and then carved by the head of the family. This dish is descriptive about the skill required in its preparation.

Fish Recheado

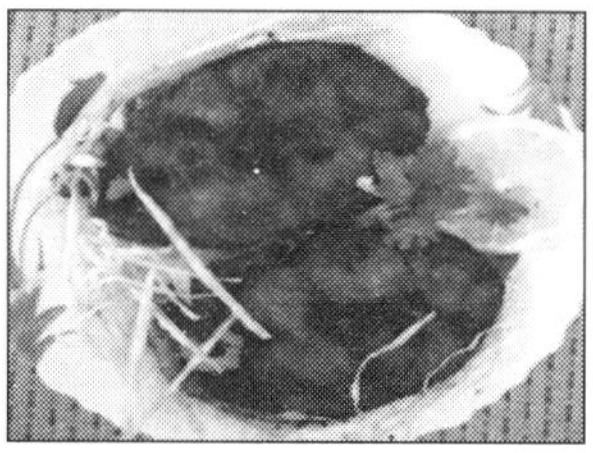

Recheado means stuffed in Portuguese. In this dish, a fresh whole fish, usually a mackerel or pomfret or any other fish, is slit down the centre and stuffed with a spicy red paste, after which it is shallow fried. Mackerel Recheado is one of Goa's most famous dishes. The fiery-red Recheado *masala* is made by grinding Kashmiri red chilies, garlic, clove, turmeric, cumin, peppercorns, sugar, fenugreek and tamarind into a smooth but thick paste using vinegar. The Recheado masala can be stored in an airtight container for months as the vinegar in it acts as a preservative. The Recheado *masala* is of vibrant red colour, and spicy and pungent spice combination.

Prawn Balchao

This Goan favourite is a great contribution of the Portuguese to the Goan cuisine. Balchão originally originated in Macao, where it is called Balichao. Balchao is a technique of cooking either fish or prawns in a dark red and tangy sauce. Balchao is very similar to pickling and can be made days in advance without reheating. The traditional Balchao uses a paste made from dried shrimp known as *galmbo* in Konkani spices and *feni*. This paste is added to fresh prawns, onion, spices and oil to prepare a Prawn Balchao. Balchao is mostly bottled, and served and eaten as an accompaniment in meals. Some people don't prefer to use the dried shrimp paste, as it bestows a fairly pungent fishy flavour to the dish in which it is used.

Pork Vindaloo

Undoubtedly, Pork Vindaloo is the signature dish of Goan cuisine, which is one of the hottest and fiercest delicacies of Goa. It is a gourmet's delight.

The name 'vindaloo' derives from the Portuguese dish 'carne de vinha d'alhos,' which is a dish basically of meat, usually pork, with wine and garlic. There are vivid renditions of the etymology for this word one being 'vinho' for wine, 'alhos' for garlic (Portuguese), 'viande' and 'aloo' for meat and potato (French and Indian).

Traditional vindaloos do not have potatoes although the word 'aloo' does signify 'potato' in Hindi. At certain places, this dish is made with chicken or lamb stock mixed with potatoes. It is a spicy concoction of lots of red chilies, garlic, cooked with chunks of pork, Goan vinegar and hard palm jaggery and is best relished with plain boiled rice. Authentic vindaloo compulsorily uses pork, marinated in vinegar (with substantial amount of garlic, chillies and other spices) in barrels, sometimes for days, even months, before being simmered to cook. Potatoes are never incorporated in the authentic vindaloo. In Goa, the pork is marinated in a *feni*, exclusively prepared in Goa.

Sorpotel

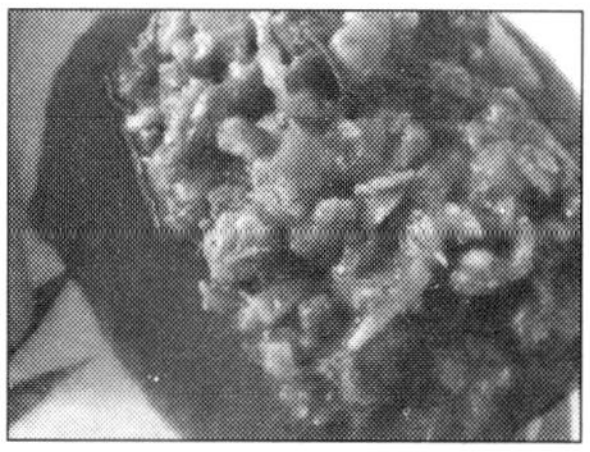

Unarguably, Sorpotel, adapted from the Portuguese dish of Sarabulho, is the heart and soul of Goan Christian cuisine. Sorpotel is one of those authoritative dishes that genuinely highlights the assemblage of Goan and Portuguese cultures in the cuisine of this state – the Goan part characterized by the generous use of spices and Portuguese part marked by the enormous use of vinegar, which is seen nowhere else. Sorpotel is basically prepared from pork and offals (liver, heart and kidney). All of them are diced and cooked in a thick and very spicy sauce flavoured with red chillies, cinnamon, cloves dipped in pungent *toddy* vinegar, which is required to balance the potent taste of pig blood, another unique traditional ingredient of this revered dish. The blood is not used in recent versions of the dish as it is not preferred and actually is also not to everyone's taste. There are many places in the region where pork has been substituted by lamb meat and even beef, depending upon the diner's preferences.

Sorpotel, like Balchao, can be kept for several days as enormous quantity of vinegar is used which acts as preservative, and is actually considered to taste even much better if left for three to four days before being reheated.

Sorpotel is often accompanied by *sanna* – 'a spongy, white, and slightly sweet steamed rice and coconut bread. However, it can also be relished with bread, on rice, or in a bun as a sandwich. Thus, Sorpotel has been the real essence of Goan Cuisine with distinctive elements.

Chicken Cafreal

Chicken Cafreal is a Goan dish which has its origin in the tribal populace. The dish emphasizes a lot on its simplicity, in taste as well as its cooking style. Cafreal means 'Africa' in Portuguese, and this dish emerged perhaps from the colonies in Angola. It was named after the African soldiers or *kaffirs* as a tribute to those who brought it to Goa centuries ago. Today, the dish is made by marinating pieces of chicken in a paste made of spices, chilies, garlic and ginger and lemon juice and then deep-fried or shallow fried till dry. The resultant dish is almost dry, but spicy. This is the dish with much resemblance to the Portuguese-style grilled chicken, and the sauce it is marinated in tastes similar to the famous Portuguese Peri-peri sauce.

Chicken Xacutti

The dish, greenish brown in colour, Xacutti (pronounced as sha-coo-ti), incorporates abundant spices like sliced or grated coconut, poppy seeds, nutmeg, coriander leaves, red and green chillies, ginger and cloves. Apart from this, tamarind and lemon juice make for a sharp acrid curry. It is thicker in consistency than the fish curry but has been recognized as rich, acute and a spicy delicacy. The meat is first dipped in a marinade with turmeric powder, large pieces of crushed ginger along with lots of herbs. The Goan Hindus specifically use lemon and Kashmiri chillies whereas the Goan Christians differentiate the taste of the dish by the use of vinegar and bicholim chillies in this preparation. The chicken can be substituted with mutton, lamb or fish. It is a real delight for spicy food lovers.

Prawn Caldeen

It is a yellow-colour curried dish in which the prawns are cooked with onion, ginger garlic paste, coconut milk, green chillies and turmeric. The distinct taste and appearance of the dish is due to rice which is used as a thickening agent in this dish. The base of the gravy is fresh white coloured coconut milk. Tamarind is added finally to render a tartness and sourness to the dish. It is a light curry preparation of prawns with mild flavours.

Khatkhate Curry

Khatkhate curry is an exotic preparation with strange and unusual combination of assorted vegetable stew of Goan cuisine. It is prepared with no less than five vegetables, with addition of grated coconut, jaggery, *kokum*, tamarind, (Sichuan pepper – a typical spice from the Konkan region), dried red chillies, *garam masala* powder, and turmeric powder. The vegetables incorporated are radish, potato, sweet potato, carrots, corn, pumpkins, and any seasonal vegetables. This dish is mostly prepared for grand events like weddings, pujas, festive occasions and many other functions. Due to the incorporation of many vegetables, it has an assemblage of taste and texture, and is nutritious as well.

Chouricos

Chouricos are essentially spicy pork sausages, which owe a sense of high obligation to the Portuguese in terms of culinary traditions. Goan sausages are highly salted and cubes of pork are typically spiced with vinegar, turmeric powder, red chillies, garlic, ginger, cloves and cinnamon. Once they are prepared, the strings of sausages are dried in the sun and then hung on the fire where they are exposed to smoking. Traditionally, they are eaten during the monsoon, when availability of fish is very less. In order to prepare them, they are soaked in water and then usually fried and served with a hot sauce and rice.

Bebinca

Bebinca, also known as *bibik* or *bebinka*, is a kind of pudding and an authentic traditional Goan dessert. It typifies the Goan dessert. The dessert is prepared with great dexterity. Typical Bebinca is a splendid concoction made from layer upon layer of coconut pancakes and it has 16 specific layers, but it can be made as per one's choice and liking. The ingredients used to make it are plain flour, sugar, ghee, egg yolk, coconut milk and almond slivers to garnish. The dessert has to be baked in layers, and one layer is baked before the next one is added. Bebinca is served warm with cold ice cream. Though making Bebinca is a very monotonous process which requires patience, the dessert is a mouth-melting delicacy. It can also be preserved for a long time or consumed fresh.

Dodol

Dodol is essentially gentle jaggery flavoured fudge made from palm, jaggery, rice flavour and coconut milk. It is allowed to cool in a flat pan and then served in slices, and is traditionally consumed during Christmas time.

Sannas

It is considered to be the Goan version of south Indian *idli*. Sannas are amazingly soft spongy, white, and slightly sweet steamed rice and coconut bread. Sanna consists of two types: *toddy* fermented *sannas* and the other prepared using the sap of the coconut palms. Sannas are popularly common amongst the Goans – both Hindus and Catholics.

Arroz Refogado

This delicacy of Goa is made by mélange of chicken, rice and seafood like prawns, squid, and clams. The chicken breasts are pan fried in oil and then the rice is sautéed along with bell peppers, onions and tomatoes and cooked in stock with addition of seafood and saffron in it. Meanwhile, the chicken is also added with desired seasoning and served.

Caldeirada

It is a mildly flavoured delicacy offering in which a wide variety of fishes or prawns are cooked into a kind of stew with vegetables (such as potatoes, onions, green peppers, tomatoes, and so on) and often flavoured with wine.

Canja de Galinha It is a type of chicken broth with rice and chicken pieces, and is originally a typical Goan preparation.	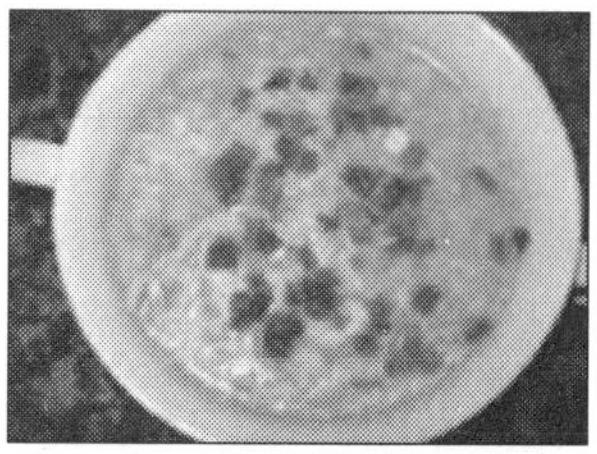
Pez Pez comprises Goan rice (also known as Ukade rice that are reddish in colour and thick grained), water and salt to taste. It is usually eaten with pickles or papads or dried and roasted fish or prawn curry (very thick). Pez is very popular in Goan homes and is usually eaten during brunch.	
Feijoada Essentially, it is a stew of beans with beef and pork. This stew is made of dried black-eyed beans, oil, onion, tomatoes, cloves, ginger, turmeric powder, tamarind pulp, chili powder/paprika powder, salt to taste and coconut milk. It is usually served with rice and assorted sausages, such as chouriços.	
Cabidela This delicacy is made up of meat, pork liver, tongue, kidneys and has spices like red dried chilies, peppers, peppercorns, cloves garlic, ginger, cumin seeds, cloves, cinnamon, vinegar, oil and sugar. Traditionally, blood is an essential constituent of this preparation and this renders a brown colour to the dish. Arroz de cabidela is a rice preparation with the same ingredients used in *cabidela* and rice.	
Alsandache Tondak It is undoubtedly a scrumptious vegetarian delicacy of red kidney beans in a spicy Xacutti masala.	
Galinha Piri-Piri This is a mouth–watering delicacy in which chicken pieces are marinated in a pleasant mixture of *piri-piri* and Goan herbs and then barbequed or fried. The piri-piri is a very spicy sauce made with red chilli peppers, citrus peel, onion, garlic, pepper, salt, lemon juice, bay leaves, paprika, pimento, basil, oregano, and tarragon.	
Bolos These are cakes made from coarsely-ground wheat flour fermented by adding *toddy* vinegar and then baked. These are made during the times of the Carnival.	

Moonga Ganthi It is a basic lentil preparation made by boiling sprouted *moong dal* with green chillies, curry leaves and tender coconut. It is flavoured with a *masala* of red chillies, coriander seeds and pepper corn, and tempered with asafeotida and mustard seeds.	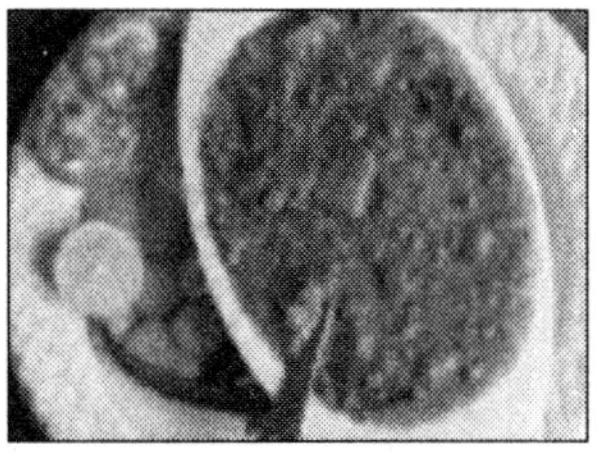
Varan It is a simple yellow lentil preparation, generally tempered with mustard seeds and red chillies.	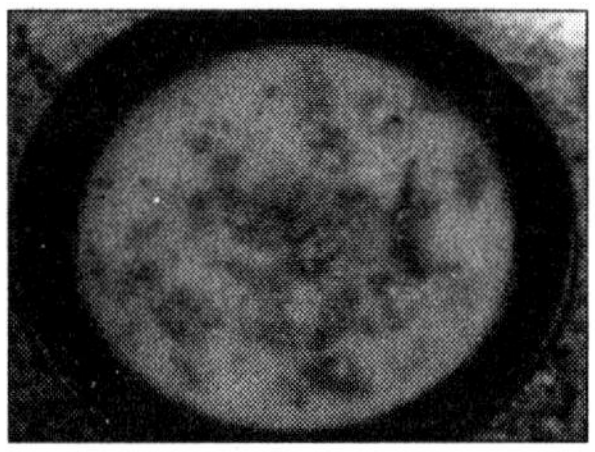

Culinary Trivia: Fruit and its Classification

Fruits:

Botanically, a fruit is an organ that develops from the ovary of a flowering plant and contains one or more seeds.

Culinarily, a fruit is the perfect snack food, the basis of a dessert, colourful sauce or soup, or an accompaniment to meat, fish, shellfish or poultry.

Classification:

Berries – Black berries, blue berries, currants, cranberries, raspberries, strawberries.
Citrus – Grapefruits, lemon, limes, oranges, tangerines, kumquats.
Exotic – Figs, gooseberries, guava, lychees, pomegranates, prickly pears, rambutans, persimmons.
Grapes – White grapes, black grapes.
Melons – Casaba melons, water melons, musk melons, honeydew melons, cantaloupes.
Pomes – Apples, pears, quince.
Stone fruits – Apricots, cherries, peaches, nectarines, plums.
Tropicals – Banana, dates, kiwis, mangoes, papaya, pineapples.

12 Gujarati Cuisine

"Not eating meat is a decision, eating meat is an instinct." – Denis Leary

Gujarat, situated on the north-west coast of India is bordered by Rajasthan on the north, Maharashtra on the south, Madhya Pradesh on the east, and the Arabian Sea as well as the Pakistani province of Sindh on the west.

Gujarati cuisine is a resplendent cuisine which radiates simplicity in all aspects. Essentially, Gujarati cuisine has been influenced and defined by the Jain vegetarian populace and Hinduism, and this influence has been the determining factor in making it largely a vegetarian cuisine. It has bestowed new shades to the stream of vegetarian culinary art.

Gujarati cuisine is delightfully an ultimate assemblage of green leafy vegetables and the world of pulses, which has subtle flavours of the spices and finally accompanied with rice preparation and a variety of breads. The authentic cuisine of Gujarat is characterized by rather bland taste and catered traditionally on large silver or stainless steel platters. It comprises one variant of *dal*, *kadhi*, two or three vegetables and pulses, salads, desserts, breads (either *puri* or *chapati*), rice preparation, *chutneys*, hot pickles and *papad*.

Gujarati cuisine is a lavish platter which renders a large variety of dishes, thereby creating a passion among the Gujarati people to love their food and feel proud about it. The Gujarati Thali is considered to be a balanced diet as it comprises all the four major components, (*dal*, *bhaat*, *rotli* and *shaak*), i.e., cereal, pulses, vegetables and rice with supplements like pickles, *chutney*, papad, buttermilk and salads. It is simply very nutritious. The people here sparingly use ginger, garlic and green chillies, and use more of jaggery instead of sugar in their preparation. It is thereby gifted with the right kind of blend of *masalas* in vegetables and *dals*, hence the food is readily digestible. The staple *dal* in Gujarat is *tuver dal*, normally served among the rich. But the use of *moong dal* is also prevalent in certain regions of Gujarat. The consumption of *chana dal* is widespread in the powdered form of *besan* – used in *farsan* and sweetmeats.

The two major factors, in fact two influences, which have defined and shaped Guajarati cuisine have been the influence of Jainism and Vaishnavism.

The Jain influence has been apparent from prior to the 6th century, when the teachings and preachings of Lord Mahavira had influenced the common people considerably. King Kumarapala, who luxuriated the consumption of meat in this period, decided to relinquish meat eating later under the influence of Jainism. Similarly, in 12th century AD, he had forbidden the slaughtering of animals in this kingdom. Jain scholars like Hemachandra preached the same philosophy during the 11th century AD, thereby discouraging everyone from eating meat. Thus, Jains prohibited animal slaughtering as a practice of non-violence and also prohibited meat eating in the society. Jains even admonished everyone for incorporation of spices like onion and garlic, which are considered to produce heat in the body.

The Vaishnavs who were the admirer and believer of Lord Vishnu also preached vegetarianism. The discourses of Vallabhacharya who formed the Pushti Marga in the 15th century AD, gave a strong force to the movement of Vaishnavism in Gujarat. At present, about two-thirds of the population in Gujarat is strictly vegetarian.

The Gujaratis have excelled and are very skilled in preparing homemade *khichdi* (rice and lentil or rice and *mung* bean), and *chaas* (buttermilk) with a wide variety of pickles as an accompaniment. Main dishes are generally based on vegetables cooked by the steaming method and added with different spices and *dals* that are added to a *vaghar*. *Vaghar* is a mixture of spices added in hot oil that varies depending on the main ingredient.

Salt, sugar, lemon, lime, and tomato are used frequently to prevent people from dehydration in the hot areas of Gujarat, where temperature reaches almost 50°C (122°F) in the shade. Gujaratis use mainly sugar or jaggery in some of their *sabzi/shaak* and *dal* dishes. The sweetness imparted by sugar or jaggery in these dishes is the main factor to counterbalance the slightly bland taste of the vegetables.

The dry climate conditions of Gujarat are not conducive to the production and cultivation of rice in the area. Rather, wheat, bajra, and maize are commonly found and therefore *rotis* or *chapatis* are preponderantly present in the Gujarati Thali.

Some renowned sweet dishes and desserts are made with local sugarcane, jaggery (a solid made from unrefined cane sugar), milk, almonds, and pistachios.

Gujarati cuisine is also unique and has been distinguished for its wide variety of *farsan*, which are readily served alongside of main meal. Certain famous Gujarati *farsans* can be served as snacks, tea time dishes or as a light meal.

In coastal areas of Gujarat, the Kharwa community has developed a unique cuisine consisting of fresh and dried fish. The most widely relished varieties of seafood are pomfrets, *khandwas, gedadas, surmai*, prawns, crabs, lobster and *narsinga* (calamari).

During summer in Gujarat, lots of pumpkins are harvested along with snake gourd, pointed gourd (*parwal*), and ridged gourd (*turiya*). The winter produce is completely different which makes the cuisine more interesting, comprising sweet potatoes, fresh green peas, a variety of radish, red and purple carrots and fenugreek (*methi*). Aubergines are common too and are available round the year. Besides these, Gujarat has a good production of chillies, cumin, fennel and garlic. Gujarat also produces banana, mango, papaya and chikoo in large quantity.

Based on geographical boundaries, Gujarat has been divided into four major regions to understand the cuisines more comprehensively. Due to the climatic changes, there are slight variations in eating habits and modes of preparation. The four regions are North and South Gujarat, Kutch and Kathiawad.

North Gujarat

This region is renowned for its traditional Gujarati Thali comprising rice, *dal*, curry, vegetables, sprouted beans, *farsan*, pickles, *chutney* and *raita*. Food is mostly non-spicy and oil is used generously. People here don't prefer to eat spicy foods and have excelled in the preparation of *farsans*. *Farsans* prepared here are varied some of which are Pathara, Khaman Dhokla, and Khandvi.

Kathiawad

It is astonishing that Kathiawad with its vast extension of dry earth and lack of water resources has high production of sugarcane, wheat, millets, peanuts, and sesame native to this region. It has high production of pulses as well and hence pulses dominate Kathiawari food. *Gur* (jaggery) is also used generously due to production of sugarcane. This region offers a wide range of delicious and mouth-watering variety of pickles.

The cuisine of Kathiawad is esteemed for its preparation like *debras* which is made with whole wheat flour, mixed with green chillies, yogurt, salt and sugar. These are consumed with Chhundo, which is a spicy and sweet shredded mango pickles made up of grated ripe mangoes. Chhundo is a variety of Indian pickles preparation also used as a condiment and also as an accompaniment. It is not just that it can be made only with mangoes but with various fruits and vegetables. It is a typical Gujarati dish but consumed all over India.

Methi Masala is a famous spice combination of this region, which is basically a dry powder made from fenugreek seeds, chilly powder and salt. This dry *masala* is used to sprinkle over raw vegetables and salads. It renders a piquant flavour to the dish.

Phafda, a flavoured assorted flour *puri* is another Kathiawari favourite.

Kathiawar is distinguished with rich and spicy dishes and not as sweet like other Gujarati dishes.

Kutch

Kutch (also spelled Kachchh) cuisine is comparatively very simple and majorly vegetarian. In the rural areas of Kutch, bajra and milk are the chief foods. *Bajra na rotla* with curds and butter milk is a common food among all the Gujarati people and they relish it. They also drink a generous portion of buttermilk during lunch. Milk is considered to be worthy of religious respect and hence offering it to someone is acknowledged a gesture of friendship and welcoming attitude. Settlement of conflict is invariably marked by offering milk to each other as a concluding remark.

Rice and pulses form the staple diet of the people in this locality, who blend these two commodities with specific spices in a number of ways to dish out delicacies of utter excellence. It is very interesting to note that this region has been inhabited by the pure Hindu vegetarian and by the Bohra community of Muslim traders, who are well-famed for their beef delicacies.

They are also famed for their superb variety of soups – hot and cold, clear and generously added with cashew nuts and diced vegetables.

Tea is undoubtedly the most popular drink in this region and is savoured regardless of sex, caste, religion or social status. The tea with milk is always preferred and offering black tea to guests is considered to be a bad gesture. Tea without milk is offered when people visit a host to mourn the death of the host's near and dear ones.

Dabeli is a unique spicy snack prepared by mixing boiled potatoes with a specific *dabeli masala* and serving the mixture between Ladi-Pav (burger bun). It is accompanied by *chutneys* made from tamarind, dates, garlic, red chilies, and so on, and finally garnished with pomegranate and roasted peanuts.

This region is also famed for the *khichdi* (a simple lentil and rice mixture) and the main dish here is consumed with *kadhi* – a savoury curry made of yogurt using bay leaves, ginger, chillies and finely chopped vegetables as garnishing-onions and pickles.

Few dishes that are popular from this region also includes *dudhi muthia, khakra, thepla, khaman dhokla,* (which is a salty steamed cake); *doodhpak*, a sweet and thickened milk delicacy and *shrikhand*, which is a dessert made of yogurt, flavoured with saffron, cardamom, nuts and candied fruit which is eaten with hot, fluffy *puris*.

The food of Kutch is non-spicy, hence to spice up the flavour of bland foods it is enjoyed with a wide collection of pickles and *chutneys*.

Alcoholic liquor made from the distillation of molasses is another popular drink and is enjoyed by most of the local people of the region. As alcoholic drink is strictly banned in entire Gujarat, it is illegal to drink or have such item in Kutch too. Women are not allowed to drink the alcoholic liquor in any circumstances.

South Gujarat

Southern Gujarat is blessed with abundant rainfall as compared to the Kathiawad region and hence green vegetables and excess of fruits dominate the cuisine of this region. This region believes in simplicity and hence doesn't have faith in the philosophy of elaborate dishes and expensive ingredients. Notwithstanding, it tastes exotically different and is genuinely scrumptious.

Popularly consumed items include a delicious vegetable mixture called *undhyoo* and *paunk*, which is a tangy delicacy. Surat is famed widespread for its bakery items like the *nankhatais, gharis* and the *saglu-baglu mithai*, which are readily available in the city's bakeries and in confectionery shops.

Despite the fact that the cuisine is characterized by the simplicity, Gujarati food is nutritionally well balanced. It includes the salads, fresh homemade preserves and pickles and beverages like *chhaas* or buttermilk and *aam ras* or fresh mango pulp. The taste of certain dishes is inclined towards the sweeter side but few have higer sugar content as compared to salt and spices. Many a times, jaggery is used as a substitute to sugar. Onion, potato and garlic are used extensively in combination of dairy products as these are a substitute of green leafy vegetables that cannot be grown in a harsh and dry climate around the year. The cuisine has a lot of scope in its range due to the change in the seasonal availability of vegetables throughout the year.

Thus, speaking without exaggeration, Gujarati cuisine ranges in its taste from very sweet items like *peda* and *jalebi* to utmost spicy taste like pickles and *chutneys*. Many Gujarati dishes are considered distinctively sweet, salty, and spicy at the same time.

A Gujarati Thali would not be complete without staples like garlic chutney, raw onions, chilli pickles or fried green chilies, *chaas*, papad, and ghee with jaggery. These have become an inseparable part and also the salient features of this cuisine.

Shaak: An assemblage of Varied Stir Fried Vegetable Preparation

It is a common term used generally for a dry and stir fried vegetable preparation such as *batata nu shaak,* (potatoes cooked with tomatoes); *kobi vatana nu shaak* (cabbage and green peas); *tuvar ringan nu shaak* (brinjal and fresh tuvar beans), *ringan nu shaak* (eggplant curry), *bhinda nu shaak* (okra curry), *tameta bataka nu rasawalu shaak* (tomato potato gravy vegetable), *kantola nu shaak* (one type of slight bitter tasting vegetable), *karela nu shaak* (bitter gourd vegetable), and so on.

Farsan: A Signature Snacks Collection

Farsan is a common term used collectively for the type of snacks in Gujarati cuisine. They are either fried snack items which are then dried and can be stored, or are fresh and steamed. Some popular farsans are:

Dhokla: It is a savoury cake which has carved a niche for itself by gaining utmost popularity in Gujarati cuisine. It is made by steaming a fermented batter of gram flour and yogurt. This delicacy is made by preparing a batter of gram flour and soda bicarb and then allowing it to ferment and then steaming it. It is then cut into pieces and then tempering it with mustard seeds, green chillies, and curry leaves on the top. Nowadays, it is instantly fermented by few using Eno powder available in sachet in medical stores. It is available in two versions in the market, one is plain *dhokla* and the other is *masala dhokla* which is bit spicy in taste.

Khandvi: It is a roll made of gram flour and yogurt topped with mustard seed, fresh coriander, and grated coconut. It is made by cooking a batter of gram flour, curds, turmeric, water, and salt on slow flame until it leaves the side of the pan. It is then spread onto a greased plate and then sprinkled with grated coconut and tempered mustard seeds. Thin lines of about 1 inches strip are cut and each strip is rolled to pipes and then served.

Ragda: It is a fried potato dish patty garnished with *sev*.

Batata vada: It is a dumpling made of boiled and mashed potato dipped in the spiced batter of gram flour and then deep fried.

Patra: It is a dish of colocasia leaves rolled up with a spiced gram flour batter and steamed and garnished like *dhoklas*.

Samosa: It is the most consumed snacks in India. It is a pyramid shaped pastry of refined flour flavoured with *ajowain*, and filled with a savoury potato mixture and then deep-fried.

Sev: It is a snack preparation which is made of gram flour dough. It has a thin shred like shape and is pressed from the *sev* machine to obtain this peculiar shape. It is commonly consumed snacks which can be stored for a longer period of time.

Ganthiya: It is also made of gram flour but from a softer dough. It has a cylindrical shape and is much thicker in size as compared to *sev*.

Muthia: The name *muthia* is derived from the way it is made, from the 'gripping' action of the hand. It is a steamed dumpling made of gram flour, fenugreek, salt, turmeric, and red chilli powder. The steamed dumpling can also be stir fried with mustard seed.

Specialty Dishes

Fulka Rotli Also referred as *rotli* or *chapati*. It is made with whole wheat flour and is rolled thin.	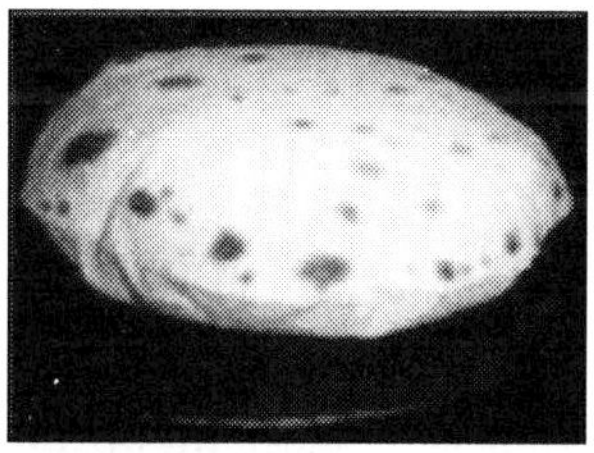
Puri It is deep-fried bread made with whole wheat flour.	
Thepla It is also called *Dhebra*. It is made with a mixture of flours. It is shallow fried, mildly spiced, and usually contains shredded vegetables. An example is *methi thepla*.	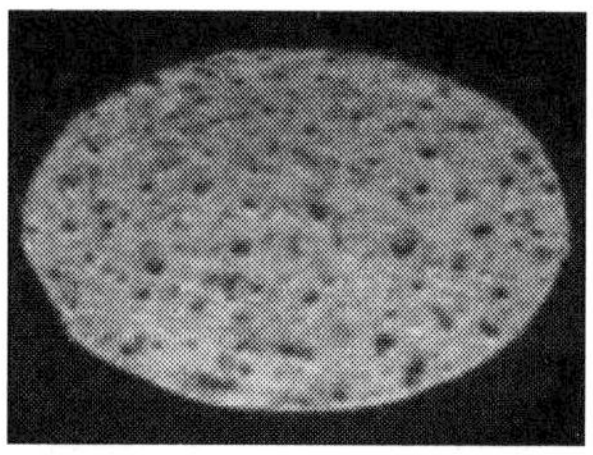
Bhakhri It is made with whole wheat flour. It is thicker and crispier than *rotli*.	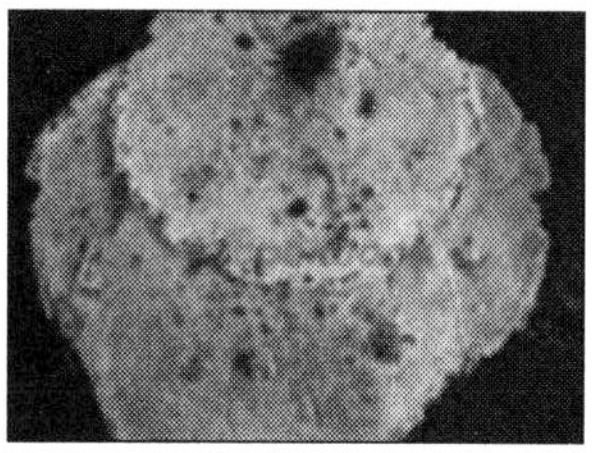
Bajri no Rotlo It is thick millets flour flatbread usually grilled over coals.	

Juvar no Rotlo It is thick sorghum flat bread and cooked in a similar manner as *bajri no rotlo.*	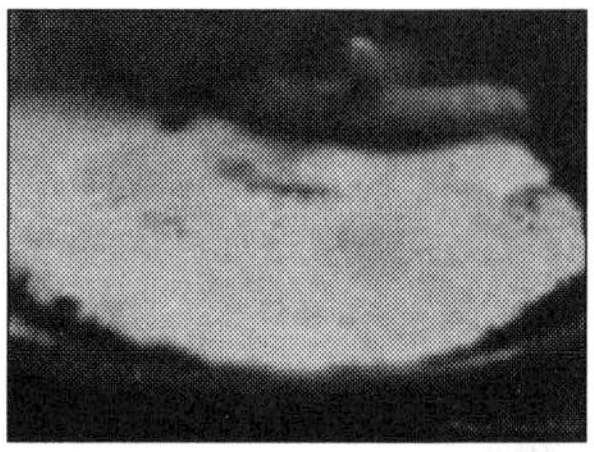
Puran Poli (Vedmi) It is whole wheat bread with sweet *moong dal* filling. It is shallow fried and usually made for special occasions.	
Vagharelu Bhaat It is rice fried along with a *baghar* (tempering) of mustard seeds, red chillies, curry leaves and turmeric.	
Khichdi It is a very simple preparation in which rice and *dal* are cooked in the porridge style. It is accompanied with ghee, curds and pickles.	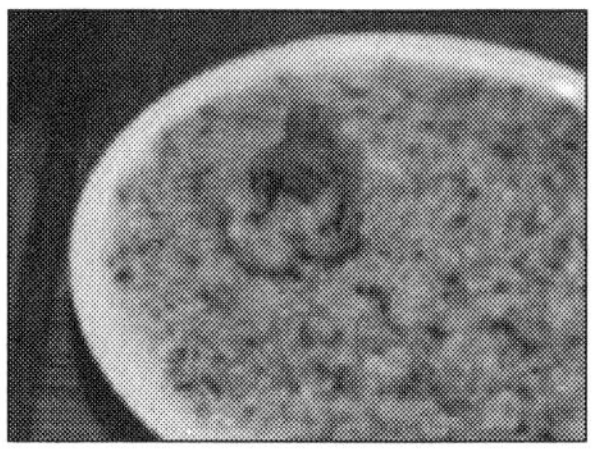
Khatta-Mittha Bhaat As the name suggests, it is sour and sweet rice preparation. Rice is boiled with potatoes and spices. It is yellow in colour and is accompanied with lemon peels.	
Undhiyu It is a combination of varied vegetables such as eggplant, tubers, and is slow cooked with special spices traditionally in a clay pot.	
Bateta nu Shaak It is a simple potato curry preparation.	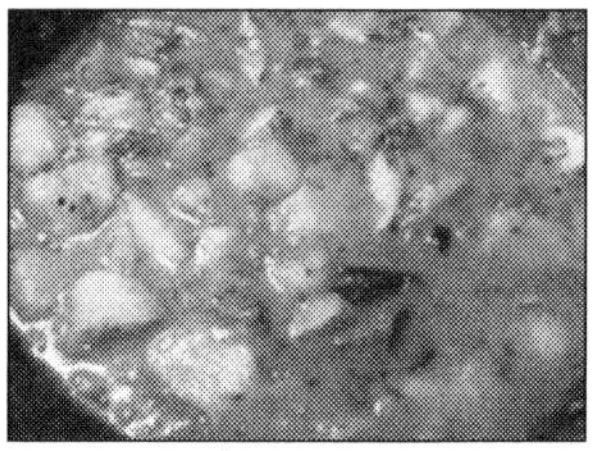

Bateta Sukhi Bhaji It is a dry potato preparation.	
Dudhi nu Shaak It is a bottle gourd or squash curry preparation.	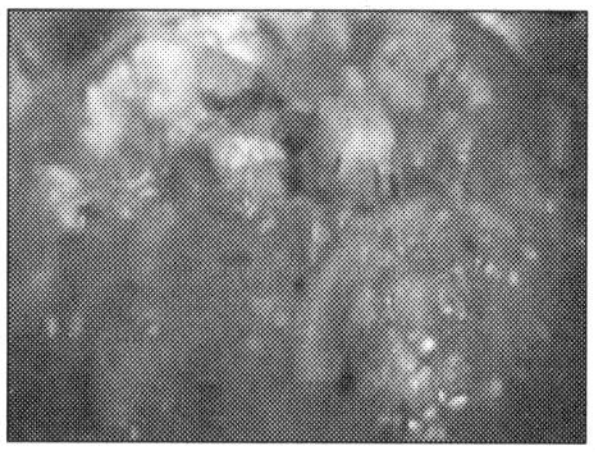
Guavar nu Shaak It is a simple dry preparation of cluster beans.	
Panchkutiyu Shaak It is a five-vegetable curry preparation and is enjoyed by all.	
Sutarfeni It is one of the irresistible sweets prepared from flaky, shredded rice dough with almonds and pistachios on top. It is prepared using refined flour, corn flour and semolina in the dough. It is relished with great sense of satisfaction.	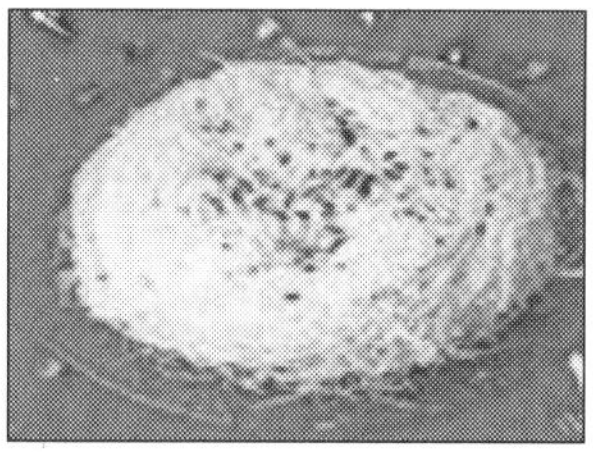
Basundi It is a dessert prepared mostly in Maharashtra, Gujarat and Karnataka. Basically, it is sweetened dense milk flavoured with cardamom and saffron. It is made by boiling milk on low heat until the milk is reduced to half. It is served chilled, garnished with charoli nuts (*chironji*), and slices of almonds and pistachios.	
Mohanthal It is a scrumptious dessert preparation prepared using gram flour, clarified butter (*desi ghee*) and sugar. It is prepared by mixing half the quantity of ghee with gram flour and then mixing it till it attains the crumbly texture. Then the remaining ghee is heated in a different pan and the gram flour with ghee in crumbly texture is added and stirred till golden brown colour. Meanwhile the sugar syrup is prepared and is added in the gram flour and mixed thoroughly. It is then poured in a greased tray and cut into squares, garnished with nuts and served.	

Gudpapdi It is dessert made from wheat flour, roasted in ghee to a golden brown colour, mixed with jaggery, flattened in a thali, sprinkled with poppy seeds, cut into square pieces and served.	
Khajoor Pak It is a sweet delicacy made from mixture of dates and dry fruits cooked together in little ghee, flattened in a *thali*, cut into squares and garnished.	
Salli Jardalao Murghi It is a very popular chicken preparation in which the chicken is cooked with apricots and finally garnished with deep fried potato straw.	
Patrani Macchi It is a unique and typical delicacy in which the fish is marinated in a spicy green chutney and then wrapped in a banana leaf and steamed. It is eaten with *chutney* and is very nutritious.	

Culinary Trivia: Chutneys

Chutney is a very famous accompaniment that complements many Indian preparations. It consists of a mixture of spices, vegetables, and/or fruits. It may be either wet or dry, and has a texture either coarse or fine. *Chutney* is a relish which is added to meals to add flavour. It is eaten and can be eaten with a wide variety of foods. It is traditionally ground with a mortar and pestle made of stone. *Chutney* is prepared by grinding certain ingredients to a paste like consistency or a little coarser one. The *chutney* such as green coriander *chutney* (*dhaniye ki chutney*), mint *chutney* (*pudine ki chutney*), *aam ki chutney, lasoon ki chutney, nariyal ki chutney, saunth ki chutney* or *imli ki chutney* (comprising tamarind, jaggery, ginger, salt, red chilli powder and dry fruits like raisins and dates) and so on has become an integral part of Indian cuisine. One can't even imagine in India dishes like *pakora* without *pudine ki chutney, idli* and *dosa* without *nariyal ki chutney, dahi bhalle* without topping of *saunth ki chutney* and *biryani* without *pudine ki chutney.*

The word "chutney" derives from the Sanskrit word *catnī*, meaning to lick. The common element of all "chutneys" is that they are added to meals to add flavour; and hence the best English "translation" of "chutney" is "relish".

13 Haryanvi Cuisine

"The only think I like better than talking about Food is eating." – John Walters

Haryana state of north India is bordered by Punjab and Himachal Pradesh on the north, by Rajasthan on the west and south and Uttar Pradesh on the east.

Haryana is a tiny state but has a sparkling dimension of very rich agricultural production heritage contributing to its growth and prosperity. It is also referred as 'the lands of rotis'. Haryana has been symbolized by the notion *'Desan me des haryana, jit doodh-dahi ka khana'* which means that amongst all countries Haryana is a country with generous production of milk and curds as the food. As major portion of Haryana has been large farming lands, it has huge counting of cattle and hence there is no scarcity of milk and milk products. Being an agricultural state, most of them are farmers. Haryana, with its dominating agrarian culture has preserved its utter simplicity in its cuisine and this can be easily realized in every aspect. Haryana was an integral part of Punjab and hence it also resembles Punjab in its cuisines.

Haryana has been pioneering in propagating the type of cattles like the Murrah buffalo and Haryana cow, which are renowned all over the country for producing large quantity of milk. People prepare *desi ghee* and butter at home and use them lavishly in every possible preparation. The home-made butter is called *tindi* or *nooni* ghee. It is a custom which has been practised from the long period for a girl's family to give her daughter gifts of ghee, *gondh* (edible gum), *laddus* (a sweetmeat made of gram flour) and dry fruits when she becomes a mother. Food is crucial in gifts also and is therefore honoured and revered.

Other common ingredients of Haryanvi cuisine are rice, wheat, bajra, and fresh vegetables. Spices such as ginger, garlic, red chilli powder, black pepper, cumin seeds, and *garam masala* are widely used.

In earlier days, rotis were made from a flour of wheat, gram and barley, which was a genuinely a nutritious and healthy combination. Then there is the *gochini atta* made from wheat and gram flour. However, with the inflation in price of gram and barley, people now prefer the wheat flour which is comparatively cheaper. This change or adaptation has been a major loss both in terms of taste and intake of nutrients.

The people of Haryana have always been portrayed to be of a simplistic nature in terms of their culinary features. They traditionally eat and savour whatever comes their way. A large population in the villages of Haryana bypass breakfast and goes for lunch forthrightly. In lunch they prefer to eat bread made from flour (either of wheat, gram or bajra). They eat lots of green chillies to enliven their taste buds. The evening meal is normally very simple and includes *khichri* (porridge made of bajra, *moong* or rice). In urban areas, the breakfast is a mandatory affair as compared to rural areas. They consume bread chiefly made from wheat. *Saag* is necessary along with milk, curds or buttermilk. *Dals* are not consumed daily. Vegetables seasoned lightly are preferred. *Tinda, ghia* (kind of sweet gourd) and other seasonal vegetables constitute a major part of the daily diet in Haryana. On special occasions, *pethe ki subzi* is a hot favourite. Fresh vegetables are the salient features of Haryanvi cuisine, which is predominantly vegetarian. Haryanvi cuisine lacks far behind in the world of non-vegetarianism as compared to other states. It doesn't have any dish in the non-vegetarian segment to exhibit or attract the food lovers.

Vegetarianism is the main trend in this state but today the number of non-vegetarians is also on the increase. It emphasizes basically on simplicity in each dish. Buttermilk and tea are the most popular drinks. In olden days, milk was preferred but the trends prevailing now have replaced it with tea. *Lassi* prepared from yogurt is also relished most. Fresh vegetables are easily available throughout the year. *Raabri* and *Bajre ki khichri* (millets porridge) with *lassi* are the two main relished dishes. *Bajre ki khichri* is also eaten with liberal amount of ghee or *kadhi* (chickpea flour beaten in spiced yogurt). Some of the popularly consumed renowned dishes of Haryanvi cuisine are *singri ki subzi, kachri ki subzi, methi gajar* (preparation of methi leaves, carrots, tomatoes and spices), mixed *dal* (an unusual combination of mixed, spiced pulses, simmered over a slow fire), *hara dhania chholia* (dish of *hara chana*), *kadhi pakora, tamatar chutney, mithe chawal, bhura roti ghee, churma, kheer* and *malpuas*. Each dish nonetheless of simplicity has been able to charm and captivate the connoisseur of the Indian food.

The highly beneficial to digestive system, *bathua-ka-raita* (green leafy *bathua* in delicately spiced yogurt) is very refreshing and mouth-watering. *Aloo ki tikiyas* (mashed, browned potatoes patties, stuffed with spicy lentils, and smothered in a sour tamarind *chutney*) are the other favourites. *Teet ka achar* is a popular pickle made of *kair* from *kair* tree is preferred by all.

The traditional breads eaten are *chapatis* (millets, corn and whole wheat breads) and *puris* (puffed, fried whole wheat breads).

The desserts prepared by the people are simple and yet very delicious. The sweet delicacies are made from easily available ingredients. Specialties include the scrumptious and very tempting *gajar ka halwa* (grated carrots simmered in sweetened milk, garnished with almond slivers and other nuts), *kheer* (rice simmered in thick sweetened milk with raisins) and the *rich raabri* (wheat flour custard, simmered in sweet buttermilk). *Malpua, peda, churma, kheer, raabri, jaleba* (similar to *jalebi* but larger in size) and *laddu* are some of the sweets made during festivities. *Jaleba* of a place called Ghuhana and *phirni* of Pundri is very famous in Haryana. *Malpua* is a deep-fried delicacy made with milk, flour, ghee, and jaggery. One very distinct typical and traditional sweet prepared here is *khees* which is made up of the first milk after the delivery of the cattle. The milk has its own flavour and the people of Haryana love this dish above all.

The *dhaba* (eating joints) culture has flourished and mushroomed a lot in Haryana. It exists on every highway in Haryana nowadays, and eating at such places is a very common affair for the Haryanvi people.

Specialty Dishes

Bajre ki Roti

This is the traditional bread made from millet flour. People mix the millets flour (*bajre ka atta*) with little wheat flour, so that it can be easily rolled. Wheat provides elasticity and holds the millets flour while rolling. Then it is shallow fried on a *tawa* plate and served with dollops of butter or *desi ghee*.

Bajre ki Khichdi

It is a common preparation in Haryana and people like to eat it frequently. It is prepared from the millets. The millets is pounded and then soaked in water for a while and the cooked with *desi ghee* and water. It is lightly seasoned and relished with *lassi* or *achaar*.

Chana Saag

This is a very nutritious preparation prepared during the winter season only due to seasonal availability of hare *chane* (*chholia*). It is a delicacy made with spinach and *cholia*, with onion and tomatoes added to it in a lesser quantity.

Maseladaar Karela

It is a scrumptious dish for all the lovers of bitter gourd. In this dish, bitter gourd is fried and kept aside and finally added in dry gravy like mixture of onion, tomato, ginger-garlic and spices.

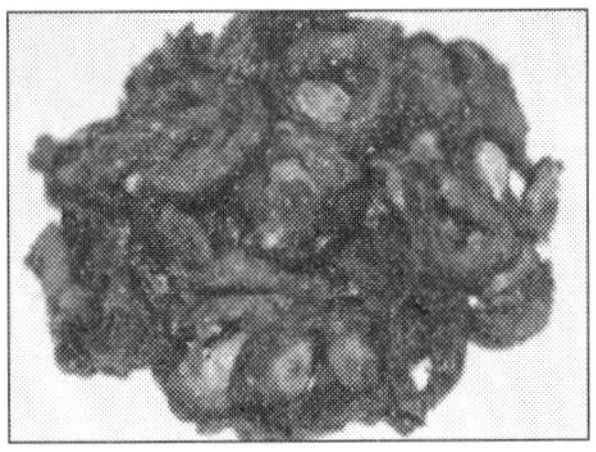

Aate ka Halwa

A simple and tasty dish in which the wheat flour is fried in clarified butter till well cooked, and then sweetened with sugar syrup and garnished with slices of dry fruits.

Ghee Boora

It is the simplest preparation, in which the clarified butter is added with unrefined brown coloured sugar. It is eaten as a side dish with great gusto.

Gajar Methi ki Subzi

It is a fragrant preparation made by the combination of fresh fenugreek leaves and baton cuts of carrots. It tastes amazingly divine and is very nutritious. This is also prepared generally during the winter season.

Aloo Gajar ki Subzi

It is an usual combination, and a perfect dish is made out of the dices of potatoes and carrots. The contrasting colour of both the ingredients makes the dish very appealing.

Bathue ka Saag

It is a scrumptious delicacy made by the leaves of *bathua* (amaranth leaves). It is also unique due to its fragrant feature.

Culinary Trivia: Balti Style Cooking

Balti is more of a style of cooking than one particular curry. The word *balti* can be translated as "bucket" (i.e. a cooking pan) and some say the style of cooking is indigenous to an area of northern Pakistan known as Baltistan. A *balti* pan is basically a *karahi* which has the shape of a Chinese wok but with 2 small round handles on either side of the pan instead of one long handle. In specialist "Balti Houses" the *balti* is a meal in itself which contains both meat and vegetables and is eaten straight from the *karahi* using curled up pieces of *naan* bread. In standard Indian restaurants, the *balti* is more of a stir-fried curry containing a plenty of fried green peppers and fresh coriander cilantro).

Culinary Trivia: Kharif Crop and Rabi Crop

Kharif Crop	Rabi Crop
Kharif crop refers to agricultural crops sown in the rainy (monsoon) season. Such crops are planted to be harvested in the autumn.	*Rabi* crop refers to agricultural crops sown in winter. Such crops are planted to be harvested in the spring.
The term *kharif* means "autumn" in Arabic.	The term rabi means "spring" in Arabic
Also referred as summer crop.	Also referred as winter crop.
Examples: bajra, jowar, sugar cane, rice, sunflower, *arhar dal*, peanut, and so on.	Examples: wheat, barley, mustard, sesame, peas, linseed, gram, and so on.

14 Himachali Cuisine

> **"Our minds are like our stomaches; they are whetted by the change of their food, and variety supplies both with fresh appetite." – Quintilian**

Himachal Pradesh, a state in Northern India and in the lap of Himalayan valley, is bordered by Jammu and Kashmir on the north, Punjab on the west and south-west, Haryana and Uttarakhand on the south-east and by the Tibet Autonomous Region on the east.

Himachal Pradesh has a cuisine which speaks very high of its uniqueness and typicality. Notwithstanding the influence from the coterminous lands of Punjab and Tibet, the geographical and climatic conditions of the state have a huge effect on the culinary arts of Himachal Pradesh. Moreover, due to a very cold weather, the inhabitants have a high nutritional requirement in order to acclimatize properly with the weather. This is one of the reasons which is accountable in preparing several dishes with high nutritional value. The cuisine is fabricated in such a fashion that it provides heat and energy to the people residing here in harsh cold conditions. The traditional or indigenous dishes are prepared using simple equipment and basic staple ingredients.

Normally, the daily cuisine of Himachal Pradesh is a quintessential cuisine which is fairly simple and highly similar to other North Indian states. Rice, paddy and maize are the staple diet of the people here. But the actual taste differs from region to region. Thus, while in the barren regions of Kinnaur and Lahaul-Spiti, locally-grown coarse grains like buckwheat, millets and barley are chiefly used, in the regions with high productivity and having pastoral tradition use generous amounts of milk and its by-products in their dishes. The state is highly blessed with a wide range of native fruits, vegetables, herbs and spices which are used munificently in the local cuisine.

There are certain sweet snacks in the state, such as *rot* which is made from the dough of whole wheat flour and jaggery and is the speciality of the areas like Una, Hamirpur and Bilaspur. It is relished during religious functions. Similarly, in Mandi and Kangra districts, a fermented wheat flour slurry is used to prepare small dumplings called *gulgule* (sweet fritters). It can be preserved for a 2 or 3 days, as its shelf life is higher. *Sancholu* or *mithdoo* is another sweet dish delicacy which is made by kneading wheat flour with sugar, ghee and grated coconut. The dough is rolled and cut into different fanciful shapes and then pressed in distinct wooden dyes to endow it with different designs and then deep-fried till golden brown.

The state of Himachal Pradesh has an exquisite cuisine which is adorned with certain non-vegetarian preparations, and with liberal usage of spices like cardamom, cinnamon, cloves and red chilies. It forms an essential part of the cuisine of Himachal Pradesh. Such dishes are produced from the kitchens of the Himachal homes in a unique fashion. The local people are not considered to be particularly fond of vegetarian fare. In the average Himachal households, various kinds of meat, lentil and cereal preparations are cooked.

Meat is prepared with an array of spices like cinnamon, red chillies, cloves, cardamom and coriander leaves. The tempting and tantalizing aroma is sufficient to whet one's appetite. Kullu trout, grilled fishes, chicken *anardana* are the popularly known non-vegetarian dishes. Originally, the Himachal cuisine is dominated by red meat and wheat bread.

Vegetarians have a distinct segment of preparations and relish dishes like *guchhi mattar*, *sepuvadi* and *kaddu ka khatta*. Rajma is also popular in vegetarian preparations and people enjoy it enthusiastically as it is prepared in the Punjabi style.

A typical day-to-day meal in the cuisine of Himachal Pradesh comprises a cluster of basic preparations like *dal-chawal-subzi-roti* (the common North Indian fare of lentil broth, rice, vegetable curry and bread). The spicy *chutney* and red hot chilies add radiance and brightness to their simple cookery.

Himachal Pradesh has diversified inhabitants and provides many dimensions to the large varieties of satisfying and mouth-watering exquisite dishes. Exemplary delicacies are prepared during festive and special occasions.

Milk and milk products are also used munificently. Himachalis have a great penchant for tea and they prepare it in a myriad ways.

The desserts of Himachal Pradesh are symbolized with sour and sweet taste. The sour desserts are generally made of tamarind or jaggery and the sweet desserts are made of sweetened rice.

Dham: A Signature Traditional Mid-day Meal of Himachal Pradesh

When festive food is being confabulated, the traditional and archetypal meal, *dham* (lunch served in traditional occasions) finds instant citation. The authentic *dham* is commemorated with great enthusiasm. Himachal Pradesh is attributable with many lip smacking and mouthwatering delicacies. The *dham* bestows one with a possibility to be familiar with a wide array of delicacies of the state. Dham is cooked specifically by *botis* (a peculiar caste of brahmins who are professional cooks by generation). The mise-en-place and preparation for this luxuriant mid-day meal begins the night before. The utensils preferred to be used for cooking the food are normally made of copper. It is served in courses to people who sit cross-legged on the floor. The food is served on washed leaf plates. The *dham* comprises plain aromatic rice, fried pulses or *dal*, spicy vegetable curry of red kidney beans and many desserts to pacify one's appetite.

The traditional *dham* portrays a different dimension of foods in every region of the state. The typical menu for *dham* would begin with rice, *moong dal* and a *madrah* of *rajma* which is cooked in yogurt which is prepared in a distinct style by adding approximately almost a galaxy of twenty spices. This is followed by *mash dal, boor ki kari* topped by *khatta* (sweet and sour sauce) made of tamarind and jaggery. The *dham* ends with the *mitha* (dessert) – sweet rice or *mithdee* (made of *boondi* or bread crumbs). The varied range of food items reflects the vivacious and dynamic yet elementary lifestyle of the people of Himachal Pradesh.

Specialty Dishes

Madrah

It is a renowned delicacy from Chamba. It is a very traditional Himachali dish and is undoubtedly, one of the most exquisite culinary delights of the state. It is made with chick peas or red kidney beans, yogurt, coconut, onion, ginger, garlic, chilli powder, coriander powder, almonds and raisins along with 20 spices cooked on slow flame. Extreme care is taken while mixing yogurt in the dish so that the yogurt added doesn't get curdsled.

Sidu

It is cooked from flour of wheat and savoured with ghee or butter. Sidu is made by kneading the flour with yeast and is permitted to rest for 4-5 hours. It is first browned over a very mild fire with slight addition of fat and then it is vaporized. Sidu is offered to most of the guests who are overwhelmed at the amazing taste of this indigenous cuisine. It is generally eaten with *desi ghee, dal* or mutton curry.

Kullu Trout

Kullu Trout is an exemplary dish which involves of properly cooked fish with the mixture of marinades and then serving it with a sauce. The marinades include crushed coriander seeds, chilli flakes, mustard oil, salt, dill leaves, and lemon juice and rind. The marinade is rubbed all over the fish and cooked properly for more than 10 minutes on a low flame. The mixture of sauce incorporates diced onion, chopped coriander, lemon juice, salt, and mustard oil and seeds. The sauce is prepared by frying the onions and the mustard seeds until it turns into light brown and then by adding all the remaining ingredients. Then, the sauce is poured all over the fried fish and thus the delectable mouth-watering Kullu Trout is prepared.

Ankolas and Aktori *Ankolas* is a cake simply made of rice flour and *aktori* is a cake made with leaves of buckwheat and wheat flour and is common in drier areas of the Lahaul-Spiti valley.	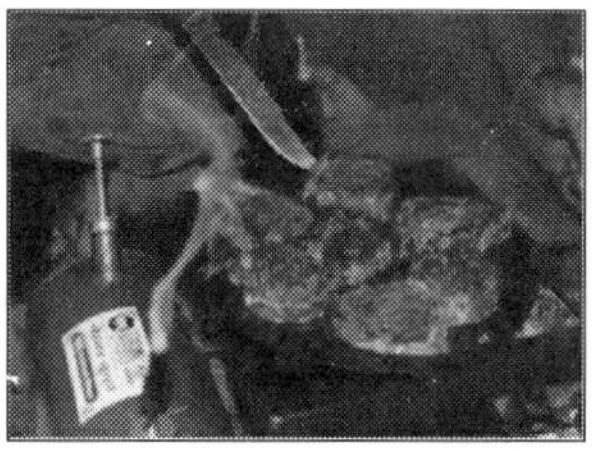
Patande *Patande* is famous dish in the Hamirpur, Chamba and Sirmour districts of the state which is made from wheat. *Patande* is like a pancake and so is popularly known as the Indian pancake of Himachal Pradesh.	
Maahni It is an *urad dal* preparation with dried mangoes in it.	
Khatta Khatta is a simple and subtle dish made with chick pea flour, dry mango powder, coriander powder, chilli powder and *boondi* (a chick pea flour based snack). It tastes similar to *kadhi* and tastes best with white rice.	
Mal Puda It is a pancake made just like *dosa*. It is made by preparing a smooth paste of jaggery by boiling it in water and then mixing it with flour and finally cooking the batter of flour and jaggery on *tawa* till both sides are cooked.	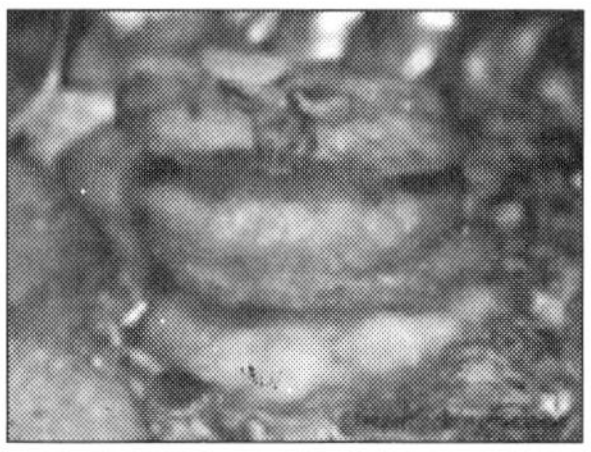
Kachalu Ka Salan This is a preparation of colocassia (*arvi*) made by boiling and then peeling the *arbi*. Then in a separate pan heat oil, add onions, ginger, garlic and spices and sauté boiled *arbi* in it and finally add lassi in it and cook till it is thick in texture. It is served garnished with green coriander. In Himachal Pradesh, *arbi* is called as *kachalu*.	
Chicken Anardana A paradigmatic delicacy of chicken prepared with soaked and grinded pomegranate seeds with other ingredients like onion, ginger, garlic, tomato and spices.	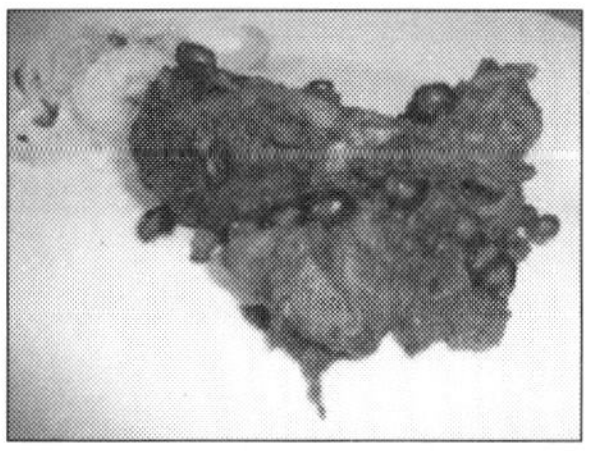

Sepu Badi

This is a typical preparation made by soaking and grinding the *urad dal* and then steaming it and cutting it into cubes. Then these cubes are cooked in a spinach paste and curds along with other spices and served. It is a simple dish but very popular in the state.

Chha Meat

This is a mutton delicacy of Himachal Pradesh made by marinating mutton with mustard oil and ginger-garlic paste and then cooking it with cloves, cardamom and few powdered spices along with buttermilk in large quantity. The meat seems to have a delectable taste with this spice combination.

Babroo

Babroo is prepared using either rice or wheat flour slurry. A batter of semi-liquid consistency is formed by mixing it with carom seeds, *garam masala* and water and it is allowed to ferment. After fermentation, the mixture is poured on a griddle and flattened using a ladle and cooked like a *dosa*. The procedure of making *babroo* is similar to preparing of *dosa*. It has many variants and the sweet variant of *babroo* made with wheat flour is referred as *dhandar* and the one with rice flour is called as *chilru*.

Chawal Atte ki Beduan Roti

Chawal atte ki beduan roti is a baked cereal and legume based preparation which is prepared by stuffing the paste of soaked and de-husked black gram mixed with *garam masala* in kneaded rice flour.

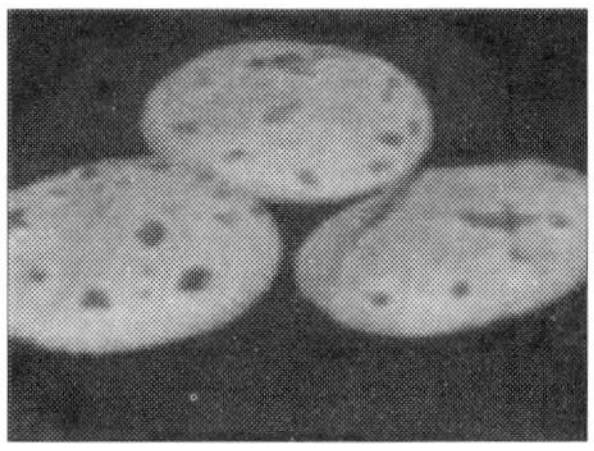

Beduan Roti

Beduan roti is a chapati stuffed with boiled and mashed colocasia (*arvi*) bulbs mixed with salt, ginger-garlic paste, and *garam masala* and chilli powder. It is then baked on a hot *tawa* and is a famous speciality of rural kitchens.

Bhruni ki Subzi

It is a very unique and nutritious preparation prepared using the tender leaves of fig. The leaves are allowed to boil in an earthern pot and then ground to a paste form. It is added with salt and pepper to heighten the flavour of the dish. It is cooked by the smoking method (referred as *dhuni* in the local dialect). In this, a few drops of ghee/oil are poured over burning coal and due to this smoke erupts from the live coal. The paste is exposed to the fumes and the fumes are allowed to be absorbed in the paste, which imparts it a unique smoky flavour.

Bhaturu

It is a fermented bread made from wheat flour. It is either roasted or deep fried, based on the preferences. It is a common preparation in Himachali day-to-day cuisine.

Culinary Trivia: Sago

Sago is a starch extracted in the spongy centre, or pith, of various tropical palm stems, especially Metroxylon sagu. It is traditionally cooked and eaten in various forms, such as rolled into balls, mixed with boiling water to form a paste, or as a pancake. *Sago* is often produced commercially in the form of "pearls". Sago pearls can be boiled with water or milk and sugar to make a sweet *sago* pudding. *Sago* pearls are similar in appearance to tapioca pearls and the two may be used interchangeably in some dishes.

In India, it is manufactured from extract of 'cassava', i.e., tapioca-root, and popularly known as Tapioca Sago or 'Sabudana'.

The fruit of palm trees from which the *sago* is produced is not allowed to ripen fully. The full ripening completes the life cycle of the tree and exhausts the starch centre to produce the seeds. It leaves a hollow shell and causes the tree to die. The palms are cut down when they are about 15 years old, just before they are ready to flower. The stems which grow up to 30 feet high splits out. The starch pith is taken from the stems and ground to powder. A single palm yields about 800 pounds (360 kilograms) of starch. The powder is kneaded in water over a cloth or sieve. It passes into a trough where it settles. After a few washings, the flour is ready to be used in cooking.

15 Hyderabadi Cuisine (Andhra Pradesh)

"Bad food is made without pride, by cooks who have no pride, and no love. Bad food is made by chefs who are indifferent, or who are trying to be everything to everybody, who are trying to please everyone... Bad food is fake food... food that shows fear and lack of confidence in people's ability to discern or to make decisions about their lives." – Anthony Bourdain

Andhra Pradesh is situated on the country's southeastern coast, which is surrounded by Maharashtra, Chhattisgarh and Orissa on the north, Bay of Bengal on the east, Tamil Nadu on the south and Karnataka on the west.

It would be unfair to state the cuisine of Andhra Pradesh as the cuisine of a specific region. Rather it is the assemblage of cuisine of Andhra, cuisine of Southern India and the cuisine of Hyderabad. Among this, Hyderabadi cuisine has its own identity and recognition all over the country. While the traditional Andhra food is spicy and fiery in nature, Hyderabadi food brings Mughal influence into the Andhra cuisine. The generous use of spices in this region is due to the impact of South Indian cooking style.

This state comprises mainly the people of both Hindu and Muslim populaces and they are almost in equal numbers, so the cuisine of the land is a stimulating aggregation of these two diverse food cultures.

The cuisine of Andhra Pradesh is a foodie's delight and a paradise for food lovers. The food of every Indian state has a certain kind of uniqueness to it and the same holds true for the cuisine of this state too. Abundant use of spices and exotic seasonings mark the cooking style of Andhra Pradesh. Rich taste and spicy flavours define the characteristic of the food of this place. This cuisine includes a salubrious motley of vegetarian and non-vegetarian items. A large chunk of the population is vegetarian and has devised brilliant vegetarian recipes. The people along the coastal areas have highly developed ravishing seafood delicacies. As Andhra Pradesh was under the rule of Mughal Emperors (Nizams), the cuisine of the land has been heavily influenced by the Mughals and this influence is mirrored in the world-famous Hyderabadi cuisine. In fact, Hyderabadi cuisine has been blessed by the impact of Mughlai cuisine and has refined and matured as a captivating cuisine with a varied bouquet of impeccable and mouth-watering dishes.

The abundance of rice in the state due to its huge production has dominated its use and has made rice the basic commodity ingredient of Andhra Pradesh which is consumed with *sambhar* (stew prepared with lentils) or *pappu* (boiled lentils) or *rasam* (stew prepared with tamarind juice) or curds. A motley of vegetables is cooked in varied styles and is accompanied with rice. As rice forms the basis of the food, a lot of rice based items are common in this state. *Idli, dosa, vada* and *uttapam* are a few of the popular rice-based delicacies of Andhra Pradesh. Chutneys and pickles are crucial elements of this cuisine. *Pachadi* (*chutney/raita*) and *ooragaya* (pickles) are two extensive varieties used at times with rice. *Pachadi* is typically made of vegetables/greens and roasted green/red chilies. It is freshly prepared and has to be consumed within a day or two. *ooragaya* is prepared in large quantity seasonally and uses bountiful portions of chilli powder, *methi* (fenugreek) powder, mustard powder and oil. *Avakkaya* or raw mango pickles is famed for its spicy and exceptional taste. Desserts are relished with great fervor and enthusiasm.

The usual items during breakfast are *dosa, pesarattu* (a *moong dal* based pan-cake or crepe fried in a flat pan laced with cooking oil and it is generally served with ginger *chutney*) or *upma,* served with saliva-generating *chutneys*.

An authentic traditional meal in Andhra Pradesh is served on a leaf of banana (*aratiaaku*) but nowadays, it has been replaced by stainless steel plates (*kancham*). Very rarely, *vistari* (a larger plate made of several leaves sewn together with minute wood sticks) is also used. Rice is served with the topping of spoonfuls of ghee. A dry curry is usually consumed with rice. *Pulihara* or tamarind rice is a the significant food of Andhra Pradesh which is savoured with green chillies and spices. The vegetable dishes are added with wide-ranging spices to bestow a delicious taste and render it more flavoursome. The meal is a suave affair with a degree of sophistication incorporating at least five kinds of dishes in the spread. Traditional Andhra Pradesh cuisine also has a wide range of non-vegetarian dishes to offer. The most common items undoubtedly are fishes and prawns spiced with ground pepper and cooked in sesame and coconut oil, which gives the items a unique and spicy taste. The meal is compulsorily accompanied by a variety of famous hot pickles and *chutneys*. The meal is finished by having curds, which compensates the fiery taste of the dishes and adds a cool note to the spread.

The magnitude of the regional variation of Andhra Pradesh cuisine is diverse and multifarious. The primary factors to affect the variation are the substantial influences of the Hindu imperial families and the Muslim Nawabi Imperial families. Topographic variations have also contributed to the variation in the cuisine. The cuisines of Andhra Pradesh can be categorically classified based by its regions like Kosta (Coastal) Andhra, Telangana, Rayalaseema, Uttarandhra and Hyderabadi cuisine. Andhra Pradesh lies in close proximity with and neighborhood of Western, Central and Eastern India, which makes the cuisine of these border regions more diverse and distinctive.

Kosta (Coastal Andhra) Cuisine

This region chiefly comprises the area having Krishna Delta, Godavari Delta and the long coastline of the Bay of Bengal.

Rice, *dal* and seafood are the primary and essential food of the people living in this coastal region. Rice being the chief staple item, the preparation of most of the food items are centred on rice.

The populace here has a huge variety of curries, lentil stews, spicy pickles and delicious chutneys popular in their diet. This area is also the largest producer of chillies, and hence the taste of the food of this region has an inclination towards spicy and fiery flavour.

Very spicy dishes like Gongoora Mutton, Bommidaila Pulusu, Natukodi Chicken are a few non-vegetarian specialties of the region.

Avakkaya is the most loved pickle here and is made of raw mangoes and has a sourish taste.

In the southern part of this coastal area lies the Nellore region, which is acknowledged for some staggeringly distinctive recipes.

Uttarandhra Cuisine

Uttarandhra is recognized for a varied and remarkable culinary art, comprises the districts of Srikakulam, Vizianagaram and Visakhapatnam that lie in the north eastern portion of the Coastal Andhra region coterminous to Odisha. Uttarandhra is also popularly known as Kalinga Andhra.

Even though the delicacies of this region have very distinct flavour and taste but it shares a lot of similarities with the Kosta Andhra cuisine.

The people here relish certain preparations like *murku, booralu, appadams, putharekulu, anabshahi* and *pulihara*.

Idlis, upmas, dosas, pickles and *chutneys* are hugely enjoyed in this part of Andhra Pradesh and such dishes have created a special place in the cuisine of this region.

Avakkaya is the front-runner mango pickle, just as it is throughout the state. *Gongoora* is a green chutney made of chilli as the main ingredient is a peculiarity of the region.

In Visakhapatnam, a snack item called *Murri* mixture is very popular along the sea-beaches. *Murri* mixture is a finger-licking snack item made up of puffed rice, chopped onions, chopped green chillies, tomatoes, boiled peas and fresh coriander leaves, lemon juice and it has a splendid taste.

The cooking style of this region is distinctive as compared to the rest of the region, which renders it an entirely different taste. They cook vegetables in widely different flavoured gravies like gravies of fenugreek seed paste (referred as *menthipettinakura*), mustard seed paste (referred as *avapettinakura*), and sesame paste (referred as *nuvvugundakura*).

They have specialized in cooking dishes of corn seeds or vegetables flavoured in onion paste, again in a completely different style (referred as *ullikaram*).

The people of this region mostly prefer to eat almost many of their dishes having sweet taste, which is uncommon in the rest of Andhra Pradesh and hence they often cook lentils in jaggery (referred as *bellampappu*), which is consumed with butter and steamed rice.

When it comes to the items consumed during breakfast time, *puri* and *patoli* are mostly preferred and are liked by all as well.

Patoli is simply soaked up split black chickpeas (*senagapappu* or *chana dal*), ground to a coarse paste and then seasoned and added with crushed coriander seeds, onions and at times with cluster beans (*goruchikkudukayi*) and then cooked.

Uppupindi is coarsely broken rice *upma* steamed with vegetables and tempered with whole red chilli, mustard seeds, curry leaves and so on. This dish is an essential item prepared during festive occasions, when people would fast during the day and then consume it in the night with great relish.

As far as stew preparation is concerned, a very unique sweet and sour stew consisting of tamarind and *hing* (referred as *inguvacharu*) is popular among kids and grown-ups alike. It can be consumed with rice or *uppupindi.*

A special kind of sweet stew comprising rice flour, jaggery for sweetener, corn cobs cut to even lengths, and whole shallots is also very popular and is called *bellam pulusu.* It is known for its thick consistency, sweet taste, and a full-bodied flavour.

The pickles of the region are entirely different from the rest of India and even the other regions of Andhra Pradesh. They dry their raw mango pieces with mustard powder, red pepper powder and salt soaked in sesame oil under the sun for certain days which gives the pickles a larger shelf-life, a darker shade of colour and a sweet taste. This technique of pickling was started several centuries ago with the intention to retain the raw mangoes from being spoilt due to the high content of moisture in the atmosphere in the region that is adjacent to the coast of the Bay of Bengal.

Rayalaseema Cuisine

The area of Rayalaseema is located in the southern part of Andhra Pradesh. It is in close vicinity to Tamil Nadu and southern part of Karnataka. Due to its location, it is heavily influenced by the cooking styles and trends of both these places. The cuisine is excellent in taste and varied.

The very common dishes famed all across are *alsandalavada, ulavacharu, peetalakura,* brain fry, liver fry and prawn *iguru* which can be combined with *sajja* or *jonna* rotis and *raagisangati.*

Attirasaalu (Aresalu), *baadusha, jaangri, jilebi, pakamundalu* (prepared by the concoction of steam rice flour, ground nuts, and jaggery), *boruguundalu* (a sweet delicacy prepared form corn of jowar and jaggery), *palakova,* and *ravaladdu* are some of the splendid sweets also referred as *bakshalu* in this region.

Masala borugulu (snacks), *ponganaalu* wet rice flour fried in oil with addition of carrots, onions, chillies are the other popular savoury specialities in these districts.

Telangana Cuisine

Telangana is the region (now a new state) located in the western part of Andhra Pradesh.

The cuisine of this place has an apparent impact of the Persian and Afghan cuisines, as this region was under the control of Muslim rulers for a long time. Such impact has made the cuisine of this region more lively and interesting.

Jonna rotte (sorghum), *sajja rotte* (penisetum), *uppudi pindi* (broken rice) are a few of the common preparations of this region. This region is renowned for certain tasty vegetarian delicacies like *ulliakkukura* (spring onion curry), *kakarayapulusu* (gravy made of bitter gourd), *rasam, karapu annam* (chilli rice), and so on.

For the people having a strong liking for non-vegetarian dishes, this region has many unique items like *chapala pulusu* (fish gravy), *kodi kura, guddu pulusu* (also known as *egg pulusu*) to offer.

Snacks include *sakinalu* which is prepared with rice flour, spices and sesame seeds and is generally prepared for the festive occasion of the Sankranti festival. *Poornalu* is also one such snack made of rice flour stuffed with the concoction of jaggery, mixed *dal* paste and dry fruits mixture. It is often served hot with ghee. It is called *poornalu* in the Telangana region and *boorelu* in the Andhra region.

Hyderabadi Cuisine

Hyderabadi cuisine, a princely legacy of Nizams, is a well known and esteemed cuisine in the world. It has engraved a name for itself amongst the excellent global cuisines due to its brilliant taste and long lingering flavour. Hyderabadi cuisine serves as the hallmark of Andhra Pradesh cuisine. It has set a standard which is high and it firmly stands to maintain its excellence and brilliance in cuisine. The food is fundamentally rich in taste and aromatic in flavour. Its out of the world and distinct taste is the resultant of the abundant use of exotic spices and clarified butter. Fresh fruit is preferred to be used in the preparation of this cuisine as compared to dried fruits used in other cuisines of India. This cuisine is especially well-famed and illustrious for its platter of spectacular non-vegetarian delicacies. It is an amalgamation and consolidation of Muslim techniques with meat, with varied spices and also with certain unique ingredients of the predominantly local Hindu populace.

The brilliant Hyderabadi cuisine exhibits a strong and appreciable influence of the Mughlai cuisine. It is also inspired by the cuisines of Arab, Persia and Turkey. The herbs and spices incorporated in this cuisine are generally native to the Telugu and Marathwada cuisines. This cuisine originated and developed in the kitchens of the Nizams of Hyderabad who were great connoisseurs of food and transformed the preparation of food in their reign to an inspirational art form. It is a varied accumulation of several influences, but with its own distinct taste, flavour and identity. It blends the class and refinement of the North, with the sauce and spice of the South with great finesse and thus is a good example of cross-cultural interaction. This amalgamation of aromas, fragrances, flavours and tangs, colour and textures, has resulted in the evolution of a highly refined cuisine with a high degree of sophistication.

The cuisine focuses on the use of right ingredients in an accurate proportion at an appropriate time. The ingredients are selected with minute details and cooked as per the need to the exact degree and time. The emphasis is on selecting the perfect kind of meat, rice and, most significantly, the spices. The precisely accurate assemblage of the particular herbs, spices and condiments gives a distinct flavour, taste and texture to the dishes. Commodities such as coconut, tamarind, peanuts and sesame are tremendously used in this cuisine.

Hyderabad is regarded as the birthplace of the delicious *biryani* in India. It first evolved in the kitchens of the Nizam of Hyderabad as a result of the blending of the Mughlai and Andhra Pradesh cuisines. *Biryani* is undoubtedly the most esteemed dish of this cuisine which is famed throughout the length and breadth of the country as well as at the international level. Hyderabadi Biryani is a dish prepared with long grained basmati rice, lamb meat and flavoured with exotic and rich spices. Generally, mutton or chicken is used as a substitution in place of lamb meat.

The dishes are named after the herbs and spices used and the process of cooking follows. For instance, Murgh do Pyaza derives its name from the onions or *pyaz* that are added twice to the dish in two variations to achieve the accurate taste.

The *masalas* are an essential constituent of this cuisine. *Masala* is basically a rich blend of herbs, spices and condiments which provides the base for the dishes and is referred to as 'gravy'. Most of the *masalas* or blends are prepared clandestinely and that are handed down from one generation to the next or passed on to the *shagird* (student) by the *ustad* (teacher). The quantity of *masalas* blended is not disclosed to anyone outside the family and is kept a well-guarded secret. The head cooks or the *khansamas* are a respected class of people in Hyderabad due to their culinary craft.

This cuisine also has delicacies particularly related to a city like Hyderabad (Hyderabadi Biryani), Aurangabad (Naan Qalia), Bidar (Kalyani Biryani), Gulbarga (Tahari), and so on.

The first course of a Hyderabadi meal is referred as *gazak*. It is a dry preparation and was served both at lunch and dinner in old times. It could be a savoury item like *samosa, tootak, lukhmi* or even *kebab*.

A few celebrated delicacies of Hyderabadi cuisine are undoubtedly Hyderabadi Biryani (a traditional delicious meal of lamb and rice), Kachche Gosht Ki Biryani (rice and raw meat cooked over steam where the meat has been kept marinated with spices and yogurt overnight), Hyderabadi Zafrani Biryani (rice cooked with saffron), Pakki Biryani (the meat is cooked before combining it with rice and cooking over steam), Hyderabadi Haleem (wheat and meat cooked over slow flame for a long time), Bagara Khana (basmati rice delicacy), Mirchi ka Salan (green chilly curry), Paaya (bone soup), Pathar ka Gosht (mutton/lamb cooked by searing on a stone slab found in Hyderabad), Dum ka Keema (minced meat cooked over steam), Boti Kebab (minced meat delicacy), Dalcha (mutton and lentil delicacy), Bina Masale ka Murgh (chicken done with only curds, turmeric and saffron). Such an elaborate list of superbly prepared dishes has taken the Hyderabadi cuisine to the pinnacle of the superlative dishes.

Hyderabadi cuisine emphasizes on the variety souring agents, in which lemon and the tamarind play a crucial role but dishes like *korma* are mildly soured with yogurt and some dishes are soured with vinegar too. Green mango is also used as a favourite souring agent during the season, with several meat dishes and lentil preparations soured delectably with it. The dried powder of mango called *amchoor* is also used as a souring agent. The references of use of *ambada* (roselle leaves), *karonda* (*Carissa caranda*), *halfaleori, kamrak* (star fruit) and *bilamboo* is also evident and apparent.

The technique of seasoning or the *baghar*, also called *chhokna* in Hydearabad and *takda* in the North, is used in Hyderabad to an outstanding effect in order to bestow a subtle and mild difference of taste into a dish. In this *baghar* procedure, the food is seasoned by a process of adding chillies, herbs and spices into hot oil and then pouring it over the dish while it is still sizzling. The *baghar* intensifies the taste and renders it delicious.

The taste of Indian cuisine has been defined by the balanced use of herbs and spices used in its preparations and hence herbs and spices have become an integral and inseparable part of Indian cuisine. The spices and herbs have been used in same fashion in Hyderabadi cuisine as well rendering it delicious and fragrant. There are certain spices which are used rarely in other parts of India but are used frequently in Hyderabad and they are *shahi zeera* (black cumin), *khas khas* (poppy seeds), *kebab chini* (cassia buds), *pathar ka phool* (stone flower), *magaz* (melon seeds), and so on. One ingredient ignored and used scarcely all over the country is undoubtedly the *til* (sesame seeds), but it is used sparingly in this region.

Apart from *garam masala*, two different surpassing combinations of *masalas* are used in Hyderabad. They are *Potli ka masala* and *Bhojwar masala*. A magical mix of various herbs and spices called the *Bhojwar masala* contains a mix of coriander seeds, sesame seeds, cumin seeds, bay leaf, groundnut, dry coconut and *pathar ka phool*. This combination is used in dishes like *baghare baigan, mirchi ka salan*, and *mahi gosht*. Another exotic combination is *Potli ka masala*, which has herbs and spices tied in a muslin cloth and placed in a dish to make it more flavourful. It contains sandalwood powder, dried rose petals, bay leaves, coriander seeds, black cardamom, cassia buds, *pathar ka phool, kulanjan, kapur kachri, paan ki jad* (betel roots), and so on. It is used in dishes like *nehari* and in *chakna*, and a tavern (restaurant with bar) dish of meat and organ meat.

Hyderabadi cuisine is more inclined and dedicated towards non-vegetarian dishes as compared to vegetarian dishes. This hardly means that vegetarian dishes are into oblivion or disrespected. The repertoire of a few vegetarian dishes has reached great heights all over. The penchant for non-vegetarian dishes has been overwhelming, with a clear bias for goat's meat. The gourmets of Hyderabad have incorporated some dishes of other regions into their collection, and the most spectacular of these is perhaps the *Muzbi*, in which the entire goat is stuffed with pulao, chicken, boiled eggs and nuts and raisins, and cooked. One of the Arab soups which has become famous here is *Marag* soup, a rich broth of mutton and marrow. This region is not a great place for the dessert lovers, but even though it does offer some varieties of sweet dishes which are incredibly superior in taste as well as appearance. There are a few desserts like *khubani ka meetha, double ka meetha, badam ki jaali* which are renowned and acknowledged all over. A preparation is very popular, almost similar to *kheer* by the name *sheerannam*, which is flavoured with saffron and green cardamom.

Thus food is indeed viewed as a celebration and is prepared, served and eaten with grandeur and elegance.

The Hyderabadi cuisine is rightly called the 'Nawabi cuisine'. It is really tough to discover another cuisine that is so brilliant in taste, aromatic in flavour, rich in texture and perfect in temperament.

Specialty Dishes

Lukhmi Considered the exotic royal cousin of very famous North Indian preparation *samosa*, *lukhmi* comes from the word *luqma* or morsel meaning small quantity of something. It is a very famous delicacy made by filling mincemeat in a dough of refined flour, ghee and yogurt to give it a rectangular shape. This is then deep fried and served hot.	
Tootak Tootak is a mince savoury made by filling minced meat in a dough of semolina and ghee. It is given a ball shape, flat at the bottom, gentle cone-like in the middle and rounded at the top. It is then baked on live charcoal and served.	
Patthar ka Gosht A meat chunk, beaten with mallet is marinated with *kebab chini*, green chilies, ginger, garlic and raw papaya paste. Then a stone slab is heated from below with live charcoal underneath and then the marinated meat pieces is cooked on it with proper basting of oil. It is served with onion rings, lemon wedges and mint *chutney*. The stone releases few minerals which mingle with meat chunks and give the dish a unique flavour which sets it apart from other dishes.	
Taatee ka Gosht Very similar to *patthar ka gosht*, but the only difference is stone slab of *patthar ka gosht* is replaced with strips of metal interwoven like plaited *chattai* or *taatee*. This meat preparation is more spicy as compared to other *kebab* preparations. It is served with *chutney*.	

Pongali It is a preparation made of green gram cooked with rice flour and flavoured with black pepper. This porridge is then tempered with curry leaves, dry chilli, and a pinch of asafoetida. This dish is usually made on Pongal.	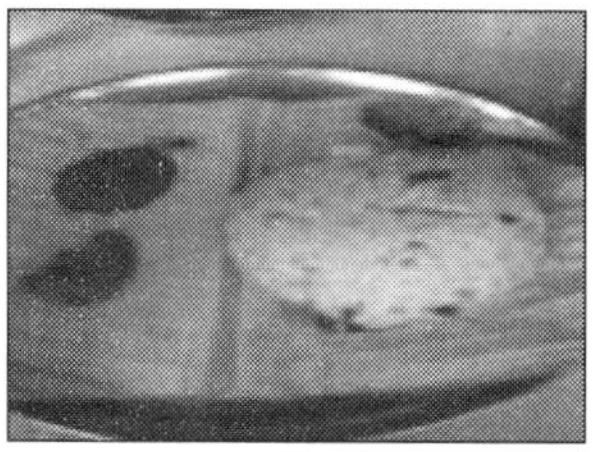
Kursi Miyane A ground-breaking dish in which the hardboiled eggs are cut lengthwise and then the egg yolk is mixed with cooked mince and is refilled in the scooped egg white pieces. The egg is then pierced with a thin stick to hold the two eggs halves together. Then it is batter fried and served hot.	
Shikampoor Literally, the word *shikampoor* means a dish that satisfies and treats the taste of a person longing for luxurious taste with ultimate elegance. It is a cigar-shaped *seekh kebab* made up of finely pounded meat and stuffed with a pleasant mixture of paneer, mint, green coriander and green chillies. It is a very succulent and *moist kebab* due to addition of curds in the mince mixture.	
Dum ke Laoz This dish is also known as *kheeme ki barfi* and resembles an indian sweetmeat or *mithai* in appearance. *Laoz* means a sweet dish. Hence, this term is used in the name of the dish. Mince is added with other ingredients like ginger-garlic paste, yogurt and egg and then the mixture is baked till it turns golden and served garnished with nuts.	
Bhuna Kheema Bhuna is first and foremost a cooking process where spices are gently fried in a plenty of oil to bring out their flavour. The dish "bhuna" is an extension of that process where meat is added to the spices and then cooked in its own juices which results in deep strong flavours but very little sauce. It is a very simple dish made by mince fried till brown along with other ingredients like onion, ginger-garlic paste, spices, green coriander, mint leaves and lemon juices.	
Chowgra It is a delicious meat dish cooked with a lot of vegetables like French beans, brinjals, potatoes, carrot, cauliflower and peas. The vegetables are deep-fried in order to preserve their flavour.	
Chippe ka Gosht It is a dry meat dish cooked in an earthen vessel called a *chippa*, hence meat cooked in it is called *chippe ka gosht.* In this, the meat gets a subtle flavour of the earthen vessel and this makes it unique. It is loved by all due to its unique taste.	

Chigur Gosht A meat preparation flavoured with refined souring agent *chigur* (tender tamarind shoots). *Chigur* is very popoular in Hyderabad and is used frequently in many other preparations too.	
Nehari The word 'nehari' derive from 'nehar' or fasting and is a popular breakfast item with the Muslim populace. It is generally had after the first namaz of the day. *Nehari* is made with the goat's head, tongue and trotters or with a combination of these ingredients. The mixture of fragrant herbs and spices, *potli ka masala* is added and is cooked overnight on slow fire till the ingredients are tender. It is had with *kulcha.* *Nalli nehari* is a variation which is made with marrow bones. It is allowed to cook overnight in various vessels, sometimes even buried underground while it is cooked, resulting in extremely tender morsels of meat, including the flavourful bone marrow. Cooked brains and bone marrow are served alongside the stew, which is sprinkled with a blend of powdered spices. Traditionally, the cooking time for *nehari* demands for 6-8 hours, in addition to the preparation of the ingredients.	
Haleem It is a dish made from the combination of pounded wheat and mutton. During the month of Ramadan, *haleem* is offered for *iftar,* when the day-long fast is formally broken. The word *haleem* means mild and the dish is gentle on the digestive system, especially after a long fast. It is served with rice.	
Dalcha It is a unique preparation made by the mélange combination of meats and lentils. It is highly nutritious. Meat is cooked along with *chana dal,* and whole spices and braised along with yogurt until the meat is soft. The dish is then tempered with ghee, garlic, and whole red chillies. It has a special place in Hyderbadi cuisine.	
Bhuna Gosht As the name suggests, the meat in this preparation is properly sauté fried till it turns brown in colour and taking care to prevent it from sticking to the bottom of the pan. The meat pieces are dry and succulent. It is served with either *khichri* or *patchipulsu* (liquid accompaniment made of tamarind, onions, green chillies, coriander, mint and curry leaves).	
Chakna It is a very popular dish made up of meat cubes, mutton chops, kidneys, sweetbread, liver and tongue cooked in a very thick gravy of onion, spices, and whey and gram flour. It is flavoured with mint leaves and green fresh coriander.	

Burhani

It is a dish of meat in which the dry cooked meat is served with the thick dollops of thick concentrated yogurt on it.

Murgh Achari

Murgh achari is an interesting aromatic dish in which the chicken is cooked in pickles spices (cumin seeds, nigella seeds/*kalonji*, whole red chillies, mustard seeds and fenugreek seeds). The meat in this preparation cooks in its own juices, in the fragrance of spices, with no tenderizer and not a drop of water is used. It tastes amazing and heavenly with *jowar ki roti*.

Methi Murgh

A popular chicken dish delicately flavoured with fresh fenugreek herbs and mildly soured with tomatoes. The dish looks pleasingly appealing due to its green colour imparted by the fenugreek leaves used in it.

Ande ka Khagina

It is simply a scrambled egg preparation with onion, green chillies, ginger, garlic, green coriander, and so on in a Hyderabadi style. It is a sort of egg *bhurjee* preparation.

Hyderabadi Biryani

It is renowned worldwide and is loved by everyone throughout for its splendid and resplendent taste. Hyderabadi Biryani is unparalleled among the connoisseurs of *biryani*. The blending of Telagana and Mughlai cuisine in the kitchens of Nizams resulted in the creation of this dish. The mutton is marinated in ginger-garlic paste with red chilli powder, coriander powder, green chillies, lemon juice and *garam masala* powder for about 2-3 hours. Basmati rice is also parboiled and kept aside. Then in a heavy bottomed pan, the parboiled rice and cooked mutton are layered with sprinkling of saffron milk and ghee in between and cooked tightly covered. Chopped mint leaves, coriander leaves are also added along with golden brown fried onion slices. This preparation has all the flavour and fragrances blended in each grain of the rice, making it an irresistible dish. It is usually accompanied by *dahi ki chutney*, *mirchi ka salan* and some vegetable salads as well.

Kachhi Biryani

It is a dish which requires a great deal of expertise and skills to prepare it to perfection. In this preparation raw meat is cooked along with raw rice and other ingredients. The meat is marinated properly with a tenderizing agent for about 4 hours and then the marinated meat is layered with the rice and its marinade. It is also referred as *kachhe gosht ki biryani*.

A *masala* is prepared with cinnamon, cardamom, cloves, bay leaves, peppercorn, and *shahi jeera*. The meat is marinated with beaten curds, ginger-garlic paste, papaya paste, chilli powder, turmeric powder, and a little fried onion paste. This mixture is kept aside for about 3 hours. The rice is cooked till almost done. The marinated meat is placed in a heavy-bottomed pan with melted ghee. The rice is spread over the meat, and saffron, ghee and lemon juice are sprinkled over the rice. The *handi* is then sealed well with flour dough. This is initially cooked on a high flame for 20-25 minutes, and then on a low flame for another 45 minutes.	
Qabooli The word *qabooli* means acceptable. It is a vegetarian *biryani* made by using yellow split gram lentils with rice.	
Mirchi ka Salan It is a signature dish of Hyderabadi cuisine made up of large green chillies as the main ingredient and then it is cooked in a unique mixture of roasted coriander seeds, sesame seeds, cumin seeds, peanut, poppy seeds, and dry coconut and fenugreek seeds. Tamarind paste and jaggery also play a very crucial role as ingredients in the gravy of this dish. The combination of spices used in this dish is representative of a composite North-South culture.	
Baghare Baigan It is a dish very similar to *mirchi ka salan*. Here, the green chillies are replaced by brinjal and rest of the ingredients are same and so is the method.	
Chapa Pulusu It is a fish preparation made by marinating the fish in garlic paste, turmeric and salt and then cooking it in gravy made of coconut milk, and tempered with curry leaves and whole red chillies.	
Tamater Kut A soupy dish in which tomatoes are cooked with onion, ginger and garlic in very less amount and excess water. It is given the *baghar* which lends it a unique Hyderabadi flavour and is served garnished with boiled eggs.	
Keoti Dal A lentil curry preparation of four lentils (*arhar dal, masoor dhuli dal, moong dhuli* and *channe ki dal*) boiled properly and mashed. Then it is given the *baghar* and is served hot. The word *keoti* means a mix of lentils.	

Dalcha It is a well-known specialty of Hyderabad consisting of lentils and meat curry in which the meats consist of tender ribs, mutton cubes and marrow bones. The dish is given the *baghar* and is soured with tamarind.	
Raughani Roti A bread very rich in cream, milk and ghee is *raughani roti*. Actually the word *raughan* means ghee, and as this is used in large quantity, it is referred as *raughani roti*. The ghee, milk and cream are kneaded with flour and then rolled and cooked on a griddle on slow flame.	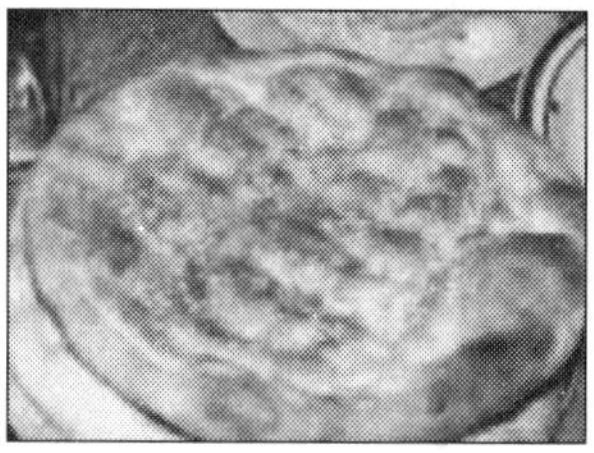
Bakharkhani Roti It is a delicately rich bread made by mixing flour with milk, ghee, sugar and nuts. The dough is made by soft kneading and dough balls are prepared, rolled and then baked in an oven with proper brushing of oil and served.	
Baadam ki Jaali This delicacy is a thin cake made up of almonds and sugar as the main ingredients. It can be either single layered or double layered and cut into small adorable and decorated patterns with the help of a fancy cutter.	
Double ka Meetha It is one of the famed preparations of this region, which is made by soaking fried pieces of diagonally cut bread in sugar syrup and reduced milk flavoured with saffron and then baking it dry. It is served garnished with slices of pistachio and almonds. It is also considered the South Indian version of *shahi tukra* from North India.	
Khubani ka Meetha A unique sweet delicacy made by soaking apricot with sugar overnight and then boiling it till the apricot pulp gets separated from the seeds and then it is served with fresh cream. *Khubani* is the Hindi term for apricot.	
Nimish A celestial dessert of Hyderabad is par excellence in culinary arts. This dish has taken Hyderabadi dessert to a level of elegance and finesse. The full cream buffalo milk is boiled with continuous stirring, so that the cream doesn't form on the top. Sugar is added and then it is cooled with stirring again to avoid the formation of cream on it. Then it is added with rose water and saffron. The pan in which it is cooled is covered with muslin cloth and kept outside in wintry night dew. Before sunrise, next morning, it is churned in an electric churner and the foam formed due to the churning is collected in an earthen saucer and served as *nimish*.	

Gil-e-Firdaus It is an amazing sweet dish of grated white pumpkin with *sago* (*sabudana*) and *khoya*, cooked in thickened milk, sugar and then served garnished with nuts (slivered almonds and pistachios) and rose petals. It is served chilled.	
Mauz-ka-Meetha A dessert made up of ripe banana mashed and cooked in brown sugar syrup till thick, and then it is spread on a plate and served topped with plenty of nuts and cream.	
Ande-ka-Piyosi A baked sweet dish made with eggs, sugar, *khoya*, saffron, almonds and purified butter. Egg white and egg yolk are separated and then the egg white is beaten till stiff and egg yolk is added with sugar and creamed. Then the egg white and egg yolk mixture is mixed slowly with slight addition of almonds and *khoya* and then it is poured in a greased baking tray and baked till done. It is cut into diamond shape when cold and served.	

Culinary Trivia: Mughlai Cuisine

Having reigned over India for so long, the Mughals left a deep and long lasting influence on Delhi's cuisine. The Mughlai cuisine is literally 'fit for royalty'. With its rich sauces, butter-based curries, ginger flavoured roast meats, and mind-blowing sweets, it has captured the fancy of food lovers all over the world. From a tangy shorba or soup to the rose petal strewn *kulfi*, Mughlai food offers a rich fare that is irresistible.

Culinary Trivia: Kebab

Kebab is a dish made from pieces of meat, fish, or vegetables roasted or grilled with a skewer on a spit. The traditional meat for *kebab* is lamb, but depending on local tastes and religious prohibitions, other meats may include beef, goat, chicken, pork or fish. Basically this dish originated in Middle East and got popular worldwide. Like other ethnic foods brought by travellers, the *kebab* has remained a part of everyday cuisine in most of the Eastern Mediterranean and South Asia. It is a popular dish among the youth as a snack after a night-out.

Kebab is a term derived by combining two words *kum* (less) and *aab* (water), as it is cooked with very less of water. *Kebabs* in India have a distinct taste which can be credited to the spices native to the Indian subcontinent.

Some popular *kebabs* are:

Kakori kebab,	*Shami kebab*
Kalmi kebab,	*Malai kebab*
Mutton seekh kebab,	*Kacche gosht ke chapli kebab*
Galawati kebab,	*Boti kebab*
Hara bhara kebab,	*Kathi kebab*
Reshmi kebab	

Culinary Trivia: Tikkas

Tikkas are a kind of *kebab* in which small chunks of either paneer or chicken or mutton pieces are marinated in curds-based marination and then skewered and cooked in a *tandoor*.

Examples: Chicken *tikka*, paneer *tikka*, and so on.

16 Karnataka Cuisine

"The food that enters the mind must be watched as closely as the food that enters the body." – Pat Buchanan

Karnataka, located in the Deccan Plateau in the south-west part of India is bordered by the Arabian Sea and the Laccadive Sea on the west, Goa on the north-west, Maharashtra on the north, Andhra Pradesh on the east, Tamil Nadu on the south-east, and Kerala on the south-west.

Karnataka is blessed with varied and productive natural resources and exemplary cuisine. The state has an amazing food culture which is extremely rich in variety and portrays sigularity in every shade of its cuisine. It has an amazing potpourri of varied mouth-watering dishes to captivate a foodie and gourmet of any kind.

The variegated cuisine of Karnataka is an amalgamation of distinct numerous vegetarian and non-vegetarian cuisines that have the impact of its neighbouring states. The region in and around the city of Mysore has an impeccable pure vegetarian meal which is popular and renowned all over. The people living in the coastal areas eat fish appreciatively, meat and a cluster of seafood. The cuisine of Karnataka is not the cuisine of a single locality but the cuisine made with the amalgamation of various regions like Udipi, Malenadu, Kodagu, Mangalorean and Navayath and hence the flavours and tastes of the cuisine of Karnataka are distinct.

Rice is the staple food of the state as this region has high production of rice due to a favourable climate. Wheat, jowar and ragi are used to prepare rotis in the northern parts of Karnataka and people consume it popularly. The populace in northern Karnataka prefers and uses more of jowar while in Mysore people generally prefer ragi.

The food of Karnataka is characteristically non-greasy and symbolizes using of oil less in quantity. Most of the food items are prepared using a stingy amount of oil. The steaming method is the most used cooking method in Karnataka which requires very minimal quantity of oil in it, thus restricting the use of oil automatically. Sesame oil and groundnut oil are usually used as the medium of cooking in the interiors of the state whereas those inhabiting the coastal areas prefer coconut oil as it is in abundance. The neighboring state Goa has influenced the cooking of food in and around the Mangalore Coast and so, the use of coconut milk is liberal here. Fruits form a crucial element of the cuisine of Karnataka. Fresh fruits as well as fruits in the pickled form are a compulsory feature of this cuisine. There are numerous methods of cooking rice here. Rice based delicacies are commonly popular in this part of India. Mangalore is a place which exhibits some of the most scrumptious and tempting rice-based delicacies in the country. The cuisine of Karnataka has not remained aloof from the influence of the Hindu and the Muslim method of preparing food.

The regional food habits in this state are defined and characterized by the availability of local ingredients; and hence the resultant cuisine is a highly distinctive cuisine. Karnataka's cuisine is symbolized by a motley of distinct textures and flavours and tastes. Karnataka's vast culinary repertoire blends the earthy and exotic flavours of North Karnataka, the traditional fare of South Karnataka, and the spicy and tempting delicacies of the coastal region, and the distinctive Kodava cuisine.

The authentic and traditional Karnataka meals (referred as *oota*) are served on a *patravali* (banana leaf) or *muttuga* (leaves stitched together). People sit cross-legged on the mats or on raised platforms to have the meal. Spoons or forks are not used as food is eaten with hands. It is a tradition existing from time immemorial to begin the meal with a delicious dessert named *payasa*.

The breakfast has numerous dishes in its bouquet and they are *uppittu, idli-sambar, thatte idlis, masala dosa, set dosa, rava dosa, puri playa, uthappam, vada sambhar, kesari bhath* and many more.

Essential menu items include highly nutritious cereal salads like *kosambari, playas, gojju, tovve, huli, and papad.* A unique cluster and varied collection of rice based dishes, including *chitranna* (rice cooked with flavoured spices, particularly oil-popped mustard seeds and turmeric), *vangi bhath* (rice preparation with brinjal), and *pulliyogare* (sour rice dish) form an inseparable part of the traditional assemblage.

Bisi bele bhath, a unique combination of rice, *dal*, tamarind, chilli powder and a dash of cinnamon in rural areas, is undoubtedly the most illustrious dish of Karnataka. Ragi served either with mutton curry or *soppina saaru* also constitute the staple diet.

The meal comes to an end with tasty dishes like *chiroti, Mysore Pak, obbattu* or *holige* (stuffed or plain sweet flat bread/pancake/crepe) and *shavige payasa*.

Desserts: Desserts are a significant aspect of the cuisine of Karnataka. People have a special liking for sweets here and love lot of sweet dishes. The commodities such as milk, vermicelli, sugar, coconut, jaggery and various dry fruits are chiefly used to prepare the sweet dishes of this state. Some of the renowned and popularly consumed delicacies of this state are *Mysore Pak, Dharwad pedha, Chiroti* (a light flaky pastry soaked in almond milk), *obbattu* or *holige* (a flat, thin wafer-like *chapati* with a filling of jaggery, coconut or copra and sugar and fried), *gokak, kardantu,* and so on. This cuisine has some wonderful kinds of *payasa* (*payasam* or *kheer*), which is made up of milk and rice. A few splendid *payasas* of the land recognized all over are *Shavige payasa* (made of vermicelli), *Gasgasa payasa* (made of poppy seeds, coconut and jaggery), *Seeme akki payasa* (prepared with tapioca, sugar and milk), and so on.

The wide array of dishes like *payasas*, different kinds of *pedhas, kesari bhath* and *chiroti* are the sweet items relished by the people of Karnataka.

Certain regional trends of cuisines of Karnataka are described below.

Mangalore

The cuisine of Mangalore is considered to be spicy and is predominantly rice based. Fruits play a very crucial role and have become inseparable due to its importance in Karnataka cuisine. The connoisseurs are of the belief that generous use of fresh coconut and chillies in the food here produces a spell-binding magic. Everyone who is a gourmet or loves food is touched by the charisma it spells. People from no other state or place in India are supposed to consume rice in such a varied and delicious way. Pancakes, *rice roti, kori roti, neer dosa,* red grain rice and *sannas* are well-famed rice delicacies of this cuisine. Spicy *kane fry* (ladyfish) and *patrode* (a dish prepared by steaming stuffed colocassia leaves), *akki* roti are few items which have added new dimensions to the cuisine.

Malnad

It is a unique cuisine which is the result of amalgamation of Coorgi and Mangalorean cuisines. This cuisine offers a lots of unbeatable dishes like *midigayi* pickles (small raw mango), *sandige, avalakki* (beaten rice), and *talipittu* (*akki roti* made of rice flour) and lots more. This cuisine is simple but genuinely amazing.

Udipi

This cuisine is quintessentially a rigorous vegetarian fare. Even the use of onions and garlic is totally prohibited. This cuisine has a prominent place for itself in the Karnataka cuisine. The iconic and very delicious ubiquitous *masala dosa* is considered to have originated from this place. *Masala dosa* is undoubtedly the most celebrated dish of the state. Not only the *masala dosa*, but a few other popular South Indian dishes have also originated from this place. *Sambar, rasam, adyes* (dumplings), *ajadinas* (dry curries), pickles and *chutneys* are some of the special delicacies of this cuisine. Pumpkins and gourds, coconut, jackfruit, colocasia leaves, raw green banana and red chillies are a few ingredients that are frequently used in this cuisine. The incorporation of such ingredients has bestowed a unique taste and character to the cuisine.

Rasam, spicy pepper water, is an essential and integral part of the menu in this region.

Kodagu

The cuisine of Kodagu adds an outstanding contrast to the other cuisines of Karnataka. This cuisine is basically a non-vegetarian fare. It has excelled tremendously with the non-vegetarian delicacies like *pandi* (pork) curry, *koli* (chicken) curry, *bembla* (bamboo shoot) curry, *kadumbuttu* (rice dumplings), *nool puttu* (rice noodles), *votti* (rice roti), and so on and has carved a niche for itself in the culinary map of Karnataka.

North Karnataka

The cuisine popular in North Karnataka has wheat and jowar rotis (unleavened bread made of millets). People enjoy a wide range of *rotis* is like *jolada roti, thali peet, khadak roti,* and *sajja roti* (*bajra roti*) in this cuisine. Variety of *chutneys* and spicy curries are served along with these items. These *rotis* are also enjoyed with dishes like *yenne badanekayi, kaalu palya, soppu palya, usli* (made from spicy sprouted gram) and *jholka* (made from *channa dal* flour).

The best feature of North Karnataka cuisine is the portrayal of sweet preparations such as *dharwad peda, gokak khardantu, belgaum khunda, shenga holidge* and *yellu holidge,* besides the local *hoornada holige*. Thus, it has its own typicality and characteristics in Karnataka cuisine.

Specialty Dishes

Akki Roti

It is a common breakfast item prepared chiefly from rice. *Akki roti* simply means rice-pancake, which is made the soft dough prepared by kneading rice flour mixed with salt and water. Certain other ingredients like sliced onions and carrots, chopped coriander, cumin seeds and sesame seeds can also be added while kneading the dough. It is shallow-fried on a griddle (*tawa*) with little oil.

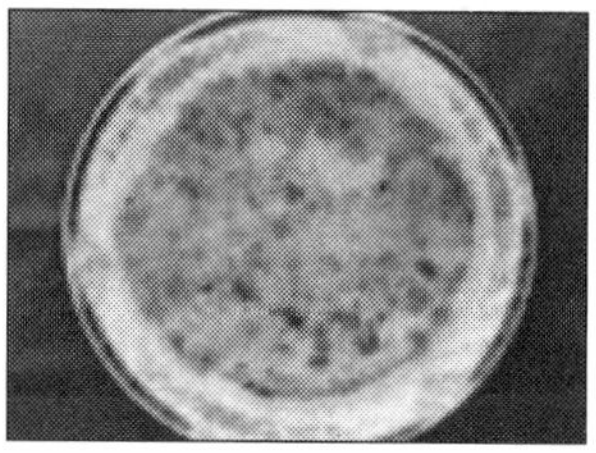

Saaru

Rasam in Karnataka is referred as *saaru*. Saaru literally means essence, and, by extension, juice or soup. It is a very significant dish and is prepared essentially with black pepper and tamarind, both ingredients are native to and are in plentitude in South India in general. It is traditionally prepared using tamarind juice as a base, with the addition of tomato, and chili pepper, pepper, cumin and other spices as seasonings. The dominance of black pepper can easily be felt while drinking or consuming it.

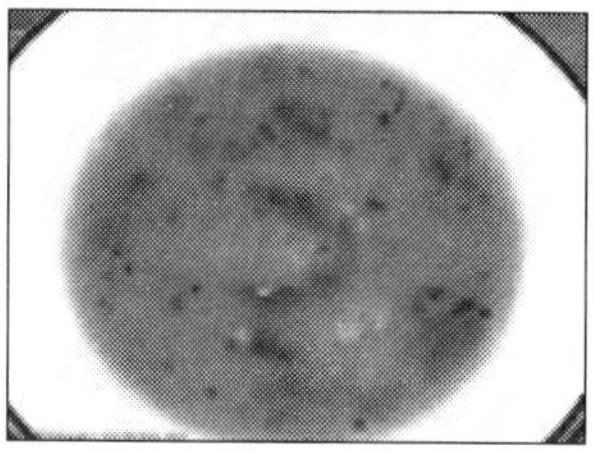

Bisi Bele Bhaat

It is a rice-based dish, with its origin in Karnataka. *Bisi bele bhaath* translates to hot lentil rice in the Kannada language. It is also known as *Bisi bele huliyanna* which translates to hot lentil sour rice. It is a preparation in which *arhar dal*, vegetables, spices, curry leaves and tamarind pulp is incorporated. It is served hot and sometimes eaten along with salads, papad or potato chips.

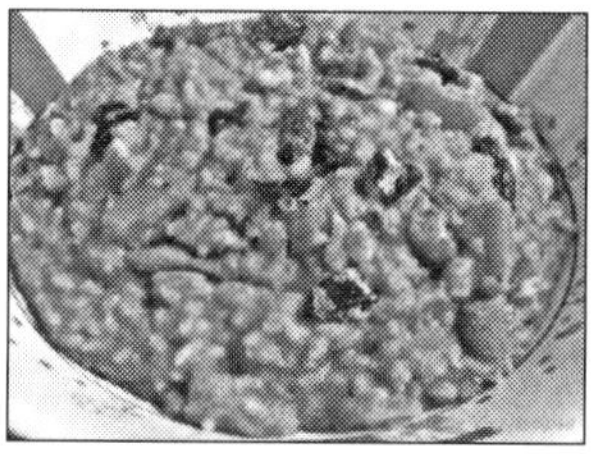

Mysore Pak

Mysore pak is an illustrious dessert which is the native of Karnataka and is made of ample amounts of ghee, sugar and gram flour. Pak means the sugar syrup in Kannada.

According to old references, it is considered that Mysore Pak was first created in the kitchens of the Mysore Palace and hence the cook gave it the name Mysore Pak signifying that it is a dish from the Mysore Palace.

Uppittu

It is a very famous variant of *upma*. The word 'uppu' means salt and 'hittu' means flour in Kannada and hence the dish is called *uppittu*. *Upma* is usually made with semolina and the taste can be distinct with the variation in spices.

Jolada Roti

It is a unique speciality from North Karnataka. It is an unleavened Indian bread made out of jowar (sorghum). The name *jolada roti* literally translates into sorghum bread. It is eaten with pulses, curries or with various types of *chutneys*.

Vangi Bath It is a dry rice but tasty dish, which originated in Karnataka and literally means, fried brinjal rice.	
Puliyogare or Puliyodharai It is a South Indian rice preparation usually eaten as a snack. *Puliyodharai* is also known as *hurianna* meaning 'sour rice'. It is traditionally made using steamed or boiled rice mixed with tamarind paste, groundnuts or peanuts, coriander, coconut, red chili, curry leaves, jaggery, pepper, mustard seeds, fenugreek, turmeric, asafoetida, *urad dal*, and cumin.	
Sambhar *Sambhar* is a vegetable stew or chowder based on a broth made with tamarind and is most symbolic curry preparation in the cooking of southern regions of India. A wide variety of assorted vegetables are added to *sambhar*. Typical vegetables included are okra, carrot, radish, pumpkin, drumstick, potatoes, tomatoes, brinjal and whole or halved shallots or onions, but many other different vegetables may be used with adequate results. It is consumed with *dosa, idli* or with rice. This preparation is highly nutritious and digestible.	

Culinary Trivia: Papad

Papad is a thin, crisp round shaped Indian food typically based on seasoned dough made from black gram, lentils, chickpeas, rice or potato. It is typically served as an accompaniment to a meal in India. It is also served as an appetizer or snack, sometimes with toppings such as chopped onions, green chillies, *chutneys* and condiments.

It is referred with various names such as *papadam, appadam, poppadom,* and so on.

It can be cooked by deep frying, roasting over an open flame, toasting, or microwaving, depending on the desired texture required. Its recipes vary from region to region and from family to family.

Arguably the most popular recipe uses *urad dal* or black gram. Black gram flour is mixed with black pepper, salt and then the mixture is kneaded together. A well-kneaded mixture is then flattened into thin rounds and kept for sun-drying. Once dried, papad can be stored for later consumption. It is then cooked by deep frying, roasting and so on. *Papad* may also contain rice, jackfruit, *sabudana,* and so on, as main ingredients. Cracked black pepper, red chilli powder, asafoetida, or cumin or sesame seeds are often used as flavouring agents.

17 Kashmiri Cuisine

"The art of the cuisine, when fully mastered, is the one human capability of which only good things can be said." – Friedrich Durrenmatt

Kashmir, located in the north-western region of the Indian subcontinent is bordered by Himachal Pradesh on the south and slightly touches Punjab. It is also surrounded by neighbouring countries like Pakistan, Afghanistan and China.

The cuisine of Kashmir is one of the oldest regional cuisines of India and has evolved and refined over a period spaning hundreds of years. The cuisine of Kashmir has its peculiar quality that differentiates it from the rest of the other regional culinary arts of India. The cuisine of Kashmir is awesome and pristine as the beauty of Kashmir per se.

Spices play a very crucial role in imparting taste and aroma to the dishes in Kashmiri cooking. Kashmiri cuisine is quite tempting and is known for its flavour and hot spicy taste. There are varieties of Kashmiri dishes made with the same spices like red chilies, aniseed, asafeotida, ginger powder, cumin seed, and curds or yogurt. White rice is the staple food which balances the spicy hot Kashmiri dishes.

One spice can completely change the taste of a dish. Quantities of spices specified in recipes are merely a guide.

Mainly, chillies and salt are the two items, which can be used according to personal taste. In fact, the secret behind the tasty Kashmiri cookery lies not in high spicing but in the delicacy of spicing. While the use of spices is traced back to the pre-Aryan era, the absence of onion and garlic in preparation of the delicious curries in Kashmir dates back to the vedic period.

The cuisine of Kashmir, which mostly comprises non-vegetarian dishes is differentiated basically by three varied style of cooking — the Kashmiri Pandit cuisine, the Muslim cuisine and the Rajput style of cooking. Each style of cooking has its own tradition of mixing and using the ingredients. For example, Kashmiri Pandits eat meat but abstain from eating garlic and onion.

Wazwan: Distinguished Signature of Kashmiri Cuisine

The traditional Wazwan takes the Kashmiri cuisine to a very different level of hospitality and more or less has become an inseparable identity of Kashmiri cuisine. Wazwan cuisine is a salient element, of the Kashmiri culture and an individuality that has evolved in the valley centuries ago and has maintained a distinct characteristic of an entity of its own unrivaled in the world.

Wazwan, means a majestic multi-course meal in the tradition of Kashmir region of the Himalayas in India. It is the splendid formal banquet in Kashmir and is treated with great esteem and reverence, because its preparation is considered an art and regarded as the dignified aspect of the Kashmiri culture. It would sound incredible but it is a fact that Wazwan has thirty-six traditional courses in its huge display. In all probability, only the Chappan Bhog (56 courses) in the world has so many courses with huge ostentatious display. It demands for substantial investment of time and endeavour for the preparation of the banquet Wazwan, but the result is worth the effort made.

Wazwan is a combination of two words: Waz meaning *chef* and wan meaning a *shop selling delicacies*. The preparation of it is traditionally done by a head chef known as *Vasta Waza. Vasta Waza* in assistance with a group of chefs referred as *wazas*, prepare the banquet meal in an open-air kitchen called *vurabal*. The history of Kashmir's traditional cuisine is not a matter of newly born cuisine, but it has refined over a period of time and Wazwan dates back to 14th century onwards, when the Mongol ruler Timur invaded India in 1348 during the historic period of Nasiruddin Muhammad, a ruler belonging to the Tughlaq dynasty.

As Wazwan is the banquet meal, it is mostly prepared on important occasions, especially marriages. It is a matter of huge concern as Wazwan is actually attached with large wastage of food, as much of the food has to be discarded. But, its dominance in the Kashmiri culture has overshadowed this aspect of concern and Wazwan is still very popular today.

The animals are slaughtered according to the Muslim custom and then butchered expertly on the spot. According to *waza* the animals to be slaughtered has seventy two parts and a most of them are cooked. Organ meats (offals) such as kidney, heart, and liver will be prepared and served in lunch to the host and family.

Basically, two tents are set up during the banquet meal pıeparation, one as the kitchen and the other is used as the dining pavilion. Earnest young men will cut meat into cubes, mince it and pound it repeatedly into a smooth paste. All of this is done with mallets and cleavers over several hours.

Once the cooking is finished, long white silk sheets called *dastarkhans* are spread out on the carpeted floor of the dining pavilion area.

Guests come in and take their respective place. Males and females sit in separate rows and then jugs of water and basins are brought so that the guests may wash their hands.

Guests are then sorted into fours for the Wazwan to be served. Prior to beginning the meal, there is a ritual to wash the hands of the diners and hence jug and basin known as *Tash-t-Nari* are passed among the guests. The food is covered with a cover (*sarposh*). While starting the meal, the cover has to be removed, and the name of Supreme Almighty God is appealed with the group uttering of word 'Bismillah' and then the eating starts.

Tash-t-nari

A large serving dish called as *trami* is piled high with gobs of rice is decorated and adorned by four *seekh kababs*, four pieces of *methi korma*, two *tabak maaz*, sides of barbecued ribs, one *safed murg*, one *zafrani murg*, along with other foods. When one *trami* is finished, it is replaced with a new one brought in, until the dinner goes on. Ladies prefer to eat food in *kinz* and men prefer *thalbana* bowl. Along with this is served yogurt in large clay bowls and sweet pumpkin *chutney* in saucers.

It is essential to have seven dishes for such occasions, and they are Rista, Roghan josh, Tabak maaz, Dhaniwal korma, Aab gosht, Marchwangan korma and Gushtaba. The meal comes to an end with Gushtaba. After the main course desserts are served in *turpiyali*.

In Wazwan, the vegetarian dishes are not preferred and only one or two dishes find a place in the lavish banquet. It is the dream and wish of every Kashmiri citizen to organize and arrange the royal Wazwan once in his life time for their relatives.

Salient Features of Kashmiri Cuisine

Kashmiri cuisine is very peculiar with the richness and redolence of the spices used in it - cinnamon, cardamom, cloves, saffron, and so on.

Mutton, chicken or fish are of utmost importance in the Kashmiri meal and everyday the cooking mostly combines vegetable and meat in the same dish. Few combinations of non-vegetarian ingredients with vegetarian ingredients include the combination of mutton and turnips, chicken and spinach, fish and lotus root. All these combinations are very popular and are relished with great enthusiasm.

Kashmiris do not have a sweet tooth and hence desserts do not play an important role in Kashmiri cuisine. Unlike other regional cuisines, *kahva* (*kehwa*) or green tea is used to wash down a meal. *Kahva* is served or poured from a large unique metal kettle known as *samovar*.

Samovar

Kashmiris have a special liking for breads such as *sheermal* and *baquerkhani*, without which the Kashmiri breakfast is considered incomplete.

The variety of breads consumed here is rarely seen elsewhere. *Tsot* and *tsochvoru* are basically small round breads, topped with poppy and sesame seeds and is traditionally washed down with salt tea. *Lavas* is a cream colored unleavened bread. *Baquerkhani* is the rough puff pastry bread of Kashmir and *kulcha* is a variety of shortbread, sweet or savoury, which melts in the mouth. It is topped with poppy seeds.

Styles of Cooking

The Kashmiri cuisine is distinguished mainly by three different patterns of cooking, in which the Kashmiri Pandit and the Muslims have some similarity and the other distinguishing style of cooking is that of the Rajputs.

The core difference between the two styles of cooking is that of the ample use of *heeng* (asafoetida) and curds among the Hindus and the open-handed use of onion and garlic by the Muslims. The cooking style of Muslims has been described well in the section Wazwan.

Hindu Brahmins or Kashmiri Pandits are not opposed to the concept of eating meat and they are in fact voracious meat eaters. They prefer goat meat in their meal and that too taken from a young one. The meat is mostly chosen from the legs, neck, breast, ribs and shoulders and cut into large pieces. Almost every dish, be it vegetarian or non-vegetarian, except certain *kebabs*, is cooked with curds as its main ingredient. The Kashmiris mostly cook their food by providing heat on it from two sides, i.e., from both top and bottom, in order to gain the most-sought after distinctive taste. During the ancient period, they used charcoal fire for such tasks but today's era of modernization, oven has replaced the use of charcoal fire.

Originally, Kashmiri Pandits did not incorporate onions and garlic in their meals, but now many of them have developed a taste for them and have started including them in various preparations as optional items.

When it comes to the cooking principles of the Pandit families, though they are by and large similar but few Pandit families have come up with minor changes in using ingredients and also in the method of cooking. The factor which has not seen any change is the substantial use of aromatic spices and prohibition of onion and garlic in some households. Curds is used in almost all preparations, in order to provide a creamy silky consistency to the dish and this is one of the unique features of Kashmiri cuisine.

Kashmiris also add asafoetida to flavour to their meat dishes.

Kashmiri Pandits are highly particular about the procurement of vegetables used for preparation of *saal* (feast in Kashmiri) throughout the fetivity and celebration. It would not be unfair to state that a Kashmiri Pandit wedding is a genuine vegetarian affair since the marriage ceremony is associated with sacred and hallowed rituals. The Kashmiri people are so particular about such functions that they consider to take a *mahurat* (checking whether the stars and planet are favourable or not, known as *saath* in Kashmiri) for buying all these commodities, from vegetables to numerous spices.

Kashmiri Pandits have a strong penchant for tea. Three types of tea are vastly popular amongst Kashmiri Pandits – the *kahwa* (considered to be the wonderful cousin of our green tea), the *sheer chai* (or the *noon chai*) and the milk tea (a sweet milky tea). *Kahwa* is an aromatic clear tea which is enriched with dry fruits, whereas *sheer chai* is a red milky tea with salt in it in place of sugar and is supposed to help in the process of digestion.

Two spices, *saunf* (aniseed) and dry ginger are referred to as additive spices and are used tactfully to enhance the taste of the cuisines. For example, some dishes get pungent in taste due to little excess of dry ginger in it and hence care has to be taken while adding dry ginger in any preparation.

Few other dishes have no spices except a little *saunf* added to them for flavour.

Local Chief Produce of Kashmir

Kashmir, also considered the land of fruits and nuts, uses dry fruits in the Kashmiri curries due to its abundant availability. For example, walnuts, almonds and raisins are added to the curries. Ghee is the medium of cooking, probably because the fat is required to impart heat to the body, though mustard oil is also used.

The varieties of rice grown locally here are mildly fragrant and very light. All the dishes are centred on the main course of rice. All the year round, a thick-leafed green vegetable known as *haak* is grown and is used in the preparation of delicious *saag*. Lotus root is also an important local produce for people having boat as their abode and it makes a very good alternative for meat.

Fresh vegetables are used in season as per the availability. Morel mushrooms called as *gucchi* are harvested and consumed fresh in summer with great gusto. They are somewhat expensive and this is the reason why it is used mostly for specific events such as religious and wedding feasts. Their full-bodied flavour heightens the flavour of *pilafs* and other meatless dishes. Corn bread is used as a substitute for rice.

Apples are grown in plenty and hence are available in copious quantities. The fruits are preserved by method of canning or as pickles. It is taken care that they are used in as many dishes as possible. Apples include sweet and tart variety and are available in various colours like red apples and yellow crab apples. The fruits like *nadra* cherries and plums (*alu bukhara*) are also grown in plenty.

The Kashmiri cuisine has also been influenced by streams and lakes. Fresh fish is a favourite. Multitudinous meat dishes are served on the occasion of traditional feasts. Lamb and poultry are served as accompaniments. Smoked meat, dried fish and certain vegetables are stored for use in winter.

Traditionally, rice is the staple crop of the valley, which forms the primary food of the people. Succeeding rice, corn comes next, which is followed by wheat, barley and oats. Kashmir is blessed with a temperate climate unlike other states of the Indian subcontinent, and hence it is suited to crops like asparagus, artichoke, seakale, broad beans, scarlet runners, beetroot, cauliflower and cabbage. Fruit trees are common in the valley, and the cultivated orchards yield pears, apples, peaches, and cherries, which are of fine quality. The abundant trees found in the valley are *deodar*, firs and pines, maple, birch and walnut. Large quantities of water-chestnuts (*singhade*), commonly called *golus*, are a main produce of Kashmir's Wullar Lake.

Singhara (Water-chestnut)

Musk and water melons, cucumbers and almost all varieties of fruit, tuber, root and leafy vegetables are also grown in abundance. A blood-red variety of pomegranate is also found and is referred as *kabuli anar*. The seeds are dried and then powdered and it is used to sprinkle over preparation of vegetables. The winters in the region are very harsh and hence it becomes difficult to cultivate any vegetable during this period. The vegetables grown here are dried during autumn (referred as *sheengri*) and are used during the winter season. The vegetables preserved in the dried form are brinjals, tomatoes, white gourd and so on.

The first snowfall of the season in Kashmir is celebrated by the Muslim community with a dish *harissa* which is kind of porridge made by meat and grains. It is consumed with delicious *girda* bread. Hindus enjoy hearty bowls of *razma gogji* (red kidney beans simmered with turnips) during snowfall.

Unique Kashmiri Ingredients

Ver

It is a peculiar *masala* 'cake' which is made from the combination of spice-blends, onions and locally grown chillies that can be stored for longer period of time. It is only in Kashmir that the spice is preserved in the form of cake and a part of it is used whenever required. It is used in flavouring various curries. This masala cake is dough-nut shaped and has a strong and acrid aroma. It comprises garlic and *praan* (Kashmiri onion, which is a strange cross between a spring onion or scallion and shallot) by the Muslims, whereas asafoetida and fenugreek is used by the Hindus, along with lots of freshly ground red chillies, cumin, coriander, dried ginger, cloves, cardamom and turmeric. All these spices mentioned are ground and then made into a patty. It is then left to dry on wooden boards under shade. Here it is turned over skilfully many times until it is quite hard, after which it is strung and kept for the rest of the year for further use. As per the requirement, small amounts are broken off from the patty cake pieces, crumbled and then sprinkled over many foods to render them a recognizably special Kashmiri flavour.

Praan (Kashmiri onion)

Kanaguchhi (Morel Mushroom)

This is an imperial dish which is mostly prepared on grand occasions like marriages, *ghar-achan saal*, and so on. This species of mushroom is rare, uncommon and wild. It is not easily available like the other species. It is very challenging to cultivate this for commercial purpose because the spores are not easily available and it needs great care, attention and complicated scientific methods. As the quantity of it is less, it is very expensive (costs between Rs. 15000-20000/kg). It can be prepared in various delicacies like *guchh yakhni, mitha guchh, guchh pulao,* and so on.

Saffron

Kashmir is also referred as the Land of Saffron. Fifteen kilometres from Srinagar is a place Pampore, which is famous worldwide for its production of high grade saffron. It is also grown in Kishtwar of Jammu, but in very limited quantity. Pampore and its surrounding neighbouring areas produce an average of 2200 kilograms of saffron every year. It is normally sown in August till the 15th of September. The flowers are plucked in October and November. During harvesting or plucking of flowers, the atmosphere must not be hot but pleasing. So, this process is completed early in the morning to avoid high temperature. The ideal time for the plucking of flower is from early sunrise to 10 am. After harvesting, the flowers are allowed to dry for about 5-6 days. Then, they are kept in an airy container so that the quality of the produce does not degenerate. In days of modernization, solar drier is also used. It takes only seven, eight hours to dry the produce. As saffron is in abundance, it is used to flavour certain pulaos, curries and sweets.

Haak

Haak is a thick leafy green vegetable from. The leaves seem to appear like outer cabbage leaves and much darker in colour. The aroma and taste bear a resemblance to the taste of something between cabbage and mustard leaves. Even after cooking, the leaves never got mushy and soft as the leaves of spinach gets.

In Kashmir, there are several varieties of *haak* or seasonal greens found and they are: *Monjji haak* (kohlrabi greens), *Kadam haak, Mujj haak* (radish greens), *Vappal haak* (dandelion greens), *Wasta haak* (red in colour), *Hernj haak* and *Aaram haak*.

No similar cuisines could be found in Portuguese and Kashmiri cuisines, yet they have a common link the *haak*.

Known in English as collard greens, this member of the vast *Brassica* genus has a distinct personality with its trademark crinkly blue-green leaves along a central stem and its pronounced taste.

Haak is also referred as *karam ka sag* in Kashmir and is an essential commodity used in the diet of almost all Kashmiris on a daily basis. It is consumed with plain cooked rice, throughout the year, as a green leafy vegetable. It is the best source of vitamins and minerals in Kashmiri diet. It is said that all Kashmiris crave for *haak* and *bhaat* (plain cooked rice), in their prayers. It is assumed that *haak* is a divine godly leaf, and a blessed food article gifted to us by Rishi Kashyap, and his progeny, and it is called *shakh ambari*. Even in feasts and special events, *haak* is compulsorily prepared and served. Whole leaves are boiled in water, with a little dash of mustard oil, whole red Kashmiri chilies, and salt, and then spiced with a little Ver Masala. The whole mature red chilies are preserved by sun-dried in autumn, when these are available, and then stocked by every house in Kashmir for the year's future consumption. The cooked *haak* is a tasty vegetable delicacy, enjoyed by the poor and as well as the affluent and rich. Haak is mostly cooked by Kashmiris in a special earthenware cooking vessel called *leij*.

Haak leaves, dried in shade, are preserved and cooked during winter, when fresh *haak* is not available at many places. Dried leaves are reconstituted by boiling before cooking. Nowadays fresh *haak* is available almost throughout the year. *Haak* has added a new and altogether a different dimension to Kashmiri cuisine.

Knol Khol

Also known as *kohlrabi, navalkol* or *ganth gobhi, knol-khol* is a vegetable under the *brassica* family very popular in Kashmir. It is a greenish white coloured large and round vegetable, somewhat similar to cabbage, although it does not have leafy covering. There are long light green coloured extrusions, which come out as its shoots. It is large and woody or hard and comes in late winters. It is used to prepare vegetables or salads dishes.

Specialty Dishes

Mutton Roganjosh (Neni Roghanjosh)

Roganjosh is a combination of two words: *Rogan* which literally means *'meat fat'* and *josh* literally means *'heat'*, though in a figurative sense, it means intensity. Traditionally meat with lots of fat content on the bone is used for making *Rogan Josh* and it was slow-cooked in its own fat, with extra fat added for an intense flavour. With the application of heat, the fat content melts the fat and the dish gets intense oil floating on it. In these days of cholesterol-consciousness, however, animal fat is avoided and a minimum amount of oil is used. The dish gets its heat and fieriness from the overgenerous use of body heat-inducing spices such as large black cardamoms and cloves. The authenticity of the dish as cooked in Kashmir is the unsparing use of the true Kashmiri red chilli, which has a very mild flavour but render an attractive and appealing bright red colour. The Muslims there use *praan*, a Kashmiri shallot that has a flavour resembling garlic, and *maval*, the petals of the cock's comb flower. The latter gives the curry an even brighter red colour and is believed to have cooling and soothing characteristics. The Hindus of Kashmir do not use *praan* or onion or garlic like the Muslims but they give body or flavour to the curry by the adding yogurt. The spice that distinguishes Kashmiri Rogan Josh from those made in other parts of India is fennel powder. The curry is mildly spicy and has a ravishing flavour. Traditionally, it is consumed with boiled rice but can also be eaten with rotis or a saffron *pulao*.

Gushtaba

Gushtaba is called by Muslims as 'the king of dishes' or 'dish of kings'. It is famous for its flavour and taste. It is served as the last meat dish in a Wazwan feasts, before the dessert. The preparation of this dish demands a lot of effort, as boneless cubes of lamb are beaten along with lamb fat with a wooden mallet on a coarse stone so that the fibres break down, yielding a paste of meat. It is then flavoured with powdered spices like black cardamom seeds, fennel and black pepper corns, Kashmiri *garam masala*, and ginger powder. Small meat balls (*goshtabas*) are prepared from this spiced meat paste. Then thin delicious gravy is made by combining yogurt, ghee, salt, and Kashmiri spices. The *goshtabas* are poached in it until spongy and tender and are served in gravy.

Rishta

Undoubtedly, Rishta is one of the most famous and a mouth-watering dish of Kashmiri Wazwan. Lamb dumplings are prepared and then poached in a rich bright red gravy, flavoured with saffron and an extract of *maval* petal of cock's comb flower (basically used for colouring). It is prepared in the spice combination of red chili powder, fennel seeds, cardamom and other spices in a very special manner. The resultant preparation is worth the time.

Tabak Maaz

This is again a lamb delicacy prepared from the ribs of lamb. The lamb ribs are allowed to boil in a mixture of milk and water, spiced with aniseed powder, ginger, turmeric, asafoetida, and cinnamon powder, till the meat absorbs all the water. After that, the meat pieces are taken out and cut into pieces, and then pan-fried in hot ghee flavoured with cardamom, fennel, and cinnamon. The pieces of meat are then fried till they are crisp and golden brown in colour. It short, it is a deep-fried dry lamb rib preparation.

Kabargaah

This preparation is very similar to *tabak maaz,* but the only difference is that in Kabargaah, the tender boiled pieces of lamb ribs are dipped into a batter made with gram flour and spices, and then fried until crisp and served.

Methi Maaz

This is a preparation which is served as an appetizer. In this, small boneless pieces of lamb (*boti*) are combined with offals such as the stomach of lamb, the oesophagus or the food pipe, and lungs. These are cooked with spices and a paste of boiled fenugreek (*methi*) leaves.

Heddar

It is a dry preparation of mushrooms in spices consisting of fennel powder and ginger powder along with chopped tomatoes. It is very nutritious and a tasty dish of this state.

Aab Gosht

This is a very unique preparation which literally is made by the combination of two words. Aab Gosht literally meaning 'water meat'. In this the lamb stock is cut in pieces to be portioned and then boiled in water along with ginger-garlic, aniseed powder and salt till tender. Then the gravy is prepared separately by cooking fried onion paste in ghee with the addition of black pepper powder and reduced milk. The milk is cardamom flavoured as it is boiled with milk and hence the cardamom flavour is completely infused in the milk.

Dhaniwaal Korma

It is a rich preparation of lamb or chicken cooked in gravy dominated by the addition of yogurt and coriander leaves. The preparation for the gravy is started by heating pure ghee to which ingredients such as garlic paste, cloves, and green cardamom are added. Once they are done, the gravy is finished by adding cooked yogurt, turmeric, and coriander powder, and then garnished with lots of coriander leaves.

Marzwaangan Korma

It is a spicy mutton curry prepared with mutton pieces and spices like aniseed, cardamom, cloves, cinnamon, gingerroot powder, and tamarind pulp, and is usually served with rice and *naan*. It is normally hot and spicy as compared to other mutton preparations.

Gosht ke Kofte (Machh)

There are several dishes made of minced meat. The fashion of mincing, and pounding into different textures, and spices used, varies according to different varieties of dishes to be cooked. Different dishes are prepared with application of different degree of pounding and mincing. *Machh,* also called *Ganda Machh* or *Kofta,* is a famous preparation made for serving in banquet dinners and feasts, and is also a welcome change in daily domestic menus.

The lean meat of leg, shank or shoulder, is generally used for mincing. The mincing is done with a chopping knife on a wooden crosscut block, usually of mulberry or apricot wood. This mode of mincing makes the *Machh* fine and granular.

If mincing is done by means of a machine, then such minced meat is later on pounded with spices in a mortar with a pestle. This *Machh* becomes fine but becomes compact like dough.

Mutton Yakhni (Neni Yakhni)

Mutton Yakhni has a thick whitish curds gravy which is highly flavoured with spices such as fennel seeds, cinnamon, cardamom, cloves, and red Kashmiri chilli powder. Curds is an integeral part in this preparation which has no chillies or turmeric used in it. When mutton is replaced with chicken, it is referred as Chicken Yakhni.

Yakhni Pulao

Essentially, *yakhni* is a yogurt and saffron based mutton broth. The broth/ stock of *yakhni* is made using mutton and aromatic spices like whole garam masala, tied in a bouquet *garni*. Aromatic spices like fennel seeds, dry ginger powder, cinnamon, cloves, black and green cardamom are the essence of this *pulao* or *pilaf*. Yogurt is another ingredient which plays a key role in bringing all these flavours together and giving this *pulao* its unique flavour. In this preparation, rice is cooked in the mutton broth along with the partially cooked mutton.

Shyami (Shyaem)

It is a minced meat cutlet preparation. First of all the minced meat stock is rolled into a cylindrical form and then boiled in water and then cut into roundels. Later on it is cooked in a gravy very similar to *yakhni*.

Chamani Qaliya/Paneer Qaliya

This is a very delicious preparation of paneer in which paneer is diced, fried and boiled with ingredients like milk, broken dry ginger or sliced green ginger, aniseeds, turmeric, salt and half a pinch of asafoetida. Then, the paneer pieces are strained and cooked in gravy. The gravy used in this is flavoured with spices like cloves, cardamom, cinnamon, black pepper, *garam masala* and most importantly curds. Paneer is served in this gravy.

Veth Chaman

This is a preparation very similar to Chamani Qaliya. Paneer is cut into oblong shaped pieces of 3″× 2″ size. The gravy of this preparation is thick enough and includes spices like cumin seeds, aniseed, and all spices of whole *garam masala*.

Tsaman Pulao

It is a *pulao* preparation in which the rice is cooked with milk and *garam masala* and finished on *dum* with raisins, almonds. It is tempered with ghee, cumin, fried paneer, and peas. Finally, it is flavoured with saffron and *kewra*. The same rice dish when added with more nuts and glazed cherries is referred as Kashmiri Pulao.

Bhaz Bhaat

It is a rice preparation made in the fashion of *pulao* using cauliflower and fried potatoes as the main ingredients. The preparation is simple. Ghee is heated in a pan and then added with whole spices, sliced onions, ginger juliennes and then soaked rice. It is then cooked till slightly overdone.

Rwangan Tsaman

Cottage cheese known as *tsaman* is commonly eaten. *Tsaman* in Kashmir has many variations. *Rwangan* refers to tomatoes. In this preparation, the cottage cheese is stewed in tomato gravy flavoured with *ver* and other spices. When this preparation is cooked with fresh fenugreek leaves it is called *methi tsaman.*

Kamal ke Jadh ki Yakhni (Nadeir Yakhean)

This dish is almost mandatory in vegetarian banquet dinners and feasts, with grand menus, and is mostly cooked in an earthen pot called *deg*. It is also prepared in an earthen smaller pot, a *leij*, or in a steel *patila,* for domestic meals. Each person takes 3 or 4 pieces, with a liberal serving of its delicious gravy, with plain cooked rice.

Note: A stalk of lotus roots is called a *nadur* in Kashmir, and more than one stalk *nadeir*.

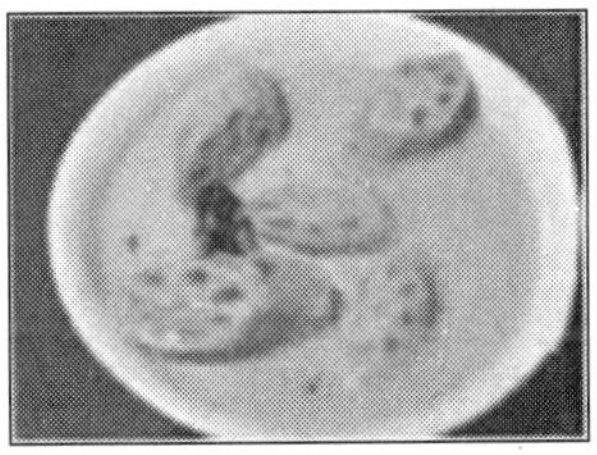

Khate Baingan (Choek Vangan)

It is a dish generally served in wedding vegetarian dinners and feasts, a piece or two to each guest. It is also prepared in small quantities for domestic meals, usually as a side dish like a pickles. It is a preparation of brinjals cooked in curds and tomato. *Vangun* is one Brinjal, and *vangan* more than one. When fresh brinjals are not available, even dried brinjal slices (*vangan hachi*), after soaking these in hot water for about 15 minutes, are used.

Note: Radish slices are also cooked as above, and the dish is called Choeki Muji/ Khatti Muli.

Dama Oluv/Dum Aloo

Very popular vegetarian preparation with potato as the main ingredient in which the boiled and fried potatoes are cooked in a gravy made of few spices. Many times, the potatoes are stuffed with paneer are used in this preparation.

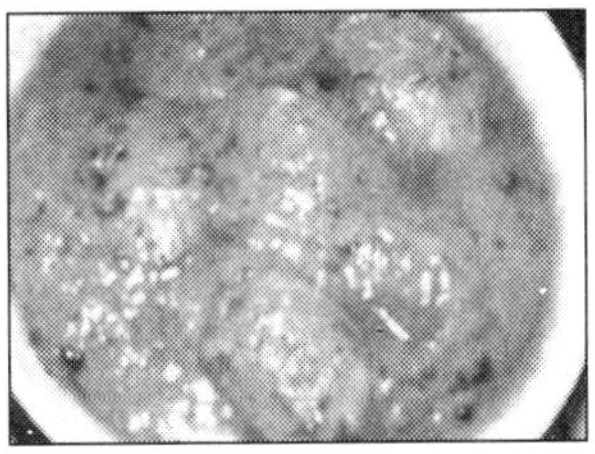

Rajma Shaljam (Rajma Gogji)

This is a favourite dish of this region and is very nutritious, as well as delicious. This preparation has red kidney beans (*rajma*) cooked with turnips as the main ingredients, flavoured with fennel and *saunth* (dry ginger powder). It is a satisfying vegetable dish and goes very well with plain cooked rice.

Roth

Roth is a type of sweet *puri* about 1/2"thick and 6" in diameter. The size can vary as per the choice and convenience and its main ingredients are wheat flour, sugar and coconut. *Roth* are prepared generally on certain rituals, auspicious occasions and particularly, in the month of August/September, when new wheat crop is harvested. Kashmiri Pandits prepare these on Vinayaka Chaturathi or on any other auspicious day of that month, to offer these as *naveid* to Shri Ganesha. This *prasad* after puja is distributed to all relatives and neighbours, and is also consumed by all family members. Kashmiri Pandits also send big *Roth* to the in-laws of their daughters after their wedding, as a *prasad* and as a token and mark of gratitude and appreciation to God. *Roth* is both singular and plural.

Mooli ka raita (Muji Chetein)

This is a side dish and serves as an appetizer. It is served in dinner banquets, and also used in domestic meals. White round radishes are generally used. Sometimes long or red varieties are also used.

Ranith Gada (Fish in Kashmiri Style)

This is a splendid preparation of Kashmiri Pandits but is enjoyed and savoured both by Hindus and Muslims alike. Fish of bigger size, each weighing about one kilogram or even more, are used usually in making the curry. The fish is cut and then deep fried in oil. Then the cooking liquor is prepared by boiling ingredients like red chilli powder, asafoetida, cloves, aniseed and ginger powder. Then in this liquid, *garam masala* is added with tamarind, tomatoes, tart apples, prunes, fresh plums, or fresh or dry apricots to impart a pleasant tart taste to the curry.

Kashmir Gaad

It is a fish delicacy in which cut deep fried pieces of fish is cooked in a thick gravy comprising red chilli powder, turmeric, badiyan, asafoetida and cloves. This fish is cooked on religious occasions and is enjoyed most by everyone in Kashmir.

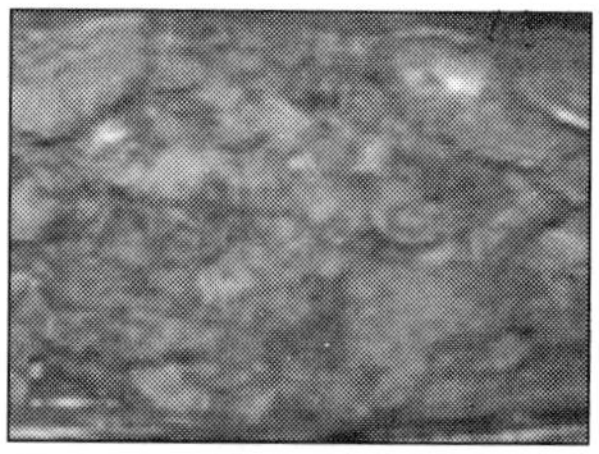

Girda

It is a flat leavened bread with equal quantities of whole whaet flour and refined flour kneaded separately and then mixed in single dough and then baked in a *tandoor* or on a griddle. It is oval shaped like *naan* and poppy seeds or *kalonji* are used on it from outside while cooking.

Tahaer

Tahaer is generally prepared by Pandits on auspicious days as *prasad*. Muslims also prepare it on certain occasions. Generally non-vegetarian people eat Tahaer with cooked liver. It is referred as Charvan in Kashmir and is condimented preponderantly with red chilli powder.

Firni (Firun)

Firun, also called *firni* is a form of plain custard prepared from milk and rice soaked in water for 12 hours and then mashed with palm. *Firun* is even nowadays sometimes prepared as a dessert, in feasts on big occasions, both by Kashmiri Pandits and Muslims.

Shufta

Shufta is basically a sweet dish consisting of paneer, dry fruits and condiments, cooked in thick sugar syrup and served as a side dish. Small dices of paneer are deep-fried and then it is cooked along with a mixture of *munnakas*, apricot, dates, coconut and few condiments along with sugar syrup and cooked till done.

Laed

It is a small spherical sweet *laddoo* prepared from wheat flour and then deep-fried in *desi ghee*, and these are made as offering to Shri Ganesha during his pooja.

Hogaad Bum

Hogaad are the dried fish mostly cooked and eaten in winters. It is also cooked in combinations with other ingredients. *Hogaad* is available in plenty during winters. The fish can be dried easily at home in summer by keeping them in direct sunlight after washing them properly. In order to save the dried fish from insects, kites, hawks and other pilferers, they should be wrapped in *malmal* cloth (muslin cloth) and hanged outside the balcony or terrace till dry. *Bum* is a plant mostly found near the shallow waters of ponds and lakes. It resembles the dried straw or hay of rice. It is nutritious for health as it has large quantity of fibre in it. It is beneficial for liver, kidneys and heart as well. It is also prepared in various combinations.

Maesh Crari

Maesh crari, also called Kalyadi, is a milk product very rich in fats, proteins and carbohydrates. These can be fried on low flame and eaten as snacks or with rice. Pure, perfect and real *maesh crari* is available in villages near Pahalgam. The cost is about Rs. 600/kg. The advantage of the *crari* of Kashmir is that they are dry, more tasty and are easily fried in oil in the same manner as cheese is fried. *Crari* of Jammu is wet and resembles normal cheese. These are very difficult to prepare.

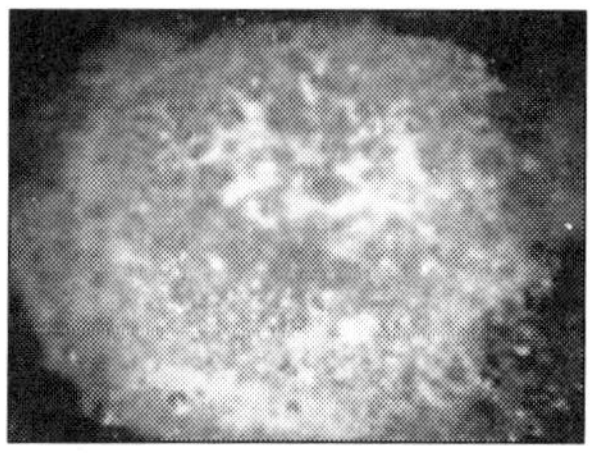

Mechama

It is a delicious dessert in which rice is cooked with sugar syrup and then milk is added at the later stage and flavoured with saffron and *kewra* water with lots of nuts and raisins.

Modur Polav

This is a sweet condimented *pulao* of *basmati* rice and it includes almond, raisin, dry dates, coconut, ginger, saffron, *kewra* essence and many whole spices with ghee and a large quantity of sugar as well.

Sheer Chai/Noon Chai/Kashmiri Tea

It is a traditional and authentic tea beverage from Kashmir. *Noon chai* is made from special tea leaves, milk, salt, pistachios, almonds, and cardamom. Cinnamon is sometimes also added for flavour. A pinch of baking soda is added to give it more of a pronounced pink colour. This preparation of tea is enjoyed throughout by every Kashmiri.

Kehwa

Kehwa is made with Kashmiri green tea leaves but any other green tea would do. Traditionally in Kashmir, this tea is made in a *samovar* which is a brass kettle. To make the tea aromatic, spices such as saffron, cinnamon, cloves and cardamom are infused and the concoction is then served in tiny shallow cups with crushed nuts such as walnuts or almonds along with sugar or honey.

Culinary Trivia: Korma

Korma is a mild creamy meat stew made with yogurt, saffron and spices. From *Akbarnama*, it appears that *korma* was created in the royal kitchen of Akbar during mid 1500s. It is surmised that *korma* was a fusion of Persian and Indian cuisine brought by Rajputs employed in the service of Jodhabai. Rajputs are credited with creating Murgh Musallam. Rajputs created *korma* and named it after *kurma*, a well known Rajput tribe. Most likely ingredients were: mutton (boneless meat, and bone-in meat), curds, cardamom, black peppercorn, ginger, and lots of saffron. The almonds were soaked in water overnight, peeled and ground, and added to give it a thick creamy texture. Turmeric was rarely used in the royal kitchen to cook meat dishes. The meat was braised just like making Rogan Josh with little bit of water at a time, on very low heat till the meat was tender. Korma however is not a part of 30 recipes documented in *Ain-i-Akbari*.

18 Kerala Cuisine

> **"Flowers always make people better, happier, and more helpful; they are sunshine, food and medicine for the soul." – Luther Burbank**

Kerala, a state in the south-western region of India on the Malabar Coast is bordered by Karnataka on the north and northeast, Tamil Nadu on the east and south, and the Lakshadweep Sea on the west.

Kerala, considered as God's own country, is also referred to as the land of spices. The state has a distinguished and delectable culinary assemblage of its own and is highly famed worldwide for its hot and spicy delicacies. The amazing platter of Kerala is bestowed with not only the dishes which are spicy, but it has an assorted repertoire of vegetarian and non-vegetarian fare along with a few sweet delicacies as well. All the preparations are appreciated a lot by connoisseurs all over the country.

The very typical traditional Kerala meal for special occasions is referred to as *sadya* meaning feast. It is served on freshly cut banana leaves called *vazhaillai*. The food is eaten using the right hand. There is a prescribed format of serving various dishes on the banana leaf. People usually sit cross-legged in rows of mats at the time of the *sadya* as a tradition.

It has a very tempting concoction of spicy vegetable delicacies like *kaalan, olan, aviyal, thoran* and so on.

The land of Kerala has been blessed and enriched by a mixed populace having their own traditions and cooking techniques. This mingling of cooking practices has made the cuisine of Kerala unique and has imparted it with distinctive attributes. The Hindu populace in the state is adept in preparing resplendent vegetarian dishes while kitchens of Muslim households are skilled in producing a luxuriant variety of non-vegetarian dishes. Christians on the other hand have come up with few interesting fish recipes for the coastal state.

The cuisine of Kerala differs from region to region and place to place. People living in coastal Kerala prefer to consume seafood frequently, while those residing in the plains are dependent more on vegetables in their regular meals. However, the tribal community and people living in the northern part of the state have taken meat as their main course. Impacts of voyagers from various parts of the world like Greece, Italy, France, China and Africa have also contributed in shaping the cuisine of coastal Kerala. Due to the repetitive visit of ocean-voyagers and due to the absorption of their culinary trends and cooking practices, the cuisine of Kerala has emerged as the ultimate amalgamation of indigenous and foreign dishes.

The influence of the culinary style of the princely states of Travancore and Kochi in the south, and Malabar District in the north is easily visible. It is because of such adaption from various cooking style and their impact, Kerala cuisine incorporates a large variety of vegetarian dishes using many vegetables and fruits that are usually not used in curries elsewhere in India. It includes plantains, bitter-gourd, yam, colocassia, ash gourd, and so on. In northern Kerala, tamarind and lime are used to impart sourness to the sauces whereas in the south only *kodampuli* is used to give a distinct sourness to the dish. The community of Muslims and Syrian Christians were essentially meat eaters and hence they promoted chiefly the unique non-vegetarian dishes, whereas Hindus especially brahmins were steadfast vegetarians in nature, and abstained from eating non-vegetarian dishes. But with the passage of time and because of their high absorbing attitude, few Hindu brahmins have nowadays started taking non-vegetarian dishes as well.

Rice is abundant here. Rice and cassava (tapioca) forms the staple diet of Kerala. All the main dishes are prepared using them and are served along with *kootan*, the side dishes which may be made from vegetables, meat, fish or a mix of all of them. The food is relished with lip-smacking *chutneys* and mouth-watering pickles. The people here are highly educated and hence put a great stress on the health aspects of their food. The use of oil, sugar and artificial additives is always under the eye of scrutiny and hence is always used minimally. The Kerala cuisine is archetypal in nature and is characterized by mildly flavoured food, which is gently cooked with sophistication and has a salubrious effect. Being located on the coastal area of the country, seafood is also in plenty and hence is one of the main essences in the daily diets of the common man and the locals. The weather is highly conducive to the production of spices and the availability of spices is extensive. The Kerala cuisine is luxuriantly spicy specifically by the incorporation of the spices hot in nature like chilli, black pepper, cardamom, cloves, ginger, and cinnamon. It is due to this attribute that the state is also referred as the land of spices. The spices like coriander, turmeric, cumin seeds are not far behind in consumption and are also used sparingly in various preparations.

The food is generally characterized and has gained fame due to its mind-blowing freshness, sensuous aroma and captivating flavour emanating from it. Keralites are mostly acknowledged to be fish and rice eating people. Being close to the coastal area, Kerala has huge production of coconut as well and nobody can envisage Kerala food without the commodities like chillies, curry leaf, mustard seed, tamarind and asafoetida. A large pinch of tamarind often replaces tomatoes, but there is hardly any genuine alternative for curry leaf. Curry leaf has also emerged as an indispensible commodity of this resplendent cuisine. Since time immemorial, coconut has been an integral and essential constituent of the cuisine of Kerala and is considered to be an inseparable commodity of almost all dishes prepared in Kerala. The Kerala cuisine is also defined by the local produce available here, similar to the other states of India.

Coconut being abundant, is incorporated in every possible form possible, i.e., coconut kernel, (sliced or grated) coconut cream and coconut milk in their dishes for thickening and flavouring. Coconut has been an indispensable ingredient of the state. The spices used here enhance the flavour of the dish and tamarind imparts sourness to it, while coconut imparts it richness, and helps in absorbing some of the tongue teasing peppery hot flavours. Tender coconut water is genuinely one of the best refreshing natural thrust quencher on the earth. The fresh creamy flesh of a coconut is referred as *elaneer* and is used in many delectable desserts. The coconut milk or *thenga pal* is used as a base for certain curries and desserts.

The breakfast of Kerala is exemplary and has been declared as the 'best breakfast of the world'. The typical breakfast of Kerala is reckoned with splendid delicacies. It has *appam* with egg curry, *puttu* with *kadala* curry or *idiyappam* with chicken curry. Other South Indian dishes such as *Dosa*, and *Idli*, have also added a feather in the cap of Kerala.

Kerala exhibits a huge display of certain popular vegetarian dishes like *sambhar, aviyal, kaalan, thoran, Poduthol* (dry curry), *pulisherry, olan, erisherry, puliinji, cherupayaru* (*mung* bean), and *kappa* (tapioca) and has marked an indelible niche in the world of vegetarian fare. The excellence in vegetarian dishes has been a real delight to all food lovers. Vegetarian dishes mostly comprise fresh spices that are absorbed in water and crushed to make a paste-like mixture to dampen rice.

The usual non-vegetarian dishes include stew (using chicken, mutton, and fish) or chicken curry (*nadan kozhi curry*), chicken fry (*kozhi porichathu/varuthathu*), beef fry, fish/chicken/mutton molly (fish or meat in light gravy), fish curry (*meen curry*), fish fry (*meen porichathu/ varuthathu*), prawn fry (*konchu varuthathu*), spicy steamed fish (*meen pollichathu*), and so on.

The Kerala cuisine also has an opulent selection of varied array of *chutneys* and pickles to enliven and spice up the taste buds. It has an ultimate variety of pickles and *chutneys*, and crunchy *pappadums*, banana chips, jackfruit chips, *pakka vada* (crunchy gram and rice flour chips), *kalathappam, kinnathappam kozhalappam, achappam, cheeda,* and *churuttu*. The crunchy *papadum*, banana chips (*upperi*), sweetened banana chips (*sarkkara varatty*) and jackfruit chips can even beat French fries in every sense. Many kinds of banana are available and used in Kerala. *Nethrakya* is a variety of banana that is used for making banana chips, while Mysore *Pazham* is a tart flavoured banana mostly consumed with *puttu* in breakfast.

The utensils used are also unique and are quite different from the utensils of the other cuisines and they are crucial to Kerala cuisine. An *aduppu* is a square hearth, *mun chatti* is cooking pot made from clay, *cheena chatti* (literally Chinese pot) is a deep frying pan or a wok.

The Keralite people are adept in using the commodities available to them in the best possible manner. The result is very obvious in the form of marvellous cuisine that is simple yet palate tickling. They carry same passion for the dish as simple as *kanji* (rice porridge) or as luxuriant as the *sadya* (traditional banquet feast). Coffee and tea (both hot) drunk black, or with milk and white sugar or unrefined palm sugar (*karippatti*). They have excelled in this segment of the cuisine appreciatively. Highly nutritious and tender coconut water is also a very popularly consumed beverage in Kerala.

The Muslim communities in Kerala are referred to as *moplahs* or *mappilas*. The cuisine of the Muslim community is known as *moplah* cuisine in Kerala. This cuisine is totally different in features from the Hindu community's cuisine and is largely centred on meat preparation. It is a normal tradition to have at least one or two dishes in a meal. The dishes prepared here are light and spicy. The gravies are preponderantly flavoured with coconut pastes and milk.

Being a coastal area, fish and seafood play a very crucial role, and is a significant constituent of the cuisine. Vegetables are generally eaten in the form of pickles and lentils so as to accompany rice. During Ramadan, feast is laid out where breakfast is also lavish with porridges and other preparations like *pathiris*.

Thus, the Kerala cuisine is an excellent display of exquisite cuisine in the form of combination of variegated vegetables, meats and seafood flavoured with a variety of spices, amazing snacks and pickles and beverages.

Breakfast

Appam is unanimously considered to be favourite Kerala breakfast. It has variants like *idiyappam, paal-appam,* and so on, which adds a new dimension to this peculiar preparation. This pancake is usually made from the batter of rice flour and toddy and is consumed during breakfast. It has been characterized by a thick, spongy centre and very fine lace-like outer section. It is mostly accompanied with spiced sauce, and at times with fruit.

Many varieties of *appam* are made in Kerala. When held over a stone or metal plate and boiled over water *kal-appam* is made. *Yare* (or leaf) *appam* is basically made from a mixture of rice batter, grated coconut, jaggery and jackfruit pulp and is traditionally steamed in banana leaf.

Kuzhal appam is another famous variety of *appam* which is a crisp, tube-like fried product whereas *nai-appam* (the *athirasam* of Tamil Nadu) is a dark, chewy, deep-fried doughnut fashioned from a *toddy*-fermented rice and jaggery mixture. *Acch appam* is a crisp appam in which a metal frame (*accha*) is dipped in batter and then immersed in hot oil, which fries the cookie and frees it from the frame. It represents the crisp kind of *appam* preparation.

Puttu is another popularly consumed breakfast delicacy which is prepared from rice flour dough combined with shredded coconut steamed in a bamboo stick. It is served with banana or served plain with sugar. It is a unique item which has some uniqueness as it is steamed using bamboo stick.

Idiyappam is basically rice noodles usually served with coconut milk and is accompanied with meat dishes like mutton stew or chicken stew.

Desserts

The lavish and irresistibly attractive desserts form an essential and quintessential part of the meals. It has a huge consolidation of ultimate desserts. These are served midway through the meals.

The most popular representative of this segment is undoubtedly the *payasam*, a thick fluid preparation of milk, coconut extract, sugar, cashews, dry grapes, and so on. *Payasam* can be made with many base constituents, including *paal payasam* (made from rice), *ada payasam* (with *ada*, broken strips of baked starch from various sources), *ari unda* (made from rice powder), *parippu payasam* (made from *dal*), *pazham pradhaman* (made from banana), *palada pradhaman* (made of flakes of cooked rice, milk, and sugar), *chakka prathaman* (made of jackfruit), *kadala prathaman* (made from black gram), *gothambu payasam* (made from wheat). But the most famous is *semiya payasam*, which is made of *semiya* (vermicelli) and milk. *Ada payasam* is popular mostly during the festive occasions of Vishu and Onam. Most *payasams* can also be consumed chilled. Jaggery or molasses is a common sweetening ingredient, although white sugar is not far behind and is gaining popularity. There could be a chronological sequence of *payasams,* such as the lentil *payasam* and the jackfruit *payasam*, bengal gram *payasam,* and so on, though *ada pradhaman*, a rich *payasam* with thin rice wafers, is arguably an amazing and sumptuous delicacy.

Pal payasam, made with sugar, ghee and spices, brewed in creamy white milk is regarded as the supreme delicacy in the sweet dishes. This is served with a golden yellow sweet pancake known as *boli*. *Pradhaman* is essentially a sweet dish in the form of a thick liquid, similar to *payasam*, but much varied in terms of ingredients and is made much intricately. It is made with white sugar or jaggery to which milk or coconut milk is added.

Other popularly consumed sweets include *unniappam* (fried rice cake), *pazham pori/ethakka appam* (plantain slices covered with a fried crust made of sweetened flour), *kozhakkatta* (rice dumplings stuffed with a sweet mixture of molasses, and coconut) and *ilayappam* (rice, jaggery and coconut mixture covered in banana leaf). Thus, the world of Kerala dessert is a wonderful aggregation of mouth-watering delicacies.

Sadya: Distinguished Signature Feast

Speaking without exaggeration, Sadya simply means banquet in Malayalam. It is a simple vegetarian fare served on a banana leaf.

The community of Nambudiris are staunch followers of vegetarianism. Traditionally, the temples in Kerala served meals to all followers and devotees visiting the temples and the food was cooked by Nambudiris. This is how Sadya came into existence.

The typical and authentic Kerala Hindu feast served on a banana leaf is an exhibition of lavish and sumptuous spread of rice and more than 14 vegetables (about 24-28 dishes), topped with *payasam*, the delicious sweet dessert cooked in milk.

Each dish to be served has been allotted a specified area on the plantain leaf. The top half of the leaf is reserved for accessories, the lower half for the rice, and in some communities, the rice is served only after the guest has been seated. The lower right part of the leaf may have a ladle of warm sweet, milky *payasam*, which should be eaten quickly. On top left a pinch of salt, a dash of pickles and a thimbleful of salads, or a small but noticeable portion of *chutney* is kept. In the middle of the leaf there may be a cluster of fried items like small round chips of either banana, yam or potato, hard round dices of spiced, ground *dal* known as thin *papads*, or frilly wafers or vada, and banana at the bottom left.

The top right hand corner is reserved for the most crucial and defining dishes, the curries, hot, sweet, or sour, and the dry items. If it is a vegetarian meal, the vegetables are carefully chosen from the villages or countrysides comprising native vegetables such as gourds, drumsticks, brinjals and non-native ones, which could be carrot, cabbage, and cauliflower. If non-vegetarian meal is also served, then in some cases, a separate leaf is provided for the fried meats, chicken, fish, crab, and so on. But again, the variations are presented with extreme care, one dry item next to a gravied one.

The central dish is plain boiled rice, served along with other dishes collectively called *kootan* which incorporates curries like *parippu, sambhar, rasam, pulisseri* and others like *kaalan, avial, thoran, olan, pachadi,* mango pickles, *naranga* curry, as well as *papadum,* banana, plain yogurt or buttermilk, and plantain chips.

Traditionally, one of the important features is that onion and garlic are strictly left out in the preparation of any dish.

Certain dishes create curiosity and are much-awaited such as a *puran poli,* made up of sweetened *dal* stuffed into a pancake, *puris,* sweet rice or any one of the famous rice preparations such as *pulisadam,* or *bisibela baath.*

After having worked through the overtures, the long journey commences with the rice, which is generously drenched with the ghee. *Sambhar,* the highly spiced *dal*-based dish containing whatever the appropriate vegetables are in the season follows, and this is succeeded by the peppery flavoured *rasam.*

The *kootans* are made with vareigated vegetables and have a potpourri of amazing flavours. Some say the reason for including so many dishes in the Sadya is to make sure that the diners will like at least two or three dishes and hence would have something of his own liking in the meal.

After the final serving of rice and curds, or buttermilk or both, a traditional meal concludes with a small banana, a few betel leaves and areca nuts to digest the meal and cleanse the palate.

The banana leaf on which a meal is served should be folded and closed by the eater once finished. Closing the leaf inwards signifies a sense of contentment with the food and closing it away would indicate a signal to the cooks that it needs improvement.

Specialty Dishes

Naimeen Vevichathu

It is a delicacy of fish in which the fish is cooked along with onion, ginger, red chilli powder, fenugreek seeds and tamarind pulp. It is cooked till desired consistency is reached and then removed from fire.

Ada Pradhaman

It is a classic mouth-watering dessert or traditional *payasam* of Kerala. This is a sweet delicacy made by rice which is sweetened by cooking it in the syrup of jaggery and then added with coconut milk, cardamom powder and fried nuts at the end.

Note: *Ada* is rice paste soaked in water and steamed in banana leaves.

Aattirachi Ularthiyathu

Aattirachi means mutton. This dish is prepared by sautéing sliced onion and green chillies in oil and then added with red chilli powder, coriander powder and turmeric powder. Then add crushed ginger-garlic and mutton cubes and cook with sufficient water. Finally, add sautéed tomatoes and cook till done and serve.

Vegetable Manga Mappas

It is a mixed vegetable preparation consisting of carrots, cauliflower, French beans, potatoes, green peas, and so on and cooked in oil tempered with mustard seeds, chopped onions and spices. Then add second extract of coconut milk and dices of raw mango in it and cook. Finally, add the first extract of coconut milk and cook till gravy thickens and serve hot.

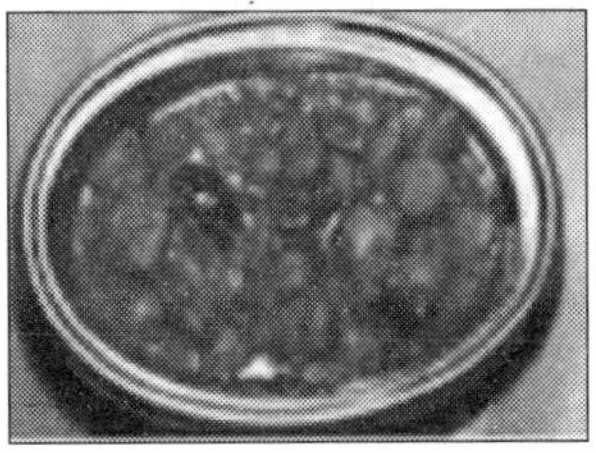

Kozhi Peralan

It is a chicken delicacy prepared by marinating the chicken with a paste of powdered spices along with curry leaves and vinegar. Then onions are sautéed and cooked with spices (spices kept aside after marinating the chicken) and chopped tomato is added in it and cooked. Then, marinated chicken is added and cooked till done.

Thalassery Biryani

It is also known as Kerala Biryani or Malabari Biryani. It is the *biryani* variant of Kerala and is treated with great respect in Malabari cuisine for its outstanding taste and aroma. In this preparation, *khaima* rice is preferred as compared to *basmati* rice of North India. Chicken is mostly preferred as meat in this *biryani*, but nowadays mutton and egg have also found place in this preparation.

Olan

It is prepared with white gourd, beans, coconut milk and ginger seasoned with coconut oil and it is usually a part of Sadya. This is prepared by cooking the soaked beans till done and adding it with chopped pumpkins and then cooking it till done and tempered with other ingredients.

Thoran

Thoran is a dry dish traditionally made of finely chopped vegetables such as yard-long bean, unripe jackfruit, bitter gourd, and so on. The chopped vegetable is mixed together with grated coconut, mustard seeds, curry leaves and turmeric powder and briefly stirred on a pan over a very hot fire. Nowadays, it is also made with carrots, green beans, cabbage, green tomatoes or spinach, vegetables that were traditionally not available in Kerala. It is served with rice.

Kaalan

It is a typical Keralite dish made of yogurt, coconut and one vegetable like plantain (raw banana) or a tuber-like yam. It is very thick in consistency and sourer in taste as compared to *aviyal*.

Avial

The word 'avial' is used to signify 'boiled' or 'cooked in water'. This sense is derived from the way the dish is made. It is a famed side dish that is common in Kerala as well as Tamil and Udupi cuisines. It is a thick concoction of assorted vegetables like elephant yam, plantain, pumpkin, carrots, beans, brinjals, drumsticks, snake gourd, cucumber, and so on. Curds and coconut, seasoned with coconut oil and curry leaves are added. Curds in this preparation can be substituted with raw mango or tamarind pulp. It is generally eaten with rice.

Pazhampori

It is an amazing delicacy in which ripe and peeled bananas are dipped in a batter of flour, sugar, cumin seeds and yellow colouring agent and then deep-fried. It is served hot.

Nadan Kozhi Curry

This heavily spiced chicken curry of Kerala has regional variations in terms of ingredients used, but nevertheless has the same combination of spices that add to its flavour. It is a chicken dish characterized by basic spices used along with (first) and extract of coconut milk (second). The addition of coconut milk adds a new aspect to the curried dish.

Cheru Payar

It is a simple yet tasty *dal* preparation in which green gram is boiled and tempered with mustard seeds, red chilli, curry leaves and small onion in coconut oil. It is served hot by mixing grated coconut at the end.

Erachi Vada

In this preparation minced meat of beef is mixed with garlic, ginger, green chillies, powdered cinnamon, cloves, fennel, little lime juice and coriander leaves. The mixture is given the shape of *vada* (ring-shaped) and deep fried in oil. It is served hot.

Kappa

This delicacy is made by boiling peeled tapioca and then adding the drained tapioca with salt, ground coconut, green chili and turmeric. Prepare a tempering of mustard seeds, onions and curry leaves and add this on stirred tapioca and serve hot.

Karimeen Pollichathu

The fish is marinated in ginger-garlic paste, red chilli powder, coriander powder, crushed pepper corns and lime juice, wrapped in banana leaf and grilled on a hot tawa till it cooks. It is served on banana leaf with lemon wedges beside it.

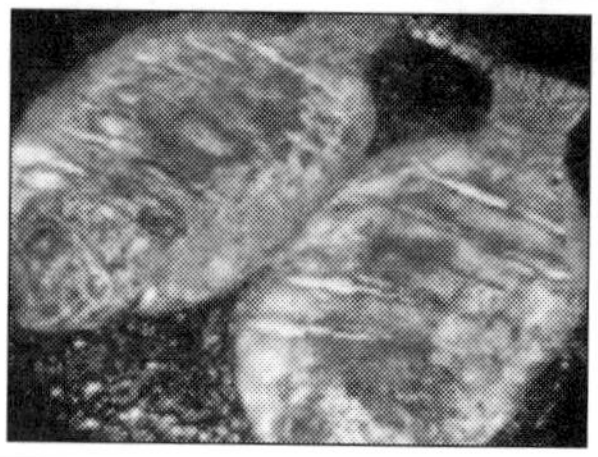

Erachi Ishtu

It is a beef meat stew of *moplah* cuisine in which meat cubes and potatoes are cooked with coconut milk, ginger-garlic paste, chillies and spices.

Kadala Curry

It is a preparation of black bengal gram and spiced up with the paste of sauted grated coconut, shallots, red chillies, coriander, curry leaves and garlic in a small amount of coconut oil till golden brown. It is finally tempered with mustard seeds, sliced onions, coriander powder, chilli powder, and *garam masala* powder.

Kozhi Varutharacha Curry

It is a mouth-watering dish of chicken, in which the chicken is cooked with potato, onion and spices like coriander seeds, red chillies and pepper, fried grated coconut, and curry leaves. Once the chicken is cooked, it is tempered with curry leaves and small onions in coconut oil.

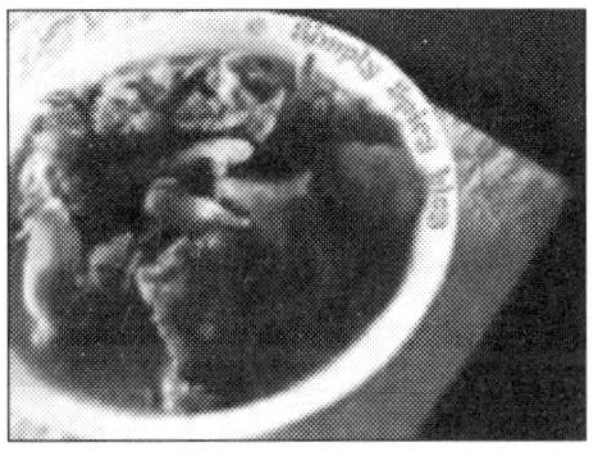

Chemmeen Varuthathu

It is an outstanding delicacy of prawns marinated with spices in the paste of lemon juice, red chilli paste, turmeric powder, cumin powder, ginger-garlic paste and then shallow-fried till cooked and served along with onion rings and fried curry leaves.

Malabari Paratha

These are flaky shallow-fried *parathas* often served with beef masala. The dough is kneaded to a very soft consistency and then flattened by flipping it on a clean table. Oil is then applied on the thin dough and rolled like a *lacchha paratha*. It is then shallow-fried until crisp and served.

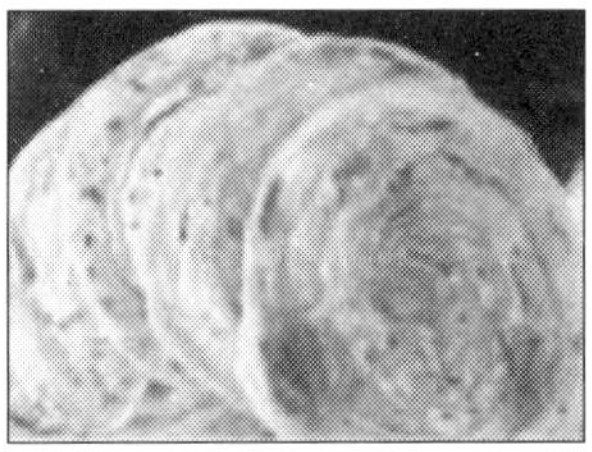

Muttamala

This is a specialty dessert of the Muslim community made during Ramadan months and weddings. These are strands of egg poached in sugar syrup. It is a mouth-watering delicacy.

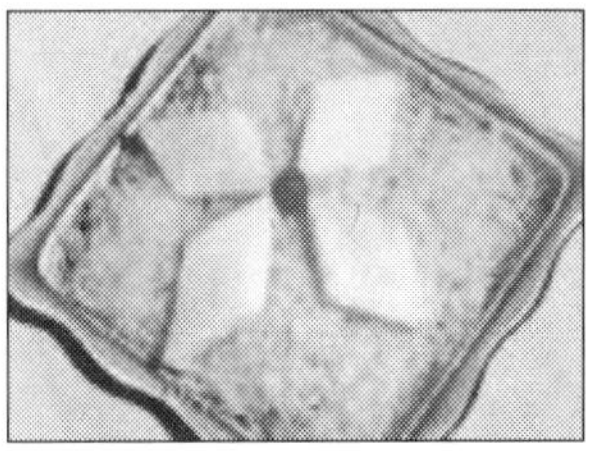

Erachi Varattiyathu

Erachi means beef. It is a very popular beef preparation in which beef cubes are boiled with salt, turmeric and green chillies. It is cooked till done. The excess water is drained and the beef cubes are kept aside. Sliced onion is sauted along with ginger-garlic paste and powered *masala*. Then tomato is added and when the gravy is ready beef cubes are added.

Note: *Erachi ularthiyathu* is same preparation as *erachi varattiyathu*. The only difference is that turmeric is replaced by aniseed.

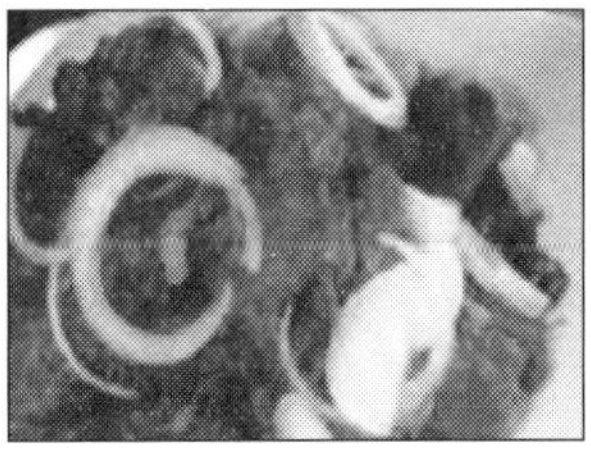

Meen Porichathu

The fish for this preparation is marinated with turmeric, lime juice, and salt and kept aside for 20-30 minutes. A special *Malabari garam masala* powder is prepared for the fish using red chillies, curry leaves, ginger-garlic, aniseed, cloves, cinnamon, green cardamom, turmeric and salt. The fish is shallow fried on both sides in coconut oil using the spices mentioned. It is then garnished with lemon wedges, onion roundels and fried curry leaves and served.

Culinary Trivia: Pickles

Pickles are referred as *achaar* in Hindi. It is belived to have been derived from items like *axi* or *achi* used for the chilli. They are made from certain individual varieties of ingredients like vegetables and fruits that are chopped into small pieces and cooked in edible oils with many different spices. Spices used for pickling are referred as pickling spices. Vegetables can also be combined in pickles to make mixed vegetable pickles. The spices used for picking are fenugreek seeds, mustard seeds, cumin seeds, *kalonji* (onion seeds), asafoetida, fennel seeds, turmeric powder, red chilli powder, coriander powder, salt and so on.

The most common ingredients used for pickles in India are raw mango, lemon, and so on. Other ingredients like carrot cauliflower, raddish, tomato, onion, pumpkin, ginger, garlic, *amla, zimikand, karonda* are also used for the same purpose.

Homemade pickles are prepared in the summer and kept under the sun while stored in porcelain or glass jars with airtight lids. In pickles, high usage of salt, oil, spices acts as preservatives whereas many commercially made pickles use preservatives like citric acid and sodium benzoate. The taste of some pickles made in North India may appear different in taste made in South India due to difference of oil used. Sesame oil is used in South India whereas mustard oil is used in North India.

19 Madhya Pradesh Cuisine

> "Food can become such a point of anxiety - not because it's food, but just because you have anxiety. That's how eating disorders develop." – Vanessa Carlton

Madhya Pradesh, a state located in Central India, is bordered by the states of Uttar Pradesh on the northeast, Chhattisgarh on the southeast, Maharashtra on the south, Gujarat on the west, and Rajasthan on the northwest.

Madhya Pradesh has an elegant cuisine which is so lavish in terms of it gastronomic features that it speaks a lot about its exquisite taste and entrancing essence. The culinary feature of Madhya Pradesh has been influenced tremendously by its climatic conditions. It offers a high-toned blend of both vegetarian and non-vegetarian dishes. The culinary habits is a culmination of traditions followed in the past and which prevails in the present with slight alteration due to its absorbing nature. The cuisine has gracefully refined and added much to it with the adaptation of new changes and experimentations done.

The food habits are relatively changed as the season alters. The dishes and the meals rely much on the availability of the seasonal vegetables and the weather. The cuisine of Madhya Pradesh also reflects the mild touch of its neighbouring state's cuisines like those of Rajasthan and Gujarat.

The cuisine of Madhya Pradesh is varied and it is dissimilar from one part of the state to the other. The northern part and the western part of Madhya Pradesh have their delicacies concentrated around wheat and meat, whereas the southern and the eastern part of the state primarily focus on rice and fish as their staple diet.

The cities of Gwalior and Indore offer a wide array of sumptuous delicacies made from milk and milk products. Bhopal is the capital city where people have inculcated worthy efforts to prepare excellent fish and meat dishes. The platter of the dishes chiefly centre on fish and the meat dishes consists of *rogan josh, korma, keema, biryani pilaf* and *kebabs* such as *shami kababs* and *seekh kebabs.* These dishes are extremely spicy and stimulate the taste buds of the diners. There is a street named Chatori Gali in old Bhopal where one savours traditional Muslim non-vegetarian fares like *paya soup, bun kebab, nalli nihari,* to name a certain amazing specialities.

Bafla is another dish which is the specialty of Madhya Pradesh and is made of wheat. This dish is made by dipping wheat cakes in ghee and is eaten with *dal.* This dish has gained wide appreciation and has achieved immense popularity.

Bhutte ka kees is a typical dish made with corn and milk and is served with roti. It is a specialty dish of Indore city. It is a seasonal dish prepared when fresh corn is readily available. *Butte* means corn and *Kees* means the grated part. Traditionally, the corn kernels are grated and then used in the recipe. But nowadays, the corn available in frozen state throughout the year can be blended coarsely and can be used to prepare the delicacy. The grated corn is tempered with mustard seeds and spiced with finely chopped green chillies and later cooked in milk. It is garnished with freshly grated coconut and chopped coriander leaves to add mild sweetness and captivating aroma of the herbs.

Chakki ki shaak is another unique delicacy made of steamed wheat dough and curds. *Amli ki kadhi* is one distinct preparation where instead of curds, tamarind is used sparingly.

Rice, wheat, sorghum, gram flour, millets, lentils, and sago are few of the common ingredients used frequently in Madhya Pradesh cuisine. Milk, meat, and fish are also used extensively. The seasonal vegetables and fruits are used aplenty. Fruits available abundantly such as water melon, mango, banana, guava, and papaya are also used in cooking as well as consumed after meals.

The land of Madhya Pradesh has been the home of largest population of tribes, thereby giving birth to tribal cuisine. Tribal cuisines are an exotic amalgamation of locally produced ingredients such as wheat, vegetables, meat and dairy products. Tribal festivals speak well about how food plays an integral part in everyday life. It is claimed that the smaller tribes of Abujhmar people relish red ants and rats as delicacies with their meals, but this claim is not substantiated on the basis of evidence.

A typical day commences with aromatic tea, accompanied by hot fuming *poha* (flattened rice) and a sweet delicacy like *jalebi. Roti, paratha, puri, dosa, naan* are also consumed during breakfast. *Sabudana khichdi* is unanimously the most popular breakfast dish of the state. Lunch comprises steamed rice with curries, *dals*, and vegetable dishes. *Chapati* with *dal* is another common food. *Namkeens* and sweets are an indispensable and inseparable item of the state food. Different types of *chaats, samosa,* and *kachori* are liked by all and are eaten as snacks. *Lassi*, date palm *toddy,* sugar cane juice, beer and rum produced from sugar cane are some of the common beverages of this region.

Palak puri is a nutritious dish in which the wheat flour is kneaded with boiled paste of spinach puree and then deep fried. It is an excellent dish which has its origin in this state, but is very popular throughout the country. It has created its place in the daily meal of the state. The rice has been uniquely modified by frying it with green peas, carrot and nuts and this dish is referred as *pilaf* rice.

This state has many rivers flowing through it and hence fish has been the major ingredient used here. Also, the forest area provides uncountable meats like those of deer, wild boar, lamb and chicken.

The non-vegetarian section is flooded with fish items of several kinds. It is used generously in many delicacies and is used in various varieties of forms like cutlets, barbeque and curries. Fishes commonly used are *rohu, pavda,* glaskat and *singhada*. Some illustrious dishes are *bhunji macharia* (roasted fish), *macharia ke kebab* (fish kebabs) and *machariya tarkari* (fish with vegetables). Fish has become an inseparable and integral part of the cuisine such that when even the rivers dry up, the supply of fish never ceases. It is regularly harvested in artificial lakes such as the Vijay Sagar reservoir in Mahoba.

The *Bundeli gosht* is a celebrated dish of the state (tender lamb shank pot-roasted with cardamom, mace and other fragrant herbs), *bhindi gosht* (lamb cooked with ladyfinger), *kukra ka jhol* (a unique chicken curry) and *Sighdi wala kukra* (barbequed roast chicken) are some delicacies that are eaten with *masala* rice.

This state has some sweet delights for all the food lovers, especially those with a sweet tooth. Some of the sweets popularly consumed are *gulab jamun, mawa bati, laddoo, raabri, malpua, khopra pak, moong dal halwa, gajar ka halwa, ras malai,* and *rasgulla. Mawa bati* is a scrumptious dessert made of *mawa* (condensed milk), jaggery, and *til* seeds. *Khopra pak* a superb preparation made by using freshly grated coconut, milk, and sugar. *Ras malai* and *rabri* are luxuriant desserts made with milk, nuts, and sugar. *Malpua* is made with milk, semolina, refined flour and sugar syrup. All the desserts are delectable and fulfill the craving for desserts delightfully. One very renowned sweet delicacy is *Raas kheer* which is prepared by mixing the extracts of the *mahua* flower with milk and millets. In this dish, no sugar is added.

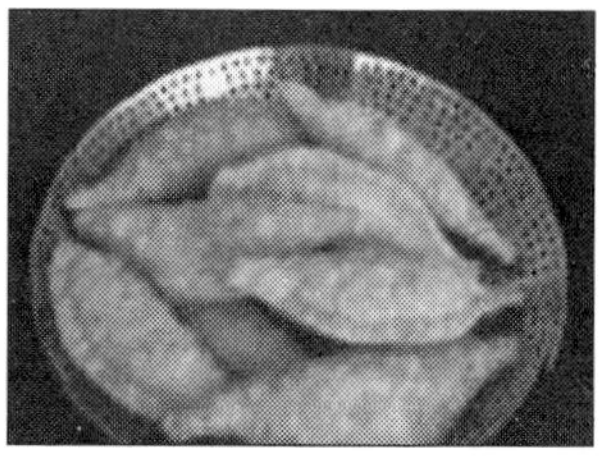

Kusli is an exceptional preparation with *huge* repute among the people of Madhya Pradesh and even Chattisgarh. It is made with *maida* (refined flour), ghee and *sooji* (semolina). It resembles to the Gujiya preparation.

The city of Indore can also be adjudged as 'the city of *chaat*' or as a unique food destination, which has a famed food junctions called *Chappan Dukan,* which has 56 shops all selling the famous *chaats*, savouries, and juices. The other famous food junction is *Sarafa Bazar*, which sells a huge variety of street food. *Dahi bhalla, aloo patis, aloo kachori, pohe jalebi, raj kachori* and *samosa chaat* are some of the tasty and popular dishes available here. The tantalizing taste of the street food of Indore makes street food an unforgettable experience.

The outstanding gastronomic aspect of this cuisine is the typical and impeccable assemblage of wheat and milk which makes for perfect local culinary products. The cuisine has an exotic native flavour due to the food being cooked in a clay pot and the fuel being used is firewood. The famed dishes of this region are *kunde ka bhatta, murar ke kebab* and *tapu* (sweet cakes made from varieties of wheat). A special sweet cereal called *thulli* is also consumed with milk or yogurt. The rice variety is also not common and is distinct from other regions of India, one being the *kodu til ka bhaat* which is a renowned rice preparation with black sesame seeds. The two variants of rice used extensively in this region are *kodu* and *kudki*.

The dishes are extraordinarily plain with little oil in it and strictly use no artificial flavours. The *dal* preparation prepared from green sprouts is also very popular. One renowned preparation of this region is the *kunde ka bhatta,* almost similar to the authentic *baigan ka bharta.* They use the green eggplant in it which endows it a perfect taste. The *puris* of the region are made from *bajra* and *jowar.* During festive occasions or on special events, one preparation well-famed is the *chikeriya tarkari* (a pot of treasured fresh vegetables available during the season).

In summer, there is a tradition to finish the meal with any of the fruits like the luscious mangoes (especially Dussehri), juicy melons and watermelons, custard apples, bananas, papayas and guavas.

Sulfi is the local liquor, distilled from the flowers of the *mahua* tree, is popular here. The date palm *toddy* is also common and popular among a large section of the people of this state.

Cuisine of Bundelkhand

Bundelkhand is the area which covers certain districts of this large state as well that as of the neighbouring state Uttar Pradesh. The cuisine of Bundelkhand is referred to as 'tribal cuisine' and it has contributed much in shaping the cuisine of Madhya Pradesh. The uniqueness of its taste is characterized by the style of preparation used, the use of raw materials and commodities and excessive use of various kinds of millets in it. It is asserted that its root originated from the Jain cuisine. It is a cuisine that has come to existence from the food preferences of its historic rulers and also the defining factor of geo-climatic availability of the ingredients involved. It is considered to be an impeccable aggregation of excellent Rajput-Jain history and the harsh reality of residing forests where meat eating is an essential necessity for living. Apparently, the culinary practices infused very deep into civilian households and blended with their local but amazing flavours.

The cuisine has been influenced largely due to altering geographies. Jowar (known as *jundi* in Bundelkhand) was considered to be a significant cereal in ancient times, but today wheat has replaced its utility and has emerged as a chief ingredient. The cuisine has been defined by the extensive use of different millets cultivated in this area. Wheat and milk are the chief local ingredients which are used generously in the cuisine.

The Bundeli *gosht* is a celebrated dish of the state in which tender lamb shank is pot-roasted with cardamom, mace and other fragrant herbs.

Deer meat was once a supreme delicacy from Bundelkhand, until its hunting was strictly forbidden by government. Wild game was also hunted, and pigeons, jungle fowl and quails were seen often on the menu. Wild boar is still consumed at times in the deep wilderness and forests but rarely among the villagers.

Culinary Trivia: Samosa

A *samosa* is a fried or baked pastry with savoury filling, such as spiced potatoes, onions, peas, lentils and sometimes ground lamb, ground beef or ground chicken. They may or may not contain pine nuts. They were introduced to South Asia (India and Pakistan) during the Muslim Delhi Sultanate when cooks from Middle East and Central Asia migrated to work in the kitchens of the Sultan and the noblity. Its size and consistency may vary, but it is distinctly triangular in shape. Indian *samosas* are usually vegetarian, and often accompanied by a mint sauce or *chutney.* With its origins in Uttar Pradesh, they are a popular appetizer or snack.

Samosa contains a *maida* flour shell stuffed with some filling, generally a mixture of mashed boiled potato, onion, green peas, spices and green chili. The entire pastry is then deep-fried to a golden brown colour, in vegetable oil. It is served hot and is often eaten with fresh Indian *chutney,* such as mint, coriander or tamarind. It can also be prepared in a sweet form, rather than as a savory one. *Samosas* are often served in *chaat,* along with the traditional accompaniments of yogurt, *chutney,* chopped onions, coriander, and *chaat masala.* The size, shape and consistency may vary, but typically, they are distinctly triangular.

Amir Khushro (1253–1325), a scholar and a royal poet of the Delhi Sultanate, wrote around 1300 AD that the princes and nobles enjoyed the "samosa prepared from meat, ghee, onion, and so on".

Ibn-Batuta, the 14th-century traveller and explorer, describes a meal at the court of Muhammad-bin-Tughluq, where the *samushak* or *sambusak,* a small pie stuffed with minced meat, almonds, pistachio, walnuts and spices, was served before the third course, of *pulao.*

The *Ain-i-Akbari,* a 16th-century Mughal document, mentions the recipe for *qutab,* which it says, "the people of Hindustan call *sanbúsah*".

20 Maharashtrian Cuisine

"I'm into very colorful food. Obviously lots of flavour, but I think we eat with our eyes first, so it has to look great. The presentation has to be great." – Giada De Laurentiis

Maharashtra is bordered by the Arabian Sea on the west, Gujarat and the Union Territory of Dadra and Nagar Haveli on the northwest, Madhya Pradesh on the north and northeast, Chhattisgarh on the east, Karnataka on the south, Andhra Pradesh on the southeast and Goa on the southwest.

Maharashtra is a Brobdingnagian state and its name itself signifies its gigantic connotation. The cuisine of Maharashtra is largely dominated by the landscape, the people and the crops grown in various regions. Maharashtrian cuisine has a broad spectrum of cuisine from being mild to very spicy dishes. Wheat, rice, *jowar, bajri* (bread made from millets like *jowar* and *bajra*), vegetables, lentils and fruit form important constitutents of Maharashtrian diet.

Maharashtra is famed not only for its panoptic array of subtle variety and robust taste but also for the significance given to the food. The saying *anna he poornabrahma* succinctly summarises what Maharashtrian feel about the food they cook and eat. They consider *anna*, or food, equal to *Brahma*, or the creator of the universe. Simply saying, Food is God, and hence is worthy to be worshipped. In formal meals, it is a practice to sing sacred verses to dedicate the meal to the God. This also connotes the importance of meal and God.

The Maharashtrian cuisine emphasizes and puts a lot of stress on the use of pounded *masalas* and lots of chillies, setting it apart from the rest of the regional cuisines. It has an incredible variation in snacks, assorted vegetarian and non-vegetarian dishes, lovely soups, pickles and desserts.

The cuisine derives a special taste due to the two unique spice combinations, i.e. *goda masala* and *kala masala*. The cuisine includes subtly flavoured vegetarian delicacies and hot, aromatic meat and fish curries. Their crackling and crisp sweets are made usually from rice and jaggery.

Charmed by the aesthetic presentation of food, people add extra grace to the feasts. The guests sit on floor rugs or red wooden seats and eat from silver or metal *thalis* and bowls placed on a raised '*chowrang*', or a short decorative table. *Rangolis* (auspicious patterns of coloured powder) are drawn around the *thali* or the *chowrang*. During the meal, each guest is given a bowl of saffron-scented water to dip the fingers in, before switching on to the next course, in order to avoid mixing of flavours. There is a particular order of serving the savouries and sweets, curries and rice or *rotis*, and a person unaware of this is not considered to be proficient in the art of hospitality. *Agarbattis* (incense sticks) spread fragrance everywhere and the host believes the satisfaction of his guests is his prime responsibility. This creates an altogether a unique atmosphere and a heavenly ambience in and around the dining area.

Maharashtrian meals (primarily lunch and dinner) are served on *thali*. Each food item served on the *thali* has an explicit place allotted to it. The *bhaaji* is served in the plate on the right hand side while the *chutney*, and *koshimbir* are served from left running along the outer boundary of the circular plate. The *papad, bhaaji* are served below the *koshimbir* with the rice and *poli* are served at the bottom of the circle close to the diner's hand. *Puran* is served at the top in the inner concentric circle. *Amti* and *rassa* are served in reparate bowls arranged on the right hand side of the diner. Water is always kept on the left hand side of the plate. Traditionally, the food is consumed using the right hand rather than using any cutlery. It is considered socially incorrect to involve left hand while eating. The left hand is only used to pick the glass of water. When everything is being served, the women of the house will serve the rice, pour a little *toop* (clarified butter) and *varan* (lentil) on the top of the rice and then the meal starts after a brief thanksgiving.

The vegetable preparations made from any peculiar vegetable or with a combination of vegetables are simply called *bhaajis*. A peculiar variant of the *bhaaji* is referred to as *rassa* or curry. Vegetarians here are very innovative in ideas to make the *rassa* or curry of potatoes and or caulifower with tomatoes or fresh coconut kernel and plenty of water to produce a soup-like preparation of a different form than *bhaaji*. The *rassa* has an excellent taste and texture, which is liked by all. In the vegetarian section, the most popular vegetables are brinjals. A popular technique of cooking brinjals is *bharli vangi* or baby brinjals stuffed with coconut. French beans vegetable (*farasbichi bhaaji*), jackfruit vegetable (*phansachi bhaaji*), spinach and buttermilk vegetable (*palakachi ta katli bhaaji*), banana flower vegetable (*kel phulachi bhaaji*) and *bombli batata bhaaji* are all popular Marathi recipes. The Maharashtrian fare seems to be incomplete without *papads*, which are eaten roasted or fried. *Papad* has been an indispensable item in the meal.

Varan is simply a plain *dal*, a common Indian lentil stew. *Aamti* is similarly a variant of *dal* preparation made interesting with the combination of sweet and sour flavours of jaggery and tamarind in it.

This state has proved its supremacy in the field of producing non-vegetarian dishes. The people primarily use chicken, mutton (mainly goat), fish and other seafood in their preparation. The *Kolhapuri taambda rassa* (red curry) and *pandhra rassa* (white curry) of chicken and mutton from the southern city of Kolhapur and the *varhadi rassa* or (*varhadi* chicken curry) from the Vidarbha region are dishes considered to be excellent and beyond comparison in this segment throughout Maharashtra. All non-vegetarian and vegetarian dishes are eaten with boiled rice or with *bhakris*, which are soft *rotis* made of rice flour. Unique rice *puri* called *vada* and *amboli*, which is a sort of pancake made of fermented rice, *urad dal*, and semolina, are also consumed as a part of the main meal.

The coastal regions of Konkan are renowned for its fish and seafood dishes and have contributed a lot in the shaping the Maharashtrian cuisine. Amongst seafood, the most popularly consumed fish is unarguably, *bombil* or the Bombay duck, which is normally, served batter fried and crisp.

Koshimbir is a very popular and healthy addition to the plate and has been a significant part in the meal. Typically, it is made from variety of raw vegetables like cucumbers, tomatoes, onion and spinach, mixed with yogurt and garnished with coriander and ground roasted peanuts (*danyache kut*) and it is also lightly seasoned with *phodni* (spices in hot oil). *Raitas* made with distinct vegetables such as cucumber or carrots are variants of *koshimbir*.

The cuisine of the state has witnessed grated coconut spicing with many kinds of dishes, but coconut oil is not very widely used as a cooking medium. Peanuts and cashew nuts are extensively used in vegetables and peanut oil is the main cooking medium.

The most unique and symbolic feature is the use of *kokum* in various delicacies. The *kokum* is a deep purple berry that has a pleasing sweet and sour taste. *Kokum*, most commonly used in an appetizer-digestive called the *sol kadhi*, is served chilled.

The people here are very religious in temperament and they keep fasting on certain occasions. Fasting time is also treated as a festive feast as the people in Maharashtra prepare an extensive array of dishes during this period. They prepare *sabudana chi khichadi* (*khichadi* made up of sago), *sabudana wada* (a deep fried snack), *batata chi khees* (grated-potato seasoned) during fasting. Peanuts find a special place in almost all preparations in one form or the other.

The most famed desserts of Maharashtra are the *puranpoli*, which is *roti* stuffed with a sweet mixture of jaggery and gram flour and the shreekhand, which is sweetened curds flavoured with cardamom and saffron.

Heavily based on traditions followed by family, majorly depending on the caste or specific religion; onion and garlic are also forbidden in the cooking. For example, a section of Hindu community in Maharashtra and other parts of India abstain from eating onion and garlic, specifically during *Chaturmas* (generally equates to the rainy or monsoon season).

Pickles are also an important factor in the meals of Maharashtrians and the people here prepare a vast variety of distinguished and remarkable pickles. Pickles are called *lonche* here. The main pickles are mustard pickles (*moharicha loncha*), *amla* pickles (*awlyacha loncha*), mango pickles (*ambycha loncha*), lemon pickles (*limbacha loncha*), *thecha* (basically meaning pounding, is a spicy *chutney* made by pounding green chillies and garlic and is accompanied during meal with bread), *papad*, and *daangar* (made of *urad dal* and buttermilk ground to paste and tempered with spices and is had with tamarind rice as an accompaniment).

Maharashtra has an extraordinarily unique culinary assemblage which is highly appreciated by every Indian. It is characterized by the tremendous usage of spices along with ginger-garlic and onion as well. Many appetizers have rose to prominence in Maharashtra and are relished with great gusto. It has *pohe*, *vada-pav*, *pav-bhaaji*, *misal-pav*, *zunkabhakar*, and so on.

As per the geographic location and on the basis of culinary distinction, this large state is divided into 5 main regions, namely Konkan, Vidarbha, Marathawad, Kolhapur and the Western Ghats.

Konkan

It is the coastal area comprising Raigarh, Sindhurgarh and Ratnagiri. It primarily comprises fish and coconut as the chief ingredient. A unique spice *tirphal* acts as a souring agent and is used almost in every fish preparation here. Sindhurgarh is renowned for pancakes such as *ambodi*, prepared from fermented batter of rice and *urad dal*. *Sabudana khichdi* is a very illustrious savoury pudding made of sago and groundnuts. *Thalipith* is another type of pancake usually made with a mixture of rice and various pulses and is mostly eaten during breakfast. *Usals*, a nutritious item, prepared from cereals, are often accompanied with fish curries in this part of the state. The populace of Konkanastha Brahmins sparingly use tamarind, jaggery and asafoetida to add new flavour to their food as compared to other.

Ratnagiri is famous all over the world for the mango variety considered to the king of mangoes, Alphanso or *Hapus*. It is also famed for the celebrated dish *sukhe mutton* or dried lamb.

Vidarbha

Situated in the north-eastern part, this area comprises districts like Nagpur, Chandrapur, and so on. The farmers eat a dish prepared with raw *jowar* that is roasted and mixed with curds, and is known as *hurda*. Spicy food is preferred. It is common to consume raw onion, green chillies with almost any meal they eat. *Poha* is a wonderful dish of this region and is famed all across Maharashtra. Nagpur is renowned in the world for the production of best oranges.

Kolhapur

Situated in south of Maharashtra, this area comprises Satera, Sangli, Solhapur and Kolhapur. This area has been known and characterized by the famous non-vegetarian dishes. This region witnesses scanty rainfall, leading to hardships in the life of people residing here, due to dearth of water. *Jowar* is the staple crop and hence the *bhakri* made from *jowar* is consumed commonly. The consumption of spices, in all preparations, is on the higher side and hence the dishes are spicy and fiery red in colour. *Larangi mirchi* belongs to this region. Mutton Kolhapuri is the highly esteemed dish of this region. The popular snacks are *poha, sheera, kurdai* and *malpuas*, consumed with tea during evening.

Marathwad

Situated in the east of Maharashtra, this area comprises cities like Aurangabad, Nander and Latur. The people here prefer moderately spiced food and they use freshly ground *masalas* and ingredients for the preparation of various dishes.

Western Ghats

Located on the northwest coastline along the Arabian Sea, this area includes Nasik, Pune and Mumbai. The food is preferred moderately spiced or with very less spices. Bombil or Bombay duck is a dried variety of fish, which has a very unique smell. It is prepared in gravy or is just stir-fried and served. Pickles, *chutney, papad, koshimbir* (an Indian version of salads) is a popular accompaniment to food in this region. *Dadpe poha* is made from pressed rice, onions, salt, green chillies, green coriander, and lime juice and then tempered with asafoetida, curry leaves and mustard seed. This is consumed with great gusto during breakfast.

The main meal comprises boiled rice, *varan* (plain *arhar dal*) with some ghee in it, *polis* (local term for breads made from flour), two or three vegetable dishes, *koshimbir* (salads), *chutneys* of garlic or peanuts, and a lemon wedges. *Goda masala* is a common spice concoction used in Maharashtrian cooking which comes from this area.

Maharashtra is a large state with a motley of exemplary cuisines that can also be broadly bifurcated into two major division, viz. the coastal and interior regions.

A major part of Maharashtra, which lies on the coast of the Arabian Sea is called the Konkani and highly appreciates its own Konkani cuisine, which is a homogeneous consolidation of Malvani, Gaud Saraswat Brahmin, and Goan cuisines. The core of Maharashtra cuisine is referred as Varadi cuisine.

Konkani Cuisine: The cuisine of Konkan is very exquisite in nature. The coastal area of Konkan is rich in terms of ingredients produced here, like coconuts, mangoes, cashew nut, rice and a variety of pulses. The region is also capable of growing *kokum* aplenty, which is a sweet-sour fruit. It is chiefly used as the souring agent in curries as a substitute of tamarind or tomatoes. *Kokum* is versatile in its use as it is also used in making soups as well. A special spice *tirphal* is used as an ingredient to sour the fish dishes in the region of Konkan. Fish and seafood are available in aplenty. All these ingredients have contributed a lot in defining Konkani food. A typical Konkani meal, therefore, will compulsorily have fish curry served with rice. The populaces which are lacto-vegetarians will have rice as their chief staple with vegetables and lentils in their diets. *Popadams* prepared from rice floor are also a Konkani specialty. Besides these fish, crabs, prawns, shellfish, and lobsters are also relished by the coastal Maharashtrians.

Malvani Cuisine: Malvan is the area in the southernmost district of Maharashtra – Sindhudurg.

The food from Malvan and its surrounding areas are known as Malvani cuisine. Despite being a part of the Konkan region, it has created an entirely different cuisine with a revered identity. The Malvan region has its border with Goa on the south and Kolhapur on the east. The west coast is the Arabian Sea. The sea heavily influences the food. Hence, heavy consumption of fresh coconut and seafood is easily visible and reflected in the cuisine. The Malvani prawn *pulao* is a typical Malvan delectable delicacy in which the prawn is marinated in a fresh green paste and then steamed along with the rice. Similarly, *dalitoy* which is a vegetarian lentil soup made up of vegetables and coconut is also known for its greatness in the culinary section. It is highly respected in every home-made meal.

Certain breads from this region are also popular like *ghavan* which is a pancake having a net-like appearance and is enjoyed hugely by the people. The other is *dhonda* or cucumber cake which is a wonderfully tasting dish baked from cucumber and jaggery. Sweet dishes like *khaproli* which is a light-weight pancake dipped in sweetened and yellow coloured syrup and *Malvani malpua* is a sweet item deep fried in oil and is enjoyed by the Muslim populace during the Ramzan festival takes the cuisine of this region to a very different level altogether. Thus, Malvani cuisine has bestowed certain preparations, which are of high repute in the world of culinary fare.

Varadi Cuisine: Besides the coastal cuisine, the interior region of Maharashtra, the Vidarbha area has sprung up with a typical and distinctive cuisine known as the Varadi cuisine. The Varadi cuisine has been known for the superb equilibrium it has maintained in between spices and the extensive use of powdered coconut and *besan* (gram flour) – the latter being used more in the vegetarian dishes. Chicken and mutton are distinctively popular in this region since seafood is scantily available. Commonly used spices in this area are black pepper, dry coriander, bay leaves, cardamom, cinnamon and cloves. The food is cooked mainly in earthern pots, which lends it a rusty and robust flavour. Some of the distinguishing features of this cuisine are that it includes many dishes made of *besan* (gram flour) like *zunka bhakar* and *pathawadi* and *vada bhat*. *Varadi rassa* (*Saoji* curry) is the splendid gravy chiefly used in preparing meat dishes. This gravy is commonly used in preparing chicken and mutton curries. However, it is also used to prepare vegetarian dishes, using potato, paneer or soya chunks as well. *Saoji* chicken or mutton is known for its spicy taste.

Bombay has its own collection of amazing dishes like *vadapav*, *misal* and *pavbhaaji*. *Chaat* is perhaps the most widely consumed street food in the city, ensued by *bhelpuri*, *panipuri*, *pavbhaaji*, and *dosa*. The non-vegetarian people are delighted with the vast collection of snacks items, such as *kebabs*, *baida roti*, *tandoori* chicken, *seekh kebabs* and *fish koliwada*. In Mumbai, the entire meal is often followed by *paan*. *Paan* is an assortment of dates, beetle nut, dry grated coconut, saunf, rose petal jam, some spices like clove or cardamom wrapped in betel leaf. It is considered to be blessed with a digestive and coolant features.

Specialty Dishes

Pohe

Pohe is a simple and fragrant preparation consumed in breakfast. It is made of flattened rice, chopped onion, green chillies, peanut, green peas, mustard seeds, asafoetida, lemon juice, turmeric powder, a pinch of sugar and salt. It is made lively by the incorporation of fresh fragrant curry leaves in it. Other variants are *batata pohe* (where diced potatoes are used), *dadpe pohe*, a mixture of raw *pohe* with shredded fresh coconut, green chillies, ginger and lemon juice; and so on.

Vada Pav

Vada pav is undoubtedly the most popular food of the state. *Vada pav* consists of deep fried mashed potato dumpling (*vada*), eaten sandwiched in a wheat bun (*pav*) and is almost always accompanied with the famous red chutney made from garlic and chillies, and fried green chillies. *Batata vada* refers in Marathi, to a *vada* (fritter) made out of *batata*, the latter referring to a potato and *pav* to unsweetened bread or bun.

Sabudana Vada

It is a traditional deep fried snack and is consumed with spicy *chutney* and tea. The *sabudana* (sago) is soaked overnight, potato is boiled and mashed, and peanuts are roasted and ground to a coarse powder after removing the husk. Then all these three ingredients are mixed properly with red chilli powder, chopped green chillies and coriander leaves with salt. Balls are made out of it and flattened slightly to give it shape of a disc and then it is deep fried and served hot and fresh.

Pav-Bhaaji

This special dish from Mumbai made of mashed and steamed mixed vegetables concoction (mainly potatoes, capsicum, peas, tomatoes, onions and green pepper) cooked in spices and butter. The assorted vegetable mix in tomato dominated gravy is served with soft wheat bun, shallow fried in butter, and chopped onions.

Misal Pav

It is a delicacy from Kolhapur which is a curried mix of sprouted lentils, topped with *batata bhaaji, pohe, chivda, sev, farsaan,* raw chopped onions and tomato. It is sometimes eaten with yogurt and is served with wheat bread bun.

Tilgud Ladoo

This is specialty during the festive period of Makar Sankranti and is made using jaggery and sesame seeds. It is shaped into round dumplings. It is distributed during Makar Sankranti and while distributing 'tilgud ghya ani godh godh bola' is chanted, meaning 'take tilgud and speak as sweet as possible' in English. It is relished by everyone with great delight. It is nutritious as it has all the goodness of sesame seeds.

Zunka Bhakar

A native Maharashtrian chick pea flour delicacy eaten with *bhakri* (flat bread) made either with *bajri* (pearl millets) or *jwari* (millets). It is considered to be the food of the poor people at one time, as it is low in cost.

Dalimbi

It is a traditional preparation in which field beans are cooked with *kokum* which imparts a subtlety of sour flavours that are distinctly different from the tartness of tamarind or lemon. *Kokum* is the dried peel of the fruit which is grown along the coast.

Methi Che Varan

It is a simple *toovar dal* preparation in which the *dal* is cooked by chopped fresh fenugreek leaves and tempered with garlic, jaggery, mustard seeds and asafoetida. It is cooked in no time and is served with steamed rice or *rotis*. The addition of fenugreek leaves takes this dish to a different level.

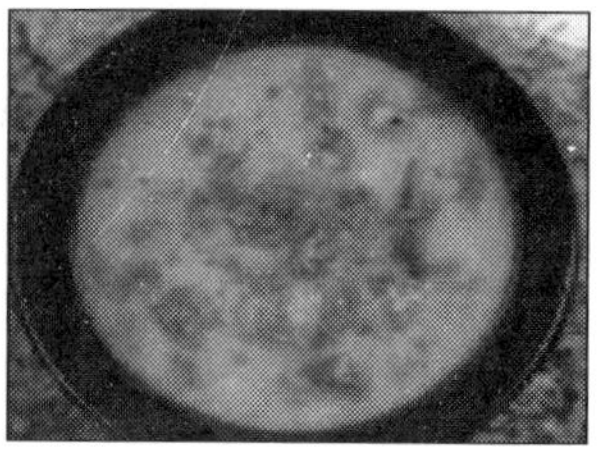

Malvani Chana Masala It is a special preparation of green *chana*, which is cooked and crushed to a very convenient consistency before being used in the gravy. In this dish, tamarind is used instead of tomatoes, which adds uniqueness and pungency to the dish. Also, in this dish a mixture of *malvani masala* is used, which is prepared by grinding all the roasted ingredients.	
Batata Chi Bhaaji It is a simple dish of boiled potatoes tempered with green chillies and curry leaves and spiced up with crushed peanuts. Also referred as *Puneri aloo*, this is also enjoyed during fasting days. It is one of the simplest potato dishes, yet consumed with great gusto.	
Bharleli Vaangi It is a delicacy with small brinjals stuffed with a sweet and spicy peanut flavoured concoction bringing out all the authentic flavours of Maharashtrian cooking. The brinjals have to be cooked over a slow flame with great care in order to retain the natural flavours of this dish.	
Faraali Misal The marvellous *sabudana khichdi* is topped with a peanut-potato mixture and *faraali chivda* to get the most desired Faraali Misal. This dish is enjoyed during fasting days.	
Danyachi Usal It is a sumptuous preparation of boiled peanuts flavoured with a coconut-based paste. A simple seasoning of cumin seeds enhances the flavour and aroma of the curry manifold.	
Masala Bhaat This traditional rice preparation is an amazing combination of spicy flavours and mouth-watering textures. When served with curds or *raita*, it is considered to be a complete meal in itself. Vegetables like brinjals and *tendli* are used but other vegetables can also be used depending upon the availability during the season, to make the meal more nutritious.	
Kothimbir Vadi In this dish chick pea flour is mixed with red chilli powder, turmeric and coriander powder and a batter is prepared. Then a casserole is greased and the batter mixture is poured into it with sprinkling of sesame seeds on it and then it is steamed. After steaming it is cut into pieces and then deep fried.	

Amti

Aamti is a variant of curry, typically consisting of a *lentil* (toovar) stock, flavoured with *goda masala,* tamarind and jaggery and in some cases coconut as well. Simply stated this is sweet and sour flavoured *toovar dal* dish.

Tambda Rassa

It is a spicy and delectable red curried Kolhapuri dish prepared using mutton and spicy stock. It is very aromatic due to the use of fresh spices and gets perfect blends of flavours and taste as it is prepared with mutton stock. It is very spicy and cannot be tolerated by mild spice eater.

Pandhra Rassa

Pandhra means white curry and it is a liked by all in Kolhapur. It is a soup like dish of water used to boil the mutton along with spices such as coriander, ginger and garlic and so on. This is a very tasty item consumed before the meal. This *rassa* is also used to cure certain cough and throat related ailments.

Sungtachi Jhinga Kodi

It is a popular prawn dish which consists of prawns in coconut gravy, blended with spices and asafoetida.

Sol Kadhi

Sol kadhi is the most refreshing appetizer drink of this state, which originated in the Konkan region of Maharashtra. It is made of *kokum* fruit, coconut milk and flavoured with garlic and cumin. Konkani or Malvani cuisine is little spicy and *sol kadhi* gives soothing effect after a hot and spicy and delicious meal. It can be had as an effective appetizer just before the meals and during meals, or even as a digestive after meals. *Sol kadhi* can be served chilled or lukewarm.

Tomato Saar

Tomato *saar* is a spicy flavoured tomato broth and is a classic culinary creation of the state of Maharashtra. It portrays an impeccable balance in combination of flavours – slightly sweet, slightly tangy, slightly spicy and slightly salty. Maharashtrians like to pour it over steamed white rice or *masale bhaat* or simply slurp it all up like a soup. It has a unique fragrance that comes out of it.

Kokam Saar

It is a mouth-watering soup prepared from dried *kokam.* The alkaline properties of *kokum saar* neutralizes the pH and helps restore gastric balance and hence is very useful in acidity disorders.

Puran Poli

It is one of the most popular sweet items in the Maharashtrian cuisine. It is made from jaggery, yellow gram (*chana*) *dal*, plain flour, cardamom powder and ghee. It is made by stuffing sweet *dal* mixture in flour dough and then cooking it by shallow frying. This is prepared during almost all festivals.

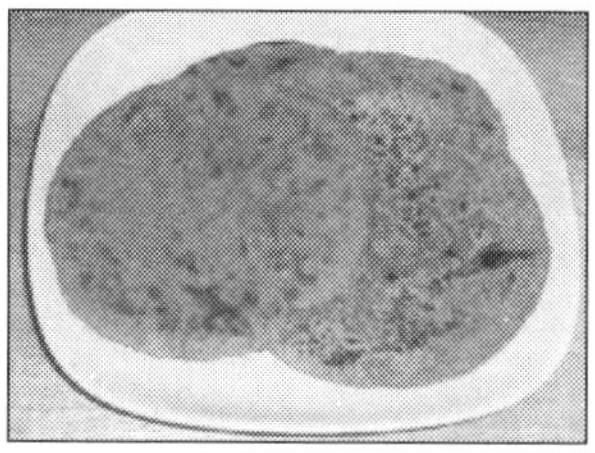

Modak

Modak is a sweet dumpling made by stuffing the sweet filling of fresh grated coconut and jaggery in the soft shell which is made from rice flour, or wheat flour. The dumpling can be fried or steamed. The steamed version, called *ukdi che modak*, is consumed hot with ghee. It is considered the favourite food of Lord Ganesha and hence this food is offered to him during Ganesh Chaturthi.

Karanji

It is a deep-fried dumpling with a filling of grated coconut sweetened with jaggery and flavoured with powdered cardamom seeds. It is crescent in shape and it is a common sweet during Diwali. It is also known as *gujiya* in North India.

Anarsa

It is the preparation which is made by soaking rice for 3-4 days in fresh water daily. After this, the rice needs to be dried till it has slight moisture. The moist rice is then ground into a fine powder and pressed with the palm of the hand into pressed dumpling. It tends to take the shape of a *Pithi*. After this, the *Pithi* is added with sugar or jaggery and small lumps are created. The *pithi* retains the shape given, as rice has little moisture when added in sugar or jaggery. This mixture can be stored for a few days at room temperature as long as the moisture is retained in airtight container during storage. Small flat discs with about 2 inches in diameter are created by flattening a small ball of the dough over a layer of poppy seeds, just on one side. These disks are fried with the poppy coated side first into hot ghee. It is then ready to be served. *Anarsa* is a little difficult to prepare, due to tedious tasks attached to it. It is made during festive occasions.

Shevaya chi Kheer

It is prepared by cooking *shevaya* (vermicelli) in milk. The preparation is sweetened with jaggery or sugar, flavoured with powdered cardamom seeds and finally garnished with chopped nuts.

Narali Bhaat

This is a sweet rice preparation made using coconut with special flavouring of cardamom and cloves. This is the special dish for the festive occasions of Narali Pornima, which falls on the Full Moon day in the Hindu month of Shravan (August).

Shrikhand It is sweetened yogurt flavoured with saffron, cardamom and *charoli* nuts. Here it is consumed with *puri*. The strained yogurt is referred to as *chakka*. It is then added with sugar and mixed thoroughly in a deep bowl. Cardamom, saffron, and other flavouring agents are then added and mixed properly. It is then left in the refrigerator to cool. The dish is served chilled. Nowadays, the *shrikhand* is available in many flavours like saffron flavoured, pista flavoured and mango flavour as well.	
Shankarpali In this dish, sweetened flour is cut into various fancy shapes like diamond and is square and then deep fried. It is prepared from a dough of milk, sugar, ghee, refined flour, semolina and salt. The mixture is made into a dough and then cut into diamond shaped pieces which are deep fried in ghee or butter. It is traditionally enjoyed as a treat on the Diwali festival.	
Gulachi Poli This preparation is made especially on the occasion of Makar Sankranti in typical Brahmin households. *Gulachi poli* is made with a stuffing of soft and shredded jaggery mixed with toasted, ground *til* (white sesame seeds) and some gram flour which has been toasted to golden colour in plenty of pure ghee. The dish is made like a *paratha* like that of a stuffed *roti* fried on pure ghee till crisp on both sides. Its taste seems to be heavenly when eaten slightly warm with liberal amount of desi ghee.	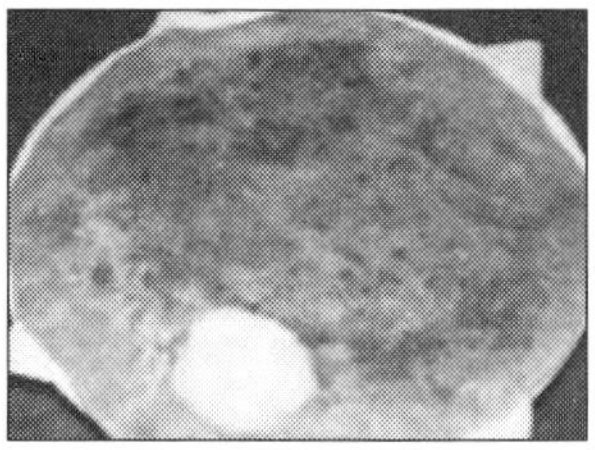
Amras This dish is made from mangoes. The term is inderived from the combination of *aam* (mango) and *ras* (juice), *Aamras* or *amras*. This is the pulp of the tropical fruit Mango and the pulp of ripe mangoes is extracted usually by hand and consumed along with *chapati* or *puri*. In order to enhance the flavour, ghee, milk and sugar are added to the pulp. It can be made during the period when the market is flooded with fresh mangoes.	
Chitranna This is a preparation made up of green gram *dal* and rice soaked together. It is boiled and then tempered with ginger, green chillies, mustard seeds, cumin seeds, curry leaves and turmeric. The preparation when done is finished with sprinkling of grated coconut and lemon juice on it.	
Vaangi Bhaat This is a simple and basic brinjal-rice preparation. A tempering is prepared done mustard seeds, black gram *dal*, bengal gram *dal*, and dry chillies in ghee. Brinjals cooked in buttermilk are then added to it. The rice is added with the required water to cook. The rice needs to be seasoned well. Turmeric and green chillies are also added. Finally, a spice powder prepared with black pepper, cloves, cinnamon, coriander, and cumin seeds are added. It tastes amazingly great due to the combination of brinjals and rice in it.	

Culinary Trivia: Kulfi

Kulfi is a popular frozen dairy dessert from the Indian subcontinent and is often described as "traditional Indian ice cream". It is denser and creamier as compared to normal ice cream. It comes in various flavours. The more traditional ones are cream (*malai*), rose, mango, cardamom (*elaichi*), saffron (*kesar* or *zafran*), and pistachio. *Kulfi* is not whipped and hence results in a solid, dense frozen dessert similar to traditional custard based ice cream. Thus, it is sometimes considered a distinct category of frozen dairy-based dessert. Due to its density, *kulfi* takes a longer time to melt than Western ice creams.

Kulfi was traditionally prepared by evaporating sweetened and flavoured milk via slow cooking with almost continuous stirring to keep milk from sticking to the bottom of the vessel where it might burn, until its volume was reduced by half, thus thickening it, increasing its fat, protein and lactose density. It has a distinctive taste due to caramelization of lactose and sugar during the lengthy cooking process. The semi-condensed mix is then frozen in tightly sealed moulds (often *kulhars* with their mouths sealed) that are then submerged in ice mixed with salt to speed up the freezing process. The ice/salt mixes, along with its submerged *kulfi* moulds, is placed in a *matka* or an earthen pot that provides insulation from the external heat and slow down the melting of ice. *Kulfi* prepared in this manner is hence called Matka Kulfi.

Kulfi is also served with *faloodeh* (vermicelli noodles made from starch). Traditionally in India, *kulfi* is sold by vendors called *kulfiwala* who keep the *kulfi* frozen by placing the moulds inside a large earthenware pot called *matka,* filled with ice and salt. It is served on a leaf or frozen onto a stick. Often it is served as *falooda kulfi,* which is *kulfi* with rice noodles, rose or any flavour sugar syrup and other ingredients.

21 North-Eastern Cuisine of India

"I have an enormous fondness for delicious food. It's very comforting." – Teri Garr

The North-East Zone of India comprises seven states. These are popularly called 'Seven Sisters of India'.

The states which come under this zone are:

- Arunachal Pradesh
- Assam
- Manipur
- Meghalaya
- Mizoram
- Nagaland
- Tripura

Arunachal Pradesh

Arunachal Pradesh, situated in northeast India is bordered by Assam and Nagaland on the south, and shares international borders with Bhutan on the west, Myanmar on the east and the People's Republic of China on the north.

Arunachal Pradesh means the 'land of the dawn-lit mountains' or the 'land of the rising sun'. The sun rays hit the land of this state before spreading to other states of India, due to its geographical location.

Arunachal Pradesh is a vivid coalescesence of varied tribal communities and individual preferences of the various tribes and these are mirrored in the cuisine of the state. The chasteness of the tribal culture, their ultimate lifestyle and the availability of the local ingredients has been the defining criterion of the resplendent and recherché cuisine of Arunachal Pradesh. The cuisine is unarguably varied, similar to the different tribal communities living in this hilly state. The state has many tribes, which are further divided into sub-tribes and each has its own style of cooking, contributing to the richness and vastness to the cuisine. Speaking without any ornamentation, the cuisine is characterized by a subtle taste often described as bland but has its own unique flavours to mesmerize the diner with its tarrying flavours and amazing taste. It has non-spicy food which is seldom aromatic and is rarely fried. The dishes are mostly seasoned with the locally available bamboo shoots, which is a significant ingredient in their cooking patterns. Certain edible herbs are incorporated to enhance the taste and flavour the dishes.

Arunachal Pradesh is an agrarian state, blessed with the appreciable production of cereal crops. Rice, buckwheat, soya bean, wheat, millets, sugarcane, oilseeds and maize are the common crops produced and cultivated in the state. These crops are used in a variety of ways in the day-to-day meals as well as in meals that are cooked on any grand opulent event. Fruits and vegetables of distinct varieties are largely cultivated throughout the state and popularly consumed by the people. Oranges, plum, peach, pineapple and cherries are heavily produced and consumed in the state. Its lettuce is tremendously famed. Nonetheless, leafy vegetables and maize are common in their food. They are essentially non-vegetarian and consume meat on a large scale. The collection of non-vegetarian dishes forms the integral part of their cuisine. The inhabitants of this state also love to relish various fish and egg preparation besides the meat varieties like chicken, pork and mutton.

Rice is chief staple food of the people, as its production is very high in the state. *Apong* is a very popularly consumed rice beer made from fermented rice and millets. It is the preferred local drink consumed with the intention to relieve stress. Rice is a multifaceted ingredient and hence it is used in the boiled state to prepare a variety of snacks and delicacies, like rice cakes.

Chhurpi is simply the paneer prepared from the milk of the yak. The presence of *chhurpi* in the homes of Arunachal Pradesh is an indication of its opulent social status. Based on the classification of age, *chhurpi* is majorly of three types, i.e., *chhur singba, chhur chirpen* and *chhur pupu*. The fresh *chhurpi* is called *chhur singba* or *chhur minga*. It is the similar to paneer like product made from yak milk after fermentation of the milk by addition of extract of crab apple fruits. The *Chhurpi* which is 3-4 days old are referred to as *chhur chirpen* whereas the *chhurpi* which is 4-5 years old and kept in bags made of yak skin is termed *chhur pupu*.

The authentic cuisine of Arunachal Pradesh is considered to be highly nutritional. The dishes are very simple to prepare and delicious. Characterized by non use of oil and Indian spices, it is cooked by mostly steaming and boiling method to preserve the natural goodness of the ingredients used. The nutritional value of the food is highly enhanced by the use of local herbs packed with medicinal properties and also by fresh spices which are grown in the region. The cuisine of this state has been conferred with a typical taste and indistinguishability, due to the use of very fresh organic vegetables, fragrant herbs with medicinal powers and tender bamboo shoots and various scented leaves. Meat, fish and eggs are a good source of protein and hence they contribute in meliorating the cuisine with features of good health.

Brass utensils are used by common populace in the state to cook food.

Alcohol is a significant constituent of the cuisine of Arunachal Pradesh and is mostly served after every meal.

Thus, the cuisine of Arunachal Pradesh is exquisite and requires a deep sense of culinary knowledge to appreciate the cuisine.

Specialty Dishes

Momo

It is unarguably the signature dish of the state and the whole country is really delighted with the taste of this delicacy. Momo has been famed to such a level that it would be be next to impossible to find any nook and corner of the country without a sale counter of steaming momos with bright spicy red sauce. It has been a matter of uncertainty about its origin, but it is certain that it was the *monpa* tribe of Arunachal Pradesh that is solely responsible for bringing this dish to the cutting edge perspective and hence, contributing in its immense popularity. This dish is either available as a steamed or in a fried form. It is basically dough stuffed with a mixture of onion and meat served steaming hot accompanied with spicy chilly sauce and tasty soup. This dish is delicious and is one of the most famous dishes available all across the country.

Zan

It is the chief food of the *monpa* tribe and is a popular preparation made using millets or flour with boiling water.

Khura

It is a popularly consumed snack relished with tea, which is essentially a pancake made of little *chang*, water and flour.

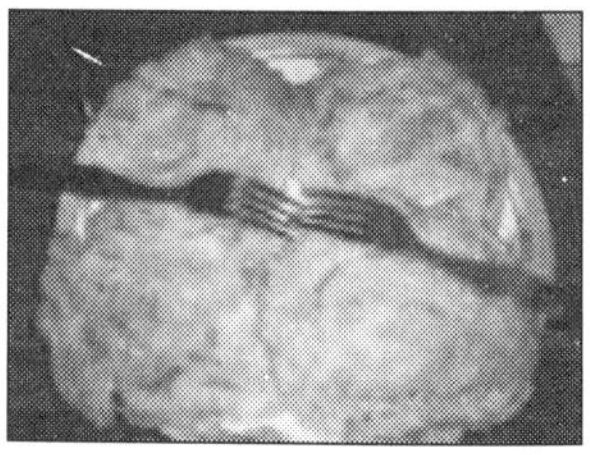

Thukpa

It can be mentioned as one of the most famous dishes. Thukpa is an amazing preparation made with noodles, minced meat and soup. This is a light and highly nutritious dish. It is available in three forms:

- ***Dre thuk:*** It is prepared from noodles, minced meat and soup.
- ***Ashum thukpa***: It is prepared from maize, beans and meat.
- ***Bak tza:*** It is prepared from flat rectangular shaped dough, minced meat and soup.

Wungwut Ngam It is an extraordinarily good dish involving chicken and rice powder and is cooked in a traditional style.	
Ngatok It is an ethnic fish curry prepared in a distinct method using a heated stone, charcoal or wood coal or ashes. It is cooked with local spices which imparts it a unique flavour and taste.	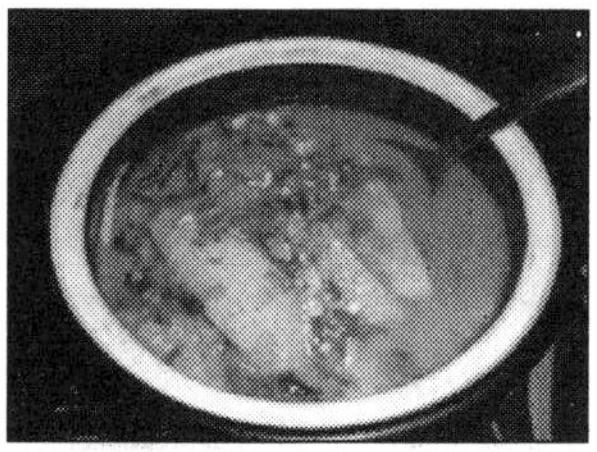
Pasa This tribal soup is a wonderful dish prepared using raw fish with the addition of various spices and leaves.	

Assam

Assam, situated in the north-eastern region of India is surrounded by six of the other Seven Sister States: Arunachal Pradesh, Nagaland, Manipur, Mizoram, Tripura and Meghalaya.

Assam has an endearing beauty and is mesmerizing land gifted with adorable hills, lovely valleys, wonderful landscape, dense green forests and the vast River Brahmaputra.

Assam, acknowledged worldwide for being the largest tea growing area, is hugely famed all across the world for its splendid collection of amazing flavoured tea. The food of Assam depicts the impact of the climatic conditions as well as the cultural variation among the people. The cuisine of Assam is characterized by simplistic features and is convenient to cook. Nonetheless, this simple cuisine is distinguished by its typical flavour and unique taste and is like by the populace to a great extent.

The kitchen was considered to be the demesne, especially of the women. Women were actually superior in the tasks associated with the kitchen. Women carried a great competency related with the kitchen associated tasks and have mastered their culinary proficiency. The kitchen of the Ahom king was taken great care and managed by the Sangmais. They basically hailed from the Barahi community, famed for their culinary and faithfulness. The person authorized to supervise the kitchen were referred as Sangmai Barua. The Sangmais had no documentation which can be used as a reference to follow. They mastered their culinary expertise to cater to the distinct taste preferences of all kings and queens.

The Assamese cuisine has adopted a cooking pattern which seems to be agile and elementary in nature. The Assamese people have a strong preference for non-spicy food prepared with less consumption oil. The popularly used spices in the preparation of the cuisine of this state are ginger, mustard, garlic, coriander, cardamom, cumin, and the *pas phoron* (*panch phoran*) which consists of fenugreek seeds, nigella seeds, fennel seeds, cumin seeds and black mustard seeds. Rice is the chief staple item of the Assamese cuisine and all other dishes are mostly based on it. Simply speaking, it can be said that rice is an essential part of all meals in Assam. The Assamase people generally take three meals a day. They take the first meal of the day, early in the morning. The tradition of consuming *poita bhat* was usual in most of the families. The first meal of the day here is the cooked rice kept overnight in cold water. It is consumed with additions of pickles, roasted fish, roasted vegetables, green chilly, salt, mustard oil, and so on. The people here prepare a special kind of sauce named as *kharoli*, with ground mustard seed and salt. It is prepared in most households. In a few parts of the valley, there was the tradition of consuming *maar bhat*. It is essentially rice cooked without draining the starch and boiled along with few vegetables and salt. Certain other preparations based on rice were also consumed and they were *komal chaul*, a sort of tiffin rice, *cira*, simple pounded parched rice and eaten as food, *akhai*, parched paddy free from the husk, *muri*, puffed rice, *sandoh guri*, essentially a coarse powder of parched rice, *pitha guri*, powdered rice, and so on. All these preparations were consumed with milk and *gur* or molasses. As it is an agrarian state, in the rural areas, the first meal of the day was packed and carried to the field for the working farmers who left home early in the morning. The farmers used to start their work before sunrise. The chief meal of the day was supposed to be consumed during the noon. Simple and plain boiled rice was eaten with many different accompaniments. Thus, rice has been an essential and integral part of a traditional breakfast and snacks. During special functions or occasions, a distinct class of rice cake delicacy called *pitha* is dished up. Taste has been the mainstay of the Assamese cuisine and it is an assemblage of all six tastes sweet, sour, salty, pungent, bitter and astringent.

Fish has been a keystone ingredient of the Assamese food culture. Being a hilly region, a huge variety of fruits and green vegetables are available here, which form an essential part of the everyday meal.

The Assamese people have a unique style of eating and tasting each dish. They separately eat each dish with an appropriate quantity of rice in order to actually savour the individualistic taste of each preparation. Rice never dominates the taste of any preparation. The meal starts with the delicate tasting ones and gradually shifts to dominating ones. An Assamese meal is traditionally served in bell metal utensils. In the centre of a bell metal utensil dish called *kahi*, in which a small pile up of piping hot rice served along with pieces of lime, whole green chillies and about a spoonful of side dishes like *kharoli* made of mustard paste, and *khorisa*, made from mashed fermented bamboo shoots.

A traditional Assamese fare commences with *khar* or alkali and finishes with tenga or sour ones. *Khar* is a celebrated dish prepared by using the banana plant and is traditional and unique to the state of Assam. It is the first course to be served taken with rice. The ashes of dried bark and root of the plantain tree is alkaline in properties. The people used to preserve the ash-leach for its salty and alkaline properties. A dish enhanced with the seasoning of that liquid is referred to as *khar*. This home prepared alkali was used in various curries of vegetables like papaya, gourds, black gram, and leafy vegetables. *Pasala* was another distinctive and unique item prepared with *khar*. *Pasala* was made with the tender part of plantain sapling. It is suggested to eat *khar* once in a while for its medicinal properties.

Tenga is also an assorted group of preparation which is a light and sour dish incorporating fish. Tenga has become such a preparation that it has to be there in a proper Assamese meal. Fish and vegetable curries are seasoned either with lemon juice, tamarind or *thekera*, a locally available citric fruit, are popularly consumed *tenga* items. *Khar* is ensued by *xaak bhaaji* (dry green leafy vegetables). Then *pitika* is served, which is basically a side dish prepared with steamed and mashed vegetables, seasoned particularly with mustard oil and spices. *Aloo pitika* (mashed potato) is a very popular item consumed here and hence people eat it with great gusto. Potato has been the most popular vegetable of Assam. After this, *daali* (pulses) accompanied by *pokori* (fritters) and *bhaaji* (fries of fish and vegetables) is served. Then it is followed by *torkari* (vegetable dishes) and *manxor jhul* (meat preparation). *Haanh* (duck), *manxo* (mutton), *kukura* (chicken), *gahori* (pork) are the most favourite varieties of meat here. The meal is summed up by the most crucial *maasor tenga*.

The bitter tasting item *teeta* is prepared with vegetables having bitter taste like bitter gourd, neem leaves, cane shoots, *teeta phool*, *teeta bhekuri*, and so on. *Shokota* is another bitter item consumed here. It is prepared with dried tender leaves of the jute plant. It is mandatory to consume *teeta* was once in a fortnight only because of its medicinal properties. These bitter items are present in the kitchen of both the affluent and the poor.

Curry is an absolute essential accompaniment to rice. Curries can be both vegetarian and non-vegetarian. The Assamese people have a great liking towards non-vegetarian dishes and hence are mostly non-vegetarian. Fish, meat and eggs all have contributed to their non-vegetarian resource. The Hindus, even the brahmins of Assam are generally non-vegetarian and are dissimilar to the brahmins from the rest of India. This difference has been due to the non-Aryan influence over the Assamese culture. Assamese curries are mild and subtle in taste by nature. The humid climate prevailing in the region has encouraged them to follow certain practices, in order to keep their stomach cool and also to avoid the digestive disturbances. Hot spices are not grown here and hence are not available. The traditional Assamese delicacies hence use minimal quantity of spices. Condiments and spices like turmeric, ginger, garlic, mustard seeds, black pepper, hing (asafoetida) were easily available in pre-colonial Assam. One or two items of curry had to be served with vegetable or fish delicacies. The ladies looking after the kitchen would take extra care to balance the flavour and texture of the meal. Most of the women have mastered this art of blending the taste and also in the presentation. This sort of professionalism has been passed down to their successors.

The vegetarian dishes are essentially the simple curries of mixed vegetables. In Assam, the collective term used for vegetables is *Saak Pachali*. This term is very broad and comprehensive and it encompasses the ripe vegetables, leaves, herbs, tubes, roots, flowers and pods. The green vegetables in the diet consists more of leaves and tender stems than fruits and roots. Here, one can experience the several varieties of local potatoes like *kaath aloo* or hard yam, *moa aloo* or sweet yam, *mitha aloo* or sweet potato, *ada aloo, miri aloo* and *sina aloo.* Varied kinds of gourds are also cultivated here, namely, *panilau* (bottle gourd), *rangalau* (pumpkin), *komora* (white gourd melon), and *jika, bhul.* Even brinjals of distinct sizes are very common with the people. Both leaves and roots are most used in various curries.

Jolpan or snacks are an unavoidable and inseparable part of the Assamese cuisine. Though *jolpan* is usually served at breakfast, it is even served during the occasions of festivals and weddings too. *Jolpan* is again centred on rice which is the quintessential ingredient. It may comprise *bora saul* (a variety of rice, boiled and served as *jolpan* with curds or milk, jaggery or sugar), *Komal saul* (a very unique variety of rice from Assam that can be eaten without cooking but just by soaking in water for sometime), *xandoh, chira* (flattened rice), *muri* (puffed rice), *akhoi,* along with curds, jaggery, yogurt and assorted kinds of *pitha* (rice cake or pan cake), *laru* (sweet balls) and tea.

Assamese cuisine has excelled in the preparation of delicacy *pithas.* Amazing motley of unique *pitha* is popular in Assam which includes *til pitha, ghila pitha, sunga pitha, uhuwa pitha, tekeli pitha, deksi pitha,* and so on. *Laskara* (coconut sweet balls) and *tilor laru* (sesame sweet balls) are famous delicacies savoured by the Assamese along with tea.

Tamul (betel nut) and *paan* (betel leaves) is traditionally served at the end of the meal. *Tamol paan* or areca nut and betel leaf are the basic traditional elements of the Assamese culture. *Tamul* is eaten with paan, lime and tobacco. It is a custom to eat it by chewing after every meal.

Dining habit has also become a part of cultural norms as eating is acknowledged as culturally ordered interaction. All classes of people, be it rich or poor, followed some simple etiquette and mannerism during dining. In Assam, meals are traditionally served on a large circular bell metal dish called *kahi* and bowls called *bati.* People sit on the floor or on a tool called *pira.* The flooring area close to the kitchen is always kept clean. The affluent class used to have a raised earthen platform on which food was served to the head of the family. People use only the right hand while eating. It is a custom not to leave the dining place when others are still eating. A pot full of water with a *gamocha* (towel to wipe hands) and a bowl are kept in a corner of the floor. A guest is generally received by offering *tamul paan* served humbly in a *xarai* or a *bata* (traditional bell-metal utensils). It is also considered that a ceremony cannot be completed without a respectful offering of *tamul paan* to the concerned deity. The lady looking after the kitchen mostly eats only after all the members have dined out. The adult female members also had the practice of taking meal after the male members of the family had their meal. In community feasts and wedding parties, plantain leaf cups called *dona* are used in place of utensils. As every household took good care of the guest, the guest had to sincerely admire the food served by the host. This tradition is still existent.

Thus, authentic Assamese cuisine is resplendent and excellent from the health point of view also as it uses quantity of oil, ghee, butter or spices sparingly. Even though this cuisine is undoubtedly rustic and bland, but the raw flavour captivates everyone with its delicious taste and flavours. The eating habits, culinary traditions and cooking customs prevalent have added a new and unique dimension to this food deemed to be simple.

Manipur

Manipur, located in northeastern India is bordered by Nagaland on the north, Mizoram on the south, Assam on the west; and Burma on the east.

Manipur is named as 'the land of jewels' due to its vast tradition and specialization in all the cultural aspects like martial arts, dance, theatre, sculpture and the cuisine of the land. The green lush environment, superb climate and exquisite cuisine make Manipur a worthy land.

Manipur has a specific and unique individuality in terms of culinary culture and features. The cuisine is symbolized by hot and spicy nature. The Manipuri cuisine has an array of delectable dishes that are very simple to cook and are healthy for consumption. The cuisine is vast and it is surprising to know that this cuisine has the variety of dishes not less than 200 in number.

The chief food of Manipur consists of rice, fish and leafy vegetables. Rice being the staple diet, rice beer (*Yu*) is the most significant alcoholic beverage of this state, renowned all over. Generally, the people of Manipur create a kitchen garden where they grow vegetables and a pond where they cultivate fish. Thus, they always have a great supply of organic vegetables which is very healthy and fresh. This also turns the cuisine seasonal as the cuisine depends heavily on the different vegetables grown according to the season in the kitchen gardens or acquired from the local market. Assorted aromatic herbs, roots and certain vegetables found only in this region lend this state a unique cuisine. Dried fish is eaten by all ethnic groups of people. They are fond of eating meat of dogs, locust, and all kinds of birds and frog.

A few of such herbs and roots are *maroi napakpi, maroi nakuppi, awa phadigom, mayang ton, toning khok,* and so on and some of the vegetables particular to the region are *yendem* (a kind of taro), *chawai, hawai mana, koukha* (a herb root), *loklei, pulei, komprek,* and so on.

Mushrooms of many kinds are also a significant part of the Manipuri cuisine. Some varieties are *uyen* (similar to *shittake* mushroom), *uchina* (black slimy mushroom), *chengum, kanglayen* (lichen).

Some unique and distinct ingredients of the cuisine are *hawaijar* (fermented soya bean), *soibum, shoidon* and *soijin* (fermented bamboo shoot), and *ngari* and *hentak* (fermented fish). *Hawaijar* is acknowledged and renowned for its unique organoleptic features. It has a characteristic flavour and distinct aroma. It is consumed on a regular basis as food in every household. It is added in many of the celebrated dishes of Manipur. It is heavily incorporated as a condiment with vegetables. It is consumed directly or used as a flavouring agent in vegetable items making it softer, tender and delicious. A special delicacy of this state is called *chagempomba*, which is prepared using *Hawaijar*, rice and other vegetables. It is also eaten as accompaniment eaten as paste with chilli and salt known as *ametpa*.

Fish has a significant place in the cuisine of Manipur. *Ngari* is one of the most loved delicacies of fish which is a hot favourite among the locals. Its popularity can be described with the notion that a Manipuri could live without a meal a day but could not survive without an Ngari a day. They use a special small kind of fish locally called *phabou nga* for the preparation of *Ngari*. The *phabou nga* is washed properly in water and then sun-dried till it becomes crispy. The fish head is crushed properly with the help of a hammer. A special vessel is used for the preparation of *Ngari*, in which mustard oil is plastered and then the dried fish is stacked in it in proper order. The container is closed airtight after filling. It takes approximate about 3 to 6 months to get mature and then is ready to eat. It has a typical odour which indicates the fish is fermented properly and is now ready for consumption. *Nga aiyaba* or dried fish is another loved dish of the locals.

Hentak is another distinct preparation prepared from fishes like *phabou nga* or *ngakha*. The fish is sun-dried till the moisture content of the fish is at the lowest and then it is crushed into a powdered form. Wild colocassia stem is also crushed after washing properly and then cutting it into pieces. The powdered fishes and crushed wild colocassia stems are properly mixed and then rolled in round forms and stored in a container, which after 3 days, is again crushed with the help of a pestle and mortar. This is how *hentak* is prepared.

The dishes of the state are typically spicy, and locally grown chillies and herbs contribute to make the dishes hot and spicy. *Iromba* is an assemblage of fresh vegetables, bamboo shoots, fermented fish called *ngari* and chillies. Chicken is also savoured with great zest by the natives.

The cuisine is traditionally served on banana leaves and eaten by sitting on the floor cross-legged.

Some delectable and wonderful dishes of this cuisine include *kanghou*, a dish made with assorted vegetables fried in oil along with traditional spices, *paknam* which is a mixture of *ngari* cake and gram flour, *chagem pomba, alu kangmet* which involves mashing of boiled potato with fried red chillies and topped with mustard oil, *nga thongba* (fish curry), *ooti* (a typical Manipuri vegetarian dish), *pakora thongba, chagem pomba* (made with fermented soya, mustard leaves, dry fish and other herbs), keli chana, and so on.

Shuktani is a side dish made especially during religious festive days and occasions consisting of neem leaves, basak leaves and sugar. *Chamfoot* or *anganba* is used to cool the stomach.

Heithongba is a very pungent dish of lemon, sugar, salt, aonla and tamarind. *Maroi morok thongba* is another unique speciality of the state. *Morok* stands for green chilli. As a result, this dish is quite hot in taste.

Manipuri cuisine has a special place for desserts and the people here have mastered their skills in preparing dessert items. The dessert items comprise *madhurjan, chahou kheer, khamen ashinba athoomba, kheer angouba,* and so on. Hei Thongba (fruit dish) is the most celebrated dessert and is considered to be the best. It is mostly served at the end of a meal. This dish helps in digesting a heavy meal.

Thus, Manipur is blessed with abundant and distinct varied ingredients and has great culinary features.

Specialty Dishes

Iromba

It is a signature dish made by boiling potatoes and vegetables together with an excess of *umorok* (literally meaning *tree chilli*, *u* stands for tree and *morok* stands for chilli) or red tree chillies. Fermented fish and dry fish are added later and seasoned with coriander leaves, toning *khok tilhou, maroi napakpi, maroi nakuppi, mayang ton* and *awa phadigom* among others. This dish is indeed a lovely preparation and is enjoyed by all.

Singju It is a nutritious salad made of finely chopped cabbage, raw papaya, onions, lotus stems, tree beans, coriander leaves, *sinju pan*, ginger, and *heibi mana*. *Ngari* along with abundant quantities of seasonal vegetables are added in it. The dish is given a unique taste by tempering with salt, red chilli, red roasted sesame powder and chick pea powder.	
Chamthong or Kangshoi This is a dish made with a combination of seasonal vegetables and *ngari*, onions, *maroi* and salt. The dish is tempered with fried fish pieces and topped with dried fish, *ngari* and water. This dish is soupy in texture and is relished with rice.	
Morok Metpa It is a lavish dish made in the form of a coarse paste with a mixture of dry red chillies or green chillies, onions and coriander leaves. The chillies are usually crushed or boiled with *ngari*. The item is finally topped with fried fish pieces.	

Meghalaya

Meghalaya, located in northeast India, is surrounded by Bangladesh on the south and the Assam on the north.

Meghalaya also popularly named as 'Abode of Clouds', is a ravishing land which spells it mesmerizing charms of natural beauty. It experiences heavy rainfall during the monsoons which adds to its splendid greenery.

The cuisine of Meghalaya is symbolic of a special distinct flavour and incomparable taste of its own. Meghalaya is the home of three Mongoloid tribes, namely Khasi, Garo and Jaintia and their cuisine have contributed a lot in fabricating the cuisine of this state. The cuisine of Meghalaya is chiefly non-vegetarian in nature and represents a hot and spicy food.

Rice is the chief and staple food of the natives, accompanied by heavily spiced meat and fish dishes. In fact, rice is inseparable from this cuisine. A peculiar variety of rice called the red rice is grown locally and is relished by the people for its amazingly delicious taste. The local people domesticate ducks, cows, goats, pigs, fowls and prefer their meat in their meals. Along with these, dry fish, meat of bison and deer are also popularly relished by the local populace. Even pork is extremely popular among the people of all the three tribes. The cooking style and traditions of the Khasi and Jaintia community have few similarities and they specifically use black sesame seeds to temper the pork dishes as well as other preparations. A cold salad prepared from shredded pork, onion and ginger is also quite common among the natives.

The cultivation of mushrooms during the monsoons is a usual affair and enjoyed in the entire state. Many different kinds of mushroom varieties are cultivated here and hence used in the local cuisine. They are simply fried and served as fried delicacies. It is also cooked along with meat to enhance the taste of the meat dishes. Rice being a popular item, many rice based dishes and snacks are commonly eaten in this hilly state. *Putharo* is a rice cake which is popular among the natives. *Pumaloi* is another variety of dry and flaky rice cake made from rice flour. Among the snacks deep fried, jaggery sweetened *pukhiein* and steamed *pusla* are popular delicacies, enjoyed with tea.

Meghalaya is blessed with a huge production of different fruits like oranges, lemons, bananas, guavas, pineapples, and so on. and the people of the state love eating all these fruits.

The aboriginal people of Meghalaya have a great liking towards chewing unripe betel nut and tobacco along with a dash of lime after having their meals. The locally brewed drinks are popularly consumed by the people in daily life, as well as on all the festive and other occasions.

The cuisine of Meghalaya has a common cuisine and food pattern all over, but the three major communities have some uniqueness and typicality in cooking and eating pattern.

- **Garo Cuisine**

The cuisine of the Garo tribe is symbolized by the simplistic nature of the food in nature which is delectable. This elementary cuisine has a unique flavour which is obtained by adding slight variations to the food. Meat and fish has a crucial place in this cuisine. A typical Garo meal comprises rice, a few tempting meat and fish delicacies and an alluring dry fish soup. This community has mastered its cooking arts in the preparation of *chutneys* which are made from different herbs. Fermented fish and fermented soya beans are also popular with them. This tribal community is very skilled in preserving fish and meat by the traditional technique of drying in the sun and also by smoking it over the fire. *Khapa* is one of the most celebrated dishes of the tribal community, which is basically a chicken delicacy. *Nakham Bitchi* is delectable hot and spicy soup made by incorporating dry fish or *nakham* and then flavoured with chillies.

- **Khasi Cuisine**

The food preferences of this tribe are dissimilar to the Garo tribe. The food of the Khasi tribe is centrally based on rice. They love the meat of beef, pork, chicken and others. Along with meat items, fresh and dried fish are also a very popular non-vegetarian fare. Red meat is essentially incorporated in the meal, and pork is undoubtedly the most popular food of animal origin. The only spices used by this tribe in the traditionally distinct preparation are turmeric, ginger, salt, green chillies and sesame seeds. Rice is either cooked plain or is combined with onions, ginger and turmeric, bestowing a yellow colour to the rice which is referred as *jastem*. Rice cooked in combination with pork yields *jadoh*. A splendid pork salad, *Dohkhlieh* is also popular in this tribe. *Mylliem chicken* is another unique chicken dish cooked in combination with Khasi peppers. *Tungrymbai* is traditional fermented food product prepared using fermented soya beans, and it is a cheap source of high protein and other nutrients in the local diet. *Dohneiiong* is another popularly consumed pork dish tempered with black sesame seeds.

- **Jaintia Cuisine**

The Jaintia tribe has emphasized heavily on the consumption of delicious mushroom dishes. This tribe cultivates varied, unique and indigenous mushrooms which are incorporated in the preparation of dishes. *Tit Tung* is the common term for mushroom in this tribal area. The aboriginal people combine mushroom with pork and temper the dish with black sesame seeds to give the preparation a distinct touch and unique flavour.

Thus, the cult cuisine of Meghalaya has many tastes trapped in it and is unarguably an exquisite cuisine.

Mizoram

Mizoram, located in Northeast India, is bordered by the states of Tripura, Assam, Manipur and with the neighbouring countries of Bangladesh and Burma.

Mizoram is a splendid state blessed with mesmerizing hills, lovely valleys, whirling rivers and pristine lakes. Mizoram has a distinctive food culture and is entirely different from the other state cuisines of India. It not only shares some of the food features that are similar to the other northeastern states but also retains a flavour and taste that is unique. Vestige of Chinese food culture as well as North Indian style of cuisine has mingled to create the Mizo food culture.

Non-vegetarian delicacies are the primal attractions of the Mizo cuisine. Vegetables are also preferred among the local population but non-vegetarian items have a special place in the meal of Mizoram. Rice is the staple food item and is accompanied by certain other vegetarian and non-vegetarian fare. Fish is also one of the main non-vegetarian items widely relished by the Mizo people. Pork and chicken are other non-vegetarian items consumed popularly by the locals in this state. Even duck meat has a distinct place in the Mizo cuisine. Bamboo shoots and local herbs are the significant constituents of this cuisine.

Mustard oil is the preferred cooking medium. People do not prefer to eat oily food and hence less oil is used in the almost all preparations. Characterized by its simplistic nature, the food is very delicious. The food is beneficial from the nutritional aspect as the dishes are primarily cooked by boiling or steaming. Spices and locally produced herbs are used so are the bamboo shoots used to flavour the dishes of this state. The commonly used spices are ginger, garlic, onion and chillies. The food is traditionally served on fresh banana leaves. The people of Mizoram do not prefer to eat dessert after the meals, but they prefer to have fresh fruit after the meals. *Zu* or tea is undoubtedly the popular beverage relished by the people. Locally made wines are enjoyed by the aboriginals after dinner. *Lubrusca* grape wine is very popular among the local section of the people.

Mizoram has its own cuisine which has a huge collection of many indigenous dishes, imparting it an altogether distinct look and a delectable taste. Among the popular items are *Bai*, a dish prepared in combination with boiled spinach, pork and bamboo shoots in significant quantity. *Sawchair* is another favorite dish prepared from rice and pork or chicken. Vawksa Rep or Smoked Pork is relished by the people. It is a dish made from cubes of pork smoked in an open fire to render it a unique smoky taste and is flavoured with bamboo shoots and locally produced herbs. *Arsa Buhchiar* or chicken with sticky rice is a unique and common dish where a whole chicken is cooked by roasting it in open fire and then cooked with an addition of sticky rice and locally produced herbs. *Misa Mach Poora* is a shrimp delicacy well-famed in the state. *Panch Phoron Tarkari* is a delightful vegetable item to eat. *Dal* with eggs is a combination dish of pulses and eggs. *Poora Mach* and *Koat Pitha* are also famous dishes of the Mizo cuisine.

Thus, the cuisine of Mizoram has its own distinctive features and is bestowed with certain good culinary aspects, which makes it truly mesmerizing.

Nagaland

Nagaland is a state situated in the extreme north-eastern part of India. It is bordered by Assam on the west, Arunachal Pradesh and part of Assam on the north, Myanmar on the east and Manipur on the south.

Nagaland is a beautiful state, mostly covered by lush mountains. This state has a wonderful and exemplary cuisine which has attracted everyone towards its incomparable flavour and taste.

Nagaland is a state bestowed with a rich culture and an exquisite cuisine. The state comprises various Naga tribes and each tribe has its unique dishes. The tribal cuisine is so diverse and varied that the cuisine is never similar for any two of the tribes.

A typical Naga meal comprises rice accompanied by a meat preparation, few boiled vegetable dishes and *chutney* (*tathu*). A distinct feature of the Naga cuisine is that dishes are cooked by boiling the ingredients and not by frying them. The people of Nagaland are staunch non-vegetarians. The food is characterized by a hot and spicy taste. The dishes in this cuisine are flavoured by locally produced ingredients.

Meat forms the main base of the meals of this cuisine and it is cooked by different methods. Mostly the meat and fish are smoked, dried or fermented. Pork is another highly recommended item in this cuisine. Pork is cooked along with bamboo shoots is a well-famed dish of this cuisine. Smoked meat is preserved by keeping the meat above the fire or allowing it to hang on the wall of the kitchen for 2 weeks or longer, which could even last for the whole year ahead. The garlic and ginger leaves are also incorporated in meat preparations.

Being a spicy cuisine, seasoning plays a crucial role in this cuisine. Chillies are an essential and integral part of the cuisine of this state and are used in most of the dishes. The variety of ginger used in the Naga cuisine is spicy, aromatic and is distinct from the common ginger available. A motley of local herbs and leaves are also used to spice up and flavour the dishes.

The cuisine of Nagaland is indigenous as it has remained free from the touch and influence of other cuisines. As hunting is the main occupation of the people, meat has become an inseparable element of the Naga cuisine. The dishes and the food have remained unchanged from time immemorial.

The basic and chief components of this cuisine are rice, potatoes, and other vegetables and meat. The variations of meat in the Naga cuisine are quite extensive and have a lot of items in its bouquet. The range of meat enjoyed by them is very vast and it includes meat of hunted animals like bovines, pigs, fish, chicken, crabs, frog, snail, spider, insects, bee larvae, dog, cat, rat, birds, snake, spider, monkey, bear, and even elephant.

Besides meat bamboo shoots, lettuce, soya beans, mustard leaves, and yam leaves are also used in cooking. These ingredients are fermented and are used to prepare various traditional preparations.

The cuisine of Nagaland has adopted the technique of fermenting the food just to preserve the food for a longer period of time. The food item to be preserved is first boiled and then allowed to be dried under the sun or near the fire. It is then wrapped in a banana leaf and stored for future use.

Meat of dog and other wild animals is considered a delicacy in Nagaland, which is uncommon in other states of India. One of the typical dishes of Nagaland is smoke-dried pork curry with *akhuni* and snails. *Akhuni* is the term used to refer the fermented soya beans. Chicken *chutney*, made with shredded chicken, king chilli, garlic, and green onion is another popularly consumed food here. Rice beer is also very common and is a traditional drink in this state. *Zutho, dzutse,* and *ruhi* are a few examples of other types of drinks consumed here.

The people of Nagaland are of the belief that certain meats have high medicinal and curative power. They strongly believe that the meat of a stone bird is very effective in treating renal diseases (kidney disease). Similarly, for treating pneumonia, dog's meat is considered the best available medicine. In case of injuries, bee larvae, snails, and frogs are considered to cure the skin and bone diseases. It might seem strange but they even believe that a snake bite can be treated by drinking a fluid full of earthworms. Such beliefs attached with their curative features have increased the consumption of meats of various animals and even insects in the state, but the popularity of items as meat has remained unchanged over the ages.

However, there are certain prohibitions regarding the consumption of peculiar kinds of meat as they are considered to be unhygienic and believed to be harmful to human beings. Though strange, but a woman is forbidden from consuming the meat of a monkey as the Naga people believe that meat of monkey turns a woman extravagant. Pregnant woman are restricted from consuming the meat of a bear as bear is considered to be an animal symbolized with lots of stupidity. The meat of tigers and leopards are not consumed by the people as they are of the belief that the tiger was the brother of man when the world was created.

Such strange and unique features have characterized the culinary aspects of the state Nagaland, but it has still managed to retain its age-old traditions and have remained largely unaffected by the modernization of the food culture in the country.

Tripura

Tripura, located in Northeast India is bordered by Bangladesh on the north, south, and west, and with Indian states of Assam and Mizoram on the east.

Tripura is a lovely state with a rich cultural heritage and culinary elements. The cuisine of Tripura is extremely varied and symbolizes a distinct taste.

The food pattern of Tripura is primarily non-vegetarian in temperament, of notwithstanding the fact that the Vaishnavite section of the people follows a strict vegetarian diet. Meat prepared in a traditional way is a significant element of the cuisine. Certain other dishes make use of vegetables as well as fish.

The Tripuri cuisine is referred as *Mui Borok* in the traditional language. One of the most popular anchor dishes of the Tripuri cuisine is a dish called *Berma* which is prepared using dried and fermented fish which is made without oil and is flavoured with local spices.

The culinary tradition of Tripura is defined by the various sections of the people comprising the tribal and non-tribal population. The staple food of the non-tribal Bengalis residing in the state basically consists of rice, fish, chicken, mutton and pork. The non-tribal Bengali populations are famed to relish a large collection of fish dishes prepared from a wide section of fish available in the state. Such preparations of curries and dishes are usually spicy in nature. The fish *hilsa* has contributed in the preparation of a famous delicacy of the state in which the fish is prepared in gravy of mustard seeds and is tempered with green chilly to render it an aromatic and spicy taste. The people are fond of its smell and taste. A few other famed dishes of this cuisine include Bangui rice and fish stew, delicate bamboo shoots, fermented fish, locally produced herbs, and delectable meat roasts.

Rice is the central base of many preparations in the state. The dominance and significance of the rice can be experienced in every aspect of the cuisine. Rice is cooked in combination with other dishes to produce wholesome meals and sumptuous food items. Vegetable oil and mustard oil are the preferred cooking mediums of the people. Mustard oil is primarily used to cook fish and meat and is used to deep fry any item. The cuisine of Tripura depends heavily on the usage of various spices to render the dishes a tempting taste. The spices most commonly used are mustard seeds, *paanch phoron* (a blend of five spices used to temper the dishes which comprises onion seeds, white cumin seeds, fenugreek seeds, fennel seeds and mustard seeds), green and red chillies, turmeric, and so on. Yogurt, coconut, gram flour and maize are also the main key ingredients in the cooking of Tripuri cuisine.

Cuisines have been the mainstay aspects of cultural fabric of every place and every community. This statement is predominantly supported by the cuisine of Tripura which reminds everyone with the fact that the inhabitants of this place have created a special mark for their tribal identity even in this age of modernization.

The state has an abundant crop of green vegetables. Commonly found vegetables of this cuisine are eggplants, chillies, pumpkins, bamboo shoots and corn.

Certain traditional and typical dishes of the cuisine of Tripura are *awandru, chakhwi, chakhwtwi kwthwng, thokni, chatang, mosodeng, deng, gudok, hang, ik, muitru, hontali, muhr, mwkhwi, napek, peng, rabra, ruk, ser, sok, yohk and yaksapk* among others.

The beautiful state of Tripura depicts a rich cuisine that is characterized by ancient tradition, varied in taste and also cares for nutritional aspects. Thus, this elegant cuisine is also representative of the fact that the people of Tripura have gracefully retained their cultural identity and food diversity withstanding in the age of modernization.

Culinary Trivia: Special Days

1st June is celebrated as World Milk Day.

1st July is celebrated as International Fruit Day.

22 Odiya Cuisine

"A house is not a home unless it contains food and fire for the mind as well as the body." – Benjamin Franklin

Odisha, formerly Orissa, situated near the Bay of Bengal, is surrounded by West Bengal on the northeast and in the east, Jharkhand on the north, Chhattisgarh on the west and northwest and Andhra Pradesh on the south.

The cuisine of the state is known as 'Oriya cuisine'. The land is characterized by a rich production of various green vegetables and the proximity to the Bay of Bengal ensures the huge availability of fresh seafood. The Oriya cuisine is renowned and known for the preponderant production of varied vegetables and its incorporation in preparing delicious dishes that renders it a varied taste and distinguished flavour. This cuisine uses seafood, chicken and meat impeccably to enhance the spectrum of variety in the Oriya cuisine. This cuisine is a quintessential and paradigmatic fusion of varied incorporation of the spices and locally produced ingredients, which makes the *Oriya* food lavish in temperament. Coconut milk and yoghurt is also used frequently with combination of spices and less oil. A blend of coconut milk and yoghurt imparts a vibrant colour and creamy texture to the delicacies, thereby enhancing the appearance and taste of the items. The cuisine of Odisha is spicy but not at all fiery in nature. The gravies or curries are subtle in taste and are fragrant without any touch of fieriness in it.

This cuisine is the resultant cuisine of the influences of the neighbouring states of Bihar and West Bengal due to the close proximity and similarity in geographical conditions. The people of Odisha are equally fond of both vegetarian and non-vegetarian fares but certain conformist families strictly stick to vegetarianism. The one who adheres to non-vegetarianism also avoid non-vegetarian food during the religious ceremonies and festive occasions. They are so passionate about religious sentiments that they don't even prefer to eat and consume onion and garlic on such days as they are also considered non-vegetarian items. In current days of modernization, certain restaurants in major cities of Odisha, for instance Puri, serve only vegetarian food that too without the use of onion and garlic, as the owners are strictly vegetarian brahmins.

As this state is near the Bay of Bengal, seafood is very popular and one can relish seafood like crabs and prawns and other fresh varieties like salmon, lobsters, and so on. The consumption of meat is less as compared to seafood consumption in the state due to the religious inclination of the people. But if someone wishes to eat meat at any point of time, he or she can easily get it. Mustard oil is the usual cooking medium for daily cooking and it is replaced by clarified butter on special occasions. This state has mastered the art to deliver an impeccable taste and texture by using rich creamy curds with coconut milk to prepare fresh seafood. Such delicacies are amazingly refreshing and mouth-watering and have taken the Oriya cuisine to a different level.

Odisha's cuisine has been blessed with a wide spectrum of tastes ranging from hot and spicy to sweets and wholesome, personifying the spirit of the state. Odisha is unarguably a land of divine delicious delicacies where the food preparation is simple, economical and hygienic.

Like all other states, spices are used to temper and flavour the dishes. The most popular spice mixture is *Pancha phutana* and *garam masala*. *Pancha phutana* is a mixture of five kinds of spices, namely, cumin seeds (*jeera*), mustard seeds (*rye*), fennel seeds (*saunf*), fenugreek seeds (*methi*) and nigella seeds (*kalonji*). *Pancha phutana* is used to temper vegetables and *dals* and is chiefly used for vegetarian dishes. *Garam masala* is a fragrant combination of the rich spices of cardamom, clove and cinnamon. *Garam masala* is commonly used to spice up the non-vegetarian dishes.

Rice is the staple and the principal crop of Odisha. Wheat comes to rice in terms of popularity and productivity. Common dishes are cooked using a variety of legumes and fresh vegetables like brinjal, pumpkin, gourd, cauliflower, cabbage, tomato, papaya, beans, lady finger, potato, peas, arum, and so on. The people are very fond of green leafy vegetables, and different kinds of roots, and hence are consumed by the people on a regular basis.

A traditional Oriya meal is presented in a unique fashion. All the dishes are served at once and the meal begins after it, rather than serving the meal course by course. The main dish of the meal is served on a large *thali* (plate) and the other dishes are arranged in small bowls and placed surrounding the large plate. Traditionally, on festive occasions and other functions, the meal is served on banana leaves. People mostly use their right hand to eat rather than with eating spoons and forks. Food is mostly served on palm leaves or several small leaves sewn together to form a large disposable plate.

A typical Oriya meal mainly comprises *saaga* (green leaf-based dish), *bhaaji* (fried vegetable dish), *bhaat* (rice), *dal* (pulse), *besara* or *mahura* (curry tempered with spices), *machha tarkari* (fish curry) and *khatta* (*chutney*). *Channa dali* is a common preferred tasty *dal* preparation, which is a sweetened pulse delicacy tempered with coconut, raisins, dry fruits and spices. *Dalma* is a nutritional dish which is another favourite item prepared by the mixture of lentils and motley of vegetables. *Pakhala* is a preparation with fermented rice seasoned with yoghurt and spices and is enjoyed especially during the summer season. *Mitha bhaat* is simply the sweetened rice tempered with lots of spices. People also love the *pulao* preparation made of rice cooked with butter, nuts, raisins, vegetables and spices. *Khichari* is a simple dish mostly served in religious festivals and is a dish of rice and lentils cooked with a variety of vegetables and then flavoured with dry red chillies, bay leaves and cumin seeds. It is a wonderful dish which is digested easily. *Besara* is a dish of combination of vegetables tempered with *panch phutana* and flavoured with spices. It is also relished by the people of Odisha with enthuthiasm.

Certain other vegetarian delights of Odisha include *jeera pakhala, bhendi bhaja, kakharu phula bhaja, aalu palak saag, kadali bhaja, alu matara, alu phulakobi bhaja, dahi bhindi, dahi baigana, posta, santula, badi dahi,* and so on.

Among the non-vegetarian delicacies are *chhencheda, chingudi malai, kankada kalia, kankada jhola, dahi machha, soriso maccha, maccha jhola, maccha bihana, chingudi jhola, machha besara,* and many more.

The cuisine offers few amazing and incomparable meat dishes like *maansha jhol, maansha soriso, maansha chana dali, and maansha kasha,* and so on.

The Oriya people have excelled in their art of preparing ultimate variations of *chutneys*, pickles and sweets. *Ouu khatta, patalghanta chutney, coriander chutney,* coconut *chutney*, mango *chutney*, tomato *chutney*, dried fish *chutney*, sweet fruit *chutney*, and so on are the common *chutneys* of this cuisine. These *chutneys* add new dimension to the Oriya meal and kills the bland taste of the dish if any.

It is a tradition to serve *paan* (betel leaf), after the completion of the meal. The cuisine of Odisha is renowned for its utter simplicity. It is mild on the stomach and has many nutritional benefits.

The people of Odisha are great lovers and creators of sweets. Sweet delicacies and sweet meats are a regular and essential constituent of their meals. The desserts prepared speak volumes about the artistic feature of professional cooks to have produced such great conglomeration of desserts. Certain great milk preparations like *rasagolla, rasmalai, khirmohan, rajbhog, rabidi, rasabali,* ricotta cheese preparations like *chhena gaja, chhena poda, chhena kheeri, chhena jilebi* are enjoyed by the people in this state. Odisha has many desserts which are equally mouth-watering such as *kalakand* (a delicacy made from condensed milk), *khaja* (a sweet made with dough and fried before dipped in sugar syrup), *kheersagar* (a dessert of cheese dumplings in condensed milk), *meetha dahi* (simply sweetened curds), *malpua* (fried and sweetened delicacy of refined flour and bananas), and many more. Kheeri or rice pudding is a resplendent delicacy that is supposed to have originated in Odisha more than two thousand years ago.

Pitha is the local name attributed to various cakes which are made following traditional techniques and demand a lot of skill and patience. Popular *pithas* of Odisha are *manda, peda, chitau, kakara, arisa, chakuli, poda, tala, enduri, bhaga pitha,* and so on.

Tea is the most preferred beverage enjoyed by the locals and coffee is also equally popular. Tender coconut water and fresh sugarcane juices provide great relief during the extreme summer months. *Bel pana* is another popularly common drink prepared with the milk and the pulp of wood apple, sweetened with sugar and flavoured with black pepper. *Nabata pana* is one such typical drink prepared with *chhena* (ricotta cheese), jaggery, banana, grated coconut and black pepper. Such beverages are taken to bring relief to the people from scorching heat. Fresh fruits like mangoes, jackfruits, watermelons, bananas, and so on are commonly savoured by the people in Odisha with gusto.

The cuisine of Odisha is renowned worldwide with the preparation of most revered Mahaprasad (*Avada*) of the Sri Jagannath temple situated at Puri. The food offered to the deities of the temple, namely, Jagannath, Subhadra and Balabhadra are known as the Mahaprasad. This Mahaprasad is a motivational factor and serves as the base for preparation of many of the food items of the Oriya cuisine. Mahaprasad associated with religious sentiments has been prepared since time immemorial in the temple kitchen and offered to the Lord. This kitchen is acknowledged as the place where lots of the dishes are supposed to have their origin. The temple kitchen is considered to be the largest kitchen in the world. It would sound strange but about a thousand of professional cooks work on about 752 clay hearths lighted by firewood to prepare the Mahaprasad in clay bowls. The food is prepared in a unique style where the bowls are stacked one over the other in stacks of five and then cooked by a unique steaming process maintaining a purified mind and body. About 10,000 people approximately partake in the Mahaprasad daily in the temple premises. The number of the devotees increases tremendously during the festive season. It goes without saying that the food is strictly vegetarian without any trace of onion or garlic in it. Even vegetables of non-Indian origin like tomatoes and potatoes are prohibited in the preparation of the Prasad. The varied lists of vegetarian dishes are accompanied by extensive sweet dishes and desserts for the Lord. The dishes generally number up to 56 items and are called Chappan Bhog of Sri Jagannath. This bhog, after being offered to the Lord Jagannath, is sent to the Ananda Market situated within the temple premises from where devotees are offered the most-sought Mahaprasad.

ChhapanBhog: It is an extensive collection of 56 dish items and is the largest collection of dish under one title in India.

Chhapan Bhog comprises of 56 sacred items offered to Lord Jagannath in Jagannath Temple, Puri and they are as such:

1. Ukhuda (Sugar coated puffed rice)
2. Nadia Kora (Coconut ladoo)
3. Khua (Condensed milk)
4. Dahi (Yogurt)
5. Pachilakadali (Ripe banana)
6. Kanika (Flavoured rice)
7. Tata Khechudi (Dry khechudi)
8. Mendha Mundia (A kind of cake)
9. Bada Kanti (Fried cake)
10. Matha Puli (A kind of pan cake)
11. Hamsa Keli (A sort of sweet cake)
12. Jhili (Thin pan cake like *dosa*)
13. Enduri (*Idli*)
14. Adapachedi (Ginger paste)
15. Saga Bhaja (Fried leafy vegetables)
16. Kadali Bhaja (Fried plantain)
17. Maric Ladoo (Chilli ladoo)
18. San Pitha (Small size cake)
19. Bara (Dumplings)
20. Arisha (Sweet fried cake made of rice flour)
21. Bundia (Sweet granules made of gram flour)
22. Pakhal (Water rice)
23. Khiri (Milk rice)
24. Kadamba (A kind of sweet)
25. Pat Manohar (Name of a sweet)
26. Takuaa (Sweets shaped like tongue)
27. Bhaga Pitha (A kind of cake)
28. Gotai (A kind of salty cake)
29. Dalma (*Dal* with vegetables)
30. Bada Kakara (Large fried sweet cake)
31. Luni Khuruma (Salty biscuits)
32. Amalu (Malpua, Sweet puri)
33. Suar Pitha (Podapitha, Baked cake)
34. Biri Buha (Black gram cake)
35 Jhadai Nadaa (Small ball-shaped cakes)
36. Khasta Puri (Strong fried cakes)
37. Kadali Bara (Fried plantain)
38. Sana Arisha (Small fried cakes)
39. Sakar (Chutney)
40. Podo Pitha (Panned cake)
41. Kanji (Sour rice)
42. Dahi Pakhal (Curd rice)
43. Bada Arisha (Large size fried cake)
44. Tipuri (Three-stage fillings)
45. Sakara (Sugar candy)
46. Suji Khir (Milk with semolina)
47. Muga Sijha (Boiled green gram)
48. Manohar (A kind of sweet)
49. Magaja Laodo (A kind of sweet)
50. Pana (Sweet drink)
51. Anna (Rice)
52. Ghia Anna (Ghee rice)
53. Dali (Sweet *dal*)
54. Besar (Mixed veg. curry)
55. Mahur (Vegetable curry with mustard seeds)
56. Saag (Leafy vegetables)

Specialty Dishes

Dalma A nutritious preparation made by the combination of *arhar dal*, raw papaya, pear gourd (*parwal*), brinjal, plaintain (raw banana) and potato cooked together and then tempered with mustard seeds, cumin seeds and spices. It is served with rice or *chapati.*	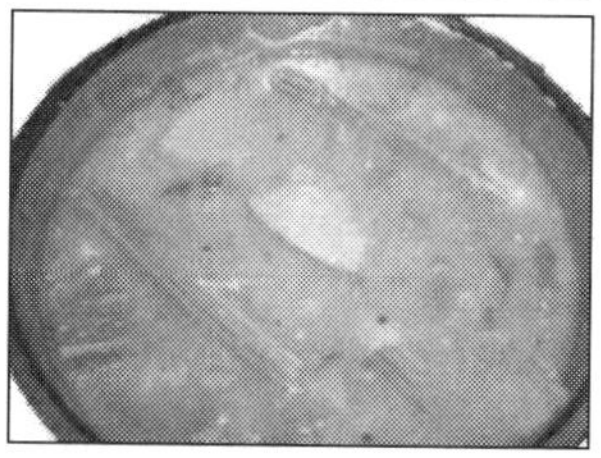
Santula It is a colorful preparation with a motley of vegetables like brinjal, potato, ridge-gourd, raw papaya tempered with onion, cloves, mustard, green chillies and boiled milk. It is also recommended for people suffering from several ailments, due to its high vegetable content, absence of hot spices, and minimal oil content.	
Machha Besara It is a fish preparation simply cut into darne and fried. Then, the fish is cooked in a thin curry of onion, tomatoes, garlic paste, cumin seeds and mustard seeds. It is garnished with coriander leaves and served with rice.	
Pithau Bhaja A very unique vegetable preparation which comprises of yam, pumpkin, brinjal, lotus stem, potato are dipped in the batter of rice with spices and then fried in oil. This kind of dry fried vegetables in rice paste is popular and common in Odisha.	
Chingudi Mahura A unique potpourri of fried prawns and vegetables cooked in a onion spiced curry. It is served with rice.	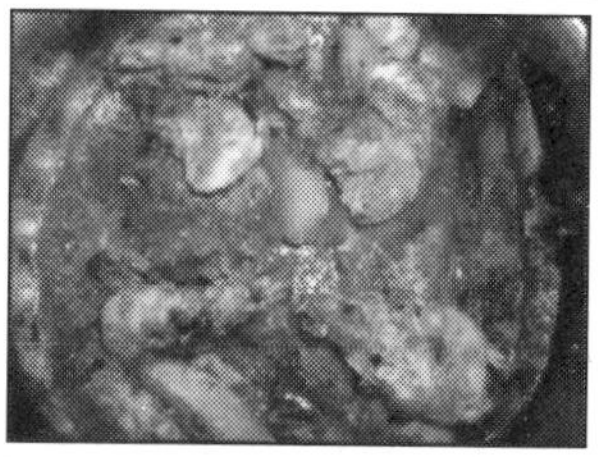
Ghanta It is a preparation of mixed vegetables like potato, yam, pumpkin, pear gourd and so on with lots of pulse seeds added to it. It tastes amazingly great with coconut flavoured curry and is served with rice.	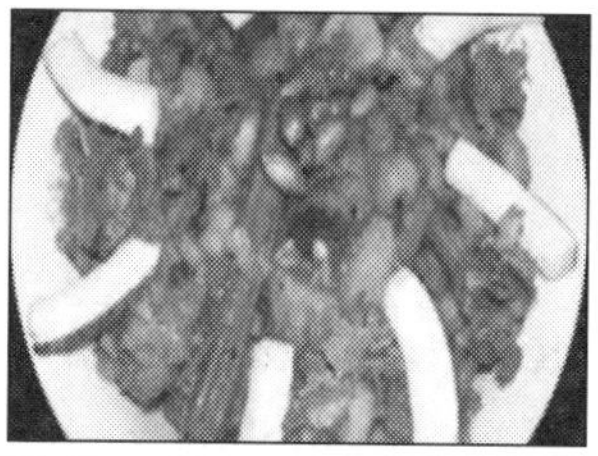
Dahi Baigana It is a simple dish in which the brinjals are fried and then dipped in whipped curds tempered with mustard seeds, cumin seeds, green chillies and curry leaves. It is served cold with hot steaming rice.	

Tomato Khajura Khata

It is a mouth-watering delicacy made of date palm and tomatoes cooked together in oil with red chillies, grated coconut and crushed ginger. It is garnished with coriander leaves.

Machha Thukuthuka

It is a typical fish curry preparation in which the marinated fish is cooked in a curry tempered with *panch phootan* (*panch phoran*). This famous dish is from Berhampur.

Ghia Anna

A dish similar to *khichadi* of North India, this is made by boiling rice and split bengal gram and then tempering it with lots of ghee, cumin seeds and curry leaves. It is served with *dalma* or any vegetable curry. This dish is very popular in the Puri district.

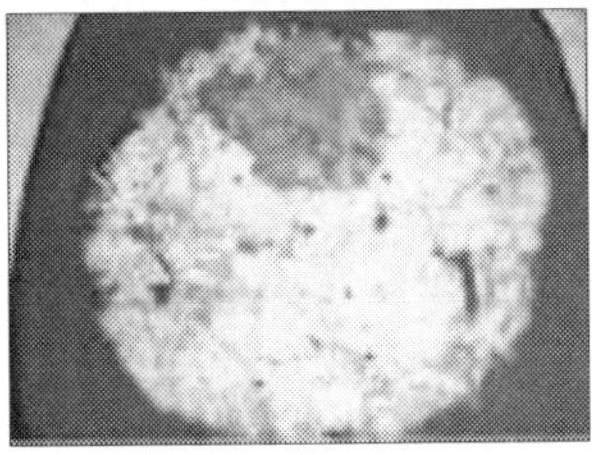

Chingudi Chadchadi

It is a dry preparation of tiny prawns cooked with mustard paste, turmeric powder, green chillies and mustard oil. All the ingredients are cooked together and it is served with rice.

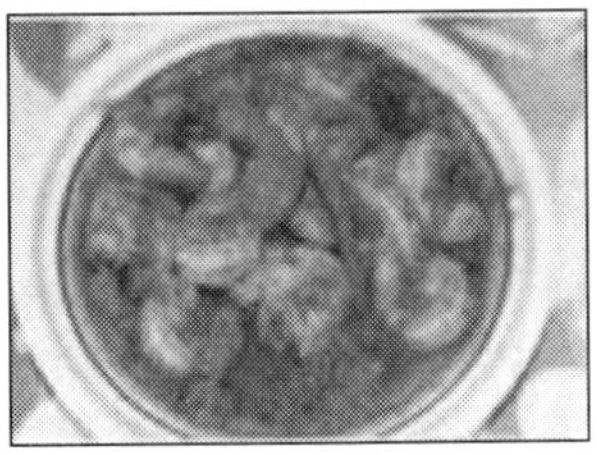

Maansha Kasha

A delicious preparation of meat in which semi-fried potatoes are added while cooking it with dry *masala* made up of onion, sugar, garlic, and spices. If the same dish is prepared in gravy form, it is referred to as *maansha jhollo.*

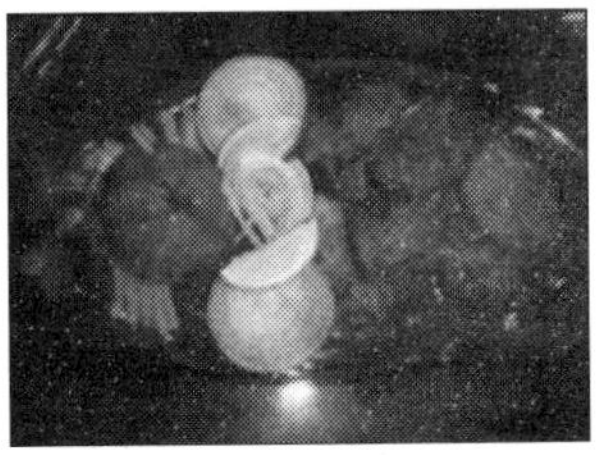

Chhena Tarkari

It is a very unusual flavourful preparation in which the dumpling of fresh *chenna* and gram flour is cooked with potato cubes cooked in a gravy of onion and tomatoes with lots of spices.

Kancha Kadali Bara

It is a dumpling made by mashing boiled plantain and potatoes and then mixing it with gram-flour, chopped green chillies, chopped onion, chilli powder, coriander leaves, grated coconut, and salt. The dumplings are then shallow-fried and served hot.

Potala Rasa

It is a delicacy which is made with combination of pear gourd and potatoes cooked in onion gravy flavoured with lots of coconut milk and spices.

Pani Kakharu Sakara

It is a dish prepared by cooking chopped white gourd in curry flavoured with grated coconut, tamarind water and jaggery, and tempered with *panch phootan* spices. This unique dish is sweet and sour in taste.

Mula Raita

It is a dish acknowledged as very old which is made by adding grated radish in curds along with cut black grapes, chopped green chillies, small pieces of apple and orange, pomegranate seeds, coriander leaves. This dish tastes great with vegetarian preparation and is even offered to deities.

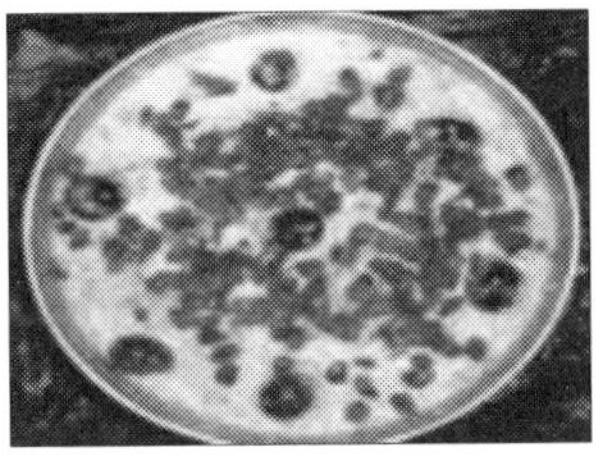

Aarisa Pitha

It is an Oriya delicacy which is made from rice, sugar and refined flour. In this preparation, the rice is soaked for about 2–3 hours and then the drained rice is ground to achieve a powdered form. Sugar syrup is also prepared meanwhile and then the rice powder is added into the boiling syrup and stirred continuously to form a batter. The batter is then taken into small portions to make small *puris* or *kachoris* (*pithas*). The *pithas* are then deep-fried in refined oil and served.

Manda Pitha

In this preparation, the *pitha* is made using milk and crushed rice. A mixture of grated coconut and sugar is prepared using cardamom and black pepper powder for added flavour. This mixture is stuffed in the *pitha* and then the stuffed balls are steamed in a steamer. It is served at room temperature. A variation of *manda pitha* is prepared by replacing crushed rice with *sooji* and this *pitha* therefore is called *sooji manda.*

Chhena Poda

It is a special sweet dish from Odisha made of *chenna*, *sooji*, sugar and nuts as the main ingredients. It is prepared by preparing a batter of *chenna, sooji*, and sugar in a bowl by proper whisking. In this batter cardamom powder, roasted nuts and raisins are added. This batter is poured in a greased tray and baked it till done and brown in colour in a preheated oven. It is then cut into even pieces and served as *chenna poda*.

Rasabali

A famous delicacy from Kendrapara, in this preparation *paneer* is mashed with wheat flour, sugar and cardamom powder. Small round balls are made from the mash and then deep fried in oil and then the fried *rasabalis* are dipped in sweetened milk and cooked for about a minute on very low flame.

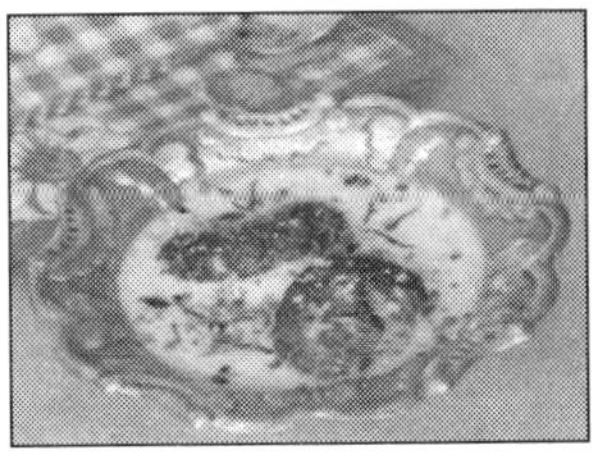

Saru Chakuli

This is a preparation very similar to *Dosa* from South India. Soaked rice and black gram is ground to make a fine paste and water is added in it to make a semi-liquid batter. Then pancake is made using this batter on a non-stick pan kept on medium flame. It is served with *dalama* or coconut *chutney*.

When the pancake is made of thicker batter, the pancake is called *chakuli*.

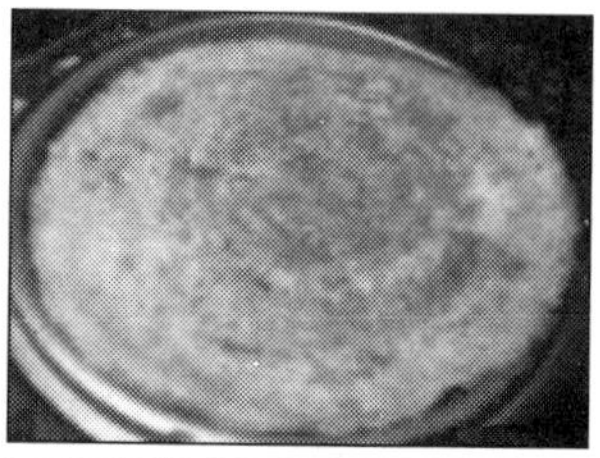

Budha Chakuli

It is a very ancient traditional Oriya dish, which is made up of rice, black gram, molasses, grated coconut and banana. Soaked rice and black gram is ground to make a fine paste and grated coconut, molasses and ripe banana are added to it to make a batter. Then this batter is used to make pancakes on a non-stick pan kept on medium flame.

Khiri

Earlier known as *bhat payasa*, it is a common dessert made using rice, milk, nuts and sugar. One of the popular writers, Yamuna Devi came across the fact that this *kheer* preparation originated from Puri in Odisha and this dessert is about a 2000 year old recipe, hence acknowledged to be one of the oldest preparations in Indian cuisine.

Khaja

A reputed dish of Odisha, which is prepared in the kitchen of Jagannath temple of Puri daily for being served as *prasad*. This is prepared by mixing equal quantity of ghee and flour to a paste consistency. A stift dough of flour, ghee with little water and salt is made. After this, the dough is rolled into rectangular shape as thick as *chapati*. Then ghee-flour paste is evenly spread on the rectangular dough and this is rolled from one side to give it a rope like shape. This is then cut into 1 inch pieces and rolled again to make it about 5 inches long *khaja*. This is fried in hot oil and then is dipped in sticky sugar syrup. This is then removed after some time and served cold.

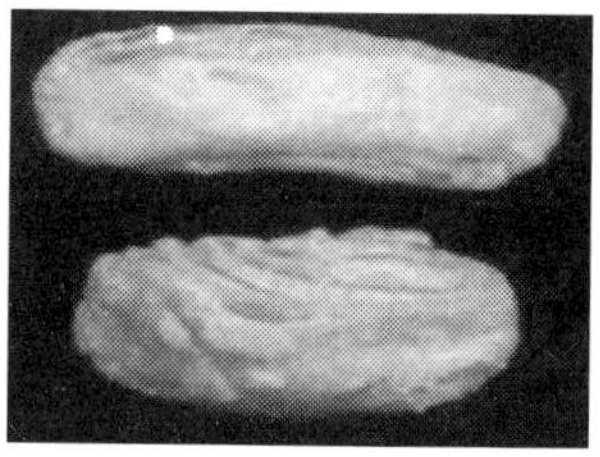

Attakali

It is a famous dish made by boiling balls of rice powder, scrubbed coconut, pepper powder and salt in rice powder in a semi-liquid form sweetened with sugar. It is served on the auspicious occasions of Bakula Amabashya and Manabasa Gurubar in Odisha.

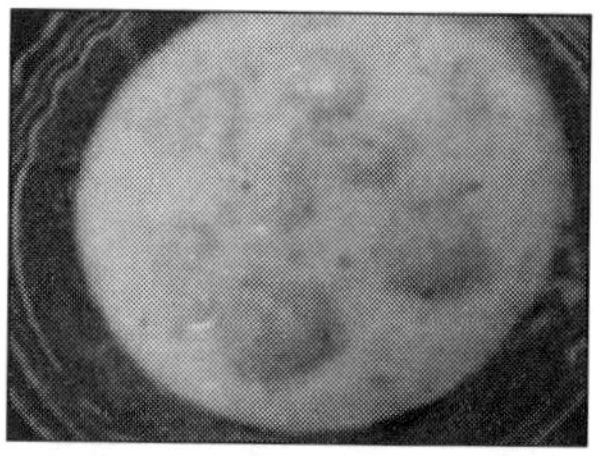

Enduri Pitha

It is a special delicacy made in the Prathamastami festival and also during many other Oriya festivities. It is prepared by grinding the mixture of rice and black gram coarsely soaked in water for about 5 hours and then letting it to ferment. Once it is fermented, the fermented mixture is applied on a green turmeric leaf and then a stuffing of grated coconut, cottage cheese, jaggery and spices is laid on the fermented layer and leaves folded, so as to sandwich the stuffing properly. It is steam cooked and served.

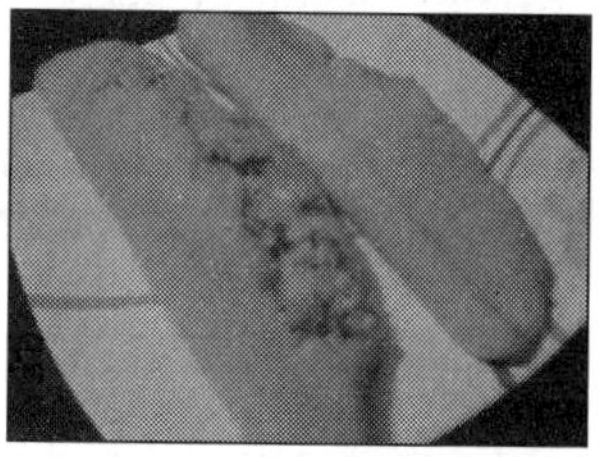

Culinary Trivia: Farra or Goojha or Peetha or Gointha

It is simply a steamed lentil-stuffed dumpling made of rice flour. It is a labour intensive and time consuming delicacy but worth all the efforts. Rice flour is kneaded with sufficient water to form a soft dough and it is kept aside. *Urad dhuli dal* and *channa dal* are soaked in water for about 4-5 hours and then ground to a coarse consistency along with garlic, ginger, red chilli powder, *garam masala* powder, turmeric powder and salt. Then, rice flour balls are made out of it and rolled like *chapati* of about 5 inch diameter. On half the side of it is kept the coarsely grinded stuffing and is covered with rest of rice flour dough portions. It is crescent shaped at this stage. Then it is steamed till done properly. It is consumed with a vegetable preparation of red pumpkin or *aloo baingan ki subzi*. *Kheer* is a must in accompaniment with this *farra* dish. Green *chutney* or *saunth ki chutney* is also served with this preparation.

23 Punjabi Cuisine

> **"Tell me what you eat, and I will tell you what you are." – Anthelme Brillat Savarin**

Punjab, located in the northwestern region of the Indian subcontinent is a state bordered by Himachal Pradesh on the east, Haryana on the south and southeast and Rajasthan on the southwest as well as the Pakistani province of Punjab on the west. It is also surrounded on the north by the Indian state of Jammu and Kashmir.

Punjab is a land of abundance, fascinating everyone with utter simplicity and robustness. Punjab can be split into two words, i.e., Punj (five) and Ab (waters). As the name suggests, Punjab is the land of the five rivers — Beas, Satluj, Chenab, Ravi and Jhelum. It is also referred as 'the land of milk and honey' and 'the bread basket of India'.

In 1947, Greater Punjab (British Punjab of 1903) was divided into two regions: Pakistani Punjab and Indian Punjab.

Possessing a robust climate, this region has been bestowed with immense dividends in terms of agricultural produce. The production of the seasonal grains and vegetables has been very high due to its fertile lands. This aspect of high productivity has successively made the cuisine of this region so lavish and rich that it is easily reflected in every element of its culinary experience. Here milk, milk products like curds, cream, ghee, and *paneer*; honey, wheat, mustard, corn, and so on are grown in abundance and can be easily seen in its cuisine.

This regional cuisine reflects the creative influence of the Mughal invasion, and the popularity of *tandoor* and its adaption in the cuisine, justifies this statement. Punjab has thus assimilated some aspects of its cuisine from external influences. The great experts in the field of culinary world are of the view that even the gravy component of Punjabi cuisine came from the Mughals. The popularity of *tandoor* throughout the country has been credited to Punjab. *Tandoori* cooking flourished here and spread all across.

Punjabi cuisine is heavily spiced to please the taste buds and hence the spices have been the key player in shaping this regional cuisine. It has full-bodied *masalas* (spices) cooked with liberal amount of *desi ghee* (clarified butter) always served with a liberal helping of butter or cream. The generous use of spices like coriander, cardamom, clove, cumin, black pepper, turmeric, mustard and red chilli are the hallmark and authentication of this exquisite cuisine.

Some dishes have gained immense popularity and have become most illustrious dish of Punjabi cuisine and are in demand all across when it comes to Punjabi cuisine. *Sarson ka saag* and *makki di roti* are two such crucial dishes, and most importantly they complement each other so well that in no other regional cuisine of India any dish complements any other dish in such a manner. Whereas there are many dishes in Punjab that go in combination with other preparations like *pindi chole* and *bhature, rajma* or *kadhi* with *jeera rice, aloo paratha* and *dahi,* and so on.

Milk and its products are abundant and hence become an essential part of everyday cookery. Curds and buttermilk are also essential components in every Punjabi meal. No meal is considered complete in a true sense without a serving of *lassi* (sweet or salted drink made with curds) or fresh curds and white butter which is consumed in large quantities. Butter is the fundamental cooking medium apart from being consumed raw along with the food.

Wheat is grown in abundance, hence the Punjabi populace are wheat eaters. They consume rice rarely mainly on festive or special occasions. Rice is never eaten plain, but with a flavouring of cumin seeds or fried onions or with *rajma* curry or *kadhi. Rajma masala* with rice or rice with *kadhi* is eaten or holidays or on festive days. In winter, rice is cooked with fresh peas called *matar-wale chawal* or cooked as a delicacy called *rao ki kheer* in which rice is cooked on very slow fire for several hours together with sugar cane juice. This *kheer* renders a special taste to the dish.

The *dal* preparations are undoubtedly the specialty of Punjabi cuisine. The *dals* are made of whole pulses like black gram, green gram and bengal gram. These are generally soaked overnight or for at least 8 hours and gently simmered on the hot embers of a *tandoor* along with ginger, garlic and other *masalas.* These are then combined with a tangy masala base which could include tomato or dried mango or pomegranate seeds. The character typical to the bean or whole lentil preparation is that the shape is retained intact, but slightest pressure would turn it into a paste and then it is rounded off with malai (cream) for that rich finish.

The Punjabi cuisine has maintained a great balance between non-vegetarian dishes and vegetarian dishes. The menu is prepared depending upon the preferences of the diners and has varied dishes in both the cases. The level of spices varies from being minimal to dominating. There are many mouth-watering dishes in the Punjabi cuisine. *Murg makhani* and *paneer makhani* are very good examples of lavish and remarkable dishes and are relished all over.

Punjab being the 'bread basket of India', the breads of this region are numerous and varied and have a different identity. Many types of bread are flat bread meaning unleavened bread and few are leavened breads. The breads here are also made up of different ingredients, i.e., of different kinds of flour. They also have different methods of preparation for various breads, like few breads are *tandoor* baked like *tandoori* naan, *tandoori roti* and *lacchha parantha;* a few are griddle baked like *phulka, bajre ki roti, makke ki roti;* a few are deep fried like *puri* and *bhatura* and a few are shallow fried like *parantha.* One of the popular ways of consuming bread is in the form of stuffed breads like *aloo parantha, gobhi ke paranthe, mooli ke paranthe,* and so on. The breads of this region are multifaceted and are incomparable from the breads of other regions.

One of the unique and typical products of this state is *wadiyan* and Punjab again has mastered the skill to prepare these to perfection. The skinned *urad dal* is ground with little water and fermented overnight and then mixed with grated *petha* (ash gourd) and coarse ground spices especially whole black peppercorn, and crushed hot chilies. The spiced mixture is formed into a hollow ball with a diameter of 2 inches. These dumplings are then dried in hot sun. Amritsar is the capital of making *wadiyan.* Smaller and milder dried dumplings are made of skinless *mung* beans, and these are referred to as *mongodiyan.* These *wadiyan* and *mongodiyan* are used in curry preparation and consumed accordingly.

The *dhaba* (roadside eatery) culture boomed mainly in Punjab culture and has marked its strong presence all over the country by becoming a significant feature on national and state highways. The eating out trends in Punjab has been one reason to give birth to the *dhaba* culture and allow it to flourish so vigorously. The food prepared in the *dhabas* is superbly tasty and delicious and is actually made and spiced according to the need and preferences of the diners. There are a lot large number of *dhabas* in every city and people enjoy eating there. The menu consists of a salad plate (sliced onions and tomatoes, fresh green chilies, wedge of lime), *tandoori roti, tandoori paratha, dal* (*mah, makhani*), vegetable curry (*aloo rasedar, aloo gobhi, aloo wadi, mattar paneer*), mutton *kaleji,* mutton *bheja, keema* (ground goat meat with green peas), and chicken curry. Eating out in a *dhaba* is treated as a grand occasion and people enjoy every aspect of it.

Tandoor: A Signature Cooking Equipment of Punjab

Tandoor is the most significant equipment and has its origin long back in Afghanistan. It came to India with the Mughals during their invasion on India. The Punjabi *tandoori* cooking is celebrated as one of the most popular cuisines in India and also throughout the world. *Tandoor* is a huge earthen oven half buried in the ground and heated with a coal fire lit below. Once it is hot, it is used for cooking breads, *kebabs, tikkas,* snacks and various delicious items. Nowadays many different types of *tandoor* are available such as traditional *tandoor,* gas operated and electric operated tandoors, and so on. Many signature dishes are prepared in *tandoor* and are liked by all.

Specialty Dishes

Rajma Masala

A well-famed dish from Punjab is *rajma masala,* it is made up of red kidney beans as the main ingredient. It is prepared by soaking the *rajma* beans overnight and then boiling it till done and cooking it in a onion tomato gravy, in which tomato has a dominating taste.

Chhole Masala

This preparation is made up of white chick peas (*kabuli chana*), prepared by soaking *kabuli chana* overnight and then boiling it till done and then cooking it in a onion-tomato gravy. It has tamarind pulp added to it in minimal quantity, which gives it a special sour taste. It is served garnished with onion roundels, tomato slices and fresh green coriander.

Pindi Chane

It is a tangy and spicy preparation of chick peas made dry in Rawalpindi style and is topped with onion rings and chopped fresh coriander. It is a dry preparation and is great in taste.

Tandoori Murg

It is a mouth-watering dish and is a signature preparation of *tandoor* and is among the most illustrious delicacies of Punjab. It is prepared by cleaning the whole chicken properly and then cut marks are made on the chicken (breasts and drumsticks), to absorbs the marination more efficiently.

Then the chicken is marinated for about 2-3 hours in a special red colour marinade made of hung curds, mustard oil, vinegar, red chilli powder, green cardamom powder, fennel powder, mace powder, whole garam masala powder, salt, and so on. Once the chicken is marinated properly, it is skewered and roasted in *tandoor* with proper basting of oil or butter in between. Extreme care is taken not to get the chicken pieces dry and also till it is properly done. Then it is cut into pieces and served with lemon wedges, onion roundels and mint chutney. It won't be an exaggeration to state that it is one among the most revered dishes of Punjab.

Sarson da Saag

Sarson da saag is a very special preparation made up of mustard leaves added with fenugreek leaves (*methi*) and cooked on a slow fire for hours with a minimum quantity of spices so that the fresh taste can be retained. In fact, the longer it takes to cook the *saag*, the better it tastes. It is a dish which is complemented best with *makki di roti*.

Makki di Roti

It is unleavened bread made up of maize flour and is griddle fried. It tastes out of the world with *sarson da saag*.

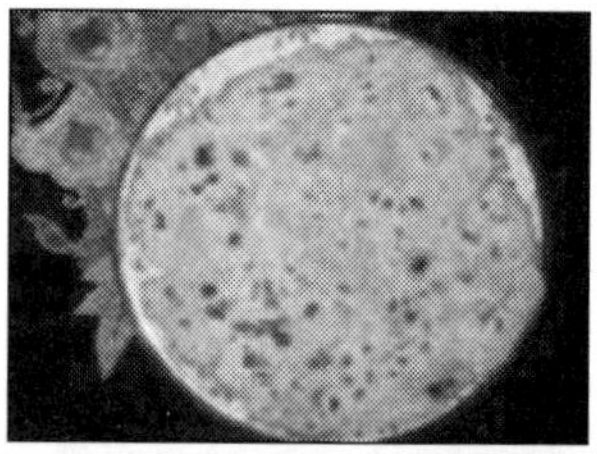

Punjabi Lobia

It is a preparation of black-eyed beans soaked in water for some time and then cooked in a tomato onion *masala* gravy with a slight spicy hint of red chillies.

Phirni

It is a typical Punjabi dessert, which is made of milk, rice and sugar, lightly flavoured with cardamom, garnished with flaked nuts, and served chilled in earthenware dishes.

Vegetable Jalfarezi

This is a sizzling vegetable preparation with an array of vegetables like carrots, peas, capsicum, cauliflower, and so on and prepared in a mildly spiced up tomato gravy.

Kadhai Paneer

It is an authentic Punjabi dish made with cottage cheese simmered in tomato *masala* gravy with an appropriate quantity of dices of bell peppers, tomatoes and onions in it.

Shahi Paneer

Shahi translates to 'royal' in English. In this preparation, *paneer* is cooked in a very rich gravy made up of boiled onion, cashew nut paste and yogurt and loads of cream. It is referred as *shahi* due to the richness of ingredients like cream, cashew nut in large quantity.

Rara Gosht

This delicacy uses mutton in two forms like mutton, leg pieces and mutton mince. The mutton is steeped in gravy of spicy mince, and soaked with rare spices. This dish is very rich in taste and texture.

Baigan ka Bharta

It is a preparation of brinjal in which it is roasted on cow-dung cakes and then mashed and mixed with chopped green chillies, ginger, garlic, tomatoes, and spices. The roasting of whole brinjal on cow-dung cakes or in *tandoor* gives this preparation a smoky flavour, which makes it different and distinct. It is loved across the country and can be said that it is this preparation in which brinjal is loved and relished most.

Navratan Korma

This is a preparation made from nine ingredients including vegetables like cauliflower, green peas, carrots, French beans, and so on), nuts (dry fruits), *paneer* and is served in rich onion gravy flavoured with cream.

Malai Kofta

This is a lovely and tasty dish, in which the dumplings of grated paneer are stewed in a mild tomato gravy garnished with cream. The *paneer* is mixed with chopped green coriander, *garam masala* powder, chopped green chillies, and chopped ginger, and so on to prepare the dumplings.

Gajar ka Halwa

It is a sweet dessert pudding associated mainly with the state of Punjab. It is made by placing bright red grated carrot in a jar containing a specific amount of milk and sugar and then cooked, stirring regularly. It is often served with a garnish of cashew nuts, raisins, almonds and pistachios. The nuts and other items used are first sautéd in ghee to add richness to the *halwa*. Then *khoya* is added in the end to the *halwa* and then it is served hot. As carrot is easily and readily available in winters, it is prepared during winter season only. It is a must in all wedding functions during the winter season.

Gulab Jamun

Gulab jamun is one of the most popular desserts of India. It is a deep-fried dumpling of *khoya* and refined flour, dipped in rose-saffron flavoured sugar syrup. The name *gulab jamun* literally translates to rose berries.

This dessert also has few variations and is stuffed with chopped nuts, raisins, *khoya* and cardamom powder for variety.

Paneer Makhani

It is one of the most loved and popular preparation of *paneer* all across the country. In this delicacy, the chunks of *paneer* are cut into cubes and cooked in silky textured tomato based gravy, enriched with dollops of butter and cream. If the tomato used is sour then it is sweetened by adding a dash of honey in it, at the end. It is also referred as Paneer Butter Masala.

Butter Chicken

It is a delicacy which has a different identity altogether in Indian cuisine. It is so popular that it has to be present in almost all non-vegetarian menus in North India. The chicken is marinated and then it is roasted in a *tandoor* (clay oven). It is then cut into pieces and simmered in smooth textured tomato based *makhani* gravy which is flavoured with butter, cream and *kasoori methi* in the end. The dish has a lovely taste and is appreciated all over.

Murg Makhani

It literally translates to 'butter chicken' in English. But the only difference in *Murg Makhani* and Butter Chicken is that the former delicacy is prepared by using boneless pieces of chicken and the latter one with chicken pieces with bone in a tomato based *makhani* gravy.

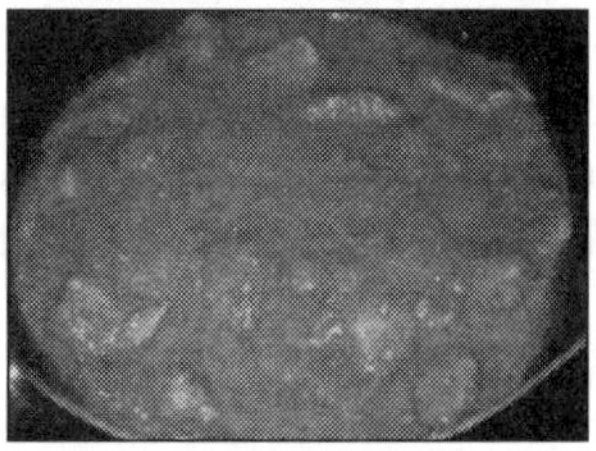

Keema Matar

It is a unique dry preparation in which ground minced meat is cooked with or tossed with peas in a onion-tomato masala and served with rice or hot *chapatis*.

Dal Makhani

It is one of the staple food preparations of Punjab and is prepared by keeping *sabut urad dal* and, red kidney beans on the embers to let it simmer overnight. Many of the recipes also call for *chana dal* in it, but in small quantity. This *dal* preparation is done with lots of tomatoes and with no onions. It has a silky and smooth texture and is served garnished with cream and butter. At the end, it is sprinkled with lots of crushed *kasoori methi*.

Punj Ratni Dal

It is a mixture of five *dals* and all these *dals* are soaked in water a day before. The *dals* preferred are *chana dal, sabut moong dal, sabut urad dal, masoor sabut* and *arhar dal*. Then they are simmered on the embers of a *tandoor* along with spices like chilly, onion, ginger, cardamom, cinnamom, mace and bay leaf. It has a great flavour and has a silky texture as well.

Mah ki Dal

It is a *dal* preparation of black *urad dal* soaked overnight and flavoured with tangy tomatoes, garlic, ginger, curds, lemon and many spices like cumin powder, coriander powder, red chilli powder, and so on. It is served garnished with cream, butter and fine chopped coriander leaves.

Dal Amritsari

Also referred to as *langarwali dal* and is very popular in Punjabi cuisine. It is prepared by the combination of two *dals* like split black *urad dal* and *chana dal*. It is tempered with sufficient quantity of onions, tomatoes, ginger and garlic with generous amount of ghee in it. It is flavoured with chopped green coriander leaves.

Amritsari Machhi

It is a unique fish preparation from Amritsar. The fish is cut across the bones (darne cut) and then dipped in a batter of gram flour and is flavoured with *ajwain*. It is then deep fried and served with mint *chutney* or spicy sauces.

Chicken Tikka Masala

It is a chicken delicacy which is cooked in *tandoor* and then cooked in onion-tomato masala gravy. In this, the chicken is deboned and chunks of chicken are marinated and the skewered and cooked in a *tandoor*. These roasted chunks are further cooked in gravy and served. The roasting process in tandoor lends a unique feature to this dish. The chicken is cooked in such a fashion that it gets so tender that it easily melts in the mouth while eating it.

Palak Paneer

It is a delicacy in which dices of paneer are cooked in a spinach paste, tempered with coriander seeds, red chilli flakes and lots of chopped ginger and garlic. It is finally garnished with cream.

Naan

This fermented teardrop oval shaped bread is made with refined flour. The dough is kneaded with flour, milk, eggs, sugar, salt, oil and curds. The dough is kneaded until smooth and elastic and is allowed to ferment for about 2 hours. Then the dough is divided into dough balls and is stretched by tossing the piece of dough quickly from one palm to the other to form a thin oval flat bread, slightly thicker around the edges than in the centre. Traditionally naan is baked on the walls of a *tandoor* oven, brushed with a thin coating of oil or ghee and served hot. At certain places, onion seeds are sprinkled on the dough, and butter is applied later on.

Lacchha Parantha

This is a flat unleavened bread made up of wheat flour dough with concentric circle shaped rolls are made by craftsmen to ensure pervasion and trapping of heat in between the layers. The layers are easily visible while eating. It is brushed with a profuse quantity of butter.

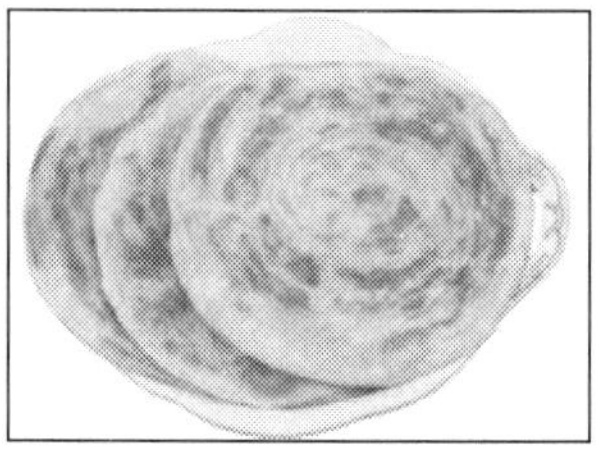

Kulcha

Kulcha refers to *naan* stuffed with any kind of mixture such as that of potatoes, cottage cheese or vegetables and cooked in a *tandoor*. It is served brushed with melted butter. In simple words, *kulcha* is a stuffed butter naan.

Missi Roti

It is a very popular bread from North India and the dough for it is prepared using gram flour, wheat flour with cumin seeds, coriander leaves, chopped onions, green chillies, turmeric and salt. It is very heavy and a highly nutritious bread.

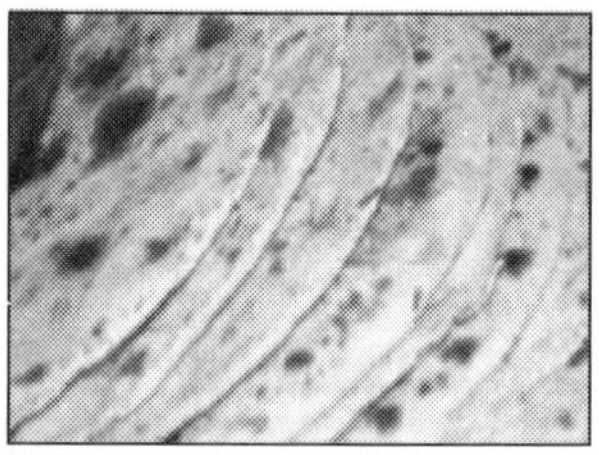

Bhature

It is a deep-fried leavened bread made of refined flour and is most enjoyed with *chhole masala*. It puffs up when it is deep-fried.

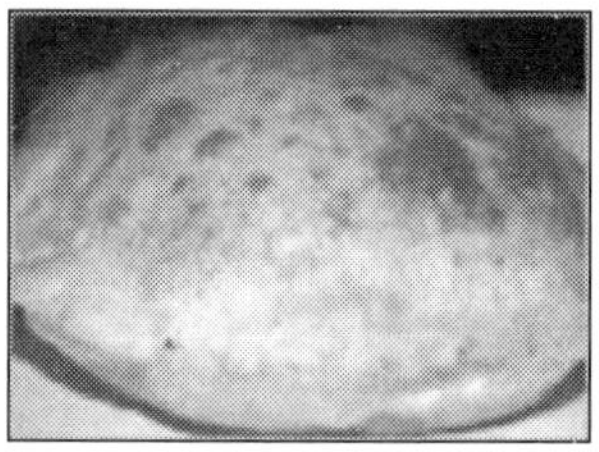

Dahi Bhalle

In this dish the deep fried dumplings made of *urad dal* are served in a dip of curds with lots of sweet-sour *chutney* and sprinkling of powdered red chilli and cumin powder. It is a preparation which is made during festive occasions and also during functions. It looks amazingly great in its presentation.

Paneer Pakoda

It is a dish in which chunks of *paneer* are dipped in the batter of gram flour with *ajwain*, red chilli powder, ginger-garlic paste and a few other spices and then deep fried. It is eaten with spicy green coriander *chutney*.

Lassi

It is made of yogurt and tempered with either salt or sugar. It is a popular drink of Punjabi origin with 'cooling' properties but it is quite popular all over the country. Many a places in India, *lassi* is served with a layer of *malai* topped with dry fruits. It is a must have in Punjabi meals during lunch.

Culinary Trivia: Kofta

Kofta is simply a meat ball. In its simplest form, *koftas* consist of balls and minced or ground meat mixed with spices and/or onions. *Koftas* were introduced to India with the Muslim conquests. *Koftas* in Indian cuisine are normally cooked in a spiced gravy or curry.

They are often shaped into balls which are prepared with a mixture of minced meat, or vegetables, rice and leeks, and served dry or in a gravy or curry. In India, vegetarian varieties, like *malai kofta, lauki kofta, kathal ke kofte* and *shahi aloo kofta,* are popular, as religious beliefs generally forbid consumption of meat. The vegetables are grated and mixed with dry spices and bound by cornflour and shaped into balls and then deep fried. Shrimp and fish *koftas* are found in South India and West Bengal.

Koftas are sometimes made with fish or vegetables rather than red meat, especially in India. They can be grilled, fried, steamed, poached, baked or marinated, and may be served with a rich spicy sauce.

Culinary Trivia: Saag

Saag are annual herbs and their green leaves are consumed as a vegetable. *Saag* is a generic term used for variety of greens consumed in India. The leaves are very nutritious and tasty. There are many varieties of *saag* available in India.

Few examples are *palak* (spinach), *chaulai, bathuaa* (amaranth leaves), *methi* (fenugreek leaves), *soaa* (dill leaves), *mooli ka saag* (radish leaves), *sarson ka saag* (mustard leaves), *todiya ka saag, marsa ka saag, kulfa* (purslane leaves), *arui ke patte ka saag, chakwad ka saag, poi ka sagg, karumva ka saag, channe ka saag,* and so on.

24 Rajasthani Cuisine

"Wit is the salt of conversation, not the food." – William Hazlitt

Rajasthan is a state in the northwestern region of India, bordered with Pakistan on the west, Gujarat on the southwest, Madhya Pradesh on the southeast, Uttar Pradesh and Haryana on the northeast and Punjab on the north.

Each region in India has its own traditional dishes and specialities and Rajasthan is no exception to it.

The cuisine and culinary arts of this charming state is judged as the most majestic and royal by the connoisseurs of food. The exquisite cuisine of Rajasthan is extraordinarily weaved with mouth-watering dishes and sumptuous meals. Each dish of this state is a class apart and contributes in defining the Rajasthani cuisine. The history of Rajasthan's cuisine is a success story of the ultimate determination and struggle faced by people of Rajasthan against conquerors along with all odds of nature and its barren lands.

Notwithstanding the harsh reality to which Rajasthan is exposed to with unproductive barren lands and extreme weather conditions, Rajasthani cuisine has been capable enough to devise culinary elements which define and shape the regional cuisine, is indeed a matter worthy of appreciation. Ingredients used frequently in these recipes have been carefully selected not by choice but more out of hard geographical compulsion rather than for the taste. The ingredients are limited in numbers and even in quantity too.

Rajasthani cooking is the resultant cuisine born out of struggle prevailing among the lifestyle of its inhabitants and most importantly based on the availability of ingredients in this harsh terrain region. Because of scarcity of food, preservation of the food was the main concern in Rajasthan. As nothing could be cultivated in the infertile lands facing the hot and stormy sand-dunes, thought provoking tasks for the cooks were to create recipes which required minimum use of water, and could be stored for longer periods of time without requiring re-heating. The cooks came out with flying colours to achieve this objective with great sense of accomplishment. It has been a paradigm for the entire world to witness such a rich cuisine with less usage of ingredients, that has come only from the lands of Rajasthan. While the eastern region of Rajasthan has fertile soil capable of growing crops ranging from wheat and maize to millets and corn, for much part the desert's dry terrain, prone to droughts, has been incapable of producing even basic necessities for sustenance.

The ancient luxurious state of Rajasthan gave birth to a truly majestic cuisine. The Rajas (kings) who went on hunting excursions ate the meat or the fowls that they brought back. Even today, Rajasthani deluxe feasts ostentatiously display meat cuisines that are incomparable and, in contrast, they are the vegetarian also. Their food is cooked in pure ghee. Rajasthan's flavoursome curries are based on the use of pulses or gram flour. Dry fruits, spices and yogurt are used in many delicacies. Rajasthan compulsorily portrays a vast array of savouries and sun-dried snacks.

Rajasthan is the Land of Princes, which boasts of many elegant gastronomic dishes both within the palaces and outside. The preparation of food was indeed a complex matter in the imperial kitchens of Rajasthan and was raised to the level of an art form. Thus the *khansamas* (the royal cooks) worked in the stately palaces and never disclosed their most enigmatic recipes to anyone. Some recipes were passed on to their next generation and the rest were passed on as skills to the chefs of semi-states and also the branded hotel companies.

The cuisine of Rajasthan is primarily vegetarian and has a varied assemblage of fabulous mouth-watering dishes. The spice content is quite high in comparison with other Indian cuisines, but the food is absolutely scrumptious. Ghee is the cooking medium for cooking most of the dishes. Rajasthani food is renowned all over for its spicy curries and delicious sweets.

Rajasthani cooking is symbolized for its distinctly typical and unique flavour and for being simple. Most elementary ingredients go into the preparation of most of the dishes in Rajasthan. The craving and passion of the Maharajas of Rajasthan for *shikar* (hunting) has been largely responsible for shaping the distinct culinary art in Rajasthan. In terms of gastronomic features, game cooking is undoubtedly the most esteemed art form in Rajasthan, largely because the skills required to clean, cut and cook the game are not easily gained. The lean mutton of the desert goats of Bikaner region too is considered a great item. The region of Mewar or Udaipur in Rajasthan is believed to have come up with a famous barbeque preparation called *sooley*.

With Pathani intrusions, came in the art of barbecuing which has now been honed to perfection and the quintessential *sula*-smoked *kebabs* or skewered boneless lamb is considered to be prepared in 11 distinct ways. On the other hand, the vegetarian cooking aspect of the Maheshwaris of Marwar or Jodhpur in Rajasthan, who do not use even garlic and onion, is no less in respect in the world of cookery. The reason for not using onion and garlic is that its are considered to excite the blood. The Vaishnavas, followers of Krishna, were also strict vegetarian, and so were the Bishnois, a community known for its passion to conserve both animal and plant life. Thus the art of vegetarian cooking has also flourished much in this state due to a great liking for vegetarianism.

The personal recipes of the Royal *khansamas* are still seen with their generations and are the highlights of royal gatherings of Rajasthan. Each state of Rajasthan had its own style of recipes which they could boast of. Many of these are still continued in Rajput households. It was primarily the men members of the family that prepared the non-vegetarian dishes. Certain Maharajas apart from being great hunters relished the passion of cooking the *shikars* by themselves for their selected esteemed guests and this unique trend continues among the generations of Rajasthan.

The desert belt of Jaisalmer, Barmer and Bikaner of Rajasthan has arid land and hence the cooks are compelled to use minimum water as much as they can. This feature has gifted them with an option to use more of milk, buttermilk and clarified butter, which is available in plentitude in this region. The Maheshwari cooking is characterized by abundant use of mango powder in place where tomatoes are rare, and asafoetida is substituted for onion and garlic to enhance the taste of the dish. In this region, one finds specific kinds of berries and beans from the indigenous plants like *ker, sangria,* and so on are also used liberally in certain preparations. Dried lentils are also used in several preparations. Gram flour is an essential constituent of this regional cuisine and is used to make some of the delicacies like *khata, gatte ki sabzi, pakodi* and so on. Powdered lentils are used for *mangodi, papad,* and so on. Vegetable preparations like *kikoda ki subzi* and *moranga ki subzi* make the cuisine of Rajasthan very distinct and unique at the same time.

The day-to-day food in Rajasthan essentially comprises unleavened bread, made of wheat, barley, millet or maize. Bajra and corn is used all over the state for preparations of *rabri, kheechdi* and *roti*. Several kinds of *chutneys* are made from locally available spices like turmeric, coriander, mint and garlic. Perhaps the best known Rajasthani food is the ultimate combination of *dal, bati* and *churma* but it offers a lot of variety if one is willing to experiment and play with the recipes.

The dishes that are prepared are based on the criteria of the availability of ingredients in the state. Among these, gram flour is the most versatile ingredient and one of the best examples. Gram flour is a major ingredient produce here and used to make some of the delicacies like *khatta, gatte ki subzi, kadhi,* and *pakodi.* Powdered lentils are used for *mangodi* and *papad*. They are used in preparation of dessert as well like *besan ki chakki* or *mohanthal*.

Jodhpur is the place acknowledged for the origin of several Indian delicacies and illustrations of this are Makhaniya Lassi, Mawa Kachori, Pyaaz Kachori, hot and spicy Mirchi bada, Lapsi (a unique sort of pudding type of dessert made with wheat, jaggery, and ghee) and so on. Similarly, Bikaner has its world-famed savouries, especially *bhujiya*, which has accounted for its popularity, and the quality of its *papads* and *badi* remains non-paralleled.

The Kachchwaaha family of Jaipur in Rajasthan is the considered the originator of the most popular meat delicacy called *safed maans* or white meat. The preparation of gravy for this is white in colour and is prepared from white mutton. The curry is prepared from cashew nuts, onion, almonds, fresh coconut kernel paste, curds, cream, white pepper and poppy seeds.

The unique creation of the Maharaja of Salwar is the *junglee maans* and is relished all across. *Junglee maans* was a great favourite among the Maharajas and due to paucity of exotic ingredients in the camp kitchens, the game brought in from the hunt was simply cooked in pure ghee, salt and plenty of red chillies. This dish incorporates very less number of ingredients and yet is very delicious.

During summer, an appetizing drink *Aanch* is very common and popular as well. It is very similar to *aam ka panna* in which raw mangoes are roasted directly over the fire and are then peeled and pureed. Then it is added with spices and dried mint powder for extra flavour.

Desserts of Rajasthan

Each region boasts of its own special food item which is popularly identified with the town or city. Each region, each district has mastered the art of preparing incomparable and outstanding dessert delicacies. Jaipur in Rajasthan has excelled in the art of preparing a few world class desserts. Its specialties include *gulab sakri* (a delicious mixture of *khoya*, sugar and fat cooked and set into a thaali and garnished with saffron), *misri mawa* (made of milk, sugar and cardamom, it resembles a *burfi* and is typically served in green leaf with a wooden spoon), *kalakand* which is amazing in taste and is similar to tender *burfi* like dessert. A Rajasthani delicacy, linked with the monsoon festival of Teej, is called *ghevar*, consisting of round cakes of white flour over which sweetened syrup is poured. Today, variations include lacings with cream and *khoya* in *ghevar*, making it a delightful concoction.

Bikaner is also famous for *gund pak* (a famous dessert made of wheat, gund, nuts and ghee). In Bharatpur, milk sweets, rarely commercially available, occupy a niche by themselves.

The region of Mewar or Udaipur in Rajasthan is renowned all across for its famous sweet *dil jani*. The region of Jaisalmer is famous for *laddoos* and *gotma* (small *besan boondis* are dipped in sugar syrup and then mashed with a wooden spatula and this method was called *ghotna* and hence the dessert is named as *gotma*), Pushkar for *malpua* (type of pancake made with *rabri* and kept in sugar syrup), Ajmer for *sohan halwa*, Alwar for milk cake (milk is boiled till all moisture is removed and mould into a cake which is finally brownish in colour from inside and whitish yellow from outside) and *kangan* (*imerti*), Kishangarh for *balushahi* or *makhan bade* (a round ball made of refined flour and white butter dough slightly flattened at the centre, fried in ghee and dipped in saffron flavoured sugar syrup), Dausa for *deoti*, Ganganagar for *khir mon*, Sambhar for *phini*, Amer for *gunjia*, Pillani for *chidawa ke pede*, Bharatpur for *gajak* (a famous dessert prepared from sesame seeds and jaggery by a very complex process) and Beawar for *til papdi* (a flattened dessert made by sesame seeds and sugar in very thin paper sheets). Hot *jalebies* are available in most towns and cities of Rajasthan.

Specialty Dishes

Dal Baati and Churma

It is the most popular and distinctive dish of the state, in fact a signature dish of the state, without which no Rajasthani meal can be considered to be complete. A delicious, rich, flavourful and a whole meal in itself consisting of three items, *baati* is a hard, round whole-wheat ball/roll, cooked in a *tandoor* oven or baked over firewood or over *kandas* (i.e. cow dung cakes) or roasted over hot coals, served after dipping in enormous amount of ghee (clarified butter) accompanied with *dal* and *churma*. Nowadays it is made by deep frying also in clarified butter. *Dal* is a thin curry of two or more lentils tempered with moderate quantity of spices and more of *desi ghee*. *Churma* is prepared deep-fried *baatis* of unsalted dough, crushed and cooked with ghee, nuts and sugar or jaggery. The three together, simple though they sound and appear, make a very filling and delicious meal. **Note:** *Bafla* is a kind of *baati*, which is softer, has a filling and instead of being cooked in oven is fried in *desi ghee*. *Keema baati* is a non-vegetarian version on *baati*. *Keema baati* is a hard, unleavened round ball made of wheat flour and cooked in *tandoor*. It is a substitute for bread and has a *keema* filling. *Keema* is a minced meat cooked with mild spices.

Ker Sangri Kumatia Ker Sangri Kumatia is a lovely concoction of three unique ingredients which are used to produce this typical dish. *Ker* is a small, round unripe fruit which grows on a prickly shrub, whereas *sangri* is dried wild beans or dried out untamed leaves, and *kumatia* is a dried flat pod. The seeds, beans and pods are soaked overnight in water, boiled and then fried in oil, to prepare a mouth-watering exotic delicacy flavoured dish with tints of dried dates, raisins, cashew nuts, red chillies, turmeric powder, shredded dried mango, salt, coriander seeds, cumin seeds and lots of yogurt. *Note*: When only *ker* and *sangri* are used in preparation, the preparation is called *Ker Sangri*. Also when *ker-sangri-kumatia* is combined with whole red chillies and raw mango powder, the concoction is given the name of Paanchkuta.	
Besan ke Gatte These are steamed pieces of *besan* (chickpea flour) in a rich curds gravy made with ingredients like garlic, lots of yogurt and various indian spices. First of all, a dough is prepared from *besan*, crushed coriander seeds, curds, baking powder, oil and other spices and then the dough is rolled in cylindrical shape, boiled and cut into small pieces (called *gatte*) and is sometimes fried post boiling. It is then further cooked in a gravy made up of yogurt as the main ingredient. *Gatta Pulao* is a rice preparation in which the *gatte* is tempered with rice with cumin seeds and red chilli powder.	
Govind Gatta Curry It is similar to the Gatta Masala, but a much richer and complicated version. Here the *gatta* (the gramflour dumplings) are stuffed with *paneer* and nuts and instead of boiling the dumplings, they are deep fried. It is a heavy spicy food that goes well with all kinds of Indian breads. The gravy of this is similar to that of *Besan ke Gatte.*	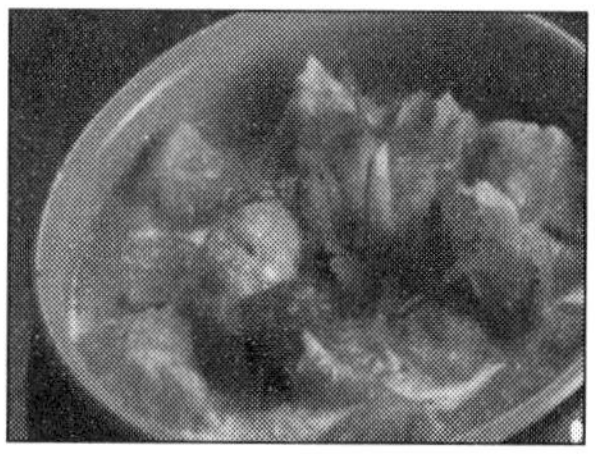
Lal Maans The most spicy and famous non-vegetarian preparation of Rajasthan is indeed Lal Maans which is made of mutton pieces cooked with lots of onions, garlic and red chillies. The thick, semi-dry tangy curry is prepared using buttermilk or curds instead of tomatoes and is delicately smoked with charcoal in the end. The deep red colour of the dish comes from a special chilli from Jodhpur called the Mathania Red Chilly.	
Safed Maans A genuinely descended version of a *korma* curry, this dish basically comprises meat cooked in a curds and cashew nut gravy with lots of onion as well. This dish is usually prepared during the special occasions. It has a delectable combination of spices such as cardamom, cinnamon, cumin and coriander seeds and all these spices have their own distinct flavours, but come beautifully together. Unlike many *kormas,* it doesn't contain any coconut. Instead the flavours are distinctly nutty, somewhat sweet and delicious. This is a main dish, it is non-spicy and goes well with all kinds of Indian breads.	
Junglee Maans This is a superb preparation of meat which is cooked with huge quantity of *desi ghee.* It has very less ingredients added to it like whole red chilli, garlic, salt and *desi ghee.* It doesn't have water and other spices. The resultant gravy is very rich due to excess usage of ghee in it. The royal families used to prepare this dish during their hunting sessions as there were very less resources and ingredients in jungle for the cooking.	

Mohan Maans

This is again a very distinct meat preparation, in which the mutton is cooked with milk and subtle mild spices. Its thick gravy is truly combined with delicate flavours of *khus khus* (poppy seeds), *khoya,* lemon, cloves and cardamom.

Khud Khargosh

Khud Khargosh is a real imperial Rajput specialty prepared during summer, when the meat (hare or rabbit meat) is tender and lean. In order to prepare this exotic dish, a whole rabbit is stuffed with spices and wrapped in dough and cooked in an open spit. The people nurtured the passion to cook this dish in jungle after hunting expedititious.

Maans ke Soole

It is tender and moist meat chunk preparation, in which the meat is marinated in flavourful fragrant spices mixed with yogurt and roasted over an open charcoal fire. After being well-done, hot ghee is poured over it, the resulting smoke becoming the source of the flavour. It is considered that there are about 11 ways to prepare smoked *soola*. It goes well with mint *chutney*. This dish is assumed to have originated in Mewar or Udaipur in Rajasthan. The meat chunks melt in the mouth while eating this delicacy.

Maans ka Soweta

It is an unusual mutton preparation in which the mutton is cooked with addition of broken corn kernels. The result of blending of two unique ingredients, meat and corn kernel is really adorable. Dices of capsicum are also added in the gravy while cooking.

Murg ka Mokul

Murg ka Mokul is a brilliant crispy fried snack dish made with chicken breasts coated with refined flour and deep fried until golden in colour and crispy in texture, tossed with some aromatic and flavourful spices to make the dish alluring and fragrant.

Haldi ki Subzi

This is a delicious preparation of fresh turmeric rhizomes available during the season and cooked in a gravy prepared with curds and spices like cumin seeds, turmeric powder and little bit of red chilli powder with asafoetida.

Gulab Jamun ki Subzi

This famous vegetarian specialty of Jodhpur is dumplings of *gulab jamun* balls which, rather than dipping in sweet syrup, is dipped in rich savoury gravy made of curds as the main ingredient.

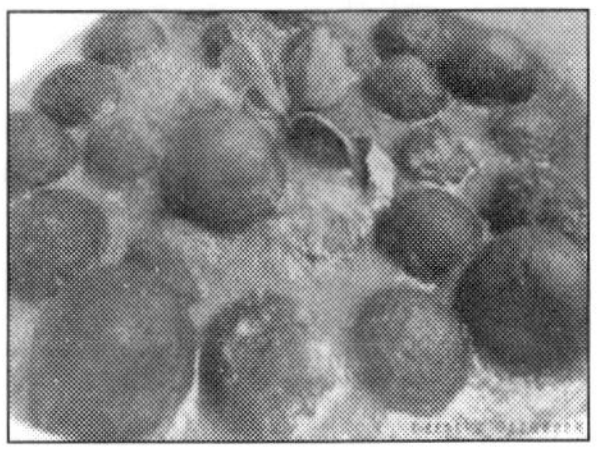

Pithorey

These are fritters made by combining gram flour, curds, turmeric, chilli powder, mustard seeds, and ghee. They can be eaten as snacks, or even stewed in a *kadhi* to make *Pithorey ki Kadhi*. In both the forms, it is very delicious and tastes great.

Papad/Rabodi ki Subzi

It is a traditional preparation which is made up of *papad* or *rabodi* (*papad* soaked in buttermilk). The *papad* could be either *besan* (gram flour) or *makka* (corn flour) based. The preparation is again based on curds as the main ingredient of the gravy.

Aloo Mangodi ki Subzi

Mangodis are small spicy dehydrated dumplings made by drying a thick spicy batter with pre-soaked and ground split green lentils, red chilli and salt in direct sunlight. These *mangodis* can be kept in kitchens just like other lentils for more than a year. Required amount of *mangodis* are deep fried and added in potato curry to make the simple, yet famous Aloo Mangodi ki Sabzi.

Rajasthani Kadhi

It is a soury simple buttermilk and gram flour based curry with less ingredients and amazing taste. In Rajasthan, it is made without any addition of dumplings (*pakodas*) or vegetables or *boondi*. It is tempered with red chilli whole flakes, mustard seeds, asafoetida, fenugreek seeds, curry leaves and so on.

Bajre ka Sogra

Bajre ka Sogra are flat breads made from millet flour. A tight hard dough is prepared by mixing *bajra* flour with small amount of wheat flour and salt. *Sogra* is an authentic word used in Rajsthan for thick *bajra* rotis, brushed with lots of pure ghee. Authentically, these *sogras* are cooked over *kandas* (cow dung cakes) in the villages to impart these thick breads with a smoky flavour. *Bajra roti, Lahsun ki Chutney* and onions are the staple diet of the Rajasthani farmers.

Khad ka Panda

This is a preparation in which a rabbit is marinated with spices in large amount and wrapped in a jute cloth. It is then covered with clay and cooked buried in the ground with live wood charcoals simmering on top.

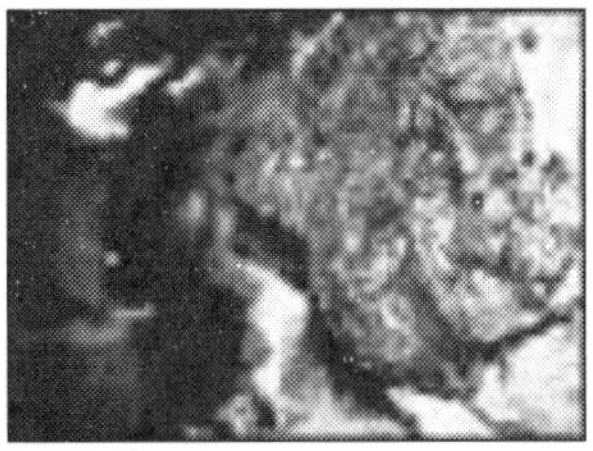

Gawar ki Phalli

It is the preparation in which cluster bean (*gwar phalli*) is cooked with spices. It is mostly finished in a curds gravy to make it a semi-dry preparation.

Raab (Makki ki Raab/Gur ki Raab/Bajre ki Raab)

This preparation is enjoyed most during winters and is prepared in 2 or 3 versions.

Makki ki Raab is made by mixing and blending boiled corn with sour butter milk. It is hot, sour and tempting and is called 'sour corn soup' and, unlike soup, it is served after the meals, dinner or lunch.

Another form of *raab* is Gur ki Raab, which is made up of *gur*, i.e. jaggery. It is a sweet dish and is also taken after meals. *Raab* made using *bajra* flour and buttermilk is called Bajre ki Raab.

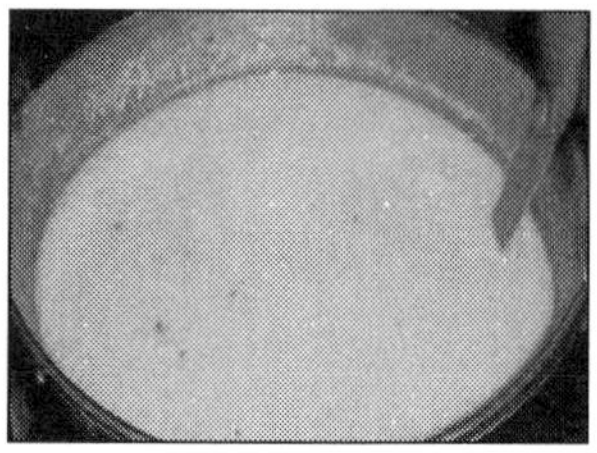

Goonda/Cordia/Lasode ki Subzi

Goonda is a kind of wild berry with a very sticky seed inside which needs to be removed before use. These can be boiled and de-seeded or else, *goondas* can be cut by striking the *goonda* with a pestic and splitting it halfway and then removing the seed using a paring knife dipped in salt water. Salt helps to remove the stickiness. After cutting a few *goondas*, fingers are dipped in salt and rubed them together. After removing the seeds, the *subzi* is prepared using these this seedless *goondas*. It is a very unique preparation and is based entirely on the availability of *goondas*.

Jhajariya

Jhajhariya is a lovely delicacy made of corn, milk, ghee and sugar garnished with raisins and nuts. In this preparation, grated or coarsely ground fresh sweetcorn is slowly roasted in ghee for few hours until it loses most of its moisture and assumes a dry granular form.

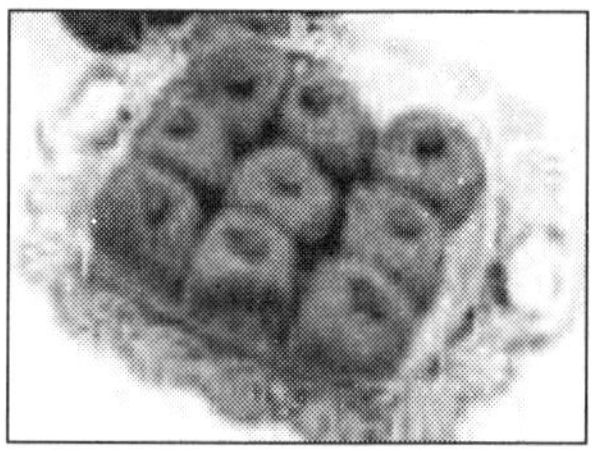

Doodh Feeni

This is a sort of very thin slightly crunchy sweet noodles made of flour. It is garnished with dry fruits like almonds and pistachios and either eaten with a sugar syrup or is dipped in hot sweet milk.

Raabdi

It is a sweet dish which is made up of wheat flour, sugar, raisins, milk cream, almonds and pistachio nuts. This group is also used for the hot drink prepared using *bajre ka atta* and curds and is a perfect drink during the cold weather.

Missi Roti

It is Rajasthani bread made in *tandoor* with wheat flour mixed with *besan*, ghee, and Indian spices. It is eaten with dollops of butter on it.

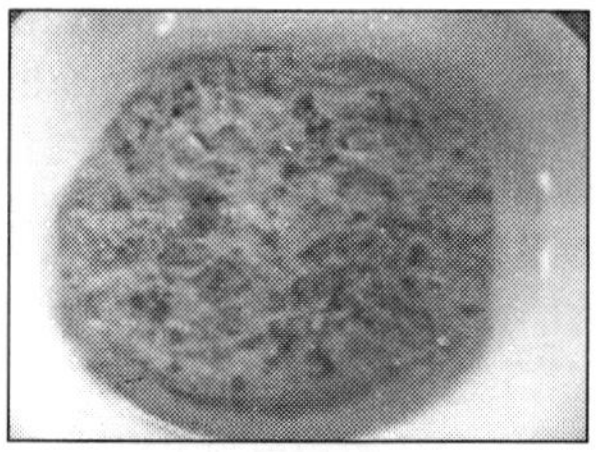

Lahsun ki Chutney

Lahsun ki Chutney is semi-dry *chutney* which is an essential part of any Rajasthani kitchen. This *chutney* is prepared with fresh garlic pods and *Jodhpuri mathania* whole red chillies and is eaten with Bajre ka Sogra or any other preparation according to individual taste. It is spicy in taste due to *mathania* red chilli and pungent due to garlic in it.

Laapsi

It is another traditional Rajasthani sweet, usually prepared at homes on festive occasions. It is made with cracked wheat, jaggery, nuts, raisins, dried fruits and lots of pure ghee. It is mostly served in the winter months and has a sweet porridge sort of look and feel.

Pyaz ki Kachori

This is one of the well-famed delicacies prepared as snacks. It is a circular shaped deep-fried snack from Jodhpur. It is a very crisp and flaky savoury pastry from outside and stuffed with a lightly caramelized and exceptionally seasoned onion filling. The filling of onion makes it splendid in its taste.

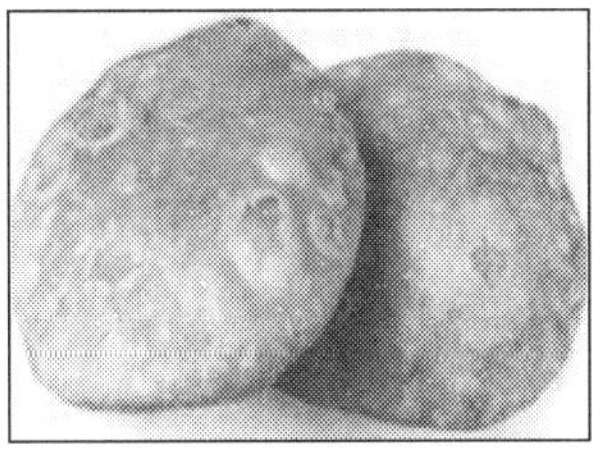

Mirchi Vada

It is a lovely and spicy snack from Jodhpur. The traditional Jodhpuri Mirchi Vadas can be imagined as a giant *pakora* with the heat of a large green chilli, tenderness of boiled and mashed potato mix, calming texture of gram flour and an excellent combination of spices that makes everybody crave for it. It is served with a tangy tomato sauce or simply with plain white bread. This preparation stimulates the taste buds of the eater.

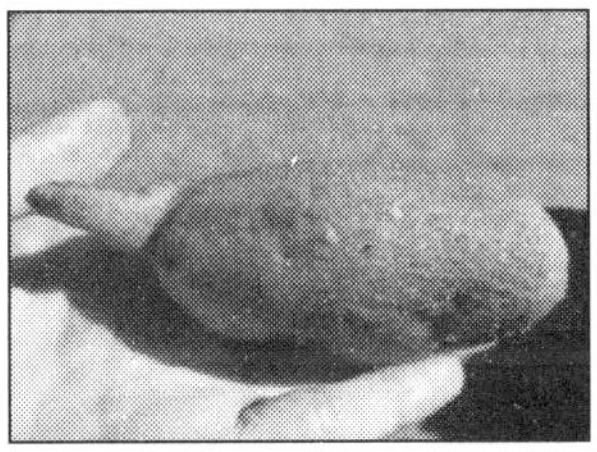

Makki ki Raab

In winter season a hot, sour and tempting delicacy, Makki ki Raab is made from ingredients which could be easily found in this tough desert region. It can be called 'sour corn soup'. But unlike soups it is followed after the meals, may it be dinner or lunch. It is prepared by mixing and blending boiled corn with sour butter milk (*chachh*).

Note: There are some other varieties of *raab* like Gur Raab, which is made up of *gur* and Bajre ki Raab which is made of *baajra* flour and buttermilk.

Mawa Kachori

It is a very special and prestigious dish that originated from Jodhpur and is made by stuffing *mawa* in *kachori*. Normally, *kachoris* are savory in taste but this *mawa kachori* is a sweet version.

Ghewar

It can be described as the signature dessert delicacy of Rajasthan. *Ghewar* is a delicious and indeed a very unique Rajasthani delicacy. A disc shaped heavenly dessert this consists of rounded cakes of wheat flour loaded with sugar syrup, condensed milk and dry fruits. *Ghewar* sweet known for its matchless sweetness comes in varieties such as Plain Ghewar, Desi Ghee Ghewar, Paneer Ghewar, Malai Ghewar and Mawa Ghewar. Paneer Ghewar is garnished with *paneer* and is highly demanded for its tasty flavuor and nutrition. It is generally prepared in January for Makar Sankranti, in March-April for Gangaur and in July-August for the Teej festival.

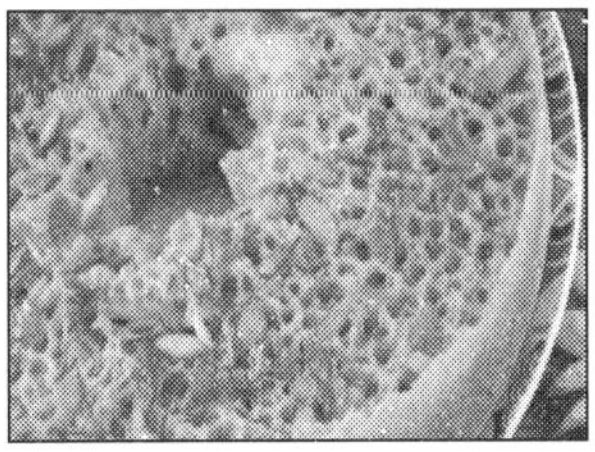

Mishri Mawa

It is also known as Kalakand and at some places as milk cake. It is a popular Indian sweet, which originated from Alwar, is made out of solidified, sweetened milk and cottage cheese.

Moong Dal Halwa

Moong *Dal* Halwa is a unique and rich sweet dish of lentils sweetened with milk and sugar. It is often prepared during the winter months, as it is supposed to keep the body warm and protect it from the bitter winter cold. It popularity has spread across and is nowadays prepared all around in North India.

Sohan Halwa

It is a sweet delicacy from Ajmer and its taste and texture is undoubtedly amazing.

Dilkhusaal

It is a Marwari sweet from Jodhpur also known as *Dal* Badaam Chakki. It mainly consists of almond, gram flour, mawa, ghee and sugar.

Besan Ki Chakki

It is basically a chickpea flour fudge made by cooking gram flour on a very low flame for long hours along with *khoya* and cardamom powder and then further adding sugar. This is a much softer version of Besan Laddoo.

Khushka

This is a kind of *biryani* which is made with basmati rice and dry fruits such as almonds, cashew nuts, and pistachios. It is made by the absorption method. The rice is sautéd along with sweet spices such as green cardamom, bay leaves, and cinnamon as well as nuts such as cashew nuts, almonds, and raisins.

Mirch Ke Tapore

It is made from diced chillies in a tangy spice combination prepared with fennel seeds, fenugreek seeds, salt, red chilli powder, mustard seeds, and so on in mustard oil. It is served as a side dish like Lehsun ki Chutney. As it has green chilli as its main ingredient, it is spicy in taste and stimulates the taste buds of the diners.

Culinary Trivia: Murabbas

Murabba is a very popular preparation and also a technique to preserve several fruits in the best possible manner. It is traditionally a sweet, prepared with fruits such as raw mangoes, plums, apricots, apple, *bael*, gooseberry (*amla*), and so on as the main ingredient. The fruit candied by this way can be preserved for long periods both as a wet *murabba* and a dry version, and they have certain medicinal properties as well.

Amla Murabba: Good quality ripe *amla* is taken and is soaked in water for two days. Then it is removed and pricked with a fork and soaked in alum water for another two days. After removing the *amla* from alum water, it is washed properly. The water is boiled in another pan and the pricked washed *amla* is put in it to boil. The flame is switched off and allowed to rest it for another 10 minutes. Then the *amla* is removed and the water is let to drain completely through a strainer. Then sugar syrup is prepared and added and cooked *amla* till it is tender and sugar syrup is thick enough. It is allowed to cool and then after 2 days cardamom powder, black pepper powder, black salt and saffron are added in it. It is preserved in glass containers and relished as and when required.

25 Sikkimese Cuisine

"Civilization as it is known today could not have evolved, nor can it survive, without an adequate food supply."
– Norman Borlaug

Sikkim, located in the Himalayan mountains, is bordered by Nepal on the west, China's Tibet Region on the north and east, and Bhutan on the east. The Indian state of West Bengal lies on the south.

Sikkim is a small naturally beautiful state with adorable landscapes. It has its own individuality and identity in the field of culinary expertise. It is a state with an entirely distinct cuisine which is interesting in all aspects. Blessed with the resplendent blend of the cultures and traditions of Nepal, Bhutan, India and Tibet, it renders a very luxurious outcome in the context of a variegated cuisine. The gilded amalgamation of all these cuisines has resulted in an entirely distinctive cuisine which is referred to as the cuisine of Sikkim.

Sikkim has attained such a status where it can ostentatiously display and portray its food culture, which can be acknowledged as the distinct cuisine of the state. The culinary characteristics of Sikkim have been appealing to the *hoi polloi* and have begun to achieve popularity among the people across the country.

Sikkim is located in the lap of the Himalayas and hence it is heavily influenced by the traditional food and food culture of the Himalayas. Rice is the chief staple food of this Himalayan state. Meat and dairy products form an essential part of the cuisine subject to their availability. Apart from these, several types of fermented foods and beverages have also been a significant constituent of this state cuisine for ages. The choice of food and the food elements popular in the cuisine is largely based on the location of the state. The high altitude of the state and the extreme climatic conditions as well as the weather of the land has put unavoidable restrictions on the cultivation of certain crops in the state. But in spite of this, certain crops like finger millets, wheat, buckwheat, barley, vegetables, potato, soybeans, so on are grown and cultivated in Sikkim.

The cuisine has been defined and shaped with the inclusion of several kinds of lentils, fresh vegetables, bamboo shoots and mushrooms. It would sound strange but it is true that certain wild flowers and nettle leaves have also been incorporated in the cuisine. The people of Sikkim are die-hard fans of non-vegetarian items and love and appreciate dishes of beef, pork and fish.

The unique characteristic of the cuisine of Sikkim is that it developed under unwanted restriction of geographical and climatic conditions. To cater to the specific needs the aboriginal people adopted the necessary aspects of cooking food from other cultures and developed them to fit their own requirements in such a fashion that it emerged as a distinctive cuisine and food culture. They embraced only those techniques and modes of food culture from the neighbouring areas and environment which proved beneficial for incorporating the available ingredients and suited their lifestyle. They generally incorporated the same ingredients like onion, ginger, garlic, turmeric, cumin, chillies, and mustard seeds. However, the cuisine seems to call for a lighter and milder finish than that needed to master the bold, dominating flavours of other regional Indian cuisines.

Sikkim has been exposed to a spine-chilling weather which affects the growth and cultivation of crops. This has compelled them to excel themselves immensely in the art of fermenting the vegetables and beverages in order to use them during the period when they won't be available a fresh. The consumption of alcoholic drinks has become the need due to such extreme cold weather, just in order to provide warmth to the body. Both men and women prefer to have such drinks frequently. Soups and pickles add new dimension to the exquisite cuisine and make it more tempting and appealing for the taste buds.

Momos and *thukpas* are two famed dishes of this state throughout the whole country.

But the cuisine of Sikkim is not limited only to *momos* and *thukpas*. There are indeed certain other specialties that transform this cuisine into a distinct and delectable affair. Tomato *achar* is a tangy and spicy tomato pickle that tantalizes the taste bud and this accompaniment changes any bland food into an interesting food.

Sikkim is flooded with the people of Nepali origin and they are highly proficient in preparing a unique kind of special bread called Selroti. This bread is a preparation of fermented rice batter deep fried in ring shape in oil and is enjoyed either as single item or in combination with spicy potato curries.

The paucity of fresh food products throughout the year has made fermented food as being a significant constituent of the cuisine of Sikkim. Chhurpi is a traditional cottage cheese made from fermented cow's milk and is slightly sour in taste. It is mostly used to make soups and pickles. Chhurpi is concocted with a wild but edible fern called Ningro to prepare tasty curries. Vatamas ko Achar is another delicious pickle prepared with non-fermented soya bean and flavoured with spices. Gundruk and Sinki are two fermented vegetables that are incorporated in the preparation of various items like soup, curries and pickles. Bamboo shoot is another crucial item that is used extensively in the cuisine of Sikkim. Bamboo shoots are used either fresh or in the fermented form. The fresh bamboo shoots are known as *tama* and are basically amalgamated with pork to prepare delicious dishes. The fermented bamboo shoots are called *mesu* and they are used to prepare incomparable pickles.

One of the irresistible local dishes of the state is Sishnu soup which is prepared from the leaves of the edible variety of the wild nettle. Pakku is a usual mutton curry relished with rice or Selroti. Kodo ko Roti is elementarily a pancake made from the locally grown finger millets called *kodo* and is relished with different kinds of pickles.

Generally, the meals are accompanied by the alcoholic beverage called Chaang which is a fermented cereal-based drink and is immensely popular in the Himalayan region. Many versions of it can be prepared, depending on the grain used to make it, e.g., Kodo ko Chaang, a beer obtained from finger millets (*ragi*) fermented with a local yeast. It is sipped from a bamboo receptacle with the help of a thin bamboo pipe. The receptacle which has millets in it is topped with warm water several times until the millets lose flavour. Raksi, a homemade indigenous alcoholic liquor distilled from rice (it is not a rice wine), has a very subtle flavour and is very popular in the state.

Specialty Dishes

Momo

It is essentially a steamed dumpling made of dough and stuffed with ingredients like chicken, onion and so on. It is always served piping hot with a bowl of hot soup and chilly sauce. It can unarguably and undoubtedly be declared the most popular item of the state as it can be found at every roadside eatery as well as at every street-side joint all across the country. The people prefer to eat it with great liking and zest.

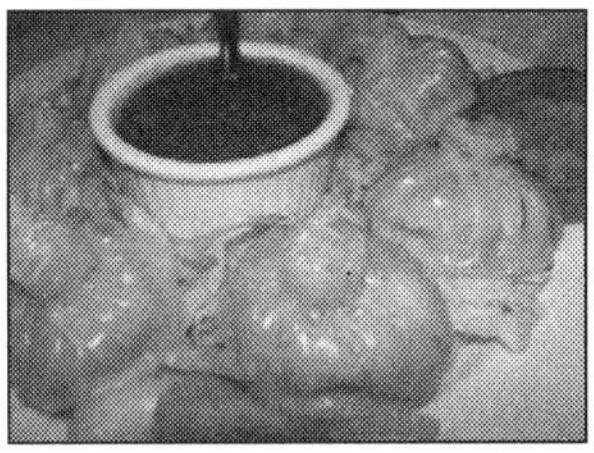

Thukpa or Gya-Thuk

This is a typical kind of soup containing noodles and is well-famed. It is characterized to be similar to the Tibetan style noodle soups.

Pork Shaphalay

It is an irresistible savory preparation stuffed with meat and deep fried, and it resembles an over-sized *samosa*. The *shaphalay* are moderately spiced and is consumed immediately after being fried, otherwise the outer crust gets soggy and chewy.

Kinema Curry It is a curried dish containing fermented soya bean. This dish is often used as a substitute for meat and savoured with rice. This dish is a rich source of protein derived from the plants and hence considered to be very nutritious.	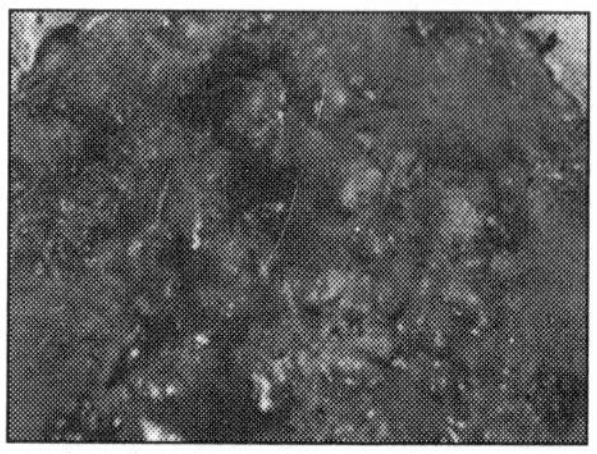
Pork Gyari *Gyari* literally translates to steak, and is one of the well-famed curry-style dishes. There are many versions of *gyari* and the similarity which exists is that all have the same smoky undertone of barbecued pork. It can also be cooked with tender bamboo shoots.	
Phing This dish consists of a glass-noodle soup which comprises mushrooms, meat (usually pork or beef), and the locally grown cherry peppers (*dallae khursani* chillies). These chillies are red, round, and fiery hot, lending dish a fiery spicy taste.	
Phulaurah It is a buckwheat-based fritter eaten as snacks with an accompaniment of Silam ko Achar. Silam ko Achar is a type of pickle made from the seeds of *silam*.	

Culinary Trivia: Pattal

It is a kind of plate which is used in India for eating in many rural areas in the country. It is made up of sal or banyan tree leaves or *dhaak* leaves, and it is simply joined with small wooden sticks which one can take from brooms stick, toothpick, and so on. Once it is used, it is disposed of. Similarly, small *katoris* made of same material, known as *donas*, are used along with *pattals*.

26 Tamil Nadu Cuisine

> "And what, Socrates, is the food of the soul? Surely, I said, Knowledge is the food of the soul." – Plato

Tamil Nadu, located in the southernmost part of the Indian Peninsula is bordered by the Union Territory of Puducherry and the Bay of Bengal on the east and the states of Kerala on the west; Karnataka on the northwest and Andhra Pradesh on the north and by the Indian Ocean on the south.

The cuisine of this state is famed and known for its distinctive taste. It offers an immense variation of vegetarian as well as non-vegetarian food items in its culinary bouquet. The taste of all the dishes is characterized by a unique taste due to coconut oil which is used as a cooking medium.

The cuisine of Tamil Nadu has certain common ingredients which are used in all the dishes. They are generally red chillies, fresh coconut, tamarind, turmeric and pinch of asafoetida. The most popular and illustrious dishes of the state are *dosas*, which are essentially crepes made from fermented batter of rice and *urad dal* (black gram), *idli* (steamed cakes, prepared from fermented batter of rice and *urad dal*), and *upama*.

Furthermore, Pongal and Uttappam served with *sambar, milagai podi* and coconut *chutney* is delicious and light. These light items are mostly served along with a cup of hot coffee that concludes a typical Tamil cuisine which is savoured by the people of this southern part of India.

Speaking about the main course, the Tamil Nadu cuisine is centred around rice along with the regular side dishes which comprises large varieties of *poriyals* (also called curries), *kootu, avial, kozhambu* (stews), *rasam* (lentil soup with pepper, coriander and cumin seeds), *sambar* (a thick stew of lentils with vegetables and seasoned with exotic spices), *thayir sadam* (steamed rice with curds), and *thayir* (yogurt or curds).

Breakfast has numerous delicious items to be served and mostly comprises *idli, pongal, dosai, aval* (flattened rice), *puttu, idiyappam, appam* with sweetened coconut milk, *chapathi, sevai* and *vadai* which are of two kinds (*medhu vadai* meaning soft *vadai* and *paruppu vadai* meaning lentils *vadai*) are served along with coconut *chutney, sambar* and *milagai podi.*

Chettinad Cuisine

The Chettinad cuisine is a sub-section of the cuisine of the state and peculiarly comes from the southern region of the state. It offers an entirely different cuisine and is distinct from the bland food of traditional Tamilian Brahmins as it is considered to be among the spiciest, oiliest and intensely aromatic cuisine in India. Notwithstanding the fact that the Chettiyar community is famed for its delicious and highly specialized vegetarian preparations, its varied assemblage of food items is renowned and incorporates a wide spectrum of numerous fish, fowl and meats. It also includes delicate noodle-like dishes and also the cautiously preserved sun-dried legumes and berries that the Chettiar ladies make into curries. Oil and spices are generously used in cooking and most dishes are fragrant with liberal amounts of peppercorn, cinnamon, bay leaves, cardamom, nutmeg, green and red chillies, and so on. The most celebrated delicacies of the Chettinad cuisines is the Varuval that is a dish fried and mixed with spices and onions, Poriyal (curry), Pepper Chicken, and Kuzambu with ingredients cooked in spices and fresh milk of coconut gravy. The appetite for Mughlai items is also quite different and that can be realized in the regional *biryani* and *payaa. Payaa* is basically a spicy form of stock made with trotters and is eaten along with *parathas*; sometimes also with *appam.* Thus, the Chettiyar community has mastered their art of culinary aspect to develop such a unique and most-sought cuisine with a delectable flavour and tempting taste, perfect enough to tantalize the taste.

During the festivals, it is a custom to prepare the important and tasty, savoury dishes. *Chedai* (crunchy crisps from rice flour), and *murukkus*, and are the most popular savouries that are provided as snacks. It is believed that eating of savouries make the gums stronger. The people are blessed with the skill to prepare numerous varieties of *payasam* made from rice, *dal*, *semiya* (vermicelli), milk, jaggery or sugar. Here, the sweets are also made according to festivals and mostly offered to gods.

Tamil Nadu, especially Chennai, is renowned for its filter coffee as most Tamils have a subtle contempt and disdain for instant coffee. The making of the filter coffee is almost a ritual. The coffee beans have to be first roasted and then ground. The powder is put into a filter set and hot boiling water is added to prepare the decoction and then allowed to set for about 15 minutes. The decoction is then added into milk with sugar to taste. The final drink is poured from one container to another in rapid succession to make the ideal frothy cup of filter coffee. Here, the people are expert in pouring coffee from one container to another from as large a distance as possible within both hands with perfection. It is a sort of showmanship and draws the attention of the people. The last process makes one wonder whether the brew could be bought 'by the yard'.

Virundhu Sappadu: The Distinguished Signature Feast of Tamil Nadu

In Tamil 'virundhu' simply means 'feast' and 'sappadu' means a full course meal, which will usually either be a lunch or dinner fare. The main course meal of a Tamil food is referred as a Virundhu Sappadu and it is specifically served traditionally on banana leaves. The reason behind the logic to serve the meal on banana leaves is that the banana leaves has flavours which sharpen the appetite. Traditionally, the banana leaf is always kept in such a fashion that the leaf tip is pointed left. Then, before the meal commences, the diners sprinkle water with their hands to clean the leaf, even if it is already cleaned. Now, in days of modernization, the *sappadu* is served on stainless steel plates with curries served in bowls made of the same material. Each dish to be served is allotted a specific place on the banana leaf. On the tender banana leaves, the upper half of the leaf is for the side dishes, while the staple item of the meal is to be served on the bottom half. The leaf's lower end corner is reserved for the desserts, which comprise a sweet, milky white preparation of rice called the *payasam*, along with *kesari* and sweet *pongal*. While the right upper end of the plate is reserved for some pickles or *chutney* or a touch of salt, the centre of the plate is reserved for fried items such as yam, banana chips, potato, vadai and *appalams* (crispy *papads*).

The vegetarian items are chosen from items like gourds, brinjals, drumsticks, carrots, French beans, cauliflower, and cabbage. For the non-vegetarian fare in the meal another separate leaf is arranged to serve chicken, fried meats, crab, fish, and so on. The region, being in a coastal area, the main section of the course for side dishes in their meals is fish. In the state, varied variety of fishes are available and are liked by the people. The huge availability of coconuts also enhances the extensive use of coconuts and its oil as the primary base for preparations of most of the items prepared in Tamil Nadu. *Paayasam*, is mostly provided at the end of the meal as a dessert or a sweet to announce the completion of all the courses of the meal. In the end, *virundu sappadu* is finished by serving *beeda*, banana, and glass of buttermilk.

Specialty Dishes

Rasam

It is essentially a soupy preparation which is had with rice or like a soup. It is prepared using tamarind juice as a base, with the addition of tomato, chili pepper, pepper, cumin and other spices as seasoning. It has many variations depending upon the ingredients used in it.

Kolambhu

Kolambhu or *kozhambu* is a very tempting thin stew of vegetables with fragrant spices. It can be prepared as many versions. The most common type is Moar Kolambhu, where buttermilk is used as the base and is thickened with a paste of rice and lentils to make it into a spicy stew with vegetables. This item is had during all meals in this region.

Thuvail This is a type of *chutney* made by addition of tamarind pulp. It is tempered with coarsely ground asafoetida, red chillies, *urad dal* and mustard seeds. The *chutney* can be made from ingredients like tomato, ridge gourd, and so on.	
Pongal It is usually a sweet preparation but can be made savoury also. It is made by concoction of rice, lentils, milk, and nuts, and flavoured with green cardamom.	
Vadai It is simply a fritter made using varied ingredients. *Ulundhu vada:* It is prepared by making a coarse paste of soaked *urad dal* and combining the same with chopped onions, green chillies, coriander, and asafoetida. This paste is then shaped as roundels and a hole is created in the centre using wet hands. These are then fried in hot oil, until crisp. *Kola vadai:* Flaked rice is soaked in water and then squeezed out. It is then kneaded into a dough and combined with grated coconut, green chillies, and ginger. They are then rolled into small balls and then cut into half inch thick slices. Each slice is shallow fried until crisp and then served.	
Poriyal Poriyal is the word used for fried or sometimes sautéd vegetable dish. It is usually made by shallow frying shredded or diced vegetables along with spices. It serves as a side dish to a three-course meal of rice with *sambhar, rasam* and curds. It can also be prepared with various vegetables. *Potato poriyal:* It is made of potatoes. *Bean poriyal:* It is made of green or string beans.	
Koozh It is a delectable porridge-like preparation. It is also called Kanji (rice *congee*) and is made using cereals.	
Avial It is a delicious stew of vegetables made with a motley of vegetables like carrots, beans, potato, yam, and so on with fresh coconut, and coconut oil which makes for a side dish in a meal consisting of rice, *sambhar, rasam* and also equally for dishes like Adai and Thosai.	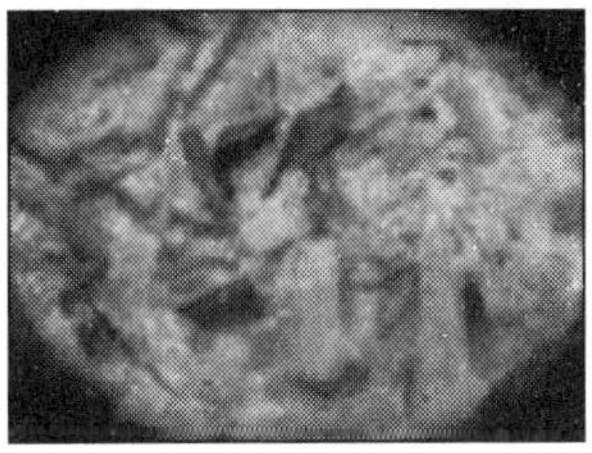

Kozhukkattai

It is a unique and most-sought after steamed dumpling made with rice flour and has a filling which are varied, i.e., from grated coconut and jaggery to various savoury preparations.

Idiyappam (String Hoppers)

It is a traditional and typical Tamil food consisting of rice flour pressed into noodle form and then steamed. The name *idiyappam* derives from the Tamil words *idi*, meaning 'broken down', and *appam*, meaning 'pancake'. The dish is also referred, less frequently as *noolappam* or *noolputtu* from the Tamil word *nool*, meaning 'string or thread'. It is eaten with spicy curies.

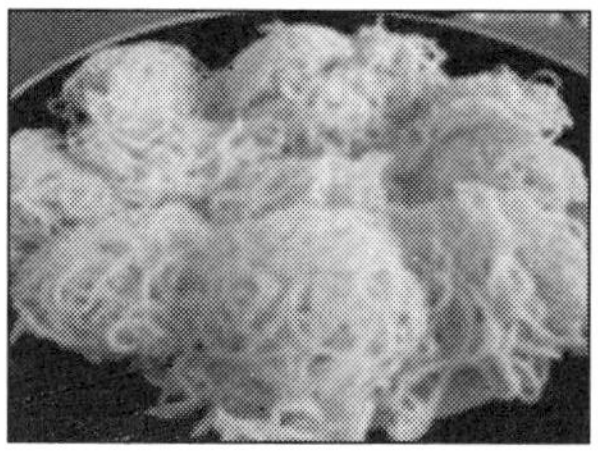

Uttapam/Ooththappam/Uthappa

It literally means 'poured appam' in Tamil, and is a *dosa*-like dish made by cooking ingredients in a batter. Uttapam is a thick pancake, with toppings cooked right into the batter and not crisp and crepe like pancake. The *uttapam* batter is made of a 1:3 ratio of *urad dal* and rice. The rice should be a combination of a boiled variety and another variety such as basmati. The *dal* and rice are subsequently ground and fermented. The outer surface is crisp and the inner layers are like that of *idli*. Uttapam is traditionally made with toppings such as tomatoes, onion, chillies, capsicum and cabbage mix. Other common choices are coconut or mixed vegetables. It is mostly eaten with *sambhar* or *chutney*.

Kootu

Kootu literally means 'add' in Tamil. It is a nutritious stew of vegetables, usually added with lentils, and spices which makes for a side dish for a meal consisting of rice, *sambhar* and *rasam*. It is less watery than *sambhar*, but drier as compared to curries.

Many variations of *kootu* exist:

Poricha Kootu: A *kootu* made with *urad dal* and pepper is called *poricha* (means 'fried' in Tamil) *kootu*.

Araichivita Kootu: A *kootu* which has a ground (freshly powdered) *masala* in it; the word *araichivita* in Tamil literally translates to 'the one which has been ground and poured.' The ground paste is made from the mixture of fried *urad dal*, gram *dal*, coriander seeds and coconut. The chopped vegetables and *arhar dal* are cooked separately. Then, the ground paste, cooked vegetables and *dal* are heated together.

Curd Rice (Thayir Sadam)

It is a very popular and aromatic preparation using unsweetened yogurt. It is popular in the South Indian states and is offered to the God in many Shiva and Vaishnavite temples, and later on distributed as *prasadam* (blessed food) to devotees. Here this is called by a different name not in common parlance (*dadhiannam/dadyodanam*) but is universally known as *thayir sadam*, literally curds rice. It is prepared with rice mixed with curds and finally tempered with curry leaves, whole red chilli, mustard seeds, asafoetida, *chana dal* (bengal gram *dal*) and washed *urad dal* (black gram *dal*).

Lemon Rice (Elumichampazha Sadam)

This famous preparation is made with rice, coloured yellow with turmeric, and then tempered with peanuts, cashew nuts, bengal gram *dal*, black gram *dal*, asafoetida, curry leaves, mustard seeds and finished with a generous sprinkling of lemon juice. As the name suggest, it is sour in taste and is very tempting. People have a special liking for it.

Puttu It is a South Indian breakfast dish made of steamed cylinders of ground rice layered with coconut. Puttu means 'portioned' in Tamil. *Puttu* is served with side dishes such as palm sugar or chickpea curry or banana, topped with ghee or oil. It is eaten with coconut *chutney*, or with *sambhar* or with a spiced pulse-based powder called *molaga*.	
Dosa *Dosa* or *dosai* is the most popular and undoubtedly the signature dish of the south Indian preparation, consumed even in North India with same intensity of liking. It is eaten as a main course or even as a snack. They are made from rice and *urad dal*. Both are soaked in water and ground and the batter is allowed to ferment. Then it is cooked on a large *tawa* in shape of pancakes. It is served with either *sambhar* or coconut *chutney*. Then they are filled with various types of fillings. These are prepared in few versions and they are: *Kal dosai*: The batter of this dosa is same as normal *dosa* batter, but the consistency of this batter is thick and it is cooked on a thick iron pan to resemble *anuttapam*. *Rava dosai:* The *dosa* batter is made by combining semolina with rice flour. This batter is slightly spiced with grated ginger and green chillies. The batter is really thin and sprinkled over a large *tawa* to prepare *rava dosa*. It is really a crisp and crunchy *dosa* as compared to the other *dosa* varieties. *Adai:* In this, the batter is prepared by grinding soaked parboiled rice, black gram, and bengal gram. It is cooked on both sides.	
Idli *Idli* is a white, spongy, swollen, circlet, about 3-4 inch in diameter and can be described as the most illustrious dish of the state. It is loved all across the country, especially North India. *Idli* is a delicacy prepared with the fermented batter of *urad dal* and parboiled rice. It is prepared in various kinds and each has its own unique ingredients. The batter is made by grinding *urad dal* and parboiled rice separately and leaving it overnight to ferment. The next day, it is steamed in the *idli* making vessel. It is also served with either *sambhar* or coconut *chutney*. *Rava idli:* In this, the fried semolina is added in the batter and then cooked in the same fashion.	

Similar Dishes in South Indian States

• Rasam

It is referred as Rasam in Tamil Nadu and Kerala, whereas Saaru in Karnataka and Chaaru in Andhra Pradesh.

It is essentially a South Indian soup with a dominating peppery flavour. It is traditionally prepared with tamarind juice as a base, with the addition of tomato, and chilli pepper, pepper, cumin and other spices as seasonings.

It is either taken with rice or as an individual dish like soup. The authentic variety is prepared chiefly with black pepper and tamarind, both ingredients being grown and found aplenty in South India.

Rasam is the basically the vitiated version of a Tamil word 'Milagu-t-tannir' literally meaning pepper water (In Tamil *milagu* means black pepper and *tannir* means water) for Mulligatawny soup (considered and revered to be the national soup of India).

There is a minute difference between Rasam and Saaru, as Saaru has many ingredients and is quite thicker in consistency and considered to be more nutritious than Rasam.

Based on the ingredients used, Rasam has numerous different variants:

- *Thakkali rasam:* made with tomato puree as the main ingredient.
- *Inji rasam:* made with ginger.

- *Poondu rasam:* made with garlic.
- *Parupu rasam or Pappu saaru:* made with pulses and tomato stock.
- *Baellae saaru:* made with *toor dal*, coconut and tamarind juice.
- *Nellikkai rasam:* made with Indian gooseberry (*amla*), hence it is sour in taste.
- *Milagu rasam or milagu saaru:* made with pepper and is known in the West as Mulligatawny soup
- *Jeera rasam:* made with cumin and tamarind.
- *Tamarind saaru:* made with tamarind extract and without lentils.
- *Majjiga saaru:* made with seasoned buttermilk and is soupy in texture.
- *Kattu saaru:* made with water of cooked *dal* and *kattu* it basically refers to the water drained from the cooked *dal*.
- *Kattina saaru:* a semi-sweet rasam made with jaggery.
- *Mysore rasam:* made with fried grams/*dals* and is a fragrant soup.
- *Kundapura koli saaru:* made with chicken.
- *Kottambari jeerige saaru:* made with coriander and cumin seeds.
- *Lemon rasam:* made with lemon juice and hence it is sour in taste.

• Poriyal

It is referred to as Poriyal in Tamil Nadu, Palya in Karnataka and Porutu in Andra Pradesh.

It is usually a simple preparation made by shallow frying shredded or diced vegetables along with spices. The preparation normally involves frying mustard seeds, *urad dal*, onions and then the main vegetable, and finally adding turmeric, spices, dried red chillies and coriander.

Poriyal serves as a side dish to a three-course meal of rice with *sambhar, rasam* and curds.

Potato poriyal: made of potatoes.

Bean poriyal: made out of green or string beans.

Palya, a very common dish in Karnataka is very similar to the *poriyal*. Few variations of the *palya* involve incorporation of *chana dal* instead of *urad dal*.

Porutu in Andhra region is prepared in almost similar manner, but the name has become alternative to Guddu Porutu, egg poriyal.

• Upama

It is referred to as Upama, Uppuma and Uppumavu in Tamil Nadu, Uppittu in Karnataka, Uppumavu in Kerala; and Upma and Uppindi in Andhra Pradesh.

It is essentially a salty preparation made up of sooji (semolina) as the main ingredient. A variety of vegetables are added during the cooking, depending on individual preferences, availability and taste.

• Curd Rice

It is referred as Mosaru Anna in Karnataka, Thayir Sadam in Tamil Nadu and Curd Rice in Andhra Pradesh.

It is a rice preparation in which a sufficient quantity of curds is added and then finally tempered with mustard seeds, curry leaves, red chilli flakes and asafoetida.

• Tamarind Rice

It is referred as Puliyogare or Hulianna in Karnataka, Puliyodharai in Tamil Nadu, and Pulihora in Andhra Pradesh.

In simple language, it is tamarind rice.

It is traditionally made using steamed or boiled rice mixed with tamarind paste, groundnuts, coriander seeds, coconut, jaggery, curry leaves, pepper, mustard seeds, fenugreek, turmeric, asafoetida, *urad dal*, and cumin.

• Sambar or Sambhar or Sambaaru

Sambar is a lentil based vegetable stew or broth made with tamarind and is most popular in the cooking of southern states of India.

Vegetables, turmeric, salt, asafoetida and a mixture of ground spices known as *sambar* powder (which contains roasted coriander seeds, chillies, lentils, and other spices) are initially boiled together. After the vegetables in the tamarind water are slightly cooked, the lentils and ground coconut mixture are added and allowed to cook until the vegetables are done. Motley of vegetables may be added to *sambar*. Typical vegetables include ladyfinger, carrot, brinjal, drumstick, pumpkin, potatoes, tomatoes, and whole or halved shallots or onions. The cooked *sambar* is typically tempered with an oil-fried spice mixture containing ingredients such as mustard seeds, black gram, dried red chilies, curry leaves, fenugreek seeds, coriander seeds, and asafoetida. Fresh curry leaves or coriander leaves may be added at the end to enhance the flavour. Curry leaves are an essential element of authentic *sambar*, which provide a distinct and pleasant herbal essence.

Culinary Trivia: Coconut

The Sanskrit term for the coconut is *narikela* (in Hindi *nariyal*) is believed to be derived from the two words of South-East Asian onion, *niyor* for oil and *kolai* for nut.

It is also referred to as *sriphala*, the blessed fruit. It is a sin to cut down the palm tree. In Indian rituals, the de-husked coconut is an auspicious symbol. It is offered to guests, used in marriage ceremonies and also during sacred functions.

Various coconut products are used in various forms. They are:

- *Coconut water:* The liquid in fresh tender coconut is a delicious natural drink all along the coast, particularly in South India. With the maturing of the nut, the volume of liquid is reduced considerably. A drink called *munnir*, made of equal quantities of green coconut water, sugarcane juice and fresh *neera*.
- *Coconut milk:* It is a hand extract of fresh coconut gratings mixed with hot water. The first extract gives thick milk and the second a thin one.
- *Coconut honey:* It is the product obtained by boiling down the sweet extract of several palms.
- *Coconut oil:* It is the fat obtained by boiling with water either the shreds of fresh coconut copra. It is used for various purposes.
- *Coconut flower:* It is the flower of the palm tree and it has a few uses. It is edible and is beneficial to the diabetics and is also used as an aphrodisiac.
- *Coconut kernel:* Copra is the kernel of the coconut, which is the drying hemisphere of the nut.

27 Uttarakhand Cuisine

"Work is the meat of life, pleasure the dessert." – B.C. Forbes

Uttarakhand, formerly a part of Uttar Pardesh, is a state situated in Central Himalaya, i.e., North India. It is bordered by the Tibet Autonomous Region on the north, Nepal on the east, and Uttar Pradesh on the south, and Himachal Pradesh on the northwest.

Uttarakhand is a hilly state which is different from the plains in terms of topography and agricultural features. Hence it offers a broad avenue and scope for cultivation of a wide range of crops — cereals, millets, pulses, oilseeds, vegetables, and so on. The rich natural diversity, in amalgamation with specific climatic conditions, lands the state an impeccable situation to cultivate edible plants and spices, thus contributing to the unique culinary of the state. The food commodities of Uttarakhand are noted for their exceedingly high nutrient significance and delectable taste. The climatic conditions here have forced the inhabitants to look for local commodities which can be eaten and would help them to live comfortably. This search has transformed certain ingredients of wild plant origin to be identified by local people for their consumption. Therefore, such wild edible plants constitute a major portion of food consumed by local populace in tribal and hilly areas of the state. The local people are gifted with incredible skill to recognize a large number of wild edible plant species, and enchance their palatability, use, nutrition, products and preparation.

Variety in food preparation is a typical characteristic of the region. They have created certain recipes in which the substitutes of the items are used, as they are meagerly produced in the region. Extensive numbers of crops have been introduced in this region by early settlers which have created a large diversity in crop plants as compared to the plains, thereby enriching the cuisine of this hilly area.

The common meal during breakfast, lunch and dinner is simple and comprises rice, *roti*, *dal* and vegetables. People prefer to eat rice and *roti*, and hence these the staple food items, whereas pulses are rarely eaten as these are very meager in availability due to low production.

Apart from the common vegetables produced in northern India, there are certain vegetables which are found only in the hilly state of Uttarkahand. When some vegetables are produced in plentitude, the farmers keeping in mind the crisis situation, preserve certain products to use it during hard times. Desiccation technique of vegetable preservation is existent from the time immemorial in Uttarakhand. This is a simple technique of securing food in the state. There are seven different vegetables stored by agriculturists by the sun-drying technique. These sun-dried vegetables are consumed in times of paucity during the winter season. The locally sun-dried vegetables are known as *khwaire* in local dialect.

In Uttarakhand, during very hard and critical period of scarcity, people are left with no option but to use salts as an alternative for vegetables. Even during busy hours, people take meal with salts on a frequent basis. With this intention, local communities have prepared flavoured salts, blended with roasted seeds of linseed, mustard, garlic, cloves, apricot nuts, coriander, cumin, chillies and turmeric.

Uttarakhand is famed for its wide range of pulses. *Bhatt* or black soyabean is an all-time favourite with the local people. *Bhatt* is rich in proteins and iron, and are authentically prepared in an iron *kadhai* to make *chudkani*, *bhatwani* and *thatwani*.

Traditionally, *chapatis/rotis* or breads are prepared from flour obtained from *mandua* (finger millets seeds) and buckwheat. *Mandua roti*, having high calcium content, is generally consumed during the cold and harsh winters. Some species of millets such as *kauni* (fox-tail millets) and *jhangora* (barnyard millets) replace rice *and kheer* as staple food. These millets are known to contain medicinal properties, and are easy on the stomach.

Typical condiments in the state include *jamboo, kala jeera, gandrayani* and *jakhiya*. Chutneys are made specifically from *bhangjeera* and *til* (sesame).

Thus, the cuisine of Uttarakhand is a perfect example of cuisine which uses local herbs and spices in the best possible manner as taste enhancers.

Specialty Dishes

Mandua Ki Roti

These delicious and highly nutritious *chapatis* are made from *mandua* flour (finger millets). It is especially eaten in Uttarakhand during the season of winter and holds a key position in the list of Uttarakhand's delicacies. It is eaten with ghee or butter and is very rich in calcium content.

Lesu

This stuffed bread is popular both in Kumaon as well as Garhwal, which is prepared by stuffing *mandua* dough into wheat flour dough and eaten with ghee or butter.

Gahat (Kulath) Ki Dal

This delicious *dal* of *gahat* (*kulath*) is tempered with *gandharein*, asafoetida and cumin seeds. It is garnished with either little boiled rice or with lots of butter and coriander leaves. *Gahat* or *kulath* is also well known for its positive impact on kidneys and other medicinal values.

Gahat (Kulath) Soup

It is a delicious and nutritious soup prepared from *gahat* grains.

Urad Ke Pakore (Wada)

These spicy *pakoras* are prepared with *urad dal* and taken as snacks, served during breakfast or with evening tea. It is also served during family and social functions.

Bhangjeera Ki Chatni

It is a tasty sour *chutney* prepared with roasted *bhangjeera* seeds and cumin seeds, mixed with *darim* (a local variety of pomegranate).

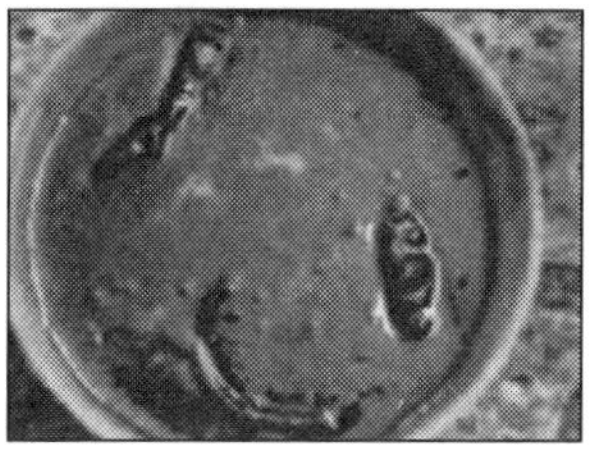

Rus It is an appetizing and highly nutritious dish made from a mixture of *dals*. It consists of a mixture of various pulses and rice as well. It is prepared by preparing a rice paste from rice soaked overnight and mixing it with properly boiled mixed *dal* extract and then it is tempered with roasted spices. It is typically eaten in winters along with steamed rice and *bhang ki chutney*. *Rus* is garnished with chopped green coriander and served with boiled rice. Ghee, also served with *Rus*, adds a magical twist to the tingling taste.	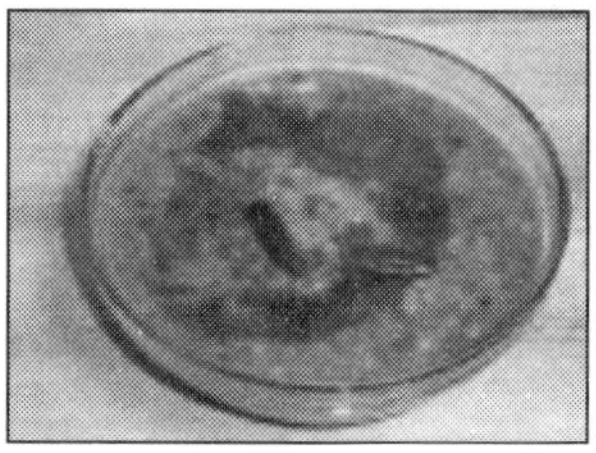
Aloo ke Gutke This famous snack has almost acquired a legendary status, and is prepared from boiled *pahari* potatoes. This is prepared by cutting cubes of potatoes and then boiling then, after which they are tempered with spices like cumin seeds, red chilli powder, coriander powder and turmeric powder and garnished with fresh coriander and fried red whole chilli.	
Jhangore ki Kheer A delectable sweet dish prepared with *jhangora* (barnyard millets) and milk and then finally garnished with nuts.	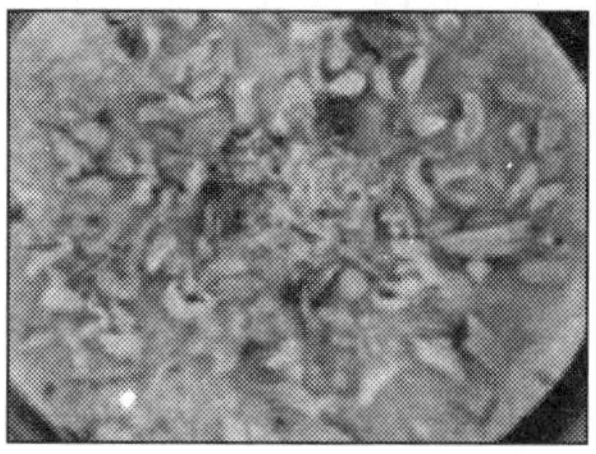
Mixed Bhaddu Dal Bhaddu is a heavy bottomed and narrow necked pot. In order to prepare this dish, *rajma* and *urad dal* are soaked in water for an overnight and then boiled with whole *garam masala* and salt. Then it is tempered with spices and tomato puree and garnished with cream before serving.	
Kafuli Kafuli is a unique thick gravy preparation made from green leafy vegetables like spinach and fenugreek leaves. Rice powder paste is added in the preparation to make it thick and then cooked. Kafuli made of spinach leaves is the most common preparation.	
Sani Hui Mooli aur Nimbu It is a mouth-watering dish which has a flavour of refreshing and tempting mixture of radish, lemon, curds and paste of *bhang* seeds. The batons of radish and lemon segments are tossed in curds and paste of *bhang* seeds, garlic and green chillies. It is usually eaten during the winter season.	
Sisunak Saag Sisunak (nettle) *saag* is famed for its high nutritious value. The leaves where this *saag* is prepared is locally known as *Bichhu Ghas* there. It is a green leafy vegetable dish, garnished with butter and tomatoes and is appreciated by everyone.	

Chainsoo

Chainsoo is a delicacy of Garhwal and is prepared using black gram *dal*. Normally, due to the high protein content in this *dal*, it is difficult to digest. It is garnished with fresh coriander and ghee. Similar preparation with slight variation is made out of black *bhat* (a variety of soyabean), but in that case it is called *bhatwani*.

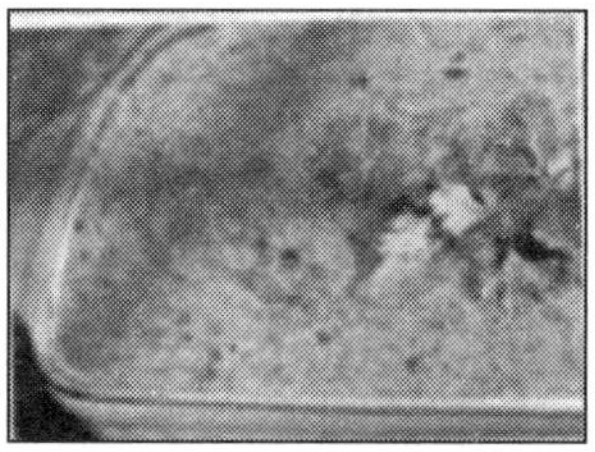

Phaanu

Phaanu is simple preparation made of *dals* and is similar to Chainsoo, but in this case the *dals* are soaked in water for about 4 to 6 hours before its cooking. A varied variety of *dals* like *gahat, arhar* or green *mung* can be used to prepare Phaanu.

Alu Dal Pakora

Alu *Dal* Pakora is served as a snack and is one of the most liked snacks of the locality of the Kumaon. It is prepared using potatoes and mixed *dal* dumplings dipped in egg white and then crumb fried. It is served with *chutney* or tomato ketchup. It is a creatively innovated food of Kumaon.

Alu Tamatar Ka Jhol

This potato gravy cooked with ample amount of tomatoes is a delicious curry which serves well with steamed rice, chapatis and *paranthas*. It is the simplest dish of the cuisine which tastes great and is a undoubtedly a very good option when hungry guests suddenly drop by at lunch/dinner.

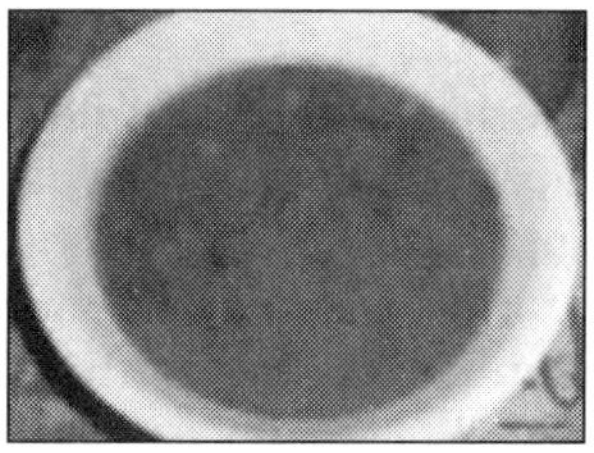

Kaapa

This is a delicious green curry prepared from spinach as the main ingredient and curds, which is served in lunch or dinner and is eaten with bread, *pita, roti* and boiled rice. This dish holds a special place in the cuisine of this state and is considered to be very nutritious.

Thechwani

Thechwani can be prepared using radish root (*pahari mula* having round roots) or potatoes. The preparation is called by this name as the radish root or potato is never cut, but crushed (*thinchao*) into pieces. In this preparation, the radish and potatoes are crushed and then tempered with spices and tomatoes. Then it is slow cooked till the radish is properly done.

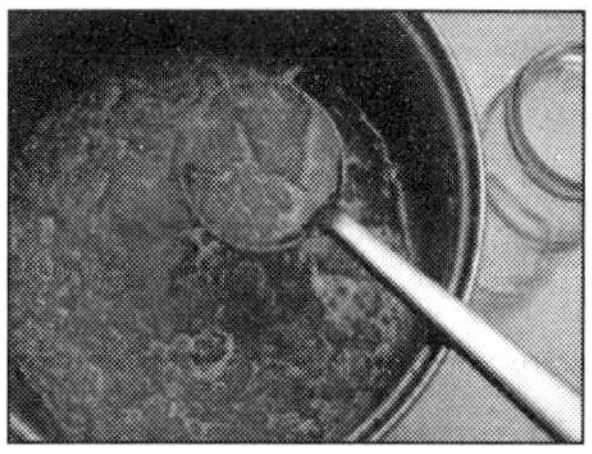

Baadi

Baadi is made from Kwada ka Aata (also known as *choon* or *mandua* flour and is black in colour). It is very simple to prepare this dish. Water is boiled and then the flour is added in it and cooked for about 2 mins and served hot with ghee. Baadi is best eaten with Gahat ki *Dal* or Phaanu. Hot Baadi and hot Phaanu are very popular foods in Uttarakhand.

Bhatt ki Churkani Made with black soyabean, this sour preparation is dark greenish black in colour and is eaten with rice and is well known for its unique taste and high nutritious value. The soaked *bhatt* is cooked with plain flour with sufficient water in it, till the *bhatt* is soft and properly done.	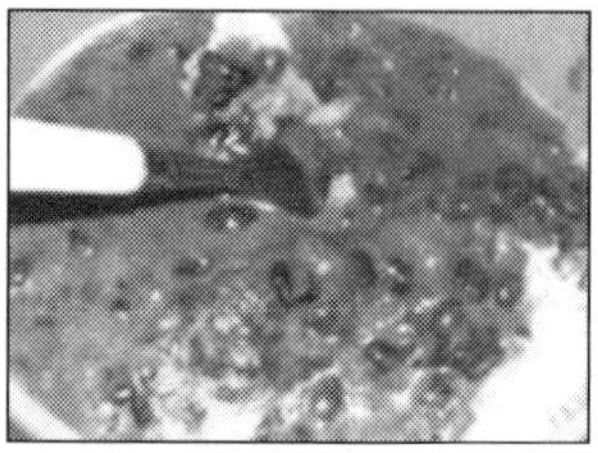
Dubka It is a typical Kumaoni dish which is made with lentils like *urad* or *moong*. In this dish, the *dals* are soaked and then ground to form a paste. This paste is cooked in oil with spices like cumin, mustard seeds, green chillies, turmeric powder, and so on.	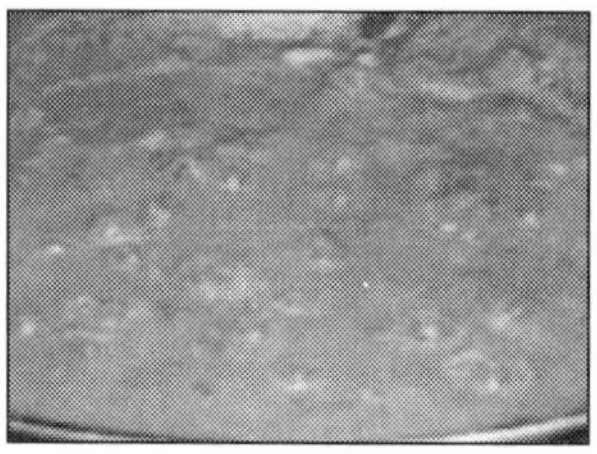
Gaderi ki Sabji It is a sumptuous vegetable preparation which is prepared from boiled Gaderi from the hills with the taste of sauted *jamboo* and garlic. It is used as a *sabji* with normal meals or snacks with tea.	
Badeel Badeel is a very popular snack of Uttarakhand. It is made from *pahari masoor* by preparing a paste of soaked *masoor dal* and grinding it, then mixing it with a few ingredients and then cooking it for a while in a pan. Then a greased thali is taken and the paste of *dal* is poured in it and cut uniformly when cooled. These small cakes are called *badeel* and they are deep-fried to be served with sweet and sour *chutney*.	
Lal Chawal ki Kheer Traditionally grown in Uttarakhand Himalayas, red rice is very high on nutritive content and is cooked with milk to prepare this special dish.	

Culinary Trivia: Gluten

It is a protein unique to the bread wheat which gives wheat dough its sticky, rubbery and elastic quality. It is essential in the making of baked products that holds the starch in place.

Culinary Trivia: Solanine

Toxic solanine in potatoes makes it green.

28 Community Cuisine

> "Part of the secret of a success in life is to eat what you like and let the food fight it out inside." – Mark Twain

A community is fundamentally a societal and gregarious group of any size that has similarity in common values, liking and interest. The community holds together the people with same purpose, belief, intention, resources, preferences, requirements, aim or any such attribute. The word 'community' is obtained from the old French *comunete* which, in turn, derives from the Latin *communitas* (from Latin *communis*, things held in common), a broad term for fellowship or the association of people who have common beliefs or activities.

Udipi Cuisine

Udipi cuisine is the cuisine of a beautiful town Udipi in Karnataka, situated on the southwest coast of India. It is renowned for its utter simplicity and its nature of revitalization. In simple language, it is the cuisine of Udipi Brahmins. This cuisine has been distinctive enough to be noticed all across the world and has left its unique imprint. This cuisine has gifted the world with its unique creation and, in fact, the most celebrated dish of the cuisine is Masala Dosa. This dish has been so popular that it hardly needs any description. It has become synonymous with the entire South Indian dish in almost every south Indian restaurant in North India and has attracted diners in these restaurants.

Masala Dosa has invigorated the fading vegetarianism of Udipi Brahmins. The typical taste of this cuisine has made it alive and popular all across the world.

With respect to the origin of this stringently enforced vegetarian cuisine, it roots perpetuated from the Ashta Mathas or Eight Monasteries formed by the Honourable Sri Madhvacharya during the 13th century. This cuisine was developed, carried over and made popular by the Tulu speaking Shivalli Brahmins who cooked for Lord Krishna at the Krishna Matha. These specific populaces of Brahmins inhabited the Udupi region in Karnataka. These Brahmins are particularly either the Madhvas, following the Madhvacharaya's traditions and teachings, or the Saivites, following the Advaita traditions of Adi Sankaracharya and are referred to as the Sthanika Brahmins.

These Brahmins, particularly, took immense care to prepare food in hygienic conditions. They also adapted the traditional methods and also used the locally available food in the best possible manner. They cooked meals in *mathas* with meticulous care and then served it to the Lord with allegiance and devotion. This tradition has helped them to carve their mastery in the art and craft in an incredibly perfect way. Certain skilled Brahmin cooks in Udipi cuisine left their town and promulgated their impeccable art of cooking in the world market, which made them popular all across. The incomparable fragrance of Udipi cuisine has cost its spell on everyone in the world market and blessed the traditional cuisine of an old remote area with an immense popularity.

The elementary ingredients of this cuisine are grains, beans, vegetables and fruits. This cuisine is renowned for its rich assemblage of delicacies. The exemplary delicacy like Masala Dosa has marked its impressive presence on the world culinary map. The divine feature of this cuisine is that it still follows the Vedic tradition in the strictest possible way and hence can be considered a staunch vegetarian cuisine. They are so particular about their food that they don't even use onions and garlic in their dishes. The main vegetables used commonly are pumpkins and gourds, and coconut oil is the chief medium of cooking. Saaru (*rasam*), a spicy peppery soup which has become an inseparable part of the menu and so are jackfruit, colocassia leaves, raw green bananas, red chillies, mango pickles and salt. *Adyes* (dumplings), *ajadinas* (dry curries), and *chutneys*, including the one made of the skin of the ridge gourd, are specialities and are acknowledged throughout.

The traditional Udipi meal is compulsorily served in a very auspicious way on hygienic banana leaf. The leaf is placed on the floor and people sit cross-legged beside it to dine. The dishes have their sequences decided and are served accordingly. Each dish has got a special place on the banana leaf as well. All the people start their meal at the same time and finish it as well at the same time. It is considered to be very rude and harsh for anyone to leave the eating row in between during a meal, even if he has finished his meal. Such behaviour is unacceptable. It is a custom to start and end the meal by uttering 'Govinda' (name of Lord Krishna).

Some of the specialty delicacies of the Udupi cuisine are:

- Sajjige and *bajil* (*upama* prepared from coarse semolina and seasoned beaten rice)
- Uddinahittu (*urad* flour mixed in curds and seasoned)
- Kosambari (salads of black gram or bengal gram lentils, seasoned)
- Different types of spicy rice, such as *chitranna* or Bisi Bele Bath
- Dosa, Masala Dosa, Neer Dosa
- Sweet dishes like Maddi, Kaai Holige, Undae (*laddu*)
- Puddings or *parammanna* or *payasa* or *kheer*
- Mangalore Bajji or Golibaje
- Kashi Halva from musk pumpkin, jackfruit, banana, and bottle gourd
- Pelakai Gatti/Gidde (jackfruit dumpling)
- Pelakai Appa (fried dumplings made from jackfruit)
- Pelakai Halwa (jackfruit halwa)
- Gashi or Ghasi (thick gravy like dish made by use of peas or pulses with coconut)
- Patrode (colacasia leaves dipped in batter and steamed cooked)
- Menaskai (especially made of *amtekai* or *ambade*)
- Putnis
- Kadubu.

The traditional method of serving a meal on plantain leaves in the Udupi style is described below:

- Uppu (salt)
- Uppinakai (pickles)
- Chutney Pudi (chutney powder)
- Kosumbri (green gram salads)
- Kosumbri (bengal gram salads)
- Kayi Chutney (coconut *chutney*)
- Beans Pallya (foogath)
- Gujje Pallya (jackfruit foogath)
- Chitranna (lemon rice)
- Happala (papad)
- Sandige (crispies)
- Kadubu (steamed rice cake)
- Anna (rice)
- Thovve (*dal*)
- Sihigojju (*raitha*)
- Saru (*rasam*)
- Uddinahittu (black gram paste)
- Badane Podi (brinjal *pakoda*)
- Menaskai (sweet and sour gravy)
- Goli Baje (maida fry)
- Avial (vegetable mix)
- Gatti Baje (lady finger *pakoda*)
- Gulla Koddel (brinjal *sambar*)
- Chiroti Milk (sweet)
- Gojjambade (*masalwada* curry)
- Kayi Holige (sweet coconut chapati)
- Vangi Bath (vegetable *upma*)
- Bharatha (sour ginger gravy)
- Paradi Payasa (sweet)
- Mosaru (curds)
- Majjige (buttermilk)

Chettinad Cuisine

Chettinad cuisine is a renowned cuisine of the Chettiyar community of the Chettinad region in Tamil Nadu. Chettiyar are in majority in this region and are the most successful trading populace. This cuisine has been acknowledged as one of the oiliest, spiciest and most aromatic cuisines of India.

This cuisine is typically characterized by the wide use of varied spices in preparing chiefly non-vegetarian dishes. The dishes are hot and pungent in taste and nature with the incorporation of freshly ground *masalas*, and then topped with a boiled egg which is an essential component of the meal. Chettinad being one of the driest regions of South India, it incorporates a variety of sun-dried meats and salted vegetables. The meat consumed is chiefly chicken, mutton, fish, prawn, lobster and crab. They do not prefer to eat beef and pork.

Rice is the main staple diet and hence a wide variety of rice-based accompaniments such as *dosais, appams, idiyappams, adais* and *idlis* are popularly consumed here. A rice pudding made of sticky red rice is also very popular in this region.

Chettinad cuisine offers a huge assemblage of tempting and mouth-watering vegetarian and non-vegetarian dishes. Some of the popular vegetarian dishes include *idiyappam, paniyaram, vellai paniyaram, karuppatti paniyaram, paal paniyaram, kuzhi paniyaram, kozhakattai, masala paniyaram, adikoozh, kandharappam, seeyam, masala seeyam, kavuni arisi* and *athirasam*.

Chettinad food has been characterized by the usage of typical and most important spices like Marathi *mokku* (dried flower pods), *anasipoo* (star aniseed) and *kalpasi* (a lichen known as the 'black stone flower' also known as *dagad phool*). Apart from this, tamarind, whole red chillies and fennel seeds are also used along with cinnamon, cloves, bay leaf, peppercorn, cumin seeds and fenugreek in this specific cuisine. Chettinad cuisine is characterized and is different from other cuisines due to liberal use of oil and spices. Most of the Chettinad dishes have lavish amounts of peppercorn, cinnamon, bay leaves, cardamom, nutmeg, green and red chilies in it, which lends it a unique flavour and distinct taste.

Following are the main dishes of the Chettinad community.

- **Chicken Chettinad**

This is a preparation in which the chicken pieces are cooked along with a special combination of spices including grated coconut, red chillies, coriander seeds, ginger, garlic, cinnamon, cardamom, cloves, black *kalpaasi* (stone flower), anise seed, black pepper, curry leaves, turmeric powder and roasted *chana dal* (*pottukadalai*).

- **Chettinad Mutton Kola Urundai or Kari Kola Urundai (Chettinad Mutton Balls)**

This is a preparation of minced meat with the Chettinad masala, mixed and mashed properly in it. Then, small balls are made out of it and then these meat balls are cooked by deep-frying till done.

- **Kathirikkai Murungakkai Masala**

This is a preparation which has brinjal and drumstick in it in along with many spices. Brinjal is *kathirikkai* and drumstick is *murungakkai* in Ttamil.

- **Karunai Kilangu Masiyal**

It is a semi-dry preparation of yam cooked with jaggery and is seasoned with mustard seeds, *chana dal, urad dal*, asafoetida, red chilli and curry leaves. It is served with rice.

- **Keerai Masiyal**

It is a spinach preparation with tomatoes, green chillies, onion, *toovar dal*, tamarind, mustard seeds and is usually served as an accompaniment to rice. *Keerai* is spinach in Tamil.

- **Karuvepilai Kulambu**

It is a stew based on broth made up of curry leaves and tamarind and other ingredients as well. It may also include vegetables as other ingredients. *Karuvepilai* means curry leaves in Tamil.

- **Muttai Kulambu**

It is a unique egg preparation with onion, tomato, ginger-garlic paste as the other ingredients. In this preparation, egg can be added as boiled egg or it can be added as egg drop also.

- **Paruppu Masiyal**

It is a *dal* preparation in which *toovar dal* or moong *dal* can be used and it is tempered with asafoetida, garlic, mustard seeds, red chilli flakes, curry leaves and so on.

- **Paal Paniyaram**

It is a sweet preparation made with a thick batter of *urad dal* and rice in 1:1 ratio. It is deep fried as balls and soaked in coconut milk first and then in milk. *Paal* is milk in Tamil.

- **Vella Mangai Pachadi**

It is simply a side dish preparation made with raw mango as the chief ingredient. In this, the mango is boiled and mashed and then jaggery is added and finally tempered with mustard seeds, fenugreek seeds, curry leaves and so on.

- **Summa Kulambu**

This is essentially a spicy and tart tamarind gravy with no other vegetables, and is an accompaniment with *idli, dosa,* rice or *upama*.

- **Vazhakkai Pulikulambu**

It is a preparation of raw plantain or raw banana with tamarind in it to provide a sour taste to the dish. *Vazhakkai* is raw banana in Tamil.

- **Keerai Koottu**

It is a simple preparation of spinach cooked in combination with *dal*.

- **Carrot Thayir Pachadi**

This is a delicacy made with the concoction of carrot and curds and it is amazing in its taste.

- **Parangikkai Pulikulambu**

It is a preparation of pumpkin curry tempered with mustard seeds, curry leaves, asafoetida, fenugreek seeds, red chilli, green chilli, and so on. *Parangikkai* is pumpkin in Tamil.

- **Seeyam**

This is a special and unique preparation which is made up of green gram and *dal*. The *dal* is boiled and is then mixed with jaggery, and then balls are made out of it, which are deep-fried, dipped in a batter of rice and urad *dal* in 2:1 ratio.

Iyengar Cuisine

The cuisine of the Iyengar community is referred to as Iyengar cuisine. Iyengars are the Brahmins of Tamil Nadu. The Iyengar cuisine is typically pure vegetarian, and symbolizes a perfect balanced diet with a distinct and unique taste. They refrain from using garlic and uses onion in very minute quantity. They follow a very restricted use of oil. They don't prefer to use colouring agents and artificial additives in their food. The famous and peculiar preparations of Iyengars symbolize the customs of the traditional Iyengar community. Iyengars are famed for their resplendent food preparations.

An Iyengar feast is referred as Sapaadu and their wedding feast is termed Kalayana Sapaadu. The wedding feast finds a special mention when the cuisine of the Iyengars is talked about.

The Iyengar wedding is a complex affair and the specific three-day wedding rituals commences with Mana Pongal and Nalangu ceremonies that take place almost simultaneously at the groom and the bride's house. A yellow Pongal cooked with *toor dal* is served along with the auspicious yellow pumpkin, *vatha kuzhambu,* and a *kesari*. On the second day, the groom's family arrives at the wedding hall for a simple breakfast and a relatively simple Sappadu is served with a delicious *payasam*. The food service begins from early evening with a heavy 'tiffin' and it is common to see guests going directly to the dining hall as soon as they arrive. Potato Bonda or assorted *bhaajis* are served along with a rice *sevai* (rice noodles) and a *halwa*. Traditionally, the wheat *halwa* was served in olden days but as it involved a lot of efforts and labour to prepare, it has been replaced by pumpkin *halwa* or the Asokam Halwa (with fried green gram), which are prepared comparatively with less efforts. Dinner is served which is a typical Ela Sappadu (plantain leaf meal). Some typical dinner specialties include Sambar Satham (Bisi Bel Bath) and Vadam (rice crispies), which are eaten with great zeal.

On the final wedding day, the breakfast is usually kept very simple. It includes *idli, pongal* and *kesari* or *halwa*. This is followed with an elaborate wedding lunch, which is served almost immediately, as early as 10 a.m. The Iyengars boast about their unique heritage and cuisine and many of them refer to this feast as Alangara Thaligai (ornamental cuisine).

The Iyengars are subdivided into two broad sections: the Thengalai Iyengars and the Vadagalai Iyengars. In both the sections, while the meal is almost the same the serving sequence is quite distinct. The typical Vadagalai Iyengar wedding feast begins with rice, *dal* and *sambar* and the rest of the meal is served thereafter. The Thengalai feast commences with a small piece of banana and a sprinkling of sugar, typically served at the left extreme of the leaf. The Kosumbari, considered to be their own salads, made with carrot is served after that. In fact, the conventional Iyengars prefer a *satvic* vegetable diet that excludes onion and garlic. Even the Iyengars, wedding menus also abstain from using onion and garlic. Koshumbari is followed with a cucumber *pachadi* (*raita*), which, in turn, is followed by the Vazhakai Karamadu. Iyengars use Amudu (nectar) termed suffix to almost many dishes from *poriyal* to *rasam* to *payasam*.

Raw banana (*vazhakai*) holds a significant place in all Iyengar meals and in this version one is allowed to cook in tamarind water before being fried with a sprinkling of bengal gram and curry leaves. It is followed by the beans, *parupu usili*, a dish almost typical to Iyengars in which *toor dal* is steamed and mashed and cooked along with beans. It is one of the most delicious accompaniments for a South Indian meal. A white pumpkin *kootu* prepared along with green peas is the next course. The Parangika Karamathu is a semi-solid vegetable delicacy prepared using jaggery, red chillies and coconut. It has a unique and attractive sweet flavour. It is followed by Varuval (wafers) a popular course which is made with potato or yam after which the ubiquitous Appalam makes its appearance. Avial is served just before the *toor dal* and rice are served. Kuzhambu (usually with okra) and *sambar* are served almost simultaneously followed by *rasam*. Thayir Vada (curds *vada*) considered to be a celebrated dish comes just before the sweet such as *jangri*, *Mysore pak* and *ladoo*. Such desserts are the common favourites. Kaara Sevai (savoury sticks with pepper) are served along with the sweets and then comes the famed Iyengar Puliyogare, the strongly flavoured tamarind rice. Some traditionalists and orthodox serve Pongal after the *puliyogare* preparation.

The sumptuous meal comes to an end with the traditional Akkara Vadasal, which is an heavenly dessert made of a concoction of rice with *moong dal* and is cooked in milk with ghee, jaggery, cashew, saffron, raisins and at times with *khoya*. This is followed by the heavy course of Iyengar curds rice *dodiyonam* which can be accompanied with the pickles of the day (usually made of mango or lime). This curd rice is again lavish and rich with plenty of milk and butter in it and is mashed for it to attain the smooth texture.

The kitchen of Iyengar offers a huge platter of varied and mouth-watering dishes. This includes Nuchina Unde, which is a steamed ground *toor dal* delicacy served with Majjige Huli which is buttermilk based pumpkin curry. Adai Dosa is a *dosa* of mixed lentils whereas Pacha Kolambu Sadham is a concoction of varied vegetables in rice preparation without using any sour ingredient but with a dominant mustard tang. Gasgase Payasam is simply a delicious *kheer* with poppy seeds and ground nuts (finely ground) whereas Tarkari Akki Roti is a rice floor *chapatti* with vegetables. Kadambam is another rice delicacy prepared with raw bananas and sweet pumpkin, with a dash of fried *rasam* powder sprinkled on top and Molagu Kootu is prepared with *toor dal* and pepper and certain mixed vegetables. Sajjappa is prepared of *bansi rava*, coconut, ghee and cardamom whereas Thuni Thengol is made of rice and *urad dal*. Uland Ogare is made up of rice, *urad dal*, *chana dal* and dry coconut whereas Ambode is quiet similar to Maddur Vada but without garlic and onion.

Following are the main dishes of the Iyengar community.

- **Puliyogare (Tamarind Rice)**

Puliyogare is a famous and distinct preparation made with a concoction of rice, tamarind pulp and a variety of spices. Addition of roasted peanuts adds a new dimension to the dish providing it a tangy taste. It makes a lovely combination with fresh curds. It holds a crucial place and is considered to be synonymous with the Iyengars and Iyengar cuisine. It is also the preferred *prasadam* in South Indian temples. Iyengars from the Melkote region are famed for this recipe.

- **Ven Pongal**

It is an amazing delicacy made with a combination of rice, green gram and is heavily spiced with pepper, cumin and cashew nut, giving it that unique delectable flavour. It is a good digestive, especially when accompanied by the lip-smacking fenugreek-tamarind *gojju* (sauce).

It is mostly prepared early in the morning during Dhanurmasa and offered as *prasadam* in almost every Vaishnavite temple.

- **Sakkar Pongal**

It is a tempting and mouth watering preparation of jaggery, rice and *dal*. This lovely dish is topped with ghee, roasted raisins and cashew nuts. Other fruits like almond add a new vibrancy to the dish, if added in sufficient amount.

- **Kancheepuram Idli**

This dish can be described as the exotic cousin of the common *idli*. The fermented rice and *urad* dough is spiced up with pepper, cumin, coconut pieces, *chana dal*, and so on. It is an exquisite snack dish which is served with lip-smacking *chutney*.

Malabari Cuisine

Malabari cuisine is simply the cuisine of the Mappila community in Malabar which is situated in North Kerala. It is also referred as Mappila cuisine. The Mappila community is the largest Muslim populace group in Kerala and they are also called Malabaris.

Malabari cuisine is a rich cuisine which is an alluring amalgamation of vegetables, meats and seafood preparation and especially flavoured with a wide variety of spices cooked in coconut milk. It is renowned all over for its immense usage of a wide variety of spices.

This cuisine has been heavily influenced and shaped by the impact of the various voyagers and travellers from Italy, Greece, China, France and Africa in the recent past, with the intention of spice trade to the coast of Malabar, located in southwestern region of India.

Malabari cuisine highlights and reminds us of the foreign impact on India's southwest coast, with its enthralling panoply of fish and meat delicacies. Being situated on the coastal line, Malabari cuisine is very rich in seafood, coconut and spices. These have become an inseparable part of Malabar cuisine.

It gasconades of a typical flavour and an everlasting taste which has been influenced by the Arabs as well as by the locally produced spices, products and cooking traditions. The authentic Malabar cuisine is genuinely spicy, symbolized by the constant use of spices like black pepper, clove, and cardamom, mandatorily cooked in fragrant coconut oil.

Malabari Biryani is the most celebrated delicacy of this cuisine which was introduced in India by the Arab seafarers. *Biryani* is basically a Mughlai rice dish cooked with meat, onions, chilies and other flavourful spices. The mutton is cooked tender, the rice flaky and delicately spiced with the impeccable conflate of seasonings, to create a lingering taste in the mouth. The Malabar Muslims have a distinct culinary culture, symbolized by a impressive influence of Arab, Mughal and local Kerala cuisine.

Malabar cuisine, emphasizing on the subtle flavour and gently cooked nature, is also renowned for its wide variety of pancakes and steamed rice cakes made from pounded rice. Pathiri is a very popular pancake basically made of rice flour. Some other mouth-watering Malabar dishes include Thoran, Appam, Avial, Milagu Kari, Mango Pulisheri, Vazhaa Halwa (banana Halwa), Ada Prathaman, and so on.

Some other illustrious dishes are Meen Pathiri (steamed rice flour pie with fish), Adaku Pathiri (layered delicacy of rice and egg), Kohzi Curry (simply a chicken curry) and Alsa – a traditional and authentic Arabian delicacy made of wheat, meat (or chicken) and salt.

Certain other renowned delicacies of the Malabar cuisine include Beef/Erachi Varatiyathu, which is a flavoured meat preparation with little gravy, and Aadu Porichathu is a whole roasted goat stuffed with chicken, which are already stuffed with eggs.

Sindhi Cuisine

Sindhi cuisine is essentially the cuisine of the people hailing from the Sindh province of Pakistan and genuinely belonging to the Indus Valley civilization. The people of the Sindh province are known as Sindhis. During the period of partition of India many Sindhis migrated to India and settled permanently in India and hence with the passage of time, Sindhi cuisine became an integral part of the diverse culinary of India.

Sindhi cuisine has been enriched vastly with the influence of the Mughlai, Arabian and Turkhani cuisines. The authentic and traditional Sindhi cuisine is purely vegetarian and even abstains from the use of onions and garlic. Sindhi cuisine is an exquisite cuisine with a wide collection of warm flavours, an amazing assortment of tasty sweets, delicious spicy curries, superbly balanced gravies, rich *biryanis*, fresh vegetables and varied kinds of flat breads or *papads*. The pickles and *papads* of this cuisine have added a new dimension to Sindhi cuisine thereby earning a high reputation worldwide.

Sindhi cuisine resembles a lot with northern Indian cuisine but is quite distinct in the feature that differentiates it with the cuisines of rest of India. The chief element it depicts is that it is based on the flavours of fresh vegetables, whereas in other North Indian cuisines, spices play the crucial part in the cuisine. The Sindhis are particular of spices and use them sparingly. The most commonly used spices are turmeric, coriander powder and *garam masala* (which is basically a mixture of spices containing mainly cardamom, clove and cinnamon). The spices never dominate the curries but it just flavours the delicacies in which it is used. *Amchoor* or mango powder is the most abundantly used spice in almost every household. They also prefer to use dried seeds of pomegranate in their dishes in extensive quantity. The gravies are imparted a spicy and tangy taste by using certain commodities like ginger, garlic, tomatoes or tamarind. These ingredients are used as the primary items in most of the Sindhi curries and gravies.

Sindhis are of the opinion that the first meal of the day, i.e., breakfast should compulsorily be heavy and filling and hence they prefer to consume heavy breakfast.

Dal Pakwan is among the commonly consumed breakfast which is basically a crisp fried refined flour flat bread served with *chana dal*, and it is rich in protein. Generally, *chutney* is also served with this delicacy. Some people prefer to have a salad comprising onions, carrots and lemon with this item.

Sindhi Koki is simply whole-wheat flour based bread which is combined with onion, garlic, chilies, dried pomegranate seeds, cumin and then cooked on griddle. One version of Koki is Bori, which is actually sweet in taste. Lolo is also another form of sweetened bread.

Dodo is again a variety of bread prepared from millet flour or *jowar* or *bajra* and is considered to be nutritious as it is high in fibre. *Bhaat* is also a common preparation made from broken wheat porridge.

The contemporary Sindhis have changed their eating pattern due to fast paced life and have modified certain recipes as per the demand of time. Delicacies like Chola Dhabhala or bread soaked in chickpea curry have become the most preferred breakfast item in many households. This is made using *moong dal* or split yellow gram and is considered to be packed with high nutrition.

Lunch is also a grand affair in this cuisine and speaks volumes about the eating style of Sindhis. A simple Sindhi lunch comprises rice, *dal* and vegetable curry. They have adopted certain cooking techniques and styles. Daagh is one such peculiar style in which the curry is cooked with browned onions. Seyal is another style of cooking dishes with the combination of ginger and garlic and scanty use of water. Then they also have another style of cooking dishes in tomato gravy.

Sindhis have an immense penchant for certain stuffed vegetables during the lunch. Stuffed lady finger, stuffed capsicum, stuffed gourd are illustrations for this. Sindhis also have special love for green leafy vegetables and Sindhi Palak is one such delicacy of green leafy vegetables relished at lunch. Lentils play a crucial part in this cuisine and hence have various side dishes like Chilra Kadhi. Aani ji Bhaaji is another side dish comprising gram flour (*besan*) dumplings.

Sindhi Kadhi is relished by all Sindhis. It is essentially made with a gram flour based curry flavoured with tamarind and containing beans, lady finger, drumsticks, and so on in it. It is consumed with boiled rice and accompanied with a side dish of *boondis*, which is a sweet delicacy of the Sindhis.

As Sindhis have an inclination towards spicy food, Amritsari Wadi is one such item that portrays their love for spices. This delicacy is made with potatoes and seasoned with spices. The tempting Sindhi Sai Bhaji, which is made with spinach, fenugreek leaves, sorrel leaves, beans, potatoes, carrot, eggplant, okra, *chana dal* is also a spicy item and liked by the Sindhis.

During the special and festive occasions, unique and typical ingredients are used to prepare the dishes. Lotus stem is one such commodity, which is used to cook the dishes on such ceremonies. They prefer to eat lotus stem over *paneer*. Bheepatata and Degh Waara

Chaanwara are two traditional and authentic delicacies of the Sindhi cuisine. Degh, which is cooked with lotus stems, potatoes, peas, onions and tomatoes is liked by all and relished with great tempo. This spicy curry is accompanied with distinct traditionally rice dish called *pulav*.

The Sindhis have mastered their skills for snack preparation as well. Aloo Tikki is basically a Sindhi snack which is enjoyed by the people all over India. They have other preparation like Sanna Pakoda, Batan Papdi, Sindhi Kheecha and Chilli Pakora which make the collection of snacks complete.

They also love *papads* and pickles. Grated mango pickles is the most favourite of any Sindhi. Pickles are very varied as they are prepared with a motley of fruits and vegetables like onions, turnips, carrots, chillies, lemons and of course, raw mangoes. The Sindhis have gained expertise in preparing even pickles.

The Sindhi cuisine also offers a huge variety of sweet dishes like Tosha, Praghuree, Khuskhus Halwa, Carrot Halwa, Gulab Jamun, Coconut Barfi and Laddoo, to name a few items. Vermicelli is combined with sugar and other items and served as a dessert item. They have excelled their art of making desserts as well.

Generally, the Sindhis prefer to have a rich taste even in their beverages and the influence of Mughlai style can be easily realized. Thandai, Sherbet, Falooda, and Rose Sherbet, are certain popular beverages of the Sindhis.

The Sindhi cuisine has certain dishes consecrated to festive and special occasions. Chiti Kuni is a preparation with seven vegetable dishes and prepared especially during the occasion of Diwali. It is a custom that if anyone suffers from chicken pox, then after recovering he or she makes an offering and prepares Mitho Lolo, a sweet griddle-roasted flat bread.

Bohra Cuisine

Bohri cuisine is the cuisine of Dawoodi Bohra (who originated from Yemen) is a sub-section of Islamili Shia Islam, now settled in Gujarat. This community is widely scattered all across the globe, from the Middle East, Pakistan, Iran, Iraq, Africa, Egypt, India to the western world, and hence the cuisine mirrors the influence of all the cuisines in its feature. The Bohras settled in Gujarat, particularly Surat, and hence also reflects the Gujarati influences in their cuisine.

The Bohra families are renowned for their wide variety of Mughlai delicacies like *kebabs* and *tikkas* all over.

Food holds a crucial role in the Bohras' culture and has become an inseparable part of their culture. Certain authentic delicacies are prepared by traditional ways which bestows the dish a distinct and delectable quality. They stick with the custom to eat in *thal*. *Thal* is simply a large round metal plate, where the family sits around it helping them from the same dish, course by course to have any meal of the day. Such style of eating food symbolizes unity, equality and sharing in the family and society. A square cloth called *safra* is placed on the carpet, and raised metal or wooden round called *kundali* is placed on it and then the *thal* is kept over it. The food is given prime importance and hence, if a dish has been placed on the *thal*, the person dining should sit till the time all have finished their meal and the person can't leave the dining area even if he is done with his food.

They are of the belief that salt clears the taste bud and heals many diseases, and hence they have a strange custom to start and end every meal with a grain of salt. They also have another tradition to eat *sodanna* which is basically cooked rice sprinkled with granulated sugar and ghee to commence the meal on certain religious occasions.

It would seem strange but the fact is that the Bohra community commences their meal with desserts. They have certain desserts that are belong typically and distinguishably only to the Bohras like Malida (a sweet made with wheat and jaggery), Lacchka (a pounded wheat *halwa*, mostly prepared on first day of the year of Bohra calendar) and Kalamro (a yogurt based rice pudding). Sancha (hand cranked) ice creams are churned and prepared on special occasions. The common desserts popular with this community are *kheer* (delectable rice pudding) and Khajur no Halwo (a tempting date pudding).

The dessert is ensued with savory appetizers and then a full course meal is served mostly accompanied with nutritious salads. The Bohras have mastered their culinary art in the stream of rice dishes ranging from *biryani* to all sorts of *pulaos*. Bohra Khichda (delicacy made mutton and beaten wheat), Kheema Khichdi (minced meat pulao), Lagan ya Seekh (delicacy of layered minced meat topped with eggs), Kheema na Samosa (typical minced meat samosas), Mutton Kari Chawal (spiced coconut milk based stew served with fragrant basmati rice studded with peas) are some unique specialties of the Bohra community.

Bohras are also very proficient in making soup as well mostly to have it with rice preparations. Soups can be cold as well as hot, depending on their preferences like soups like Sarki (made with *toovar dal* garnished with cucumber, tomatoes, spring onions and whisked curds) are cold whereas the soups like Sarka (made of *toovar dal*, groundnut and coconut) are cold soups. They also prepare spiced tomato soups, which are very tasty.

Bohri cuisine is an excellent amalgamation of both vegetarian and non-vegetarian specialties even though non-vegetarian fare is liked and preferred much as compared to vegetarian dishes. Nonetheless, Daal Chawaal Palidu is a pure vegetarian dish which seems to be the most celebrated dish the community. This unique specialty which comprises two main parts; basically a *pulao*-like rice preparation which has a base of boiled *dal* with perfect seasoning, topped by chopped onions fried to golden brown with fresh steaming basmati rice is accompanied by Palidu. Palidu is a essentially a curry-like preparation made out of a flour base much like the North Indian *pakoda* curry with *dudhi* (bottle gourd) or drumstick stewed in it. Generally, Palidu is been flavoured with the sour taste of typical *kokum* in it. Here, it is very common to add boiled mutton into the *dal*, thus making it non-vegetarian.

Certain preparations like Kefti *Dal*, which is mixed lentil soup, Patwalya which is colocassia leaf rolls, Gavarfali ni Sabzi which is a delicacy of cluster beans cooked in spices and tomato sauce and Dudhi ni Tarkari, which is a bottle gourd soup are loved most by this community and is savoured with great zest.

There is a belief existing in the Bohra community that the families that eat together stay together and hence they carry the practice. Due to this belief, all meals are taken together in a large dish called the *thal*, with the purpose to promote a sense of sharing and equality. The *thal* is mostly kept on a raised metal or wooden board called the *kundali*.

They generally prefer to go with the boiling method of cooking with meat and not the western practice of grilling, roasting or searing. They mostly boil meat with ginger, garlic and chilly paste. They don't refrain from eating beef but it is rarely eaten and preferred. While preparing meat, they prepare the sauce or gravy first and then they add boiled meat into it, which tenders the chicken or mutton. This seems to have been adapted from the Arabic style of cooking meat, which mostly involves boiling the meat.

They don't have lavish style of eating food. At times, the food can be very less, meaning only one sweet dish, one aperitif followed by the main course; or elaborated into two sweet dishes, two appetizers followed by a main course filled with salads, cold drinks and followed by paan and *gutkha*. Thus the Bohri cuisine is quite interesting in itself.

Parsi Cuisine

Essentially, it is the cuisine of Parsi populace who came from Persia around 1300 years back and then settled on the coastline of Gujarat. This is why, the Parsi food is an impeccable combination of Persian and Gujarati culinary patterns. The vegetarian segment is dominated by Indian influence and non-vegetarian fare by Persian influence.

They have mainstreamed Indian style of culinary system into their food culture and have shaped an innovative food culture for themselves.

The Parsi people are great food connoisseurs and give a lot of endeavours, time and passion in cooking ultimate dishes and delectable delicacies. The Parsi food is symbolized with a distinctive and typical flavour and simplistic taste. Spices are used with great skill to get best results in the flavours in the dish. Varied spices conflate together to yield a typical flavour and taste to the Parsi cuisine.

Rice is the staple food of Parsi food. Lentils and curries are usual features in this cuisine. It would be quite difficult to segregate this cuisine into either vegetarian or non-vegetarian section. In fact, they lay much emphasis on the nutritive value of the food. Parsis have a unique style of presenting dishes which makes it a class apart from other cuisines.

The Parsi cuisine is healthy as it is cooked with commodities and ingredients conducive to good health. This cuisine is exceptionally good with the sound usage of selected spices and rose water in a wide variety of dishes. Curry is a significant feature of this cuisine and is consumed with rice. *Ras* is also very popular in this unique cuisine. There is a slight distinction between *ras* and curry and that is due to usage of coconut. While curry requires coconut in its preparation, *ras* does not need coconut and is more liquefied in form than curry. Both curry and *ras* can be served with rice preparation in any meal.

The people of this populace love to eat meat in general. The style of cooking meat and chicken dishes are influenced by the Iranian style of cooking. They prefer to cook meat with much spices and vegetables. Salads also hold a key place in the Parsi cuisine. Kachumbar is one such salads which is prepared with onion and cucumber. All the ingredients of the salads are finely chopped and mixed and savoured with high spirits. This salad accompanies most of the dishes in the Parsi cuisine. This nutritious salad is excellent for health and enlivens the taste buds as well.

Salli Murgh is on of the celebrated delicacies of the Parsi cuisine, which is a chicken dish cooked with apricots and garnished with fine potato crisps. Khichri is a simple yet smooth dish of this community. This dish is easily digestible as it is very light and hence served to people with weak digestive system and also to those with stomach upset. Bhakras (a type of fried scone) and Sadhnas (steamed rice pancakes) are Parsi snacks. Both prepared with *toddy* are other typical and unique Parsi dishes. Other popular Parsi snacks include *batasa* which are flour and butter tea biscuits, *dar ni pori* which are simply sweetened lentils stuffed in a light pastry, *kummas* is a cake made with yogurt, *kopra paak* is a delicacy of coconut, *gharik kajoor ni* (a fried date pie) and *khaman na lavda* which are dumplings stuffed with sweetened coconut.

Dhansak is the renowned dish prepared with mutton, lentil and vegetable and this miscellanea is eaten with brown rice and consumed with a pint of lager beer. Certain other illustrious mouth-watering delicacies are Chicken Farcha (fried chicken), Patra ni Machhi (steamed fish wrapped in banana leaf and served with green *chutney*), Jinga nu Pathio (spicy shrimp curry), Saas ni Machhi (yellow rice with pomfret fish fillets in white gravy), Jardaloo Salli Boti (boneless mutton in an onion and tomato gravy with apricots and fine deep fried potato strips), Tamota ni Russ Chaval (mutton cutlets with white rice and tomato gravy), Koimino Patio (essentially a sweet and sour prawn curry) and Dhandal Patio (fish curry served with rice and lentils).

Egg is also a significant element of this cuisine. Akuri is scrambled eggs with spices and the pora is simply a Parsi omelette are popular items of this community. Egg these is also used as topping for several main dishes.

The Parsi people are great lovers of sweets, which are very simple in nature. They prepare *sev* (vermicelli) which is cooked with milk and certain dry fruits. Faluda is also loved by all in the Parsi cuisine. Usually, it is eaten at the end of a meal. It is easy on the stomach and is relished when served cold. *Ravo* (semolina) and *Kulfi* are other famed desserts of this cuisine. Parsi Mitthu Dahi is a traditional and authentic Parsi dish for auspicious occasions. Mitthu Dahi (sweet curds) is served cold with Sev, Ravo or just by itself.

Saraswat Cuisine

Saraswat cuisine is basically the cuisine of the Saraswat Brahmins from the Konkan region on the west coast of India. Saraswat Brahmins are generally pesco-vegetarian (a segment in which fish eating is not considered non-vegetarian, but treated as vegetarian), while in certain sections it is strictly non-vegetarian.

Heavily influenced by South Indian cuisine, it bears a slight resemblance to the Konkani and Udipi cuisines. The cuisine here has also been shaped and influenced by the Portuguese cuisine than the cuisine of their Goan Catholic counterparts. This cuisine is less spicy and their curries extensively use coconut, coconut oil, tamarind, and curry leaves in their food.

Hooman and Xit (*hooman* is fish curry and xit is parboiled rice) are the staple food of the Saraswat Brahmins of Goa, whereas the regular consumption of Indian breads such as *puris, chapatis* and *parathas* are seen chiefly among them.

The cuisine of Satvik Brahmin (sub-sect of Saraswat Brahmins) is similar to Jain cuisine, as they are purely vegetarian cuisines and do not use even vegetables that are plucked from under the ground like onions, potatoes, garlic, and so on and dishes such as Savalem Ranapp are commonly prepared among the Bhats (priests), conventional Goud Saraswat Brahmins and Chitrapur Saraswat Brahmins.

The families where the Kuldev (family deity) is Lord Shiva, all Saraswat Brahmins eat only vegetarian food on all Mondays in particular. Generally, Saraswat Brahmins are routinely vegetarian.

Khatkhatem, a stew with miscellanea preparation of at least 6 vegetables, is commonly prepared. The preparations like Bhaaji or shaak (delicacy of different vegetables and fruits), Usal (tempting spiced pulses in a thin watery gravy), Misal (Usal garnished and topped with fried snacks), Tondak (Rajma beans cooked with cashew nuts), Ross (coconut-based dishes), *hoomans* (varied types of curries), *karams* (vegetable salads), Lonche (pickles) and *papads* (flat bread) are savoured by them. Fast foods include Moongacho Gathi (curried green gram), Botatyache Patal Bhaji (potato curry), and Tur *Dal* Ross (split pigeon pea curry), are also their specialities.

This cuisine comprises either curries or vegetables made with ground fresh coconut gratings or tempered beans, sprouts, pulses (*dals*) garnished with grated coconut. However, due to health awareness, nowadays, the use of coconut has been minimalised. Typical dishes are Batata Song (potatoes prepared with tamarind, onions, garlic, chili powder and turmeric), Kairus (ground coconut base with spices, capsicum, potatoes, tamarind, peanuts and cashews), Sukke (ground coconut base, spices and a motley of vegetables like potatoes and, *knolkhol* (*kohlrabi*), peas, cauliflower, okra). Ghashees and Ambats, are both coconut based preparations. Apinmedi pickles made with several varieties of raw mango was a staple food, but the younger generations have not developed their taste for these.

There is a fable that once the river Saraswati dried up and due to this the Sawaswats were unable to farm and hence allowed to eat seafood/fish. Therefore, many Saraswat Brahmins are pesco-vegetarians in temperament. The fishes were euphemistically referred to as Sea Vegetable. Oysters, for illustration, are at times called *samudra phalam* meaning sea fruit.

The breakfast in a Saraswat home is unique and distinct. It includes Pez (congee) made up of Ukdem Tandhul (par-boiled rice) and Nonche (pickles) and *papad*. The affluent society would prefer to consume *dosa, idli* or *sannas* (in Goa), along with *chutney* and/or *sambhar* in their breakfast. Generally, *rotis* and *bhakries* also are types of bread consumed along with *tondak* or seasoned *batata bhaji* (potato stir fried preparation).

A typical Saraswat vegetarian lunch would have the great and unique collection of Sheeth, Roass or Varann, and if it is non-vegetarian then it would be Hoomann, Bhaji, Tondak, Lonche, Papodd, and Toi or Kadhi. The last style of cookery is not to be confused with curry, as it is the Saraswat equivalent of the Tamil *rasam*, and is prepared to serve the dual purpose of *mukha shuddhhi* (mouth purification, perhaps after the consumption of all the relatively spicy stuff) and *jeervonn* (digestive *kadhis* include asafoetida, cumin, and fennel seed). Sometimes, the *kadhis* are seasoned simply with *karivel* and *sanswam* (mustard seeds).

Sol Kadi is a raw *kokum* curry especially made with coconut milk and coconut paste, garlic paste and green chilly paste, Dali Thoye is a spiced up *tuvar dal* curry, Potato Upkari is stir-fried potato with coconut, Potato Talsani is dry and stir fried potatoes, served as an accompaniment to rice and curry. Kadgi Sukke is essentially a raw jackfruit curry, and mango uddamethi is a thick chunky curry where raw mango is cooked with coconut milk, fenugreek and jaggery. These are some of the specialities of this community.

Thus, the Saraswat cuisine also has a nice potpourri of delicacies which has been the matter of attraction to all the food lovers.

Konkan Cuisine

Konkan cuisine is simply the cuisine of the people residing in Konkan, which is situated on the western coast of India. Their mother tongue is the Konkani and they generally hail from Goa.

Malvan is the town in Sindhudurg district of Maharashtra which also comes under the domain of Konkan cuisine and is referred to as the Malvani cuisine or Konkani cuisine.

Widely appreciated for its taste, the Konkani cuisine is very distinctive in its culinary feature. The method of cooking plays a key role in developing taste in the Konkani cuisine and has a huge influence at the end product prepared.

The Konkanastha Brahmin style of food is a matter of delectation in vegetarian food and can captivate anyone with its simple yet very impressive taste.

Being located on the coastal line, abundance of seafood, fish and prawns are apparent along with chicken and beef. The Konkani cuisine relies on the technique of marination for cooking meat to the right degree. The process of marinating or seasoning meats yields better end product (of the meat) and they use tamarind or even lemon as the marinade. This renders them perfectly cooked (tender) product.

This cuisine is blessed with plentiful abundance of coconut, as coconut is mainly found in coastal regions. They use coconut in various forms, such as grated, dry grated, fried, coconut paste and coconut milk to let the cuisine develop its own unique taste. The cuisine is characterized as spicy in nature and incorporates a lot of spices like dried red chilies, coriander seeds, peppercorns, cumin, cardamom, ginger, garlic, and so on. This cuisine is also peculiar for using certain fruits while preparing dishes like fruits of *kokum*, dried *kokum*, tamarind and raw mango, to make the dishes more delectable and tasty.

One unique technique of this coastal cuisine is the style of adding spices in the dishes. The addition of spices helps to overcome of unpleasant odours, tenderizes meat, and also meliorates taste of the dishes. In certain dishes, all spices are added at once, while in few dishes they are added at some intervals, whereas in some dishes spices are added at the very end, after the meat has softened to great extent.

The Konkan cuisine can be symbolized as very spicy and fiery in taste. So, in order to pacify the spicy taste, an appetizing dish called Sol Kadhi is served to soothe the taste buds. Sol Kadhi is made from coconut milk and *kokum* fruit and generally served either as an appetizer or as a main course dish. This dish is also referred to as the Kokum Kadhi.

A typical Konkani meal comprises rice, Dalitoy, which is a lentil soup; and Upkari, which is a mouth-watering vegetable dish made from vegetables and coconut. Dalitoy is a compulsory dish in the day-to-day meal of this region. This cuisine relies more on locally produced seasonal vegetables and fruits, and the use of dairy products are also very less.

Certain celebrated delicacies of the cuisine are Bangda Fry (delicious fried macakrel), Khavda Curry (a delectable dish made from the meat of the local Konkani bird called Khavda), Phanasa Chi Bhaji (a dish of jackfruit with certain spices and chillies), Kaju Chi Aamti (a curry of cashews and spices), Khaproli (a sweet dish in which a lightweight pancake is dipped in sweetened yellow colour syrup) and Dhondas or Cucumber Cake (a mouth-watering baked preparation from cucumber and jaggery).

The Konkani people have mastered their art in providing variety to their food. Notwithstanding their scanty resources and the limitations of seasonal produce, they have successfully evolved the cuisine which comprises delectable items made with the same kind of vegetables used differently during various periods of the year. For example, mangoes are used in vegetable dishes, to cook dishes made of mangoes only, and even as *chutneys*. They also prepare various kinds of pickles. The Konkani people are very creative and innovative to use certain ingredients in the best possible manner.

There are certain common equipment found in the kitchen of any Konkani household. The equipment like Aadoli or Addoli (traditional and unique equipment used to cut and grate vegetables), Daantey or Zaatey in Goa (traditional grinding or milling stone used to extensively grind spices and other ingredients) and Chulha (cooking equipment for an open flame and is made up of bricks, cow dung, mud, and so on; generally charcoal, wood, coal or cow dung cakes are used as fuel in it) are easily found.

Thus, Konkani cuisine has many features to appreciate it and hence has attracted every sincere food lovers towards its simplicity, creativity and authenticity of culinary elements.

Culinary Trivia: Pani Puri

Pani Puri renowned all over India with various names such as golgappa, *pani ke batashe, phuchka, pani puri, gup chup,* and so on. It can be said undoubtedly that it is the most popular street food of India. It comprises a round, hollow puri, fried crisp and filled with a mixture of flavoured water (*pani*), tamarind *chutney*, chilli *chaat masala*, boiled potato, chopped onion and boiled mashed chickpeas. The filling is made by lightly mashing boiled potatoes with black salt, salt, some spices, a generous portion of tamarind pulp, chilli powder, and so on. The tamarind water is made by mixing tamarind and spices/salt and making a light and tart liquid with water. It is generally small enough to fit completely into one's mouth.

It is referred as *gol gappa* as it is sphere (*gol*) in shape and can be placed in the mouth and eaten (*gappa*) at once. It is also referred as *pani puri* as *pani* is the Hindi is water and *puri* is the name of an Indian bread made by deep frying in oil.

Part C
The Soul of Indian Cuisine

29 Spices: Heartbeat and Essence of Indian Cuisine

"If you combine good flavours, food turns into an orchestra." – Joey Fatone

"The spices are to Indian cuisine, what grammar is to language". Spices can be considered the heart-beat of Indian cuisine and it would be unfair and illogical to think or even imagine of an Indian cuisine without spices. Spices are an integral part of Indian cuisine, which adds a new dimension to the taste of Indian cuisine. It is diverse variations and impeccable combination of spices which creates a magical impact and variety in the dishes from the various states of India.

Spices are highly flavoured and aromatic natural products of vegetable origin, which are added in minimal amount to foods for zestiness, tanginess and savouriness, and for enhancing their flavour and aroma.

They are essentially dried parts of aromatic plants and mostly include flowers, seeds, leaves, bark, berries and roots. They are free from foreign matter and are used basically for flavouring, seasoning or imparting aroma to food.

According to Paul Hamlyn as mentioned in *Larousse Gastronomique*, spices are "one of many substances derived from plants that have a fragrant or sharp flavour and are used to season food".

Spices may be obtained and derived from varied parts of the plants: bark, buds, flowers, fruits, leaves, rhizomes, roots, seeds, stigmas and styles or the entire plant tops.

In fact, the very commonly used word 'aroma' is the ancient Greek word for spice. The word spice is coined from latin *species*, meaning a commodity of value and distinction.

The term 'herb' is used as a subset of spice and refers to plants with aromatic leaves; fresh or dried. Herbs are leafy spices, and few, like dill and coriander, can provide both spice seeds and leafy herbs as well.

Since time immemorial and great antiquity, spices have played a significant and crucial role in human history. At one period of time, it was valued as high as gold; governments in countries with a big spice trade became affluent on the taxes they imposed on spices. It is recorded that the Queen of Sheba brought with her spices, among other gifts, for King Solomon.

The impeccable conflate of spices has the capability to create magic if the balance and harmony are properly maintained while spicing food. In India, where spices are an integral constituent, the art of blending is hereditarily transferred by mother to their daughters. Strong and dominating spices are generally not used for their own. Most spices are dried and roasted before incorporating it in a dish. In India, the spices that are in abundance and plentitude are pepper, fennel, cumin, coriander, cinnamon, *ajwain* (Bishop's weed), cassia, clove, nutmeg and mace. It is genuinely interesting and strange to known that each spice has its own unique and distinct flavour, medicinal value and other alluring facts to go along with it.

Probably, Indian cuisine is symbolized as the most highly spiced in the world and the spices have a delightful association with almost every Indian food. It is not only that the spices are used only in curried preparation, but spices like green cardamom are used in certain dessert delicacies. In North India, spices are mostly dry-roasted and ground before use, warming mixtures such as *garam masala* are used as a seasoning and chillies are not always important. In South India, spices are ground with coconut or fresh herbs to yield a wet paste and a seasoning (*tarka*) of mustard seeds, curry leaves and dried chilli, all fried in oil, and may be stirred into the dish at the end of cooking.

Apart from being used as a preservative, spices and herbs are also used as medicines in certain cases. Before the industrially prepared medicines came into being, herbal remedies were commonly prescribed by ancient doctors and were found effective, as some practitioners and Ayurvedic scholars are now rediscovering this fact. The Ayurveda is the latest trend nowadays and it has laid extensive emphasis on this.

As the use of spices is very broad in spectrum in Indian cuisine, spices are never allowed to kill or destroy the nutritive value as well as the actual flavour of the food. Their judicious incorporation in the diet has worked magic on appetite and digestion. They actually react during digestion and stimulate the production of natural juices which maintain the normal functioning of the body.

Role of Spices

The very basic quality a common man searches and desires for in a food preparation is its organoleptic qualities (a sense of taste), rather than its nutritive value. Spices heighten the actual graph of the organoleptic properties to the peak in the food product in which it is used. Diverse, distinct and multi-colour cuisines of India and also all across the world are characterized by specific and wonderful combination of spices, condiments and herbs.

It has the following main functions:

- It improves the flavour and palatability of the dish.
- It improves the appearance and cosmetic value of the dish by giving colour to the food.
- It has certain medicinal values (therapeutic values) and also acts as aphrodisiacs (exciting sexual desire).
- It acts as preservative (increasing shelf-life).
- It enhances and heightens the flavour.
- It adds zest to the food and delights the gourmet.
- It also serves as a thickening agent in the preparation of curries.
- It contributes in improving the overall appearance of the dish.
- It has a physiological action beneficial to our system. They act as a stimulus to the digestive system; stimulate secretion of saliva thereby helping digestion in many ways.

Table 1: State-Wise Production of Spices in India

S. No.	State	Spices Grown
1.	Andhra Pradesh	Chilli, Ginger, Mustard and Turmeric
2.	Arunachal Pradesh	Turmeric, Bayleaf and Ginger
3.	Assam	Turmeric and Aniseed
4.	Bihar	Turmeric, Mustard, Garlic and Ajwain
5.	Gujarat	Chilli, Cumin Seed, Dill, Fennel, Fenugreek and Garlic
6.	Haryana	Garlic
7.	Himachal Pradesh	Ginger
8.	Jammu & Kashmir	Saffron and Ajwain
9.	Karnataka	Vanilla, Turmeric, Pepper, Mace and Nutmeg, Kokum, Ginger, Garlic, Clove Chilli and Cardamom (Small)
10.	Kerala	Vanilla, Turmeric, Pepper, Mace, Nutmeg, Ginger, Cinnamon and Cassia and Cardamom (Small)
11.	Madhya Pradesh	Ginger, Garlic and Chilli
12.	Maharashtra	Turmeric, Pomegranate Seed, Garlic and Chilli
13.	Meghalaya	Turmeric and Ginger
14.	Mizoram	Ginger
15.	Odisha	Chilli, Garlic, Ginger and Turmeric
16.	Punjab	Aniseed and Celery
17.	Rajasthan	Garlic, Fenugreek, Fennel, Dill Seed, Coriander, Cumin and Chilli

18.	Sikkim	Bayleaf, Ginger and Cardamom (large)
19.	Tamil Nadu	Vanilla, Turmeric, Pomegranate Seed, Pepper, Nutmeg and Mace, Ginger, Clove, Chilli and Cardamom (small)
20.	Tripura	Turmeric
21.	Uttar Pradesh	Aniseed, Celery, Chilli, Coriander, Cumin, Fennel, Fenugreek, Garlic, Mustard and Turmeric
22.	West Bengal	Turmeric, Ginger, Chilli and Cardamom (large)

Table 2: Spice-Wise Production in Various States of India

S. No.	Spice	Indian States where grown
1.	Pepper	Kerala, Karnataka, Tamil Nadu
2.	Cardamom (small)	Kerala, Karnataka, Tamil Nadu
3.	Cardamom (big)	Sikkim, West Bengal
4.	Chilli	Andhra Pradesh, Gujarat, Karnataka, Maharashtra, Odisha, Rajasthan , Tamil Nadu, Uttar Pradesh, West Bengal, Madhya Pradesh, Uttarakhand
5.	Coriander	Rajasthan, Uttar Pradesh, Uttarakhand
6.	Cumin	Rajasthan, Uttar Pradesh, Gujarat
7.	Fennel	Rajasthan, Uttar Pradesh, Gujarat
8.	Celery	Punjab, Uttar Pradesh
9.	Clove	Kerala, Karnataka, Tamil Nadu
10.	Nutmeg and Mace	Kerala, Karnataka, Tamil Nadu
11.	Cinnamon	Kerala, Tamil Nadu
12.	Saffron	Jammu & Kashmir
13.	Aniseed	Punjab, Uttar Pradesh, Assam, Uttarakhand
14.	Vanilla	Kerala, Karnataka, Tamil Nadu
15.	Ajwain	Bihar, Jammu & Kashmir
16.	Dill seeds	Gujarat, Rajasthan
17.	Kokam	Karnataka
18.	Mustard Seeds	Uttar Pradesh, Bihar, Andhra Pradesh
19.	Bayleaf	Arunachal Pradesh, Sikkim
20.	Cambodge	Kerala, Karnataka
21.	Fenugreek	Rajasthan, Uttar Pradesh, Gujarat
22.	Turmeric	Andhra Pradesh, Karnataka, Odisha, Tamil Nadu, West Bengal, Maharashtra, Kerala, Assam, Bihar, Meghalaya, Uttar Pradesh, Tripura, Arunachal Pradesh
23.	Ginger	Andhra Pradesh, Karnataka, Kerala, Madhya Pradesh, Meghalaya, Odisha, Arunachal Pradesh, West Bengal, Sikkim, Mizoram, Himachal Pradesh, Tamil Nadu, Uttarakhand, Jharkhand
24.	Garlic	Haryana, Madhya Pradesh, Maharashtra, Odisha, Uttar Pradesh, Gujarat, Karnataka, Rajasthan, Gujarat

Table 3: Spices Derived from Various Parts of the Plant

Parts of Plants	Name of Spices
Seeds	Aniseed, coriander, nigella, fennel, mustard, cumin, caraway, and so on
Bracket or aril	Mace
Berries	Allspice, black pepper, and so on
Buds	Cloves
Fruits	Cardamom, chillies
Kernels	Nutmeg
Leaves	Bay leaf, curry leaves, coriander, basil, and so on
Underground stem	Turmeric
Latex	Asafeotida
Barks	Cinnamon
Floral parts	Saffron

Table 4: Hindi Names of Spices

English Names	Hindi Names
All spice	*Kebab cheeni*
Aniseed	*Saunf*
Basil	*Tulsi*
Bayleaf	*Tej-patta*
Cambodge	*Malabari Imli / Tamarind*
Caraway	*Shahi jeera*
Green cardamom	*Choti elaichi*
Black cardamom	*Badi elaichi*
Red Chilli	*Lal mirch*
Cinnamon	*Dalchini*
Clove	*Laung*
Coriander	*Dhania*
Cumin	*Jeera*
Curry leaves	*Curry Patta*
Fennel	*Saunf*
Fenugreek	*Methi dana*
Asafoetida	*Hing*
Mustard	*Sarson*
Nutmeg	*Jaiphal*
Mace	*Javitri*
Black Pepper	*Kali Mirch*
Saffron	*Kesar or Zaffran*
Star Anise	*Chakri phool*
Turmeric	*Haldi*
Nigella Seeds	*Kalonji*

Table 5: Medicinal Uses of Indian Spices

Spices	Use	Benefits
Asafoetida	It is used for seasoning food especially snacks, certain curries and has high medicinal uses.	An effective curative for severe cough and stomach ache caused due to flatulation gas.
Bay leaf	It is used in cooking to add a unique and specific flavour to food. It has some medicinal properties as well.	Bay leaf oil is attributed with antifungal, anti-microbial and anti-bacterial characteristics. The chief functional properties are to treat hypoglycaemia a (low blood sugar), and so on.
Cardamom	It is used in most of the Indian and other sweet dishes to give a good flavour and aroma. It is also used extensively in the pharmaceutical sector.	Helps to control bad breath and digestive disorder. A whole cardamom chewed is suggested for mitigating diabetes effect.
Chilli	It is a key ingredient used for adding a hot and spicy flavour to the food. It stimulates the taste buds.	The antioxidants present in chilli help to reduce cholesterol. It also helps in burning calories. As a medicine it is used as a counter irritant in Lumbargo (backache), Neuralgia (acute spasmodic pain), and Rheumatic (joint pain) disorders. Dehydrated green chilly is considered a good source of Vitamin C.
Cinnamon	It is used primarily for seasoning food and preparing *masalas*. It has medicinal uses too.	It helps in the natural production of insulin and thereby reduces blood cholesterol as well. It has astringent; stimulant and anti-flatulent properties and can control nausea and vomiting as well. The cinnamon bark oil has anti-fungal properties.
Clove	It is chiefly used as a seasoning and preparing *masalas*.	Clove oil is beneficial in toothache and sore gums. It is also beneficial in treating chest pains, fever, digestive problems, cough and cold. It is highly prized in medicine as a carminative and stimulant. The antiseptic and antibiotic properties of clove oil are used in medicines especially in dentistry, oral and pharyngeal (related to throat) treatments. It has wider applications in preparations of toothpaste and mouthwashes, soaps and perfumes. It is also reported to help diabetics as well.
Coriander	Both its seeds and leaves are used in cooking. It is also blessed with some medicinal qualities.	It can be used externally on joint pains and rheumatism. It is also good for treating sore throat, certain allergies, digestion problems, hay fever, and so on. In household medicines, it is used against seasonal fever, stomach disorders, and nausea.
Cumin	It is used for mostly tempering in cooking and it attributed with medicinal properties.	Considered to be the good source or iron and also keeps the immune system healthy. Water boiled with cumin seeds is good for curing dysentery. In the world of medicine, it is used as a stimulant, carminative, treating stomach-ache, and so on.
Curry leaves	It is used as a main ingredient for seasoning in some countries. It is one of the main ingredients for tempering certain dishes in South India. It has certain medicinal uses.	They are beneficial for reducing blood sugar. The dried leaves are extensively used in herbal medicines. Volatile oil is used as a fixative for soap perfume. The leaves, bark and root of the plant are used in the indigenous medicine as a tonic, stimulant, and treating flatulence and stomachache.

Fenugreek	It is mainly used as a green leafy vegetable and seeds are used for seasoning and preparing *masalas*. It also has medicinal uses.	Fenugreek seed tea or sweet fudge is helpful in increasing breast milk. It is helpful in treating diabetes and lowering cholesterol. The seeds are used in acute pain of flatulence, dysentery, diarrhea, dyspepsia (indigestion), chronic cough and enlargement of liver and spleen, rickets and diabetes. It is also used as a tonic and aphrodisiac.
Garlic	It is used for cooking as well as for the medicinal purposes. It is also considered the best aphrodisiac.	It is useful for treating cough and cold. It also has antibiotic features and is effective in joint pains.
Ginger	It is used for giving a specific typical flavour to food and has many medicinal uses.	Helps to avoid digestive problems. It is beneficial for treating severe cough and cold. It is good for the heart.
Mustard	Its seed are used for seasoning and tempering whereas green leafy vegetable for vegetable preparation. The use of mustard oil is extensive in India but it is banned in some countries.	Mustard oil is good for body massage and even for getting a good hair. It consists of omega-3 fatty acids and is a rich source of mono-unsaturated fatty acids. It is an excellent source of iron, zinc, manganese, calcium, protein, and so on.
Nutmeg	It is used in powdered form for garnishing and also for *masala* preparation.	It is beneficial for the treatments of asthma, heart disorder and bad breath. It also benefits the spleen and relieves any bad cold. It is a well-known narcotic, not dangerous in small quantities, but even a little is considered to aid sleep. It is used as a drug in eastern countries because of its stimulant, carminative, astringent and aphrodisiac properties.
Pepper	It is extensively used in cooking, especially for garnishing and providing pungency to the dish. It is has many medicinal uses too.	It helps curing cold, cough, infections, and so on. It helps to deal with muscle pains and digestive problems also. Piperine, the pungent principle in pepper oleoresin helps to increase the bio-availability and therefore used in pharmaceuticals.
Saffron	It is used for cooking as well as in beauty products. It is mainly used in sweet dishes. It has good medicinal properties.	It is used for certain skin diseases and as a perfume in cosmetics. It is a good remedy for cough, cold and asthma. It is a very effective stimulant and anti-spasmodic and is used by the doctor as a remedy for jaundice, dysentery, measles, and so on. It is also used as an aphrodisiac. It is considered to rejuvenate the juvenile feature in the individual. In Ayurvedic medicine, it is used to heal arthritis, impotence and infertility.
Star anise	It is used in cooking and also for medicinal purposes.	Star anise oil is beneficial for rheumatism (painful disorder of joints). It is helpful for digestion and also controls bad breath.
Turmeric	It is almost used in all curry preparations and in cooking and skincare products. It also has certain medicinal uses.	It has certain antibiotic properties and is anti-cancerous in nature. It helps deal with skin problems. Turmeric powder can be used for healing cuts and wounds. It also treats diabetes. Turmeric is also used as a dye in textile industry. It is used in the preparation of medicinal oils and ointments. It is used as a carminative, tonic, blood purifier and an antiseptic.

Fennel	It is used in seed form and dry-fried or ground as required. It is used as main ingredient in curry powder and in five-spice powder as well.	It is believed to be a cure-all and to make people young, strong and healthy. Drinking hot water infused with fennel seeds is said to restore a jaded palate.

Table 6: Description of Spices

Ajwain Bishop's weed is a plant in India which produces a seed fruit, commonly known as *ajowan, ajwain* or carom seeds, or thymol seeds. Due to their seed-like appearance, the fruit pods are at times referred as seeds; they are oval-shaped and greyish in colour. Even a minimal quantity of raw fruit pods of *ajwain* manage to dominate the flavour of the dish. *Ajwain* is used to flavour savoury doughs in India in the preparations ranging from *naan* to *puri* to *poppadams*. The baking or frying process tends to burst open the flavour from the seeds and render slightly bitter components to the flavour. India has been one of the largest producers of *ajwain*. The seed has its botanical origins in India and is still cultivated extensively in most provinces. *Ajwain* has marked a unique place in the world of vegetarian cuisine that anything which needs a touch of savoury subtleness benefits most from *ajwain* in small doses.	
Allspice Allspice trees are evergreen trees and grow up to a height of 8 to 10 metres, basically found in Caribbean regions. In India, it is cultivated in Maharashtra, Tamil Nadu, Karnataka and Kerala. It is with a slim upright trunk and smooth greyish bark. The trees produce only numbered fruits. The fruits are collected before they are ripe, and then are allowed to dry with utmost care. The dried berries (cubebs) resemble to black pepper, but with stalks attached – it is termed 'tailed pepper'. It has a dominating odour of nutmeg, cinnamon and cloves. The dried berries range in size (mostly from 6.5 to 9.5 mm in diameter) and one gram has only 13 to 14 berries. The attribute of pimento is affected by factors like growing area, stage of maturity of berries at harvest and storage conditions. It is used frequently in Western cooking and less suitable for Eastern cooking. It has medicinal, anti-microbial, insecticidal, anti-oxidant and deodorant properties. It is used in marinades for meat and game cooking. The spice is crushed lightly to liberate the aroma and then used in soups, curries, sauces, *biryanis*, and so on.	
Amchoor Essentially, dried mango powder is used by cooks to render a sour character to their cuisine. *Amchoor* is the unripe mangoes, dried in sun and ground into a powder form for the cooking purposes. It is used in Indian *chutneys*, pickles and *masalas*. Vegetarian cuisine in India uses the powder to add vibrancy to the root vegetables and curries. It is also used as a meat tenderizer.	
Aniseed Aniseed is an annual plant of the parsley family with an average height of 30 to 50 cm. The plant is completely covered with fine hairs and aniseed ranges from ground - grey to greyish brown in colour, 3 to 5 mm in length, and oval in shape with short stalk attached. Five longitudinal ridges are apparently seen on each pericarp. It has been blessed with a symbolic agreeable odour and a pleasant and aromatic taste.	

It is cultivated and is native to the East Mediterranean Region. In India, it is grown on a very small scale to be used as a culinary herb or as a garden plant. It is primarily used as flavouring, preservative, culinary, household, cosmetic and medicinal element. The fruit of anis, commercially called aniseed is extensively used for motley of things such as flavouring curries, bread, soups, baked goods, dried figs, desserts, cream cheese, pickles, egg dishes, non-alcoholic and alcoholic beverages. In Indian homes, it is mostly roasted and eaten after meals to aid digestion. It is also consumed as a mouth-freshener.

In Indian cuisine, no specific distinction is made between anise and fennel. Therefore, the same name (*saunf*) is attributed to both of them. Certain people use the term *patli* (thin) *saunf* or *velayati* (foreign) *saunf* to distinguish anise from fennel.

Asafoetida

Asafetida is dried latex (gum oleoresin) released in drops from the living underground rhizome or tap root of several species of Ferula (three of which grow in India), which is a perennial (recurring repetitively) herb with a height of 1 to 1.5 m.

In India, it is grown in Kashmir and in few parts of Punjab. Asafoetida is imported to India from Afghanistan and Iran. Kandahari hing is the most superior and commercially prized product, which is followed by Irani hing, and Pathani hing.

There are two prime varieties of asafoetida, i.e., Hing Kabuli Sufaid (milky white asafoetida) and *hing lal* (red asafoetida). Asafetida is vitriolic, sulfurous and bitter in taste and gives out a strong disgusting pungent odour due to the presence of sulphur compounds therein. It is available in three configurations, i.e., tears, mass and paste. Tears are regarded as the purest form of resin, rounded or flattened, 5 to 30 mm in diameter and a greyish or dull yellow in colour. Mass asafoetida is the common commercial form which is uniform in mass; whereas the paste form contains extraneous matter.

Asafoetida is heavily used for flavouring curries, sauces, and pickles. It is used in Indian cuisine as an anti-flatulent and especially by the Brahmins. A small amount is necessary and, rather than adding it to the food itself, the resin is often shaped into a little ball and stuck to the lid of the cooking pot. The ardent followers of Jainism restrict themselves from eating root vegetables and use asafoetida in substitute of garlic and onion. The aromatic components in it resemble more or less that of onion and garlic. It is also regarded high in the sector of medicines because of its antibiotic properties.

Its name is derived from the Latin term *foetida*, which translates as 'foul smelling'. It is also referred as Devil's dung. The unknown secret of the spice's culinary use, however is that the sulfurous compounds in it evaporate under slight effect of heat, leaving behind a wonderfully complex garlic-and-onion flavour.

Basil

Basil, also referred as French basil or sweet basil or *tulsi,* is an erect glabrous (with no hair) herb; 30-90 cm high, is native to India. The leaves of basil have legion oil glands with highly aromatic volatile oil. The freshly picked bright green leaves turn brownish green when dried and become brittle and curled. The major common varieties are American basil, French basil, Egyptian basil and Indian basil.

It is indigenous especially to the lower hills of Punjab and Himachal Pradesh and is cultivated throughout India.

The dried leaves and tender four sided stems are used as prized spice for flavouring and for extraction of essential oil. Apart from flavouring certain foods, it is used for seasoning in tomato paste products. It has application in areas of medicine and also used as an insecticide and bactericide. The Indian basil is also considered sacred in society and it is a custom to water basil plant attached with religious sentiments.

Bay leaf

Bay leaf or Laurel leaf is dried leaves or an evergreen woody bush or more rarely a tree of about a height of 15 to 20 m. The upper surface of the leaf is glabrous (with no hairs) and shiny, olive green, and lower surface is dull olive to brown with a marked rib and veins. The aroma of the crushed leaves is delicate and fragrant whereas the taste is aromatic and bitter. The size of the leaves ranges from 2.5 to 7.5 cm in length and 1.6 to 2.5 cm in breadth. The shape is elliptic and tapering to a point at the base and tip of the leaves.

Indian cassia also referred as *tejpatta* is a small to moderately sized evergreen tree. The leaf of this tree is the spice resembling taste of clove and a faintly pepper like odour. It is mostly grown in the tropical and sub-tropical Himalayas extending to northeast India up to an altitude of 2000 m. The leaves are harvested when the tree reaches an age of 10 years and is continued till a century. Mature leaves are collected during October to March. It adds a unique and typical twist to the local sweet *masalas* and seems to contribute more delicate perfume than any significant flavour.

Bay leaves are used as flavouring in soups, stews, meat, fish and sauces and in confectioneries. Both leaves and fruits possess aromatic, stimulant and narcotic properties. The essential oil from the leaves is also used as spice and food flavouring agent and has numerous application in traditional medicines of certain countries.

Cambodge

Cambodge is essentially a tropical fruit commonly known as 'Malabar tamarind'. It is a medium size evergreen tree with rounded crown and horizontal or drooping branches reaching a height of 18 m. Fruit is an apple-sized berry, yellow or red, 6 to 8 grooves, forming blunt lobes with tough rind, 6 to 8 seeds and succulent arils. Fruit weighs around 50 to 180 gm.

It is a native of the Western Ghats of Kerala (India). Its suitable environment ranges from Konkan southward to Travancore and into the Shola forests of Nilgiris. The dried rind is used as a condiment for flavouring certain curries.

Caraway

Caraway is the fruit of a biennial (having a life cycle lasting two years) herb. The plant has a fleshy root and delicate branched stem that gains a height of 0.5 to 0.6 m, with small white flowers in compound umbels. The fruit when ripened splits into narrow elongated pistil, 4 to 6.5 mm long, curved, pointed at ends with 5 longitudinal ridges on the surface. The dried fruit brown in colour has pleasurable odour with sharp taste. Seeds are hard and sharp in texture.

It is cultivated in the hills of Kashmir and Kumaon at an altitude of above 2750 MSL as a cold season crop.

Cardamom (Small)

Cardamom also referred as the "queen of spices" is the dried ripe fruit (capsules of cardamom plant). Cardamom is a perennial and rhizomatous plant (2 to 3 m height) with hairy leaves (on the dorsal side) and spherical fruits in the case of Malabar, whereas the plant is robust (3 to 4 m height) with hairy leaves on both sides with ovoid capsules in the case of Mysore.

Cultivation of cardamom is generally concentrated in the evergreen forests of the Western Ghats in South India including Kerala.

Cardamom is widely used as a flavouring material in whole and ground form. It renders a lingering sparkle to every kind of dish both traditional and modern. Rice is perfumed with a few cardamom pods during cooking in Indian cuisine.

Cardamom oil has versatile applications in flavouring processed foods, cordials, and liquors and in perfumery and in Ayurvedic medicines.

The 'Alleppey Green' cardamom of India is considered the best grade available in the world.

Cardamom (Large)

Large cardamom is a perennial herb with underground rhizomes and 50 - 140 aerial leafy shoots. Each shoot has height of 1.7 to 2.6 m with 9 to 13 leaves in each cultivar. Leaves are hairy on both sides with an apparent midrib. The flower is a condensed spike with yellowish floral envelope. Each spike has 10-15 fruits. The fruit is round or oval shape, capsule with reddish brown colour.

Large cardamom is cultivated in the sub-Himalayan region of northeastern India.

It is used as a flavouring agent in dishes like *pulao, biryanis* and meat preparations. It is an ingredient in curry powder and spice *masala* mixtures and is also used extensively in ayurvedic and unani medicines.

Red Chilli

Chilli is the dried ripe fruit of the genus *Capsicum. Capsicum annum* is an annual sub–shrub and the flowers of which are borne singly and fruits provide red peppers, cayenne, paprika and chillies and sweet pepper (bell pepper). There are over 300 different sub-species cultivated today, ranging across all heat flavours, colour and shape spectra.

It was first introduced in India by the Portuguese towards the end of 15th century.

Dry chilli is extensively used as spice in curry dishes. It is also used as an ingredient in curry powder and in seasonings. This colour is highly popular among food and beverage processors for its use as a colourant, since this being a 'natural plant colour'.

Chillies are fruits that contain a very special compound capsaicin, the chemical that causes the palate to perceive 'heat'. Dave Dewitt from Albuquerque, author of *The Whole Chile Pepper* defines capsaicin as 'an incredibly powerful and stable alkaloid seemingly unaffected by cold or heat, which retains its original potency over time, cooking, or freezing. Because it has no flavour, colour, or odour, the precise amount of capsaicin present in chillies can only be measured by a specialized laboratory procedure'.

Cinnamon

The cinnamon is essentially the dried inner bark of plants, which grows in bushes and is about 2 m high, when it is 2 years old.

In India, it is grown at one or two places in Kerala. The ideal temperature for growing cinnamon is between 20°-30° C and rainfall between 1250 to 2500 mm is desirable.

Cinnamon 'chips' are rough barks which cannot be peeled and are scraped off from the thicker stems. Cinnamon leaf and bark oil are acquired by distilling the leaf and bark separately. Cinnamon bark is a popular spice with a delicate fragrance and a warm agreeable taste. It is used in the form of small pieces or powder. It is found to help diabetics in the digestion of sugar.

Clove

Clove is the air-dried unopened flower bud obtained from evergreen medium sized tree which grows to a height of 10-12 m and starts flowering in about 7 years. It continues to produce flower buds for 80 or more years. Clove clusters are plucked by hand when the buds are fully developed with a pronounced pink flush and then dried over several days in the sun. Unopened flower buds, leaves and stalks yield essential oils.

The condition conducive to the clove tree is well drained rich soil with high moisture in soil throughout the year, high temperature (25° to 35°C) with bright sun light, heavy rainfall (above 150 cm) and high humidity (above 70%).

Clove is used in whole or ground form in kitchen and as a flavouring agent in food industry. Its flavour mingles well with both sweets and savoury dishes.

Cumin Seeds

Cumin is the dried, white fruit with greyish brown colour of a small delicate annual herb plant, which is 15 to 50 cm high. The aromatic seed-like fruit is elongated, oval and 3 to 6 mm long, slightly bitter and has a warm flavour. Cumin is a tropical plant and is cultivated as a *rabi* crop in areas where atmospheric humidity during February-March is low.

Cumin seed features and releases an aromatic odour and bitter taste. It is used as a condiment, and is a primary ingredient in curry powders, seasonings of breads, cakes and cheese.

Coriander (Leaves and Seeds)

Coriander is an important spice crop having a prime position in flavouring food. The plant is a thin stemmed, small, bushy herb, 25 to 50 cm in height with many branches and umbels. Leaves are compound. The whole plant has a captivating aroma. The fruit is globular, 3 to 4 mm diameter, when pressed breaks into two lobules each having one seed. The fruit has delicate fragrance; seeds are pale white to light brown in colour.

Coriander is a tropical crop and can be successfully cultivated as *rabi* season crop in an area free from severe frost during February when the crop flowers and sets its seeds. The root has a more intense flavour than the leaves.

The young plant is used for flavouring and garnishing curries and soups. The leaves are used in making green *chutneys* along with mint leaves.

As fresh coriander is one of the most important herbs of Indian cuisine, the seeds of the coriander plant are also not far behind in the culinary world. The coriander seeds look like tiny, pale, creamy-brown peppercorns. When they are dry-fried, the seeds have a heady, slightly burnt orange aroma which is very alluring. The ground seeds have a pleasing, mild and sweet taste that is not overwhelming. The fruits (seeds) are widely used as condiments with or without roasting in the preparation of curry powders and seasonings.

Curry Leaves

The leaves of curry leaf tree are considered to be a spice. The tree is an aromatic 1-5 m, in height, 15-40 cm in diameter. It is cultivated mainly in home gardens but to a certain extent on a plantation scale.

Curry leaf is highly aromatic and is found almost throughout India up to an altitude of 1500 m.

Perhaps the most common use of curry leaf is as a finishing aromatic component (rather than a base ingredient) in the curries of central and southern India. It is extensively used in vegetarian cuisine, as the flavour blends well with the lighter fare. It is used in southern India as a natural flavouring agent in various curries. It is an essential component for flavouring and tempering curds-based *kadhi* preparation.

Fennel

It is an aromatic and biennial plant with a height of 1.5 to 1.8 m. The ripe fruit is small, cylindrical in shape, 6-8 mm long, and coloured greenish yellow and having an agreeable aroma.

It is cultivated extensively in northern India as a cold weather crop. The dry and cold weather favours high seed production. It is used extensively in India, Pakistan, Afghanistan, Iran and the Middle East in their cookery. It is one of the significant ingredients in Kashmiri *pandit* cooking as well as in Gujarati cooking. It has become an integral constitutent of the Assamese/Bengali/Odiya spice mixture *panch phoran* and also in Chinese five-spice powders. Sugar-coated and uncoated fennel seeds are used in India as *mukhwas* (mouth-fresheners), after consumption of meal and also as breath freshener.

Fenugreek

Fenugreek seed is the ripe fruit of an annual robust herb. This herb has light green leaves and produces 10-15 cm long delicate pods, and each pod comprises 10-20 small hard seeds of yellowish brown colour.

It is a cold season crop and is fairly comfortable to frost and extreme low temperatures.

Fenugreek leaf has been characterized with a typical nutty smell and taste. It is quite bitter in nature and is commonly used in many dishes in India.

The fresh tender pods, leaves and shoots are consumed as delectable curried vegetable. Powder of dried leaves is also used for garnishing and flavouring wide variety of food preparations. It is one of the principal constituents of curry powder.

Turmeric

Turmeric is a dried, cleaned and polished rhizome. The plant is an herbaceous perennial with a short stem and decorated leaf. It is a native of India. Turmeric is a tropical crop cultivated from sea level to 1200 m above MSL. The crop cannot stand water-logging or alkalinity.

Turmeric is used to flavour and to colour certain foodstuffs. It is a principal constituent of curry powder. The colour *curcumin* extracted from turmeric is used as a colourant.

Nutmeg and Mace

Nutmeg and mace are two distinct varied spices produced from a fruit of an evergreen tree usually 9-12 m high. Inside the bitter fruit of the nutmeg tree lies two precious gems: the nutmeg nut, and the covering around its outer shell, called mace. Mace is the dried envelope forming a network of the fruit and nutmeg is the dried seed kernel of the fruit.

Both nutmeg and mace are used as condiment particularly in sweet foods. Nutmeg has a wide array of use in the preparation of meat products, soups, sauces, baked foods, confectioneries, puddings, seasoning of meat and vegetable, and so on. In Indian cuisine, nutmeg is used in numerous sweet as well as savoury dishes (preponderantly in Mughlai cuisine). It is used in small quantities in *garam masala* also. Ground nutmeg is also smoked in India.

Mustard Seeds

Mustard is an annual herb cultivated primarily for its oil seed crop or as a vegetable or as fodder. Three species are known for its condiment value and they are pale yellow or white mustard seeds (*Brassica hirta*), brown mustard seeds (*Brassica juncea*) and black mustard seeds (*Brassica nigra*). The yellow and white seeds are slightly larger than their brown and black counterparts, but all are perfectly round and roughly the size of a pinhead. The leaves of the plant are alternate, long, and hairy on both sides. Flowers are small and yellow whereas seeds are 1.5–3 mm in length.

It is grown as *rabi* crop in northern India. It is cultivated during rainy season in southern India.

The major processed products are mustard powder, mustard leaves, whole mustard seeds, and so on. Whole mustard is used as a flavouring agent in Indian cooking, whereas ground mustard flavours Bengali fish curries.

Mustard flour has preservative and antioxidant properties as well.

Nigella Nigella seeds are more of a triangular in shape. The heat in cooking usually pops up the seeds and thus releases their flavours. The traditional *naan*, the Indian flatbread cooked in tandoor ovens, will have some of the tiny seeds mixed into its dough. Even the multi-seed mixes like *phanch phoran* incorporate nigella seeds in the whole form.	
Black Pepper Black pepper is the dried mature berry of a climbing, perennial shrub mostly found in hot and moist region of southern India. Flowers are minute, white or pale yellow, arranged spirally on fleshy fanfare display. The fruit is a single seeded stone fruit mostly called berry. It is spherical in shape, green in colour, changing to red on ripping. Black pepper is considered to have originated in the hills of south-western ghats of India. Black pepper is highly used by meat packers and is known for its preservative value. It has the quality to check the seasoning of the dishes, therefore are used as a final touch item at the end of cooking for a balanced flavour. It is a chief constituent of culinary seasoning and is a prime ingredient in certain commercial foodstuffs. It is also used as an ingredient in spice mixes.	
Saffron Saffron, also referred as the 'king of spices', is unarguably the most expensive spice in the world. It is derived from the dry stigmata of the plant *Crocus sativus*. The plant is a bulbous, perennial with globular underground stem, 15-20 cm high. It has 6 to 10 leaves at the time of budding, and one to two flowers with a lilac-purple colour of 3.5–5 cm and style branches of 2.5–3.2 cm. Each flower yields only three saffron hairs and hence over 75,000 flowers have to be harvested to produce about 500 g of saffron. In India, it is cultivated in Jammu & Kashmir and in Himachal Pradesh. Saffron has numerous uses in culinary segment of India, as a culinary seasoning and to colour cottage cheese, chicken and meat, liquors and cordials. It is also used in speciality breads, cakes, confectionery and *kehwa* and certain Mughlai dishes.	
Star Anise It derives its name from its star-shaped pods that comprises small brown to orange seeds. Eight to ten boat-shaped pods join in the centre to form a star. Star Anise has typical sweet and nutty aroma and pairs up well with fruits and meats. It is used as a spice and can be used whole or in a powdered form. The whole star anise is used to flavour curries, rice and lentils and the powder form can be used in *kebabs*. Broil the star anise before pounding it. Star anise also forms the basis of certain *masalas* and can also be added to sweets due to its pleasing sweet aroma.	
Garlic Garlic is basically a bulbous, rooted, perennial plant with narrow flat leaves and has small white flowers and bulbils. The whole underground bulb is called head of garlic and each segment is called a clove. It is undoubtedly the most pungent flavoured ingredient in the entire kitchen. Pungent aroma is caused by cellular disturbance due to sulphur-containing 'allicin'. It is used in pickles, curry powders, curried vegetables, meat preparations and in numerous Indian gravy preparations.	

Ginger

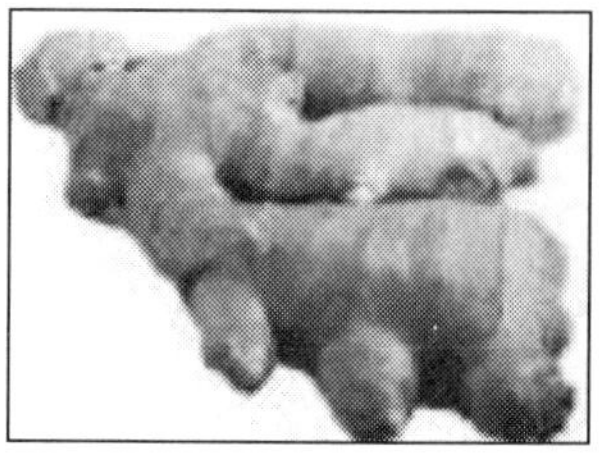

Ginger is a rhizome at the top of its family, *Zingiber*, with edible roots lying just underground and branching out horizontally. The crop is cultivated in rows from the previous year's root cuttings that have been allowed to sprout. This should be peeled away whenever the roots have to be consumed.

Ginger holds a special place in Indian cuisine, the root of ginger is either finely chopped or grated, or ground together with onion and garlic, forms the crucial basis of many curries and gravies. The whole plant is refreshingly aromatic and the underground rhizome, raw or processed, is highly valued as a spice. In India, it is used for giving a special and unique flavour to *masala* tea also and this tea is loved and desired by all across the country.

Black Salt

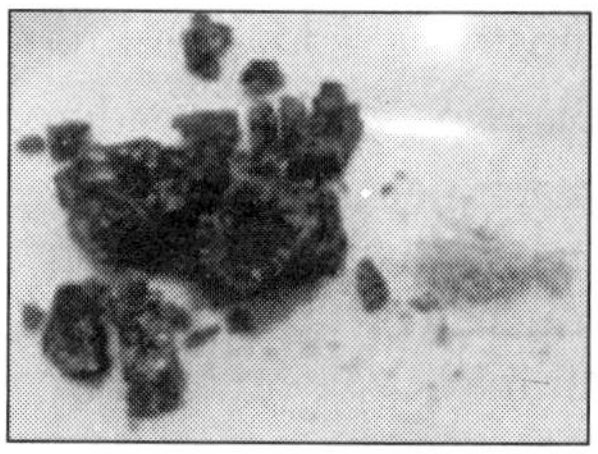

It is an assemblage of certain complex mineral compounds with salt as one prime component. As the name suggests, it is not even perfectly black, but the colour varies from grey to pink to purple. It has a malodorous aroma resembling asafoetida.

This is the usual name for the mineral 'halite'. Rock salt is a form of NaCl or the common table salt with some impurities in them. The slightly pungent smell in the salt is due to the sulphate present in it. The salt comes in the form of varied hued crystals and is ground to a powder form before using it for culinary purposes. This salt is used as a final garnish by sprinkling on the fresh fruits and vegetables, salads and fried savouries most of the time, though it is even used during the cooking process in certain dishes. It is also used as a preserving agent and also for seasoning. The significant *chaat masala* cannot be completed without the base flavour and strong aroma of black salt.

Sesame Seed

The sesame seeds are indigenous to India. The dried fruits of the sesame plant are randomly used to flavour and garnish breads, and even to make oil. It is available in black and white varieties and is cultivated for much valued spice trade. Both the white and black varieties are blessed with high richness in flavour that comes from the oil content within. Sesame oil has long been used as flavouring. Ground sesame seeds are the essential ingredients in certain preparations like *salan* gravy.

Tamarind

The large bean pods of tamarind tree have a squashy mass surrounding several exceedingly hard seeds. It has a sticky pulp that is symbolic of tartness and sweetness as well. The fresh pods may be peeled and mixed with any hot or lukewarm liquid medium, as long as the finished dish will undergo some straining to remove the seeds to get the pulp. The pulp mass is pounded and mixed only with adequate water to aid in the seed removal.

It is available as pulp, paste or powder to add the typical and lovely sour flavour. It is used in Indian curries like *cholle, salan* gravy, *sambhar* and in endless other preparations. The paste and powder are used in any preparation only after dissolving it properly in liquid.

Blending of Spices

Each spice has its own individuality and uniqueness of its own peculiar taste, aroma and symbolic flavour. Hence, utmost care must be taken while blending the spices. The spices are treated in various ways before blending. They can be broiled, fried in oil, grated, and ground into powder form or crushed, according to the need.

Each region has its own production and cultivation of spices that are marked by the climatic condition of that particular region. The blending of spices desires and demands immense understanding of the characteristic features of each spice, as blending of spices requires mingling of flavours as well.

In India, varied combinations of spices can be seen and are enjoyed with great gusto in several recipes. It is the spice, which flavours the entire Indian cuisine and

Table 7: Calorific Value of Indian Spices (Per 100 gm Edible Portion)

Spice	Calorific value (in Kilo Calories)
Asafoetida	297
Chillies (dry)	246
Chillies (green)	29
Cloves (dry)	286
Cloves (fresh)	159
Coriander seeds	288
Cumin seeds	356
Curry leaves	108
Fenugreek seeds	333
Garlic (dry)	145
Ginger (fresh)	67
Cardamom	229
Mace	437
Mint	48
Mustard seeds	541
Nutmeg fruit	472
Nutmeg rind	52
Bishops weed	363
Parsley	87
Pepper black (dry)	304
Pepper green	98
Poppy seeds	408
Tamarind pulp	283
Turmeric	349

gives a particular taste and flavour to dishes. Examples include *rajma masala, sambhar, chicken chettinad, rasam, vindaloo, rechado* preparation and the list is endless.

The blending of spices in Indian cuisine takes place in varied forms. If the *masala* is used in dry form, it is referred as dry form *masala* and if wet paste form is made then it is referred as wet *masala*. The wet *masala* is easily mixed with the gravy preparation uniformly and doesn't gets burnt in the preparation. Dry form *masala* are those which are in their dry form and no liquid component is added to them.

Following are the great combination of spices used frequently in Indian cuisine and they have worked wonders in taste and flavour as well.

Khada Masala

Basic Ingredients: Bay leaf, cloves, black pepper, cinnamon, green cardamom, cumin, mace, black cardamom.

Khada in Hindi means "whole". In this combination of spices, the spices are used in whole form and this is used for tempering in hot oil. The whole spices added to hot oil, actually flavour the oil by infusing the essence in hot oil. Many regions use whole spices like green cardamom, cinnamon to flavour the rice while boiling in water and then the whole spices are discarded thereof. In many kitchens, the whole spices are soaked in water overnight and then the whole spices are removed and flavoured water is sprinkled on the desired preparation to flavour the dish suitably.

Phanch Phoran Masala

Basic Ingredients: Aniseeds, cumin seeds, mustard seeds, fenugreek seeds, nigella seeds.

As the name suggests, it is a multi-seed combination of five spice seeds. Basically, this is a regional spice combination from Bengal and is used in tempering of various preparations like vegetables, lentils, and fish. This combination is also referred as *achari masala* as well, as it lends a unique aroma of flavour of pickled spices to the dish.

Garam Masala

Basic Ingredients: Bay leaf, cloves, black pepper, cinnamon, coriander seeds, green cardamom, cumin, mace, nutmeg and black cardamom.

Garam masala literally translates to 'hot spices'. The entire Indian cuisine revolves around this aromatic combination of spices and this is the centre point of Indian cuisine. This spice mix flavours the dish and bestows them the superior feature of delectable taste. Each spice is broiled individually and then they are powdered and mixed. There can be slight variation in spice combination, depending upon the preferences of region and also the user. The *garam masala* is generally sprinkled on top of every dish at the time of finishing. This is the most widely used spice combination across the country.

Potli ka Masala

Basic Ingredients: Coriander seeds, dry rose petals, sandalwood powder, *pathar ka phool* (stone flower), bay leaves, black cardamom, cinnamon, galingale (*pan ki jadi*), *kapur kachri.*

This is a unique spice mixture from Hyderabad. All the spices are tied in a muslin cloth or in any thin cloth and a *potli* (bag) of spices is made. This potli is used or boiled in any preparation for the dish to have flavour. After cooking the *potli* is removed and discarded.

Sambhar Masala

Basic Ingredients: Coriander seeds, cumin, asafoetida, dry red chilli, black pepper, fenugreek seeds, curry leaves, coconut grated, *channa dal, urad dal*, turmeric.

This is a typical regional *masala* from the south Indian cuisine. It is used in *sambhar*, a lentil curry made with motley of fresh vegetables. Each dry spice is broiled separately. *Chana dal* and *urad dal* are sautéd in a minimum quantity of oil and all the ingredients are ground along with fresh curry leaves to a fine powder. This *masala* lends a typical flavour and taste to *Sambhar*.

Lazzat-e-Taam

Basic Ingredients: Clove, green cardamom, large cardamom, mace, cinnamon, nutmeg, black pepper, coriander seeds, allspice, coconut, lemongrass, cumin, caraway seeds, sandalwood powder, dry rose petals, *makhana* (fox-nut), bay leaf, poppy seeds, fennel seeds, anise seeds, *kewra* water (vetivier), and *ittr*.

This is a flavoursome assemblage of spices from Awadh. *Lazzat-e-taam* literally means a substance which enhances the taste of the food. This unique combination of *masala* when dry roasted on a griddle emanates and exudes a subtle aroma. It is then removed from the fire and pounded or ground in a grinder. It is then mixed with *kewra jal* or *ittr* and is stored in an airtight container and used as per the requirement.

Bhojwar Masala

Basic ingredients: Coriander seeds, bay leaves, sesame seeds, cumin seeds, dry coconut, groundnut, *pathar ka phool* (stone flower), *putane ki dal*.

It is an amazing combination of masala from Hyderabadi cuisine. All the ingredients are powdered and mixed together and used in preparation as required. This spice combination is used specifically in Hyderabad only and is a rarity in other regions.

Xacutti Masala

Basic Ingredients: Dry red chilli, poppy seeds, sesame seeds, coriander seeds, cumin, fenugreek seeds, mustard seeds, black peppers, aniseed, ajwain, green cardamom, black cardamom, cloves and cinnamon.

All the ingredients mentioned above are dry roasted and ground to a powder form. They are used in Goan cuisine in various preparations like chicken, mutton, pork, seafood, egg, and in vegetarian *xacutti* preparation also.

This spice combination lends a unique taste to the dish in which it is added.

Rechado Masala

Basic ingredients: Kashmiri chillies, garlic, cloves, turmeric, cumin seeds, mustard seeds, black pepper, tamarind, ginger, sugar and vinegar.

This is a bright red coloured spice mixture and is used in Konkani cuisine and Goan cuisine as well. All the ingredients are mixed with vinegar and then ground into a paste. It is a wet form of *masala* mixture. It might seem strange but Kashmiri mirch used in it indicates less spiciness and more of red bright colour.

Salan Masala

Basic Ingredients: Desiccated coconut, sesame seeds, coriander seeds, cinnamon stick, whole cloves, green cardamom pods, cumin seeds, chilli powder, and ground turmeric.

This is a very famous spice combination from Hyderabad and is used in preparations like *mirchi ka salan, arbi ka salan, baghare baigan,* and so on. All the ingredients are dry roasted or broiled and then cooled and mixed. All the spices are then ground to a powder form and are used in various preparations as per the requirement. This combination adds richness to the dish in which it is used.

Goda Masala

Basic Ingredients: Coriander seeds, dry coconut, white sesame seeds, black sesame seeds, cumin seeds, black cumin seeds, asafoetida, cinnamon, cloves, black cardamom, dry red chilies, turmeric powder, salt and oil.

This unique combination of spices is from the Maharashtrian cuisine and is generally used in Konkani cuisine. All the above ingredients are roasted in very little oil. After this, they are drained and ground into a powder form. This spice blend can be used for flavouring numerous preparations of meats and vegetables.

Chettinad Masala

Basic Ingredients: Grated coconut, red chillies, coriander seeds, ginger, garlic, cinnamon, cardamom, cloves, black *kalpaasi* (stone flower), anise seed, black pepper, roasted *channa dal* (*pottukadalai*), curry leaves and turmeric powder.

All these ingredients are shallow-fried in very little oil and ground to a thick paste. This is also a very important combination of spice mixture and is used in the preparation of very famous and signature dish of Cheetinad cuisine, i.e., Chicken Chettinad.

Ver Masala

Basic Ingredients: It has two variations with very slight difference, one is for Hindus and other is for Muslims.

For Hindus: Asafoetida, fenugreek seeds, red chillies, cumin, coriander, dried ginger, cloves, cardamom and turmeric.

For Muslims: Garlic, *praan*, red chillies, cumin seeds, coriander seeds, dried ginger, cloves, cardamom and turmeric.

This is a Kashmiri special *masala* cake, in which all the spices are ground, then made into patties and are left to dry on wooden boards under shade. Once it is dry, small amounts are broken from the cake and used accordingly to flavour certain Kashmiri dishes.

Kaala Masala

Basic Ingredients: Cumin seeds, coriander seeds, cloves, cinnamon sticks, *kalpasi*, coconut, sesame seeds and chillies.

'Kaala' means 'black' in the Marathi language and this refers to both the colour of the final *masala* and the ingredients which it contains. Typically, it is prepared from dark spices such as cloves and cinnamon and the spices will be roasted until they obtain a dark colour. This spice mixture is basically from Maharashtra and is used in the preparations like *usal, varan* and *masala bhat*.

Rasam Powder

Basic Ingredients: Coriander seeds, cumin seeds, black pepper, red chilli powder, mustard seeds, fenugreek seeds, asafoetida, turmeric and curry leaves.

This is a very popular south Indian combination of *masalas* and is used very commonly in *Udipi* cuisine, Kerala cuisine and other south Indian dishes. All the ingredients except turmeric and asafoetida are dry-roasted and then all ingredients are mixed and ground into a powdered form. The *rasam* powder is kept in an air-tight container. It imparts a nice aroma and taste to the dish.

Culinary Trivia: Scoville Heat Scale

In early 20th century, American pharmacist, Wilbur Scoville was fascinated by the charateristics of capsicum. So, he formulated a scale that directly measures the heat-causing component of chilies. The scale starts at zero for no heat, as with bell peppers, and reaches to the high point of 280,000 Scoville Units (SU) for chillies like *habanero*. A good reference point for us is the common *jalapeno*, at roughly 50,000 SU.

Culinary Trivia: The Bhut Jolokia

It is also called ghost pepper, is a chilli hybrid cultivated in Assam and Nagaland. In 2007, Guinness World Records certified that the it was the world's hottest chilli pepper, considered to be around 400 times hotter than Tabasco sauce; however, in 2013 the Guinness World Records confirmed the Carolina Reaper, the world's hottest pepper.

Culinary Trivia: Oleoresins

Spice oleoresins (a mixture of natural resin and oil) express the complete flavour profile of the spice. It contains the volatile as well as non-volatile constituents of spices. Oleoresins can be defined as the true essence of the spices and can replace whole/ ground spices without damaging any flavour and aroma characteristic. Oleoresins are obtained from spices by extraction with a non-aqueous solvent followed by removal of the solvent by evaporation. Spice oleoresins assure best quality of flavour and aroma. They are complete and balanced, consistent and standardized.

Culinary Trivia: Alkanna Tinctoria

Alkanet root is the English term for *ratanjot* which is herb grown in Kashmir and is originally responsible for red colour of *roganjosh* and *tandoori* chicken. The root of it is ground to a powder and used as a natural food colouring. It is vibrant red in colour and look flaming hot but are not hot to taste as chilli powder.

30 Basic Gravies and Pastes

"Salt is born of the purest of parents: the sun and the sea." – Pythagoras

The culinary element which distinguishes Indian cuisines from the rest of international cuisines is unarguably the gravy. Gravy is undoubtedly the core of the Indian cuisine. If spices are referred as the heart-beat of Indian cuisine, then gravies can easily be referred as the body of main course preparation in this cuisine.

Gravies provide the body, texture, flavour and appearance to the main dish. It is the gravy combination with impeccable spices that creates magic on every food lover or diner.

Basic Gravies

In general, gravies are categorized into four different varieties, such as:

• Onion-Tomato Gravy

As the name suggests, the most important ingredient of this gravy is onion and tomato. Onion and tomato are used in the ratio of 3:1.

The key ingredients of this gravy are: Oil, ginger-garlic paste, onion, red chilli powder, coriander powder, turmeric powder, water, tomato.

Water can be replaced by curds while mixing the spices.

Method of preparation: Oil is heated in a heavy bottomed utensil and then the whole *garam masala* is added, till it splutters and emanates its flavour in oil. Then onion is added either chopped or in a paste form or a mixture of both the forms. It is then stirred and cooked till it is light brown in colour. Then ginger-garlic paste is added and cooked, taking care that it doesn't stick to the bottom of the pan or utensil. After this, powdered spices are added by mixing these in water or curds. It is cooked till oil comes on top and then pureed tomato is added and cooked. Finally, it is finished with finely chopped green coriander, and/or juliennes of ginger as well.

Many renowned preparations are served in this gravy like *matar paneer, matar* mushroom, chicken curry, chicken *masala,* and mutton *masala,* mixed vegetable, and so on.

• Brown-Onion Gravy

Onion is the main ingredient of this gravy. As onions used are deep fried till brown in colour, it is named as brown-onion gravy. Onion and tomato are used in the ratio of 5:1.

The key ingredients of this gravy are: Oil, onion, ginger-garlic paste, curds, red chilli powder, coriander powder, tomato puree and cashewnut paste (optional).

Method of preparation: Oil is heated in a *kadhai* and then sliced onions are put into it and then deep fried till brown in colour. Once they are golden brown in colour, they are removed and spread on kitchen paper to absorb excess oil in it and is cooled as soon as possible. If it is not spread and kept in a form of lump, onions will stick into each other and will have too much of oil. Due to absorption of excess oil and cooling, the onion turns crispy. This golden fried onion can be kept in a stainless steel container for one or two days, if required. When the gravy is to be prepared, the onions fried are mixed with curds and ground into a thick paste. Then the heavy bottom pan is taken with fresh oil in it and is kept on flame. Then ginger-garlic paste is added and stirred till light brown. After this the red chilli powder and coriander powder are mixed in water and added in ginger-garlic paste. Once spices are cooked, the brown onion-curds paste is added into it and cooked, till it starts releasing excess oil. After this, tomato puree is added and cooked till done. If the onion gives burnt flavour, then it can be rectified with the addition of cashew nut paste in it. The cashew nut paste also provides richness to the dish. It is finished with finely sliced juliennes of ginger.

Many renowned preparations are made with this gravy like: Mutton *roghan josh*, vegetable *kofta*, and so on.

• White Onion Gravy/White Gravy/ Shahi Gravy

Onion again plays a key role in this gravy. It is referred as white gravy as it is white in colour. It is also referred as *shahi* gravy due to its excess of richness.

The key ingredients of this gravy are: oil, bay leaf, green cardamom, ginger-garlic paste, onion, cashew nut, melon seeds, curds, coconut paste, cream, salt and white pepper powder.

Method of preparation: First of all peeled onion, cashew nut and melon seeds, all three ingredients are boiled in sufficient quantity of water in an open pan. The ratio of onion, cashew nut and melon seeds are 5:1:1. When the melon seeds are soft enough, prepare a smooth paste of all the three ingredients by draining the water and also washing it properly in running water and then grinding it in a mixer. Keep this paste aside.

Then take a heavy bottomed pan, heat oil in it and add the bay leaf and green cardamom in it. In this the ginger-garlic paste is added, and is continuously stirred, so that the ginger-garlic paste doesn't stick to the bottom of the pan. After this, add the boiled paste of the three ingredients and cook, till oil comes on the top. Then curds, coconut paste and cream can be added in the end and cooked for a short while. Finally, it is seasoned with salt and white pepper. This gravy is also garnished with whipped cream.

Note: Many cooks add red chilli powder, turmeric powder in small amount in the start of the gravy, so that it attains a light colour, apart from actual white colour.

Preparations made in this gravy are: safed *maas, murg kali mirch,* chicken *rizala, murg wajid ali* and so on.

• Makhani Gravy

Tomato is the key ingredient in this gravy. *Makhan* means butter. This gravy has silky texture and is called *makhani* gravy as butter is used in large quantity.

The key ingredients of this gravy are: oil, bay leaf, green cardamom, ginger, garlic, green chillies, red tomatoes, red chilli powder, butter, cream.

Method of preparation: Heat the oil in a heavy bottomed pan and add slices of ginger, garlic, green chillies, bay leaf, green cardamom and whole ripe red tomatoes. Keep on stirring in between, so that the ingredients do not stick to the bottom of the pan and also tomatoes are properly mashed to puree. Then the cooked mixture is strained and the mixture that is left in the strainer is ground to paste in a mixer and then again it is strained to all to the previous strained mixture.

Then, oil is taken in another *patila;* ginger-garlic paste is added with red chilli powder and fried. Then, the tomato puree obtained earlier is added and allowed to cook for long, till all oil comes on the top of the tomato gravy. Seasoning is added accordingly and crushed *kasoori methi,* broiled on a griddle is also added. The *makhani* gravy is ready. Cream and butter is added in the end.

Note: If the tomato gives sour taste, then honey is added to adjust the sourness of the gravy. In this gravy, onion, turmeric and coriander powder is not used at all.

Many preparations served in this gravy are as follows: butter chicken, *murg makhani, paneer butter masala,* and so on.

These are the four main gravies on which the other gravies are based on.

The gravies based on the main four gravies are either added or flavoured with other dominating ingredients or are mixed with other gravy to produce a different gravy as the end product.

Subsidiary Gravies

• Lababdaar Gravy

This is not a gravy of its own but a derivative of *makhani* gravy added with the paste of cashew nut. The addition of cashew nut in *makhani* gravy makes the gravy rich in taste and consistency. The addition of cashew nut also helps in overcoming the sourness of the *makhani* gravy.

• Hariyali Gravy/Green Gravy

This again is a derivative of one of the main gravies, i.e., onion-tomato gravy. The paste of boiled spinach is added in it. The puree of spinach gives it a green colour, as its name suggests. It is also referred as *palak* gravy. In this, the quantity of onion-tomato gravy is much less as compared to spinach paste. At certain places, only onion paste cooked with spices is added to the spinach paste and not the tomato *masala.*

Preparations like *palak paneer, palak matar, saag gosht, palak* mushroom, *aloo palak, aloo tamater,* and so on are served in this gravy.

- **Kesari Gravy**

This is a combination of two main gravies, i.e., onion-tomato gravy and white onion gravy with addition of saffron in it. When the guest in the restaurant demands for two preparations in similar gravy, then the chefs or cooks blend the two said gravies to create altogether different end product. In such situation, *kesari* gravy is of great help.

- **Achari Gravy**

This is a derivative of onion-tomato gravy in which panch-phoran (pickling spices) is added and slight paste of *achar masala*. This gravy tastes almost similar to the pickles. This gravy is used for preparation like *gosht achari, paneer achari, subz achari, khumb achari,* and so on.

The region and methods of preparation keeps on changing from region to region, and also from chef to chef (cook to cook).

There are many preparations across India in which the gravy is prepared but they differ from all the above mentioned gravies.

Like in Rajasthan, the ingredient which plays a crucial role in providing body to the main dish is curds. There are many preparations in Rajasthan which are solely cooked in curds and the preparations are like *gatte ki subzi, haldi ki subzi, papad ki subzi,* and so on. Similarly, in south India, coconut milk plays the same role.

So a gravy has its own identity and its own special features. It is all about the creativity of the chef and the ingredients available.

Pastes

In the context of Indian cuisine, paste is a term which is used to denote the ground mix of either one ingredient or a combination of ingredients, to be used in various preparations, gravies and so on. In kitchens we have many types of pastes available like ginger and garlic paste, red chilli paste, spinach paste, cashew nut paste and so on. The pastes made in the kitchen are of great help to the person working in kitchen. It helps the kitchen personnel to perform with great ease and efficiency.

Following are the various pastes used in the kitchens of India.

- **Ginger Paste**

One of the most frequently used pastes in the kitchens across the whole country is ginger paste. This paste is prepared by scrapping the skin of the fresh ginger and then cutting it into very thin slices so that it can be grounded into fine paste in a grinder. This paste is used in various gravy preparations and also in various marinades of *kebabs* and *tikkas*.

- **Garlic Paste**

The other paste used most is garlic paste. This paste is prepared by peeling garlic and grinding it into a fine paste. It also has the same use as ginger paste. It is also used along with ginger for marinating *kebabs*.

- **Boiled Onion Paste**

The onion is boiled in sufficient water and then drained and washed in fresh running water to remove all the dirt and dust it carries. Once it is cooled, it is ground in a grinder to form a fine paste. This boiled onion paste is used in certain gravies and then in many preparations of Mughlai cuisine.

- **Brown Onion Paste**

The onion slices are deep fried in hot oil till light golden brown in colour and then cooled on an absorbent paper. After cooling it gets crisp and then it is mixed with curds to provide moisture to it and then ground into fine paste in a grinder. This paste of brown onion is used in brown onion gravy.

- **Cashew Nut Paste**

This paste is made by soaking the cashew nut overnight and then grinding it into a fine paste. Many cooks use the technique of boiling the cashew nut in water and then making smooth paste out of it. This paste provides richness to the dish and also at times to overcome the spiciness and sourness of the dish. There are many preparations in *halwai* section that calls for cashew nut paste like *kaju ki barfi, kaju katli,* and so on.

- **Red Chilli Paste**

A red chilli paste can be prepared in numerous different ways. It can be boiled in water and paste can be prepared. It can be soaked in oil or vinegar and paste can be prepared. If the paste required is with less pungency then the seeds of red chilli have to be removed. The main purpose of this paste is to make any dish extra spicy or to provide bright red colour. This paste cuts the monotonous bland taste and gives a spicy tinge.

- **Tamarind Pulp**

This is basically a pulp and not a paste, but comes under this section of classification. Tamarind is dipped in lukewarm water and then mashed with hand and sieved through a strainer. It is also used in numerous preparations like *chhole masala,* many *chutney* preparations and in many south Indian dishes.

- **Melon Seeds Paste**

This is the boiled paste of melon seeds and is used in various gravy preparations. The main intention of using this paste is to cut down the cost factor. As cashew nut is slightly expensive, it is used as a substitute and serves the same purpose in gravy. It is one of the main ingredients of *shahi* white onion gravy.

- **Spinach Paste**

This is a paste of boiled and refreshed spinach and is used as chief ingredient of *palak* gravy. It is used in preparation like *palak paneer, gosht palak, palak matar,* and so on.

Culinary Trivia: Loab

It is a term referring to the final stage of cooking when the oil used during cooking rises to the top surface giving the dish a finished appearance. Oil floating in curries are *loab* and *rogan josh* is a good example of it.

Culinary Trivia: Moin

This term refers to the shortening of dough. In this process, fat is rubbed into the flour and made into dough for *puris, parathas* or *kachoris*. This addition makes the final product crisp, flaky and crumbly.

31 Tandoor, Marinades and Tenderizers

"Sharing food with another human being is an intimate act that should not be indulged in lightly." – M. F. K. Fisher

Introduction

The *tandoor* is a multifaceted cooking appliance which is assumed to be the oldest kitchen equipment of great antiquity. Its roots can be dated back about 5000 years in Iran. It is a very efficient and useful for various preparations in Indian cuisine.

India has witnessed a lot of technological changes and due to this, many modern and advanced cooking equipment with excellent output have been introduced in recent times, but still the *tandoor* has maintained its significant position and it is a permanent utility in Indian kitchens. It can be defined as a cylindrical clay oven in which food products like breads, snacks, starters, and so on can be cooked, baked or roasted using charcoal and wood as the fuel. Some modern-day *tandoors* use electricity or gas instead of charcoal.

The heat in *tandoor* was traditionally generated by a charcoal fire or wood fire, burning within the *tandoor* itself, thus exposing the food to both live-fire, radiant heat cooking, and hot-air convection cooking. Temperatures in a *tandoor* can reach to a maximum of 480°C (900°F), and it is very common for tandoor ovens to remain lit for long periods of time to maintain the high cooking temperature.

Tandoor was found during the digging and excavation of archeological sites such as Harappan and pre-Harappan sites. It is very difficult to find the place actually where it originated. It is speculated and contemplated that it originated in ancient India or a nearby area.

Origin of Word Tandoor

Several theories have been put forward which gives a brief idea regarding the origin of the *tandoor*. The first hypothesis is related to the Sanskrit word *kandu*. The word *tandoor* is actually considered to be derived from the term *kund* which literally means a large bowl-shaped vessel, either countersunk or above the ground, as a permanent fixture or with the option to be in mobile cofiguration.

The *kund* could have been used for the storage of water and grain or as a *havan kund*, to organise a sacred ritual fire in vedic times. With the passage of time, the word *kund* transformed to *kandu* in conversational usage, and from *kandu* it became *kandoor*, also *kandoora*. Then the 'k' sound got converted into the't' sound, and so we finally have had the word *tandoor*.

The other theory describes and emphasizes that it is derived from conversational Pashtu (essentially the official language of Afghanistan) or Persian Pidgin (artificial language), from the word 'tat' meaning hot and 'andar' meaning inside. Through this channel of conversational usage, the word emerged as *tandoor*.

Origin and History of Tandoor

Whenever the genesis of cooked foods has been pursued the spit roast, on which game cooking was performed, comes to the mind. It is believed that when fortunate survivors of a forest fire in pre-historic times returned to collect stock and valuate the magnitude of scathe in forest fire, they found a pleasant smell of animal flesh roasted in fire circumstantially. They tasted it somehow and were surprised to find it palatable and easily chewable.

Probably, this could have been the beginning of game cooking by spit roasting technique, initially on a spear. But with progression of time, the sophistication creeped in and spear got substituted with a *seekh* or skewer. One may easily come across certain historical references to animal sacrifice, which apparently mentions that the animals were pierced to death on a spear and then spit roasted to make it favourably edible. The cooked meat was being distributed as *prashad* or 'sacred gift'. As far as fruits and vegetables were concerned, in those times of antiquity they were consumed in their natural form of raw state or when ripe, but mostly uncooked.

As people began to lead on more settled existence, showing inclination towards farming and cultivation, they became more mechanized and thereby discovered leisure and developed ideas as well.

Grain was already being consumed extensively. It was pounded and mixed with water, kneaded into dough and baked on hot stones or what is considered to a very ancient and crude hearth.

This period of time witnessed the development and glorification in the Egyptian, the Mesopotamian and the Indus Valley civilizations constituting the 'fertile crescent', each developing severally of their self but with almost similar basic needs. Even though the *tandoor* has been discovered earlier in the pre-Harappan culture, it is quite evident that in Egypt too the evolution of the *tandoor* and grinding stone took place simultaneously.

It is apparently anticipated that during the period of construction of the monumental pyramids, there was an obvious and continuous huge demand for large amounts of food and bread for the workers employed in the construction. It is also considered that the Egyptians were well aware of fire and way to create it, but all they required was finely ground grain. On the other hand, it is unclear who really invented the quern (a primitive stone mill), but assembling two and two stones together, it becomes quite clear that the same stone used for the pyramids was used to make a quern, by actually placing one stone on top of the other. Thus, with the availability of freshly ground wheat and fire, the bakery was assumed to be born, and was able to provide bread on a massive scale.

In India, as per the existing evidence, it is assumed that three types of quern seem to have been in use. One of these was the rotary (moving in circular motion) quern, the illustrations of which have been found at Taxila, dating way back to around 100 BC. The design of this specific quern or grinding wheel was very simple and was technically effective. It essentially had two circular discs ranging from ten to thirty inches in diameter with an eccentric stone handle at one point.

There was an orifice at the centre through which wheat was dropped in. Certain historical referential records indicate that grinding wheels of such pattern were as large as three to four feet in diameter with two long handles. Two strong muscular men were required, one pushing it halfway, and the other complementing to complete the circle in a kind of relay action. This peculiar technique resulted in a lot more fine ground wheat for dough. The dough ready was rolled out and patted into shape in almost the same way as it is done today. Then it was baked in the *tandoor*.

Thus, it becomes evident that India has all the elements required to operate a primitive bakery and nothing was required to be outsourced. The main element needed was simply beam of any kind of wood. Thus, we have been bestowed with the grinding wheel as flour machine and *tandoor* as the baking oven.

Kalibangan, located in the Ganganagar district of Rajasthan has been of great culinary importance to India as the earliest *tandoor* in India was unearthed here as the evidence points out. This place has been named 'Kalibangan', literally meaning black bangle because many broken terracotta bangles that had turned black over a period of time were found scattered around here. The excavations carried out here at the site dates back to almost 2600 BC All such evidence suggest to the fact that they been a part of the highly advanced and glorious Harappan culture.

Journey of Tandoor

The golden vedic period found its way with the declivity of the Indus or the Harappan cultures in India.

The sacred and most revered vedas have emphasized on the prominence to food, as it is spoken of in all texts except for the *Rigveda*. Wheat, the bestower of life, was regarded the most significant. Besides this, the people ate rice, *dals* (*masur, chana, arhar*, and so on) and *masa* (meat), curds and butter. *Ghee*, the 'divine' core and essence of food, was also commonly used. Meat was marinated in curds to tenderize and then roasted on spits. It was even cooked, boiled with spices and curried.

Around 800-300 BC, the reliable sources mentions a piece of broken pot (*kapala*) was being used to bake *roti*. The *Ashtanga Samgraha* (AD 25) mentions wide varieties of wheat *roti* with varied cooking technique.

Kukula pakva:	Bread cooked in a pit heated with chaff and husk fire
Karpara pakva:	Bread cooked specifically on an earthenware plate
Bhrastra pakva:	Simply fried bread
Kandu pakva:	Bread baked in a *kandu* (*tandoor*)
Angara pakva:	Bread cooked on live charcoals.

As per the credentials of written and codified chronicles, the first mention of meat is cooked in *tandoor* by the noted physician Sushruta and is described elaborately in the *Sushruta Samhita Sutrasthanam*.

Such written chronicles also mention about the varied and distinct techniques of meat preparation. They are as listed as such:

Ulluptam:	It is a minced meat preparation.
Pishtam:	It is meat ground into paste and then made into balls and cooked on skewers.
Prataptam:	Meat in this is cooked by roasting with clarified butter over charcoal fire.
Kandu pachitam:	Simply cooked in the *tandoor.*
Parishushkam:	It is seasoned meat.
Pradigdham:	In this, the meat is cooked with milk and clarified butter.
Shulyam:	Basically meat roasted on spits.

Similarly, certain articles and chronological records have described food that are dry-fried on broken vessels of baked clay or that are cooked over a charcoal fire is considered light with respect to digestion. Certainly, the *tandoor* was a very dominating and an integral part of the lives of the people of these ancient times.

The Buddhist texts, known as the *Jataka,* are regarded to be a great assemblage and vast ocean of knowledge. Even this, also mentions of wheat *roti* and *khajjaka* cakes made from wheat flour and cooked in the *tandoor.* It is occasionally coated with *gur* (jaggery), and is liked by people with huge passion and appreciation.

About 326 BC, when Alexander the Great led and monitored the Greek invasion towards the prosperous kingdom of Magadha (present-day Bihar), they somehow managed to cross the Indus, but then the situation did not allow them to advance any further as the soldiers were weary and tired and hence they all were forced to go back. They carried along with them the rotary quern for ease of food making during their war phase. The writings of generals indicate the thorough insight into the habits practised and also the rituals of that time. The writings describe the Greeks as the expert bakers of bread and archaeologists are of the belief that the rotary quern was brought by them to India. Two such rotary querns was found in Taxila. Thus unknowingly, Greeks have gifted Indian culinary system the valuable rotary querns. Wheat was the most important grain of that period. This provision of quern has introduced *tandoor* as the cooking oven considered to be the most convenient for baking breads of wheat.

After Alexander, a period of great turmoil ensued, till the Kushan kings took over the charge around 165 BC.

The channel of the Silk Route traders moving outwards from Punjab and the North-Western Frontier Provinces also propagated their knowledge of food to other regions of the world. They popularized the conceptualization and the art of cooking in the *tandoor.* They even carried a *tandoor* with them as it was easy to make and carry. Thus, *tandoor* spread all across.

Charaka, the court medical practitioner to the Kushan king Kanishka, is the author of an Ayurvedic formal treatise who, in companionship with great scholar Sushruta, penned down a number of valuable books on Indian system of medicine. This exposition gives an elaborated perception and minute detailing of food, and tenderization and marination.

Sushruta mentions and gives a detailed account of a dish referred to as *prataptam.* The meat is first fried in *ghee,* then flavoured with the addition of yogurt, lemon juice, pomegranate juice, and so on and is again cooked with *ghee* and *samudra* salt (sea salt) over a charcoal fire over a gridiron (a cooking utensil with parallel metal bars in order to grill meat). The ingredients added to flavour meat are added after certain interval during the period of cooking. Sushruta also describes meats that are cooked with sesame or mustard paste and with condiments to a honey colour in a *tandoor* and named them as *kandu pakvam.*

Along with this, Sushruta also describes of another meat preparation called *shulyam,* in which the meat has to be soaked in asafeotida water and then cooked over a gridiron on a smokeless fire. During its cooking, a concoction of water and pomegranate juice is sprinkled over the meat.

Stein, the great archaeologist, while at work in a place called Lou-lon along the silk route, discovered manuscripts which were noted down in an ancient Indian script. They revealed that the trader's community, especially from Punjab, commuting on this route, had left the traces of food legacy even in Lou-lon. Stein described this work of his as his most thrilling and adventurous discovery. Until then, hardly anyone had the slightest knowledge of how far the Indian trading community had spread during the rule of the Kushan kings. The group of caravans travelling to these parts from India carried with them their *tandoors* to ease the cooking functionality. As the group of travellers was huge, the womenfolk always had their hands full. In the afternoons, when the caravans had their stoppage, the *tandoors* were lighted. In a hurry, everyone had bread (*roti*) to eat. Subsequently, the breakfast was of *navala,* the stale bread.

The declivity of the Kushan Empire marked the decline of trade. The traders transformed into the local populace of the region. But they still relished the taste of food eaten in earlier years and it was taken care of the fact that the fire under the *tandoor* was still lit in the homes of these traders-turned-settlers.

At this period of time, the Buddhist culture started to gain popularity. As they were strict vegetarian, the preference shifted towards baking of breads. The diet comprised vegetarian components like wheat, rice, pulses, vegetables, milk and milk products. Only certain class of warriors and low caste people ate meat during this period of time.

Around AD 320-540, during the reign of Gupta period, the best of the Buddhist and the Hindu traditions were restored to life with utmost vigour. The peace and prosperity flourished; and great literatures were written and traditional values related with food were upheld tightly.

With the arrival of Islam in power, Kabul and Ghazi were occupied by Turks. The local population adopted Islam. In AD 711, Mohammed Bin Kassim extended Sindh up to Multan, a great centre for commercial buzz of trade and industry at that time. No major invasion took place between AD 711 and 1175 and people prospered tremendously. Prosperity led to degeneration of moral values in every sphere of life. Fortunately, food acquired huge prominence. The art of cooking got elaborated and it fascinated people as well. Food was made presentable in varied ways with the incorporation of more spices, ingredients, colours and decorations into it.

Turning certain pages of glorious Indian heritage history, the first 'cookery book' that emerged to give us this piece of valuable information was *Manasollasa,* which literally meant 'joy fulfillment' and was written by King Someshwara in AD 1127. It chronologically mentions certain methods of cooking, dealing especially with food habits of the nobility. It describes both the vegetarian and non-vegetarian sections of kitchens in real depth.

Around AD 1175, Mohammad Ghori conquered Multan, Kutch and Sindh from the Arabs, and also annexed Punjab from the Ghaznavi ancestry. During the period of continuous and tremendous change, Delhi witnessed a series of dynasties acquiring power including the Slave kings, Khiljis, Tughlaqs, Sayyads and the Lodis.

During this time, AD 1200-1500, Punjab had its own description of its story. Accordingly, the conditions in Punjab were quite unstable and the local populaces were domineered by the local *jagirdars,* who were considered to be the representatives of the governors. Only some who had certain approach to royalty could maintain large and lavish kitchen.

During this period of hardship, Guru Nanak (AD 1469-1539) founded a new religion in Punjab called Sikhism. His teachings greatly influenced people. His thoughts were simple, and he advocated against superstition, idol worship, the caste system, and the hypocrisy of the priests, amongst other things. The most crucial step he took with relation to culinary segment was to bring all people together under the concept of *langar,* where people of all castes sat and ate together. The *tandoor* was utilized to its maximum potential and was used to cater hot, freshly baked bread to large number of people at a time. The Guru requested people to have common *tandoors* in their lanes. The main intention behind this was to abolish the distinction between high and low castes and along with it was a great fuel saver. The *sanjha chulha* or common oven as it was called emerged to be extremely popular with the local womenfolk. It proved economical and provided them a common unique platform to exchange ideas and daily news.

This concept mushroomed all over Punjab and the North-West Frontier Province. The *tandoor* was lit at certain places to allow all to bake their bread conveniently. People of varied castes, creed and colour were merged into one and no distinction was made amongst them. The goal was one and common: to bake fresh bread for the hungry stomach.

Then arrived Mughals. Actually the real perception of the eating habits of the Mughal emperors is from the tenure of Akbar's time. It is described that the Akbar had deputed a massive number of employees to look after the different sections of the kitchen. The chronicle *Ain-i-Akbari* acknowledges the various kinds of breads of varied shapes and sizes. One version of bread was baked in the *tandoor,* and another type on skillets. Every major locality had a *nanbai* in the bazaar. *Nanbais* were actually the bakers selling a variety of breads freshly baked in the tandoor.

Writings during the tenure of Emperor Shah Jahan describe three new varieties of breads, one of which was called *roghni* which was prepared using finely ground flour and clarified butter and then baked in the *tandoor.* It was very thin and appeared as thin leaves and the other two varieties were salty and sweet.

The noted author Francoise Bernier wrote during the reign of Aurangzeb, that the *rotis* available in the bazaars were not fit to be eaten. Hence, the kings and noblemen invented metallic *tandoors* that were carried on camel back, to give them good, hot freshly baked bread and this thereby accentuated on the eating quality of the breads.

The dominance of the Mughal Empire witnessed prosperity which resulted in ensured lavish standards of living. The affluent class had large and well-equipped kitchen and food was given due importance. Notwithstanding with the disintegration of the Mughal Empire, the food habits didn't change and the nawabs maintained their lifestyle of luxurious eating, wining and dining as before.

In a literary work in Urdu, the writer describes that the *tandoor* was the popular oven to bake breads. Each affluent and rich man had specialist and skilled cooks to prepare these breads. New breads evolved – plain breads, leavened breads, sweet breads as well as stuffed breads.

The Mughal period witnessed tremendous changes in India. They always accentuated on the good food. They improved the transportation facility. Road transportation was the main means by which people could move from one town to another. Sher Shah Suri constructed the Grand Trunk road which made the movement of people and goods safe and faster. People carried with them the means of their culture, tradition, their spices, herbs, the cooking techniques and their food to various regions of India, which shaped Indian food and thus the Mughal food culture also became an essential constituent of Indian culinary system. The Grand Trunk Road played a significant role in popularizing Mughal culture and their food habits in varied parts of India. Thus, the food, knowledge, and accomplishments have become an integral part of India cuisine.

The decline of Mughals was followed by the British people. They also adopted the food system of India. They ruled India for about 250 years. At the moment of leaving India, they took along them the food cooking techniques, skills and the knowledge of our country like *tandoori* dishes, *tandoor* and the *spiciness*, which Indian people loved most.

Then, after independence, a renowned personality Kundan Lal Gujral brought a great revolution in the arena of *tandoori* cooking. He invented certain dishes and bestowed this gift to the entire world and is still savoured most by all food lovers. He invented wonderful and delectable delights like *tandoori* chicken and *dal makhani* (black lentil cooked slowly overnight and mixed with tomato puree and topped with fresh cream). He proved to be a trendsetter.

Types of Tandoor

The advent of modernization and technological changes experienced new invention and development in the world of *tandoor*. There are many types of *tandoor* available in the current Indian market:

- Coal *Tandoor*
- Gas *Tandoor*
- Solar *Tandoor*
- Iron *Tandoor*
- Meter *Tandoor*

Coal Tandoor: This type of *tandoor* is further divided in two varieties:

Stone coal *tandoor*: In this type of *tandoor*, the net like structure is created in the bottom of the *tandoor* which provisions the ash to automatically fall down and once the *tandoor* cools it can easily be removed.

Wood coal *tandoor*: This type of *tandoor* doesn't have any net-like structure in the bottom. In this *tandoor*, the timber of woods is inserted directly into the bottom of the *tandoor* and lit and then after the ash is collected and removed from the bottom of the *tandoor*.

Charcoal *tandoors* are available in various configurations of shapes and sizes, depending upon the requirement. Traditionally, such *tandoor* uses non-smoky, non-resinous wood as fuel but in current scenario, wooden charcoal is the fuel used most abundantly. The food prepared in such *tandoors* are characterized as highly flavoured and have a rustic aroma as well.

Gas *Tandoor*: This *tandoor* is portable. In this, the burner is at the bottom of the *tandoor* and lit during use, which facilitates the generation of proper heat in the *tandoor*. It works on butane gas, LPG or natural propane. The food cooked in this type of *tandoor* doesn't have any specific aroma and flavour of the food prepared in charcoal-lit *tandoor*.

Solar *Tandoor*: In this *tandoor*, the sunlight energy is stored in the equipment and this facilitates the cooking of the food. In this type of *tandoor*, the actual cost is the cost of the equipment and it takes longer time to cook the food. Cost of maintenance of this *tandoor* is low and quantity of the food should be decided. It is not very popular and is seen rarely.

Iron *Tandoor*: It is a variation of the traditional clay *tandoor* and it is made of metallic *tandoor*. It is made of a special iron-alloy sheet and was introduced on an experimental basis, and it worked to be a great success.

Its basic construction and proportions are similar. Sizes differ according to requirement and it bakes just as good as the mud *tandoor*. The main difference is that this *tandoor* works on the principle of 'hot air circulation', and the fuel used is cooking gas.

Meter *Tandoor*: This *tandoor* is same as the coal *tandoor* but it is installed with meter (thermostat) to control the temperature of the *tandoor* and if the temperature is higher, it can be controlled. The temperature inside the *tandoor* is indicated by a meter.

Manufacturing a Tandoor

Tandoor is basically a very effective equipment which is prepared from the basic material like clay. Utmost care is taken care of that the clay used should not contain any sand in it.

The clay used is usually mixed with a specific kind of grass such as *munj* along with certain natural binders like horse dung and so on. The plastic clay should be thoroughly avoided as it is characterized to develop cracks once it is dried. The clay is made ready by beating it with a simple and flat broad piece of wood or stone. Binders are mixed with water and then added with the clay. The mixture is kneaded with hands or feet, covered with a sack and then kept wet for three or four days.

Then the next stage involves the shaping of the clay by hand. The *tandoor* is usually assembled in sections. There are two methods of making the *tandoor*: the more common 'modelling' technique and the uncommon 'coiling' technique.

The Modelling Method

The modeling method involves several stages:

Stage 1: After the clay is ready to use; slabs are prepared which are about 12-15 cm wide, 50-60 cm long and 2-3 cm thick. Some dry clay is sieved onto these and then they are rolled into cylinders, which are then unrolled into a kind of semicircle. Two or three such unrolled cylinders are moulded together into a circle and this circle forms the base of the *tandoor.*

Stage 2: Once the base is prepared, the uppermost part of this ring is attached at certain intervals to create little notches. It is then allowed to dry overnight; in order to make it hard and capable enough to bear the weight of the next ring.

Stage 3: Another ring is placed on top of this ring and fused properly, once the clay has dried to desired hardness. This soft and wet clay ring gets properly placed on top of the earlier ring. This design provides the *tandoor* substantial firmness and stability. Consequently, subsequent sections are added accordingly till the required height is attained. The standard height of the *tandoor* is about 34-36 inches, but can be altered and modified as per the need and requirement to the specification of the customers.

Stage 4: This phase is marked with the shaping of the last section on top, which is turned inwards by hand and shaped like the upper part of a pitcher. Two hand held wooden spatulas, referred to as *pindi* and *thapa,* are used to beat the clay to smoothen out the surface and along with strengthen the *tandoor.* After this, a jute cloth is dipped in clay water and wrapped around the *tandoor,* after which it is left to dry. The construction of *tandoor* is hereby considered to be complete now.

The Coiling Method

Going with the name of the method, this indicates that this method incorporates clay rolled into a long rope that is coiled upon it very carefully until the required height is attained. The top part of the *tandoor* is shaped in the same fashion as the rest. The sides are beaten slightly with the hand and it is ensured that the finished *tandoor* should bear no sign of ridges or elevation. Once the *tandoor* is ready, it is allowed to dry. Later on, an opening of about 10 cm is made at the bottom of *tandoor* to facilitate proper circulation of air. This is considered to be crucial as to control temperature and to facilitate easy removal of ashes.

Curing of Tandoor

Once the *tandoor* is ready and before it is fired, certain process of curing is desired for its efficient usage. A new and proficient *tandoor* has to be smooth from inside. The boiled paste of green leafy vegetable, usually spinach, are used to coat the inside walls. Next day, a mixture of buttermilk or *khatti lassi,* oil, and salt is rubbed all over the inner walls and left to cure overnight. This process prevents the *rotis* and other breads from sticking to the walls of the *tandoor,* while they are being cooked.

A coating of molasses also serves the same purpose and can be used as a substitute of above-mentioned ingredients.

After the crucial process of curing, the *tandoor* should be lit with very low heat on the first and second day for a short duration of about half an hour each day. It becomes perfectly ready to be used on the third day and then on. In order to keep the *tandoor* in good working order, the inner walls are coated with the paste of greens or molasses on a regular basis at least once a fortnight.

Equipment and Tools Used With Tandoor

- *Seekhs*
- Hooks
- Pad
- Iron covers
- Wooden plank
- Needle and thread

• Skewers (Seekhs)

Seekhs are the key tool supporting the system. These are made from wrought iron. The length varies depending on the depth of the *tandoor.*

Different types of *seekhs* are made for various purposes.

Seekhs for *roti, naan,* and so on come in a pair. The end of one *seekh* is bent at a right angle (about as inch). The end of other paired seek is flattened like a spatula. When a *roti* or *naan* is cooked, the bent end of *seekh* is inserted in it and a *seekh* with flat end is used to scrape and separate it from the walls of the *tandoor.*

Seekhs used for the preparation of *kebab* like *seekh kebab,* are kept pointed at both the ends. This facilitates the *tandoori* cook to remove the *kebab* from either side.

Thinner *seekhs* are required for vegetable preparation and meats like fish, prawns, and so on.

In order to get best results, care must be taken to always grease and rub the *seekh* with a cloth before putting anything on them.

• Hooks

Hooks are used in a way that one hook can be linked to another (like a chain).

These can be suspended with the food to be cooked, in the *tandoor*. The upper hook is suspended on a *seekh* rested across the top of the *tandoor*.

- ### Pads

It is a kind of cushion used for making breads in the *tandoor*. Generally, it is stuffed with coconut coir. The prepared dough of the bread is flattened by palm and is placed on this cushion and then slapped on to the inner side walls of the *tandoor*. The bigger the bread prepared, the larger is the cushion required. It is used to place *roti* or *naan* on to the inner walls of the *tandoor*. A couple of clean dusters are tied around a wad of coir to make this. It is also referred as *gaddi* in Hindi.

- ### Iron Covers

An iron cover of convex shape is used to cover the top of the *tandoor*. Besides this, another small iron plate is used to shut off the small opening at the bottom of the *tandoor*. These help in regulating the heat, once *tandoor* is heated. When the temperature of the *tandoor* decreases, both the covers are put on for a while.

- ### Wooden Plank

It is a rectangular piece of wooden board and it is used for flattening the dough balls of bread and also to place the dough balls on it till they are prepared.

- ### Needle and Thread

A trussing needle and kitchen thread is used to stitch and tie the ingredients properly on the skewer. For example, whole stuffed chicken requires to be stitched properly and same is the case with whole stuffed vegetables.

Precautions and Care taken while Cooking on Tandoor

The smooth functioning at *tandoor* is only possible if the workstation near the *tandoor* is organized efficiently. The proper placing of ingredients and tools of *tandoor* at their desired places ensures the quickest delivery of the guest order without any hassle. Everything has to be planned properly before operation, to carry the entire task more effectively.

When a recipe demands for a whole stuffed chicken, then the chicken stock has to be stitched up before being suspended in the *tandoor* with utmost care and precision. Few cooks insert tooth-picks in chicken stock at opposite ends to hold the thread while it is being wrapped around and this also has proved to be very successful.

It should always be noted that the aluminium dishes should never be used to marinate or keep marinated foods. Aluminium imparts an unpleasant metallic taste to the food. Non-metallic and lead-free ceramic dishes are ideal for marination. Stainless steel is also popular today.

The addition of salt during marination needs special mention. The white meats and vegetables can be marinated with salt added together with spices, and so on at the beginning, but for the marination of red meats, salt should never be added in the first marinade, as the addition of salt releases water and juices from the meat, making it stringy. This also results in loss of certain amount of flavour. In such meats, salt can be added to the marinade just before fifteen to twenty minutes prior to cooking.

The food being cooked in the *tandoor* is brushed regularly with hot melted butter or oil and this process is known as basting. This process facilitates the sealing of the juices inside the meat, thereby preventing the food from drying.

Care Related to Skewering

Certain things are to be taken into account before and while skewering the meat being cooked to derive best possible results. The pieces of flesh when skewered should have some gap in between and not pack to pack from one end to other. *Ghee* or any edible oil should be applied to clean and lubricate the skewers before threading and then it has to be wiped clean.

While threading the meat, the skewer should not be pushed straight by force but it has to be woven with efficient up and down movement of hands. This ensures that the meat fibres are on different levels and it cannot slip off easily.

A whole chicken also needs to be skewered carefully. It should be skewered from the neck end and skewer should come out near the tail. Care should be taken not to break the backbone of the chicken.

The ready-threaded skewered item should be allowed to stand for a short period of about ten to fifteen minutes. This resting allows the marinade to dry completely. But if it is found to be too dry, oil may be applied at that stage. Cooking time is usually anywhere between 10-35 minutes, till the aroma of the meat spreads. The skewer should then be taken out of the *tandoor* and the juices are allowed to drip for 4-5 minutes while the meats are still on the skewer. The half-cooked skewered item can be kept up to 3-4 hours.

However, in hot climates, the meat should not be kept half-prepared for more than two hours.

In order to remove meats from the skewers one can use any of the breads — *naan*, *roti*, and so on. The meat can firmly be held with these and with a twisting motion; it can be taken off from the skewer. It is convenient to take off meat pieces from the skewer when it is hot. This technique can easily be judged and mastered well with efforts.

Marination and Marinades

Marination

Marination is a technique that involves marinating the food in a mixture of certain ingredients. The marinated food has to be cooked – either grilled, barbequed, or in a *tandoor* – with the coating of marinade in it. The process of marination renders the marinated food tender and spiced as well. It can be done for all types of vegetables, meat, game, poultry, beef and fish.

Marinades

A marinade is a concoction of certain ingredients like tenderizers (typically vinegar, lemon juice or wine), oils, herbs, spices, and curds, and so on.

In simple words, it is essentially a mixture of curds, vinegar, wine, oil, spices, herbs in which meat, fish and poultry is soaked before cooking. In particular, it is used and applied to *kebabs*.

The principal aim of a marinade is to season the food infused in it by impregnating it with the flavour of its spices and condiments. It also softens and tenderizes the fibre of the meat and facilitates efficient cooking.

Precautions to be Taken During Marinating

- Marinating should be done at a very low temperature in order to restrict bacterial growth as raw red meat may have the possibility to contain harmful bacteria which may contaminate the whole marinade.
- The used marinade should not be incorporated in any other preparation, unless and until it is rendered safe by boiling directly before use. The fresh or set-aside marinade that has not come in contact with meat should be used.
- The glass or food-grade plastic container should be used for marinating. The marinade should be transferred to a new container the very next day itself for long shelf life.
- Metal, including pottery glazes usually contains lead, and which reacts with the acid in the marinade and hence should be avoided.

Basic marination can be categorized as below:

- Based on ingredients
  - Curds-based marination
  - Cream-based marination
- Based on colouring agent
  - Red marination
  - Green marination
  - Yellow marination
  - White marination

Marination based on ingredients:

- **Curds-based marination:** Hung curds or thick yogurt is blended with ginger-garlic paste, spices, and tenderizing agents. The processed commodity is then marinated well and chilled in the refrigerator for at least 6 hours. This helps the marinade to stick to the *kebabs* and not fall off when put in a hot *tandoor*.
- **Cream-based marination:** In this marination, dairy cream is used to marinate the *kebabs* along with spices and flavouring agents. Some use binding agents like nut paste, roasted gram flour, and so on in order to let the marinade stick properly to the stock. This marination renders a smooth texture to the dish prepared.

Marination based on colouring agents:

- **Red marination:** Basic ingredients: Hung curds, ginger-garlic paste, red chilli paste, *kasoori methi* powder, *garam masala* powder, lemon juice, refined oil, salt.

  All the ingredients are whisked together until smooth paste. It is used for chicken, mutton and *paneer*, and so on. The red chilli paste used renders red colour to the marination.
- **Yellow marination:** Basic ingredients: Hung curds, ginger-garlic paste, yellow chilli paste, *garam masala* powder, mustard oil, turmeric, salt.

  All the ingredients are whisked together until a smooth paste is obtained. Yellow chilli paste can be replaced by turmeric powder or saffron, depending upon the requirement of the dish prepared. It is used for tender meats like prawns, fish, *paneer*, and so on.
- **Green marination:** Basic ingredients: Hung curds, coriander leaves, mint leaves, spinach paste, ginger-garlic paste, yellow chilli powder, *kasoori methi* powder, *garam masala*, mustard oil, salt.

  Mint leaves, coriander leaves and spinach paste are mixed and ground to form a green paste. Then all the rest of ingredients are whisked properly to a smooth paste with the green paste. This marination is used for tender meats like chicken, fish and *paneer kebabs*.
- **White marination:** Basic ingredients: Processed cheese grated, egg white, cream, cashew nut paste, ginger-garlic paste, green chilli, coriander roots, white pepper powder, mace powder, and green cardamom powder, salt.

Mix grated cheese and egg white properly. Add cream in cheese and then add remaining ingredients and mix them thoroughly. This marination is mild and rich in taste and is used mainly for chicken *kebabs*.

Tenderizers

Tenderizers play a crucial role in *tandoori* cooking as it tenderizes the meat to be cooked in *tandoor*.

There are three ways of tenderizing a meat pieces and they are:

- Mechanical tenderization such as pounding. Mostly lamb is beaten with a wooden or rubber mallet to facilitate the tenderizing process. The beating breaks the muscle fibres and makes them tender.
- The tenderization that occurs through cooking, such as braising.
- Tenderizing by using various enzymes such as papain in papaya, bromelain in pineapple, actinidin in kiwi fruits, and so on.

The essential charcteristics of all tenderizers depends upon the acid content and the enzymes. These function by readily dissolving the sinews, hard tissues and muscle fibres, thereby rendering softness to the meat. Meat consists of muscles and connective tissues that are made up of proteins. Proteins contain lots of amino acids linked together in chains to make large molecules. Meat tenderizers act by breaking the amino acids apart. Marinades designed to tenderize meat usually contain acids or enzymes.

Raw fruits can be used to tenderize meat before cooking because they contain enzymes that break down proteins.

The tenderizer in marinade is either acidic or enzymatic in nature.

Acidic ingredients in marinades like vinegar, wine and lemon juice will tenderize meat by denaturing or unwinding the long protein in the muscles. The meat should not be left with an acidic marinade for long as it will eventually break down all the proteins - leaving behind a mushy mess.

Enzymes can speed up or catalyze the breakdown of proteins into amino acids. For example, fruits like papaya, kiwi fruit, pineapple, fig and mango are a good source of enzymes that can break down meat proteins. These fruits all contain a type of enzyme called protease.

The most commonly used tenderizers are curds, raw papaya, *kachri*, vinegar, lime juice, and raw pineapple.

Curds

It is basically fresh milk impregnated with a culture of lactobacillus. The lactic acid present in curds helps to break down the meat fibres and renders the product soft and succulent, when cooked.

Raw Papaya

It is an oblong melon-like fruit and is obtained from a fully grown tree and is used in the raw state. Papaya contains a protein-digesting enzyme called papain that gives it the tenderizing property.

Kachri

It is a wild variety of the cucunis family. It is used in powder form and is used as a tenderizing agent for meats.

Lime

The citric acid content in lime gives it the tenderizing property. It is also used for marinating meat for *kebab* preparation. Other citrus fruits, such as orange or sweet lime can also be used as tenderizers.

Raw Pineapple

It is an oval, spiky-looking fruit with a pungent taste. The active enzyme found in pineapple is bromelain, which bestows it the tenderizing property.

Raw Fig

The enzyme found in fig is ficin, which is responsible for their tenderizing property. It is used rarely due to its seasonal availability.

Tamarind

The ripe fruit of tamarind has two acids - citric acid and tartaric acid. Both give this fruit a sour taste as well as tenderizing feature.

Vinegar

Vinegar contains acetic acid in it. The acetic acid acts as a tenderizer. Malt vinegar is the most commonly used vinegar in making *kebabs*.

Ginger

Ginger contains a proteolytic enzyme that naturally breaks down protein. Ginger paste is used in marination to tenderize meats.

Tea

It contains tannins which are a natural tenderizer. The tea liquor is used as a marinade as per the requirement.

Thus, in short, both the factors of tenderizing and marinating are very crucial in *tandoori* cuisine and hence the marinades have become an essential constituent of *tandoori* cooking.

Culinary Trivia: Food Colour

Food colour is an important element in providing food a distinctive and appealing appearance. Food colour adds appeal to the dish and stimulates appetite as well. They are of two types: natural colours like chlorophyll, caramel and annatto; and synthetic ones that are chemically synthesised and have high tinctorial strength (colouring capacity). Synthetic colours are classified as "food colours" and "non-food colours". The first are those that can be used in foods after thorough toxicological evaluation. Use of non-permitted colours can result in severe gastrointestinal side effects; allergy and can even damage some vital organs.

There are eight food colours permitted in India: "Tartrazine" and "Sunset Yellow" for yellow; "Carmosine", "Ponceau - 4R" and "Erithrosine" for red; "Brilliant Blue" and "Indigo Carmine" for blue; and "Fast Green" for Green.

The usage of colour is regulated by Prevention of Food Adulteration Act (PFA). The maximum permitted limit in foods is 100 mg per kg of food or one gm in 10 kg.

Culinary Trivia: Enzymes

Enzymes in our bodies tend to work best around 37°C. However, enzymes from fruits, such as papaya or pineapple work best between 50–70°C. If left for too long on the meat, they can completely digest it.

32 Biryani and Pulao

"I have a great love for cuisine, so I'm always interested in local food, and there are so many interesting dishes, spices and ingredients in India." – Romain Grosjean

Biryani

The term *biryani* is derived from the Persian word *birian* which literally means 'fried before cooking'. *Biryani* is the most popular and famed rice based wholesome dish from India. It has also become an integral meal of southern Asia.

According to one legendary fable, *biryani* is considered to have been brought to North India by invader Taimur Lang, or Taimur, the crippled person from Kazakhstan, via the route of Afganistan. Another fable describes that Begam Mumtaj Mahal the one considered as the inspiration to build the wonderful monument Taj Mahal has prepared the *biryani* as a wholesome meal for the entire army. Few people are of the opinion that the dish was introduced in West Asia. It is said that the migrants used to bury the huge earthenware pots with rice and meat in a pit with certain flavourful spices. After some time, the pot was brought out from the pit and the dish which emerged from the resultant concoction of all ingredients was the incomparable and luscious *biryani*.

One segment of the *biryani* is considered to have originated from the Mughals, who brought the dish from Persia and later on, during their rule in India, the *biryani* established itself firmly in certain cities like Lucknow, Hyderabad, and so on.

The other segment of *biryani* is supposed to have been brought to India by Arab traders who crossed the Arabian Sea and landed in Calicut. The Calicut *biryani* is usually served with vinegar pickles and *papads* fried in coconut oil, and is a softer version as compared to the others. It is also light on the stomach and has no relation in context of taste to the other *biryanis* in the country.

Biryani has attained such a huge popularity that nearly every community has prepared and popularized its own version of *biryani*. From the northwestern region comes the *memoni biryani* (people who occupied the area between Sindh, Gujarat and Pakistan) which is a tremendously spicy *biryani*, whereas the Sindhi mutton *biryani* is typically different.

The populace of Iran have their own version of the Iranian *biryani* whereas the Bohris have their version of *Biryani*. The Bohris *biryani* is usually prepared during their wedding functions and is characterized to have obtained its flavour from tomatoes. The Kashmiri *bhuna gosht biryani* and the Kashmiri *kacchhe gosht ki biryani* symbolise the benefaction of the Mughal rulers to the northern-most state of India.

The Lucknawi or Awadhi *biryani* is the footmark and the Mughlai essence. The Mughals left on the eastern part of India. According to the version of History, in 1856, Nawab Wajid Ali Shah was forced to leave Lucknow by the British and hence the *biryani* travelled from Lucknow to Calcutta with him. The team of expert royal cooks shifted with him and so did the *biryani*. At one period of time, in Calcutta (present-day Kolkata) the *biryani* made its way into the homes of poorer people, as they could not afford meat every day. So the meat was replaced by potatoes.

Aurangzeb is considered to have encroached the South and appointed the *Nizam-ul-Mulk* who later as the Asaf Jahi ruler became the Nizam of Hyderabad. This describes the journey of *biryani* down towards South India.

It is noted that the marriages held between the families of the Nizams of Hyderabad and the Nawab of Arcot gave birth to a new sort of *biryani* which is popularized as Arcot *biryani*, another distinct type of *biryani*, which demands for smaller grains of rice variety.

Tipu Sultan of Karnataka propagated *biryani* and brought it to Mysore. They hired the Hindu vegetarians as bookkeepers that led to the worthy invention of *tahiri biryani* in their kitchens. The vegetable *biryani* is the *tarkari* version, which was basically made for the cashiers and financiers working for the Nawabs, and they were Mahajan Hindus. The Hyderabadi version of the mixed *vegetable biryani* is also referred as the *tahiri biryani.*

Preparation of Biryani

Biryani is the wonderful concoction of rice and meat that is fried before cooking. In early days, the rice was fried in clarified butter (*desi ghee*) even without washing it. The logic behind doing so was that frying rice in *ghee,* rendered them the much desired nutty flavour. The second logic was that, frying of rice burnt the starch resulting in gelatinizing the outer layer. After that the rice was boiled with spices till it was half cooked. The meat was marinated with a mixture of curds, papaya, and spices and then it was cooked.

After cooking the two chief ingredients separately, they are cooked together in an earthen pot, i.e., *handi.* Then the meat and rice are layered in the *handi.* Always the bottom and top layers are that of the rice and middle layer contains the meat. Some condiments like saffron, mace, screw pine and rose essence or rose water and cardamom are added while layering the *biryani.* All these condiments render a flowery sweet aroma to the dish. Then, this *handi* is sealed and placed on the live coal for cooking. Longer period of time is desired to cook, as longer cooking at low temperatures would mingle the taste, which is no less than the magic. The seal of the *handi* is broken only when it was to be served.

Certain versions of *biryani* delicacies are popular across India and some of them are given below.

Calcutta Biryani

It is characterized as being less spicy compared to the other varieties. It has marked an imprint for its own place in the heart of *biryani* lovers and food connoisseurs. It comprises rice, meat, potato and at times egg. Because of high expense of meat, potato is used as a substitute which has become a unique and distinct feature of Calcutta *Biryani.*

Awadhi Biryani

The Lucknow Biryani is undoubtedly the most celebrated dish of the Muslims and that of Lucknow as well. It is also referred as *pukka biryani* as the rice and meat are cooked separately and then layered. It is a complete and wholesome meal in itself which every individual of Lucknow boasts of it.

Hyderabadi Biryani

This exotic and much discussed *biryani* resulted due to the perfect conglomeration of Mughlai cuisine and Andhra Pradesh cuisine in the kitchens of Hyderabadi Nizam. Two versions of this are highly famed and they are *kacchi* (raw) *biryani* and the *pakki biryani.* It is accompanied with a nutty flavoured *mirchi ka salan* and *boorani raita.*

Kachchi Gosht ki Biryani

It is prepared with meat marinated with spices in yogurt before cooking. The meat is sandwiched between layers of fragrant long grained *basmati* rice, and is cooked on *dum.* This is genuinely a challenging method as it requires punctilious attention on time and temperature to avoid over- or under-cooking of the meat. It is a very flavourful *biryani.*

Pakki Biryani

In this, the meat is marinated for a shorter period of time, and the meat is cooked before being layered with the rice and cooked in a dough- sealed vessel by typical *dum* technique. In *pakki biryani, yakhni* (gravy) and the other ingredients are cooked before baking. This is the most common version of *biryani* consumed all across India.

Pulao

Pulao is simply a rice dish essentially cooked in seasoned broth. It is considered that *pulao* was first documented by the illustrious and famed Persian scholar Abu Ali Ibn Sina in the 10th century. It is apparent that *pulao* is a very common rice dish of the Muslims and journeyed with them from one civilization to another for many centuries. In the current scenario, pulao depicts itself as a resplendent element of the cuisine of various countries like Iran, Afghanistan, Bangladesh, Uzbekistan, Turkey, Arabia, Kazakhstan, Pakistan, Azerbaijan, India, and so on, and has gained varied names like *pilaf, palao, pulao, pilau,* and so on.

Pulao is an inseparable element of formal and informal meal of Asian and Middle-Eastern cuisines. *Pulao* is essentially and mostly made of best quality rice like *basmati* rice or jasmine rice, cooked in a broth seasoned with a few or all of the following basic ingredients—onion, tomatoes, ginger, garlic, allspice, coriander seeds, dry fruits, saffron and salt. *Pulao* can be made from a wide selection of ingredients like meat, lentils and beans or vegetables. Meat, lentils, beans and vegetables are also cooked in the broth for a while to release and exude amazing flavours. For non-vegetarian meaty *pulao,* meat pieces with bones are usually preferred as they release more flavour and makes the broth richer. In the most basic and simplest technique of cooking *pulao,* rice is just cooked in seasoned broth and then covered and steamed. It results in a perfectly cooked, grain-separated, flavourful and rich pot of rice buzzing with flavour.

A wide variety of *pulao* dishes are famous all across the world and some of them are given below.

Kabuli Pulao

Kabuli Pulao is a renowned recipe and it originates from Tajikistan, Afghanistan, Iran, Uzbekistan, and Turkmenistan and is a matter of great delight all over the world. Kabuli Pulao is simply prepared with rice, meat, onion, allspice and white cumin seeds. The rice is cooked in meat stock, and then allowed to be baked in the oven with the meat pieces on the top. The baked *pulao* is then served with the topping of a motley of ingredients like fried carrots, raisins, almonds, pistachio, green cardamom and sugar.

Persian Pulao

Persian Pulao, popularly known as Polo is cooked by a slightly different technique. Rice is first partially cooked in salted water and then layered in a pan with prepared meat and dry fruit gravy, and then it is covered tightly and steamed over very low heat until done. Persian Polo is prepared with a concoction of a wide variety of ingredients like spinach, lentils, beans, meat, fenugreek, nuts, dry fruit, and so on.

Turkish Pilaf

Turkish Pilaf, basically from Turkey, is a simple flagrant rice dish, which complements impeccably well with certain Turkish savouries. Turkish Pilaf incorporates many flavourful ingredients like stock, nuts, dry fruit, saffron, allspice and butter. In the elementary Turkish Pilaf recipe, the rice is first fried in butter until brown and then cooked in stock. The cooked rice is then garnished with fried nuts and a variety of dry fruits.

Mughlai Pulao

Mughlai Pulao is the celebrated dish of the Muslim populace of Pakistan, Bangladesh and India. As Mughals were royals, their food was no exception. The most famed version of Mughlai Pulao was made with rice, chicken, mince (*keema*), allspice, onion, ginger, garlic, saffron, curds, almonds, cumin seeds, coriander seeds and turmeric. The rice was initially fried with certain spices and then cooked. Cooked rice was then layered with prepared chicken and *keema* curry in a serving dish and garnished with slivers of fried almonds.

Shahjahani Pulao

Shahjhani Pulao is an exquisite delicacy of Mughlai cuisine and is named after the Mughal Emperor Shahjahan. The Shahjahani Pulao is attributed with an imperial taste and majestic flavour. It is prepared with rice, meat, chillies, onion, tomatoes, curds, green chilies, potatoes, ginger, garlic, allspice, fresh coriander and almonds. In Shahjahani Pulao, the cooked rice is layered with prepared meat curry and yogurt in a dish and finally garnished with boiled eggs, fried almond slivers and chopped fresh coriander.

Arabian Pulao

Arabian Pulao is considered to be the noted and exotic rice dish of the Middle East region. Despite being simple in cooking technique, it is bestowed with rich and captivating flavours. The basic ingredients of it are rice, meat, onions, garlic, allspice, certain nuts, dry fruits and fresh mint leaves. The meat is half cooked in spices and stock, then the meat is removed and baked. The rice is cooked in stock and then served with the baked meat garnished with fried nuts, dry fruit and fresh mint leaves on top. It is a custom to serve Arabian Pulao in a large platter and the entire family eats directly from that platter with hands.

Other Popular Pulaos

Apart from the *pulao* delicacies listed above, certain famed *pulao* preparations are as such: Shahi Pulao, Yakhni Pulao, Simple Pulao and Pea Pulao. They all are cooked by almost the similar technique and method but are made distinct by incorporation of different ingredients.

Culinary Trivia: Basmati

It is a long variety of long grain rice. *Basmati* is a Sanskrit word meaning fragrant. It has been cultivated in India for thousands of years and India has been the largest cultivator of this variety. Its typical flavour is due to the aroma compound 2-acetyl-1-pyrroline. There are several varieties cultivated in India and few popular varieties are: Basmati 370, Basmati 385, Basmati 198, Basmati 217, Basmati 370, Kasturi, Mahi Suganda, Pusa, and so on. It has been used in *biryani* and *pulao* preparations and has set a benchmark for other rice variety regarding quality.

Culinary Trivia: Cook

The cooks were referred by various names in Sanskrit, such as *supakara, bhojanadatr, alarika, odanaka* and *sudas.* The one who specialized in frying were called a *pupika* and one with the baking skill was called *kandavika.* The *avalika* was the person who was expert in spicing.

33 Breads

> "There are people in the world so hungry, that God cannot appear to them except in the form of bread." – Mahatma Gandhi

Indian cuisine is a bouquet of myriad remarkable delicacies and amidst this vibrant variety, one food item that stands out is its breads. Bread is the most basic food element in almost all cultures, and in a country with so much heterogeneity it is interesting to have a wide assortment of multitudinous breads.

The bread is essentially the base of Indian cuisine and has gained such a prominence that no meal is considered to be consummate in the absence of bread in the menu. Almost all the gravy preparations or curry preparations in India are consumed with either bread or with rice dishes. Thus, bread plays a crucial role in Indian food. Bread is a decisive factor while deciding the menu in any grand function or even in small events. Bread provides a true sense of contentment to the diner and it is very gratifying indeed.

In India, it is very difficult to define bread. There is a wide variety of available flatbreads such as – unleavened, yeasted, fermented breads, crepes, stuffed breads with a variety of textures and shapes. These breads may be cooked on an iron griddle (*tawa*), or in a hot *tandoor* or clay oven, or deep-fried in a *kadhai* until puffy and soft.

Flat breads like *rotis, parathas* and *naans* are more popular in the northern regions of India, while *dosas* or crepes made with a batter of grains and/or lentils are more popularly consumed in South India.

Breads can be classified depending upon three factors:

- **Main ingredient (grain) used**
  - **Wheat flour based:** *Roti, paratha, puri, lacchha paratha.*
  - **Refined flour based:** *Naan, kulcha, roomali roti, malabari paratha, lucchi, pav.*
  - **Gram flour based:** *Missi roti.*
  - **Bajre/Jowar/Ragi based, and so on:** *Bajre ki roti, makki ki roti,* etc.
- **Cooking method applied**
  - **Pan Fried Bread**
  - **Tandoor Baked**
  - **Deep Fried**
  - **Oven Baked.**
- **Leavening agent used**
  - **Leavened Bread:** Those in which leavening agent is used to let the dough of bread ferment. Examples of leavening agent are curds, yeast, baking powder, and so on.
  - **Unleavened bread:** Those in which no leavening agent is used and the breads are unfermented.

Description of Various Breads

Akki Roti

It is a rice flour bread from Karnataka. *Akki* means rice in Karnataka.

It is made by mixing sliced onions, carrots, chopped coriander, cumin seeds, sesame seeds with salt and water and kneaded well to make a soft dough. Oil is spread over a griddle (*tava*) and a small amount of the dough is neatly spread over it to resemble a thin pancake (*roti*).

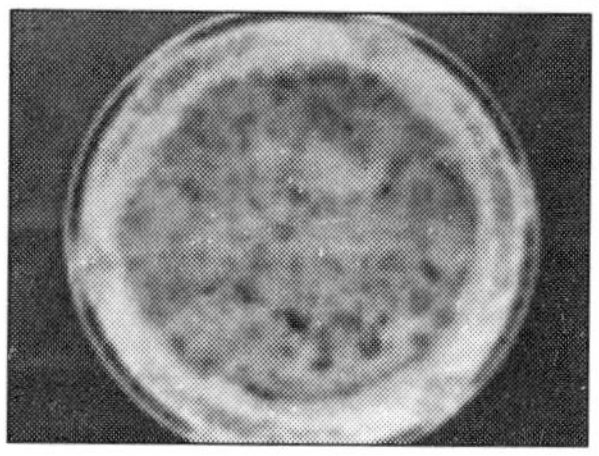

A small amount of oil is spread over it and the griddle is placed over heat till the *roti* turns golden brown. Akki Roti is served hot and is eaten along with chutney. A dash of butter or *ghee* with Akki Roti is also preferred.

Another way of making Akki Roti is to spread the dough over a plantain leaf and then cook it over the griddle with the plantain leaf on the top.

Anda Paratha

Anda is the Hindi term for egg. Anda Paratha reveals itself in many versions. The simplest version has a crisp coating of whipped egg, while the fancier recipe involves filling the half-fried bread with a mixture of beaten egg, finely chopped green chillies, onions, ginger and coriander via a cut made with a sharp knife in its belly.

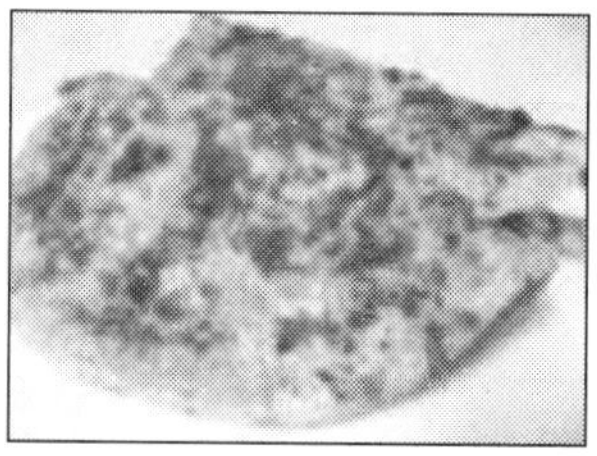

Baati

The Baati is an authentic and unique bread, designed to last. It was the staple travel food of the Rajput warriors and Marwari traders in Rajasthan. Tomato sized balls of whole wheat dough are roasted over hot coals and are eaten dipped in *ghee*. They can also be cooked in an electric *tandoor*. Smaller Baatis can be cooked without leavening. They may also be cooked in boiling water first and then baked accordingly.

Baida Paratha

This is a bread from Bohra muslim community and it is a *paratha* that is stuffed with mince meat mixture in refined flour dough and cooked. The bread is eaten with great gusto and passion.

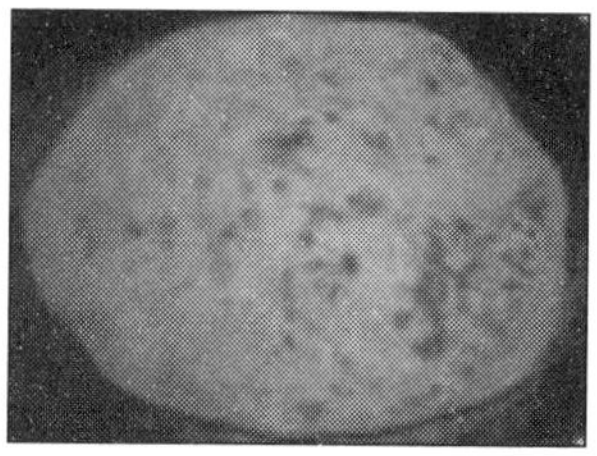

Bajre ki Roti

This is a traditional bread made from the millet flour. It is bit difficult to bake as it doesn't have gluten in its flour that binds it to hold its shape while cooking. At times, the millets flour is mixed with a small quantity of wheat flour to facilitate easy rolling of the dough. It is served with garlic *chutney* and sliced onion in Rajasthan.

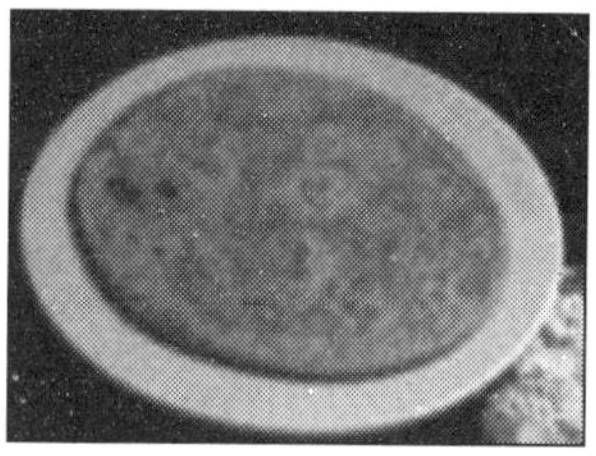

Bakharkhani

This is a soft rich leavened bread and is a specialty from Hyderabad. The dough of this bread is enriched with milk, *ghee*, melon seeds, sugar, and saffron. It can be leavened with yeast or baking powder. The dough is made by soft kneading and dough balls are prepared, rolled and then baked in oven with proper brushing of oil. The top of the bread is garnished with slivered almonds and crushed fennel. It is consumed with *nehari*.

Bhakri

Bhakri is a famous round and flat unleavened bread mostly used in the cuisine of western and central India, especially in the states of Gujarat, Maharashtra and northern Karnataka.

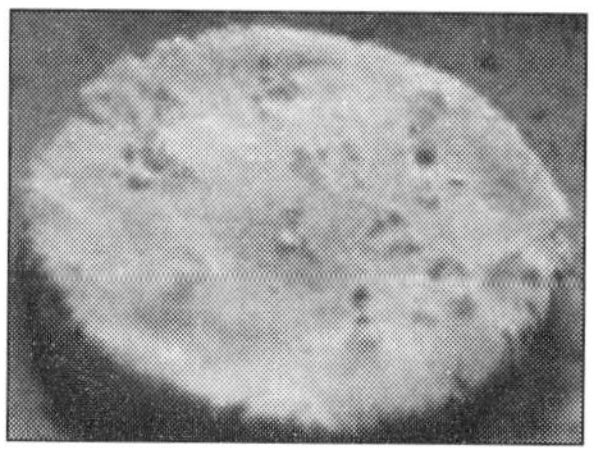

It is made mostly from *jowar* flour, *bajra* flour and even rice flour (in the Konkan region). Bhakri are made primarily with oil, water, and flour. Bhakri has traditionally been the farmer's food which would be carried to the farm at the crack of dawn and make up for both breakfast and lunch. In modern days however, Bhakri has been replaced by *rotis* and *phulkas* but still has its own passionate fan-following. Typically Bhakri is accompanied by various curries, chutney (*thecha* - a thick paste of really hot green or red chilies) and raw onion.	
Bhatura It is made from refined flour and is leavened with yeast or curds which results in a softer and fluffier deep-fried bread.	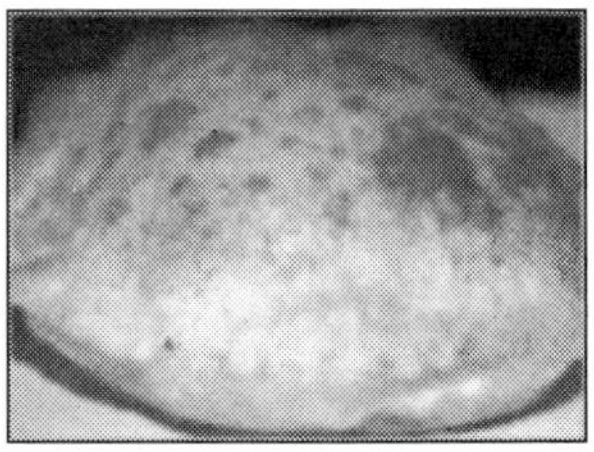
Bidari Paratha This *paratha* is made using the dough of wheat flour, refined flour and semolina with water all together. Semolina provides a nice grainy texture. The dough is firm and pliable and is allowed to rest for 20 minutes covered with a damp wet cloth. Then, the dough is divided into small balls and rolled into oval shape and deep-fried in hot piping oil and served fluffy hot with spicy preparations.	
Dhakai Paratha This is a bread made with refined flour, wheat flour, salt and curds kneaded into dough. The dough is allowed to rest for about half an hour and then rolled into round shape. Oil is applied on top of the rolled dough and folded into half from the diameter. Then oil is applied on it again and folded again to get the quarters of it. Then it is rolled to triangle shape and shallow fried in *ghee*, till golden brown in colour.	
Dosa It is a flat bread made with flours like rice flour and legumes and cooked like a pancake. The rice and *urad dal* are soaked in water overnight and then ground into a coarse paste and is left to ferment. This fermented paste is used for preparing crepe *dosa*. It may be filled with a spicy mixture of potatoes and lots of spices and it is known as *masala dosa*.	
Gilafi Kulcha It is a speciality bread from Awadh. *Gilaf* means cover in Urdu. It is made by wrapping a kind of firm *naan* dough with a layer of dough that is rich in fat content. This bread is baked in a *tandoor* and after baking, the top layer separates out as a crisp outer layer. This layer has a soft bread inside and hence the name Gilafi Kulcha.	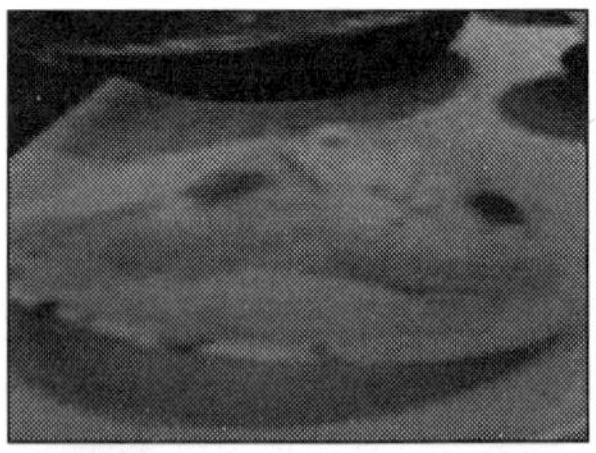
Jolada Roti It is a speciality from northern Karnataka and is an unleavened Indian bread made out of *jowar* (sorghum). The name Jolada Roti literally translates into sorghum bread. It is eaten with pulse, curries or with assorted *chutnies*.	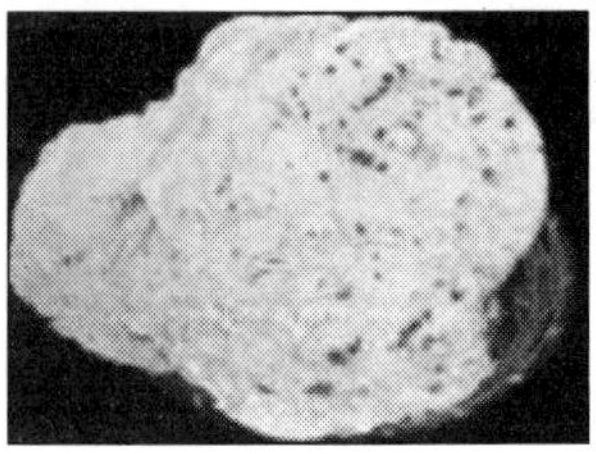

Kerala Porotta Kerala Porotta is a south Indian flat bread made with refined flour, eggs and fat. These are prepared by a technique which involves waving and puffing the dough in order to form the layers. It is named after the south Indian state of Kerala, where it is a common menu item. It is usually served with a curry dishes.	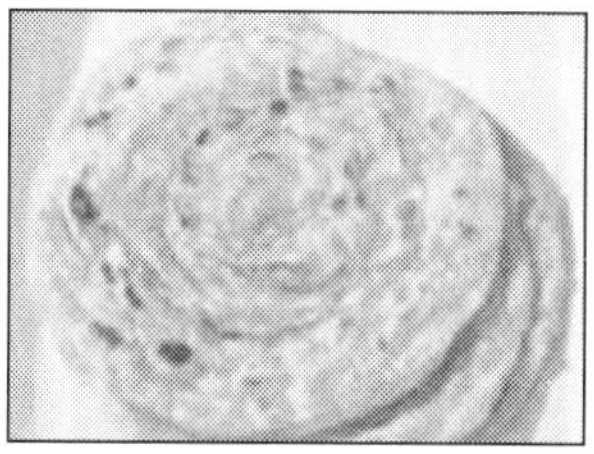
Khameeri Roti *Khameer* translates to fermentation. It is made up of whole wheat flour kneaded with curds, salt and left to ferment in a warm place and to get sour. The natural fermentation in the dough gives it a pleasing aroma and creates a natural leavening. It has been characterized by slight sour taste and is puffed as well.	
Khasta Roti *Khasta* translates to crispy in English. This bread is made by using semolina and refined flour dough. The fat used is also high and this along with semolina gives it a crispy texture. It is baked in a *tandoor* and served hot with a brushing of butter on it.	
Kulcha Kulcha refers to *naan* dough stuffed with any kind of mixture such as that of potatoes, cottage cheese or vegetables and then baked in a *tandoor*. It is served brushed with melted butter. Speaking without any exaggeration, Kulcha is simply a stuffed *naan*. Amritsari Kulcha is the most popular version of this bread and is stuffed with a boiled and spiced potato mixture and is served with *chhole*, onion roundels and lemon wedges.	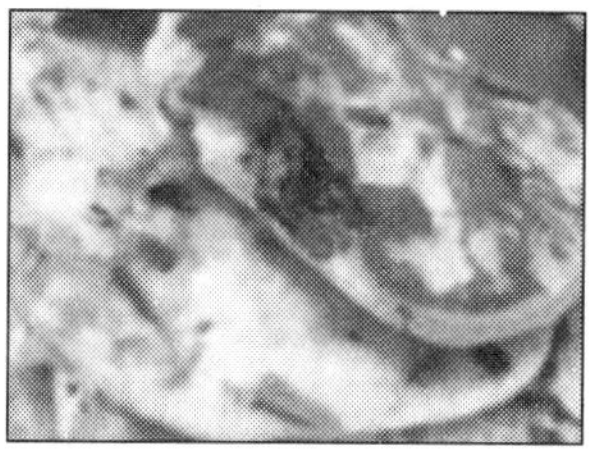
Laccha Paratha *Laccha* means flakes and this effect is created by flattening out whole wheat dough to a thin circular cane. Then the flattened dough cake is applied with melted butter and also sprinkled with whole wheat flour. Then it is rolled like a rope and made into a dough ball by spiral fold and then again flattened and baked in a *tandoor*. This rolling creates flakes in it when it is crushed between the palms of the hand. It is brushed with melted butter and served hot. It also has few variations like Pudina Paratha if smeared with dried mint on top before baking and Methi Paratha if smeared with dried fenugreek leaves.	
Lucchi It is a deep-fried Bengali bread that resembles *puri* in appearance and is made from refined flour and fried without any colour. Luchi that is stuffed is called *kochuri*, and *kochuri* stuffed with mashed peas (Koraishutir Kochuri) is one remarkable bread variety.	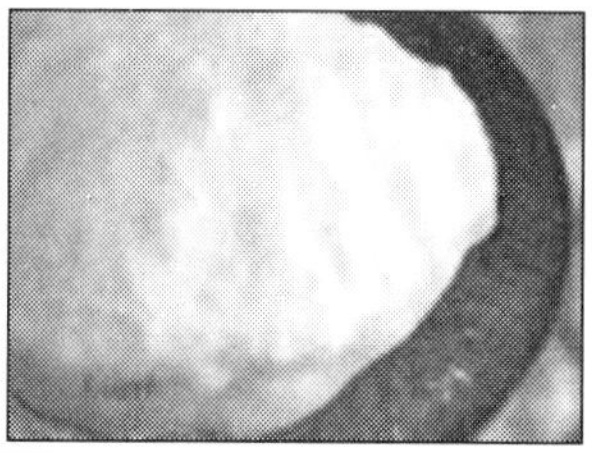
Makhuni Roti This is a stuffed *paratha* in wheat flour dough from Bihar. The stuffing is different from other breads and includes *sattu* (roasted black gram powder), chopped onion, green coriander, green chillies, garlic, *ajwain*, mustard oil and salt. It is shallow-fried using oil in a pan.	

Makki ki Roti

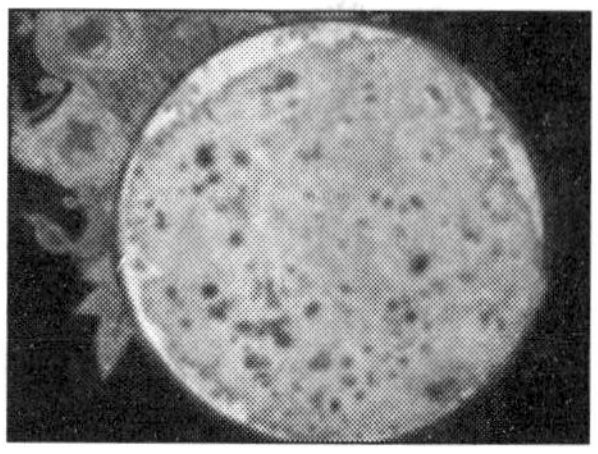

It is an unleavened Punjabi bread. It refers to a special *roti* in which, unlike the usual wheat flour, cornflour is used. The name Makki ki Roti literally means '*roti* made from cornflour'.

Makki ki Roti is yellow in colour when ready, and it also has comparatively less binding strength, which makes it difficult to handle and even difficult to cook as compared to wheat flour dough.

Makki ki Roti is cooked in Punjab during winters and is a world famous delicacy and compliments greatly especially Saag or Sarson Ka Saag (cooked mustard green leaves) and *lassi* (buttermilk).

Malabari Paratha

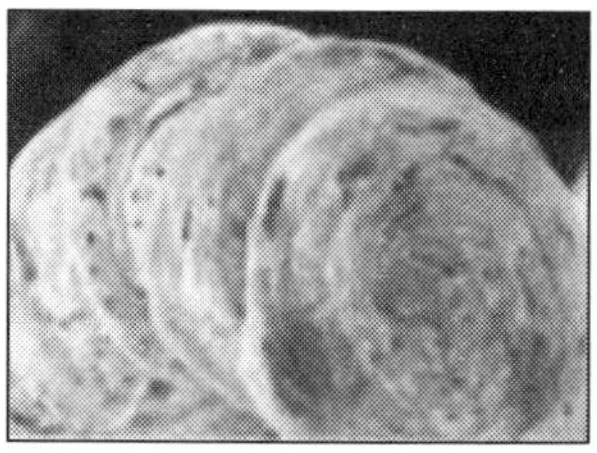

These are flaky shallow-fried *parathas* made by Malayalees (sometimes referred as Malabaries), who are the aboriginals of Kerala. The dough is kneaded to a very soft consistency and then flattened by flipping it on a table. Oil is then applied on the thin dough and rolled like a *laccha paratha*. It is then shallow-fried until crisp and is often served with beef masala.

Missi Roti

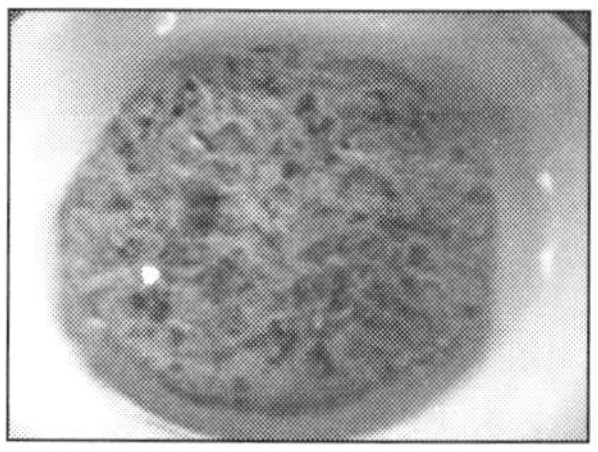

It is a very popular item from North India and the dough is prepared using gram flour, wheat flour with cumin seeds, coriander leaves, chopped onions, green chillies, turmeric and salt.

It can be shallow fried on a *tawa* or can be baked in a *tandoor* as well.

Mughlai Paratha

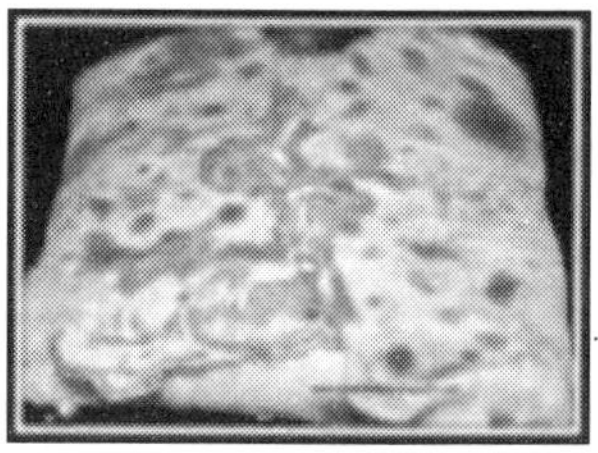

It is also referred to as "egg *paratha*". In Bengal, it is referred as Dim Paratha as 'dim' stands for egg. It is a *paratha* basically with egg. Refined flour is kneaded into dough with water and a pinch of salt. It is then rolled into thin *rotis* and cooked mildly on both sides on a non-stick pan. Then the egg mixture containing beaten egg, chopped onion, ginger, tomato and green chillies is poured in the centre and then spread all over. Oil is poured at the corner of *tawa* and two ends of the *roti* are folded and cooked till done. It is served with tomato ketchup or some other spicy sauce.

Naan

This fermented oval-shaped bread is made with refined flour. The dough is kneaded with fiour, milk, eggs, sugar, salt, oil and curds. The dough is kneaded until smooth and elastic and is allowed to ferment for about 2-3 hours. Then the dough is divided into dough balls and these are stretched by tossing the balls of dough quickly from one palm to the other to form a thin oval flat breads, slightly thicker around the edges than in the centre. Traditionally *naan* is baked on the walls of a *tandoor*, brushed with a thin coating of oil or ghee and served hot.

Generally, the *naan* dough is sprinkled with poppy or sesame seeds or nigella seeds before being baked. Chopped onion or fresh coriander can also be added to the dough, according to the cook's creativity.

It has many variations like Butter Naan if smeared with butter on top, Garlic Naan if smeared with chopped garlic or Khurmi Naan if smeared with tomato puree paste and cheese on it. Each variation has its own peculiar taste and appeal.

Paratha

Paratha originated in ancient vedic times. The word *paratha* originated from the vedic Sanskrit word (*purodhasha*). *Purodhasha* are offered to the fire God during *yogna* ceremonies. At that time, they were considered to have been stuffed with ingredients like powdered lentils and chopped vegetables.

It is also believed that *paratha* derives its name from word *parat*, translated as layer. In simple words, it is a layered bread.

Paratha is a richer version of *chapati*, crispy and is cooked in *ghee* on a griddle. Dough for this is prepared using whole wheat flour and water. The dough is rolled into flattened disc and it is folded four times with slight oil application in between and then re-rolled, giving it a flaky, layered texture and shallow fried in oil on a *tawa*.

Stuffed parathas are made by stuffing various things in the dough like Gobhi Paratha (cauliflower stuffed), Aloo Paratha (potato stuffed), Paneer Paratha (cottage cheese stuffed), Methi Paratha (fresh fenugreek stuffed), Matar Paratha (crushed green peas stuffed), Mooli Paratha (grated raddish stuffed), Keema Paratha (minced meat stuffed), and so on. Stuffed *parathas* are served with a slice of pickles and a small portion of curds as well.

Pathiri

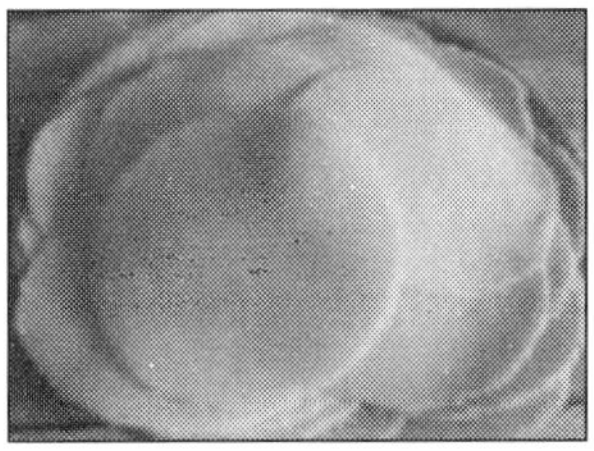

Pathiri is a unique pancake made of rice flour. It is part of the local cuisine in Kerala. Crushed rice is made into a white dough and baked on pans. After preparation it is sometimes soaked in coconut milk to keep it soft and to improve the flavour.

Today, *pathiri* is still a popular dish among the Muslim populace in Kerala. It is usually prepared for dinner and served with meat or fish. In some regions, *pathiri* is regularly served during Iftar in the fasting month of Ramadan of the Muslims.

Variants of *pathiri* include Neypathiri (made with ghee), Poricha Pathiri (fried rather than baked), Meen Pathiri (stuffed with fish), and Irachi Pathiri (stuffed with meat).

Pav

Pav is simply a soft bread roll that is baked in an oven. It has a great combination with certain dishes like Vada Pav, Misal Pav, Pav Bhaji, and so on.

Puri

It is a classic deep fried bread made from dough using wheat flour, salt, oil, *ajwain* and water. It originated in Orissa. The dough is then rolled out into small, flat circular shapes or into a larger form from which small circular portions are cut. These are then deep-fried in *ghee* or vegetable oil.

Puri can be made into two ways: flat or puffed. To prepare flat *puris*, prick several holes into the rolled dough before frying to allow steam to escape. To prepare puffed-up *puri*, leave the dough as it is. The *puri* puffs up like a ball when it is fried, due to moisture in the dough, which transforms into steam that expands.

Puran Poli

It is a bread as well as a sweet preparation of Maharashtra. It is made from jaggery, yellow gram (*chana*) *dal*, plain wheat flour, cardamom powder and ghee. It is made by stuffing a boiled sweet *dal* mixture in flour dough and then cooking it by shallow-frying and this is prepared during almost all festivals.

Rajgira Roti

This is a bread made with amaranth flour. Amaranth flour is consumed during the fasting days. This flour doesn't contain gluten in it and hence potatoes can be used as binding agent in it. This flour also absorbs lot of oil during frying and hence it is fried in very hot oil.

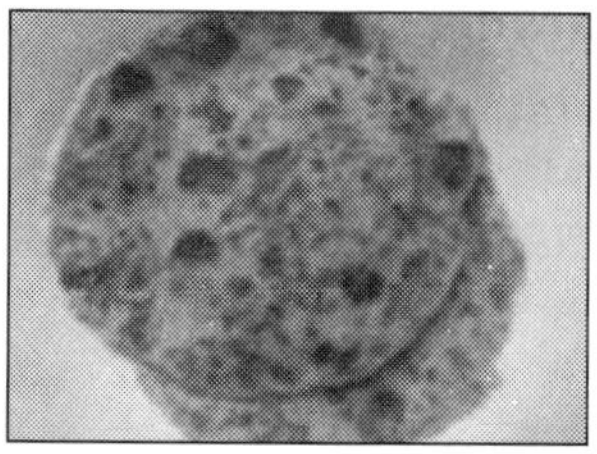

Roghani Roti

It is a bread which is very rich in content of cream, milk and ghee. Actually the word *roghan* means ghee, and as this is used in large quantity and hence it is referred as Roghani Roti. The *ghee*, milk and cream are kneaded with flour and then rolled balls are cooked on a griddle on slow flame. It can also be cooked in a *tandoor* as well. After cooking in *tandoor*, *roghan* is applied on the *roti* before serving and is served hot.

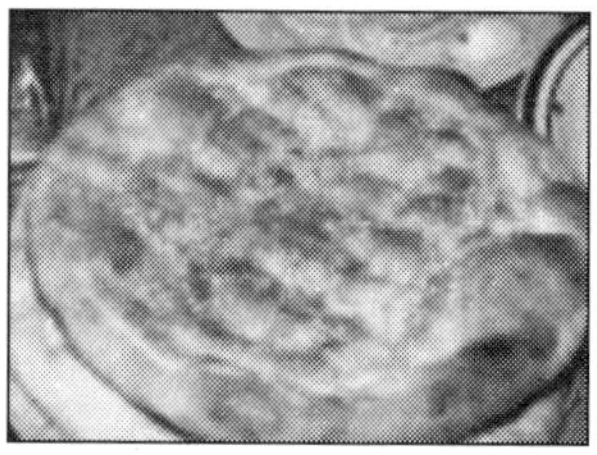

Roomali Roti

As the name suggests, this bread resembles handkerchief in appearance. It is shaped without rolling on a board and is given the shape by flying it high with the hands and finally cooked on a convex iron griddle. It is very light and thin in texture. It can only be prepared by cooks with great expertise and skills. Its preparation in public depicts showmanship of the cook and becomes the centre of attraction.

Roti/Phulka/Chapati

The term *roti* derives from the Sanskrit word *rotikā*, meaning 'bread'. Also, the name is related to the French word 'rôtie', meaning toasted bread.

This flat bread is made from a dough comprising whole-wheat or *atta* flour and water. The kneaded dough is divided into small portions of dough balls which are then rolled into a thin, flat disc with a rolling pin. The rolled-out dough ball is cooked on a dry *tawa*, or skillet. In some regions, after several minutes on the skillet, it is then put directly on a flame, making it puff up like a disc balloon.

This unleavened flatbread is served with almost every meal in India and is often eaten three times a day. *Chapati* or *roti* is eaten in such a fashion that it replaces spoons in most parts of India; i.e., a piece of roti is used to scoop up a portion of the side dish while eating.

Sheermal

It is a variety of refined flour dough invented by Muhammadan, a top notch bread maker and is a specialty of the Awadh region. The refined flour is kneaded into a dough with milk, ghee, sugar and *kewra* essence. The bread is then rolled and brushed with saffron water before being baked. After baking, the bread is brushed with melted *ghee* and served. It is traditionally cooked in a *tandoor* but can also be cooked in a *mahi tawa* by covering with a lid and applying heat from the top and bottom. It is a special *Mughlai* bread.

Taftan

Taftan is a leavened flour bread from the Awadh region and enriched with saffron and small cardamom powder baked in a clay oven. The bread is very rich in its texture.

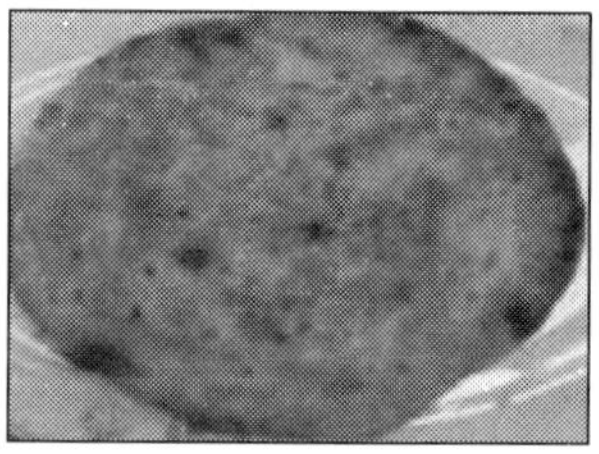

Tandoori Roti It is an unleavened bread made with whole wheat flour. The dough is prepared by kneading flour and water and then the dough is divided into small dough balls. These dough balls are flattened with hands and baked on the walls of a hot tandoor. It can be eaten plain or smeared with a dollop of butter on it.	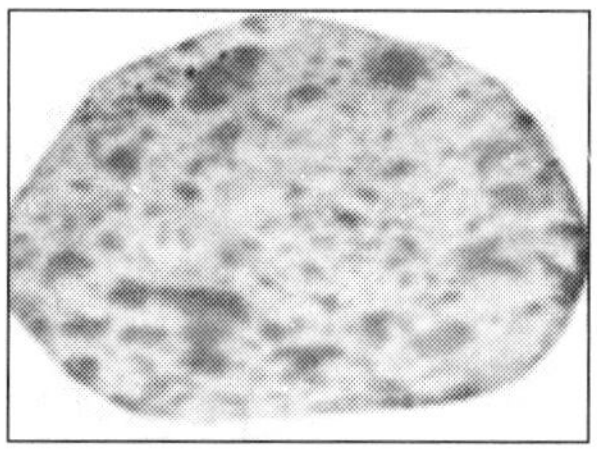
Varqi Paratha This is a bread with many layers in it. They are prepared with a mixture of wheat flour and plain flour. The flour is kneaded with salt, ghee, sugar and water into a soft dough. It is then allowed to rest for about an hour and rolled into rectangular shape. After resting for a while, the ghee is incorporated into the rolled dough by folding method into various layers or fold. It is then refrigerated and cut into round shape by a cutter and then pan-fried at very low flame with extreme care till it turns golden brown in colour.	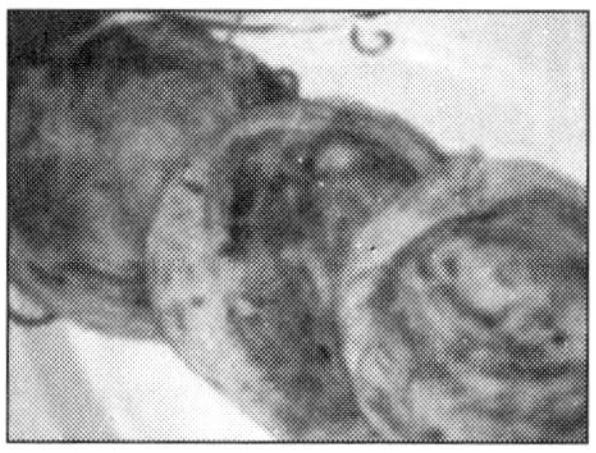

Culinary Trivia: Biggest Naan

According to the Guinness Book of World Records, the Bengal Brasserie in Hither Green, London, baked a *naan* measuring 5 cm thick, 66 cm long, 58.4 cm wide, and weighing 4 kg.

Culinary Trivia: World Bread Day

Sixteenth October is celebrated as World Bread Day every year.

Culinary Trivia: Baking Soda and Baking Powder

Baking Soda: It is also referred as soda bicarbonate. When baking soda is combined with moisture and an acidic ingredient (example yogurt, chocolate, buttermilk, and honey), the resulting chemical reaction produces bubbles of CO_2 that expands under oven temperature, causing baked items to rise. The reaction begins immediately upon mixing the ingredients, so one need to bake recipes which calls for immediate cooking.

Baking Powder: It contains sodium bicarbonate, but it includes the acidifying agent already (cream of tartar), and it is also a drying agent (usually starch).

Cream of Tartar: It is a byproduct of wine making. It is also known as potassium bitartrate and also potassium hydrogen tartrate.

34 Sweets

> "Food is for eating, and good food is to be enjoyed... I think food is, actually, very beautiful in itself." – Delia Smith

Indian cuisine is widely varied and Indian desserts are no exception to it. India has a broad spectrum of enormous collection of sweets from each region and state. Sweets fascinate every food epicurean from all across the globe. Sweets play a cardinal role in Indian cuisine and the best way to finish a meal is with a lingering sweet taste. It won't be an exaggeration to state that any of the special ceremonies, festivals, jovial occasions and celebrations is considered to be incomplete and meaningless without the presence of sweets. It is an old custom to distribute sweets during festivities and other such functions. The sweets have gained so much of popularity that these have become an integral part of and synonymous to the festivals.

Sweets have gained utmost popularity in every nook and corner of India and due to this the confectionery industry has flourished vigorously in India. The availability of ingredients and changing taste preferences of the diners have contributed to the creation of many new wonderful sweet varieties. The making of Indian sweets demands a great skill and expertise in the cook. The Indian cuisine has been considered the sweetest cuisine of the world by many gourmets. The logic for this is that many preparations are inclined towards the sweet taste like those in Gujarat and Bengal; as they prefer to add sugar or jaggery in almost many savoury dish.

It would seem exceptionally strange that the sweets prepared don't have a standard recipe and hence they are prepared according to the creativity of the cooks or the ingredients available. The recipes are kept a secret by the cooks and are not revealed easily to anyone. The preparation of the sweets requires a lot of skills and expertise, which are gained by severe practice. The fundamental essence of sweets lies in its texture, its flavour, its appearance, its taste rather than its method of preparation. The sweets have become an integral part of Indian diet and people love to consume it. Sweets in India are mostly consumed after the meals, as a dessert course.

Few states in India, like Rajasthan, Bengal, Odisha and Uttar Pradesh have created a niche in the world of sweets and have subsequently mastered their art to prepare and create noteworthy desserts. Rajasthan has bestowed India with certain impeccable dishes like Ghevar, Mishri Mawa, Milk Cake, and so on, while Bengal has gifted India with refined taste of Rasogulla, Rasmalai, Cham-Cham, Sandesh, and so on. Odisha is the birthplace of most-sought after desserts like Rasogulla whereas Uttar Pradesh has been blessed with desserts par excellence such as Petha and Lal Peda which the generations will relish throughout.

The tradition of Indian sweets traces its history long back and it dates back to more than 3000 years ago. India is a diverse country where every state has been associated with availability of certain distinct ingredients, climatic conditions and cultural diversity of the people residing there. This can be better understood by the base (basic ingredient) of the desserts prepared in North, South, East and West India. The desserts in North India are mostly based on *khoya* (reduced milk), whereas in the eastern states like Bengal, desserts are primarily based on *chhena* (fresh cottage cheese) and South India uses rice, jaggery and coconut in their desserts. Thus, the produce and availability of ingredients has been the most defining and decisive factor in making of desserts, region wise.

The world of Indian sweets has also been influenced by the invasions and the rulers as well. Several Indian desserts depict an apparent influence of the Portuguese, Mughals, and British. Many desserts have been endowed as a gift from the Mughal rulers to India and same is with the Portuguese as in Goan desserts.

The tradition of making and eating desserts has been age old. In Hindu mythology, it is believed that Lord

Ganesha enjoyed eating *modak* and had a great penchant for it. It is for this reason, during Ganesh Chaturthi, *modak* is compulsorily prepared and served as *prasad* and is distributed among all the devotees.

The ancient texts describe and mention about a dessert known as *kundalika* which is now popular as *jalebi*. This explains that sweets have been prevailing in India gloriously from the ancient period.

Description of Various Sweets

Ada Pradaman It is a sweet preparation which is made by cooking pressed rice (also known as *poha* or *chivda*) with jaggery, thin extract of coconut milk and water. The mixture is cooked till it thickens. Then thick coconut extract is added in it and is removed as soon as it boils. Then the dish is garnished with fried coconut flakes, cashew nuts and raisins. It can be served hot or cold.	
Ariselu or Adhirasam or Kajaya It is a sweet dish preparation from Odisha, Andhra Pradesh and Tamil Nadu comprising rice flour, ghee and jaggery as the chief ingredients. In Andhra Pradesh it is referred as Ariselu; in Karnataka as Kajaya, whereas in Tamil Nadu, it is referred as Adhirasam. It is prepared during the festive occasions of Makar Sankranti and Diwali. Its authentic preparation takes about a week. Rice is soaked in water and then sun-dried. It is then ground into fine powder. In order to make it sweet, the jaggery is dissolved and boiled in water and then added in the rice flour. Then it is kept in an earthen ware pot and allowed to ferment for next 3-5 days in sunlight during day time. When batter is ready, small balls of dough is taken and rolled into *puri* shape and then deep-fried till golden brown in colour.	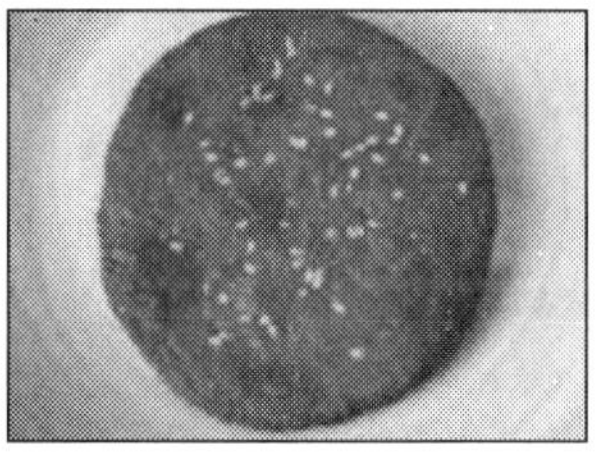
Balu Shahi or Makkhan Wada This is a dessert which is also referred as Makkhan Wada. This is prepared by mixing flour and *ghee* by rubbing them with light hands and then kneading the mixture into a dough with curds and soda bicarbonate. The dough is allowed to rest for about an hour and then after it is shaped into balls and an impression is made in the centre with the help of the thumb. The balls are then fried in *ghee* until golden brown. As soon as they are removed from *ghee*, it is dipped into sugar syrup. The soaked balls absorbs the sugar syrup gradually, and finally they are served garnished with *chandi ka varq*.	
Basundi *Basundi* is sweetened dense milk made by boiling milk on low heat until milk is reduced by half. Thick cream may be added during the boiling process to hasten the thickening process. At the end, a little sugar, cardamom powder, *chironji* (charoli nuts), and saffron are added to it. It is served chilled garnished with slices of almonds and pistachios. It is a dessert from Gujarat and Maharashtra.	
Bibinca This is the multi-layered sweetmeat specialty of Goa. It is prepared by adding extract of coconut milk to flour, sugar and other flavourings. Then from this mixture, pancakes are prepared. The pancakes are layered and are baked before adding the next one over the other. The traditional version has almost 16 layers.	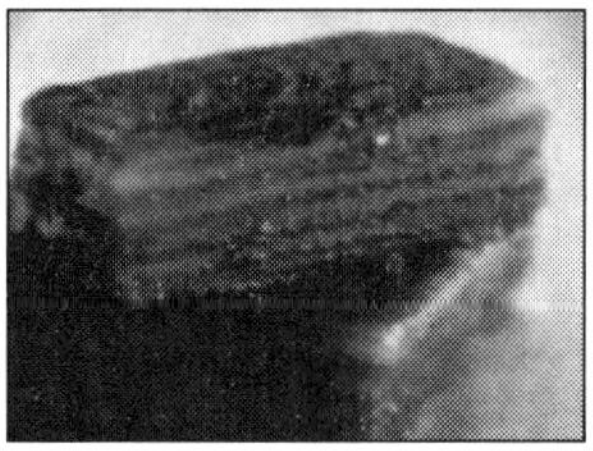

Bolinas

Bolinas are Goan coconut cookies made from grated coconut, sugar, semolina, egg yolks, and butter. All the ingredients are mixed and are baked into small round shapes. It is enjoyed very much with tea as snacks.

Burfi

Burfi is a wide array of sweets which are made with *khoya* as the base and then set into slabs in a greased tray and cut into various shapes like lozenge and square. Plain burfi is made with condensed milk and sugar and cooked until it solidifies. It is flavoured with rose water or cardamom powder and it is customary to garnish it with *chandi ka varq*.

It has many variants, depending upon the flavour and chief ingredient used. The famous variants are: *Kaju Katli* (cashew nut burfi), Besan Burfi (gram flour based), Anjeer Burfi (fig based), Pineapple Burfi (pineapple based), Akhrot Burfi (walnut based), Coconut Burfi (made with grated coconut), Dodha Burfi (wheat flour based), Kesari Burfi (saffron based), Chocolate Burfi (chocolate based), and so on.

Belgrami

It is a sweet preparation of Bihar, which is made from cheese, sugar and *ghee*. It is famous from a small town Udwantnagar, which is situated in between Arrah and Buxar.

Chhena Gaja

It is a sweet delicacy from Odisha. It is prepared by combining *chhena* (cottage cheese) and semolina and kneading it into a dough. Water is then squeezed out from the dough and is dried to a right consistency. It is then molded into rectangular shapes (*gajas*), boiled and then deep fried in oil. The fried *gajas* are then coated with sugar syrup and then served. The ingredients used are same as Rasgulla. It is a fried version of Rasgulla. The Chhena Gaja of Pahala, near Bhubaneshwar is famed all over.

Chhena Poda

Chhena Poda literally means burnt cheese in Odiya language. It represents the cheese dessert of Odisha. It is the only well known Indian dessert whose flavour is preponderantly obtained from caramelization of sugar. It is made by kneading well homemade cottage cheese or *chhena*, sugar, cashew nuts and raisins and then baking a it for a few hours till it attains a brown colour. It is believed that Chhena Poda originated in the Odiya town of Nayagarh in the first half of the twentieth century.

Chikki

This is a traditional sweet made from groundnuts and jaggery. A variety of ingredients can be added to the *chikki* such as puffed rice, sesame and desiccated coconut. Some *chikkis* are made from pistachios, almonds and cashew nuts.

In order to prepare *chikkis*, a hot syrup is made from the jaggery and the nuts are then transferred using a wooden mould and then the *chikkis* are further rolled into 6-8 mm size using a wooden roller. Once cooled and hardened, the *chikkis* are then cut into squares and served. It is prepared especially during the winter season and is liked by all due to its excellent taste and crunchy texture.

Dodol

This is a Goan specialty which depicts Portuguese influence on this delicacy. In order to prepare this dish, rice flour is mixed with fresh coconut milk and cooked on low flame till it gets thick in consistency. Meanwhile, jaggery and other ingredients like dry fruits are added into it and then it is poured into a greased tray and allowed to set. After this, it is cooled and cut into squares and served.

Doodh Pak

Doodh Pak, basically a Gujarati dessert a rice pudding made from milk, rice, saffron and nuts. The milk is slow-boiled to a thickened and sweetened consistency and the dish is garnished with chopped almonds. It is consumed with *puris*.

Double ka Meetha

It is a bread pudding dessert comprising fried bread slices soaked in hot milk infused with spices like saffron and cardamom. It is garnished with slivers or pistachios and almonds. It is typically a Hyderabadi dessert which refers to milk bread, called Double Roti in the local Indian dialect because it swells up to almost twice its original size after baking. This dish is very similar to Shahi Tukda.

Ghevar

Traditionally a Rajasthani sweet of great repute it is associated with the Teej festival. It is disc-shaped, and made from oil, flour and sugar syrup. A thin batter is prepared of all the ingredients with water and then it is poured in a thin stream, into a tall ring that is placed inside the pan containing hot oil. The moisture present in batter evaporates eventually when it is poured in hot oil leaving behind large holes in the resulting flat disc-like structure with raised edges. This disc shaped item is called *ghevar* and is removed on a wired rack. It is then soaked in sugar syrup and garnished accordingly.

There are many varieties of *ghevar*, including Plain Ghevar, Paneer Ghevar, Mawa Ghevar, and Malai Ghevar.

Gulab Jamun

It won't be an overstatement to that Gulab Jamun is the most popular dessert of India. It is a deep-fried dumpling made of *khoya* and refined flour, dipped in rose-saffron flavoured sugar syrup. The name Gulab Jamun simply translates to rose berries.

This dessert also has few variations and is stuffed with chopped nuts, raisins, *khoya* and cardamom powder for variety.

Kala Jamun: It is the most popular version of Gulab Jamun. The dumplings here are fried till a deep dark colour is achieved. It is allowed to absorb the sugar syrup but is not served with sugar syrup like Gulab Jamun.

Zauq-e-Shahi: This variance of Gulab Jamun is from Awadh and it is made into marble size and served with *rabri*, pistachios and saffron on it.

Halwa

Halwa refers to various kinds of dense, sweet confection prepared from wide variation of ingredients. The *halwas* in India have a huge spectrum of variations and are distinguished by the region it belongs to and the ingredients from which they are prepared.

Gajar ka Halwa: A delectable sweet dessert pudding this is this is chiefly associated with the state of Punjab. It is made by cooking bright red grated carrot with a particular quantity of milk and sugar with continuous stirring. It is served with a garnish of cashew nuts, raisins, almonds and pistachios. The nuts and other items used are first sautéd in ghee to add richness to the *halwa*. Then *khoya* is added in the end to the *halwa* and then it is served hot. As carrot is easily and readily available in winters, it is prepared during the winter season only.

Gajrela is a dish very similar to Gajar ka Halwa and the ingredients of both are the same. The ingredients used to make Gajrela are full shredded carrots, cream milk, sugar, cardamom powder, saffron, *ghee* and chopped almonds and pistachio used for the garnish. The sweet is available in small rectangular pieces. It is also referred as Gajar ke Halwe ki Burfi.

Moong Dal Halwa: This resplendent delicacy is time consuming, but the end result is splendid in its taste and is worth the effort to prepare it. It is a preparation of *dhuli moong dal*, in which the *dal* is soaked in water and then ground into paste known as *peethi*. The *peethi* is then fried in ghee until golden brown. Milk and sugar are added later on and *halwa* is allowed to be cooked till the ghee floats on top. The *halwa* is garnished with slivers of nuts and is served hot.

Sooji ka Halwa: This is the most prepared *halwa* in households throughout India. It is made by frying semolina in *desi* ghee and then adding sugar syrup in it and cooking it till it thickens. It is easy to prepare and gets prepared quickly as compared to other *halwas*. It is served garnished with desiccated coconut and dry fruits.

There are other halwas like: *Aate ka Halwa* (made of wheat flour), *Lauki ka Halwa* (made of white pumpkin), *Matar ka Halwa* (made of green peas) and so on.

Imarti

Imarti is also referred as Jhangri. This noteworthy dish is made by deep-frying *urad* flour batter in a kind of circular flower shape, and then soaked in sugar syrup. This dessert is of Mughal origin and was brought to fame by them. Generally, it is consumed with *rabri*. The district of Jaunpur in Uttar Pradesh is renowned for its scrumptious *imartis* throughout.

Jalebi

It is assumed to be a dessert from ancient India and has also found references in vedic texts under the name *kundalika*. It is prepared by making a batter of flour, water, curds and baking powder. This batter is allowed to ferment overnight and then it is poured in a circular motion through a thick cloth called *ratna*, which has a hole in centre, into the hot oil in Jalebi Kadhai. The batter is poured in circles to form the particular Jalebi shape. Once it is fried till crisp, it is dipped into sugar syrup flavoured with saffron. It is served hot with *rabri* or even with fresh curds.

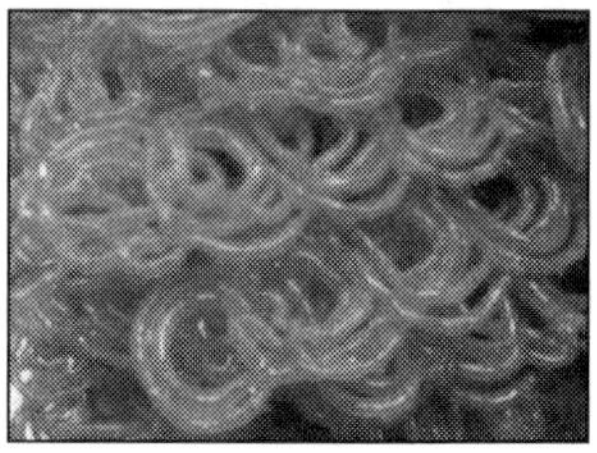

Kakara

This is a lovely dessert of Odisha. It is prepared from the dough of rice flour, refined flour, and jaggery. The dough is then stuffed with a mixture of grated coconut, black pepper and jaggery and shaped into dumplings. The dumplings are then deep-fried until crisp.

Kalakand

It is one of the popular desserts of North India, made by reducing milk on a slow flame and then adding a drop of tartaric acid in it to let it curdle partially. It attains a granular texture and then sugar is added and set into slabs and cut into square shapes, when cooled.

It is also called Milk Cake, if it is cooked for a longer period of time to have a caramelized texture.

Kalathappam

Kalathappam is basically a sweet rice cake. The rice is soaked and then ground into a fine powdered form. It is then added with jaggery and cooked on a slow flame from the bottom, and burning charcoals kept on top of the lid as well. By this technique, the desserts get baked and are served hot. It can also be baked in an oven.

Karanji or Gujiya

Karanji is a semicircular shaped stuffed sweet dessert and is also eaten as a snack. The dough for Karanji is made using refined flour, *desi ghee,* and water. Then a stuffing is prepared by roasting semolina, coconut, jaggery, and raisins until brown. *Khoya* can also be added in the filling, according to the taste preference. Then a small ball of the dough is rolled in circular shape and the filling is placed in the centre. It is then folded into a half-moon shapes and the sides are pressed to give it a design. In the market, the metallic or plastic moulds are also available to give the desired shape with convenience while preparing *gujiyas*. The *gujiyas* prepared are then deep fried in oil on medium flame till golden brown in colour. This dish is prepared during the festive occasions of Holi and Diwali in almost all households.

Several regional cuisines in India feature dishes similar to Gujiya, but with different fillings.

Gujiyas are called *Pedukiya* in Bihar. *Pedukiyas* are very popular in Bihar and are savoured by everyone. There are two types of Pedukiya made in Bihar – one with *suji/rawa* (semolina) and other with *khoya*. In *Suji Pedukiya* – the *suji* is roasted in ghee with sugar, cashew nut, grated coconut, cardamom, raisins and other nuts and then deep fried in ghee. In *Khoya Pedukiya* – pure *khoya* is mixed with nuts and sugar and then deep fried.

Karanji (Marathi) in Maharashtra, *Ghughra* (Gujarati) in Gujarat, *Karachika* (Tamil) in Tamil Nadu *Karjikayi* (Kannada and Telugu) in Andhra Pradesh and Karnataka are all fried sweet dumplings and are made of wheat flour and stuffed with dry or moist coconut delicacies. In Goa, Goan Hindus prepare it on the occasion of Ganesh Chaturthi and call it Nevris.

Khaja

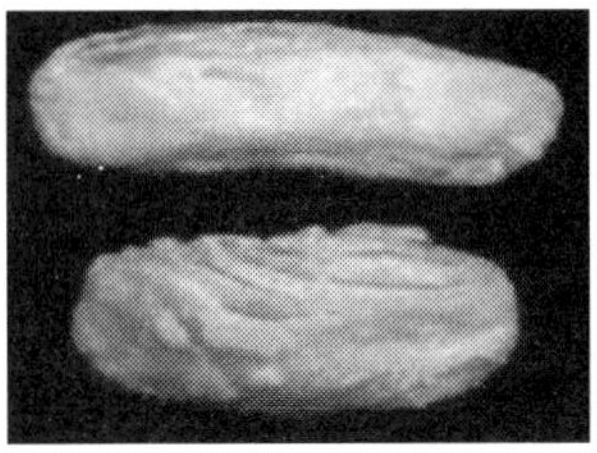

This is a splendid dessert of Bihar made by stuffing *khoya* in the dough of wheat flour and then deep frying it till crisp. After deep frying, the fried crescent shaped roll is soaked in sugar syrup known as *pak*, till it absorbs the syrup. Khaja is usually dry from outside and full of sugar syrup from inside and is juicy.

In South India, a similar sweet is known as Badushahi is prepared.

When Khaja is stuffed with dried fruits, it is known as *Chandrakala* (half round) or *Suryakala* (full round).

Kheer

Kheer is unarguably the most prepared Indian dessert at homes by housewives and all. In simple terms, it is rice boiled and cooked in sweetened milk and finally garnished with nuts.

In order to prepare this dessert, rice (about one-twelfth the quantity of milk) is sautéd in *desi ghee* for a short while and then is added with milk and boiled. After this it is added with sugar and cooked to a right consistency and degree. Finally, it is garnished with nuts and served.

Kesari Kheer: When the *kheer* is flavoured with saffron, it is called Kesari Kheer.

Kheer Kadam

This is a unique, delicious and delectable dessert from Bengal. Rasgulla is a squeezed and the sugar syrup is removed from it and then the Rasgulla balls are mixed and cooked. In a separate pan, *khoya* and sugar and mixed and cooked for 8-10 minutes. Small balls are made from this cooked mixture and then flattened. The squeezed Rasgulla is kept on it and *khoya*-sugar mixture is folded in such a way that the Rasgulla gets stuffed in it.

Kheersagar

It is a dish from Odisha. Kheersagar literally means 'ocean of milk'. It comprises small *chhena* cheese balls soaked in sweetened and condensed milk. The milk used in this delicacy is flavoured with saffron and cardamom. This dish is served at room temperature or chilled. This delicacy holds a place of high repute in the culinary world of sweets in Odisha.

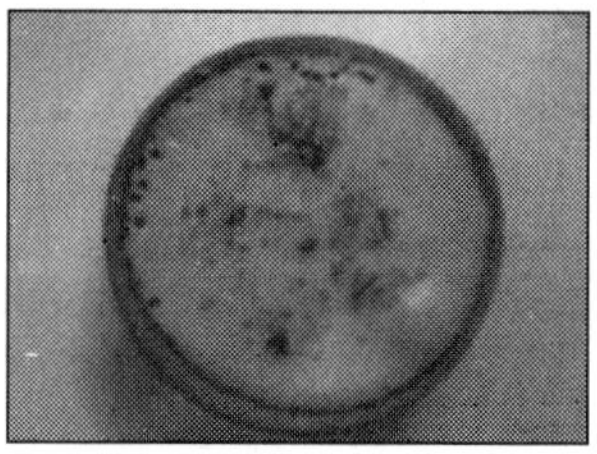

Kozhukkattai or Kozhukatta or Modak

It is a sweet dumpling preparation prepared in many regions of India, with varied names and slight variations in recipes. Rice flour is kneaded into dough by adding hot water and then this dough is rolled and stuffed with a concoction of jaggery, coconut and dry fruits. It is shaped like a *potli* and is steamed. This special dish attached with religious sentiments is offered to Lord Ganesha during the festive occasion of Ganesh Chaturthi in Maharashtra.

In Tamil Nadu and in Kerala, this same dish is prepared by inserting into young palm leaves and is known as Thennai Kozhakattai.

Manda Pitha is a similar preparation of Odisha.

Laddu or Laddoo

Laddu is a very popular ball-shaped sweet and undoubtedly the most loved dessert of India. Laddu is derived from the Sanskrit word *ladduka* or *lattika,* meaning a small ball. It is prepared using different flours and sugar. It is mostly served on festive occasions and religious occasions as well. It is believed that this sweet delicacy originated from the Mithilanchal region of Bihar, during the tenure of Chandragupta Maurya.

Besan ke Laddu: It is prepared by frying gram flour in *ghee* and adding it with powdered sugar and shaping it into round balls of Besan ke Laddu.

Motichoor ke Laddu: This *laddu* is very popular in northern India and especially in the states like Rajasthan and Madhya Pradesh. It is prepared by dropping the batter of gram flour into hot *ghee* through a spoon having small perforations. The fried dropped balls are then removed and immersed in sugar syrup flavoured with saffron. When the fried balls are added to the warm sugar syrup, they absorb the sugar syrup and swell accordingly. All these fried soaked balls are slightly mashed and then shaped into rounds using the palm and served as Motichoor ke Ladoo. It is garnished with *chandi ka varq*.

Gond ka Laddu: It is prepared by frying small pieces of *gond* in oil at low flame till it is fried properly. After this allow it to cool and crush it to powder form and keep aside. Fry the wheat flour in remaining oil till it gets lightly coloured. Mix this fried wheat with fried gond. Sugar syrup of thick consistency is prepared and mixed with both fried item along with cut dried fruits in it. Then small balls are portioned out of it and shaped like *laddus*. Thus, Gond ke Laddu is prepared. It is especially consumed during the winter season and is very nutritious and energy providing.

Pinni: It is a *laddu* made by roasting whole wheat flour with clarified butter. Dry fruits are crushed and added with roasted flour and then shaped into *laddus*.

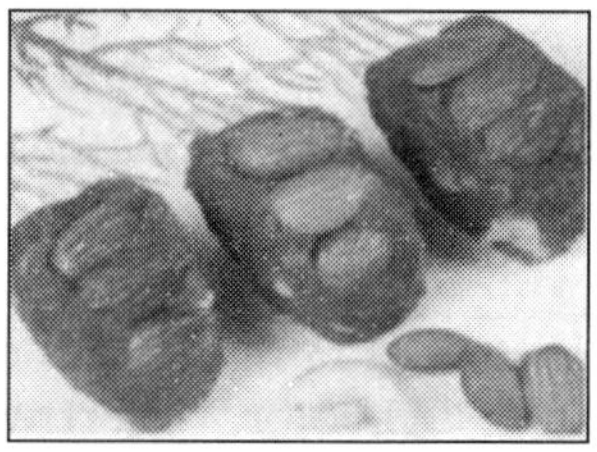

Lady Kenny

This sweet has a short story attached to it. The wife of former Viceroy of India, Lady Canning requested the sweet makers of Kolkata to make *gulab jamun* of North India. But as in North, they use *khoya* in its preparation, the sweet makers in Kolkata made the same dish with *chhena* for Lady Canning and she appreciated it a lot. Hence, this item got named after her and has become famous as Lady Kenny.

Desserts of varying sizes and shapes are prepared using the same dough and are named differently, like *Pantua, Lengcha,* and *Chennar Jalepi*.

Laganu Custard

This is a special dish of the Parsi community and a must item in the Parsi wedding menu. Milk is boiled and reduced to half. Then it is added with powdered nutmeg for flavouring and when the mixture is cool enough, eggs are beaten in it and it is baked in a oven set to moderate temperature, until its top is golden brown in colour and the custard is firm.

Lavang Latika

This is a very special sweet made across Uttar Pradesh, Bihar and Bengal as well. The dough is prepared from flour, ghee, sugar and salt by lightly mixing it with finger tips till it attains crumbly texture and then kneading it with water to form a dough. The dough is allowed to rest and meanwhile a stuffing is prepared of *khoya*, cardamom powder, and desiccated coconut, and all are mixed together properly. The dough is divided into small balls and then these are rolled and the stuffing is laid in the centre and then it is covered with rest of the rolled dough ball circumference by a folding action. Then a clove is inserted in the centre of folded dough to lock the fold and each piece is deep-fried properly and then dipped in sugar syrup to let it coat with sugar syrup and get sweetened.

Malpua

It is a specialty of Rajasthani cuisine and is made using flour, semolina, milk and sugar. A thick batter is prepared of flour, semolina and milk and then it is dropped like a pancake in hot *ghee* and fried till crisp. The fried pancakes are then soaked in hot sugar syrup flavoured with saffron. It is served usually with *rabri* and at many places it is had with ice cream also nowadays.

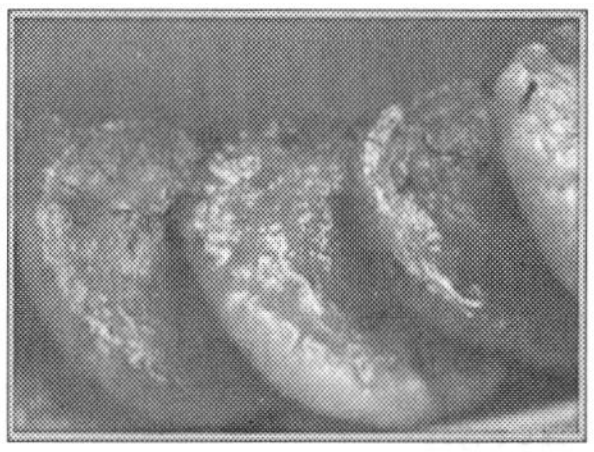

Misti Doi

It is a sweet delicacy of Bengal eaten with high zeal. Misti Doi simply means 'sweet curds'. It is prepared like a regular curds with sweet addition of palm jaggery. Palm jaggery used in it assigns this dish a unique taste and colour.

Muttamala

This is an egg-based nest shaped dessert from Kerala. The egg yolks are separated from the egg whites and are whisked properly and then passed through a muslin cloth. Sugar syrup is prepared and clarified using egg whites. The whisked egg yolk is then poured on to hot sugar syrup in hot rotary motion to form rings of egg yolks in hot syrup. Egg strings are then removed from the syrup taking care not to break the rings of egg yolk, and then they are kept on top of a wire rack to drain off excess sugar syrup.

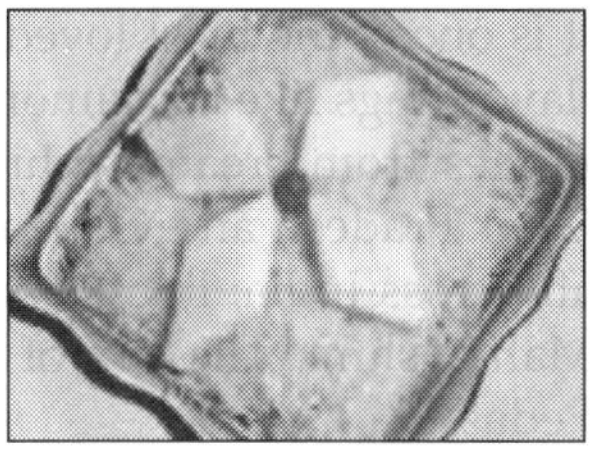

Mysore Pak

Mysore Pak is a remarkable sweet delicacy of Mysore, Karnataka. It is made with bounteous amounts of *ghee*, sugar and gram flour. *Pak* means sugar syrup in Karnataka. According to fable, the birth of Mysore Pak took place in the kitchens of the Mysore Palace by a palace cook named Kakasura Madappa out of the above mentioned ingredients. The cook at the Mysore Palace kitchen simply made a concoction of *besan*, ghee and sugar and cooked it to a right degree. The sweet prepared delighted the royalties so much that it transformed into *Royal Sweet*. When Madappa was asked its name, he apparently didn't have its name, and simply called it Mysore Pak, a delicacy from the Mysore Palace.

Parwal ki Mithai

This is a sweet made by stuffing *parwal* (pointed gourds) with the mixture of dry fruits and *khoya* flavoured with cardamom powder. First, the *parwal* is scooped and boiled in water and then in sugar syrup till soft and done. Then it is drained and stuffed with filling and served cold garnished with *chandi ka varq*.

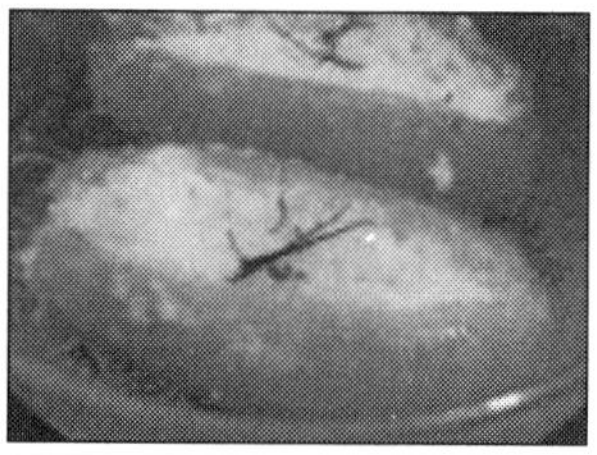

Patishapta

It is a pancake made of refined flour or rice flour, sugar and milk with a stuffing made of sweet concoction of grated coconut, sugar or jaggery and green cardamom powder. The pancakes are then rolled with the filling inside and are also garnished with the same filling. It is a typical popular Bengali cuisine.

Payasam

The word *payasam* derives from *peeyusham* meaning nectar or ambrosia. *Payasam* is the south Indian version of North Indian *Kheer*.

It has many variations like:

Semiya Payasam: made with vermicelli and milk.

Paruppu Payasam: made with *chana dal* paste, jaggery and milk.

Ada Payasam: made with rice flour paste, jaggery and milk.

Payesh

Payesh is a Bengali version of North Indian *Kheer*. It is short grain rice cooked with milk sweetened with jaggery. It is served garnished with cashew nuts and raisins.

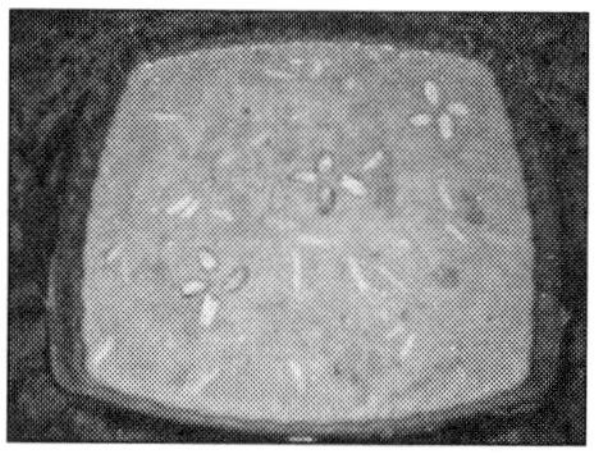

Pedha or Peda

It is one of the most loved sweets, essentially prepared with *khoya*, sugar and traditional flavourings like cardamom seeds, pistachio nuts and saffron. The colour of this dessert ranges from creamy white to caramel. It is considered that this sweet originated in Uttar Pradesh and Gujarat simultaneously. There are many variants of Peda available all across India; like Dharwad Pedha in Karnataka and Satari Kandi Peda in Western Maharashtra. The city of Mathura in Uttar Pradesh is famed all over for its delicious Pedas.

It is referred as Chenna Murki in Odisha.

Petha

It is a splendid sweet delicacy made using ash gourd (also known as winter melon) and sugar. It is a semi-transparent soft candy, usually rectangular or cylindrical in shape.

It is available in a wide array of taste like Kesari Petha (saffron flavoured), Angoori Petha (citrus fruit flavoured), Chocolate Petha (chocolate flavoured), Paan Petha (*paan* and *gulkand* flavoured), Strawberry Petha (strawberry flavoured) and so on.

One shop in Agra, Uttar Pradesh named Panchi Petha is acknowledged the best shop for this sweet delicacy.

Phirnee

It is an impeccable creamy dessert of Punjab made essentially with rice flour and milk. The milk is boiled and reduced along with sugar and a coarse paste of soaked rice is added to the milk. It is allowed to cook till it thickens. It is mildly flavoured with green cardamom powder or rose water and is served in an earthenware bowl known as *sakora*, which absorbs the extra moisture from Phirnee and makes it firm. The earthenware dish lends a typical and unique aroma to the dish, which makes it genuinely special. It is served chilled.

In Kashmir, when this dessert is made with semolina instead of rice, it is known as Kong Phiren.

Poothareku

It is a wafer-like sweet dish of Andhra Pradesh and is made by two words 'pootha' meaning coating and 'reku' meaning 'sheet' in Telugu, and it is also referred as 'paper sheets' as it gives the appearance of folded paper. Pootharekulu is the plural term of the same dish. It is believed to have been invented by the Brahmin families of the Rajamundry region.

It is prepared with rice starch/finely ground soaked black gram (*minapappu*), powdered sugar and ghee. There are two versions of this sweet – one using powdered sugar and the other one using jaggery. This sweet is prepared by making wrappers from rice flour, and filled with sugar/jaggery inside them and then folding them.

The preparation of this sweet demands tremendous labour and hence is taken care by the economically weaker sections of people.

Qubani ka Meetha

It is a Hyderabadi dish which is essentially made up of apricot. *Qubani* is an Urdu word for apricot. It is made by stewing apricots in sugar syrup and then finally flavouring it with honey.

Rabdi

The milk in this dish is boiled on a slow flame for a long period of time until it becomes thick and changes its colour to pinkish. This simple condensed milk is called Rabdi. It is added with sugar and nuts to give it a nice flavour. It is the fundamental ingredient in certain preparations like Rasmalai, Rasabali, Chhena Kheer, and so on. It is usually served chilled.

Rasabali

This sweet luscious delicacy comprises deep-fried flattened reddish brown patties of *chhena*, soaked in cardamom flavoured sweetened thick milk. The *chhena* balls are flattened so that it absorbs more milk promptly.

It originated from Kendrapara, Odisha and is offered to the God as a part of Chappan Bhog.

Rasgulla

It is a dish which originated in Odisha but attained popularity in Bengal. It is a cheese-based, syrupy dessert which is made from ball-shaped dumplings of *chhena* and semolina dough, cooked in light sugar syrup. The syrup penetrates into the dumplings. It is made in various sizes and is flavoured differently.

Some variants are:

Raj Bhog: This is a larger version of Rasgulla with a diameter of about 3-4 inches.

Kamala Bhog: This large Rasugulla is orange flavoured and is yellow coloured.

Malai Chop: It comprises prepared *chhena* sandwiched with a layer of sweetened cream.

Ras Malai

Ras Malai is simply a combination of two words *ras* meaning juice and *malai* meaning cream. It is a rich *chhena* cake without crust and is very similar to Rasgulla. It is basically sugary white, cream or yellow coloured (or flattened) balls of *paneer* poached in syrup until cooked and then soaked in the *malai* flavoured with saffron and green cardamom. It is garnished with chopped pieces of pistachios and served chilled. It is also believed that this noteworthy delicacy has originated in Odisha.

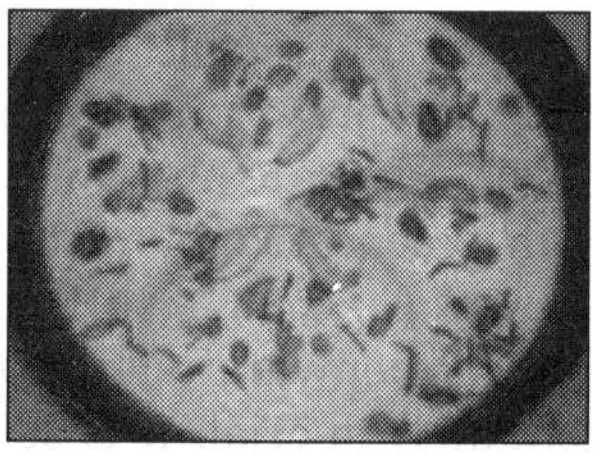

Sandesh

It is a Bengali dessert, which is made using *chhena* or *paneer* kneaded with fine ground sugar or molasses. Profoundly honoured for its excellence of delicate making, method and widely applauded by the food connoisseurs, this portrays sweet making in its finest form.

Sandesh comes in two basic varieties, Norom Pak (the softer version) and Koda Pak (the harder version). The softer version although considered better, is highly fragile. The harder version is robust and often easier for storage. Certain variations of Sandesh can be prepared by changing the flavour like Noleen Gurher Sandesh (a Sandesh made from Noleen Gurh or molasses from dates) or simply Nolen Sandesh.

The elementary version of Sandesh is Kanchagolla, which is prepared by tossing the *chhena* lightly with sugar over low heat and this version is slightly granular in texture. It is prepared by cooking fresh curds, milk and condensed milk together. The boiling curds along with milk results in a curdsled texture. The mixture is cooked till sticky and then shaped into round dumplings.

The more complex versions of Sandesh calls for *chenna* which are shaped into balls, dried and pressed, flavoured with essence of fruits. At times, the *chhena* balls are filled with syrup and mingled with coconut or *kheer* and then moulded into a wide variety of shapes.

Shahi Tukda

Shahi means 'royal' and *tukda* means 'piece', thus it translates into 'royal piece'. It is an illustrious dessert from the Awadh region. The crust of bread is removed and then it is deep-fried in ghee, until golden brown in colour. This fried bread piece is soaked in *rabri* (thickened milk) flavoured with saffron. It is served chilled, garnished with slivers of pistachios.

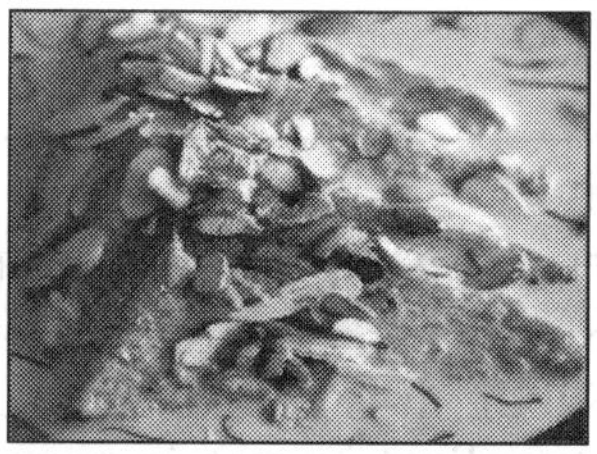

Sheer Khurma

Sheer Khurma is Mughal delicacy from the Bohra community and it literally means 'milk with dates' in Urdu. It is a sweet vermicelli pudding prepared with dried dates and milk. It is added with nuts, saffron and rose water and garnished with *chandi ka varq*. It is a special dish of the Muslims.

Soan Papdi or Patisa

This famous square shaped dessert has a crisp and flaky texture, and is served either in whole pieces or in flakes. The chief ingredients are sugar, gram flour, ghee, milk, and cardamom. The gram flour is roasted with clarified butter until fragrant and then the sugar syrup is poured and stirred until thin strands are formed. It is then flavoured with green cardamom powder, melon seeds, slivers of pistachio, and so on.

It is called Soan Papdi in Uttar Pradesh and Patisa in Jammu. Many are of the belief that Patisa is softer and darker in colour whereas Soan Papdi is hard, fibrous and flaky.

This dessert is believed to have originated in a small locality called Najibabad, situated in Bijnor district, Uttar Pradesh.

Sohan Halwa

This is a traditional Persian sweet dish very popular in India. It is made by boiling a concoction of water, sugar, milk, and corn flour until it becomes solid. Ghee is used to prevent it from sticking to the pan. Saffron is added to flavour it. Nuts are also added in this preparation, which bestows it a rich feature.

Thekua

It is a dessert from Bihar. The ingredients like whole wheat flour, jaggery, ghee, cardamom powder and so on are mixed together and then balls of this mixture are shaped in a mould (*sancha*) and deep fried in ghee, till done and turns reddish brown. These are then cooled and served. It can also be stored for a long period of time.

Unni Appam

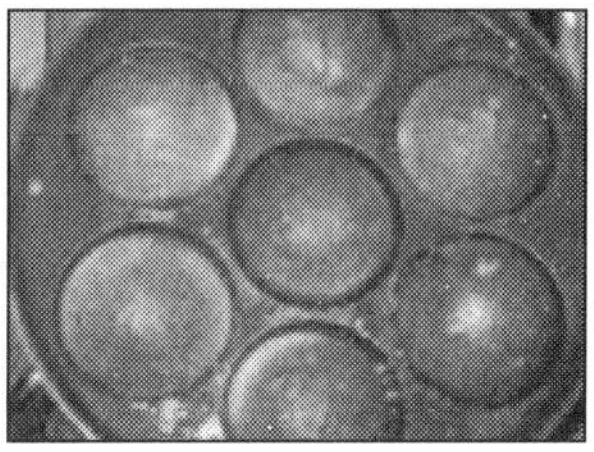

In Malayalam, *unni* means 'small' and *appam* means 'rice cake'. It is small round-shaped rice cake made from a batter of rice, jaggery, banana, roasted coconut pieces, roasted sesame seeds, ghee and cardamom powder, fried in oil. It is very popularly consumed in Kerala.

Culinary Trivia: Sugar Syrup

Sugar syrup is used in a lot of Indian sweets and desserts in varying consistencies. Terms like one- or two-thread consistency are often used in connection with this syrup and it can be confusing. This simple yet very effective technique is used, to tell when the syrup is ready for a particular dessert. Sugar is taken double the quantity of water and is boiled on medium flame to form sugar syrup. The scum is removed with a metal sieve.

The consistency of syrup is checked by dipping a wooden spatula in the syrup and lifting it out. Then it is allowed to cool and the syrup is torched with clean forefinger and then the thumb and forefinger are pressed together and pull apart gently. The syrup is kept boiling gently till right consistency for the recipe is reached. Stages progress fairly quickly after a point, so one needs to check frequently.

Half-thread consistency is reached when a single thread is formed and breaks immediately when the forefinger and thumb are pulled apart gently.

One-thread consistency is reached when a single thread is formed (and does not break) when the forefinger and thumb are pulled apart gently.

Two-thread consistency is reached when two threads are formed (and do not break) when the forefinger and thumb are pulled apart gently. This stage is also called the soft ball stage, when a drop of syrup of this consistency is dropped into a bowl of cold water, it forms a soft ball.

Three-thread consistency is when three threads are formed (and do not break) when the forefinger and thumb are pulled apart gently. This stage is also called the hard ball stage, when a drop of syrup of this consistency is dropped into a bowl of cold water, it forms a hard ball.

35 Beverages

> "Food, love, career and mothers; the four major guilt groups." – Cathy Guisewite

Beverages are an essential and inseparable component of Indian cuisine as well as human life. Beverages of varied sorts are consumed by a human being since early days in the form of fruit juices, squashes, milk and milk-based drinks, tea, coffee, and so on.

In the period of prehistoric ancient times, milk was regarded a beverage of immense repute and honour. But the milk-based product buttermilk was even more common than milk and it was of two kinds: one was *lassi* and other was *chhach*.

Juices of sweet fruits like mango, citrus, grape, date, banana, apricot, jackfruit, pomegranate and *ber* were termed as *panaka*. Three such fruit juices when blended with honey and water which resulted in *panchamrutha* of high reverence, whereas a *panaka* (fruit juice of sweet fruits) thickened by boiling down yielded *yasa* and sour fruit juices reduced over heat was termed as *savhava*.

In southern India, beverages were primarily made up of two chief ingredients, tamarind and *nellikai* (*amla*). The water of tender coconut was undoubtedly the thirst-quencher since long in the southern region. An impeccable blend of coconut water, sugarcane juice and the sweet sap of the *palmyra* palm yielded *munnir*. A popular beverage for morning here was the water from boiled rice and which was soured overnight by fermentation to produce *kanji* or *kanjika*, and it was usually consumed salted and spiced.

When it comes to the natural sweet beverage then sugarcane juice, mostly drunk spiced with ginger, tops the list of popularity.

The Muslim populace brought with them the incredibly soothing sweet *sherbets*, which were often coloured and flavoured with essences like rose, *kevda* (screw pine), and certain herbs. It is recorded that in 13th and 14th centuries, in the court of Delhi Sultanate, a barley based drink popularly called *fuqqa* was served.

Few beverages have gained ritual importance and hence have had a position of great veneration. *Panchagavya* is a flux of five products all obtained from the cow – its milk, curds, ghee, urine and dung, which were considered supreme purging materials. It was regarded so sacred that only Brahmins could use it and others were forbidden.

Madhuparka was a propitious ritual beverage which comprises ghee, curds, milk, honey and sugar. It was significant as it was offered to an individual when he was welcomed as a guest to one's home, given to women after five months of pregnancy, and placed at birth on the lips of the first born son, and was traditionally offered to a student when he left home for a long apprenticeship with his teacher/*guru*.

India is a land of varied climates and hence it experiences summer and winter in varied parts of it own land at the same time. Hence, the people in India require multitudinous choices to pacify their thirst appropriately, according to the weather conditions. In scorching summer they go for some sort of frosty fruit juices and *sherbets* and in the chilling winter they opt for steaming tea or coffee.

Different regions in the country serve various drinks made with an eclectic assortment of ingredients including local spices, flavours and herbs. These beverages have added a superior value to the Indian cuisine and also become an integral part of it.

Role of beverages

All beverages have been conferred with some basic qualities and specific enhanced characteristics. This is why people prefer each beverage for a particular time, place, occasion or festival. It plays a crucial role in Indian cuisine and they are given below.

- It is a thirst quencher.
- It is valued as a social drink for various parties.
- It has got some nutritional value.
- It has some medicinal values attached to it.
- It also complements certain dishes.

Classification of Beverages

Beverages are broadly classified into two types: Non-alcoholic beverages and alcoholic beverages.

Non-alcoholic beverages can further be classified into 3 segments:

- Nourishing: Milk, juices, nutritional supplements drink, and so on.
- Refreshing: Syrups, squashes, aerated water, *sherbets*, and so on.
- Stimulating: Tea, coffee, chocolate beverages and so on.

Description of Various Beverages

Aam ka Panna Aam ka Panna is a renowned North Indian beverage, made from green raw mangoes, sugar and assortments of spices. It is a great thirst quencher as well as a tasty beverage and helps to fight the scorching heat waves prevalent in North India during summers. It has been an effective remedy for heat exhaustion and heat stroke.	
Bael ka Ras It is a nutritious drink made from ripe fruit of *bael*. It is enjoyed most during summer. It acts as an antidote for sun stroke and is also beneficial in stomach problems.	
Bhaang It is a famed beverage made from the leaves and flowers (buds) of the female cannabis plant, consumed in India. This drink is also renowned for its toxic feature. It is mostly consumed during festivals of Holi and Mahashivratri. Bhang is also available in the form of Bhang Goli, which is freshly prepared from ground cannabis and water. It is not considered as a drug but is traditionally regarded as a sleeping aid and appetizer. Bhang Ki Thandai also known as Sardai is a drink popular in many parts of the subcontinent which is made by mixing *bhang* with *thandai*, a cold beverage prepared with almonds, spices (mainly black pepper), milk and sugar. Bhang Lassi is a preparation of powdered green *bhang* mixed with curds and whey put in a village blender (a hand blending operation is carried out till the butter rises). It is regarded as tasty and greatly refreshing, with one or two large glasses having little tipping effect.	
Thandai It is a very refreshing cold drink made with a motley of ingredients like almonds, fennel seeds, melon seeds, rose petals, pepper, vetiver seeds, saffron, milk, green cardamom and sugar. It is prepared during the festive occasions of Mahashivratri and Holi and consumed in large quantity. Thandai has another similar version with almost similar ingredients and it is referred to as *Mishrambu*.	

Chaach or Mattha

Chaach means buttermilk. It is the residue liquid byproduct obtained from making butter. It can also be prepared using pure yogurt or curds and then blending it with water. It is then added with salt, roasted cumin powder for added flavour and taste. It is available in various flavours like rose flavour or some spice flavour and named Masala Chaach.

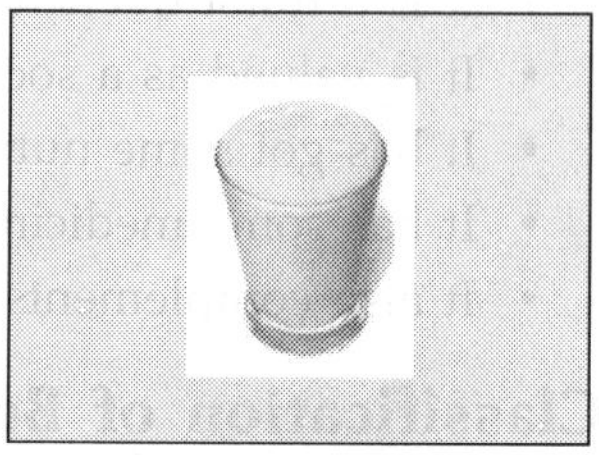

Lassi

It is a very popular and traditional, yogurt-based drink. It is prepared by blending yogurt, water, spices and sometimes fruit. It is a savoury drink, sometimes flavoured with roasted cumin powder, but can be made sweet as well. Sweet Lassi, however, contains sugar or fruits, instead of spices. Sweet Lassi is a form of *lassi* flavoured with sugar, rosewater and /or lemon, strawberry or other fruit juices. Makkhaniya Lassi is simply a *lassi* with lumps of butter in it (*makkhan* is Hindi word for butter). It is usually creamy like milkshake. Lassis are enjoyed chilled as hot-weather refreshment, mostly taken with lunch.

Lassi is served in huge metal glasses in Punjab. The *lassi* of Benaras (Varanasi) are poles apart from the refreshing *lassi* of Punjab. Here, the thick and sweetened *lassi* is topped with *malai* and a generous blob of *rabdi* over it. It is served in *kulhads* (earthenware cups), which impart it a robust flavour.

Tea

Tea is an aromatic beverage prepared from the cured leaves of the shrub *Camellia sinensis* by infusing them with either with hot water or boiling water. It is considered to be the most consumed beverage after water. Many versions of tea are preferred in India like Tulsi Tea, Ginger Tea, Cardamom Tea, Herbal Tea (tisanes), Green Tea, Flavoured Tea, Iced Tea, and so on.

Coffee

Coffee is a flavourful beverage prepared from the beans of *Coffea canephora*, made after processing, roasting and brewing in hot water. This beverage is highly rejuvenating and has addictive properties. It is preferred most in South India. It also has many variations like Cappuccino, Café latte, Café Mocha, Espresso, Ristretto, Macchiato, Affogato, and so on.

Jaljeera

Jaljeera is very popular in North India. In Hindi, *jal* means water and *jeera* means cumin. It is sometimes served as an appetizer, as it is intended to stimulate the taste buds.

Jaljeera powder generally consists of cumin, ginger, black pepper, mint, black salt, and chilli or hot pepper powder.

The cumin is a medicinal ingredient which aids digestion. The mint has a cooling effect. The black salt or rock salt acts as a digestive.

Jaljeera is believed to have cooling properties, against the temperature of the region. It is generally served with appetizers before a meal, but is also drunk between meals. Some versions do not involve any added sugar and few versions are served with *boondi* floating on it.

Kanji

Kanji is a fermented drink made in India in the festival of Holi. Kanji is made with water, carrots, beetroot, and asafeotida and mustard seeds. It may be served with *boondi* sprinkled on top. During Holi, Kanji is often added to *urad dal* dumplings or *vada;* the latter is then called Kanji Vada. It also aids to relieve problems related to stomach and digestion.

Shikanjvi

Shikanjvi is a type of traditional limeade or lemonade from North India, especially prevalent in Punjab, Himachal Pradesh, Jammu and Kashmir, Uttar Pradesh, Rajasthan, Gujarat, Maharashtra.

Alternative names include Shikanji, Shikanjbi and Shikanjbeen. While the base ingredients include lemon or lime juice, ginger juice, ice and water, Shikanjvi often contains other ingredients such as salt and cumin. It is also known as Nimbu Pani.

Ganne ka Ras

It is sugar cane juice obtained from pressed and crushed sugarcane. The juice is obtained by crushing peeled sugarcane in a mill, which can be a hand cranked machine or electrical. It is served chilled with black salt, mint leaves, roasted cumin seeds, lime juice and crushed ice. It is one of the most widely consumed drinks in India, especially in the northern states of Punjab, Haryana, Himachal Pradesh, Rajasthan, and Uttar Pradesh.

Zutho

It is a fermented drink obtained from rice and is very popular among all Naga tribes in Nagaland. It is traditionally prepared by allowing rice starch solutions to ferment and is recognized for its fruity flavour. This home-made drink has a white slurry-like appearance.

Chuak

It is the traditional rice-beer from Tripura, which is made by fermenting rice in water. It is usually drunk on social occasions of any Tripuri ceremony as a ritual. Chuak is offered to village elders on any occasion or celebration in a traditional Tripuri family.

Feni

Feni is a spirit produced solely in Goa. It is available in two forms, Cashew Feni and Coconut Feni, depending on the original ingredient. Feni is classified as 'country liquor', and is therefore not allowed to be sold outside the state of Goa. The small batch distilled Feni has a fundamental effect on its final character, still retaining some of the delicate aromas, chemical consitituent and flavour elements of the juice from which it was produced. As a thumb rule, the aroma is indicative of a carefully crafted Feni. It is generally accepted that Coconut Feni was produced before and then followed to adapt the same procedure for distilling the exotic cashew fruit. Commercially packaged Feni has 42.8% alcohol.

Sharbat or Sherbet

Sharbat is a popular West and South Asian drink. It is prepared from fruits or flower petals. It is sweet and served chilled. It can be served in a concentrated form and taken with a spoon or diluted with water to create the drink.

Popular *sharbats* are made of one or more of the following: rose, sandalwood, *bael*, *gurhal* flower (hibiscus), lemon, orange, mango, pineapple, *litchi*, *jamoon*, and so on.

It is derived from Persian word *sharbat* and Turkish word *sherbet*, which in turn is derived from Arabic word *sharba* meaning a drink. Historically, it was a cool effervescent or iced fruit soft drink

Kokum Sherbet

Kokam is essentially a deep purple colour fruit. Kokam gives tangy flavour and is used as spice in lot of Indian Cuisine especially in Goan and Malvan cuisine. Kokam Sherbet is one of the most refreshing drinks prepared from the *kokam* fruit. It is good for the digestive system and also known to provide relief from acidity and other gastric problems.

Nariyal Paani

Tender coconuts which have green shells (not the brown mature coconuts) are the ones with the most water content; and this water is referred to as coconut water or coconut juice. It has many medicinal properties attached to it and is considered auspicious as well. It is high in chlorides, potassium, and magnesium and has a moderate amount of sugar, sodium and protein. Potassium helps regulate blood pressure and heart function. Coconut water is also a good source of dietary fibre, manganese, calcium, riboflavin and Vitamin C.

Shakes

A shake is a sweet, cold beverage which is generally made from milk, fruit pulp, ice cream or iced milk, and flavourings or sweeteners. It can be prepared from various fruits available in market like banana, papaya, mango, *chikoo* (sapota), strawberry, and so on. It can also be prepared from milk and chocolate sauce, i.e., Chocolate Shake. Its preparation is very simple and all the ingredients are just blended in a blender and served chilled in a tall glass. It is a very filling beverage.

Thaati Kallu

Thaati Chettu's shoot is cut and the juice is traditionally collected in a hanging earthen pot. The juice so collected before morning is a refreshing and this light drink is called Thaati Kallu in Telugu, Neera in Marathi and Pathaneer in Tamil. It is cool in sensation with a sugary sweet taste. The juice collected in evening or after fermentation becomes sour and is called Taadi in Marathi. Taadi is consumed by Andhra Pradesh, coastal Maharashtra mostly by villagers as raw alcoholic beverage and these have some toxic values attached to it.

Gud ka Ras

Jaggery is called as *gud* in Hindi. Gud ka Ras is prepared from liquid jaggery which is prepared by boiling sugarcane juice continuously at slow flame and stirring it till it gets thick in consistency. This thick liquid is mixed with sufficient water and consumed as Gud ka Ras. It can be flavoured with lemon juice as well. This drink is consumed in North India as sugarcane in this area is grown in abundance.

Squash

It is non-alcoholic concentrated syrup which is mostly made from fruit juice, water and sugar. It is generally fruit flavoured. It is mixed with a certain amount of water before drinking.

Fruits such as pineapple, pomegranate, raspberry, strawberry, guava, *litchi,* mango, peach, blackcurrant, apple, orange, lime, lemon, and so on are used as base of squash. It is drunk chilled and is highly refreshing.

Culinary Trivia: Kulhad

A *kulhad,* sometimes called a *shikora,* is a traditional handle-less terracotta cup from North India and is meant to be disposed. Since *kulhars* are made by firing in a kiln and are almost never reused, they are inherently sterile and hygienic. Bazaars and food stalls in the Indian subcontinent traditionally served hot beverages, such as tea in *kulhad,* which suffused the beverage with an earthy aroma that was often considered appealing. Yogurt, hot milk with sugar as well as some regional desserts, such as *kulfi* (traditional ice-cream), are also served in *kulhars.*

Kulhars may have been in use in the region for the past 5000 years, since the Indus Valley Civilization.

Since *kulhars* are unglazed, a hot beverage (such as tea) partially soaks into the interior wall of the *kulhar* in which it being served. This has an enhancing effect on the beverage's taste and fragrance, which is sometimes described as "earthy".

36 Equipment

> **"The kitchen is a laboratory, and everything that happens there has to do with science. It's biology, chemistry, physics. Yes, there's history. Yes, there's artistry. Yes, to all of that. But what happened there, what actually happens to the food is all science." – Alton Brown**

Kitchen equipment is an instrument or tool that eases in smooth functioning in the kitchen. When it comes to the Indian kitchen, these are quite simple and not that complicated or sophisticated. The traditional kitchen equipment are nowadays replaced by the fancy, advanced and contemporary equipment.

Description of Various Equipment

Churner This is simply a churner mostly made up of wood, used for churning buttermilk. It is manually rotated between the palms for churning liquid food, mostly curds for making buttermilk. *Alternate names:* Mathani in North India, Ghutni in Bengal, Kavam in Andhra Pradesh.	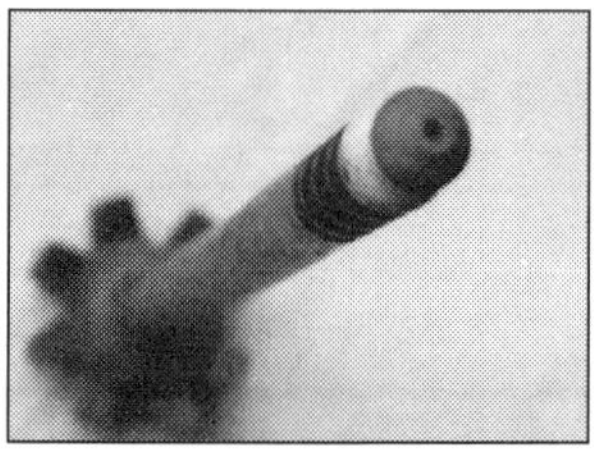
Mortar and Pestle This is an equipment used for pounding spices. It is usually made of iron, but nowadays the market is flooded with mortar and pestle made of marble, stone, bamboo, steel, brass, and iron. *Alternate names:* Hamam Dasta in North India, Rolu Pothram in Andhra Pradesh, Khalur Dula in Kashmir, Ural Ulakka in Kerala, Khal Bhatta in Maharashtra, Dori Danda in Punjab, and Haman Dista in Bengal.	
Sil-batta Sil is an extremely hard and firm rough stone slab piece and *batta* is a small, rough, conical or cylindrical stone. It is used for making paste of various masala. The ingredients to be ground are placed on the *sil* and then rubbed by the *batta* by forward and backward movement with subsequent pressure with little addition of liquid like water or vinegar. Both the *sil-batta* have to be chiseled at regular intervals after some use to provide a well-defined rough surface to ease proper grinding. *Alternate names:* Sil Nora in Bengal, Varn in Goa, Goshpar Kaen in Kashmir, Pata-warwanta in Maharashtra, Sil Pata in Bengal, and Siloutu in Uttarakhand.	

Chakla-belan

Chakla is a round marble or wooden platform used for rolling *roti* on it.

Belan is cylindrically shaped and fitted with handle and used to roll *roti*. It is made of wood or marble. Some rolling pins can move on an axis connecting the two handles. It is also termed Chauki Belan in the northern states of India.

Equipment for Cutting

It has a long semi-circular curved blade affixed on a wooden platform. The wooden platform is held by the foot with sufficient pressure, so that it doesn't move while cutting something. It is used for cutting almost anything like raw mangoes, vegetables, fish, and so on. It works like a sharp knife. In some versions, the semicircular blade cannot be moved and is fixed but in others it can move flexibly and touch the wooden platform.

Alternate names: Dantri in North India, Bothi in Bengal, Pahsul in Uttar Pradesh, Veeli in Maharashtra, Thuruvammai in Tamil Nadu, Daraati in Rajasthan, and Daatuli or Chanesoo in Uttarakhand.

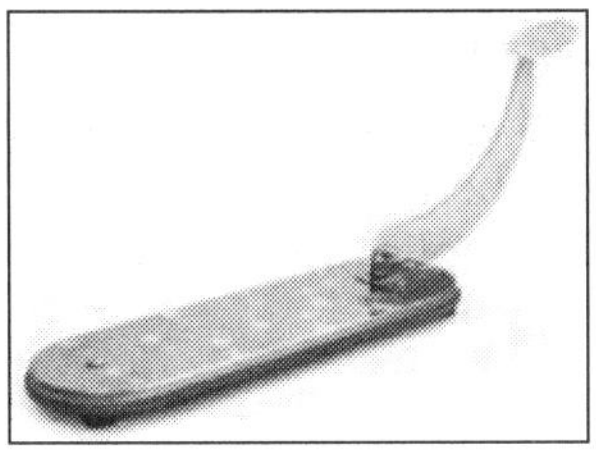

Sarasi

It is used as a pincer. It is used for holding hot vessels while removing them from flame. It is also available in various versions.

Alternate names: Sharashi in Bengal.

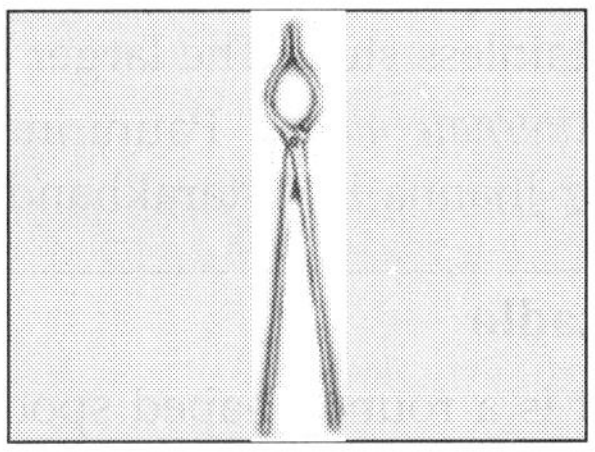

Chimta

Chimta literally means tongs. It is a flat, smooth-edged, long metal tongs. It is a flat piece of steel or iron that is pointed at both ends, and folded over in the middle. It is used for picking up live coals and for turning over bread on *tawa*. It is also used for baking *chapati* and *phulka* on the flame.

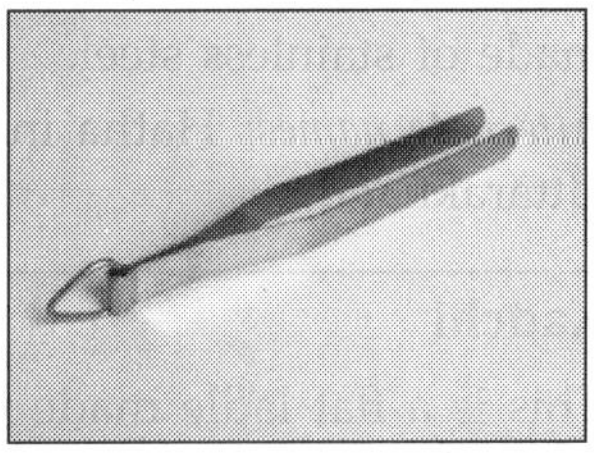

Kadhai

It is a deep concave utensil made of brass, iron, steel or aluminium. It has two handles placed diametrically opposite near the rim for holding the *kadhai* with proper grip. It is curved at the bottom and very wide at the top, rather appeasing like a half-moon. It is mostly used for deep frying but is also used for preparing certain other preparations as well.

Alternate names: Cheena Chatti in Kerala, and Korai in Bengal.

Patila/Bhagona

It is the most common used utensil or cooking pot in the kitchens of India. It is generally made of aluminium, brass, copper and stainless steel. It has straight side and flat rimmed base. It is used for various purposes like boiling, stewing, steaming or braising.

Alternate names: Thapeli in Gujarat and Toup in Uttar Pradesh.

Deg/Degchi

This is a round bottomed cooking pot that has a slightly narrow neck and a wide rim to facilitate an effective grip. The shape of this utensil is also suited for Mughlai Dum cooking.

Alternate names: Hari in Bengal, and Degul and Degcha in Kashmir.

Handi

It is a traditional pear-shaped cooking pot, available in a varied range of size. The food in this utensil is cooked on slow flame that adds to its natural and characteristic flavour, aroma and taste by preserving all to the maximum extent. It generally has thick bottom which ensures that food does not stick to the *handi*. It is made of copper, aluminium, brass, iron, and so on. Cover of the *handi* is known as *shara*.

Lagan

It is a round copper utensil with a slightly concave bottom. It is a shallow utensil of less height. It is used for cooking various types of meats or poultry especially when the application of heat is from top and bottom. It is mostly used in Mughlai cuisine.

Perforated Spoon

It is an equipment used during deep-frying any item in a *kadhai*. It is simply a spoon with perforation to let the oil or liquid drain through it. It is usually made up of stainless steel. The larger version of it is known as *channi* and is used in bulk cooking.

Alternate names: Pauni in North India, Jhanjri in Bengal, Kadchi in Rajasthan, Pannah or Jhanna in Uttarakhand, and Chakni in Bengal.

Ladle

It is a round shaped spoon with a long handle. The basic use of this equipment is to portion various curries, *dal* or any other dishes with a liquid consistency. It is generally made of stainless steel.

Alternate names: Hatha in Bengal, Chamcha in Rajasthan, and Dyadu or Kadchalu in Uttarakhand.

Kadchi

This is a flat ladle made up of stainless steel. It is used for stirring the vegetables or any other preparation while cooking. It is also used in shallow frying any items. Its larger version is known as Palta and is used in bulk cooking.

Alternate names: Khunti in Bengal.

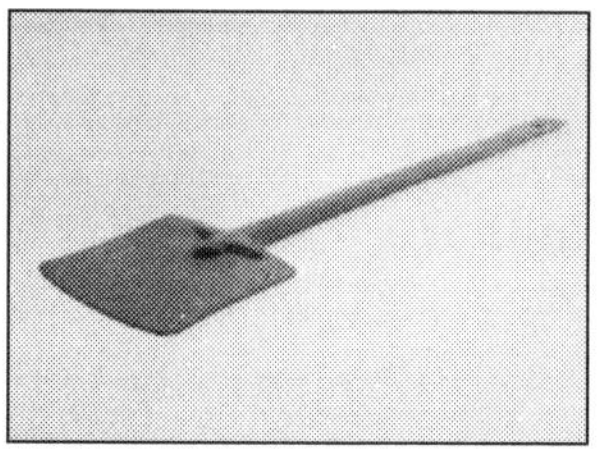

Parat

It is a deep, flat and wide-rimmed round tray made of brass or stainless steel used for kneading dough. It is made of brass or stainless steel. It is also used as serving tray during wedding functions.

Thali

It is a metal plate with or without compartments used for serving food. It is also used to keep the misc–en –place.

Alternate names: Thala in Bengal, and Thakuluu in Uttarakhand.

Katori

Small metal bowl used for serving individual portion of curries, *dal, raita* and sweets. It is available in different sizes and also used in the kitchen for storing different pastes.

Tawa

It is a slightly curved concave shaped cast iron griddle, with or without a handle. It is generally made up of iron but today many options are also available in various sizes. Generally, the *tawa* which is used in homes is of size ranging from 7 to 10 inches in diameter. This is used for making *roti* or *chapati, phulka* and *paratha.*

The *tawas* which are used commercially are bigger in size (15″ to 30″). This *tawa* is also much thicker as compared to the other one. The larger surface allows the food to be moved to the periphery. The food left at the periphery remains hot for a long time. Pav Bhaaji and *tawa* vegetables are made using this *tawa.*

Knife

It is one of the most used basic kitchen equipment and is used for cutting vegetables, meat, fish, chicken, and so on into pieces. There are many varieties of knife available in the market, varying in sizes and shapes.

Peeler

As the name suggest, it is used for peeling skin of the vegetables.

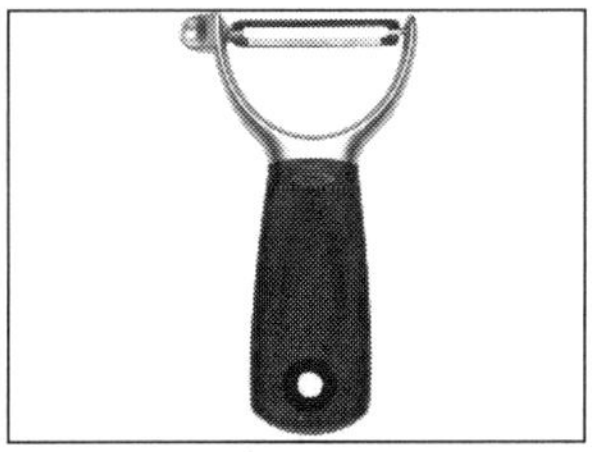

Winnow

It is a traditional equipment used for separating the grains from the chaff. It is used dexterously with perfect left and right movement of the hands in order to remove the chaff from the grains.

Alternate names: Soop in Uttar Pradesh.

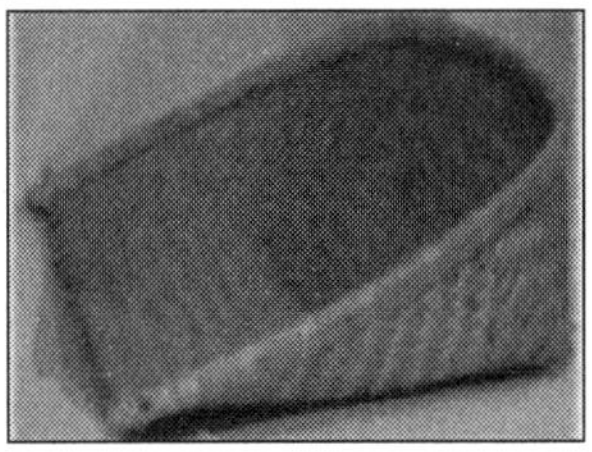

Culinary Trivia: Dung Cakes

They are made from the byproducts of animal husbandry and are traditionally used as fuel in India for making food in a domestic hearth called a *chulha.* They are made by hand by village women and are traditionally made from cow or buffalo dung. These cakes of cow dung are moulded by bare hands with a curvature to keep them stuck to the walls. Once dried, they are put in a pile and covered with thatch called *bituada.*

Index

Note: Figures in parentheses refer to the plate number where the colour image of the dish appears.

Plate 1

Kaliya (refer p. 58)

Do-Pyaza (refer p. 58)

Rizala (refer p. 58)

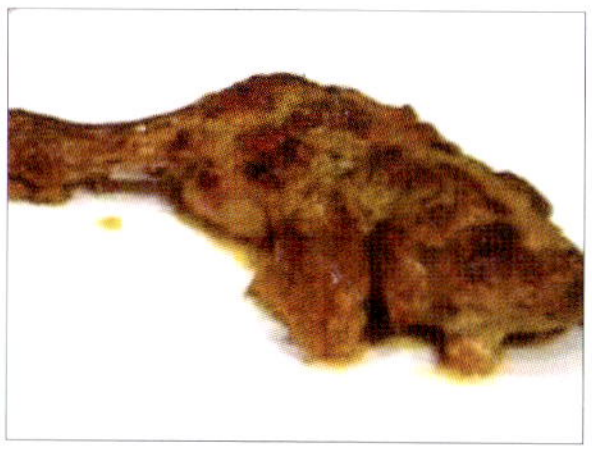
Raan (refer p. 59)

Korma (refer p. 59)

Nargisi Kofta (refer p. 59)

Shabdeg (refer p. 59)

Nehari (refer p. 59, 108)

Haleem (refer p. 60, 108)

Kakori Kebab (refer p. 60)

Shami Kebab (refer p. 60)

Gilawati Kebab (refer p. 60)

Murg Mussallam (refer p. 60)

Zamin doz Machhli (refer p. 60)

Lahm-e-Murghan (refer p. 61)

Nimona (refer p. 61)

Lazeez Lauki (refer p. 61)

Badal Jaam (refer p. 61)

Sultani Dal (refer p. 61)

Zarda (refer p. 61)

Lucknowi Biryani (refer p. 61)

Mutanjan (refer p. 62)

Roomali Roti (refer p. 62, 256)

Sheermal (refer p. 62, 256)

Plate 2

Sewain Muzaffar (refer p. 62)

Taftan (refer p. 62, 251)

Bakarkhani (refer p. 62)

Warqui Paratha (refer p. 62)

Sheer Brunj (refer p. 63)

Shukto (refer p. 69)

Bhapa Doi (refer p. 69)

Doi Macch (refer p. 69)

Aloo Posto (refer p. 70)

Shondesh (refer p. 70)

Rasmalai (refer p. 70)

Roshogolla (refer p. 70, 268)

Chumchom (refer p. 70)

Pantua (refer p. 70)

Muṛi (refer p. 71)

Jhal Muri (refer p. 71)

Moa (refer p. 71)

Radha Ballobhi (refer p. 71)

Shorshe Bata Ilish (refer p. 71)

Macher Paturi (refer p. 71)

Chingri Malai Curry (refer p. 71)

Dhokar Dalna (refer p. 72)

Kabiraji Cutlet (refer p. 72)

Kasha Mangsho (refer p. 72)

Plate 3

Litti-Choka (refer p. 75)

Sattu (refer p. 75)

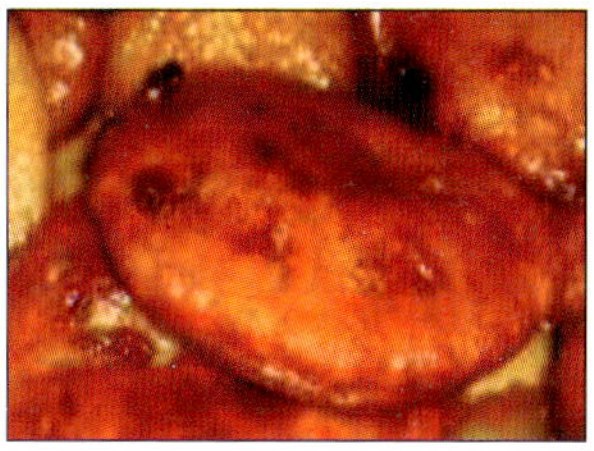
Pua (refer p. 75)

Pittha (refer p. 75)

Chiwra (refer p. 75)

Pedukia (refer p. 76)

Thekua (refer p. 76, 269)

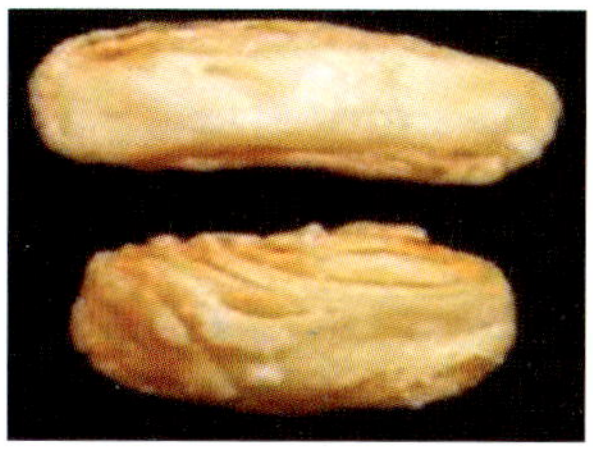
Khaja (refer p. 76, 166, 263)

Dhuska (refer p. 76)

Belgrami (refer p. 76)

Goan Fish Curry (refer p. 80)

Putte (refer p. 80)

Caldo Verda (refer p. 80)

Christmas Pudding (refer p. 80)

Leitao Assado (refer p. 81)

Fish Recheado (refer p. 81)

Prawn Balchao (refer p. 81)

Pork Vindaloo (refer p. 81)

Sorpotel (refer p. 81)

Chicken Cafreal (refer p. 82)

Chicken Xacuti (refer p. 82)

Prawn Caldeen (refer p. 82)

Khatkhate Curry (refer p. 82)

Chouricos (refer p. 83)

Plate 4

Bebinca (refer p. 83)

Dodol (refer p. 83)

Sannas (refer p. 83)

Arroz Refogado (refer p. 83)

Caldeirada (refer p. 83)

Canja de Galinha (refer p. 84)

Pez (refer p. 84)

Feijoada (refer p. 84)

Cabidela (refer p. 84)

Alsandache Tondak (refer p. 84)

Galinha Piri-Piri (refer p. 84)

Bolos (refer p. 84)

Moonga Ganthi (refer p. 85)

Varan (refer p. 85)

Fulka Rotli (refer p. 89)

Puri (refer p. 89)

Thepla (refer p. 89)

Bhakhri (refer p. 89, 251)

Bajri no Rotlo (refer p. 89)

Juvar no Rotlo (refer p. 90)

Puran Poli (Vedmi) (refer p. 90)

Vagharelu Bhaat (refer p. 90)

Khichdi (refer p. 90)

Khatta-Mittha Bhaat (refer p. 90)

Plate 5

Undhiyu (refer p. 90)

Bateta nu Shaak (refer p. 90)

Bateta Sukhi Bhaji (refer p. 91)

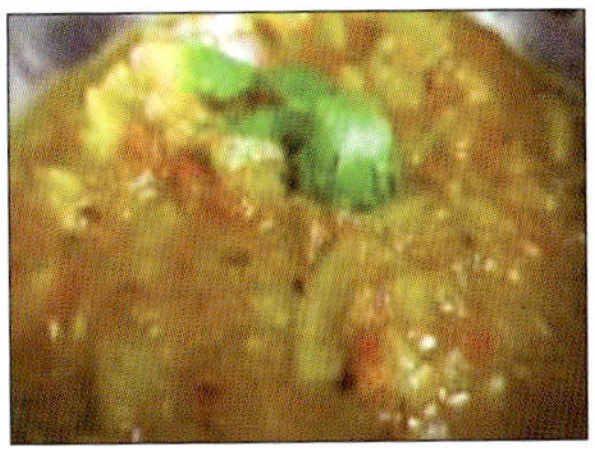

Dudhi nu Shaak (refer p. 91)

Guavar nu Shaak (refer p. 91)

Panchkutiyu Shaak (refer p. 91)

Sutarfeni (refer p. 91)

Basundi (refer p. 91, 259)

Mohanthal (refer p. 91)

Gudpapdi (refer p. 92)

Khajoor Pak (refer p. 92)

Salli Jardalao Murghi (refer p. 92)

Patrani Macchi (refer p. 92)

Bajre ki Roti (refer p. 94)

Bajre ki Khichdi (refer p. 94)

Chana Saag (refer p. 94)

Maseladaar Karela (refer p. 95)

Aate ka Halwa (refer p. 95)

Ghee Boora (refer p. 95)

Gajar Methi ki Subzi (refer p. 95)

Aloo Gajar ki Subzi (refer p. 95)

Bathue ka Saag (refer p. 95)

Madrah (refer p. 98)

Sidu (refer p. 98)

Plate 6

Kullu Trout (refer p. 98)

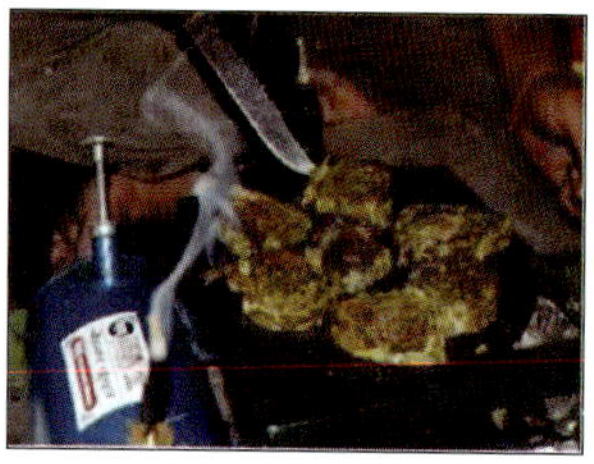
Ankolas and Aktori (refer p. 99)

Patande (refer p. 99)

Maahni (refer p. 99)

Khatta (refer p. 99)

Mal Puda (refer p. 99)

Kachalu Ka Salan (refer p. 99)

Chicken Anardana (refer p. 99)

Sepu Badi (refer p. 100)

Chha Meat (refer p. 100)

Babroo (refer p. 100)

Chawal Atte ki Beduan Roti (refer p. 100)

Beduan Roti (refer p. 100)

Bhruni ki Subzi (refer p. 100)

Lukhmi (refer p. 106)

Tootak (refer p. 106)

Patthar ka Gosht (refer p. 106)

Taatee ka Gosht (refer p. 106)

Pongali (refer p. 107)

Kursi Miyane (refer p. 107)

Shikampoor (refer p. 107)

Dum ke Laoz (refer p. 107)

Bhuna Kheema (refer p. 107)

Chowgra (refer p. 107)

Plate 7

Chippe ka Gosht (refer p. 107)

Haleem (refer p. 108)

Dalcha (refer p. 108)

Bhuna Gosht (refer p. 108)

Chakna (refer p. 108)

Burhani (refer p. 109)

Murgh Achari (refer p. 109)

Methi Murgh (refer p. 109)

Ande ka Khagina (refer p. 109)

Hyderabadi Biryani (refer p. 109)

Kachhi Biryani (refer p. 109)

Qabooli (refer p. 110)

Mirchi ka Salan (refer p. 110)

Baghare Baigan (refer p. 110)

Chapa Pulusu (refer p. 110)

Tamater Kut (refer p. 110)

Keoti Dal (refer p. 110)

Dalcha (refer p. 111)

Raughani Roti (refer p. 111)

Bakharkhani Roti (refer p. 111)

Baadam ki Jaali (refer p. 111)

Double ka Meetha (refer p. 111)

Khubani ka Meetha (refer p. 111)

Nimish (refer p. 111)

Plate 8

Gil-e-Firdaus
(refer p. 112)

Mauz-ka-Meetha
(refer p. 112)

Ande-ka-Piyosi
(refer p. 112)

Akki Roti
(refer p. 115, 150)

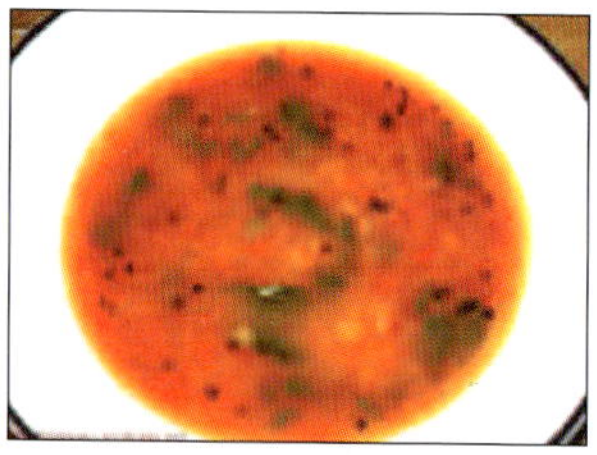

Saaru (refer p. 115)

Bisi Bele Bhaat
(refer p. 115)

Mysore Pak
(refer p. 115, 266)

Uppittu (refer p. 115)

Jolada Roti
(refer p. 115, 252)

Vangi Bath
(refer p. 116)

Puliyogare (refer p. 116)

Sambhar (refer p. 116)

Praan (Kashmiri Onion)
(refer p. 120)

Kanaguchhi
(refer p. 120)

Saffron (refer p. 121, 227)

Haak (refer p. 121)

Knol Khol (refer p. 121)

Mutton Roganjosh
(refer p. 122)

Gushtaba (refer p. 122)

Rishta (refer p. 122)

Tabak Maaz
(refer p. 122)

Kabargaah (refer p. 123)

Methi Maaz
(refer p. 123)

Heddar (refer p. 123)

Plate 9

Aab Gosht (refer p. 123)

Dhaniwaal Korma (refer p. 123)

Marzwaangan Korma (refer p. 123)

Gosht ke Kofte (refer p. 123)

Mutton Yakhni (refer p. 124)

Yakhni Pulao (refer p. 124)

Shyami (refer p. 124)

Chamani Qaliya (refer p. 124)

Veth Chaman (refer p. 124)

Tsaman Pulao (refer p. 124)

Bhaz Bhaat (refer p. 125)

Rwangan Tsaman (refer p. 125)

Nadeir Yakhean (refer p. 125)

Khate Baingan (refer p. 125)

Dama Oluv (refer p. 125)

Rajma Shaljam (refer p. 125)

Roth (refer p. 126)

Mooli ka Raita (refer p. 126)

Ranith Gada (refer p. 126)

Kashmir Gaad (refer p. 126)

Girda (refer p. 126)

Tahaer (refer p. 126)

Firni (refer p. 127)

Shufta (refer p. 127)

Plate 10

Laed (refer p. 127)

Hogaad Bum (refer p. 127)

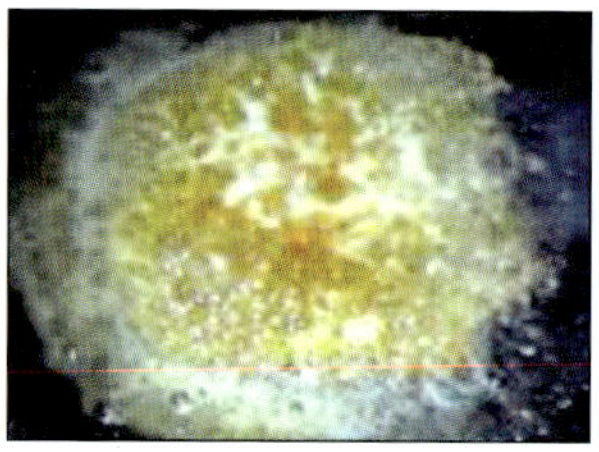

Maesh Crari (refer p. 127)

Mechama (refer p. 127)

Modur Polav (refer p. 128)

Sheer Chai (refer p. 128)

Kehwa (refer p. 128)

Naimeen Vevichathu (refer p. 132)

Ada Pradhaman (refer p. 132, 259)

Aattirachi Ularthiyathu (refer p. 133)

Vegetable Manga Mappas (refer p. 133)

Kozhi Peralan (refer p. 133)

Thalassery Biryani (refer p. 133)

Olan (refer p. 133)

Thoran (refer p. 133)

Kaalan (refer p. 133)

Avial (refer p. 134)

Pazhampori (refer p. 134)

Nadan Kozhi Curry (refer p. 134)

Cheru Payar (refer p. 134)

Erachi Vada (refer p. 134)

Kappa (refer p. 134)

Karimeen Pollichathu (refer p. 134)

Erachi Ishtu (refer p. 135)

Plate 11

Kadala Curry
(refer p. 135)

Kozhi Varutharacha
Curry (refer p. 135)

Chemmeen Varuthathu
(refer p. 135)

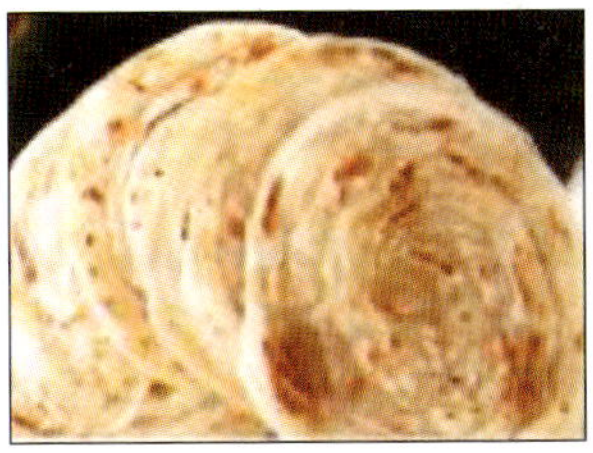

Malabari Paratha
(refer p. 135, 254)

Muttamala
(refer p. 135, 265)

Erachi Varattiyathu
(refer p. 135)

Meen Porichathu
(refer p. 136)

Pohe (refer p. 143)

Vada Pav (refer p. 143)

Sabudana Vada
(refer p. 144)

Pav-Bhaaji (refer p. 144)

Misal Pav (refer p. 144)

Tilgud Ladoo
(refer p. 144)

Zunka Bhakar
(refer p. 144)

Dalimbi (refer p. 144)

Methi Che Varan
(refer p. 144)

Malvani Chana Masala
(refer p. 145)

Batata Chi Bhaaji
(refer p. 145)

Bharleli Vaangi
(refer p. 145)

Faraali Misal
(refer p. 145)

Danyachi Usal
(refer p. 145)

Masala Bhaat
(refer p. 145)

Kothimbir Vadi
(refer p. 145)

Amti (refer p. 146)

Plate 12

Tambda Rassa (refer p. 146)

Pandhra Rassa (refer p. 146)

Sungtachi Jhinga Kodi (refer p. 146)

Sol Kadhi (refer p. 146)

Tomato Saar (refer p. 146)

Kokam Saar (refer p. 146)

Puran Poli (refer p. 147, 255)

Modak (refer p. 147, 264)

Karanji (refer p. 147, 263)

Anarsa (refer p. 147)

Shevaya chi Kheer (refer p. 147)

Narali Bhaat (refer p. 147)

Shrikhand (refer p. 148)

Shankarpali (refer p. 148)

Gulachi Poli (refer p. 148)

Amras (refer p. 148)

Chitranna (refer p. 148)

Vaangi Bhaat (refer p. 148)

Momo (refer p. 151, 187)

Zan (refer p. 151)

Khura (refer p. 151)

Wungwut Ngam (refer p. 152)

Ngatok (refer p. 152)

Pasa (refer p. 152)

Plate 13

Iromba (refer p. 155)

Singju (refer p. 156)

Chamthong (refer p. 156)

Morok Metpa (refer p. 156)

Dalma (refer p. 163)

Santula (refer p. 163)

Machha Besara (refer p. 163)

Pithau Bhaja (refer p. 163)

Chingudi Mahura (refer p. 163)

Ghanta (refer p. 163)

Dahi Baigana (refer p. 163)

Tomato Khajura Khata (refer p. 164)

Machha Thukuthuka (refer p. 164)

Ghia Anna (refer p. 164)

Chingudi Chadchadi (refer p. 164)

Maansha Kasha (refer p. 164)

Chhena Tarkari (refer p. 164)

Kancha Kadali Bara (refer p. 164)

Potala Rasa (refer p. 165)

Pani Kakharu Sakara (refer p. 165)

Mula Raita (refer p. 165)

Aarisa Pitha (refer p. 165)

Manda Pitha (refer p. 165)

Chhena Poda (refer p. 165)

Plate 14

Rasabali
(refer p. 165, 267)

Saru Chakuli
(refer p. 166)

Budha Chakuli
(refer p. 166)

Khiri (refer p. 166)

Attakali (refer p. 166)

Enduri Pitha
(refer p. 166)

Rajma Masala
(refer p. 169)

Chhole Masala
(refer p. 170)

Pindi Chane
(refer p. 170)

Tandoori Murg
(refer p. 170)

Sarson da Saag
(refer p. 170)

Makki di Roti
(refer p. 170, 254)

Punjabi Lobia
(refer p. 170)

Phirni (refer p. 171)

Vegetable Jalfarezi
(refer p. 171)

Kadhai Paneer
(refer p. 171)

Shahi Paneer
(refer p. 171)

Rara Gosht
(refer p. 171)

Baigan ka Bharta
(refer p. 171)

Navratan Korma
(refer p. 171)

Malai Kofta
(refer p. 172)

Gajar ka Halwa
(refer p. 172)

Gulab Jamun
(refer p. 172)

Paneer Makhani
(refer p. 172)

Plate 15

Butter Chicken (refer p. 172)

Murg Makhani (refer p. 172)

Keema Matar (refer p. 172)

Dal Makhani (refer p. 173)

Punj Ratni Dal (refer p. 173)

Mah ki Dal (refer p. 173)

Dal Amritsari (refer p. 173)

Amritsari Machhi (refer p. 173)

Chicken Tikka Masala (refer p. 173)

Palak Paneer (refer p. 173)

Naan (refer p. 174, 254)

Lacchha Parantha (refer p. 174, 253)

Kulcha (refer p. 174)

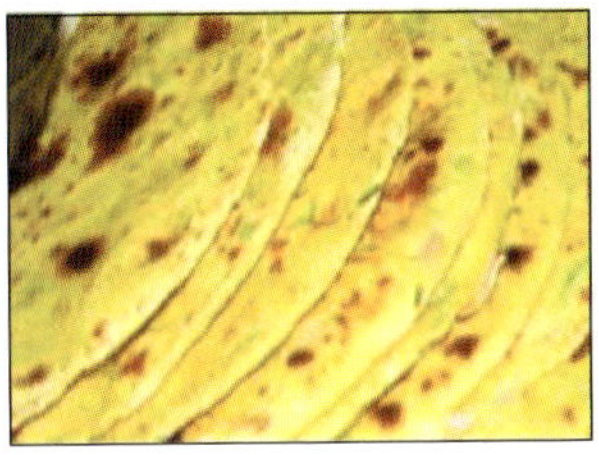
Missi Roti (refer p. 174, 254)

Bhature (refer p. 174, 100, 252)

Dahi Bhalle (refer p. 174)

Paneer Pakoda (refer p. 174)

Lassi (refer p. 175)

Dal Baati (refer p. 178)

Ker Sangri Kumatia (refer p. 179)

Besan ke Gatte (refer p. 179)

Govind Gatta Curry (refer p. 179)

Lal Maans (refer p. 179)

Safed Maans (refer p. 179)

Plate 16

Junglee Maans (refer p. 179)

Mohan Maans (refer p. 180)

Khud Khargosh (refer p. 180)

Maans ke Soole (refer p. 180)

Maans ka Soweta (refer p. 180)

Murg ka Mokul (refer p. 180)

Haldi ki Subzi (refer p. 180)

Gulab Jamun ki Subzi (refer p. 180)

Pithorey (refer p. 181)

Rabodi ki Subzi (refer p. 181)

Aloo Mangodi ki Subzi (refer p. 181)

Rajasthani Kadhi (refer p. 181)

Bajre ka Sogra (refer p. 181)

Khad ka Panda (refer p. 181)

Gawar ki Phalli (refer p. 181)

Raab (refer p. 182)

Goonda ki Subzi (refer p. 182)

Jhajariya (refer p. 182)

Doodh Feeni (refer p. 182)

Raabdi (refer p. 182)

Missi Roti (refer p. 182)

Lahsun ki Chutney (refer p. 182)

Laapsi (refer p. 183)

Pyaz ki Kachori (refer p. 183)

Plate 17

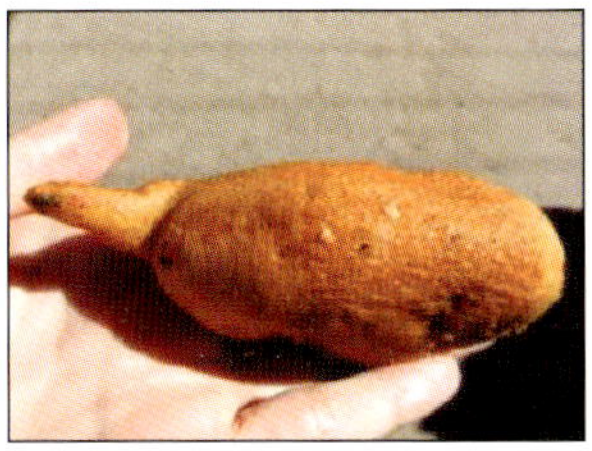

Mirchi Vada
(refer p. 183)

Makki ki Raab
(refer p. 183)

Mawa Kachori
(refer p. 183)

Ghewar (refer p. 183)

Mishri Mawa
(refer p. 183)

Moong Dal Halwa
(refer p. 184)

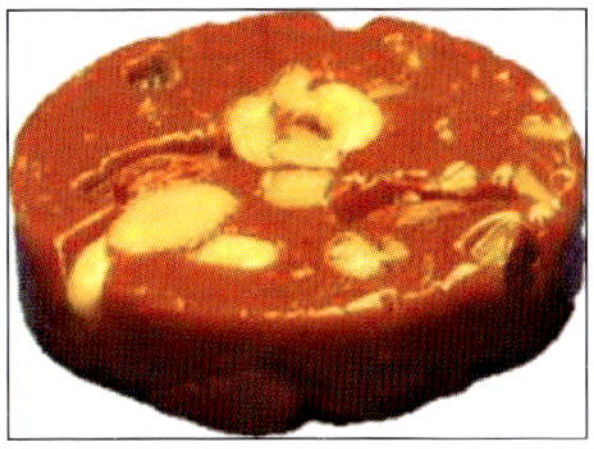

Sohan Halwa
(refer p. 184, 269)

Dilkhusaal
(refer p. 184)

Besan Ki Chakki
(refer p. 184)

Khushka (refer p. 184)

Mirch Ke Tapore
(refer p. 184)

Thukpa or Gya-Thuk
(refer p. 187)

Pork Shaphalay
(refer p. 187)

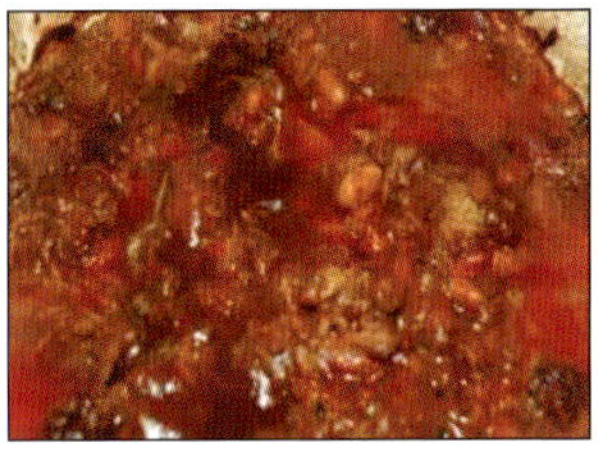

Kinema Curry
(refer p. 188)

Pork Gyari
(refer p. 188)

Phing (refer p. 188)

Phulaurah (refer p. 188)

Rasam (refer p. 190)

Kolambhu (refer p. 190)

Thuvail (refer p. 191)

Pongal (refer p. 191)

Vadai (refer p. 191)

Poriyal (refer p. 191)

Koozh (refer p. 191)

Plate 18

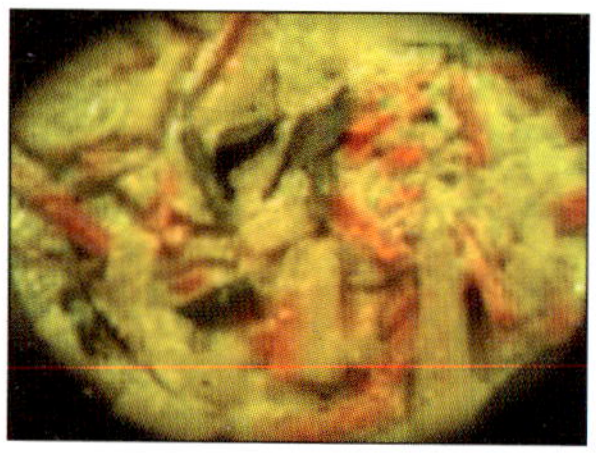
Aviyal (refer p. 191)

Kozhukkattai (refer p. 192)

Idiyappam (refer p. 192)

Uttapam (refer p. 192)

Kootu (refer p. 192)

Curd Rice (refer p. 192)

Lemon Rice (refer p. 192)

Puttu (refer p. 193)

Dosa (refer p. 193, 252)

Idli (refer p. 193)

Mandua Ki Roti (refer p. 197)

Lesu (refer p. 197)

Gahat (Kulath) Ki Dal (refer p. 197)

Gahat (Kulath) Soup (refer p. 197)

Urad Ke Pakore (Wada) (refer p. 197)

Bhangjeera Ki Chatni (refer p. 197)

Rus (refer p. 198)

Aloo ke Gutke (refer p. 198)

Jhangore ki Kheer (refer p. 198)

Mixed Bhaddu Dal (refer p. 198)

Kafuli (refer p. 198)

Sani Hui Mooli aur Nimbu (refer p. 198)

Sisunak Saag (refer p. 198)

Chainsoo (refer p. 199)

Plate 19

Phaanu (refer p. 199)

Alu Dal Pakora (refer p. 199)

Alu Tamatar Ka Jhol (refer p. 199)

Kaapa (refer p. 199)

Thechwani (refer p. 199)

Baadi (refer p. 199)

Bhatt ki Churkani (refer p. 200)

Dubka (refer p. 200)

Gaderi ki Sabji (refer p. 200)

Badeel (refer p. 200)

Lal Chawal ki Kheer (refer p. 200)

Ajwain (refer p. 221)

Allspice (refer p. 221)

Amchoor (refer p. 221)

Aniseed (refer p. 221)

Asafoetida (refer p. 222)

Basil (refer p. 222)

Bay leaf (refer p. 223)

Cambodge (refer p. 223)

Caraway (refer p. 223)

Cardamom (refer p. 223, 224)

Red Chilli (refer p. 224)

Cinnamon (refer p. 224)

Clove (refer p. 224)

Plate 20

Cumin Seeds (refer p. 225)

Coriander (refer p. 225)

Curry Leaves (refer p. 225)

Fennel (refer p. 225)

Fenugreek (refer p. 226)

Turmeric (refer p. 226)

Nutmeg (refer p. 226)

Mustard Seeds (refer p. 226)

Nigella (refer p. 227)

Black Pepper (refer p. 227)

Star Anise (refer p. 227)

Garlic (refer p. 227)

Ginger (refer p. 228)

Black Salt (refer p. 228)

Sesame Seed (refer p. 228)

Tamarind (refer p. 228)

Anda Paratha (refer p. 251)

Baati (refer p. 251)

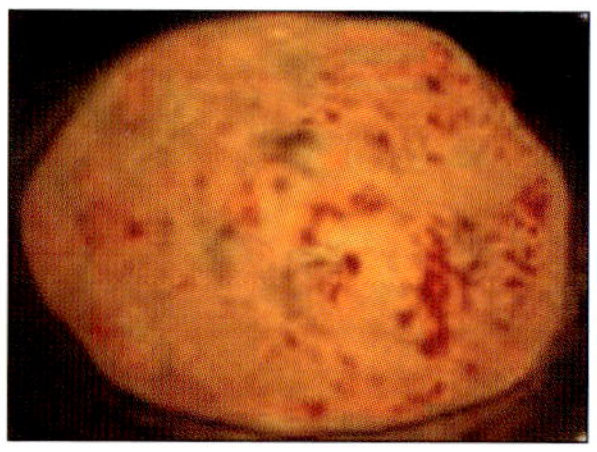

Baida Paratha (refer p. 251)

Bajre ki Roti (refer p. 251)

Bidari Paratha (refer p. 252)

Dhakai Paratha (refer p. 252)

Gilafi Kulcha (refer p. 252)

Kerala Porotta (refer p. 253)

Plate 21

Khameeri Roti (refer p. 253)

Khasta Roti (refer p. 253)

Kulcha (refer p. 253)

Lucchi (refer p. 253)

Makhuni Roti (refer p. 253)

Mughlai Paratha (refer p. 254)

Paratha (refer p. 255)

Pathiri (refer p. 255)

Pav (refer p. 255)

Poori (refer p. 255)

Roomali Roti (refer p. 256)

Roti (refer p. 256)

Sheermal (refer p. 256)

Tandoori Roti (refer p. 257)

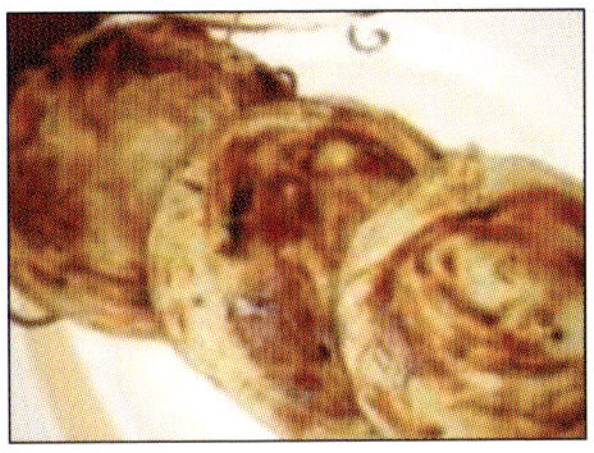
Varqi Paratha (refer p. 257)

Ariselu (refer p. 259)

Makkhan Wada (refer p. 259)

Bibinca (refer p. 259)

Bolinas (refer p. 260)

Burfi (refer p. 260)

Belgrami (refer p. 260)

Chhena Gaja (refer p. 260)

Chhena Poda (refer p. 260)

Chikki (refer p. 260)

Plate 22

Dodol (refer p. 261)

Doodh Pak (refer p. 261)

Double ka Meetha (refer p. 261)

Ghevar (refer p. 261)

Gulab Jamun (refer p. 261)

Halwa (refer p. 261)

Imarti (refer p. 262)

Jalebi (refer p. 262)

Kakara (refer p. 262)

Kalakand (refer p. 262)

Kalathappam (refer p. 263)

Kheer (refer p. 263)

Kheer Kadam (refer p. 264)

Kheersagar (refer p. 264)

Laddoo (refer p. 264)

Lady Kenny (refer p. 265)

Laganu Custard (refer p. 265)

Lavang Latika (refer p. 265)

Malpua (refer p. 265)

Misti Doi (refer p. 265)

Parwal ki Mithai (refer p. 266)

Patishapta (refer p. 266)

Payasam (refer p. 266)

Payesh (refer p. 266)

Plate 23

Peda (refer p. 266)

Petha (refer p. 267)

Phirni (refer p. 267)

Poothareku (refer p. 267)

Qubani ka Meetha (refer p. 267)

Rabdi (refer p. 267)

Rasmalai (refer p. 268)

Sandesh (refer p. 268)

Shahi Tukda (refer p. 268)

Sheer Khurma (refer p. 268)

Soan Papdi (refer p. 269)

Unni Appam (refer p. 269)

Aam ka Panna (refer p. 271)

Bael ka Ras (refer p. 271)

Bhaang (refer p. 271)

Thandai (refer p. 271)

Chaach (refer p. 272)

Lassi (refer p. 272)

Tea (refer p. 272)

Coffee (refer p. 272)

Jaljeera (refer p. 272)

Kanji (refer p. 273)

Shikanjvi (refer p. 273)

Ganne ka Ras (refer p. 273)

Plate 24

Zutho (refer p. 273)

Chuak (refer p. 273)

Feni (refer p. 273)

Sharbat (refer p. 274)

Kokum Sherbet (refer p. 274)

Nariyal Paani (refer p. 274)

Shakes (refer p. 274)

Thaati Kallu (refer p. 274)

Gud ka Ras (refer p. 274)

Squash (refer p. 275)

Churner (refer p. 276)

Mortar (refer p. 276)

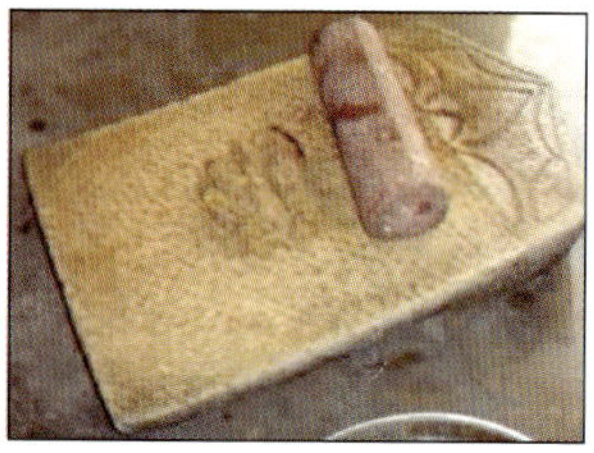
Sil-batta (refer p. 276)

Chakla-belan (refer p. 277)

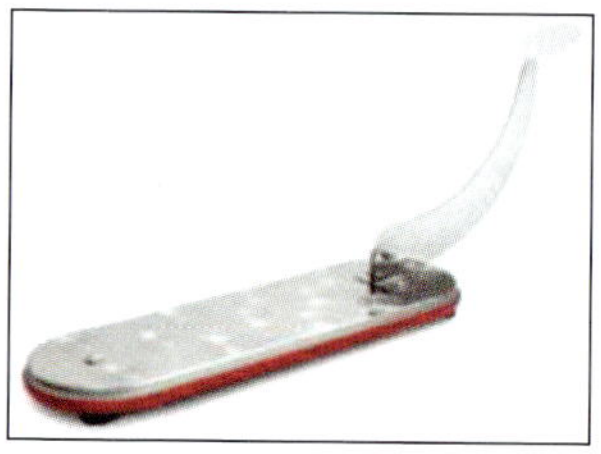
Equipment for Cutting (refer p. 277)

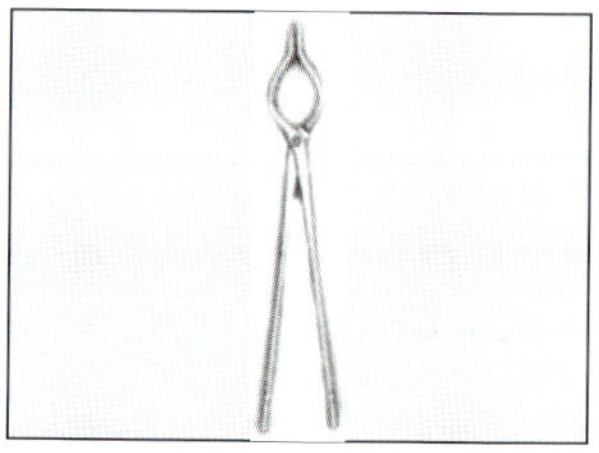
Sarasi (refer p. 277)

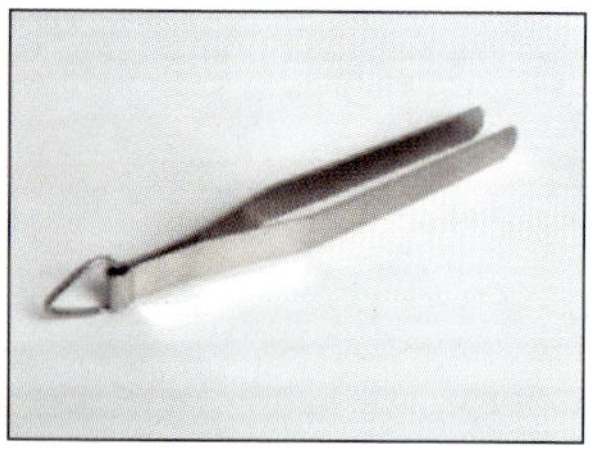
Chimta (refer p. 277)

Kadhai (refer p. 277)

Bhagona (refer p. 277)

Deg (refer p. 277)

Handi (refer p. 278)

Lagan (refer p. 278)

Perforated Spoon (refer p. 278)

Ladle (refer p. 278)

Plate 25

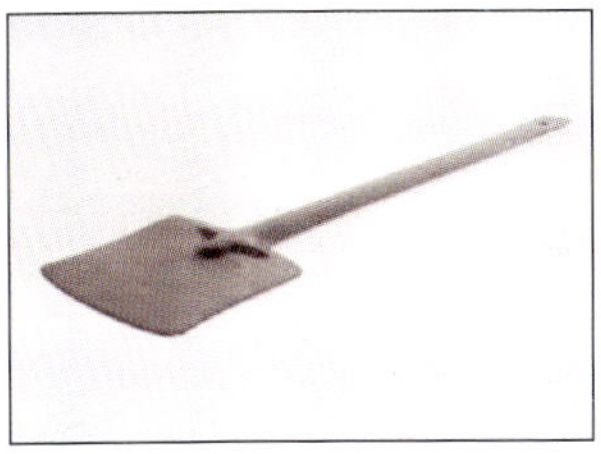

Kadchi (refer p. 278)

Parat (refer p. 278)

Thali (refer p. 278)

Peeler (refer p. 279)

Katori (refer p. 279)

Tawa (refer p. 279)

Knife (refer p. 279)

Winnow (refer p. 279)